I0832968

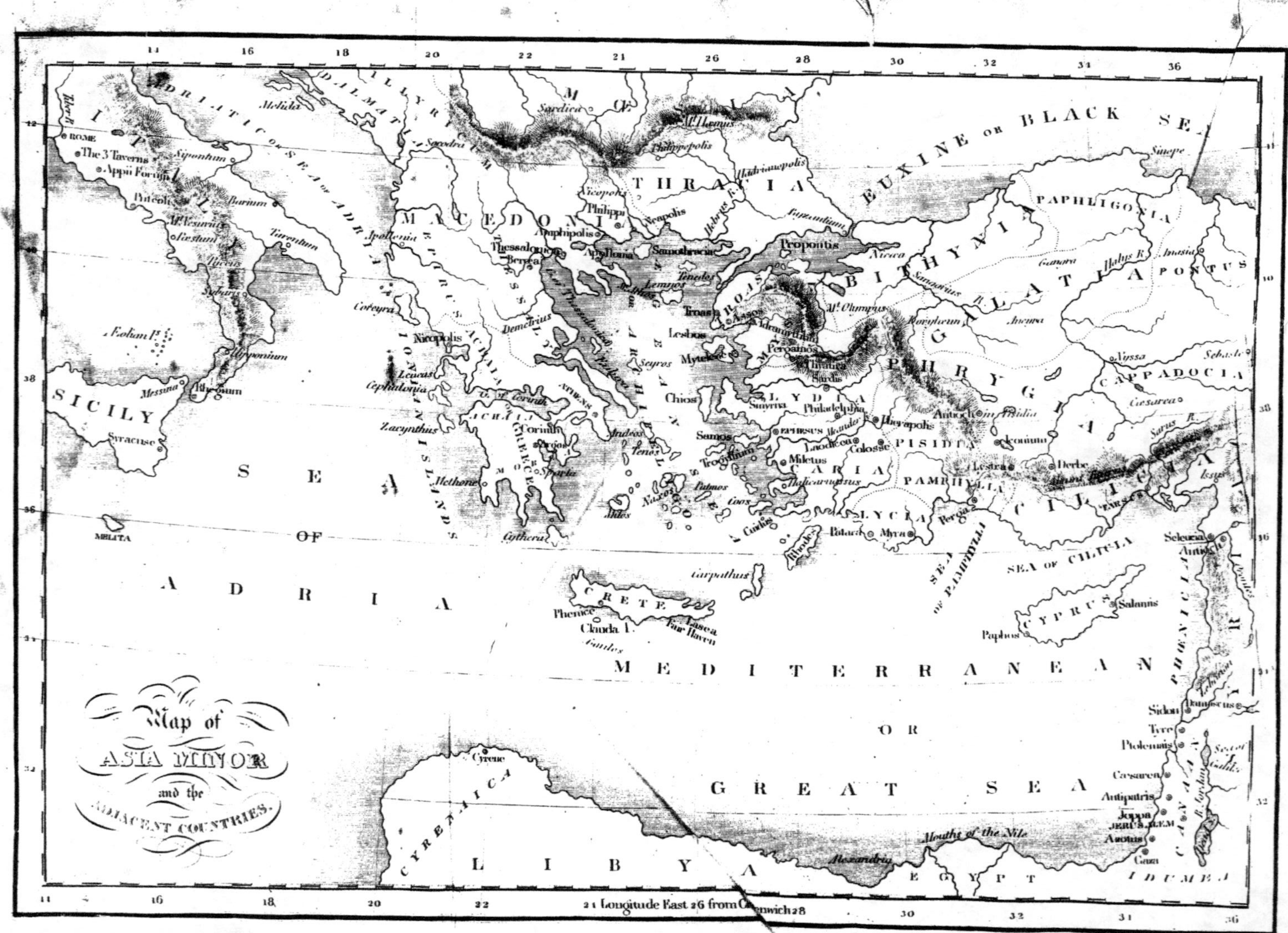
Map of
ASIA MINOR
and the
ADJACENT COUNTRIES.
EUXINE OR BLACK SEA
MEDITERRANEAN
OR
GREAT SEA
SEA OF ADRIA
SEA OF CILICIA
SEA OF PAMPHYLIA
THRACIA
MACEDONIA
BITHYNIA
GALATIA
PAPHLAGONIA
PONTUS
CAPPADOCIA
PHRYGIA
LYDIA
CARIA
LYCIA
PISIDIA
PAMPHYLIA
CILICIA
CYPRUS
CRETE
SICILY
ITALIA
DALMATIA
ILLYRICUM
EPIRUS
ACHAIA
GREECE
IONIAN ISLANDS
LIBYA
CYRENAICA
EGYPT
IDUMEA
PHOENICIA
ROME
The 3 Taverns
Appii Forum
Puteoli
Rhegium
Messina
Syracuse
MELITA
Cyrene
Alexandria
Mouths of the Nile
Philippi
Neapolis
Amphipolis
Apollonia
Thessalonica
Berea
Nicopolis
Corinth
Athens
Sparta
Troas
Assos
Mitylene
Lesbos
Chios
Samos
Miletus
Ephesus
Smyrna
Philadelphia
Sardis
Thyatira
Pergamos
Laodicea
Colosse
Hierapolis
Antioch
Iconium
Lystra
Derbe
Perga
Patara
Myra
Rhodes
Cnidus
Patmos
Salamis
Paphos
Seleucia
Antioch
Sidon
Tyre
Ptolemais
Caesarea
Antipatris
Joppa
JERUSALEM
Azotus
Gaza
Damascus
Phenice
Clauda I.
Fair Haven
Lasea
Longitude East 26 from Greenwich

NOTES,

EXPLANATORY AND PRACTICAL,

ON THE

ACTS OF THE APOSTLES.

DESIGNED FOR

BIBLE-CLASSES AND SUNDAY-SCHOOLS.

BY ALBERT BARNES.

TWELFTH EDITION.

NEW YORK:
HARPER & BROTHERS, PUBLISHERS,
329 & 331 PEARL STREET,
FRANKLIN SQUARE.
1854.

INTRODUCTION.

THERE is no evidence that the title "The Acts of the Apostles" affixed to this book, was given by divine authority, or by the writer himself. It is a title, however, which, with a little variation, has been given to it by the Christian church at all times. The term "Acts" is not used as it is sometimes with us to denote *decrees* or *laws*, but it denotes the *doings* of the apostles. It is a record of what the apostles did in founding and establishing the Christian church. It is worthy of remark, however, that it contains chiefly a record of the *doings* of Peter and Paul. Peter was commissioned to open the doors of the Christian church to both Jews and Gentiles (see Note, Matt. xvi. 18, 19); and Paul was chosen to bear the gospel especially to the pagan world. As these two apostles were the most prominent and distinguished in founding and organizing the Christian church, it was deemed proper that a special and permanent record should be made of their labours. At the same time, occasional notices are given of the other apostles; but of their labours elsewhere than in Judea, and of their death, except that of James (Acts xii. 2), the sacred writers have given no information.

All antiquity is unanimous in ascribing this book to Luke, as its author. It is repeatedly mentioned and quoted by the early Christian writers, and without a dissenting voice is mentioned as the work of Luke. The same thing is clear from the book itself. It professes to have been written by the same person who wrote the Gospel of Luke (ch. i. 1); was addressed to the same person (comp. ver. 1 with Luke i. 3); and bears manifest marks of being from the same pen. It is designed evidently as a continuation of his Gospel, as in this book he has taken up the history at the very time where he left it in the Gospel (ver. 1. 2).

Where, or at what time, this book was written is not certainly known. As the history however, is continued to the second year of the residence of Paul at Rome (Acts xxviii. 31), it was evidently written about as late as the year 62; and as it makes no mention of the further dealings with Paul, or of any other event of history, it seems clear that it was not written much *after* that time. It has been common, therefore, to fix the date of the book at about A. D. 63. It is also probable that it was written at Rome. In ch. xxviii. 16, Luke mentions *his* arrival at Rome with Paul. As he does not mention his departure from this city, it is to be presumed that it was written there. Some have supposed that it was written at Alexandria in Egypt, but of that there is no sufficient evidence.

The canonical authority of this book rests on the same foundation as that of the Gospel by the same author. Its authenticity has not been called in question at any time in the church.

This book has commonly been regarded as a history of the Christian church, and of course the first ecclesiastical history that was written.

But it cannot have been designed as a general history of the church. Many important transactions have been omitted. It gives no account of the church at Jerusalem after the conversion of Paul; it omits his journey into Arabia (Gal. i. 17); gives no account of the propagation of the gospel in Egypt, or in Babylon (1 Pet. v. 13); of the foundation of the church at Rome; of many of Paul's voyages and shipwrecks (2 Cor. xi. 25); and omits to record the labours of most of the apostles, and confines the narrative chiefly to the transactions of Peter and Paul.

The design and importance of this history may be learned from the following particulars:

1. It contains *a record of the promised descent and operations of the Holy Spirit.* The Lord Jesus promised that after he had departed to heaven, he would send the Holy Ghost to carry forward the great work of redemption. John xiv. 16, 17; xv. 26; xvi. 7—14. The apostles were directed to tarry in Jerusalem until they were endued with power from on high. Luke xxiv. 49. The four Gospels contained a record of the life, instructions, death, and resurrection of the Lord Jesus. But it is clear that he contemplated that the most signal triumphs of the gospel should take place after his ascension to heaven, and under the influence of the Holy Spirit. The descent of the Spirit, and his influence on the souls of men, was a most important part of the work of redemption. Without an authentic, an inspired record of that, the account of the operations of God the Father, Son, and Spirit, in the work of redemption, would not have been complete. The purposes of *the Father* in regard to that plan were made known clearly in the Old Testament; the record of what *the Son* did in accomplishing it, was contained in the Gospels; and some book was needful that should contain a record of the *doings* of the Holy Spirit. As the Gospels, therefore, may be regarded as a record of the work of Christ to save men, so may the Acts of the Apostles be considered as a record of the doings of the Holy Spirit in the same great work. Without that, the way in which the Spirit operates to renew and save would have been very imperfectly known.

2. This book is *an inspired account of the character of true revivals of religion.* It records the first revivals that occurred in the Christian church. The scene on the day of Pentecost was one of the most remarkable displays of divine power and mercy that the world has ever known. It was the commencement of a series of stupendous movements in the world to recover men. It was the true model of a revival of religion, and a perpetual demonstration that such scenes as have characterized our own age and nation especially, are strictly in accordance with the spirit of the New Testament. The entire book of the Acts of the Apostles records the effect of the gospel when it comes fairly in contact with the minds of men. The gospel was addressed to every class. It met the Jew and the Gentile, the bond and the free, the learned and the ignorant, the rich and the poor; and showed its power every where in subduing the mind to itself. It was proper that some record should be preserved of the displays of that power; and that record we have in this book. And it was especially proper that there should be given by an inspired man an account of the descent of the Holy Spirit, *a record of a true revival of religion.* It was certain that the gospel would produce excitement. The human mind, as all experience shows, is prone to enthusiasm and fanaticism; and men might be disposed to

pervert the gospel to scenes of wild-fire, disorder, and tumult. That the gospel *would* produce excitement, was well known to its Author. It was well therefore that there should be some record to which the church might always appeal as an infallible account of the proper effects of the gospel; some inspired standard to which might be brought all excitements on the subject of religion. If they are in accordance with the first triumphs of the gospel, they are genuine; if not, they are false.

3. It may be further remarked, that this book shows that *revivals of religion are to be expected in the church.* If they existed in the best and purest days of Christianity, they are to be expected now. If by means of revivals the Holy Spirit chose at first to bless the preaching of the truth, the same thing is to be expected still. If in this way the gospel was at first spread among the nations, then we are to infer that this will be the mode in which it will finally spread and triumph in the world.

4. The Acts of the Apostles contains a record of the organization of the Christian church. That church was founded simply by the preaching of the truth, and chiefly by a simple statement of the death and resurrection of Jesus Christ. The "Acts of the Apostles" contains the highest models of preaching, and the purest specimens of that simple, direct, and pungent manner of addressing men, which may be expected to be attended with the influences of the Holy Spirit. It contains some of the most tender, powerful, and eloquent appeals to be found in any language. If a man wishes to learn how to preach well, he can probably acquire it nowhere else so readily as by giving himself to the prayerful and profound study of the specimens contained in this book. At the same time we have here a view of the *character* of the true church of Christ. The *simplicity* of this church must strike every reader of "the Acts." Religion is represented as a work of the heart; the pure and proper effect of *truth* on the mind. It is free from pomp and splendour, and from costly and magnificent ceremonies. There is no apparatus to impress the senses, no splendour to dazzle, no external rite or parade adapted to draw the affections from the pure and spiritual worship of God. How unlike to the pomp and parade of pagan worship! How unlike the vain and pompous ceremonies which have since, alas! crept into no small part of the Christian church!

5. In this book we have many striking and impressive illustrations of what the gospel is fitted to produce, to make men self-denying and benevolent. The apostles engaged in the great enterprise of converting the world. To secure that, they cheerfully forsook all. Paul became a convert to the Christian faith, and cheerfully for that gave up all his hopes of preferment and honour, and welcomed toil and privation in foreign lands. The early converts had all things in common (ch. ii. 44); those "which had curious arts," and were gaining property by a course of iniquity, forsook their schemes of ill-gotten gain, and burned their books publicly (ch. xix. 19); Ananias and Sapphira were punished for attempting to impose on the apostles by hypocritical professed self-denials (ch. v. 1—10); and throughout the book there occur constant instances of sacrifices and toil to spread the gospel around the globe. Indeed, these great truths had manifestly seized upon the early Christians: *that the gospel was to be preached to all nations; and that whatever stood in the way of that was to be sacrificed; whatever toils and dangers were necessary, were to be borne; and even death itself was cheerfully to be met, if it would pro-*

mote the spread of true religion. This was *then* genuine Christianity; this is *still* the spirit of the gospel of Christ.

6. This book throws important light on *the Epistles.* It is a connecting link between the Gospels and the other parts of the New Testament. Instances of this will be noticed in the Notes. One of the most clear and satisfactory evidences of the genuineness of the books of the New Testament is to be found in the *undesigned coincidences* between the Acts and the Epistles. This argument was first clearly stated and illustrated by Dr. Paley. His little work illustrating it, the *Horæ Paulinæ*, is one of the most unanswerable proofs which have yet been furnished of the truth of the Christian religion.

7. This book contains unanswerable evidence of the truth of the Christian religion. It is a record of the early triumphs of Christianity. Within the space of *thirty years* after the death of Christ, the gospel had been carried to all parts of the civilized, and to no small portion of the uncivilized world. Its progress and its triumphs were not concealed. Its great transactions were not "done in a corner." It had been preached in the most splendid, powerful, and corrupt cities; churches were already founded in Jerusalem, Antioch, Corinth, Ephesus, Philippi, and at Rome. The gospel had spread in Arabia, Asia Minor, Greece, Macedon, Italy, and Africa. It had assailed the most mighty existing institutions; it had made its way over the most formidable barriers; it had encountered the most deadly and malignant opposition; it had travelled to the capital, and had secured such a hold even in the imperial city, as to make it certain that it would finally overturn the established religion, and seat itself on the ruins of paganism. Within thirty years it had settled the point that it would overturn every bloody altar; close every pagan temple; bring under its influence the men of office, rank, and power; and that "the banners of the faith would soon stream from the palaces of the Cæsars." All this would be accomplished by the instrumentality of Jews—of fishermen—of Nazarenes. They had neither wealth, armies, nor allies. With the exception of Paul, they were men without learning. They were taught only by the Holy Ghost; armed only with the power of God; victorious only because he was their captain; and the world acknowledged the presence of the messengers of the Highest, and the power of the Christian religion. Its success never has been, and never can be accounted for by any other supposition than that God attended it. And if the Christian religion be not true, the change wrought by the twelve apostles is the most inexplicable, mysterious, and wonderful event that has ever been witnessed in this world. Their success to the end of time will stand as an argument of the truth of the scheme, that shall confound the infidel, and sustain the Christian with the assured belief that *this* is a religion which has proceeded from the almighty and infinitely benevolent God.

THE ACTS OF THE APOSTLES.

CHAPTER I.

THE former treatise [a] have I made, O Theophilus, of all that Jesus began both to do and teach,

2 Until [b] the day in which he was taken up, after that he through the Holy Ghost had given commandments [c] unto the apostles whom he had chosen:

a Lu.1.1-4, &c. b Lu.24.51. ver.9. 1Ti.3.16. c Matt.28.19. Mar.16.15-19.

1. *The former treatise.* The former *book.* The Gospel by Luke is here evidently intended. Greek, 'the former *Logos,*' meaning a *discourse,* or a narrative. ¶ *O Theophilus.* See Note, Luke i. 3. As this book was written to the same individual as the former, it was evidently written with the same design—to furnish an authentic and full narrative of events concerning which there would be many imperfect and exaggerated accounts given. See Luke i. 1—4. As these events pertained to the descent of the Spirit, to the spread of the gospel, to the organization of the church by inspired authority, to the kind of preaching by which the church was collected and organized; and as those events were a full proof of the truth and power of the Christian religion, and would be a model for ministers and the church in all future times, it was of great importance that a fair and full narrative of them should be preserved. Luke was the companion of Paul in his travels, and was an eye-witness of no small part of the transactions recorded in this book. See Acts xvi. 10. 17; xx. 1–6; xxvii. xxviii. As an eye-witness, he was well qualified to make a record of the leading events of the primitive church. And as he was the companion of Paul, he had every opportunity of obtaining information about the great events of the gospel of Christ. ¶ *Of all.* That is, of the principal, or most important parts of the life and doctrines of Christ. It cannot mean that he recorded *all* that Jesus did, as he has omitted many things that have been preserved by the other Evangelists. The word *all* is frequently thus used to denote the most important or material facts. See Acts xiii. 10. 1 Tim. i. 16. James i. 2. Matt. ii. 3; iii. 5. Acts ii. 5. Rom. xi. 26. Col. i. 6. In each of these places the word here translated "all" occurs in the original, and means *many, a large part, the principal portion.* It has the same use in all languages. "This word often signifies, indefinitely, a large portion or number, or a great part." *Webster.* ¶ *That Jesus.* The Syriac version adds, "Jesus our Messiah." This version was probably made in the second century ¶ *Began to do.* This is a Hebrew form of expression, meaning the same thing as, that Jesus *did* and *taught.* See Gen. ix. 20, "Noah *began* to be an husbandman," i. e. *was* an husbandman. Gen. ii. 3, in the Septuagint: "Which God *began* to create and make;" in the Hebrew, "which God created and made." Mark vi. 7, "*Began* to send them forth by two and two," i. e. *sent* them forth. See also Mark x. 32; xiv. 65, "And some *began* to spit on him;" in the parallel place in Matt. xxvi. 67, "they *did* spit in his face." ¶ *To do.* This refers to his miracles and his acts of benevolence, including all that he *did* for man's salvation. It probably includes, therefore, his sufferings, death, and resurrection, as a part of what he has *done* to save men. ¶ *To teach.* His doctrines. As he had given an account of what the Lord Jesus did, so he was now about to give a narrative of what his apostles did in the same cause, that thus the world might be in possession of an inspired record respecting the redemption and establishment of the Christian church. The history of these events is one of the greatest blessings that God has conferred on mankind; and one of the highest privileges which men can enjoy is that which has been conferred so abundantly on this age in the possession and extension of the word of God.

2. *Until the day.* The fortieth day after his resurrection, ver. 3. See Luke xxiv. 51. ¶ *In which he was taken up.* In which he ascended to heaven. He was taken up into a cloud, and is represented as having been *borne* or carried to heaven, ver. 9. ¶ *After that, &c.* This whole passage has been variously rendered The Syriac renders it, "After he had given commandment unto the apostles whom he had chosen by the Holy Spirit." So also the Ethiopic version. Others

3 To whom also he showed himself after his passion, by many [a] infallible proofs, being seen of them forty days, and speaking of the things pertaining to the kingdom of God;

a Lu.24. Jno.c.20. & 21.

have joined the words "through the Holy Ghost" to the phrase "was taken up," making it mean that he was taken up by the Holy Ghost. But the most natural and correct translation seems to be that which is in our version. ¶ *Through the Holy Ghost.* To understand this it is necessary to call to mind the promise that Jesus made before his death, that after his departure, the Holy Ghost would descend to be a guide to his apostles. See John xvi. 7—11, and the Note on that place. It was to be *his* office to carry forward the work of redemption in applying it to the hearts of men. Whatever was done, therefore, *after* the atonement and resurrection of Jesus, *after* he had finished his great work, was to be regarded as under the peculiar influence and direction of the Holy Ghost. Even the instructions of Jesus, his commission to the apostles &c. were to be regarded as coming within the department of the sacred Spirit, within the province of *his* peculiar work. The instructions were given by divine authority, by infallible guidance, and as a part of the work which the Holy Spirit designed. Under that Spirit the apostles were to go forth; by *his* aid they were to convert the world, to organize the church, to establish its order and its doctrines. And hence the entire work was declared to be by his direction. Though in his larger and more mighty influences, the Spirit did not descend until the day of Pentecost (Luke xxiv. 49. comp. Acts ii.) yet *in some measure* his influence was imparted to them before the ascension of Christ. John xx. 22. ¶ *Had given commandments.* Particularly the command to preach the gospel to all nations. Matt. xxviii. 19. Mark xvi. 15—19. It may be worthy of remark, that the word *commandments*, as a noun in the plural number, does not occur in the original. The single word which is translated "had given commandments" is a *participle*, and means simply *having commanded*. There is no need, therefore, of supposing that there is reference here to any other command than to that great and glorious injunction to preach the gospel to every creature. That was a command of so much importance as to be worthy of a distinct record, as constituting the sum of all that the Saviour taught them after his resurrection ¶ *The apostles.* The eleven that remained after the treason and death of Judas. ¶ *Whom he had chosen.* Matt. x. Luke vi. 12—16.

3. *He shewed himself.* The *resurrection* of Jesus was the great fact on which the truth of the gospel was to be established. Hence the sacred writers so often refer to it, and establish it by so many arguments. As that *truth* lay at the foundation of all that Luke was about to record in his history, it was of importance that he should state clearly the sum of the evidence of it in the beginning of his work. ¶ *After his passion.* After he *suffered*, referring particularly to his death, as the consummation of his sufferings. The word *passion* with us means commonly excitement, or agitation of mind, as love, hope, fear, anger, &c. In the original the word means to *suffer*. The word *passion*, applied to the Saviour, denotes his last sufferings. Thus in the Litany of the Episcopal church, it is beautifully said, "by thine agony and bloody sweat; by thy cross and *passion*, good Lord, deliver us." The Greek word of the same derivation is rendered *sufferings* in 1 Pet. i. 11; iv. 13. Col. i. 24. ¶ *By many infallible proofs.* The word rendered here *infallible proofs*, does not occur elsewhere in the New Testament. In Greek authors it denotes an infallible sign or argument by which any thing can be certainly known. *Schleusner.* Here it means the same—evidence that he was alive which could not deceive, or in which they could not be mistaken. That evidence consisted in his eating with them, conversing with them, meeting them at various times and places, working miracles (John xxi. 6, 7); and uniformly showing himself to be the same friend with whom they had been familiar for more than three years. This evidence was infallible, (1.) Because it was to them unexpected. They had manifestly not believed that he would rise again. John xx. 25. Luke xxiv. There was therefore no *delusion* resulting from any *expectation* of seeing him, or from a *design* to impose on men. (2.) It was impossible that they could have been *deceived* in relation to one with whom they had been familiar for more than three years. No men could be imposed upon and made to believe that they really saw, talked with, and ate with, a friend whom they had known so

4 And [1] being assembled together with *them*, commanded [a] them
that they should not depart from Jerusalem, but wait for the promise
of the Father, which, *saith he*, Ye [b]
have heard of me:
5 For John [c] truly baptized with
water; but ye shall be baptized with

[1] or, *eating together*. a Lu.24.49. b Jno.c.14,15, & 16. c Matt.3.11.

long and familiarly, unless it was real. (3.) There were *enough* of them to avoid the possibility of deception. Though it might be pretended that *one* man could be imposed on, yet it could not be that an imposition could be practised for forty days on eleven, who were all at first incredulous. (4.) He was with them sufficient *time* to give evidence. It might be pretended, if they had seen him but *once*, that they were deceived. But they saw him often, and for the space of more than a month. (5.) They saw him in *various places* and times where there could be no deception. If they had pretended that they saw him *rise*, or saw him at twilight in the morning *when* he rose, it might have been said that they were deluded by some remarkable appearance. Or it might have been said that, *expecting* to see him rise, their hopes and agitations would have deceived them, and they would easily have *fancied* that they saw him. But it is not pretended by the sacred writers that *they saw him rise*. An impostor would have affirmed this, and *would not have omitted it*. But the sacred writers affirmed that they saw him *after* he was risen; when they were free from agitation; when they could judge coolly; in Jerusalem; in their company when at worship; when journeying to Emmaus; when in Galilee; when he went with them to mount Olivet; and when he ascended to heaven. (5.) He appeared to them as he had always done; as a friend, companion, and benefactor: he ate with them; wrought a miracle before them; was engaged in the same work as he was before he suffered; renewed the same promise of the Holy Spirit; and gave them his commands respecting the work which he had died to establish and promote. In all these circumstances it was impossible that they should be deceived. ¶ *Being seen of them forty days.* There are no less than THIRTEEN different appearances of Jesus to his disciples recorded. For an account of them see the Note at the end of the Gospel of Matthew. ¶ *Speaking to them*, &c. He was not only *seen* by them, but he *continued the same topics of discourse* as before his sufferings; thus showing that he was the *same* person that had suffered, and that his heart was still intent on the same great work. Our Saviour's heart was filled with the same design in his life and death, and when he rose; thus showing us that we should aim at the same great work in all the circumstances of our being. Afflictions, persecutions, and death never turned *him* from this great plan; nor should they be allowed to divert *our* minds from the great work of redemption. ¶ *The things pertaining to the kingdom of God.* For an explanation of this phrase, *the kingdom of God*, see the Note on Matt. iii. 2. The meaning is, Jesus gave them instructions about the organization, spread, and edification of his church.

4. *And being assembled together.* Margin, "or, *eating together*." This sense is given to this place in the Latin Vulgate, the Ethiopic, and the Syriac versions. But the Greek word has not properly this sense. It has the meaning of *congregating*, or *assembling*. It should have been, however, translated in the *active* sense, "and *having assembled* them together." The apostles were scattered after his death. But this passage denotes that *he* had assembled them together by his authority, for the purpose of giving them a charge respecting their conduct when he should have left them. *When* this occurred, does not appear from the narrative; but it is probable that it was not long before his ascension: and it is clear that the *place* where they were assembled was *Jerusalem*. ¶ *But wait for the promise of the Father.* For the *fulfilment* of the promise respecting the descent of the Holy Spirit, made by the Father. ¶ *Which ye have heard of me.* Which I have made to you. See John xiv. 16. 26; xv. 26; xvi. 7—13.

5. *For John truly baptized*, &c. These are the words of Jesus to his apostles, and he evidently has reference to what was said of John's baptism compared with his own in Matt. iii. 11. John i. 33. In those verses John is represented as baptizing with water, but the Messiah who was to come as baptizing with the Holy Ghost and with fire. This promise respecting the Messiah was now about to be fulfilled in a remarkable manner. See Acts ii. ¶ *Not many days hence.* This was probably spoken not long before his ascension, and of course not many days before the day of Pentecost.

the Holy Ghost, [a] not many days
hence.
6 When they therefore were come
together, they asked of him, saying,
Lord, wilt [b] thou at this time restore [c] again the kingdom to Israel?
7 And he said unto them, It [d] is
not for you to know the times or
the seasons which the Father hath
put in his own power.

a c.2.4;10.45;11.15. b Matt.24.3,4. c Is.1.26. Da.7.27. d Matt.24.36. 1Th.5.1,2.

6. *When they therefore were come together.* At the mount of Olives. See ver. 9. 12 ¶ *Wilt thou at this time, &c.* The apostles had entertained the common opinions of the Jews about the *temporal* dominion of the Messiah. They expected that he would reign as a prince and conqueror, and free them from the bondage of the Romans. Many instances of this expectation occur in the Gospels, notwithstanding all the efforts which the Lord Jesus made to explain to them the true nature of his kingdom. This expectation was checked, and almost destroyed by his death. Luke xxiv. 21. And it is clear that *his death* was the only means which could effectually check and change their opinions respecting the nature of his kingdom. Even his own instructions would not do it; and only his being taken from them could direct their minds effectually to the true nature of his kingdom. Yet, though his death checked their expectations, and appeared to thwart their plans, yet his return to life excited them again. They beheld him with them; they were assured it was the same Saviour; they saw now that his enemies had no power over him; that a being who could rise from the dead, could easily accomplish all his plans. And as they did not doubt now that he *would* restore the kingdom to Israel, they asked whether he would do it *at this time?* They did not ask whether he would do it at all, or whether they had correct views of his kingdom; but taking that for granted, they asked him whether *that was the time* in which he would do it. The emphasis of the inquiry lies in the expression, "*at this time,*" and hence the answer of the Saviour refers solely *to the point of their inquiry,* and not to the correctness or incorrectness of their opinions. From these expectations of the apostles we may learn, 1. That there is nothing so difficult to be removed from the mind as *prejudice in favour of erroneous opinions.* 2. That such prejudice will survive the plainest proofs to the contrary. 3. That it will often manifest itself even after all proper means have been taken to subdue it. Erroneous opinions thus maintain a secret ascendency in a man's mind, and are revived by the slightest circumstances, even long after we supposed they were overcome; and even in the face of the plainest proofs of reason or of Scripture. ¶ *Restore* Bring back; put into its former situation. Judea was formerly governed by its own kings and laws; now, it was subject to the Romans. This bondage was grievous, and the nation sighed for deliverance. The inquiry of the apostles evidently was, whether he would now free them from the bondage of the Romans, and restore them to their former state of freedom and prosperity, as in the times of David and Solomon. See Isa. i. 26. The word "restore" also may include more than a reducing it to its former state. It may mean, wilt thou now *bestow* the kingdom and dominion to Israel, according to the prediction in Dan. vii. 27. ¶ *The kingdom.* The dominion; the empire; the reign. The expectation was that the Messiah—the king of Israel—would *reign* over men, and thus the nation of the Jews extend their empire over all the earth. ¶ *To Israel.* To the Jews, and particularly to the *Jewish* followers of the Messiah. Lightfoot thinks that this question was asked in indignation against the Jews. "Wilt thou confer dominion on a nation which has just put thee to death?" But the answer of the Saviour shows that this was not the design of the question.

7. *It is not for you to know.* The question of the apostles respected the *time* of the restoration; it was not whether he *would* do it. Accordingly his answer meets precisely their inquiry; and he tells them *in general* that the *time* of the great events of God's kingdom was not to be understood by them. A similar question they had asked in Matt. xxiv. 3, "Tell us when shall these things be?" Jesus answered them *then* by showing them certain signs which should precede his coming, and by saying (ver. 36), "But of that day and that hour knoweth no man, no, not the angels of heaven, but my Father only." God has uniformly reproved a vain curiosity on such points. 1 Thess. v. 1, 2. 2 Pet. iii. 10. Luke xii. 39, 40. ¶ *The times, or the seasons.* The difference between these words is, that the former de-

8 But ye shall receive [1] power,
after that the Holy Ghost is come
upon you: and ye [a] shall be witnesses unto me, both in Jerusalem,
and in all Judea, and in Samaria,

[1] or, *the power of the Holy Ghost coming upon you.*

[a] Lu.24.47–49. Mat.28.19.

notes any time or period indefinite, or uncertain; the latter denotes a fixed, definite, or appropriate time. They seem to be used here to denote the periods of all classes of future events. ¶ *The Father hath put,* &c. So much had the Father reserved the knowledge of these, that it is said that even the Son did not know them. See Mark xiii. 32, and the Note on that place. ¶ *In his own power.* That is, he has fixed them by his own authority; he will bring them about in his own time and way; and therefore it is not proper for men anxiously to inquire into them. All prophecy is remarkably *obscure* in regard to the *time* of its fulfilment. The reasons are, (1.) To excite men to watch for the events that are to come, as the time is uncertain, and they will come "like a thief in the night." (2.) As they are to be brought about by human agency, they are so arranged as to call forth that agency. If men knew *just when* an event was to come to pass, they might be remiss, and feel that their effort was not needed. (3.) The knowledge of future scenes—of the exact *time,* might alarm men, and absorb their thoughts entirely, and prevent attendance to the present duties of life. Duty is ours now; God will provide for future scenes. (4.) Promises sufficiently clear and full are therefore given us to encourage us; but not full enough to excite a vain and idle curiosity. All this is eminently true of our own death, one of the most important future scenes through which *we* are to pass. It is *certainly* before us; it is *near; it cannot* be long avoided; it *may come* at any moment. God has fixed the time, but will not inform us when it shall be. He does not gratify a vain curiosity, or terrify us, by announcing to us the day or the hour when we are to die, as we do a man that is to be executed. This would be to make our lives like that of a criminal sentenced to die, and we should through all our life through fear of death be subject to bondage. Heb. ii. 15. He has made *enough* known to excite us to prepare, and to be always ready, having our loins girt about, and our lamps trimmed and burning. Luke xii. 35.

8. *But ye shall receive power,* &c. Literally, as it is translated in the margin, "ye shall receive the power of the Holy Ghost coming upon you." This was said to them to console them. Though they could not know the *times* which God reserved in his own appointment, yet they should receive the promised guide and comforter. The word *power* here refers to all the help or aid which the Holy Spirit would grant; the power of speaking with new tongues; of preaching the gospel with great effect; of enduring great trials, &c. See Mark xvi. 17, 18. The apostles had *impatiently* asked him if he was *then* about to restore the kingdom to Israel. Jesus by this answer rebuked their impatience; taught them to repress their ill-timed ardour; and assured them again of the coming of the Holy Ghost. ¶ *Ye shall be witnesses.* For this purpose, they were appointed; and for this design they had been with him for more than three years. They had seen his manner of life, his miracles, his meekness, his sufferings; they had listened to his instructions, had conversed and eaten with him as a friend; they had seen him after he was risen, and were about to see him ascend to heaven; and they were *qualified* to bear witness to all these things in all parts of the earth. They were so numerous, that it could not be pretended that they were deceived; they had been so intimate with him and his plans, that they could testify of him; and there was no motive but conviction of the truth, that could lead them to all these sacrifices in making known the Saviour. The original word here is μαρτυρες, *martyrs.* From this word the name *martyrs* has been given to those who suffered in times of persecution. The reason why this name was given to them was that they *bore witness* to the life, instructions, death, and resurrection of the Lord Jesus, even in the midst of persecution and death. It is commonly supposed that nearly all of the apostles thus bore witness to the Lord Jesus: of this, however, there is not clear proof. See Mosheim's Ecclesiastical History, vol. i. p. 55, 56. Still the word here does not necessarily mean that they should be *martyrs,* or be put to death in bearing witness to the Lord Jesus; but that they should every where testify to what they knew of him. The fact that this was the design of their appointment, and that they actually bore such testimony, is abundantly confirmed in the

and unto the uttermost part of the earth.

9 And when he had spoken these things, while they beheld, he was taken up; and a cloud received him out of their sight.

Acts of the Apostles, ch. i. 22; v. 32; x. 39. 42; xxii. 15. ¶ *In Jerusalem.* In the capital of the nation. See Acts ii. The great work of the Spirit on the day of Pentecost occurred there. Most of the disciples remained in Jerusalem until the persecution that arose about the death of Stephen. Acts viii. 1. 4. The apostles remained there till Herod put James to death. Comp. Acts viii. 1, with xii. 1. This was about eight years. During this time, however, Paul was called to the apostleship, and Peter had preached the gospel to Cornelius, Philip to the eunuch, &c. ¶ *In all Judea.* Judea was the southern division of the Holy Land, and included Jerusalem as the capital. See Note, Matt. ii. 22. See ch. viii. 1. ¶ *And in Samaria.* This was the *middle* portion of Palestine. Note, Matt. ii. 22. This was fulfilled by the disciples. See ch. viii. 1, "And they were all scattered abroad throughout the regions of Judea and Samaria (ver. 4), every where preaching the word." viii. 5, "Then Philip went down to the city of Samaria, and preached Christ unto them." ver. 14; ix. 31. ¶ *And unto the uttermost parts of the earth.* The word *earth*, or *land*, is sometimes taken to denote only the land of Palestine. But here, there does not seem to be a necessity for limiting it thus. If Christ had intended that, he would have mentioned *Galilee*, as being the only remaining division. But as he had expressly directed them to preach the gospel to all nations, the expression here is clearly to be considered as including the Gentile lands as well as the Jewish. The evidence that they did this, is found in the subsequent parts of this book, and in the history of the church. In this way Jesus replied to their question. Though he did not tell them the *time* when it was to be done, nor did he affirm that he would restore the kingdom to *Israel*, yet he gave them an answer that *implied* that the work should advance—should advance much farther than the land of Israel; and that *they* would have *much to do* in promoting it. All the commands of God, and all his communications are such as to call up our energy, and teach us that *we* have much to do. The uttermost parts of the earth have been given to the Saviour (Ps. ii. 8); and churches should not rest until he whose right it is shall come and reign. Ezek. xxi. 27.

9. *While they beheld.* While they *saw* him. It was of importance to state that circumstance, and to state it distinctly. It is not affirmed in the New Testament that they *saw him rise* from the dead; because the evidence of that fact could be better established by their seeing him *after* he was risen. But the truth of his *ascension to heaven* could not be confirmed in that manner. Hence it was so arranged as that he should ascend in open day; in the presence of his apostles; and that not when they were asleep, or indifferent, but when they were engaged in a conversation that should fix the attention, and when they were looking upon him. Had Jesus vanished secretly, or in the night, the apostles would have been amazed and confounded; perhaps they would even have doubted whether they had not been deceived. But when they *saw* him leave them in this manner, they could not doubt that he had risen; and when they saw him ascend *to heaven*, they could not doubt that his work was approved, and that God would carry it onward. This event was exceedingly important. (1.) It was a confirmation of the truth of the Christian religion. (2.) It enabled the apostles to state distinctly *where* the Lord Jesus was, and *at once* directed their affections and their thoughts away from the earth, and opened their eyes on the glory of the scheme of religion they were to establish. If their Saviour was *in heaven*, it settled the question about the *nature* of his kingdom. It was clear that it was not designed to be a temporal kingdom. The *reasons* why it was proper that the Lord Jesus should ascend to heaven rather than remain on earth, were, (1.) That he had *finished* the work which God gave him to do *on the earth* (John xvii. 4; xix. 30), and it was *proper* that he should be received back to the glory which he had with the Father before the world was. John xvii. 4, 5. Phil. ii. 6. 9, 10. (2.) It was proper that *he* should ascend, that the Holy Spirit might come down and perform *his* part of the work of redemption. Jesus, by his *personal* ministry, as a man, could be but in one place; the Holy Spirit could be in all places, and be present at all times, and could apply the work to all men. Note, John xvi. 7. (3.) A *part* of the work of Christ was yet to be performed in heaven. That was the work of *intercession*. The high-priest of the Jews not only made

10 And while they looked steadfastly toward heaven, as he went up, behold, two[a] men stood by them in white apparel;

11 Which also said, Ye men[b] of Galilee, why stand ye gazing up into heaven? This same Jesus, which is taken up from you into

a Jn. 20.12.

b c.2.7;13.31.

an *atonement*, but also presented the blood of sacrifice before the mercy-seat, as the priest of the people. Lev. xvi. 11—14. This was done to typify the entrance of the great High-priest of our profession into the heavens. Heb. ix. 7, 8. 11, 12. The work which he performs there is the work of *intercession*. Heb. vii. 25. This is properly the work which an advocate performs in a court of justice for his client. It means that Christ, our great High-priest, still pleads and manages our cause in heaven; secures our interests; obtains for us grace and mercy. It consists in his appearing in the presence of God for us (Heb. ix. 24); in his presenting the merits of his blood (Heb.ix.12.14); and in securing the continuance of the mercy which has been bestowed on us, and which is still needful for our welfare. The Lord Jesus also ascended that he might assume and exercise the office of *King* in the immediate seat of power. All worlds were subject to him for the welfare of the church; and it was needful that he should be solemnly invested with that power in the presence of God, as the reward of his earthly toils. 1 Cor. xv. 25. "He must reign till he hath put all enemies under his feet." Eph. i. 20—22. Phil. ii. 6—11. ¶ *A cloud received him.* He entered into the region of the clouds, and was hid from their view. But *two* others of our race have been taken bodily from earth to heaven. Enoch was translated (Gen. v. 24. Comp. Heb. xi. 5); and Elijah was taken by a whirlwind to heaven. 2 Kings ii. 11. It is remarkable that when the *return* of the Saviour is mentioned, it is uniformly said that he will return *in the clouds*. ver. 11. Matt. xxiv. 30; xxvi. 64. Mark xiii. 26. Rev. i. 7. Dan. vii. 13. The clouds are an emblem of sublimity and grandeur, and perhaps this is all that is intended by these expressions. Deut. iv. 11. 2 Sam. xxii. 12. Ps. xcvii. 2; civ. 3.

10. *Looked steadfastly.* They fixed their eyes, or gazed intently toward heaven. Luke iv. 20, "And the eyes of all them in the synagogue *were fastened* (Greek, the same word as here) on him." It means the intense gaze when we are deeply interested, and wish to see clearly and distinctly. Here they were amazed and confounded; the thing was unlooked-for; and they were even *then* inquiring whether he would not restore the kingdom to Israel. With this mingled amazement, and disappointment, and curiosity; and with the earnest desire to catch the last glimpse of their beloved master, they naturally continued to gaze on the distant clouds where he had mysteriously disappeared from their view. Never was a scene more impressive, grand, and solemn than this. ¶ *Toward heaven.* Toward the distant clouds or sky which had received him. ¶ *As he went up.* Literally, "*The ascending, or going up.*" Doubtless they continued to gaze after he had departed from their view. ¶ *Two men.* From the *raiment* of these "men" and the nature of their message, it seems clear that they were angelic beings, who were sent to meet and comfort the disciples on this occasion. They appeared in *human form*, and Luke describes them as they appeared. Angels are not unfrequently called *men*. Luke xxiv. 4, "Two *men* stood by them in shining garments," &c. Comp. John xx. 12. Matt. xxviii. 5. As *two* angels are mentioned only as addressing the apostles after the resurrection of Jesus (John xx. 12. Luke xxiv. 4), it is no unnatural supposition that these were the same who had been designated to the honourable office of bearing witness to his resurrection, and of giving them all the information about that resurrection, and of his ascension, which their circumstances needed. ¶ *In white apparel.* Angels are commonly represented as clothed in white. Note, John xx. 12. Matt. xxviii. 3. Mark xvi. 5. It is an emblem of purity; and the worshippers of heaven are represented as clothed in this manner. Rev. iii. 4, "They shall walk with me in white." 5, "He that overcometh shall be clothed in white raiment." iv. 4; vii. 9. 13, 14.

11. *Ye men of Galilee.* Galilee was the place of their former residence; and this was the name by which they were commonly known. There is no evidence that the angel intended this name in any way to reproach them. ¶ *Why stand ye,* &c. There is doubtless a *slight* degree of censure implied in this, as well as a design to call their attention away from a vain attempt to see the departed Sa-

heaven, shall[a] so come in like manner as ye have seen him go into heaven.

a Jno.14.3. 1Th.4.16.

viour. The impropriety *may* have been, (1.) In the feeling of disappointment, as if he would *not* restore the kingdom to Israel (2.) Possibly they were expecting that he would again *soon* appear; though he had often foretold them that he would ascend to heaven. (3.) There might have been an impropriety in their earnest desire for the mere *bodily presence* of the Lord Jesus, when it was more important that it should be in heaven. We may see here also that it is our duty not to stand in idleness, and to gaze *even* towards heaven. We, as well as the apostles, have a great work to do, and we should actively engage in it without delay. ¶ *Gazing up.* Looking up. ¶ *This same Jesus.* This was said to comfort them. The *same* tried friend, who had been so faithful to them, would return. They ought not therefore to look with despondency at his departure. ¶ *Into heaven.* This expression denotes into the immediate presence of God; or into the place of perpetual purity and happiness, where God peculiarly manifests his favour. The same thing is frequently designated by his sitting on the right hand of God, as emblematic of power, honour, and favour. Note, Mark xvi. 19; xiv. 62. Heb. i. 3; viii. 1. Acts vii. 55. Rom. viii. 34. Eph. i. 20. ¶ *Shall so come.* At the day of judgment. John xiv. 3, "If I go and prepare a place for you, I will come again," &c. ¶ *In like manner, &c.* In clouds, as he ascended. See Note, ver. 9. 1 Thess. iv. 16. This address was designed to comfort the disciples. Though their master and friend was taken from them, yet he was not removed for ever. He would come again with similar majesty and glory, for the vindication of his people, and to tread all his enemies under his feet. The *design* for which he will come, will be to judge the world. Matt. xxv. There will be an evident fitness and propriety in his coming. (1.) Because his appropriate work in heaven as mediator shall be accomplished; his people shall have been saved; the enemy subdued; death shall have been conquered: and the gospel shall have shown its power in subduing *all forms* of wickedness; in removing the effects of sin; in establishing the law, in vindicating the honour of God; and shall thus have done all that will be needful to be done to establish the authority of God throughout the universe. It will be proper, therefore, that this mysterious order of things shall be *wound up*, and the *results* become a matter of record in the history of the universe. It will be better than it would be to suffer an *eternal millennium* on the earth, while the saints should many of them slumber, and the wicked still be in their graves. (2.) It is proper that he should come to vindicate his people, and raise them up to glory. Here they have been persecuted, oppressed, put to death. Their character is assailed; they are poor; and the world despises them. It is fit that God should show himself to be their friend; that he should do justice to their injured names and motives; that he should bring out hidden and obscure virtue, and vindicate it; that he should enter every grave and bring forth his friends to life. (3.) It is proper that he should show his hatred of sin. Here it triumphs. The wicked are rich, and honoured, and mighty, and say, Where is the promise of his coming? 2 Pet. iii. 4. It is right that he should defend his cause. Hence the Lord Jesus will come to guard the avenues to heaven, and to see *that the universe suffers no wrong*, by the admission of an improper person to the skies. (4.) The great transactions of redemption have been public, open, often grand. The apostacy was public, in the face of angels and of the universe. Sin has been open, public, high-handed. Misery has been public, and has rolled its deep and turbid waves in the face of the universe. Death has been public; all worlds have seen the race cut down and moulder. The death of Jesus was public; the angels saw it; the heavens were clothed with mourning; the earth shook; and the dead arose. The angels have desired to look into these things (1 Pet. i. 12), and have felt an intense solicitude about men. Jesus was publicly whipped, cursed, crucified; and it is proper that he should publicly triumph, that all heaven rejoicing, and all hell at length humbled, should *see* his public victory. Hence he will come with clouds—with angels—with fire—and will raise the dead, and exhibit to all the universe the amazing close of the scheme of redemption. (5.) We are in these verses presented with the most grand and wonderful events that this world has ever known—the ascension and return of the Lord Jesus. Here is consolation for the Christian and

12 Then [a] returned they unto Jerusalem, from the mount called Olivet, which is from Jerusalem a sabbath-day's journey.
13 And when they were come in,
they went up into an upper room,
where abode both Peter, [b] and
James, and John, and Andrew, Philip, and Thomas, Bartholomew, and
Matthew, James *the son* of Alpheus, and Simon Zelotes, and Judas
the brother of James.
14 These all continued with one
accord in prayer and supplication,

a Lu.24.52. b Lu.6.13-16.

---

here is a source of ceaseless alarm to the sinner

12. *Then they returned to Jerusalem.* In Luke xxiv. 52, we are told that they *worshipped* Jesus before they returned. And it is probable that the *act* of worship to which he refers, was that which is mentioned in this chapter—their gazing intently on their departing Lord. ¶ *From the mount called Olivet.* From the mount of Olives. Note, Matt. xxi. 1. The *part* of the mountain from which he ascended was the eastern declivity, where stood the little village of Bethany. Luke xxiv. 50. ¶ *A sabbath-day's journey.* As far as might be lawfully travelled by a Jew on the Sabbath. This was two thousand paces or cubits; or seven furlongs and a half—not quite one mile. Note, Matt. xxiv. 20. The distance of a lawful journey on the Sabbath was not determined by the laws of Moses, but the Jewish teachers had fixed it at two thousand paces. This measure was determined on because it was a tradition, that in the camp of the Israelites when coming from Egypt, no part of the camp was more than two thousand paces from the tabernacle; and over this space, therefore, they were permitted to travel for worship. Perhaps, also, some countenance was given to this from the fact that this was the extent of the suburbs of the Levitical cities. Num. xxxv. 5. Mount Olivet was but *five* furlongs from Jerusalem, and Bethany was fifteen furlongs. But on the eastern declivity of the mountain the *tract* of country was called, for a considerable space, the region of Bethany; and it was from this place that the Lord Jesus ascended.

13. *Were come in.* To Jerusalem. ¶ *They went up into an upper room.* The word ὑπερῷον, here translated *upper room,* occurs but four times in the New Testament. Acts ix. 37, "She (Dorcas) was sick and died; whom when they had washed, they laid her in *an upper chamber.*" 39; xx. 8, "And there were many lights in the *upper chamber* where they were gathered together." The room so designated was an upper chamber used for devotion; or to place the dead before burial; or occasionally for conversation, &c. Here it evidently means the place where they were assembled for devotion. Luke (xxiv. 53) says they were continually *in the temple* praising and blessing God. And some have supposed that the upper room here designated, was one of the rooms in the temple. But there is no evidence of that; and it is not very probable. Such a room was a part of every house, especially in Jerusalem; and they probably selected one where they might be together, and yet so retired that they might be safe from the Jews. ¶ *Where abode.* Where were remaining. This does not mean that this was their *permanent* habitation; but they remained there waiting for the descent of the Holy Spirit. ¶ *Peter, &c.* All the apostles were there which Jesus had at first chosen, except Judas. Luke vi. 13—16.

14. *These all continued,* &c. The word *continued* denotes persevering and constant attention. The main business was devotion. Acts vi. 4, "*We* will give ourselves continually to the ministry of the word." Rom. xii. 12, "Continuing instant in prayer." xiii. 6, "Attending continually upon this very thing." It is their *main* and *constant* employment. Col. iv. 2. ¶ *With one accord.* With one mind; unitedly; unanimously. There were no schisms, no divided interests, no discordant purposes. This is a beautiful picture of devotion, and a specimen of what social worship ought now to be, and a beautiful illustration of Ps. cxxxiii. The apostles felt that they had *one* great object; and their deep grief at the loss of their master, their doubts and perplexities, led them, as all afflictions ought to lead us to the throne of grace. ¶ *In prayer and supplication.* These words are nearly synonymous, and are often interchanged. They express here petitions to God for blessings, and prayer to avert impending evils. ¶ *With the women.* The women that had followed the Lord Jesus from Galilee. Luke viii. 2 3; xxiii. 49. 55; xxiv. 10. Matt. xxvii. 55. The women particularly mentioned are Mary Magdalene

with the [a] women, and Mary the mother of Jesus, and with his brethren.

15 And in those days Peter stood up in the midst of the disciples, and said, (the number of the names together were about an hundred and twenty,)

16 Men *and* brethren: This scripture must needs have been fulfilled which [b] the Holy Ghost by the mouth of David spake before concerning

a Lu.23.49,55;24.10.

b Ps.41.9. Jno.13.18.

Mary the mother of James and Joses, the mother of Zebedee's children, Joanna the wife of Chuza, and Susanna. Besides these, there were others whose names are not mentioned. Most of them were relatives of the apostles or of our Saviour; and it is not improbable that some of them were wives of the apostles. Peter is known to have been married (Matt. viii. 14), and had his wife in attendance (1 Cor. ix. 5); and the same was doubtless true of some of the other apostles (1 Cor. ix. 5). Mary is here particularly mentioned, the mother of Jesus; showing that she now cast in her lot with the apostles. She had besides been particularly intrusted to the care of John (John xix. 26, 27), and had no other home. This is the last time she is mentioned in the New Testament. John xix. 27. ¶ *And with his brethren.* See Note, Matt. xii. 46. At first they had been unbelieving about the claims of Jesus (John vii. 5); but it seems that they had been subsequently converted.

15. *In those days.* On one of the days intervening between the ascension of Jesus and the day of Pentecost. ¶ *Peter stood up.* Peter *standing up*, or rising. This is a customary expression in the Scriptures when one begins to do a thing. Luke xv. 18. The reason why *Peter* did this may be seen in the Note on Matt. xvi. 16, 17. It is not improbable, besides, that Peter was the most aged of the apostles; and from his uniform conduct we know that he was the most ardent. It was perfectly characteristic, therefore, for him to introduce the business of the election of a new apostle. ¶ *The disciples.* This was the name which was given to them as being *learners* in the school of Christ. Note, Matt. v. 1. ¶ *The number of the names.* The number of the *persons*, or *individuals.* The word *name* is often used to denote the person. Rev. iii. 4. Acts iv. 12; xviii. 15. Eph. i. 21. In Syriac it is, "the assembly of men was about an hundred and twenty." This was the first assembly convened to transact the business of the church; and it is not a little remarkable that the vote in so important a matter as electing an apostle, was by the entire church It settles the question that the election of a minister and pastor should be by the church, and not be imposed on them by any right of presentation by individuals, or by any ecclesiastical body. If a case could ever occur where a minister should be chosen by the ministry only, such a case was here in the election of another apostle. And yet in this the entire church had a voice. Whether this was *all* the true church at this time, does not appear from the history This expression cannot mean that there were no more Christians, but that these were all that had convened in the upper room. It is almost certain that our Saviour had, by his own ministry, brought many others to be his true followers.

16. *Men* and *brethren* This is a customary mode of address, implying affection and respect. Acts xiii. 26. The Syriac has it more appropriately than by the introduction of the conjunction "and"—"Men, our brethren." ¶ *This scripture* This portion or prediction contained in the writings of the Old Testament. *Scripture*, writing. Note, John v. 39. The passage to which Peter refers is commonly supposed to be that recorded in Ps. xli. 9. "Yea, mine own familiar friend....hath lifted up his heel against me." This is expressly applied to Judas by our Saviour, in John xiii. 18. But it seems clear that the reference is not to the 41st Psalm, but to the passage which Peter proceeds to quote in ver. 20. ¶ *Must needs be fulfilled.* It would certainly happen that it would be fulfilled. Not that there was any physical necessity, or any compulsion; but it could not but occur that a prediction of God should be fulfilled. This makes no affirmation about the *freedom* of Judas in doing it. A man will be just as free in wickedness if it be *foretold* that he will be wicked, as if it had never been known to any other being. ¶ *The Holy Ghost*, &c. This is a strong attestation to the inspiration of David, and accords with the uniform testimony of the New Testament, that the sacred writers spake as they were moved by the Holy Ghost. 2 Pet. i. 21. ¶ *Concerning Judas.* In what respect this was concern

Judas, which was guide [a] to them
that took Jesus.
17 For he [b] was numbered with
us, and had obtained part of this
ministry.
18 Now [c] this man purchased a
field with the reward [d] of iniquity;
and falling headlong, he burst asun-

a Matt.26.47. Jno.18.3. b Lu.6.16.

der in the midst, and all his bowels
gushed out.
19 And it was known unto all
the dwellers at Jerusalem; insomuch as that field is called in their
proper tongue, Aceldama, that is to
say, The field of blood.
20 For it is written in the book

c Matt.27.5-10. d 2Pet.2.15.

---

ing Judas, see ver. 20. ¶ *Which was guide*, &c. Matt. xxvi. 47. John xviii. 3.

17. *He was numbered with us.* He was chosen as an apostle by the Lord Jesus. Luke vi. 13—16. This does not mean that he was a true Christian, but that he was reckoned among the apostles. Jesus knew that he never loved him. Long before he betrayed him, he declared that he was a devil. John vi. 70. He knew his whole character when he chose him. John ii. 25. If it be asked why he chose *such* a man to be an apostle; why he was made the *treasurer* of the apostles, and was admitted to the fullest confidence; we may reply, that a most important object was gained in having such a man—*a spy*—among them. It might be pretended when the apostles bore testimony to the purity of life, of doctrine, and of purpose, of the Lord Jesus, that they were interested and partial friends; that they might be disposed to *suppress* some of his real sentiments, and represent him in a light more favourable than the truth. Hence the testimony of such a man as Judas, if favourable, must be invaluable. It would be free from the charge of partiality. If Judas *knew* any thing unfavourable to the character of Jesus, he would have communicated it to the Sanhedrim. If he knew of any secret plot against the government, or seditious purpose, he had every inducement to declare it. He had every opportunity to know it: he was with him; heard him converse; was a member of his family, and admitted to terms of familiarity. Yet *even Judas* could not be *bought*, or *bribed*, to testify against the moral character of the Saviour. If he *had* done it, or *could* have done it, it would have preserved him from the charge of treason; entitled him to the reputation of a public benefactor in discovering secret sedition; and have saved him from the pangs of remorse, and from self-murder. Judas *would* have done it if he could. But he alleged no such charge; he did not even dare to lisp a word against the pure designs of the Lord Jesus; and his own pangs and death are the highest proof that can be desired of *his* conviction that the betrayed Redeemer was innocent. Judas would have been just the witness which the Jews desired of the treasonable purposes of Jesus. But *that* could not be had, even by gold; and they were compelled to *suborn* other men to testify against the Son of God. Matt. xxvi. 60. We may just add here, that the introduction of such a character as that of Judas Iscariot into the number of the apostles, and the *use* to be made of his testimony, would never have occurred to an impostor. An impostor would have said that they were *all* the true friends of the Lord Jesus. To have *invented* such a character as that of Judas, and to make him perform such a part in the plan as the sacred writers do, would have required too much art and cunning, was too refined and subtle a device to have been thought of, unless it had actually occurred.

18. *Now this man*, &c. The money which was given for betraying the Lord Jesus was thrown down in the temple, and the field was purchased with it by the Jewish priests. See Matt. xxvii. 5, 10, and the Notes on that place. A man is said often to do a thing, when he furnishes *means* for doing it. ¶ *The reward of iniquity.* The price which he had for that deed of stupendous wickedness—the betraying of the Lord Jesus. ¶ *And falling headlong.* He first hanged himself, and then fell and was burst asunder. Matt. xxvii. 5.

19. *It was known*, &c. Matt. xxvii. 8. The scene in the temple; the acts of the priests in purchasing the field, &c. would make it known; and the *name* of the field would preserve the memory of the guilt of Judas. ¶ *Their proper tongue.* The language spoken by the Jews—the *Syro-chaldaic.* ¶ *Aceldama.* This is composed of two Syro-chaldaic words, and means literally, The field of blood.

20. *For it is written*, &c. See Ps. lxix. 25. This is the prediction doubtless to which Peter refers in ver. 16.—The intermediate passage in ver. 18, 19, is probably a parenthesis; the words of Luke, not of

of Psalms, Let [a] his habitation be desolate, and let no man dwell therein: and, [b] His bishopric [1] let another take.

a Ps. 69.25. b Ps. 109.8. 1 or, *office*, or, *charge*.

Peter. It is not probable that Peter would introduce a narrative like this, with which they were all familiar, in an address to the disciples. The Hebrew in the Psalm is, 'Let their habitation (Heb. *fold, enclosure for cattle; tower, or palace*), be desolate, and let none dwell in their tents."—This quotation is not made literally from the Hebrew, nor from the Septuagint. The *plural* is changed to the *singular*, and there are some other slight variations. The Hebrew says, "let no men dwell in their *tents*." The reference to the *tents* is omitted in the quotation. The term *habitation*, in the Psalm, means evidently the dwelling place of the enemies of the writer of the Psalm. It is an image expressive of their overthrow and defeat by a just God, 'let their families be scattered, and the places where they have dwelt be without an inhabitant, as a reward for their crimes.' If the Psalm was originally composed with reference to the Messiah and his sufferings, the expression here was not intended to denote Judas *in particular*, but *one* of his foes, who was to meet the just punishment of rejecting, and betraying, and murdering him. The change, therefore, which Peter made from the plural to the singular; and the application to Judas especially, *as one of those enemies*, accords with the design of the Psalm, and is such a change as the circumstances of the case justified and required. It is an image, therefore, expressive of judgment and desolation coming upon his betrayer—an image to be literally fulfilled in relation to his habitation, drawn from the desolation when a man is discomfited, overthrown, and his dwelling place given up to desolation. It is not a little remarkable that this Psalm is repeatedly quoted as referring to the Messiah. Ver. 9, "The zeal of thine house hath eaten me up," expressly applied to Christ in John ii. 17. Ver. 21. "They gave me also gall for my meat; and in my thirst they gave me vinegar to drink." The thing which was done to Jesus on the cross. Matt. xxvii. 34. The whole Psalm is expressive of deep sorrow—of persecution, contempt, weeping, being forsaken, and is throughout applicable to the Messiah; with what is remarkable, not a single expression to be, of necessity, limited to David. It is not easy to ascertain whether the ancient Jews referred this Psalm to the Messiah. A part of the *title* to the Psalm in the *Syriac* version is, "It is called a prophecy concerning those things which Christ suffered, and concerning the casting away of the Jews." The prophecy in ver. 25 is not to be understood of *Judas alone, but of the enemies of the Messiah in general, of which Judas was one.* On this principle the application to Judas of the passage by Peter is to be defended. ¶ *And his bishopric let another take.* This is quoted from Ps. cix. 8; "Let his days be few, and let another take his office." This is called "a Psalm of David," and is of the same class as Ps. vi. xxii. xxv. xxxviii. xlii. This *class* of Psalms is commonly supposed to have expressed David's feelings in the calamitous times of the persecution by Saul, the rebellion of Absalom, &c. They are *all also* expressive of the condition of a suffering and persecuted Messiah; and are many of them applied to him in the New Testament. The *general principle* on which most of them are applicable is, not that David *personated* or *typified* the Messiah, which is nowhere affirmed, and which can be true in no intelligible sense; but that he was placed in circumstances similar to the Messiah; encompassed with like enemies; persecuted in the same manner. They are expressive of high rank, office, dignity, and piety, cast down, waylaid, and encompassed with enemies. In this way they express *general sentiments* as much applicable to the case of the Messiah as to David. They were placed in similar circumstances. The same help was needed. The same expressions would convey their feelings. The same treatment was proper for their enemies.—On this principle it was that *David* deemed his enemy, whoever he was, unworthy of his office; and desired that it should be given to another. In like manner, Judas had rendered *himself* unworthy of his office, and there was the *same propriety* that it should be given to another. And as the office had now become vacant by the death of Judas, and according to *one* declaration in the Psalms; so according to another, it was proper that it should be conferred on some other person. The word rendered "office" in the Psalm, means the *care, charge, business, oversight* of any thing. It is a word applicable to *magistrates*, whose care it is to see the laws executed; to military men who have charge of an

21 Wherefore of these men [a] which have companied with us all the time that the Lord Jesus went in and out among us,

22 Beginning from the baptism of John, unto that same day that he was taken up from us, must one be ordained to be a witness with us of his resurrection.

23 And they appointed two, Jo-

a Lu.10.1,2. Jno.15.27.

army, or a part of an army. In Job x. 12, it is rendered "thy visitation"—thy care. In Num. iv. 16; "and to the office of Eleazer," &c. 2 Kings xi. 18. In the case of David it refers to those who were intrusted with military or other offices, and who had treacherously perverted them to persecute and oppose him; and thus shown themselves unworthy of the office. The Greek word which is used here, ἐπισκοπὴν is taken from the Septuagint, and means the same thing as the Hebrew. It is well rendered in the margin "office, or charge." It means charge of any kind, or office, without in itself specifying of what kind. It is the *concrete* of the noun ἐπισκοπος, commonly translated "bishop," and means *his* office, charge, or duty. That word designates simply *having the oversight of any thing*, and as applied to the officers of the New Testament, it denotes merely *their having charge of the affairs of the church*, without specifying the *nature* or the *extent* of their jurisdiction. Hence it is often interchanged with presbyter, or elder, and expresses the discharge of the duties of the same office. Acts xx. 28. "Take heed (presbyters or elders, ver. 17) to yourselves, and to all the flock over the which the Holy Ghost hath made *you overseers*"—ἐπισκοπους—bishops. Heb. xii. 15. "Looking diligently," &c. ἐπισκοπουντες. Phil. i. 1, "with the bishops and deacons." "Paul called presbyters, bishops; for they had at that time the same name."—Theodoret, as quoted by Scheusner. 1 Pet. v. 2. "Feed the flock of God (i. e. you who are elders, or presbyters, v. 1); *taking the oversight thereof*," ἐπισκοπουντες. These passages shew that the term in the New Testament designates the supervision or care which was exercised over the church, by whomsoever performed, without specifying the nature or extent of the jurisdiction. It is scarcely necessary to add that Peter here did not intend to affirm that Judas sustained any office corresponding to what is now commonly understood by the term "*bishop*."

21, 22. *Wherefore of these men.* Of those who had witnessed the life and works of Christ, and who were therefore qualified to discharge the duties of the office from which Judas fell. Probably Peter refers to the seventy disciples Luke x. 1, 2. ¶ *Went in and out.* A phrase signifying that he was their constant companion. It expresses in general all the actions of the life. Ps. cxxi 8. Deut. xxviii. 19; xxxi. 2. ¶ *Beginning from the baptism of John.* The words "beginning from" in the original refer to the Lord Jesus. The meaning may be thus expressed, 'during all the time in which the Lord Jesus beginning (his ministry) at the time when he was baptized by John, went in and out among us, until the time when he was taken up,' &c. From those who had during that time been the constant companions of the Lord Jesus must one be taken, who would thus be a witness of *his whole ministry.* ¶ *Must one be ordained.* It is *fit* or *proper* that one should be ordained. The reason of this was, that Jesus had originally chosen the number twelve for this work, and as *one* of them had fallen, it was proper that the breach should be filled by some person equally qualified for the office. The reason why it was proper that he should be taken from the seventy disciples was, that *they* had been particularly distinguished by Jesus himself, and commanded to preach, and endowed with various powers, and had been witnesses of most of his public life. Luke x. 1—16. The word *ordained* with us has a fixed and definite meaning. It denotes to set apart to a sacred office with the proper form and solemnities, commonly by the imposition of hands. But this is not, of necessity, the meaning of this passage. The Greek word usually denoting *ordination* is not used here. The expression is literally, "must one *be*, or *become*, γενεσθαι, a witness with us of his resurrection." The expression does not imply that he must be set apart in any particular manner, but simply that one should be designated, or appointed for this specific purpose, *to be a witness* of the resurrection of Christ.

23. *And they appointed two.* They *proposed*, or as we should say, *nominated* two. Literally they *placed* two, or made them to stand forth, as persons do who are candidates for office. These two were probably more distinguished by prudence, wisdom, piety, and age than the others; and were so nearly equal in qualifications,

seph called Barsabas, [a] who was
surnamed Justus, and Matthias.
24 And they prayed, and said,
Thou, Lord, which [b] knowest the
hearts of all *men*, shew whether of
these two thou hast chosen,
25 That he may take part of this
ministry and apostleship, from

a c.15.22. b Je.17.10. Re.2.23.

that they could not determine which was the best fitted for the office. ¶ *Joseph called Barsabas*, &c. It is not certainly known what the name *Barsabas* denotes. The Syriac word *Bar* means *Son*, and the word *Sabas* has been translated *an oath*, *rest*, *quiet*, or *captivity*. Why the name was given to Joseph is not known; but probably it was the family name—*Joseph son of Sabæ*. Some have conjectured that this was the same man who, in ch. iv. 36, is called Barnabas. But of this there is no proof. Lightfoot supposes that he was the son of Alpheus, and brother of James the Less, and that he was chosen on account of his relationship to the family of the Lord Jesus. ¶ *Was surnamed Justus.* Who was *called* Justus. This is a Latin name, meaning *just*, and was probably given him on account of his distinguished integrity. It was not uncommon among the Jews for a man to have several names. Matt. x. 3 ¶ *And Matthias.* Nothing is known of the family of this man, or of his character, further than that he was numbered with the apostles, and shared their lot in the toils, and persecutions, and honours of preaching the gospel to mankind.

24. *And they prayed.* As they could not *agree* on the individual, they invoked the direction of God in their choice—an example which should be followed in every selection of an individual to exercise the duties of the sacred office of the ministry. ¶ *Which knowest the hearts of all men.* This is often declared to be the peculiar prerogative of God. Jer. xvii. 10. "*I, Jehovah, search the heart*," &c. Ps. cxxxix. 1. 23. 1 Chron. xxviii. 9. Yet this attribute is also expressly ascribed to Jesus Christ. Rev. ii. 18. Comp. 23. "These things saith the Son of God—I am he which searcheth the reins and the hearts." John ii. 25; vi. 64; xvi. 19. There are strong reasons for supposing that the apostles on this occasion addressed this prayer to the Lord Jesus Christ. (1.) The name *Lord* is the common appellation which they gave to him. Acts ii. 36; vii. 59, 60; x. 36. 1 Cor. ii. 8. Phil. ii. 11. Rev. xi. 8, &c. (2.) We are told that they *worshipped* him, or rendered him divine honours after his ascension. Luke xxiv. 52. (3.) The disciples were accustomed to address him after his crucifixion by the names Lord or God indifferently. Acts i. 6. John xx 28. Acts vii. 59. (4.) This was a matter pertaining especially to the church which the Lord Jesus had redeemed, and *to his own arrangement* in regard to it. *He* had chosen the apostles; *he* had given them their commission; *he* had fixed their number; and what is worthy of special remark here, *he* had been the companion of the very men, and knew their qualifications for their work. If the apostles *ever* called on the Lord Jesus after his ascension, this was the case in which they would be likely to do it. That it *was* done is clear from the account of the death of Stephen. Acts vii. 59. 60. And in this important matter of ordaining a new apostle to be a witness for Jesus Christ, nothing was more natural than that they should address *him*, though bodily absent, as they would assuredly have done if he were present. And if on this occasion they *did* actually address Christ, then two things clearly follow. First, that it is proper to render him divine homage, agreeably to the uniform declarations of the Scripture. John v. 23, "That all men should honour the Son even as they honour the Father." Heb. i. 6, "And let all the angels of God worship him." Phil. ii. 10, 11. Rev. v. 8—14. 1 Thess. iii. 11, 12. Secondly, he must be divine. To none other but God can religious homage be rendered; and none other can be described as *knowing the hearts of all men*. The reason why they appealed to him on this occasion *as the searcher of the heart*, was doubtless the great importance of the work to which the successor of Judas was to be called. One apostle of fair external character had proved a traitor; and with this fact full before them, they appealed to the Saviour himself, to select one who would be true to him, and not bring dishonour on his cause. ¶ *Shew whether*, &c. Shew *which* of them. ¶ *Thou hast chosen.* Not by any public declaration, but which of the two thou hast judged to be best qualified for the work, and hast fitted for it.

25. *That he may take part of this ministry.* The word rendered *part*, κλῆρον, is the same which in the next verse is rendered *lots*. It properly means a lot, or portion; the portion divided to a man, or assigned to him by casting lots; and also the instrument or means by which the lot

which Judas by transgression fell, that he might go to his own place,

is made. The former is its meaning here; the *office*, or portion of apostolic work which would fall to him by taking the place of Judas. ¶ *Ministry and apostleship*. This is an instance of the figure of speech *hendiadys*, when two words are used to express one thing. It means *the apostolic ministry*. See instances in Gen. i. 14, "Let them be for signs *and* for seasons," i. e. signs *of* seasons. Acts xxiii. 6, "Hope *and* resurrection of the dead," i. e. hope *of the* resurrection of the dead. ¶ *That he might go to his own place*. These words by different interpreters have been referred both to Matthias and Judas. Those who refer them to Matthias say that they mean, that Judas fell that Matthias might go to his own place, that is, to a place for which he was fitted, or well qualified. But to this there are many objections. 1. The apostolic office could with no propriety be called, in reference to Matthias, *his own place*, until it was actually conferred on him. 2. There is no instance in which the expression *to go to his own place*, is applied to a successor in office. 3. It is not true that the design or reason why Judas fell was to make way for another. He fell by his crimes; his avarice, his voluntary and enormous wickedness. 4. The former part of the sentence contains this sentiment: 'Another must be appointed to this office which the death of Judas has made vacant.' If this expression, "that he might go," &c., refers to the successor of Judas, it expresses the same sentiment, but more obscurely. 5. The obvious and natural meaning of the phrase is to refer it to Judas. But those who suppose it to refer to Judas differ greatly about its meaning. Some suppose it refers to his own house; that he left the apostolic office to return to his own house; and they appeal to Numbers xxiv. 25. But it is not true that Judas did this; nor is there the least proof that it was his design. Others refer it to the grave, as the place of man, where all must lie; and particularly as an ignominious place where Judas should lie. But there is no example of the word *place* being used in this sense; nor is there an instance where a man by being buried is said to return to his own, or proper place. Others have supposed that the manner of his death, by hanging, is referred to, as his own or his proper place. But this interpretation is evidently an unnatural and forced one. The word *place* cannot be applied to an *act* of self-murder. It denotes habitation, abode, situation in which to remain; not an *act*. These are the only interpretations which can be suggested of the passage, except the common and obvious one of referring it to the future abode of Judas in the world of wo. This might be said to be his *own*, as it was adapted to him; as he had prepared himself for it; and as it was proper that he who had betrayed his Lord should remain there. This interpretation may be defended by the following considerations: 1. It is the obvious and natural meaning of the words. It commends itself by its simplicity and its evident connexion with the context. It has in all ages been the common interpretation; nor has any other been adopted unless there was a theory to be defended about future punishment. Unless men had previously made up their minds *not to believe in future punishment*, no one would ever have thought of any other interpretation. This fact alone throws strong light on the meaning of the passage. 2. It accords with the crimes of Judas, and with all that we know of him. The *future doom* of Judas was not unknown to the apostles. Jesus Christ had expressly declared this; "it had been good for that man if he had not been born;" a declaration which *could* not be true if, after *any* limited period of suffering, he were at last admitted to eternal happiness. See Matt. xxvi. 24, and the Note on that place. This declaration was made in the presence of the eleven apostles, at the institution of the Lord's supper, at a time when their attention was absorbed with deep interest in what Christ said; and it was therefore a declaration which they would not be likely to forget. As they *knew* the fate of Judas, nothing was more natural for them than to speak of it familiarly as a thing which *had* actually occurred when he betrayed his Lord, hung himself, and went to his own place. 3. The expression "to go to his own place," is one which is used by the ancient writers to denote going to the eternal destiny. Thus the Jewish Tract, *Baal Turim*, on Num. xxiv 25, says, "Balaam went to his own place, i. e. to Gehenna," to hell. Thus the Targum, or Chaldee Paraphrase on Eccl. vi. 6, says, "Although the days of a man's life were two thousand years, and he did not study the law, and do justice, in the day of his death his soul shall descend to hell, to the one place where all sinners go." Thus Ignatius in the Epistle to the

26 And they gave forth their lots: and the lot fell upon Matthias; and he was numbered with the eleven apostles.

Magnesians says, "Because all things have an end, the two things death and life shall lie down together, *and each one shall go to his own place.*" The phrase *his own* place, means the place or abode which is fitted for him, which is his appropriate home. Judas was not in a place which befitted his character when he was an apostle; he was not in such a place in the church; he would not be in heaven. Hell was the only place which was fitted to the man of avarice and of treason. And if this be the true interpretation of this passage, then it follows, 1. That there will be such a thing as future, eternal punishment. One such man there certainly is in hell, and ever will be. If there is *one* there, for the same reason there may be others. All objections to the doctrine are removed by this single fact; and it cannot be true that *all* men will be saved. 2. Each individual in eternity will find his own proper place. Hell is not an arbitrary appointment. Every man will go to the place for which his character is fitted. The hypocrite is not fitted for heaven. The man of pride, and avarice, and pollution, and falsehood, is not fitted for heaven. The place *adapted* to such men is hell; and the design of the judgment will be to assign to each individual *his proper abode* in the eternal world. 3. The design of the judgment of the great day will be to assign to all the inhabitants of this world *their proper place.* It would not be fit that the holy and pure should dwell for ever in the same place with the unholy and impure; and the Lord Jesus will come to assign to each his appropriate eternal habitation. 4. The sinner will have no cause of complaint. If he is assigned to his *proper place*, he cannot complain. If he is *unfit* for heaven, he cannot complain that he is excluded. And if his character and feelings are such as make it *proper* that he should find his eternal abode among the enemies of God, then he must expect that a God of justice and equity will assign him such a doom. But, 5. This will not alleviate his pain; it will *deepen* his wo. He will have the eternal consciousness that that, and that only, is *his* place—the doom for which he is fitted. The prison is no less dreadful because a man is conscious that he deserves it. The gallows is not the less terrible, because the man knows that he *deserves* to die. And the eternal consciousness of the sinner that he is *unfit* for heaven; that there is not a solitary soul there with whom he could have sympathy or friendship; that he is fit for hell, and hell only, will be an ingredient of eternal bitterness in the cup of wo that awaits him. Let not the sinner then hope to escape; for God will assuredly appoint his residence in that world to which his character here is adapted.

The character and end of Judas is one of the most important and instructive in history. It teaches us, 1. That Christ may employ wicked men for important purposes in his kingdom. See Note on ver. 17. He does no violence to their freedom, suffers them to act as they please, but brings important ends out of their conduct. One of the most conclusive arguments for the pure character of Jesus Christ is drawn from the silent testimony of Judas. 2. The character of Judas was eminently base and wicked. He was influenced by one of the worst human passions; and yet he cloaked it from all the apostles. It was remarkable that any man should have *thought* of making money in such a band of men; but avarice will show itself every where. 3. We see the effects of avarice in the church. It led to the betraying of Jesus Christ, and to his death; and it has often betrayed the cause of pure religion since. There is no single human passion that has done so much evil in the church of God as this. It *may be* consistent with external decency and order; it is that on which the world acts, and which it approves; and it may therefore be indulged without disgrace; while open and acknowledged vices would expose their possessors to shame and ruin. And yet it paralyzes and betrays religion probably more than any single propensity of man. 4. The character of an avaricious man in the church will be developed. Opportunities will occur when it will be seen and known by what principle the man is influenced. So it was with Achan (Josh. vii. 21); so it was with Judas; and so it will be with all. Occasions will occur which will *test* the character, and show what manner of spirit a man is of. Every appeal to a man's benevolence, every call upon his charity, shows what spirit influences him, and whether he is actuated by the love of gold, or by the love of Jesus Christ and his cause.

26. ***And they gave forth their lots.*** Some

have supposed that this means they *voted*. But to this interpretation there are insuperable objections. 1. The word *lots*, κλήρους, is not used to express *votes*, or *suffrage*. 2. The expression "the lot fell upon" is not consistent with the notion of voting. It is commonly expressive of casting lots. 3. Casting lots was common among the Jews on important and difficult occasions, and it was natural that the apostles should resort to it in this. Thus David divided the priests by lot. 1 Chron. xxiv. 5. The land of Canaan was divided by lot. Num. xxvi. 55. Josh. xv. xvi. xvii. &c. Jonathan, son of Saul, was detected as having violated his father's command, and as bringing calamity on the Israelites, by lot. 1 Sam. xiv. 41, 42. Achan was detected by lot. Josh. vii. 16. 18. In these cases the use of the lot was regarded as a solemn appeal to God, for his direct interference in cases which they could not themselves decide. Prov. xvi. 33, "The lot is cast into the lap, but the whole disposing thereof is of the Lord." The choice of an apostle was an event of the same kind, and was regarded as a solemn appeal to God for his direction and guidance in a case which the apostles could not determine. The *manner* in which this was done is not certainly known. The common mode of casting lots, was to write the names of the *persons* on pieces of stone, wood, &c. and put them in one urn; and the name of the office, portion, &c. on others. These were then placed in an urn with other pieces of stone, &c. which were blank. The names were then drawn at random, and also the other pieces, and this determined the case. The casting of a lot is determined by laws of nature, as regularly as any thing else. There is properly *no chance* in it. We do not know how a die may turn up; but this does not imply that it will turn up without any regard to rule, or at haphazard. We cannot trace the influences which may determine either this or that side to come up; but still it is done by regular and proper laws, and according to the circumstances of position, force, &c. in which it is cast. Still although it does not imply any *special* or miraculous interposition of Providence; though it may not be absolutely wrong, in cases which cannot otherwise be determined, to use the lot, yet it does not follow that it is proper often to make this appeal. Almost all cases of doubt can be determined more satisfactorily in some other way than by the lot. The habit of appealing to it engenders the love of hazards and of games; leads to heart-burnings, to jealousies, to envy, to strife, and to dishonesty. Still less does the example of the apostles authorize *games* of hazard, or lotteries, which are positively evil, and attended with ruinous consequences, apart from any inquiry about the lawfulness of the lot. They either originate in, or promote, covetousness, neglect of regular industry, envy, jealousy disappointment, dissipation, bankruptcy falsehood, and despair. What is gained by one is lost by another, and both the gain and the loss promote some of the worst passions of man; boasting, triumph, self-confidence, indolence, dissipation, on the one hand; and envy, disappointment, sullenness, desire of revenge, remorse, and ruin, on the other. God intended that man should live by sober toil. All departures from this great law of our social existence lead to ruin. ¶ *Their lots.* The lots which were to decide *their* case. They are called *theirs*, because they were to determine which of them should be called to the apostolic office. ¶ *The lot fell.* This is an expression applicable to casting lots, not to voting. ¶ *He was numbered.* By the casting of the lot. συγκατεψηφίσθη. This word is from ψῆφος—*a calculus*, or *pebble*, by which votes were given, or lots were cast. It means, that *by the result of the lot*, he was reckoned as an apostle. Nothing further is related of Matthias in the New Testament. Where he laboured, and when and where he died, is unknown, nor is there any tradition on which reliance is to be placed. The election of Matthias throws some light on the organization of the church. 1. He was chosen to fill the place vacated by Judas, and for a specific purpose, to be *a witness* of the resurrection of Christ. There is no mention of any other design. It was not to ordain men exclusively, or to rule over the churches, but to be a witness to an important fact. 2. There is no intimation here that it was designed that there should be *successors* to the apostles in the *peculiar* duties of the apostolic office. The election was for a definite object, and was therefore temporary. It was to fill up the *number* originally appointed by Christ. When the purpose for which he was appointed was accomplished, the *peculiar* part of the apostolic work ceased of course. 3 There *could be* no succession in our times to the peculiar apostolic office. They were to be *witnesses* of the work of Christ. For this they were sent forth. And when the desired effect resulting from such a witnessing was accomplished, the office itself would cease. Hence there is no record

CHAPTER II.

AND when the day of Pentecost [a] was fully come, they [b] were all with one accord in one place.

a Le 23. 15. b c 1. 14.

that after this the church even pretended to appoint successors to the apostles to discharge their *peculiar* work. And hence no ministers of the gospel can now pretend to be their successors in the *peculiar* and *original* design of the appointment of the apostles. 4. The only other apostle mentioned in the New Testament is the apostle Paul, not appointed as the successor of the others, not with any peculiar design except to be an apostle to the Gentiles, as the others were to the Jews, and appointed for the same end, to testify that Jesus Christ was alive, and that *he had seen him* after he rose. 1 Cor. xv. 8; ix. 1. Acts xxii. 8, 9. 14, 15; ix. 15; xxvi. 17, 18. The ministers of religion, therefore, are successors of the apostles, not in their peculiar office as witnesses, but as preachers of the word, and as appointed to establish, to organize, and to edify and rule the churches. The *peculiar* work of the apostleship ceased with their death. The ordinary work of the ministry, which they held in common with all others who preach the gospel, will continue to the end of time.

CHAPTER II.

1. *And when the day of Pentecost.* The word *Pentecost* is a Greek word, signifying *the fiftieth* part of a thing; or the fiftieth in order. Among the Jews it was applied to one of their three great feasts which began on *the fiftieth* day after the Passover. This feast was reckoned from the sixteenth day of the month Abib, or April, or the *second day* of the Passover. The paschal lamb was slain on the fourteenth of the month at even (Lev. xxiii. 5). On the fifteenth of the month was a holy convocation—the proper beginning of the feast; on the sixteenth was the offering of the first-fruits of harvest, and *from that day* they were to reckon *seven weeks*, i. e. forty-nine days to the feast called the feast of Pentecost, so that it occurred *fifty* days after the first day of the feast of the Passover. This feast was also called *the feast of weeks*, from the circumstance that it followed a succession of weeks. Ex. xxxiv. 22. Num. xxviii. 26. Deut. xvi. 10. It was also *a harvest festival*, and was accordingly called *the feast of harvest.* And it was for this reason that two loaves made of new meal were offered on this occasion as first-fruits. Lev. xxiii. 17. 20. Num. xxviii. 27. 31. ¶ *Was fully come.* When the day had arrived. The word means here simply, *had come.* Comp. Mark i. 15. Luke i. 57. This fact is mentioned, that the time of the Pentecost had come, or fully arrived, to account for what is related afterwards, that there were so many strangers and foreigners present. The promised influences of the Spirit were withheld until the greatest possible numbers of Jews should be present at Jerusalem at the same time, and thus an opportunity be afforded of preaching the gospel to vast multitudes in the very place where the Lord Jesus was crucified, and also an opportunity be afforded of sending the gospel by them into distant parts of the earth. ¶ *They were all.* Probably not only the apostles, but also the one hundred and twenty mentioned in ch. i. 15. ¶ *With one accord.* See ch. i. 14. It is probable they had *continued* together until this time, and given themselves entirely to the business of devotion. ¶ *In one place.* Where this was cannot be known. Commentators have been much divided in their conjectures about it. Some have supposed it was in the upper room mentioned (ch. i. 13); others that it was a room in the temple; others that it was in a synagogue; others, that it was in the promiscuous multitude that assembled for devotion in the courts of the temple. See ver. 2. It has by many been supposed that this took place on the first day of the week, that is on the Christian Sabbath. But there is a difficulty in establishing this. There was probably a difference among the Jews themselves on this subject. The law said that they should reckon seven Sabbaths, that is seven weeks *from the morrow after the Sabbath.* Lev. xxiii. 15. By this Sabbath the Pharisees understood the *second day* of the Passover, on whatever day of the week it occurred, which was kept as a holy assembly, and might be called a Sabbath. But the Caraite Jews, or those who insisted on a *literal* interpretation of the Scriptures, maintained that by the *Sabbath* here was meant the *usual Sabbath* the seventh day of the week. Consequently *with them* the day of Pentecost *always* occurred on the *first day* of the week; and if the apostles fell in with their views, the day was fully come on what is now the Christian Sabbath. But if the views of the Pharisees were followed, and the Lord Jesus had with them kept the Passover on *Thursday*, as many

2 And suddenly there came a
sound from heaven, as of a rushing mighty wind, and it filled [a]
all the house where they were sit
ting.
3 And there appeared unto them

a c.4.31.

have supposed, then the day of Pentecost would have occurred on the Jewish Sabbath, that is on *Saturday*. *Kuinöel. Lightfoot.* It is impossible to determine the truth on this subject. Nor is it of much importance. The day of Pentecost was kept by the Jews also as a festival to commemorate the giving of the law on mount Sinai.

2. *And suddenly.* It burst upon them at once. Though they were waiting for the descent of the Spirit, yet it is not probable that they expected it in this manner. As this was an important event, and one on which the welfare of the church depended, it was proper that the gift of the Holy Spirit should take place in some *striking* and *sensible* manner, so as to convince their own minds that the promise was fulfilled, and so as deeply to impress others with the greatness and importance of the event. ¶ *There came a sound.* ἦχος. This word is applied to any noise or report. Heb. xii. 19 "The *sound* of a trumpet." Luke iv. 37, "The *fame* of him," &c. Comp. Mark i. 28. ¶ *From heaven.* Appearing to rush down from the sky. It was fitted therefore to attract their attention no less from the *direction* from which it came, than on account of its *suddenness* and *violence*. Tempests blow commonly horizontally. This appeared to come *from above;* and this is all that is meant by the expression "from heaven." ¶ *As of a rushing mighty wind.* Literally, "as of a violent wind or gale," borne along (φερομένης), *sweeping along like a tempest.* Such a wind is sometimes borne along so violently, and with such a noise, as to make it difficult even to hear the thunder in the gale. Such appears to have been the sound of this remarkable phenomenon. It does not appear that there was any wind; all might have been still; but the sudden sound was *like* such a sweeping tempest. It may be remarked, however, that the *wind* in the sacred Scriptures is often put as an emblem of a divine influence. It is *invisible*, yet *mighty;* and thus represents the agency of the Holy Spirit. The same word in Hebrew (רוח), and in Greek (πνεῦμα), is used to denote both. The mighty power of God may be denoted also by the violence of a mighty tempest. 1 Kings xix. 11. Ps. xxix. civ. 3; xviii. 10. And thus Jesus by *his breath* indicated to the apostles the conferring of the Holy Ghost. John xx. 22. In this place *the sound* as of a gale was emblematic of the mighty *power* of the Spirit, and of the great *effects* which his coming would accomplish among men. ¶ *And it filled.* Not the *wind* filled, but the *sound*. This is evident, (1.) Because there is no affirmation that there *was* any wind. (2.) The grammatical structure of the sentence will admit no other construction. The word "filled" has no nominative case but "the sound." And suddenly there was a sound as *of* a wind, and (the sound) filled the house. In the Greek, the word "wind" is in the genitive or possessive case. It may be remarked here, that this miracle was *really* far more striking than the common supposition makes it to have been. A *tempest* might have been terrific. A mighty *wind* might have alarmed them. But there would have been nothing unusual or remarkable in it. Such things often occurred; and the thoughts would have been directed of course to the *storm* as an ordinary, though perhaps alarming occurrence. But when all was still; when there was no storm, no wind, no rain, no thunder, such a rushing sound must have arrested their attention, and directed all minds to so unusual and unaccountable an occurrence. ¶ *All the house.* Some have supposed that this was a room in or near the temple. But as the *temple* is not expressly mentioned, this is improbable. It was probably the private dwelling mentioned in ch. i. 13. If it be said that such a dwelling could not contain so large a multitude as soon assembled, it may be replied that their houses had large central courts (see Note, Matt. ix. 2); and that it is not affirmed that the transaction recorded in this chapter occurred *in* the room which they occupied. It is probable that it took place in the court and around the house.

3. *And there appeared unto them.* There were *seen by them*, or they saw. They were first seen by them in the room before they rested on the heads of the disciples. Perhaps the fire appeared at first as scintillations or corruscations, until it became fixed on their heads. ¶ *Tongues.* γλῶσσαι. The word *tongue* occurs often in the Scriptures to denote the member which is the instrument of taste and speech, and also to denote *language* or speech itself.

cloven tongues like as of fire, and it sat upon each of them:

4 And they were all filled [a] with the Holy Ghost, and began [b] to speak with other tongues, as the Spirit gave them utterance.

a c.1.5. b Mar.16.17. c.10.46.

It is also used, as with us, to denote that which *in shape* resembles the tongue. Thus Josh. vii. 21. 24 (in Hebrew), "a tongue of gold," i. e. a *wedge* of gold. Josh. xv. 5; xviii. 19. Isa. xi. 15, "The tongue of the sea," i. e. a bay or gulf. Thus also we say, a tongue of land. The phrase "tongue of fire" occurs once, and once only, in the Old Testament (Isa. v. 24), "Therefore as the fire devoureth the stubble (Heb. *tongue of fire*), and the flame consumeth," &c. In this place the *name* tongue is given from the *resemblance* of a pointed flame to the human tongue. Any thing long, narrow, and tending to a point, is thus in the Hebrew called *a tongue*. The word here means, therefore, slender and pointed appearances of flame; perhaps at first moving irregularly around the room. ¶ *Cloven.* Divided, separated. διμεναι, from the verb to *divide*, or *distribute into parts*. Matt. xxvii. 35, "They *parted* his garments." Luke xxii. 17, "Take this (the cup), and *divide* it among yourselves." Probably the common opinion is that these *tongues* or flames were, *each one* of them, split, or forked, or cloven. But this is not the sense of the expression. It means that they were separated or divided *one from another;* not *one great flame*, but broken up, or *cloven* into many parts; and probably moving without order in the room. In the Syriac it is, "And there appeared unto them tongues which divided themselves, like fire, and sat upon each of them." The old Ethiopic version reads it, "And *fire*, as it were, appeared to them, and sat on them." ¶ *And sat upon each of them.* Or rested, in the form of a lambent or gentle flame, upon the head of each one. This evinced that the prodigy was directed to *them*, and was a very significant emblem of the promised descent of the Holy Spirit. After the rushing sound, and the appearance of the flames, they could not doubt that here was some remarkable interposition of God. The appearance of *fire*, or *flame*, has always been regarded as a most striking emblem of the Divinity. Thus, Exod. iii. 2, 3, God is said to have manifested himself to Moses in a bush which was *burning*, yet not consumed. Thus, Exod. xix. 16—20, God descended on mount Sinai in the midst of thunders, and lightnings, and smoke, and *fire*, striking emblems of his presence and power. See also Gen. xv. 17. Thus Deut. iv. 24 God is said to be "a consuming fire." Comp. Heb. xii. 29. See Ezek. i. 4. Ps. xviii. 12—14. The classic reader will also instantly recall the beautiful description in Virgil. (Æniad, b. ii. 680—691.) Other instances of a similar prodigy are also recorded in profane writers Pliny H. N. 2. 37. Livy, i. 39. These appearances to the apostles were emblematic doubtless, (1.) Of the promised Holy Spirit, as a Spirit of *purity* and of *power*. The prediction of John the Baptist, "He shall baptize with the Holy Ghost and *with fire*" (Matt. iii. 11), would probably be recalled at once to their memory. (2.) The *peculiar* appearance, that of *tongues*, was an emblem of the diversity of *languages* which they were about to be able to utter. Any *form* of fire would have denoted the presence and power of God; but a *form* was adopted expressive of *the case*. Thus *any appearance* at the baptism of Jesus might have denoted the presence and approbation of God; but the form chosen was that of *a dove* descending; expressive of the mild and gentle virtues with which he was to be imbued. So in Ezek. i. 4, any form of flame might have expressed the presence of God; but the appearance *actually* was emblematical of his providence. In the same way, the appearance here, expressed their peculiar endowments for entering on their great work—the ability to speak *powerfully* with new tongues

4. *Were all filled with the Holy Ghost.* Were entirely under his sacred influence and power. See Note, Luke i. 41. 67 To be *filled* with any thing is a phrase denoting that all the faculties are pervaded by it, engaged in it, or under its influence Acts iii. 10, "Were *filled* with wonder and amazement." v. 17, "Filled with indignation." xiii. 45, "Filled with envy." Ver. 52, "Filled with joy and the Holy Ghost." ¶ *Began to speak with other tongues.* In other languages than their native tongue. The languages which they spoke are specified in ver. 8—11. ¶ *As the Spirit gave them utterance* As the Spirit gave them power to speak. This language implies plainly that they were now endued with a faculty of speaking languages which they had not before learned. Their native tongue was

that of Galilee, a somewhat barbarous dialect of the common language used in Judea, *the Syro-Chaldaic.* It is possible that some of them might have been partially acquainted with the Greek and Latin, as both of them were spoken among the Jews to some extent; but there is not the slightest evidence that they were acquainted with the languages of the different nations afterwards specified. Various attempts have been made to account for this remarkable phenomenon without supposing it to be a miracle. But the natural and obvious meaning of the passage is, that they were endowed by the miraculous power of the Holy Ghost with ability to speak foreign languages, and languages to them before unknown. It does not appear that *each one* had the power of speaking *all* the languages which are specified (ver. 9—11), but that this ability was among them, and that together they could speak these languages; probably some one, and some another. The following remarks may perhaps throw some light on this remarkable occurrence. (1.) This ability was predicted in the Old Testament (Isa. xxviii. 11), "With....another tongue will he speak unto this people." Comp. 1 Cor. xiv. 21, where this passage is expressly applied to the power of speaking foreign languages under the gospel. (2.) It was predicted by the Lord Jesus that they should have this power. Mark xvi. 17, "These signs shall follow them that believe....they shall speak with *new tongues.*" (3.) The ability to do it existed extensively and long in the church. 1 Cor. xii. 10, 11. "To another *divers* kinds of tongues; to another the interpretation of tongues: all these worketh that one and the self-same Spirit." Ver. 28, "God hath set in the church....diversities of tongues." 30; xiv. 2. 4, 5, 6. 9. 13, 14. 18, 19. 22, 23. 27. 39. From this it appears that the power was well known in the church, and was not confined to the apostles. This also may show that in the case in the Acts, the power was conferred on other members of the church as well as the apostles. (4.) It was very important that they should be endowed with this power in their great work. They were going forth to preach to all nations; and though the Greek and Roman tongues were extensively spoken, yet their use was not universal; nor is it known that the apostles were skilled in those languages. To preach to all nations, it was indispensable that they should be able to understand their language. And it was necessary that they should be endowed with ability to speak them without the slow process of being compelled to learn them. (5.) One design was to establish the gospel by means of miracles. Yet no miracle could be more striking than the power of conveying their sentiments at once into all the languages of the earth. When it is remembered what a slow and toilsome process it is to learn a foreign tongue, this would be regarded by the heathen as one of the most striking miracles which were ever wrought in the establishment of the Christian faith. 1 Cor. xiv. 22 24, 25. (6.) The *reality* and *certainty* of this miracle is strongly attested by the early triumphs of the gospel. That the gospel was early spread over all the world, and that too by the apostles of Jesus Christ, by men of Galilee, is the clear testimony of all history. They preached it in Arabia, Greece, Syria, Asia. Persia, Africa, and Rome. Yet how *could* this have been effected without a miraculous power of speaking the languages used in all those places? *Now,* it requires the toil of many years to speak in foreign languages; and the *recorded success* of the gospel is one of the most striking attestations to the fact of the miracle that could be conceived. (7.) The *corruption* of language was one of the most decided effects of *sin,* of pride and ambition, and the source of endless embarrassments and difficulties. Gen. xi. It is not to be regarded as wonderful if *one* of the effects of the plan of recovering men should be to show the power of God over *all* evil; and thus to furnish striking evidence that the gospel *could* meet all the crimes and calamities of men. And we may add, (8.) That from this we see the necessity now of *training* men who are to be missionaries to other lands. The gift of miracles is withdrawn. The apostles, by that miracle, simply were *empowered* to speak other languages. That power must still be had if the gospel is to be preached. But it is now to be obtained, not by miracle, but by slow and careful study and toil. If possessed, men must be taught it. They must labour for it. And as the church is bound (Matt. xxviii. 19) to send the gospel to all nations, so it is bound to provide that the *teachers* who shall be sent forth shall be qualified for their work. Hence *one* of the reasons of the importance of training men for the holy ministry.

5 And there were dwelling at Jerusalem, Jews, devout men, out of every nation under heaven.

6 Now [1] when this was noised abroad, the multitude came together, and were confounded, [2] because that every man heard them speak in his own language.

7 And they were all amazed, and marvelled, saying one to another,

[1] When this voice was made.

[2] or, troubled in mind.

5. *There were dwelling at Jerusalem.* The word rendered *dwelling*, κατοικοῦντες, properly means to have a *fixed* and permanent habitation, in distinction from another word, παροικοῦντες, which means to have a *temporary* and *transient* residence in a place. But it is not always confined to this signification; and it is not improbable that many wealthy foreign Jews had a permanent residence in Jerusalem for the convenience of being near the temple. This was the more probable, as about that time the Messiah was expected to appear, Matt. ii. ¶ *Jews.* Jews by birth; of Jewish descent, and religion. ¶ *Devout men,* ἄνδρες εὐλαβεῖς. Literally men of cautious and circumspect lives, who lived in a prudent manner. The term is applied to men who were cautious about offending God; who were careful to observe his commandments. It hence is a general expression to denote *pious* or *religious* men. Acts viii. 2, "And *devout* men carried Stephen to his burial." Luke ii. 25, "And the same man (Simeon) was just, and devout." The word *devout* means, "yielding a solemn and reverential attention to God in religious exercises, particularly in prayer, pious, sincere, solemn" (*Webster*), and very well expresses the force of the original. ¶ *Out of every nation under heaven.* A general expression meaning from all parts of the earth. The countries from which they came are more particularly specified in ver. 9—11. The Jews at that time were scattered into almost all nations, and in all places had synagogues. See Note, John vii. 35. Still they would naturally desire to be present as often as possible at the great feasts of the nation in Jerusalem. Many would seek a residence there for the convenience of being present at the religious solemnities. Many who came up to the feast of the Passover would remain to the feast of the Pentecost. And the consequence was, that on such occasions, the city would be full of strangers. We are told, that when Titus besieged Jerusalem at about the feast of the Passover, there were no less than three millions of people in the city, and this great multitude greatly deepened the calamities arising from the siege. Josephus also mentions an instance where great multitudes of Jews from other nations were present at the feast of Pentecost. Jewish War, b. ii. ch. iii. § 1.

6. *When this was noised abroad.* When the rumour of this remarkable transaction was spread, as it naturally would be without delay. ¶ *Were confounded.* συνεχύθη. Were violently moved and agitated; were amazed, and astonished at the remarkable occurrence. ¶ *Every man heard them speak,* &c. Though the multitude spoke different tongues, yet they now heard *Galileans* use the language which *they* had learned in foreign nations. ¶ *His own language.* His own *dialect*, διαλέκτῳ. His own *idiom*, whether it was a foreign language, or whether it was a modification of the Hebrew. The word may mean either; but it is probable that the foreign Jews would greatly modify the Hebrew, or conform almost entirely to the language spoken in the country where they lived.—We may remark here, that *this* effect on the first descent of the Holy Ghost was not peculiar to that time. A work of grace on the hearts of men in a revival of religion will always *be noised abroad.* A multitude will come together, and God often, as he did here, makes use of this motive to bring them under the influence of religion. *Curiosity* was the motive here, and it was the *occasion* of their being brought under the influence of the truth, and of the conversion. In thousands of cases, this has occurred since. The *effect* of what they saw was to confound them. They made no complaint at first of the *irregularity* of what was done, but were all amazed and overwhelmed. So the effect of a revival of religion is often to convince the multitude that it is indeed a work of the Holy One; to amaze them by the display of his power; and to silence opposition and cavil by the manifest presence and the power of God. A *few* afterwards began to cavil (ver. 13), as some will always do in a revival; but the mass were convinced, as will be the case always, that this was a mighty display of the power of God.

7. *Galileans?* Inhabitants of Galilee. It was remarkable that *they* should speak

Behold, are not all these which speak, Galileans? [a]

8 And how hear we every man in our own tongue, wherein we were born?

9 Parthians, and Medes, and

a c.1.11.

---

in this manner, because, (1.) They were proverbially ignorant, rude, and uncivilized. John i. 46. Hence the term *Galilean* was used as an expression of the deepest reproach and contempt. Mark xiv. 70. John vii. 52. (2.) Their dialect was proverbially barbarous and corrupt. Mark xiv. 70. Matt. xxvi. 73. They were regarded as an outlandish people, unacquainted with other nations and languages, and hence the amazement that they could address them in the refined language of other people. Their native ignorance was the occasion of making the miracle more striking. The native *weakness* and inability of Christian ministers makes the grace and glory of God more remarkable in the success of the gospel. "We have this treasure in earthen vessels, that the excellency of the power may be of God, and not of us." 2 Cor. iv. 7. The *success* which God often grants to those who are of slender endowments and of little learning, though blessed with a humble and pious heart, is often amazing to the men of the world. God has chosen the foolish things of the world to confound the wise. 1 Cor. i. 27. This should teach us that no talent or attainment *is too humble* to be employed for mighty purposes, in its proper sphere, in the kingdom of Christ, and that pious effort may accomplish much, may awe and amaze the world, and then burn in heaven with increasing lustre for ever; while pride, and learning, and talent may blaze uselessly among men, or kindle up the worst passions of our nature, and then be extinguished in eternal night.

8. *Wherein we were born?* That is, as we say, in our *native* language; that which is spoken where we were born.

9. *Parthians, &c.* To show the surprising extent and power of this miracle, Luke enumerates the different nations that were represented then at Jerusalem. In this way the number of *languages* which the apostles spoke, and the extent of the miracle, can be ascertained. The enumeration of these nations begins at the east, and proceeds to the west. *Parthians* mean those Jews, or proselytes, who dwelt in *Parthia.* This country was a part of Persia, and was situated between the Persian gulf and the Tigris on the west, and the river Indus on the east. To the south it was bounded by the desert of Caramania, and it had Media on the north. Their empire lasted about four hundred years, and they were much distinguished for their manner of fighting. They usually fought on horseback, and when appearing to retreat, discharged their arrows with great execution behind them. They were a part of the vast Scythian horde of Asia, and disputed the empire of the east with the Romans. The language spoken there was that of *Persia,* and in ancient writers, *Parthia* and *Persia* often mean the same country. ¶ *Medes.* Inhabitants of *Media.* This country was situated north of Parthia, and south of the Caspian sea. It was about the size of Spain, and was one of the richest parts of Asia. In the Scriptures it is called *Madai.* Gen. x. 2. The *Medes* are often mentioned, frequently in connexion with the *Persians,* with whom they were often connected under the same government. 2 Kings xvii. 6; xviii. 11. Esther i. 19. Jer. xxv. 25. Dan. v. 28. vi. 8; ix. 1. Esther i. 3. 14. 18. Dan. viii. 20. The language spoken here was also that of Persia. In this whole region many Jews remained after the Babylonish captivity, who chose not to return with their brethren to the land of their fathers. From the descendants of these probably were those who were now assembled from those places at Jerusalem. ¶ *Elamites. Elam* is often mentioned in the Old Testament. The nation was descended from *Elam,* the son of Shem. Gen. x. 22. It is mentioned as being in alliance with Amraphel, the king of Shinar, and Arioch, king of Ellasar, and Tidal, king of nations, Gen. xiv. 1. Of these nations in alliance, Chedorlaomer, king of Elam, was the chief. ver. 4. See also Ezra ii. 7; viii. 7. Neh. vii. 12. 34. Isa. xi. 11; xxi. 2; xxii. 6. &c. They are mentioned as a part of the Persian empire, and Daniel is said to have resided *at Shushan, which is in the province of Elam.* Dan. viii. 2. The Greeks and Romans gave to this country the name of *Elymais.* It is now called *Kusistan.* It was bounded by Persia on the east; by Media on the north; by Babylonia on the west; and by the Persian gulf on the south. The Elamites were a warlike people, and celebrated for the use of the bow. Isa. xxii. 6. Jer. xlix. 35. The language of this people was of course the Persian. Its capital *Shusan,* called

Elamites, and the dwellers in Mesopotamia, and in Judea, and Cappadocia, in Pontus, and Asia,

10 Phrygia, and Pamphylia, in

by the Greeks *Susa*, was much celebrated. It is said to have been fifteen miles in circumference; and was adorned with the celebrated palace of Ahasuerus. The inhabitants still pretend to show there the tomb of the prophet Daniel. ¶ *Mesopotamia.* This name, which is Greek, signifies *between the rivers;* that is, the region lying between the rivers *Euphrates* and *Tigris.* In Hebrew it was called *Aram-Naharaim;* that is, Aram, or Syria *of the two rivers.* It was also called Padan Aram, the plain of Syria. In this region were situated some important places mentioned in the Bible:—*Ur of the Chaldees*, the birth-place of Abraham (Gen. xi. 27, 28); *Haran*, where *Terah* stopped on his journey and died (Gen. xi. 31. 32); *Carchemish* (2 Chron. xxxv. 20); *Hena* (2 Kings xix. 13); *Sepharvaim* (2 Kings xvii. 24). This region, known as Mesopotamia, extended between the two rivers from their sources to Babylon on the south. It had on the north Armenia, on the west Syria, on the east Persia, and on the south Babylonia. It was an extensive, level, and fertile country. The language spoken here was probably the *Syriac*, with perhaps a mixture of the *Chaldee.* ¶ *In Judea.* This expression has greatly perplexed commentators. It has been thought difficult to see why *Judea* should be mentioned, as if it were a matter of surprise that they could speak in this language. Some have supposed an error in the manuscripts, and have proposed to read *Armenia*, or *India*, or *Lydia*, or *Idumea*, &c. But all this has been without any authority. Others have supposed that the language of Galilee was so different from that of the other parts of Judea, as to render it remarkable that they could speak that dialect. But this is an idle supposition. This is one of the many instances in which commentators have perplexed themselves to very little purpose. Luke recorded this as any other historian would have done. In running over the languages which they spoke, he enumerated this as a matter of course, not that it was remarkable simply that they should speak the language of *Judea*, but that they should *speak so many*, meaning about the same by it as if he had said *they spoke every language in the world.* Just as if a similar miracle were to occur at this time among an assembly of native Englishmen and foreigners. In describing it, nothing would be more natural than to say, they spoke French, and German, and Spanish, and *English*, and Italian, &c. In this there would be nothing remarkable, except that they spoke *so many languages.* ¶ *Cappadocia.* This was a region of Asia Minor, and was bounded on the east by Armenia, on the north by Pontus and the Euxine sea, west by Lycaonia, and south by Cilicia. The language which was spoken here is not certainly known. It was probably, however, a mixed dialect made up of Greek and Syriac, perhaps the same as their neighbours, the Lycaonians. Acts xiv. 11. This place was formerly celebrated for iniquity, and is mentioned in Greek writers as one of the three eminently wicked places, whose name began with C. The others were *Crete* (Comp. Titus i. 12), and Cilicia. After its conversion to the Christian religion, however, it produced many eminent men, among whom were Gregory Nyssen, and Basil the Great. It was one of the places to which Peter directed an epistle. 1 Pet. i. 1. ¶ *In Pontus.* This was another province of Asia Minor, and was situated north of Cappadocia, and was bounded west by Paphlagonia. Pontus and Cappadocia under the Romans constituted one province. This was one of the places to which the apostle Peter directed his epistle. 1 Pet. i. 1. This was the birth-place of Aquila, one of the companions of Paul. Acts xviii. 2. 18. 26. Rom. xvi. 3. 1 Cor. xvi. 19. 2 Tim. iv. 19. ¶ *And Asia.* Pontus, and Cappadocia, &c. were *parts* of Asia. But the word *Asia* is doubtless used here to denote the regions or provinces *west* of these, which are not particularly enumerated. Thus it is used Acts vi. 9; xvi. 6; xx. 16. The capital of this region was Ephesus. See also 1 Pet. i. 1. This region was frequently called *Ionia*, and was afterwards the seat of the seven churches in Asia. Rev. i. 4.

10. *Phrygia and Pamphylia.* These were also two provinces of Asia Minor. Phrygia was surrounded by Galatia, Cappadocia, and Pisidia. Pamphylia was on the Mediterranean, and was bounded north by Pisidia. The language of all these places was doubtless the *Greek*, more or less pure. ¶ *In Egypt.* This was that extensive country, well known, on the south of the Mediterranean, watered by the Nile. It extends 600 miles from north to south, and from 100 to 120 east and west. The language used there was the *Coptic.* At present the Arabic is spoken. Vast numbers of Jews dwelt

Egypt, and in the parts of Libya about Cyrene, and strangers of Rome, Jews and proselytes,

11 Cretes and Arabians, we do hear them speak in our tongues [a] the wonderful works of God.

a 1Cor.12.10,28.

in Egypt; and many from that country would be present at the great feasts at Jerusalem. In this country the first translation of the Old Testament was made, which is now called the Septuagint. ¶ *In the parts of Libya.* Libya is a general name for Africa. It *properly* denoted the region which was near to Egypt; but the Greeks gave the name to all Africa. ¶ *About Cyrene.* This was a region about 500 miles west of Alexandria in Egypt. It was also called *Pentapolis*, because there were in it five celebrated cities. This country now belongs to *Tripoli.* Great numbers of Jews resided here. A Jew of this place, Simon by name, was compelled to bear our Saviour's cross after him to the place of crucifixion. Matt. xxvii. 32. Luke xxiii. 26. Some of the Cyrenians are mentioned among the earliest Christians. Acts xi. 20; xiii. 1. The language which they spoke is not certainly known. ¶ *Strangers of Rome.* This literally means "Romans dwelling, or tarrying," i. e. at Jerusalem. It may mean either that they were *permanently* fixed, or only *tarrying* at Jerusalem. οἱ ἐπιδημοῦντες Ῥωμαῖοι. They were doubtless Jews who had taken up their residence in Italy, and had come to Jerusalem to attend the great feasts. The language which they spoke was the Latin. Great numbers of Jews were at that time dwelling at Rome. Josephus says that there were eight synagogues there. The Jews are often mentioned by the Roman writers. There was a Jewish colony across the Tiber from Rome. When Judea was conquered, about sixty years before Christ, vast numbers of Jews were taken captive and carried to Rome. But they had much difficulty in managing them as slaves. They pertinaciously adhered to their religion, observed the Sabbath, and refused to join in the idolatrous rites of the Romans. Hence they were freed, and lived by themselves across the Tiber. ¶ *Jews.* Native born Jews, or descendants of Jewish families. ¶ *Proselytes.* Those who had been converted to the Jewish religion from among the Gentiles. The great zeal of the Jews to make proselytes is mentioned by our Saviour as one of the peculiar characteristics of the Pharisees. Matt. xxiii. 15. Some have supposed that the expression *Jews and proselytes* refers to the Romans only. But it is more probable that reference is made to *all* those that are mentioned. It has the appearance of a hurried enumeration; and the writer evidently mentioned them as they occurred to his mind, just as we would in giving a rapid account of so many different nations.

11. *Cretes.* *Crete*, now called *Candia*, is an island in the Mediterranean, about 200 miles in length and 50 in breadth, about 500 miles southwest of Constantinople, and about the same distance west of Syria or Palestine. The climate is mild and delightful, the sky unclouded and serene. By some this island is supposed to be the *Caphtor* of the Hebrews. Gen. x. 14. It is mentioned in the Acts as the place touched at by Paul. Acts xxvii. 7, 8. 13. This was the residence of Titus, who was left there by Paul *to set in order the things that were wanting*, &c. Titus i. 5. The Cretans among the Greeks were famous for deceit and falsehood. Titus i. 12, 13. The language spoken there was probably the Greek. ¶ *Arabians.* Arabia is the great peninsula which is bounded north by part of Syria, east by the Euphrates and the Persian gulf, south by the Indian ocean, and west by the Red sea. It is often mentioned in the Scriptures; and there were doubtless there many Jews. The language spoken there was the *Arabic.* ¶ *In our tongues.* The languages spoken by the apostles could not have been less than seven or eight, besides different dialects of the same languages. It is not certain that the Jews present from foreign nations spoke those languages perfectly; but they had doubtless so used them as to make them the common tongue in which they conversed. No miracle could be more decided than this. There was no way in which the apostles could *impose* on them, and make them *suppose* they spoke foreign languages, if they really did not; for these foreigners were abundantly able to determine that. It may be remarked that this miracle had most important effects besides that witnessed on the day of Pentecost. The gospel would be carried by those who were converted to all these places; and the way would be prepared for the labours of the apostles there. Accordingly, most of these places became afterwards celebrated by the establishment of Christian churches.

12 And they were all amazed, and were in doubt, saying one to another, What[a] meaneth this?

a c.17.20.

13 Others, mocking, said, These men are full of new wine.

14 But Peter, standing up with

and the conversion of great multitudes to the Christian faith. ¶ *The wonderful works of God.* τὰ μεγαλεῖα τοῦ Θεοῦ. The *great things* of God; that is, the great things that God had done in the gift of his Son; in his raising him from the dead; in his miracles, ascension, &c. Comp. Luke i. 49. Ps. lxxi. 19; xxvi. 7; lxvi. 3; xcii. 5; civ. 24, &c.

12. *Were in doubt.* This expression, διηπόρουν, denotes a state of *hesitancy* or *anxiety* about an event. It is applied to those who are travelling, and are ignorant of the way, or who hesitate about the road. They were *all* astonished at this; they did not know how to understand it or explain it, until some of them supposed it was merely the effect of new wine.

13. *Others mocking, said.* The word rendered "mocking" means *to cavil, to deride.* It occurs in the New Testament but in one other place. Acts xvii. 32. "And when they heard of the resurrection of the dead, some mocked." This was an effect that was not confined to the day of Pentecost. There has been seldom a revival of religion, a remarkable manifestation of the power of the Holy Spirit, that has not given occasion for profane mockery and merriment. One characteristic of wicked men is to deride those things which are done to promote their own welfare. Hence the Saviour himself was mocked; and the efforts of Christians to save others have been the subject of derision. *Derision*, and *mockery*, and *a jeer*, have been far more effectual in deterring men from becoming Christians than any attempts at sober argument. God will treat men as they treat him. Ps. xviii. 26. And hence he says to the wicked, "Because I have called and ye refused.... but ye have set at nought my counsel, I also will laugh at your calamity, I will *mock* when your fear cometh." Prov. i. 24—26 ¶ *These men are full of new wine.* These men are drunk. In such times men will have some way of accounting for the effects of the gospel; and the way is commonly about as wise and rational as this. "To escape the absurdity of acknowledging their own ignorance, they adopted the theory *that strong drink can teach languages.*"—Dr. McLelland. In modern times it has been usual to denominate such scenes fanaticism, or wild-fire, or enthusiasm. When men fail in argument, it is common to attempt to confute a doctrine or bring reproach upon a transaction by "giving it an ill name." Hence the names Puritan, Quaker, Methodist, &c. were at first given in derision, to account for some remarkable effect of religion on the world. Comp. Matt. xi. 19. John vii. 20, viii. 48. And thus men endeavour to trace revivals to ungoverned and heated passions; and they are regarded by many as the mere offspring of fanaticism. The friends of revivals should not be discouraged by this; but should remember that the very first revival of religion was by many supposed to be *the effect of a drunken frolic.* ¶ *New wine.* γλεύκους. This word properly means the juice of the grape which distils before a pressure is applied, and called *must.* It was *sweet* wine; and hence the word in Greek meaning *sweet* was given to it. The ancients, it is said, had the art of preserving their new wine with the peculiar flavour before fermentation for a considerable time, and were in the habit of drinking it in the morning. See Horace, Sat. b. ii. iv. *Sweet wine,* which was probably the same as that mentioned here, is also mentioned in the Old Testament. Isa. xlix. 26. Amos ix. 13.

14. *But Peter.* This was in accordance with the natural temperament of Peter. He was bold, forward, ardent; and he rose now to defend the apostles of Jesus Christ, and Christ himself, from an injurious charge. Not daunted by ridicule or opposition, he felt that now was the time for preaching the gospel to the crowd that had been assembled by curiosity. No ridicule should deter Christians from an honest avowal of their opinions, and a defence of the operations of the Holy Spirit. ¶ *With the eleven.* Matthias was now one of the apostles, and now appeared as one of the witnesses for the truth. They probably all arose, and took part in the discourse. Possibly Peter *began* to discourse, and either all spoke together in different languages, or one succeeded another. ¶ *Ye men of Judea.* Men who are Jews; that is, Jews by birth. The original does not mean that they were permanent dwellers *in Judea,* but that they were *Jews,* of Jewish families. Literally, "men, Jews." ¶ *And all ye that dwell, &c.* All others besides

the eleven, lifted up his voice, and
said unto them, Ye men of Judea,
and all *ye* that dwell at Jerusalem,
be this known unto you, and hearken to my words:

15 For these are not drunken, as
ye suppose, seeing [a] it is *but* the
third hour of the day.

16 But this is that which was [b]
spoken by the prophet Joel:

a 1 Th.5.7. *b* Joel 2.28,32.

native-born Jews, whether proselytes or strangers, who were abiding at Jerusalem. This comprised, of course, the whole assembly. and was a respectful and conciliatory introduction to his discourse. Though they had mocked them, yet he treated them with respect, and did not render railing for railing (1 Pet. iii. 9), but sought to *convince* them of their error. ¶ *Be this known*, &c. Peter did not intimate that this was a doubtful matter, or one that could not be explained. His address was respectful, yet firm. He proceeded calmly to *show* them their error. When the enemies of religion deride us or the gospel, we should answer them kindly and respectfully, yet firmly. We should *reason* with them coolly, and convince them of their error. Prov. xv. 1. In this case Peter acted on the principle which he afterwards enjoined on all. 1 Pet. iii. 15, "Be ready always to give an answer to every man that asketh you a reason of the hope that is in you, with meekness and fear." The design of Peter was to *vindicate* the conduct of the apostles from the reproach of intoxication. to show that this could be no other than the work of God; and to make an application of the truth to his hearers. This he did, (1.) By showing that this could not be reasonably supposed to be the effect of new wine, ver. 15. (2.) That it had been expressly predicted in the writings of the Jewish prophets, ver. 16—21. (3.) By a calm argument, proving the resurrection and ascension of Christ, and showing that this also was in accordance with the Jewish Scriptures, ver. 22—35. We are not to suppose that this was the *whole* of Peter's discourse, but that these were the topics on which he insisted, and the main points of his argument.

15. *For these are not drunken*, &c. The word *these* here includes Peter himself, as well as the others. The charge doubtless extended to all. ¶ *The third hour of the day*. The Jews divided their day into *twelve* equal parts, reckoning from sunrise to sunset. Of course the hours were longer in the summer than in the winter. The *third* hour would answer to our nine o'clock in the morning. The reasons why it was so improbable that they should be drunk at that time were the following. (1.) It was the hour of morning worship, or sacrifice. It was highly improbable, that at that early hour they would be intoxicated. (2.) It was not usual for even drunkards to become drunk in the day time. 1 Thess. v. 7. "They that be drunken, are drunken in the night." (3.) The charge was, that they had become drunk with wine. Ardent spirits, or alcohol, that curse of *our* times, was unknown. It was very improbable that so much of the weak wine commonly used in Judea, should have been taken at that early hour as to produce intoxication. (4.) It was a regular practice with the Jews, not to eat or drink *any* thing until after the third hour of the day, especially on the Sabbath, and on all festival occasions. Sometimes this abstinence was maintained until noon. So universal was this custom, that the apostle could appeal to it with confidence, as a full refutation of the charge of drunkenness at that hour. Even the intemperate were not accustomed to drink before that hour. The following testimonies on this subject from Jewish writers, are from Lightfoot. "This was the custom of pious people in ancient times, that each one should offer his morning prayers with additions in the synagogue, and then return home and take refreshment." *Maimonides, Shabb.* ch. 30. "They remained in the synagogue until the sixth hour and a half, and then each one offered the prayer of the Mincha, before he returned home, and then he ate.' "The fourth is the hour of repast, when all eat." One of the Jewish writers says, that the difference between thieves and honest men might be known by the fact that the *former* might be seen in the morning at the fourth hour, eating and sleeping, and holding a cup in his hand. But for those who made pretensions to religion, as the apostles did, such a thing was altogether improbable.

16. *This is that*. This is the *fulfilment* of that, or this was predicted. This was the *second* part of Peter's argument, to show that this was in accordance with the predictions in their own Scriptures. ¶ *By the prophet Joel*. Joel ii. 28—32. This is not quoted *literally*, either from the Hebrew or the Septuagint The substance however is preserved.

17 And it shall come to pass in the last days, (saith God,) I will pour out [a] of my Spirit upon al

a Is.44.3. Eze.36.27

17. *It shall come to pass.* It shall happen, or shall occur. ¶ *In the last days.* Heb. Chaldee, Syriac, and Arabic, *after these things*, or *afterwards*. The expression *the last days*, however, occurs frequently in the Old Testament. Gen. xlix. 1. Jacob called his sons, that he might tell them what should happen to them *in the last days*, i. e. in future times. Heb. *in after times*. Micah iv. 1. "*In the last days* (Heb. in after times) the mountain of the Lord's house," &c. Isa. ii. 2, "*In the last days* the mountain of the Lord's house shall be established in the tops of the mountains," &c. The expression then properly denoted *the future times* in general. But, as the coming of the Messiah was to the eye of a Jew the most important event in the coming ages, the great, glorious, and crowning scene in all that vast futurity, the phrase came to be regarded as properly expressive of that. And they spoke of future times, and of the last times, as the glad period which should be crowned and honoured with the presence and triumphs of the Messiah. It stood in opposition to the usual denomination of earlier times. It was a phrase in contrast with the days of the patriarch, the kings, the prophets, &c. The *last days*, or the closing period of the world, were the days of the Messiah. It does not appear from this, and it certainly is not implied in the expression, that they supposed the world would then come to an end. Their views were just the contrary. They anticipated a long and glorious time, under the dominion of the Messiah, and to this expectation they were led by the promise that his kingdom should be for ever; that of the increase of his government there should be no end, &c. This expression was understood by the writers of the New Testament as referring undoubtedly to the times of the gospel. And hence they often used it as denoting that the time of the expected Messiah had come, but *not* to imply that the world was drawing near to an end. Heb. i. 2, "God hath spoken in these last days by his Son.' 1 Pet. i. 20, "Was manifested in these last times for you." 2 Pet. iii. 3. 1 Pet. i 5. 1 John ii. 18. "Little children it is the last time," &c. Jude 18. The expression *the last day*, is applied by our Saviour to the resurrection and the day of judgment. John vi. 39, 40. 44, 45; xi. 24; xii. 48. Here the expression means simply *in those future times, when the Messiah shall have come.* ¶ *I will pour out of my Spirit.* The expression in Hebrew is, "I will pour out my Spirit." The word *pour* is commonly applied to *water*, or to blood, to pour it out, or to shed it, Isa. lvii. 6; to *tears*, to pour them out, i. e. to weep, &c. Ps. xlii. 4. 1 Sam. i. 15. It is applied to water, to wine, or to blood, in the New Testament. Matt. ix. 17. Rev. xvi. 1. Acts xxii. 20. "The blood of thy martyr Stephen *was shed*." It conveys also the idea of *communicating largely*, or *freely*, as water is poured freely from a fountain. Titus iii. 5, 6, "The renewing of the Holy Ghost, which he *shed on us abundantly*." Thus Job xxxvi. 27, "They (the clouds) pour down rain according to the vapour thereof." Isa. xliv. 3, "I will pour water on him that is thirsty." xlv. 8, "Let the skies pour down righteousness." Mal. iii. 10, "I will pour you out a blessing." It is also applied to *fury* and *anger*, when God intends to say that he will not spare, but will signally punish. Ps. lxix. 24 Jer. x. 25. It is not unfrequently applied *to the Spirit*. Prov. i. 23. Isa. xliv. 3. Zach. xii. 10. And then it means that he will bestow large measures of spiritual influences. As the *Spirit* renews and sanctifies men, so to pour out the Spirit is to grant freely his influences to renew and sanctify the soul. ¶ *My Spirit.* The *Spirit* here denotes the third person of the Trinity, promised by the Saviour, and sent to finish his work, and apply it to men. The Holy Spirit is regarded as the source, or *conveyer* of all the blessings which Christians experience. Hence he renews the heart. John iii. 5, 6. He is the source of all proper feelings and principles in Christians, or he produces the Christian graces. Gal. v. 22—25. Titus iii. 5—7. The spread and success of the gospel is attributed to him. Isa. xxxii. 15, 16. Miraculous gifts are traced to him; especially the various gifts with which the early Christians were endowed. 1 Cor. xii. 4—10. The promise that he would pour out his Spirit, means that he would in the time of the Messiah, impart a large measure of those influences, which it was his peculiar province to communicate to men. A *part* of them were communicated on the day of Pentecost, in the miraculous endowment of the power of speaking foreign languages, in the wisdom of the apostles, and in the conversion of the three thousand. ¶ *Upon all flesh.* The word *flesh* here means *persons*,

flesh: and your sons and your daughters shall prophesy, and your young men shall see visions, and your old men shall dream dreams:

or *men.* See Note, Rom. i. 3. The word *all* here does not mean every individual, but every *class* or *rank* of men. It is to be limited to the cases specified immediately. The influences were not to be confined to any class, but to be communicated to all *kinds* of persons, old men, youth, servants, &c. Comp. 1 Tim. ii. 1—4. ¶ *And your sons and your daughters.* Your children. It would seem, however, that females shared in the remarkable influences of the Holy Spirit. Philip, the Evangelist, had four daughters which did prophesy. Acts xxi. 9. It is probable also that the females of the church of Corinth partook of this gift, though they were forbidden to exercise it in public. 1 Cor. xiv. 34. The office of prophesying, whatever was meant by that, was not confined to the *men* among the Jews. Ex. xv. 20, "Miriam, the prophetess, took a timbrel," &c. Judg. iv. 4, "Deborah, a prophetess, judged Israel." 2 Kings xxii. 14. See also Luke ii. 36, 'There was one Anna, a prophetess," &c. ¶ *Shall prophesy.* The word *prophesy* is used in a great variety of senses. (1.) It means to *predict,* or *foretel* future events. Matt. xi. 13; xv. 7. (2.) To divine, to conjecture, to declare as a prophet might. Matt. xxvi. 68, "Prophesy who smote thee" (3.) To celebrate the praises of God, being under a divine influence. Luke i. 67. This seems to have been a considerable part of the employment in the ancient schools of the prophets. 1 Sam. x. 5; xix. 20; xxx. 15. (4.) To *teach*—as no small part of the office of the prophets was to teach the doctrines of religion. Matt. vii. 22, "Have we not prophesied in thy name?" (5.) It denotes then, in general, *to speak under a divine influence,* whether in foretelling future events; in celebrating the praises of God; in instructing others in the duties of religion, or *in speaking foreign languages under that influence.* In this last sense, the word is used in the New Testament, to denote those who were miraculously endowed with the power of speaking foreign languages. Acts xix. 6. The word is also used to denote *teaching,* or speaking in intelligible language, in *opposition* to speaking a foreign tongue. 1 Cor. xiv. 1—5. In this place it means that they should speak under a divine influence, and is *specially* applied to the power of speaking in a foreign tongue. ¶ *Your young men shall see visions.* The will of God in former times was communicated to the prophets in various ways. One was by *visions,* and hence one of the most usual names of the prophets was *seers.* The name *seer* was first given to that class of men, and was superseded by the name *prophet.* 1 Sam. ix. 9, "He that is now called a prophet was before time called a *Seer.*" ix. 11. 18 19. 2 Sam. xxiv. 11; xxix. 29 &c. This name was given from the *manner* in which the divine will was communicated, which seems to have been by throwing the prophet into an ecstacy, and then by causing the *vision,* or the *appearance* of the objects or events to pass before the mind. The prophet looked upon the passing scene, the often splendid diorama as it actually occurred, and recorded it as it appeared to his mind. Hence he recorded rather the *succession* of images than the *times* in which they would occur. These visions occurred sometimes when they were *asleep,* and sometimes during a prophetic ecstacy. Dan. ii. 28, vii. 1, 2. 15; viii. 2. Ezek. xi. 24. Gen. xv. 1. Num. xii. 6. Job iv. 13; vii. 14. Ezek. i. 1; viii. 3. Often the prophet seemed to be transferred, or translated to another place from where he was; and the scene in a distant *land* or *age* passed before the mind. Ezek. viii. 3; xl. 2; xi. 24. Dan. viii. 2. In this case the distant scene or time passed before the prophet, and he recorded it as it appeared to him. That this did not cease before the times of the gospel is evident. Acts ix. 10, "To Ananias said the Lord *in a vision,*" &c 12, "And hath seen (i. e. Paul) *in a vision,* a man named Ananias," &c. i. e. Paul hath seen Ananias represented to him, though absent; he has had an image of him coming in to him. Acts x. 3, Cornelius "saw in a vision evidently an angel of God coming to him," &c. This was one of the modes by which in former times God made known his will; and the language of the Jews came to express a revelation in this manner. Though there were strictly no *visions* on the day of Pentecost, yet that was one scene under the great economy of the Messiah, under which God would make known his will in a manner as clear as he did to the ancient Jews. ¶ *Your old men shall dream dreams.* The will of God in former times was made known often in this manner; and there are several instances recorded in which it was done under the gospel. God informed Abimelech in a dream, that Sarah was the wife of Abraham. Gen. xx. 3. He spoke to

18 And on my servants and on my handmaidens I will pour out, in those days, of my Spirit; and [a] they shall prophesy:

19 And I will show wonders in heaven above, and signs in the earth beneath; blood, and fire, and vapour of smoke:

[a] c.21.4,9,10. 1Cor.12.10

Jacob in a dream, Gen. xxxi. 11; to Laban, xxxi. 24; to Joseph, xxxvii. 5; to the butler and baker, xl. 5; to Pharaoh, xli. 1—7; to Solomon, 1 Kings iii. 5; to Daniel, Dan. ii. 3; vii. 1. It was prophesied by Moses that in this way God would make known his will. Num. xii. 6. It occurred even in the times of the gospel. Matt. i. 20. Joseph was warned in a dream. ii. 12, 13. 19. 22. Pilate's wife was also troubled in this manner about the conduct of the Jews to Christ. Matt. xxvii. 19. As this was one way in which the will of God was made known formerly to men, so the expression here denotes simply that his will should be made known; that it should be one characteristic of the times of the gospel that God would reveal himself to man. The ancients probably had some mode of determining whether their *dreams* were divine communications, or whether they were, as they are now, the mere erratic wanderings of the mind when unrestrained and unchecked by the will. At present no confidence is to be put in dreams.

18. *And on my servants.* The Hebrew in Joel is "upon *the* servants." The Septuagint and the Latin Vulgate, however, render it "on *my* servants." In Joel, the prophet would seem to be enumerating the different conditions and ranks of society. The influences of the Spirit would be confined to no class; they would descend on old and young, and even on servants and handmaids. So the Chaldee Paraphrase understood it. But the Septuagint and Peter evidently understood it in the sense of *servants of God;* as the worshippers of God are often called *servants* in the Scriptures. See Rom. i. 1. It is possible, however, that the Hebrew intended to refer to the servants of God. It is not "upon *your* servants," &c. as in the former expression, "*your* sons," &c.; but the form is changed, "upon *servants* and handmaids." The language, therefore, will admit the construction of the Septuagint and of Peter; and it was this variation in the Hebrew which suggested, doubtless, the mention of "*my* servants," &c. instead of *your* servants. ¶ *And handmaids.* Female servants. The name is several times given to pious women. Ps. lxxxvi. 16; cxvi. 16. Luke i. 38. 48. The meaning of this verse does not materially differ from the former. In the times of the gospel, those who were brought under its influence should be remarkably endowed with ability to declare the will of God.

19, 20. *I will show wonders.* Literally, "I will give signs." δωσω τέρατα. The word in the Hebrew, מופתים, *mophethim*, means properly *prodigies;* wonderful occurrences; miracles wrought by God or his messengers. Exod. iv. 21; vii. 3. 9; xi. 9. Deut. iv. 34, &c. It is the common word to denote a *miracle*, in the Old Testament. Here it means, however, *a portentous appearance, a prodigy, a remarkable occurrence.* It is commonly joined in the New Testament with the word *signs*, "signs and wonders." Matt. xxiv. 24. Mark xiii. 22. John iv. 48. In these places it does not of necessity mean *miracles*, but unusual and remarkable appearances. Here it is fixed to mean great and striking changes in the sky, the sun, moon, &c. The Hebrew is, "I will give signs in the heaven, and upon the earth." Peter has quoted it according to the sense, and not according to the letter. The Septuagint is here a literal translation of the Hebrew; and this is one of the instances where the New Testament writers did not quote from either.

Much of the difficulty of interpreting these verses consists in fixing the proper meaning to the expression "that great and notable *day* of the Lord." If it be limited to the day of Pentecost, it is certain that no such events occurred at that time. But there is, it is believed, no propriety in confining it to that time. The description here pertains to "the last days" (ver. 17), i. e. to the *whole* of that period of duration, however long, which was known by the prophets as *the last times.* That period might be extended through many centuries; and *during* that period *all* these events would take place. The *day of the Lord* is the day when God shall *manifest himself* in a peculiar manner; a day when *he* shall so strikingly be seen in his wonders and his judgments, that it may be called *his* day. Thus it is applied to the day of judgment, as the *day of the Son of man;* the day in which *he* will be the great attractive object, and will be signally glorified. Luke xvii. 24. 1 Thess. v. 2. Phil i. 6. 2 Pet. iii. 12. If

20 The[a] sun shall be turned into darkness, and the moon into blood, before that great and notable day of the Lord come:

a Mar.13.24. 2Pet.3.7,10.

as I suppose, "that notable day of the Lord" here denotes that future time when God shall manifest himself in judgment, then we are not to suppose that Peter meant to say that these "wonders" should take place on the day of Pentecost, or had their fulfilment then, *but would occur under that indefinite period called "the last days," the days of the Messiah, and* BEFORE *that period was closed by the great day of the Lord.* The gift of tongues was a *partial* fulfilment of the *general* prophecy pertaining to those times. And as the prophecy was thus *partially* fulfilled, it was a pledge that it would be *entirely;* and thus there was laid a foundation for the necessity of repentance, and for calling on the Lord in order to be saved. ¶ *Blood. Blood* is commonly used as an emblem of slaughter, or of battle. ¶ *Fire.* Fire is also an image of war, or the conflagration of towns and dwellings in time of war. ¶ *Vapour of smoke.* The word *vapour,* ἀτμίς, means commonly an exhalation from the earth, &c. easily moved from one place to another. Here it means (Heb. Joel) *rising columns,* or *pillars of smoke;* and is another image of the calamities of war, the smoke rising from burning towns. It has almost always been customary in war to burn the towns of an enemy, and to render him as helpless as possible. Hence the calamities denoted here are those *represented* by such scenes. To what *particular* scenes there is reference here, it may be impossible now to say. It may be remarked, however, that scenes of this kind occurred before the destruction of Jerusalem, and there is a striking resemblance between the description in Joel, and that by which our Saviour foretels the destruction of Jerusalem. See Notes on Matt. xxiv. 21—24.

20. *The sun shall be turned into darkness.* See Note, Matt. xxiv. 29. The same images used here with reference to the sun and moon, are used also there. They occur not unfrequently. Mark xiii. 24. 2 Pet. iii. 7—10. The shining of the sun is an emblem of prosperity; the withdrawing, or eclipse, or setting of the sun is an emblem of calamity, and is often thus used in the Scriptures. Isa. lx. 20. Jer. xv. 9. Ezek. xxxii. 7. Amos viii. 9. Rev. vi. 12; viii 12; ix. 2; xvi. 8. To say that the sun is darkened, or turned into darkness, is an image of calamity, and especially of the calamities of war, when the smoke of burning cities rises to heaven, and obscures his light. This is not, therefore, to be taken literally, nor does it afford any indication of what will be at the end of the world in regard to the sun. ¶ *The moon into blood.* The word *blood* here means that obscure, sanguinary colour which the moon has when the atmosphere is filled with smoke and vapour; and especially the lurid and alarming appearance which it assumes when smoke and flames are thrown up by earthquakes and fiery eruptions. Rev. vi. 12, "And I beheld when he had opened the sixth seal, and lo, there was a great earthquake, and the sun became black as sackcloth of hair, and the moon became as blood." Rev. viii. 8. In this place it denotes great calamities. The figures used are indicative of wars, and conflagrations, and unusual prodigies of earthquakes. As these things are (Matt. xxiv.) applied to the destruction of Jerusalem; as they actually occurred previous to that event (see Notes, Matt. xxiv.); it may be supposed that the prophecy in Joel had an immediate reference to that. The meaning of the quotation by Peter in this place, therefore is, that what occurred on the day of Pentecost, *was the beginning of the series of wonders that was to take place during the times of the Messiah.* It is not intimated that those scenes were to close, or to be exhausted in that age. They may precede that great day of the Lord which is yet to come in view of the whole earth. ¶ *That great and notable day of the Lord.* This is called the *great* day of the Lord because on that day he will be signally manifested, more impressively and strikingly than on other times. The word *notable,* ἐπιφανῆ, means signal, illustrious, distinguished. In Joel the word is *terrible,* or *fearful;* a word applicable to days of calamity, and trial, and judgment. The Greek word here rendered *notable,* is also in the Septuagint frequently used to denote calamity, or times of judgment. Deut. x. 21. 2 Sam. vii. 23. This will apply to *any* day in which God signally manifests himself; but particularly to a day when he shall come forth to punish men, as at the destruction of Jerusalem, or at the day of judgment. The meaning is, that those wonders should take place *before* that

21 And it shall come to pass, *that* whosoever [a] shall call on the name of the Lord, shall be saved.

a Ps.86.5. Ro.10.13. 1Cor.1.2. He.4.16.

distinguished day should arrive when God should come forth in judgment.

21. *Whosoever shall call.* In the midst of these wonders and dangers, whosoever should call on the Lord should be delivered (Joel). The *name* of the Lord is the same as the Lord himself. It is a Hebraism, signifying to call on the Lord. Ps. lxxix. 6. Zech. xiii. 9. ¶ *Shall be saved.* In Hebrew, shall be *delivered*, i. e. from impending calamities. When they threaten, and God is coming forth to judge them, it shall be that those who are characterized as those who call on the Lord, shall be delivered. This is equally true at all times. It is remarkable that no Christians perished in the siege of Jerusalem. Though more than a million of Jews perished, yet the followers of Christ who were there, having been warned by him, when they saw the signs of the Romans approaching, withdrew to *Ælia*, and were preserved. So it shall be in the day of judgment. All whose character it has been that *they called on God*, will then be saved. While the wicked shall then call on the rocks and the mountains to shelter them *from* the Lord, those who *have* invoked his *favour* and *mercy* shall then find deliverance. The use which Peter makes of this passage is this: Calamities were about to come; the day of judgment was approaching; they were passing through *the last days* of the earth's history; and therefore it became them to call on the name of the Lord, and to obtain deliver ance from the dangers which impended over the guilty. There can be little doubt that Peter intended to apply this to the Messiah, and that by the name of the Lord he meant the Lord Jesus. See 1 Cor. i. 2. Paul makes the same use of the passage, expressly applying it to the Lord Jesus Christ. Rom. x. 13, 14. In Joel, the word translated *Lord* is JEHOVAH, the incommunicable and peculiar name of God; and the use of the passage before us in the New Testament, shows how the apostles regarded the Lord Jesus Christ; and proves that they had no hesitation in applying to him names and attributes which could belong to no one but God.

This verse teaches us, 1. That in prospect of the judgments of God which are to come, we should make preparation. We shall be called to pass through the closing scene of this earth; the time when the sun shall be turned into darkness, and the moon into blood, and when the great day of the Lord shall come. 2. It is easy to be saved. All that God requires of us is to call upon him, to pray to him, to ask him, and he will answer and save. If men will not do so easy a thing as to call on God, and *ask* him for salvation, it is obviously proper that they should be cast off. The terms of salvation could not be made plainer or easier. The offer is wide, free, universal, and there is no obstacle but what exists in the heart of the sinner. And from this part of Peter's vindication of the scene on the day of Pentecost, we may learn also, 1. That revivals of religion are to be expected as a part of the history of the Christian church. He speaks of God's pouring out his Spirit, &c. as what was to take place *in the last days*, i. e. in the indefinite and large tract of time which was to come under the administration of the Messiah. His remarks are by no means limited to the day of Pentecost. They are as applicable to future periods as to that time; and we are to expect it *as a part of Christian history*, that the Holy Spirit will be sent down to awaken and convert men 2. This will also vindicate revivals from all the charges which have ever been brought against them. All the objections of irregularity, extravagance, wildfire, enthusiasm, disorder, &c. which have been alleged against revivals in modern times, *might* have been brought with equal propriety against the scene on the day of Pentecost. Yet an apostle showed that that was in accordance with the predictions of the Old Testament, and was an undoubted work of the Holy Spirit. If *that* work could be vindicated, then modern revivals may be. If that was really liable to no objections on these accounts, then modern works of grace should not be objected to for the same things. And if that excited deep interest in the apostles; if they felt deep concern to vindicate it from the charge brought against it, then Christians and Christian ministers now should feel similar solicitude to defend revivals, and not be found among their revilers, their calumniators, or their foes. There will be enemies enough of the work of the Holy Spirit without the aid of professed Christians; and that man possesses no enviable feelings or character who is found with the enemies of God and his Christ, in oppos

22 Ye men of Israel, hear these words; Jesus of Nazareth, a man approved of God among you by miracles [a] and wonders and signs, which God did, by him, in the midst of you, as ye [b] yourselves also know:

23 Him, being [c] delivered by the

a Jno.14.10,11. He.2.4. b Jno.15.24. c Lu.22.22;24.44. c.3.18.

ing the mighty work of the Holy Spirit on the human heart.

22. *Ye men of Israel.* Descendants of Israel, or Jacob, i. e. Jews. Peter proceeds now to the third part of his argument, to show that Jesus Christ had been raised up; and that the scene which had occurred was in accordance with his promise, was proof of his resurrection, and of his exaltation to be the Messiah; and that, therefore, they should repent for their great sin in having put their own Messiah to death. ¶ *A man approved of God.* A man who was *shown* or *demonstrated* to have the approbation of God, or to have been sent by him. ¶ *By miracles, and wonders, and signs.* The first of these words properly means the displays of *power* which Jesus made; the second, the unusual or remarkable events which attended him; the third, the *signs* or *proofs* that he was from God. Together, they denote the *array* or *series* of remarkable works—raising the dead, healing the sick, &c. which showed that Jesus was sent from God. The *proof* which they furnished that he was from God was this, that God would not confer such power on an impostor, and that therefore he was what he pretended to be. ¶ *Which God did by him.* The Lord Jesus himself often traced his power to do these things to his commission from the Father; but he did it in such a way as to show that he was closely united to him. John v. 19. 30. Peter here says that God did these works *by* Jesus Christ, to show that Jesus was truly *sent* by him, and that therefore he had the seal and attestation of God. The same thing Jesus himself said. John v. 36, "The work which the Father hath given me to finish, the same works that I do, bear witness of me, that the Father hath sent me." The great works which God has wrought in creation, as well as in redemption, he is represented as having done by his Son. Heb. i. 2, "By whom also he made the worlds." John i. 3. Col. i. 15—19. ¶ *In the midst of you.* In your own land. It is also probable that many of the persons present had been witnesses of his miracles. ¶ *As ye yourselves also know.* They knew it either by having witnessed them, or by the evidence which every where abounded of the truth that he had wrought them. The Jews, even in the time of Christ, did not dare to call his miracles in question. John xv. 24. While they admitted the miracle, they attempted to trace it to the influence of Beelzebub. Matt. ix. 34. Mark iii. 22. So decided and numerous were the miracles of Jesus, that Peter here appeals to them as having been known by the Jews themselves to have been performed, and with a confidence that even *they* could not deny it. On this he proceeds to rear his argument for the truth of his Messiahship.

23. *Him, being delivered.* ἔκδοτον. This word, *delivered,* is used commonly of those who are *surrendered* or delivered into the hands of enemies or adversaries. It means that Jesus was surrendered, or given up to his enemies by those who should have been his protectors. Thus he was delivered to the chief-priests. Mark x. 33. Pilate released Barabbas, and *delivered* Jesus to their will, Mark xv. 15. Luke xxiii. 25; he was delivered unto the Gentiles, Luke xviii. 32; the chief-priests delivered him to Pilate, Matt. xxvii. 2; and Pilate delivered him to be crucified, Matt. xxvii. 26. John xix. 16. In this manner was the death of Jesus accomplished, by being *surrendered* from one tribunal to another, and one demand of his countrymen to another, until they succeeded in procuring his death. It may also be implied here that he was given or surrendered by God to the hands of men. Thus he is represented to have been *given* by God. John iii. 16. 1 John iv. 9, 10. The Syriac translates this, "Him, who was destined to this by the foreknowledge and will of God, *you delivered* into the hands of wicked men," &c. The Arabic, "Him, delivered *to you* by the hands of the wicked, you received, and after you had mocked him, you slew him." ¶ *By the determinate counsel.* The word translated *determinate,* τῇ ὡρισμένῃ, means, properly, that which is *defined, marked out,* or *bounded;* as, to mark out or define the boundary of a field, &c. See Rom. i. 1. 4. In Acts x. 42, it is translated *ordained* of God; denoting *his purpose that it should be so,* i. e. that Jesus should be the judge of quick and dead. Luke xxii. 22, "The Son of man goeth as it is *determined* of him," i. e. as God has purposed or determined beforehand that he should go.

determinate counsel and foreknowledge of God, ye [a] have taken, and [b] by wicked hands have crucified and slain:

a c.5.30. b Matt.27.

Acts xi. 29, "The disciples.... *determined* to send relief unto the brethren which dwelt in Judea," i. e. they *resolved* or *purposed* beforehand to do it. Acts xvii. 26, "God.... *hath determined* the times before appointed and fixed," &c. In all these places there is the idea of a *purpose*, or *intention*, or *plan* implying *intention*, and marking out or fixing the boundaries to some future action or event. The word implies that the death of Jesus was *resolved on* by God before it took place. And this truth is established by all the predictions made in the Old Testament, and by the Saviour himself. God was not *compelled* to give up his Son. There was no *claim* on him for it. And he had a right, therefore, to determine when and how it should be done. The fact, moreover, that this was *predicted*, shows that it was fixed or resolved on. No event can be *foretold*, evidently, unless it be *certain* that it will take place. The event, therefore, must in some way be fixed or resolved on beforehand. ¶ *Counsel.* βουλῆ. This word properly denotes purpose, decree, *will.* It expresses the act of the mind in *willing*, or the purpose or design which is formed. Here it means the purpose or will of God; it was his plan or decree that Jesus should be delivered. Acts iv. 28, "For to do whatsoever thy hand and *thy counsel* (ἡ βουλή σου) determined before to be done." Eph. i. 11, "Who worketh all things after *the counsel* of his own will." Heb. vi. 17, "God, willing....to show....the immutability of *his counsel.*" See Acts xx. 27. 1 Cor. iv. 5. Luke xxiii. 51. The word here, therefore, proves that Jesus was delivered by the deliberate purpose of God; that it was according to his previous intention and design. The reason why this was insisted on by Peter, was, that he might convince the Jews that Jesus was not delivered by *weakness*, or because he was unable to rescue himself. Such an opinion would have been inconsistent with the belief that he was the Messiah. It was important, then, to assert the *dignity* of Jesus, and to show that his death was in accordance with the fixed design of God; and therefore, that it did not interfere in the least with his claims to be the Messiah. The same thing our Saviour has himself expressly affirmed. John xix. 10, 11; x. 18. Matt. xxvi. 53. ¶ *Foreknowledge.* This word denotes the seeing beforehand of an event yet to take place It implies, 1. Omniscience; and 2. That the event is fixed and certain. To foresee a contingent event, that is, to foresee that an event will take place, when it may or may not take place, is an absurdity. Foreknowledge, therefore, implies that for some reason the event *will certainly* take place. What that reason is, the word itself does not determine. As, however, *God* is represented in the Scriptures as purposing or determining future events; as they could not be *foreseen* by him unless he had so determined, so the word sometimes is used in the sense of determining beforehand, or as synonymous with decreeing. Rom. viii. 29; xi. 2. In this place the word is used to denote that the delivering up of Jesus was something more than a bare or naked decree. It implies that God did it according to his *foresight* of what would be the best time, and place, and manner of its being done. It was not the result merely of *will*; it was will directed by a wise foreknowledge of what would be best. And this is the case with all the decrees of God. It follows from this, that the conduct of the Jews was foreknown. God was not disappointed in any thing respecting their treatment of his Son. Nor will he be disappointed in any of the doings of men. Notwithstanding the wickedness of the world, his counsel shall stand, and he will do all his pleasure. Isa. xlvi. 10. ¶ *Ye have taken.* See Matt. xxvi. 57. Ye *Jews* have taken. It is possible that some were present on this occasion who had been personally concerned in taking Jesus; and many who had joined in the cry, "Crucify him." Luke xxiii. 18—21. It was, at any rate, the act *of the Jewish people* by which this had been done. This was a striking instance of the fidelity of that preaching which says, as Nathan did to David, "Thou art the man!" Peter, once so timid that he denied his Lord now charged this atrocious crime on his countrymen, regardless of their anger and his own danger. He did not deal in *general* accusations, but brought the charges home, and declared that *they* were the men who had been concerned in this amazing crime. No preaching can be successful that does not charge on men their personal guilt; and that does not fearlessly proclaim their ruin and danger ¶ *With wicked hands.* Greek, "through or by the hands of the lawless, or wicked." This refers, doubtless, to Pilate and the Roman soldiers, through whose instrumentality this had been done. The reasons for supposing that this is the true interpretation of the passage are these: (1.) The Jews had not the power of inflicting death themselves. (2.) The term used here, *wicked*, ἀνόμων, is not applicable to the *Jews*, but to the Romans. It properly means *lawless*, or those who had not the law, and is often applied to the heathen. Rom. ii. 12. 14. 1 Cor. ix. 21. (3.) The punishment which was inflicted was a Roman punishment. (4.) It was a matter of fact, that the Jews, though they had *condemned* him, yet had not put him to death themselves, but had demanded it of the Romans. But though they had employed the Romans to do it, still they were the prime movers in the deed; they had plotted, and compassed, and demanded his death; and they were therefore not the less guilty. The maxim of the common law, and of common sense, is, "he who does a deed by the instrumentality of another, is responsible for it." It was from no merit of the Jews that *they* had not put him to death themselves. It was simply because the power was taken away from them. ¶ *Have crucified.* Greek, "having affixed him to the cross, ye have put him to death." Peter here charges the crime fully on them. Their guilt was not diminished because they had employed others to do it.—From this we may remark, 1. That this was one of the most amazing and awful crimes that could be charged on any men. It was malice, and treason, and hatred, and murder combined. Nor was it any common murder. It was *their own Messiah* whom they had put to death; the hope of their fathers; he who had been long promised by God, and the prospect of whose coming had so long cheered and animated the nation. They had now imbrued their hands in his blood, and stood charged with the awful crime of having murdered the Prince of Peace. 2. It is no mitigation of guilt that we do it by the instrumentality of others. It is often, if not always, a deepening and extending of the crime. 3. We have here a striking and clear instance of the doctrine that the decrees of God do not interfere with the free agency of men. This event was certainly *determined* beforehand. Nothing is clearer than this. It is here expressly asserted; and it had been foretold with undeviating certainty by the prophets. God had, for wise and gracious purposes, purposed or decreed in his own mind that his Son should die at the time, and in the manner in which he did; for all the circumstances of his *death*, as well as of his birth and his life, were foretold. And yet, in this the Jews and the Romans never supposed or alleged that they were compelled or cramped in what they did. They *did what they chose.* If in this case the decrees of God were not inconsistent with human freedom, neither can they be in any case. Between those decrees and the freedom of man there *is* no inconsistency, unless it could be shown—what never can be—that God *compels* men to act contrary to their own will. In that case there could be no freedom. But that is *not* the case with regard to the decrees of God. An act is what it is *in itself;* it can be contemplated and measured by itself. That it was *foreseen, foreknown,* or *purposed,* does not alter its nature and more than it does that it be *remembered* after it is performed. The *memory* of what we have done does not destroy our freedom. *Our own purposes* in relation to our conduct do not destroy our freedom; nor can the purposes or designs of any other being violate one free moral action, unless he *compels* us to do a thing against our will. 4. We have here a proof that the decree of God does not take away *the moral character* of an action. It does not prove that an action is *innocent* if it is shown that it is a part of the wise plan of God to permit it. Never was there a more atrocious *crime* than the crucifixion of the Son of God. And yet it was determined on in the divine counsels. So with all the deeds of human guilt. The purpose of God to *permit* them does not destroy their nature or make them innocent. They are what they are in themselves. The purpose of God does not change their character; and if it is *right* to punish them *in fact,* they will be punished. If it is right for God to punish them, it was right to *resolve* to do it. And the sinner must answer for *his sins,* not for the plans of his Maker; nor can he take shelter in the day of wrath against *what he deserves* in the plea that God has determined future events. If any men could have done it, it would have been those whom Peter addressed; yet neither he nor they felt that their guilt was in the least diminished by the fact that Jesus was "delivered by the determinate counsel and foreknowledge of God." 5. If this event was predetermined; if that act of amazing wickedness, when the Son of God was put to death, was fixed by the determinate counsel of God, then all the events leading to it, and the circumstances at-

24 Whom [a] God hath raised up, having loosed the pains of death: because it was not possible [b] that he should be holden of it.

25 For David speaketh [c] concerning him, I foresaw the Lord always

a Lu.24. c.13.30 34. 1Cor.6.14. Ep.1.20. Col.2.12. 1Th.1.10. Heb.13.20. 1Pet.1.21. b Jno.10.18.

c Ps.16.8–11.

tending it, were also a part of the decree. The one could not be determined without the other. 6. If *that* event was determined, then others may be also consistently with human freedom and responsibility. There can be no deed of wickedness that shall surpass that of crucifying the Son of God. And if the acts of his murderers were a part of the wise counsel of God, then on the same principle are we to suppose that all events are under his direction, and ordered by a purpose infinitely wise and good. 7. If the Jews could not take shelter from the charge of wickedness under the plea that it was foreordained, then no sinners can do it. This was as clear a case as can ever occur; and yet the apostle did not intimate that an excuse or mitigation for their sin could be plead from this cause. This case, therefore, meets *all* the excuses of sinners from this plea, and *proves* that those excuses will not avail them or save them in the day of judgment.

24. *Whom God hath raised up.* This was the main point, in this part of his argument, which Peter wished to establish. He could not but admit that the Messiah had been in an ignominious manner put to death. But he now shows them that *God* had also raised him up; had thus given his attestation to his doctrine; and had sent down his Spirit according to the promise which the Lord Jesus made before his death. ¶ *Having loosed the pains of death.* The word *loosed*, λύσας, is opposed to *bind*, and is properly applied to a *cord*, or to any thing which is *bound*. See Matt. xxi. 2. Mark i. 7. Hence it means to *free*, or to *liberate*. Luke xiii. 16. 1 Cor. vii. 27. It is used in this sense here; though the idea of *untying* or loosing a band is retained, because the word translated *pains* often means a *cord* or *band*. ¶ *The pains of death.* ὠδῖνας τοῦ θανάτου. The word translated *pains* denotes properly the extreme sufferings of parturition, and then any *severe* or excruciating pangs. Hence it is applied also to *death*, as being a state of extreme suffering. A very frequent meaning of the Hebrew word, of which this is the translation, is *cord*, or *band*. This perhaps was the *original* idea of the word; and the Hebrews expressed any extreme agony under the idea of *bands* or *cords* closely drawn, binding and constricting the limbs, and producing severe pain. Thus death was represented under this image of *a band* that confined men; that pressed closely on them; that prevented escape; and produced severe suffering. For this use of the word חבל, see Ps. cxix. 61 Isa. lxvi. 7. Jer. xxii. 23. Hos. xiii. 13. It is applied to death (Ps. xviii. 5), "The *snares* of death prevented me;" answering to the word *sorrows* in the previous part of the verse. Ps. cxvi. 3, "The sorrows of death compassed me, and the *pains* of hell (*hades*, or *sheol*, the cords or pains that were *binding me down* to the grave) gat hold on me." We are not to infer from this that our Lord suffered any thing *after* death. It means simply that he could not be held by the grave, but that God loosed the *bonds* which *had* held him there, and that he now set him free who had been encompassed by these pains or bonds, until they had brought him down to the grave Pain, mighty pain, will encompass us all like the constrictions and bindings of a cord which we cannot loose, and will fasten our limbs and bodies in the grave Those bands begin to be thrown around us in early life, and they are drawn closer and closer, until we lie panting under the stricture on a bed of pain, and then are still and immoveable in the grave; subdued in a manner not a little resembling the mortal agonies of the tiger in the convolutions of the boa constrictor; or like Laocoon and his sons in the folds of the serpents from the island of Tenedos. ¶ *It was not possible.* This does not refer to any *natural* impossibility, or to any inherent efficacy or power in the *body* of Jesus itself; but simply means that *in the circumstances of the case such an event could not be. Why* it could not be, he proceeds at once to show. It could not be consistently with the promises of the Scriptures. Jesus was the *Prince of life* (Acts iii. 15), and had life in himself (John i. 4; v. 26), and had power to lay down his life, and to take it again (John x. 18); and it was indispensable that he should rise. He came, also, that through death he might destroy him that had the power of death, that is, the devil (Heb. ii. 14); and as it was his purpose to gain this victory, he could not be defeated in it by being confined to the grave.

25—28. *For David speaketh*, &c. This doctrine that the Messiah must rise from

before my face; for he is on my right hand, that I should not be moved:

26 Therefore did my heart rejoice, and my tongue was glad; moreover also my flesh shall rest in hope:

---

the dead, Peter proceeds to prove by a quotation from the Old Testament. This passage is taken from Psalm xvi. 8—11. It is made from the Greek version of the Septuagint, with only one slight and unimportant change. Nor is there any material change, as will be seen, from the Hebrew. In what sense this Psalm can be applied to Christ will be seen after we have examined the expressions which Peter alleges. ¶ *I foresaw the Lord.* This is an unhappy translation. To *foresee* the Lord always *before* us conveys no idea, though it may be a *literal* translation of the passage. The word means to *foresee*, and then to *see before us*, that is, as *present* with us, to *regard* as being near. It thus implies to put *confidence* in one; to rely on him, or expect assistance from him. This is its meaning here. The Hebrew is, *I expected*, or *waited for.* It thus expresses the petition of one who is helpless and dependent, who *waits* for help from God. It is often thus used in the Old Testament. ¶ *Always before my face.* As being always present to help me, and to deliver me out of all my troubles. ¶ *He is on my right hand.* To be *at hand* is to be *near* to afford help. The *right* hand is mentioned because that was the place of dignity and honour. And David did not design simply to say that he was *near* to help him, but that he had the place of honour, the highest place in his affections. Ps. cix. 31. In our dependence on God we should *exalt* him. We should not merely regard him as our *help*, but should at the same time give him the highest place in our affections. ¶ *That I should not be moved.* That is, that no great evil or calamity should happen to me, that I may stand firm. The phrase denotes to sink into calamities, or to fall into the power of enemies. Ps. lxii. 2. 6; xlvi. 6. This expresses the confidence of one who is in danger of great calamities and who puts his trust in the help of God alone

26. *Therefore* Peter ascribes these expressions to the Messiah. The *reason* why he would exult or rejoice was, that he would be preserved amidst the sorrows that were coming on him, and could look forward to the triumph that awaited him. Thus Paul says (Heb. xii. 2), that "Jesus.... *for the joy that was set before him*, endured the cross, despising the shame," &c. And throughout the New Testament, the shame and sorrow of his sufferings were regarded as connected with his glory and his triumph. Luke xxiv. 26. Phil. ii. 6—9. Eph. i. 20, 21. In this, our Saviour has left us an example, that we should walk in his steps. The prospect of future glory and triumph should sustain us amid all afflictions, and make us ready, like him, to lie down amid even the corruptions of the grave. ¶ *Did my heart rejoice.* In the Hebrew this is in the *present* tense, "my heart rejoices." The word *heart* here expresses the *person*, and is the same as saying *I* rejoice. The Hebrews used the different *members* to express the person. And thus *we* say, "every *soul* perished; the vessel had forty *hands*; wise *heads* do not think so; *hearts* of steel will not flinch," &c. *Prof. Stuart* on the xvith Psalm. The meaning is, because God is near me in time of calamity, and will support and deliver me I will not be agitated or fear, but will exult in the prospect of the future, in view of the "joy that is set before me." ¶ *My tongue was glad.* Hebrew, My *glory*, or my *honour* exults. The word is used to denote majesty, splendour, dignity, honour. It is also used to express the *heart* or *soul*, either because that is the chief source of man's dignity, or because the word is also expressive of the *liver*, regarded by the Hebrews as the seat of the affections. Gen. xlix. 6, "Unto their assembly, *mine honour*," i. e. my soul, or myself, "be not thou united." Ps lvii. 8, "Awake up, my glory," &c. Ps. cviii. 1, "I will sing.... even with *my glory*." This word the Septuagint translated *tongue*. The Arabic and Latin Vulgate have also done the same. Why they thus use the word is not clear. It may be because the tongue, or the gift of speech, was that which chiefly contributes to the honour of man, or distinguishes him from the brutal creation. The word *glory* is used expressly for tongue in Ps. xxx. 12; "To the end that my *glory* may sing praise to thee, and not be silent." ¶ *Moreover also.* Truly; in addition to this. ¶ *My flesh.* My body. See ver 31. 1 Cor. v. 5. It means here properly the body separate from the soul; the dead body. ¶ *Shall rest.* Shall rest or repose in the grave, free from corruption. ¶ *In hope.* In confident expectation of a resurrection. The Hebrew word rather expresses *confidence* than *hope*. The passage means,

27 Because thou wilt not leave my soul in hell, neither wilt thou suffer thine Holy One to see corruption.

My body will I commit to the grave, with a confident expectation of the future, that is, with a firm belief that it will not see corruption, but will be raised up.' It thus expresses the feelings of the dying Messiah; the assured confidence which he had that his repose in the grave would not be long, and would certainly come to an end. The death of Christians is also in the New Testament represented as a *sleep*, and as *repose* (Acts vii. 60. 1 Cor. xv. 6. 18. 1 Thess. iv. 13. 15. 2 Pet. iii. 4); and they may also, after the example of their Lord, commit their bodies to the dust, *in hope*. They shall lie in the grave under the assurance of a happy resurrection; and though their bodies, unlike his, shall moulder to their native dust, yet this corruptible shall put on incorruption, and this mortal shall put on immortality. 1 Cor. xv. 53.

27. *Thou wilt not leave my soul.* The word *soul*, with us, means the *thinking*, the *immortal* part of man, and is applied to it whether existing in connexion with the body, or whether separate from it. The Hebrew word translated *soul*, here, נפשי, *naphshi*, however, may mean, My spirit, my mind, my life; and may denote here nothing more than *me*, or *myself*. It means, properly, breath; then life, or the vital principle, a living being; then the soul, the spirit, the thinking part. Instances where it is put for the individual himself, meaning "me," or "myself," may be seen in Ps. xi. 1; xxxv. 3. 7. Job ix. 21. There is no clear instance in which it is applied to the soul in its *separate* state, or disjoined from the body. In this place it must be explained in part by the meaning of the word *hell*. If that means *grave*, then this word probably means "me;" thou wilt not leave *me in the grave*. The meaning probably is, 'Thou wilt not leave *me* in *Sheol*, neither,' &c. The word *leave* here means, 'Thou wilt not *resign me* to, or wilt not give me over to it, to be held under its power.' *In hell.* εἰς ᾅδου. The word *hell* in English, now commonly denotes the place of the future eternal punishment of the wicked. This sense it has acquired by long usage. It is a Saxon word, derived from *helan*, to cover; and denotes literally, a covered or deep place (*Webster*); then the dark and dismal abode of departed spirits; and then the place of torment. As the word is used *now* by us, it by no means expresses the force of the original; and if with *this* idea we read a passage like the one before us, it would convey an erroneous meaning altogether; although *formerly* the English word perhaps expressed no more than the original. The Greek word *Hades* means literally a place devoid of light; a dark, obscure abode; and in Greek writers was applied to the dark and obscure regions where disembodied spirits were supposed to dwell. It occurs but eleven times in the New Testament. In this place it is the translation of the Hebrew, *Sheol*. In Rev. xx. 13, 14, it is connected with *death*. "And death and hell (*Hades*) delivered up the dead which were in them." "And death and hell (*Hades*) were cast into the lake of fire." See also Rev. vi. 8. i. 18, "I have the keys of hell and of death." In 1 Cor. xv. 55, it means the grave. "O *grave* (*Hades*), where is thy victory?" In Matt. xi. 23, it means a deep, profound place, opposed to an exalted one; a condition of calamity and degradation opposed to former great prosperity. "Thou, Capernaum, which art exalted to heaven, shalt be thrust down to *hell*" (*Hades*). In Luke xvi. 23, it is applied to the place where the rich man was after death, in a state of punishment. "In hell (*Hades*) he lifted up his eyes, being *in torments*." In this place it is connected with the idea of suffering; and undoubtedly denotes a place of punishment. The Septuagint has used this word commonly to translate the word *Sheol*. Once it is used as a translation of the phrase "the stones of the pit" (Isa. xiv. 19); twice to express *silence*, particularly the silence of the grave (Ps. xciv. 17; cxv. 17); once to express the Hebrew for "the shadow of death" (Job xxxviii. 17); and *sixty* times to translate the word *Sheol*. It is remarkable that it is *never* used in the Old Testament to denote the word *keber*, קבר, which properly denotes *a grave* or *sepulchre*. The idea which was conveyed by the word *Sheol*, or *Hades*, was not properly *a grave* or *sepulchre*, but that dark, unknown state, *including the grave*, which constituted the dominions of the dead. What idea the Hebrews had of the future world, it is now difficult to explain, and is not necessary in the case before us. The word originally denoting simply the state of the dead, the insatiable demands of the grave, came at last to be extended in its meaning, in proportion as they received new

revelations or formed new opinions about the future world. Perhaps the following may be the process of thought by which the word came to have the peculiar meanings which it is found to have in the Old Testament. (1.) The word *death*, and the *grave* (*kéber*), would express the abode of a deceased *body* in the earth. (2.) Man has a soul, a thinking principle; and the inquiry *must* arise, what will be its state? Will it die also? The Hebrews never appear to have believed that. Will it ascend to heaven at once? On that subject they had at first no knowledge. Will it go at once to a place of torment? Of that also they had no information at first. Yet they supposed it would live; and the word *Sheol* expressed just this state—the dark, unknown regions of the dead; the abode of spirits, whether good or bad; the residence of departed men, whether fixed in a permanent habitation, or whether wandering about. As they were ignorant of the size and spherical structure of the earth, they seem to have supposed this region to be situated *in the earth*, far below us; and hence it is put in opposition to heaven. Ps. cxxxix. 8, "If I ascend to heaven, thou art there; if I make my bed in hell (*Sheol*), thou art there." Amos ix. 2. The most *common* meaning of the word is, therefore, to express those dark regions, *the lower world*, the region of ghosts, &c. Instances of this, almost without number, might be given. See a most striking and sublime instance of this in Isa. xiv. 9. "Hell from beneath is moved to meet thee," &c.; where the assembled dead are represented as being agitated in all their vast regions at the death of the king of Babylon. (3.) The inquiry could not but arise, whether all these beings were happy? This point revelation decided; and it was decided in the Old Testament. Yet this word would better express the state of the *wicked dead*, than the righteous. It conveyed the idea of darkness, gloom, wandering; the idea of a sad and unfixed abode, unlike heaven. Hence the word *sometimes* expresses the idea of a place of punishment. Ps. ix. 17, "The wicked shall be turned into *hell*," &c. Prov. xv. 11; xxiii. 14; xxvii. 20. Job xxvi. 6.—While, therefore, the word does not mean properly *a grave* or a sepulchre, yet it does mean often *the state of the dead*, without designating whether in happiness or wo, but implying the continued existence of the soul. In this sense it is often used in the Old Testament, where the Hebrew word is *Sheol*, and the Greek *Hades*. Gen. xxxvii. 35, "I will go down into the grave, *unto my son*, mourning.' I will go down to the dead, to *death*, to my son, still there existing. xlii. 38; xliv. 29, "He shall bring down my gray hairs with sorrow to the grave." Num. xvi. 30 33. 1 Kings ii. 6. 9, &c. &c. In the place before us, therefore, the meaning is simply, *thou wilt not leave me* AMONG THE DEAD. This conveys *all* the idea. It does not mean literally the *grave* or the *sepulchre*; that relates only to *the body*. This expression refers to the *deceased Messiah* Thou wilt not leave *him* among the dead; thou wilt raise him up. It is from this passage, perhaps, aided by two others (Rom. x. 7, and 1 Pet. iii. 19), that the doctrine originated, that Christ "descended," as it is expressed in the creed, "*into hell*;" and many have invented strange opinions about his going among lost spirits. The doctrine of the Roman Catholic church has been, that he went to *purgatory*, to deliver the spirits confined there. But if the interpretation now given be correct, then it will follow, (1.) That nothing is affirmed here about the destination of the human *soul* of Christ after his death. That *he* went to the region of the dead is implied, but nothing further. (2.) It may be remarked that the Scriptures affirm nothing about the state of his *soul* in that time which intervened between his death and resurrection. The only intimation which occurs on the subject is such as to leave us to suppose that he was in a state of happiness. To the dying thief Jesus said, "*This day* shalt thou be with me in paradise." Luke xxiii. 43. When Jesus died he said, "It is finished;" and he doubtless meant by that, that his sufferings and toils for man's redemption were at an end. All suppositions of any toils or pains after his death are fables, and without the slightest warrant in the New Testament. ¶ *Thine holy One.* The word in the Hebrew which is translated here *holy one*, properly denotes one who is tenderly and piously devoted to another; and answers to the expression used in the New Testament, "my *beloved* Son." It is also used as it is here by the Septuagint, and by Peter, to denote one that is *holy*, that is set apart to God. In this sense it is applied to Christ, either as being set apart to this office, or as so pure as to make it proper to designate him by way of eminence *the holy One*, or the *holy One of God*. It is several times used as the well-known designation of the Messiah. Mark i. 24, "I know thee, who thou art, *the holy One* of God." Luke iv. 34. Acts iii. 14, "But ye denied the *holy One*, and the just," &c. See also Luke i. 35, "That

28 Thou hast made known to me the ways of life; thou shalt make me full of joy with thy countenance.
29 Men *and* brethren, [1] let me freely speak unto you of the patriarch David, that he is both dead and buried, and his sepulchre is with us unto this day.

[1] or, *I may.*

holy thing that is born of thee shall be called the Son of God." ¶ *To see corruption.* To *see* corruption is to experience it, to be made partakers of it. The Hebrews often expressed the idea of experiencing any thing by the use of words pertaining to the senses; as, to *taste* of death, to *see* death, &c. *Corruption* here means putrefaction in the grave. The word which is used in the Psalm, שחת, *shahath*, is thus used in Job xvii. 14, "I have said to corruption, thou art my father," &c. The Greek word thus used properly denotes this. Thus it is used in Acts xiii. 34, 35, 36, 37. This meaning would be properly suggested by the Hebrew word; and thus the ancient versions understood it. The meaning *implied* in the expression is, that he of whom the Psalm was written should be restored to life again; and this meaning Peter proceeds to show that the words *must have.*

28. *Thou hast made known,* &c. The Hebrew is, "Thou *wilt* make known to me," &c. In relation to the Messiah, it means, Thou wilt *restore* me to life. ¶ *The way of life.* This properly means the path to life; as we say, the *road* to preferment or honour; the *path* to happiness; the *highway* to ruin, &c. See Prov. vii. 26, 27. It means, thou wilt make known to me *life itself,* i. e. thou wilt restore me to life. The expressions in the Psalm are capable of this interpretation without doing any violence to the text; and if the preceding verses refer to the death and burial of the Messiah, then the natural and proper meaning of this is, that he would be restored to life again. ¶ *Thou hast made me full of joy.* This expresses the feelings of the Messiah in view of the favour that would thus be showed him; the resurrection from the dead, and the elevation to the right hand of God. It was this which is represented as sustaining him—the prospect of the joy that was before him, in heaven. Heb. xii. 2. Eph. i. 20—22. ¶ *With thy countenance.* Literally, "with thy face," that is, in thy presence. The words *countenance* and *presence* mean the same thing; and denote *favour,* or the honour and happiness provided by being admitted to the presence of God. The prospect of the honour that would be bestowed on the Messiah, was that which sustained him. And this proves that the person contemplated in the Psalm *expected* to be raised from the dead, and exalted to the *presence* of God. That expectation is now fulfilled; and the Messiah is now filled with joy in his exaltation to the throne of the universe. He has "ascended to his Father and our Father;" he is "seated at the right hand of God;" he has entered on that "joy which was set before him;" he is "crowned with glory and honour;" and "all things are put under his feet." In view of this, we may remark, (1.) That the Messiah had full and confident expectation that he would rise from the dead. This the Lord Jesus always evinced, and often declared it to his disciples. (2.) If the Saviour *rejoiced* in view of the glories before him, we should also. We should anticipate with joy an everlasting dwelling in the presence of God, and the high honour of sitting "with him on *his* throne, as he overcame, and is set down with the Father on his throne." (3.) The prospect of this should sustain us, as it did him, in the midst of persecution, calamity, and trials. They will soon be ended; and if we are his friends, we shall "overcome," as he did, and be admitted to "the fulness of joy" above, and to the "right hand" of God, "where are pleasures for evermore."

29. *Men and brethren.* This passage of the Psalms Peter now proves could not relate to David, but must have reference to the Messiah. He begins his argument in a respectful manner, addressing them as his *brethren,* though they had just charged him and the others with intoxication. Christians should use the usual respectful forms of salutation, whatever contempt and reproaches they may meet with from opposers. ¶ *Let me freely speak.* That is, 'It is lawful or proper to speak with boldness, or openly, respecting David.' Though he was eminently a pious man; though venerated by us all as a king; yet it is proper to say of him, that *he* is dead, and has returned to corruption. This was a delicate way of expressing high respect for the monarch whom they all honoured; and yet evincing boldness in examining a passage of Scripture which probably many supposed to have reference solely to him. ¶ *Of the patriarch David.* The word *patriarch* properly

30 Therefore being [a] a prophet, and knowing that God had sworn [b] with an oath [c] to him, that of the fruit of his loins, according to the flesh, he would raise up Christ to sit on his throne;

a 2Sa.23.2. b 2Sa.7.12,13. Ps.132.11 c He.6.17.

means the head or ruler of a family; and then the *founder* of a family, or an illustrious ancestor. It was commonly applied to Abraham, Isaac, and Jacob, &c. by way of eminence; the illustrious founders of the Jewish nation. Heb. vii. 4. Acts vii. 8, 9. It was also applied to the heads of the families, or the chief men of the tribes of Israel. 1 Chron. xxiv. 31. 2 Chron. xix. 8, &c. It was thus a title of honour, denoting high respect. Applied to David, it means that he was the illustrious head or founder of the royal family, and implies Peter's intention not to say any thing disrespectful of such a king; at the same time that he freely canvassed a passage of Scripture which had been supposed to refer to him. ¶ *Dead and buried.* The record of that fact they had in the Old Testament. There had been no pretence that he had risen, and therefore the Psalm could not apply to him. ¶ *His sepulchre is with us.* Is *in* the city of Jerusalem. Sepulchres were commonly situated *without* the walls of cities and the limits of villages. The custom of burying *in* towns was not commonly practised. This was true of other ancient nations as well as the Hebrews, and is still in eastern countries, except in the case of kings and very distinguished men, whose ashes are permitted to repose within the walls of a city. 1 Sam. xxviii. 3, "Samuel was dead ....and Israel....buried him in Ramah, in his own city." 2 Kings xxi. 18, "Manasseh....was buried in the garden of his own house." 2 Chron. xvi. 14, "Asa was buried in the city of David." 2 Kings xiv. 20. The sepulchres of the Hebrew kings were on mount Zion. 2 Chron. xxi. 20; xxiv. 25; xxviii. 27; xxxii. 33; xxiv. 16. 2 Kings xiv. 20. David was buried in the city of David (1 Kings ii. 10), with his fathers, i. e. on mount Zion, where he built a city called after his name. 2 Sam. v. 7. Of what form the tombs of the kings were made is not certainly known. It is almost certain, however, that they would be constructed in a magnificent manner. The tombs were commonly excavations from rocks, or natural caves; and sepulchres cut out of the solid rock, of vast extent, are known to have existed. The following account of the tomb called "the sepulchre of the kings," is abridged from Maundrell. "The approach is through an entrance cut out of a solid rock, which admits you into an open court about forty paces square, cut down into the rock. On the south side is a portico nine paces long and four broad, hewn likewise out of the solid rock. At the end of the portico is the descent to the sepulchres. The descent is into a room about seven or eight yards square, cut out of the natural rock From this room there are passages into six more, all of the same fabric with the first. In every one of these rooms, except the first, were coffins placed in niches in the sides of the chamber' &c. (Maundrell's Travels, p. 76.) If the tombs of the kings were of this form, it is clear that they were works of great labour and expense. Probably also there were, as there are now, costly and splendid monuments erected to the memory of the mighty dead. ¶ *Unto this day.* That the sepulchre of David was well known and honoured, is clear from Josephus. Antiq. b. vii. c. xv. § 3. "He (David) was buried by his son Solomon *in Jerusalem* with great magnificence, and with all the other funeral pomps with which kings used to be buried. Moreover, he had immense wealth buried with him: for a thousand and three hundred years afterwards, Hyrcanus the high-priest, when he was besieged by Antiochus, and was desirous of giving him money to raise the siege, opened one room of David's sepulchre, and took out three thousand talents. Herod, many years afterward, opened another room, and took away a great deal of money," &c. See also Antiq. b. xiii. c. viii. § 4. The tomb of a monarch like David would be well known and had in reverence. Peter might, then, confidently appeal to *their own belief* and knowledge, that David had not been raised from the dead. No Jew *believed* or *supposed* it. All, by their care of his sepulchre, and by the honour with which they regarded his grave, *believed* that he had returned to corruption. The Psalm, therefore, *could* not apply to him.

30. *Therefore.* As David was dead and buried, it was clear that he could not have referred to himself in this remarkable declaration. It followed that he must have had reference to some other one. ¶ *Being a prophet.* One who foretold future events. That David was inspired, is clear. 2 Sam. xxiii. 2. Many of the prophecies relating to the Messiah

are found in the Psalms of David. Ps. xxii. 1. Comp. Matt. xxvii. 46. Luke xxiv. 44.—Ps. xxii. 18. Comp. Matt. xxvii. 35.—Ps. lxix. 21. Comp. Matt. xxvii. 34. 48.—Ps. lxix. 25 Comp. Acts i. 20 ¶ *And knowing.* Knowing by what God had said to him respecting his posterity. ¶ *Had sworn with an oath.* The places which speak of God as having sworn to David are found in Ps. lxxxix. 3, 4. "I have made a covenant with my chosen, I have sworn unto David my servant, Thy seed will I establish," &c. And Ps. cxxxii. 11, "The Lord hath sworn in truth unto David, he will not turn from it, Of the fruit of thy body will I set upon my throne." Ps. lxxxix. 35, 36. The promise to which reference is made in all these places is in 2 Sam. vii. 11—16. ¶ *Of the fruit of his loins.* Of his descendants. See 2 Sam. vii. 12. Gen. xxxv. 11; xlvi. 26. 1 Kings viii. 19, &c. ¶ *According to the flesh.* That is, so far as the human nature of the Messiah was concerned, he would be descended from David. Expressions like these are very remarkable. If the Messiah was only a *man*, they would be unmeaning. They are *never* used in relation to a mere man: and they imply that the speaker or writer supposed that there pertained to the Messiah a nature which was not according to the flesh. See Rom. i. 3, 4 ¶ *He would raise up Christ.* That is, the Messiah. To *raise up* seed, or descendants, is to give them to him. The promises made to David in all these places had immediate reference to Solomon, and to his descendants. But it is clear that the New Testament writers understood them as referring to the Messiah. And it is no less clear that the Jews understood that the Messiah was to be descended from David. Matt. xii. 23; xxi. 9; xxii. 42. 45 Mark xi. 10. John vii. 42, &c. In what way these promises that were made to David were understood as applying to the Messiah, it may not be easy to determine. The *fact*, however, is clear. The following remarks may throw some light on the subject. The kingdom which was promised to David was to have no end; it was to be established for ever. Yet his descendants died, and all other kingdoms changed. The promise likewise stood *by itself*; it was not made to any other of the Jewish kings; nor were similar declarations made of surrounding kingdoms and nations. It came, therefore, gradually to be applied to that future King and kingdom which was the hope of the nation, and their eyes were anxiously fixed on the long-expected Messiah. At the time that he came, it had become the settled doctrine of the Jews that he was to descend from David, and that his kingdom was to be perpetual. On this belief of the prophecy the apostles argued; and the opinions of the Jews furnished a strong point by which they could convince them that Jesus was the Messiah. Peter affirms that David was *aware* of this, and that he so understood the promise as referring not only to Solomon, but in a far more important sense to the Messiah. Happily, we have a commentary of David himself also, as expressing his own views of that promise. That comment is found particularly in the iid, xxiid, lxixth, and xvith Psalms. In these Psalms there can be no doubt that David looked forward to the coming of the Messiah; and there can be as little that he regarded the promise made to him as extending to his coming and his reign.

It may be remarked, that there are some important variations in the manuscripts in regard to this verse. The expression "according to the flesh" is omitted in many MSS. and is now left out by Griesbach in his New Testament. It is omitted also by the ancient Syriac and Ethiopic versions, and by the Latin Vulgate. ¶ *To sit on his throne.* To be his successor in his kingdom. Saul was the first of the kings of Israel. The kingdom was taken away from him and his posterity, and conferred on David and his descendants. It was determined that it should be continued *in the family* of David, and no more go out of his family, as it had from the family of Saul. The peculiar characteristic of David as king, or that which distinguished him from the other kings of the earth, was, that *he reigned over the people of God.* Israel was his chosen people; and the kingdom was over that nation. Hence he that should reign *over the people of God,* though in a manner somewhat different from David, would be regarded as occupying *his throne,* and as being his successor. The form of the administration might be varied, but it would still retain its prime characteristic, as being a reign *over the people of God.* In this sense the Messiah sits on the throne of David. He is his descendant and successor. He has an empire *over all the friends of the Most High.* And as that kingdom is destined to fill the earth, and to be eternal in the heavens, so it may be said that it is a kingdom which shall have no end. It is spiritual, but not the less real; defended not with carnal weapons, but not the less really defended; advanced not by the

31 He, seeing this before, [a] spake
of the resurrection of Christ, that
his soul was not left in hell, neither
his flesh did see corruption.
32 This [b] Jesus hath God raised
up, whereof [c] we all are witnesses.

a 1Pe.1.11,12. b ver.24. c Lu.24.48.

33 Therefore, [d] being by the right
hand of God exalted, and having [e]
received of the Father the promise
of the Holy Ghost, he hath shed
forth this [f] which ye now see and
hear.

d c.5.31. Ph.2.9. e Jno.16.7,13. c.1.4. f c.10.45. Ep 4.8.

sword and the din of arms, but not the less *really* advanced against principalities and powers, and spiritual wickedness in high places; not under a *visible* head and earthly monarch, but not less really under the Captain of salvation, and the King of kings.

31. *He, seeing this before,* &c. By the spirit of prophecy. From this it appears that David had distinct views of the great doctrines pertaining to the Messiah. ¶ *Spake,* &c. See Ps. xvi. ¶ *That his soul,* &c. See Note on ver. 27.

32. *This Jesus.* Peter, having shown that it was *predicted* that the Messiah would rise, now affirms that it was done in the case of Jesus. If it was a matter of prophecy, all objection to the truth of the doctrine was taken away, and the only question was, whether there was *evidence* that this had been done. The proof of this Peter now alleges, and offers his own testimony, and that of his brethren, to the truth of this great and glorious fact. ¶ *We all are witnesses.* It seems probable that Peter refers here to the whole one hundred and twenty who were present, and who were ready to attest it in any manner. The matter which was to be proved was, that Jesus was seen alive after he had been put to death. The apostles were appointed to bear witness of this. And we are told by Paul (1 Cor. xv. 6), that he was seen by more than five hundred brethren, i. e. Christians, at one time. The hundred and twenty assembled on this occasion were doubtless part of the number, and were ready to attest this. This was the proof that Peter alleged; and the strength of this proof was, and should have been, perfectly irresistible. (1.) They had *seen* him themselves. They did not conjecture it, or reason about it; but they had the evidence on which men act every day, and which must be regarded as satisfactory—the evidence of their own senses. (2.) The *number* was such they could not be imposed on. If one hundred and twenty persons could not prove a plain matter of fact, nothing could be established by testimony; there could be no way of arriving at any facts. (3.) The thing to be established was a plain matter. It was not that they *saw him rise.* That they never pretended. Impostors *would* have done thus. But it was that they saw him, talked, walked, ate, drank with him, *being alive* AFTER he had been crucified. The fact of his death was matter of Jewish record; and no one called it in question. The only fact for Christianity to make out was that he was seen *alive* afterwards; and this was attested by many witnesses. (4.) They had no interest in deceiving the world in this thing. There was no prospect of pleasure, wealth, or honour in doing it. (5.) They offered themselves now as ready to endure any sufferings, or to die, in attestation of the truth of this event.

33. *Therefore, being by the right hand.* The *right hand* among the Hebrews was often used to denote *power;* and the expression here means, not that he was exalted *to* the right hand of God, but *by* his power. He was raised from the dead by his power, and borne to heaven, triumphant over all his enemies. The use of the word right hand to denote *power* is common in the Scriptures. Job xl. 14, "Thine own right hand can save thee." Ps. xvii. 7, "Thou savest by thy right hand them that trust in thee." Ps. xviii. 35; xx. 6; xxi. 8; xliv. 3; lx. 5, &c. ¶ *Exalted.* Constituted King and Messiah in heaven. Raised up from his condition of humiliation to the glory which he had with the Father before the world was. John xvii. 5. *And having received,* &c. The Holy Ghost was promised to the disciples before his death. John xiv. 26; xv. 26; xvi. 13—15. It was expressly declared, (1.) That the Holy Ghost would not be given except the Lord Jesus should return to heaven (John xvi. 7), and (2.) That this gift was in the power of the Father, and that *he* would send him. John xiv. 26; xv. 26. This promise was now fulfilled, and those who witnessed the extraordinary scene before them could not doubt that it was the effect of divine power ¶ *Hath shed forth this,* &c. This power of speaking different languages, and declaring the truth of the gospel. In this way Peter accounts for the remarkable

34 For David is not ascended into the heavens: but he saith himself, The LORD[a] said unto my Lord, Sit thou on my right hand,

35 Until I make thy foes thy footstool.

36 Therefore let all the house[b] of Israel know assuredly, that[c] God

a Ps.110.1. Matt.22.44. b Zec.13.1. c c.5.31.

events before them. It could not be produced by new wine, ver. 15. It was expressly foretold, ver. 16—21. It was predicted that Jesus would rise, ver. 22—31. The apostles were witnesses that he *had* risen, and that he had promised that the Holy Spirit should descend; and the fulfilment of this promise was a rational way of accounting for the scene before them. It was unanswerable; and the effect on those who witnessed it was such as might be expected.

34, 35. *For David is not ascended into the heavens.* That is, David has not risen from the dead, and ascended to heaven. This further shows that Ps. xvi. could not refer to David, but must refer to the Messiah. Great as they esteemed David, and much as they were accustomed to apply these expressions of the Scripture to him, yet they could not be applicable to him. They *must* refer to some other being; and especially that passage which Peter now proceeds to quote. It was of great importance to show that these expressions could not apply to David, and also that David bore testimony to the exalted character and dignity of the Messiah. Hence Peter here adduces David himself as affirming that the Messiah was to be exalted to a dignity far above his own. This does not affirm that David was not saved, or that his spirit had not ascended to heaven, but that he had not been *exalted* in the heavens in the sense in which Peter was speaking of the Messiah. ¶ *But he saith himself.* Ps. cx. 1. ¶ *The* LORD. The small capitals used in translating the word LORD in the Bible, denote that the original word is *Jehovah.* The Hebrews regarded this as the *peculiar* name of God, a name incommunicable to any other being. It is not applied to any being but God in the Scriptures. The Jews had such a reverence for it that they never pronounced it; but when it occurred in the Scriptures they pronounced another name, *Adoni.* Here it means, *Jehovah* said, &c. ¶ *My Lord.* This is a different word in the Hebrew: it is *Adoni.* אדני. It properly is applied by a servant to his master, or a subject to his sovereign, or is used as a title of respect by an inferior to a superior. It means here, 'Jehovah said to him whom I, David, acknowledge to be *my* superior and sovereign. Thus, though he regarded him as his descendant according to the flesh, yet he regarded him also as his superior and Lord. By reference to this passage our Saviour confounded the Pharisees. Matt xxii. 42—46. That the passage in this Psalm refers to the Messiah is clear. Our Saviour, in Matt. xxii. 42, expressly applied it thus, and in such a manner as to show that this was the well-understood doctrine of the Jews. See Notes on Matt. xxii. 42, &c.

36. *Therefore, let all, &c.* 'Convinced by the prophecies; by our testimony, and by the remarkable scene exhibited on the day of Pentecost; let all be convinced that the true Messiah has come, and has been exalted to heaven.' ¶ *House of Israel.* The word *house* often means *family;* let all the family of Israel, i. e. all the nation of the Jews, know this. ¶ *Know assuredly.* Be assured, or know without any hesitation, or possibility of mistake. This is the sum of his argument, or his discourse. He had established the points which he purposed to prove; and he now applies it to his hearers. ¶ *God hath made.* God hath appointed, or constituted. See ch. v. 31. ¶ *That same Jesus.* The very person who had suffered. He was raised with the same body, and had the same soul; was the same being, as distinguished from all others. So Christians, in the resurrection, will be the *same* beings that they were before they died. ¶ *Whom ye crucified.* See ver. 23. There was nothing better fitted to show them the guilt of having done this, than the argument which Peter used. He showed them that God had sent him; that he was the Messiah; that God had showed his love for him, in raising him from the dead The Son of God, and the hope of their nation, they had put to death. He was not an impostor; nor a man sowing sedition; nor a blasphemer; but the Messiah of God; and they had imbrued their hands in his blood.—There is nothing better fitted to make sinners fear and tremble, than to show them that in rejecting Christ, they have rejected God; in refusing to serve him, they have refused to serve God. The crime of sinners has a double malignity, as committed against a kind and lovely Saviour, and against the

hath made that same Jesus, whom
ye have crucified, both Lord [a] and
Christ. [b]
37 Now when they heard *this*,
they were pricked [c] in their heart,
and said unto Peter and to the rest
of the apostles, Men *and* brethren,
what [d] shall we do?

a Jno.3.35. b Ps.2.2,6-8.

c Eze.7.16. Zec.12.10. d c.9.6;16.30.

God who loved *him*, and appointed him to save men. Comp. ch. iii. 14, 15. ¶ *Both Lord.* The word *lord* properly denotes *proprietor*, *master*, or *sovereign*. Here it means clearly that God had exalted him to be the *king* so long expected; and that he had given him dominion in the heavens; or as we should say, ruler of all things. The extent of this dominion may be seen in John xvii. 2. Eph. i. 21, &c. In the exercise of this office, he now rules in heaven and on earth; and will yet come to judge the world. This truth was particularly fitted to excite their fear. They had murdered their Sovereign, now shown to be raised from the dead, and intrusted with infinite power. They had reason, therefore, to fear that he would come forth in vengeance, and punish them for their crimes. Sinners, in opposing the Saviour, are at war with their living and mighty Sovereign and Lord. He has all power; and it is not safe to contend against the Judge of the living and the dead. ¶ *And Christ.* Messiah. They had thus crucified the hope of their nation; imbrued their hands in the blood of him to whom the prophets had looked; and put to death that Holy One, the prospect of whose coming had sustained the most holy men of the world in affliction, and cheered them when they looked on to future years. That hope of their fathers had come, and they had put him to death; and it is no wonder that the consciousness of this, that a sense of guilt, and shame, and confusion, should overwhelm their minds, and lead them to ask in deep distress what they should do?

37. *Now when they heard this.* When they heard this declaration of Peter, and this *proof* that Jesus was the Messiah. There was no fanaticism in his discourse; it was cool, close, pungent reasoning. He *proved* to them the truth of what he was saying, and thus prepared the way for this effect. ¶ *They were pricked in their heart.* The word translated *were pricked*, κατενύγησαν, is not used elsewhere in the New Testament. It properly denotes to *pierce* or *penetrate* with a needle, lancet, or sharp instrument; and then to pierce with grief, or acute pain of any kind. It answers precisely to our word *compunction.* It implies also the idea of *sudden* as well as *acute* grief. In this case it means that they were *suddenly* and *deeply* affected with anguish and alarm at what Peter had said. The causes of their grief may have been these: (1.) Their *sorrow* that the Messiah had been put to death by his own countrymen. (2.) Their deep sense of guilt in having done this. There would be mingled here a remembrance of ingratitude, and a consciousness that they had been guilty of *murder* of the most aggravated and horrid kind, that of having killed their own Messiah. (3.) The fear of his wrath. He was still alive, exalted to be their *Lord*, and intrusted with all power. They were afraid of his vengeance; they were conscious that they deserved it; and they supposed that they were exposed to it. (4.) What they had done could not be undone. The guilt remained; they could not wash it out. They had imbrued their hands in the blood of innocence; and the guilt of that oppressed their souls. This expresses the usual feelings which sinners have when they are convicted of sin. ¶ *Men and brethren.* This was an expression denoting affectionate earnestness. Just before this they mocked the disciples, and charged them with being filled with new wine. ver. 13. They now treated them with respect and confidence. The views which sinners have of Christians and Christian ministers are greatly changed when they are under conviction for sin. Before that, they may deride and oppose them: then, they are glad to be taught by the obscurest Christian; and even cling to a minister of the gospel as if he could save them by his own power. ¶ *What shall we do?* What shall we do to avoid the wrath of this crucified and exalted Messiah? They were apprehensive of his vengeance, and they wished to know how to avoid it. Never was a more important question asked than this. It is the question which all convicted sinners ask. It implies an apprehension of danger; a sense of guilt, and a readiness to *yield the will* to the claims of God. This was the same question asked by Paul (Acts ix. 6); "Lord, what wilt thou have me to do?" and by the jailer (Acts xvi. 30); "He....came trembling... and said, Sirs, what must I do to be saved?" The state of mind in this case—the case of a convicted sinner—con

sists in, (1.) A deep sense of the evil of the past life; remembrance of a thousand crimes perhaps before forgotten; a pervading and deepening conviction that the heart, and conversation, and life has been evil, and deserves condemnation. (2.) Apprehension about the justice of God; alarm when the mind looks upward to him, or onward to the day of death and judgment. (3.) An earnest wish, amounting sometimes to agony, to be delivered from this sense of condemnation, and this apprehension of the future. (4.) A readiness to sacrifice all to the will of God, to surrender the governing purpose of the mind, and to do what he requires. In this state the soul is prepared to receive the offers of eternal life; and *when* the sinner comes to this, the offers of mercy meet his case, and he yields himself to the Lord Jesus, and finds peace.

In regard to this discourse of Peter, and this remarkable result, we may observe, (1.) That this is the first discourse which was preached after the ascension of Christ, and is a model which the ministers of religion should imitate. (2.) It is a clear and close argument. There is no ranting, no declamation, nothing but *truth* presented in a clear and striking manner. It abounds with *proof* of his main point; and supposes that his hearers were rational beings, and capable of being influenced by truth. Ministers have no right to address men as incapable of reason and thought; nor to imagine that because they are speaking on religious subjects, that therefore they are at liberty to speak nonsense. (3.) Though these were eminent sinners, and had added to the crime of murdering the Messiah that of deriding the Holy Ghost and the ministers of the gospel, yet Peter *reasoned* with them coolly, and endeavoured to *convince* them of their guilt. Men should be treated as endowed with *reason*, and as capable of seeing the force and beauty of the great truths of religion. (4.) The arguments of Peter were *adapted* to make this impression on their minds, and to impress them deeply with the sense of their guilt. He *proved* to them that they had been guilty of putting the Messiah to death; that God had raised him up; and that they were now in the midst of the scenes which established one strong proof of the truth of what he was saying. No class of truths could have been so well adapted to make an impression of their guilt as these. (5.) Conviction for sin is a rational process on a sinner's mind. It is the *proper* state produced by a view of the past sins It is suffering *truth* to make an appropriate impression; suffering the mind to feel as it *ought* to feel. The man who *is* guilty, ought to be willing to see and confess it. It is no disgrace to confess an error, or to feel deeply when we know we are guilty. Disgrace consists in a hypocritical desire to conceal crime; in the *pride* that is unwilling to avow it; in the *falsehood* which denies it. To feel it, and to acknowledge it, is the mark of an open and ingenuous mind. (6.) These same truths are adapted still to produce conviction for sin. The sinner's treatment of the Messiah should produce grief and alarm. He did not murder him; but he has rejected him: he did not crown him with thorns; but he has despised him: he did not insult him when hanging on the cross; but he has a thousand times insulted him since: he did not pierce his side with the spear; but he has pierced his heart by rejecting him, and contemning his mercy. *For these things he should weep.* In the Saviour's resurrection he has also a deep interest. He rose as the pledge that we may rise: and when the sinner looks forward, he should remember that he *must* meet the ascended Son of God. The Saviour reigns; he lives, Lord of all. The sinner's deeds now are aimed at his throne, and his heart, and his crown. All his crimes are seen by his Sovereign; and it is not safe to mock the Son of God on his throne; or to despise him who will soon come to judgment. When the sinner feels these truths, he *should* tremble, and cry out, What shall I do? (7.) We see here *how* the Spirit operates in producing conviction of sin. It is not in an arbitrary manner; it is in accordance with *truth*, and by the *truth*. Nor have we a right to expect that he will convict and convert men, except as the *truth* is presented to their minds. They who desire success in the gospel should present clear, striking, and impressive truth; for such only God is accustomed to bless. (8.) We have in the conduct of Peter and the other apostles, a striking instance of the *power* of the gospel. Just before, Peter, trembling and afraid, had denied his master with an oath. Now, in the presence of the murderers of the Son of God, he boldly charged them with their crime, and dared their fury. Just before, all the disciples forsook the Lord Jesus, and fled. Now, in the presence of his murderers, they lifted their voice, and proclaimed their guilt and danger, even in the city where he had been just arraigned and put to death. What could have produced this change but the power of God? And is there not

38 Then Peter said unto them, [a]Repent, and be baptized every one of you in the name of Jesus Christ, for the remission of sins; and ye shall receive the gift of the Holy Ghost.

a Lu.24.47. c.3.19.

---

proof here that a religion which produces such changes came from heaven?

38. *Then Peter said unto them.* Peter had been the chief speaker, though others had also addressed them. He now, in the name of all, directed the multitude what to do. ¶ *Repent.* See Note, Matt. iii. 2. Repentance implies sorrow for sin as committed against God, with a purpose to forsake it. It is not merely a fear of the *consequences*, or of the wrath of God in hell. It is such a view of *sin* as evil in itself, as to lead the mind to hate it and forsake it. Laying aside *all* view of the *punishment* of sin, the true penitent hates it. Even if sin was the means of procuring him happiness; if it would promote his gratification, and be unattended with any future punishment, he would hate it and turn from it. The mere fact that it is *evil*, and that *God* hates it, is a sufficient reason why those who are truly penitent should hate it and forsake it. False repentance dreads the *consequences* of sin; true repentance dreads *sin itself.* These persons whom Peter addressed had been merely *alarmed;* they were afraid of wrath, and especially of the wrath of the Messiah. They had no true sense of sin as an evil, but were simply afraid of punishment. This *alarm* Peter did not regard as by any means genuine repentance. Such conviction for sin would soon wear off, unless *repentance* became thorough and complete. Hence he told them to *repent*, to turn from sin, to exercise sorrow for it as an evil and bitter thing, and to *express* their sorrow in the proper manner. We may learn here, (1.) That there is no safety in *mere conviction* for sin: it may soon pass off, and leave the soul as thoughtless as before. (2.) There is no *goodness* or *holiness* in mere alarm or conviction. The devils ....tremble. A man may fear, who yet has a firm purpose to do evil if he can do it with impunity. (3.) Many are greatly troubled and alarmed who yet never repent. There is no situation where souls are so easily deceived as here. *Alarm* is taken for repentance; trembling for godly sorrow; and the fear of wrath is taken to be the true fear of God. (4.) True repentance is the only thing in such a state of mind that can give any relief. An ingenuous confession of sin, a solemn purpose to forsake it, and a true *hatred* of it, is the only thing that can give the mind true composure. Such is the constitution of the mind, that nothing else will furnish relief. But the moment we are willing to make an open confession of guilt, the mind is delivered of its burden, and the convicted soul finds peace. Till this is done, and the *hold on sin* is broken, there *can be* no peace. (5.) We see here what direction is to be given to a convicted sinner. We are not to direct him to wait; nor to suppose that he is in a good way; nor to continue to seek; nor to call him a mourner; nor to take sides with him, as if God were wrong and harsh; nor to tell him to read, and search, and postpone the subject to a future time. We are to direct him to *repent;* to mourn over his sins, and to forsake them. Religion demands that he should *at once* surrender himself to God by genuine repentance, by confession that God is right, and that *he* was wrong; and by a firm purpose to live a life of holiness. ¶ *Be baptized.* See Note, Matt. iii. 6. The direction which Christ gave to his apostles was, that they should baptize all who believed Matt. xxviii. 19. Mark xvi. 16. The Jews had not been baptized; and a baptism now would be a profession of the religion of Christ, or a declaration made before the world that they embraced Jesus as their Messiah. It was equivalent to saying that they should *publicly* and *professedly* embrace Jesus Christ as their Saviour. The gospel requires such a profession; and no one is at liberty to withhold it. And a similar declaration is to be made to all who are inquiring the way to life. They are to exercise repentance; and then, without any unnecessary delay, to evince it in the ordinances of the gospel. If men are unwilling to profess religion, they have none. If they will not, in the proper way, show that they are truly attached to Christ, it is proof that they have no such attachment. Baptism is the application of water, as expressive of the need of purification, and as emblematic of the influences from God that can alone cleanse the soul. It is also a form of dedication to the service of God. ¶ *In the name of Jesus Christ.* Not εἰς, but ἐπί. The usual form of baptism is *into* the name of the Father, &c. εἰς. Here it does not mean to be baptized *by the authority* of Jesus Christ: but it means to be

39 For the promise [a] is unto you, and to your children, and [b] to all that are afar off, *even* as many as the Lord our God shall call.

a Joel 2.28. b Ep.2.13,17.

baptized *for* him and his service; to be consecrated in this way, and by this public profession, *to* him, and to his cause. The *name* of Jesus Christ means the same as Jesus Christ himself. To be baptized to his *name* is to be devoted *to him*. The word *name* is often thus used. And the profession which they were to make amounted to this: a confession of sins; a hearty purpose to turn from them; a reception of Jesus as the Messiah, and as *their* Saviour; and a determination to become *his followers*, and to be devoted to his service. Thus (1 Cor. x. 2), to be *baptized unto Moses* means to take him as the leader and guide. It does not follow that in administering the ordinance of baptism they used only the name of Jesus Christ. It is much more probable that they used the form prescribed by the Saviour himself (Matt. xxviii. 19); though as the peculiar mark of a *Christian* is that he receives and honours Jesus Christ, this name is used here as implying the whole. The same thing occurs in Acts xix. 5. ¶ *For the remission of sins.* Not merely the sin of crucifying the Messiah, but of *all* sins. There is nothing in *baptism itself* that can wash away sin. That can be done only by the pardoning mercy of God through the atonement of Christ. But baptism is expressive of a willingness to be pardoned in that way; and a solemn declaration of our conviction that there is no other way of remission. He who comes to be baptized, comes with a *professed* conviction that he is a sinner, that there is no other way of mercy but in the gospel, and with a professed willingness to comply with the terms of salvation, and receive it as it is offered through Jesus Christ. ¶ *And ye shall receive, &c.* The gift of the Holy Ghost here does not mean his *extraordinary gifts*, or the power of working miracles. But it simply means, you shall partake of the influences of the Holy Ghost *as far as they may be adapted to your case*, as far as may be needful for your comfort, and peace, and sanctification. There is no evidence that they were all endowed with the power of working miracles; nor does the connexion of the passage require us thus to understand it. Nor does it mean that they had not been awakened *by his influences*. All true conviction is from him. John xvi. 8—10. But it is also the office of the Spirit to comfort, to enlighten, to give peace, and thus to give evidence that the soul is born again. To this, probably, Peter refers; and this all who are born again, and profess faith in Christ, possess. There is peace, calmness, joy; there is *evidence* of piety, and that evidence is the product of the influences of the Spirit. "The fruit of the Spirit is love, joy, peace," &c. Gal. v. 22. 24.

39. *For the promise.* That is, the promise respecting the particular thing of which he was speaking—the influences of the Holy Ghost. This promise he had adduced in the beginning of his discourse (ver. 17), and he now applies it to them. As the Spirit was promised to descend on Jews and their sons and daughters, it was applicable to them in the circumstances in which they then were. The only hope of lost sinners is in the promises of God; and the only thing that can give comfort to a soul that is convicted of sin is the hope that *God* will pardon and save. ¶ *To you.* To you Jews, even though you have crucified the Messiah. The promise had especial reference to the Jewish people. ¶ *To your children.* In Joel, to their sons and daughters, who should, nevertheless, be old enough to prophesy. Similar promises occur in Isa. xliv. 3, "I will pour my Spirit on thy seed, and my blessing on thine offspring," and Isa. lix. 21. In these and similar places, their *descendants* or *posterity* are denoted It does not refer to children *as children*, and should not be adduced to establish the propriety of infant baptism, or as applicable particularly to infants It is a promise, indeed, to parents that the blessings of salvation shall not be confined to parents, but shall be extended also to their posterity. Under this promise parents may be encouraged to train up their children for God; to devote them to his service; believing that it is the gracious purpose of God to perpetuate the blessings of salvation from age to age. ¶ *To all.* To the whole race; not limited to Jews. ¶ *Afar off.* To those in other lands. It is probable that *Peter* here referred to *the Jews* who were scattered in other nations; for he does not seem yet to have understood that the gospel was to be preached to the Gentiles. See ch. x. Yet the promise was equally applicable to the Gentiles as the Jews; and the apostles were afterwards brought to understand it. Acts x. Rom. x. 12. 14—20; xi. The

40 And with many other words did he testify and exhort, saying, Save yourselves from this untoward generation.

Gentiles are sometimes clearly indicated by the expression "afar off," (Eph. ii. 13. 17); and they are represented as having been brought *nigh* by the blood of Christ. The phrase is equally applicable to those who have been far off from God *by their sins* and their *evil affections*. To them also the promise is extended if they will return. ¶ *Even as many*, &c. The promise is not to those who do not *hear* the gospel, nor to those who do not *obey* it; but it is to those to whom God in his gracious providence shall send it. He has the power and right to pardon. The meaning of Peter is, that the promise is ample, full, free; that it is fitted to all, and may be applied to all; that there is no defect or want in the provisions or promises; but that God *may* extend it to whomsoever he pleases. We see here how ample and full are the offers of mercy. God is not limited in the provisions of his grace; but the plan is *applicable* to all mankind. It is also the purpose of God to send it to all men; and he has given a solemn charge to his church to do it. We cannot reflect but with deep pain on the fact that these provisions have been made, fully made; that they are adapted to all men; and yet that by his people they have been extended to so small a portion of the human family. If the promise of life is to all, it is the duty of the church to send to all the message of eternal mercy.

40. *Many other words.* This discourse, though one of the longest in the New Testament, is but an outline. It contains, however, the substance of the plan of mercy; and is admirably arranged to obtain its object. ¶ *Testify.* Bear witness to. He bore witness to the promises of Christianity, to the truths pertaining to the danger of sinners; and to the truth respecting the character of that generation. ¶ *Exhort.* He entreated them by arguments and promises. ¶ *Save yourselves.* This expression here denotes, preserve yourselves from the *influence*, opinions, and fate, of this generation. It implies that they were to use diligence and effort to deliver themselves. God deals with men as free agents. He calls upon them to put forth their own power and effort to be saved. Unless men put forth their own strength and exertion, they will never be saved. When they *are* saved, they will ascribe to God the praise for having inclined them to seek him, and for the grace whereby they *are* saved. ¶ *This generation.* This age or race of men, the Jews then living. They were not to apprehend danger *from* them from which they were to deliver themselves, but they were to apprehend danger from being *with* them, united in their plans, designs, and feelings. From the influence of their opinions, &c. they were to escape. That generation was signally corrupt and wicked. See Matt. xxiii. xii. 39; xvi. 4. Mark viii. 38. They had crucified the Messiah; and they were for their sins soon to be destroyed. ¶ *Untoward.* "Perverse, refractory, not easily guided or taught." (*Webster.*) The same character our Saviour had given of that generation in Matt. xi. 16—19. This character they had shown uniformly. They were smooth, cunning, plausible; but they were corrupt in principle, and wicked in conduct. The Pharisees had a vast hold on the people. To break away from them was to set at defiance all their power and doctrines; to alienate themselves from their teachers and friends; to brave the power of those in office, and those who had long claimed the right of teaching and guiding the nation. The chief danger of those who were now awakened was from this generation; that they would deride, or denounce, or persecute them, and induce them to abandon their seriousness, and turn back to their sins. And hence Peter exhorted them at once to break off from them, and give themselves to Christ. We may hence learn, (1.) That if sinners will be saved they must make an effort. There is no promise to any unless they will exert themselves. (2.) The principal danger which besets those who are awakened arises from their former companions. They are often wicked, cunning, rich, and mighty. They may be their kindred, and will seek to drive off their serious impressions by derision, or argument, or persecution. They have a mighty hold on the affections; and they will seek to use it to prevent those who are awakened from becoming Christians. (3.) Those who are awakened should resolve at once to break off from their evil companions, and unite themselves to Christ and his people. There may be no other way in which this can be done than by resolving to forsake the society of those who are infidels, and scoffers, and profane. They should forsake the world, and give themselves up to God, and resolve to have only so much intercourse with the world as may

41 Then they that gladly received his word were baptized: and the same day there were added *unto them* about three thousand souls.

42 And [a] they continued steadfastly in the apostles' doctrine and fellowship, and in breaking of bread, and in prayers.

a 1Cor.11.2. He.10.25.

be required by duty, and as may be consistent with a supreme purpose to live to the honour of God.

41. *They that gladly received.* The word rendered *gladly* means *freely*, cheerfully, joyfully. It implies that they did it without compulsion, and with joy. Religion is not compulsion. They who become Christians do it cheerfully; and do it rejoicing in the *privilege* of becoming reconciled to God through Jesus Christ. Though so many received his word and were baptized, yet it is implied that there were others who did not. It is probable that there were multitudes assembled who were alarmed, but who did *not* receive the word with joy. In all revivals there are many who become alarmed, who are anxious about their souls, but who refuse the gospel, and again become thoughtless, and are ruined. ¶ *His word.* The message which Peter had spoken respecting the pardon of sins through Jesus Christ. ¶ *Were baptized.* That is, those who professed a readiness to embrace the offers of salvation. The narrative plainly implies that this was done the same day. Their conversion was instantaneous. The demand on them was to yield themselves at once to God. And their profession was made, and the ordinance which sealed their profession administered without delay. ¶ *And the same day.* The discourse of Peter commenced at nine o'clock in the morning. ver. 15. How long it continued it is not said; but the ceremony of admitting them to the church and of baptizing them was evidently performed on the same day. The mode in which this is done is not mentioned; but it is highly improbable that *in* the midst of the city of Jerusalem three thousand persons were wholly immersed in one day. The whole narrative supposes that it was all done *in* the city; and yet there is no probability that there were conveniences there for *immersing* so many persons in a single day. Besides, in the ordinary way of administering baptism by immersion, it is difficult to conceive that *so many persons* could have been immersed in so short a time. There is, indeed, here no positive *proof* that they were not immersed; but the narrative is one of those incidental circumstances often much more satisfactory than philological discussion, that show the extreme improbability that all this was done by wholly immersing them in water. It may be further remarked that here is an example of very quick admission to the church. It was the first great work of grace under the gospel. It was the model of all revivals of religion. And it was doubtless intended that this should be a specimen of the manner in which the ministers of religion should conduct in regard to admissions to the Christian church. Prudence is indeed required; but this example furnishes no warrant for advising persons who profess their willingness to obey Jesus Christ, to delay uniting with the church. If persons give evidence of piety, of true hatred of sin, and of attachment to the Lord Jesus, they should unite themselves to his people without delay. ¶ *There were added.* To the company of disciples, or to the followers of Christ. ¶ *Souls.* Persons. Comp. 1 Pet. iii. 20. Gen. xii. 5. It is not affirmed that all this took place in one part of Jerusalem, or that it was all done at once; but it is probable that this was what was afterwards ascertained to be the fruit of this day's labour, the result of this revival of religion. This was the first effusion of the Holy Spirit under the preaching of the gospel; and it shows that such scenes are to be expected in the church, and that the gospel is fitted to work a rapid and mighty change in the hearts of men.

42. *And they continued steadfastly.* They persevered in, or they adhered to. This is the inspired record of the result. That any of these apostatized is nowhere recorded, and is not to be presumed. Though they had been suddenly converted, though suddenly admitted to the church, though exposed to much persecution and contempt, and many trials, yet the record is that they adhered to the doctrines and duties of the Christian religion. The word rendered *continued steadfastly*, προσκαρτεροῦντες, means attending one, remaining by his side, not leaving or forsaking him. ¶ *The apostles' doctrine.* This does not mean that they held or believed the *doctrines* of the apostles, though that was true; but it means that they adhered to, or attended on, their *teaching* or *instruction*. The word *doctrine* has now a technical sense, and means a collection and arrangement of

43 And fear came upon every soul: and many [a] wonders and signs were done by the apostles.

[a] Mar.16.17

44 And all that believed were together, and [b] had all things common;

[b] c.4.32,34.

abstract views supposed to be contained in the Bible. In the Scriptures the word means simply *teaching;* and the expression here denotes that they continued to attend on their *instructions.* One evidence of conversion is a desire to be *instructed* in the doctrines and duties of religion, and a willingness to attend on the preaching of the gospel. ¶ *And fellowship.* The word rendered *fellowship,* κοινωνία, is often rendered *communion.* It properly denotes *having things in common,* or participation, society, friendship. It may apply to any thing which may be possessed in common, or in which all may partake. Thus all Christians have the same hope of heaven: the same joys; the same hatred of sin; the same enemies to contend with. Thus they have the same subjects of conversation, of feeling, and of prayer; or they have communion in these things. And thus the early Christians had their property in common. The word here may apply to either or to all, to their conversation, their prayers, their dangers, or their property; and means that they were *united* to the apostles, and participated with them in whatever befel them. It may be added that the effect of a revival of religion is to unite Christians more and more, and to bring those who were before separated to union and love. Christians feel that they are a band of brethren, and that however much they were separated *before* they became Christians, now they have great and important interests in common; united in feelings, in interest, in dangers, in conflicts, in opinions, and in the hopes of a blessed immortality. ¶ *Breaking of bread.* The Syriac renders this 'the eucharist,' or the Lord's supper. It cannot, however, be determined whether this refers to their partaking of their ordinary food together; or to feasts of charity; or to the Lord's supper. The bread of the Hebrews was made commonly into cakes, thin, hard and brittle, so that it was *broken* instead of being cut. Hence, to denote intimacy or friendship, the phrase to *break bread together* would be very expressive, in the same way as the Greeks denoted it by *drinking together,* συμπόσιον. From the expression used in ver. 44, comp. with ver. 46, that they had all things common, it would rather seem to be implied that this referred to the participation of their ordinary meals. The action of *breaking bread* was commonly performed by the master or head of a family, immediately after asking a blessing. (*Lightfoot.*) ¶ *In prayers.* This was one *effect* of the influence of the Spirit, and an evidence of their change. A genuine revival will be always followed by a love of prayer.

43. *And fear came.* That is, there was great reverence or awe. The multitude had just before derided them (ver. 13); but so striking and manifest was the power of God on this occasion, that it silenced all clamours, and produced a general veneration and awe. The effect of a great work of God's grace is commonly to produce an unusual seriousness and solemnity in a community, even among those who are not convicted. It restrains, subdues, and silences opposition. ¶ *Every soul.* Every person, or individual; that is, upon the people generally; not only on those who became Christians, but upon the multitudes who witnessed these things. All things were fitted to produce this fear: the recent crucifixion of Jesus of Nazareth; the wonders that attended that event; the events of the day of Pentecost; and the miracles performed by the apostles, were all fitted to diffuse solemnity, and thought, and anxiety through the community. ¶ *Many wonders and signs.* See Note, ver. 22. This was promised by the Saviour. Mark xvi. 17. Some of the miracles which they wrought are specified in the following chapters.

44. *All that believed.* That is, that believed that Jesus was the Messiah; for that was the distinguishing point by which they were known from others. ¶ *Were together.* ἐπὶ τὸ αὐτό. Were united, were joined in the same thing. It does not mean that they *lived* in the same house, but they were *united in the same community;* or engaged in the same thing. They were doubtless *often* together in the same place for prayer and praise. One of the best means for strengthening the faith of young converts is for them *often* to meet together for prayer, conversation, and praise. ¶ *Had all things common.* That is, all their *property* or *possessions.* See ch. iv. 32—37; v. 1—10. The apostles, in the time of the Saviour, evidently had all their property in common stock, and Judas was made their

45 And sold their possessions and goods, and [a] parted them to all *men*, as every man had need.

a Is.58.7. 2Cor.9.1,9. 1Jno.3.17.

---

treasurer. They regarded themselves as one family, having common wants; and there was no use or propriety in their possessing extensive property by themselves. Yet even then it is probable that *some* of them retained an interest in their property which was not supposed to be necessary to be devoted to the common use. It is evident that *John* thus possessed property which he retained. John xix. 27. And it is clear that the Saviour did not *command* them to give up their property into a common stock; nor did the apostles enjoin it. Acts v. 4, "While it remained, was it not thine own? and after it was sold, was it not in thine own power?" It was therefore perfectly voluntary; and was evidently adapted to the peculiar circumstances of the early converts. Many of them came from abroad. They were from Parthia, and Media, and Arabia, and Rome, and Africa, &c. It is probable, also, that they now remained longer in Jerusalem than they had at first proposed. And it is not at all improbable that they would be denied now the usual hospitalities of the Jews, and excluded from their customary kindness, because they had embraced Jesus of Nazareth, who had been just put to death. In these circumstances, it was natural and proper that they should share together their property while they remained together.

45. *And sold*. That is, they sold as much as was necessary in order to procure the means of providing for the wants of each other. ¶ *Possessions*. Property, particularly *real* estate. This word, κτήματα, refers properly to their *fixed* property, as lands, houses, vineyards, &c. The word rendered *goods*, ὑπάρξεις, refers to their *personal* or moveable property. ¶ *And parted them to all*. They *distributed* them to supply the wants of their poorer brethren, according to their necessities. ¶ *As every man had need*. This expression *limits* and fixes the meaning of what is said before. The passage does not mean that they sold *all* their possessions, or that they relinquished their title to *all* their property; but that they so far regarded all as common as to be willing to part with it IF it was needful to supply the wants of the others. Hence the property was laid at the disposal of the apostles, and they were desired to distribute it freely to meet the wants of the poor. ch. iv. 34, 35.

This was an important incident in the early propagation of religion; and it may suggest many useful reflections.

1. We see the effect of religion. The love of property is one of the strongest affections which men have. There is nothing that will overcome it but religion. That will; and one of the *first* effects of the gospel was to loosen the hold of Christians on property.

2. It is the duty of the church to provide for the wants of its poor and needy members. There can be no doubt that property should now be regarded as *so far* common as that the wants of the poor should be supplied by those who are rich. Comp. Matt. xxvi. 11.

3. If it be asked *why* the early disciples evinced this readiness to part with their property in this manner, it may be replied, (1.) That the apostles had done it before them. The family of the Saviour had all things common. (2.) It was the nature of religion to do it. (3.) The circumstances of the persons assembled on this occasion were such as to require it. They were many of them from distant regions; and probably many of them of the poorer class of the people in Jerusalem. In this they evinced what *should* be done in behalf of the poor in the church at all times.

4. If it be asked whether this was done *commonly* among the early Christians, it may be replied, that there is no evidence that it was. It is mentioned here, and in ch. iv. 32—37, and ch. v. 1—7. It does not appear that it was done even by *all* who were afterwards converted in Judea; and there is no evidence that it was done in Antioch, Ephesus, Corinth, Philippi, Rome, &c. That the effect of religion was to make men *liberal*, and willing to provide for the poor, there can be no doubt. See 2 Cor. viii. 19; ix. 2. 1 Cor. xvi. 2. Gal. ii. 10. But there is not proof that it was *common* to part with their possessions, and to lay it at the feet of the apostles. Religion does not contemplate, evidently, that men should break up all the arrangements in society; but it contemplates that those who *have* property should be ready and willing to part with it for the help of the poor and needy.

5. If it be asked whether all the arrangements of property should be broken up now, and believers have all things in common, we are prepared to answer, *No*. For, 1. This was an extraordinary case. 2. It was not even enjoined by the apostles on them. 3. It was practised nowhere

46 And they, continuing daily with one accord in the temple, and breaking[1] bread from house to house, did eat their meat with gladness and singleness of heart,

47 Praising God, and having favour [a] with all the people. And [b] the Lord added to the church daily such as should be saved.

[1] or, *at home.*

a Lu.2.52. Ro.14.18. *b* c.5.14;11.24.

else. 4. It would be impracticable. No community where all things were in common has long prospered. It has been attempted often, by pagans, by infidels, and by fanatical sects of Christians. It ends soon in anarchy, and licentiousness, and idleness, and profligacy; or the more cunning secure the mass of the property, and control the whole. Till all men are *made alike*, there could be no hope of such a community; and if there could be, it would not be desirable. God evidently intended that men should be excited to industry by the hope of gain; and *then* he demands that their gains should be devoted to *his* service. Still, this was a noble instance of Christian generosity, and evinces the power of religion in loosing the hold which men commonly have on the world. It rebukes also those professors of religion, of whom, alas, there are many, who *give* nothing to benefit either the souls or bodies of their fellow-men.

46 *With one accord.* Comp. ch. i. 14; li. 1. ¶ *In the temple.* This was the public place of worship; and the disciples were not disposed to leave the place where their fathers had so long worshipped God. This does not mean that they were *constantly* in the temple, but only at the customary hours of prayer; at 9 o'clock in the morning, and at 3 in the afternoon. ¶ *And breaking bread.* See Note, ver. 42. ¶ *From house to house.* In the margin, "at home." So the Syriac and Arabic. The common interpretation, however, is, that they did it in their various houses, now in this and now in that, as might be convenient. If it refers to their ordinary meals, then it means that they partook *in common* of what they possessed. And the expression in this verse, "did eat their meat," seems to imply that this refers to their common meals, and not to the Lord's supper. ¶ *Did eat their meat.* Did partake of their food. The word *meat* with us is applied to *flesh.* In the Bible, and in old English authors, it is applied to provision of any kind. Here it means all kinds of sustenance; that which nourished them—τροφῆς—and the use of this word *proves* that it does not refer to the Lord's supper; for that ordinance is nowhere represented as designed for an ordinary meal, or to nourish the *body.* Comp. 1 Cor. xi. 33, 34. ¶ *With gladness.* With rejoicing. This is one of the effects of religion. It is far from gloom; it diffuses joy over the mind; and it bestows additional joy in the participation of even our ordinary pleasures. ¶ *Singleness of heart.* This means with a *sincere* and pure heart. They were satisfied and thankful. They were not perplexed or anxious; nor were they solicitous for the luxurious living, or aspiring after the vain objects of the men of the world. Comp. Rom. xii. 8. 2 Cor. i. 12. Col. iii. 22. Eph. vi. 5.

47. *Praising God.* See Luke xxiv. 53. ¶ *And having favour.* See Luke ii. 52. ¶ *With all the people.* That is, with the great mass of the people; with the people generally. It does not mean that all the people had become reconciled to Christianity; but their humble, serious and devoted lives won the favour of the great mass of the community, and silenced opposition and cavil. This was a remarkable effect, but God has power to silence opposition; and there is nothing so well fitted to do this as the humble and consistent lives of his friends. ¶ *And the Lord added.* See ch. v. 14; xi. 24, &c. It was *the Lord* who did this. There was no power in man to do it; and the Christian loves to trace *all* increase of the church to the grace of God. ¶ *Added.* Caused, or inclined them to be joined to the church. ¶ *The church.* To the *assembly* of the followers of Christ. τῇ ἐκκλησίᾳ. The word *church* properly means those who are *called out*, and is applied to Christians as being *called out*, or separated from the world. It is used but three times in the Gospels. Matt. xvi 18; xviii. 17. It occurs frequently in other parts of the New Testament, and usually as applied to the followers of Christ. Comp. Acts v. 11; vii. 38; viii. 1. 3; ix. 31; xi. 22. 26; xii. 1. 5, &c. It is used in classic writers to denote an *assembly* of any kind, and is twice thus used in the New Testament (Acts xix. 39. 41), where it is translated "assembly." ¶ *Such as should be saved.* This whole phrase is a translation of a participle, τοὺς σωζομένους It does not express any *purpose* that they *should* be saved, but simply *the fact* that

CHAPTER III.

NOW Peter and John went up together into the temple at [a] the hour of prayer, *being* the ninth *hour*.
2 And a certain man, lame from his mother's womb, was carried, whom they laid daily at the gate [b] of the temple which is called Beautiful, to ask alms of them that entered into the temple;

a Ps.55.17. Da.6.10. b Jno.9.8.

they were those who *would be*, or who were about to be saved. It is clear, however, from this expression, that those who became members of the church were those who continued to adorn their profession, or who gave proof that they were sincere Christians. It is implied here, also, that those who are to be saved will join themselves to the church of God. This is every where required; and it constitutes *one* evidence of piety when they are willing to face the world, and give themselves at once to the service of the Lord Jesus.—Two remarks may be made on the last verse of this chapter; one is, that the effect of a consistent Christian life will be to command the *respect* of the world; and the other is, that the effect will be continually to increase the number of those who shall be saved. In this case they were *daily* added to it; the church was constantly increasing: and the same result may be expected in all cases where there is similar zeal self denial, consistency, and prayer.

We have now contemplated the foundation of the Christian church; and the first glorious revival of religion. This chapter deserves to be profoundly studied by all the ministers of the gospel, and by all who pray for the prosperity of the kingdom of God. It should excite our fervent gratitude that God has left this record of the first great work of grace; and our fervent prayers that he would multiply and extend such scenes until the earth shall be filled with his glory.

CHAPTER III.

1. *Peter and John went up*, &c. In Luke xxiv. 53, it is said that the apostles were continually in the temple, praising and blessing God. From Acts ii. 46, it is clear that all the disciples were accustomed daily to resort to the temple for devotion. Whether they joined in the *sacrifices* of the temple-service is not said; but the thing is not improbable. This was the place and the manner in which they and their fathers had worshipped. They came slowly to the conclusion that they were to leave the *temple;* and they would naturally resort there with their countrymen to worship the God of their fathers. In the previous chapter (ii. 43), we are told *in general* that many wonders and signs were done by the hands of the apostles. From the many miracles which were performed, Luke selects one, of which he gives a more full account; and especially as it gives him occasion to record another of the addresses of Peter to the Jews. An impostor would have been satisfied with the *general* statement that many miracles *were* performed. The sacred writers descend to particulars, and tell us where, and in relation to whom, they were performed. This is a proof that they were honest men, and did not intend to deceive. ¶ *Into the temple.* Not into the edifice properly called the temple, but into the *court* of the temple, where prayer was accustomed to be made. See Note, Matt. xxi. 12. ¶ *At the hour of prayer*, &c. The Jewish day was divided into twelve equal parts; of course, the ninth hour would be about three o'clock, P. M. This was the hour of evening prayer. Morning prayer was offered at nine o'clock. Comp. Ps. lv. 17. Dan. vi. 10.

2. *Lame*, &c. The mention of this shows that there was no deception in the case. The man had been always lame; he was obliged to be carried; and he was well known to the Jews. ¶ *Whom they laid daily.* That is, his friends laid him there *daily*. He would therefore be well known to those who were in the habit of entering the temple. Among the ancients there were no hospitals for the afflicted; and no alms-houses for the poor. The poor were dependent, therefore, on the charity of those who were in better circumstances. It became an important matter for them to be placed where they would see many people. Hence it was customary to place them at the gates of rich men (Luke xvi. 20); and they also sat by the side of the highway to beg where many persons would pass. Mark x. 46. Luke xviii. 35. John ix. 1—8. The entrance to the *temple* would be a favourable place for begging; for, (1.) great multitudes were accustomed to enter there; and (2.) when going up for the purposes of religion, they would be more inclined to give alms than at other times and especially was this true of the Pharisees, who were particularly desirous of *publicity* in bestowing charity. It is re

3 Who, seeing Peter and John about to go into the temple, asked an alms.
4 And Peter, fastening his eyes upon him, with John, said, Look on us.
5 And he gave heed unto them, expecting to receive something of them.
6 Then Peter said, Silver and gold have I none: but such as I have give I thee: In [a] the name of Jesus Christ of Nazareth, rise up and walk.

a c.4.10.

corded by Martial (i. 112.), that this custom prevailed among the Romans of placing the poor by the gates of the temples; and the custom was also observed a long time in the Christian churches. ¶ *At the gate of the temple which is called Beautiful.* In regard to this gate there have been two opinions, one of which supposes that this was the gate commonly called *Nicanor*, which led from the court of the Gentiles to the court of the women (see Plan in Notes on Matt. xxi. 12), and the other, that it was the gate at the eastern entrance of the temple, commonly called *Susan*. It is not easy to determine which is intended; though from the fact that it occurred near Solomon's porch (ver. 11, comp. Plan of the temple, Matt. xxi. 12), it seems probable that the latter was intended. This gate was large and splendid. It was made of Corinthian brass, a most valuable metal, and made a magnificent appearance. *Josephus, Jewish War*, b v. ch. v. § 3. ¶ *To ask alms.* Charity.

3. *Who, seeing Peter*, &c. There is no evidence that he was acquainted with them, or knew who they were. He asked of them as he was accustomed to do of the multitude that entered the temple.

4. *Fastening his eyes.* The word used here denotes to look *intently*, or with fixed attention. It is one of the peculiar words which *Luke* uses. Luke iv. 20; xxii. 56; Acts i. 10; iii. 12; vi. 15; vii. 55; x. 4, &c in all twelve times. It is used by no other writer in the New Testament, except by Paul twice, 2 Cor. iii. 7. 13. ¶ *Look on us.* All this was done to fix the attention. He wished to call the attention of the man distinctly to himself, and to what he was about to do. It was also done that the man might be fully apprised that his restoration to health came from him.

6. *Silver and gold have I none.* The man had asked for money; Peter assures him that he had not that to give; it was done, however, in such a way as to show his *willingness* to aid him, if he *had* possessed it. ¶ *Such as I have.* Such as is in my power. It is not to be supposed that he meant to say that he originated this power himself, but only that it was intrusted to him. He immediately adds that it was derived solely from the Lord Jesus Christ. ¶ *In the name.* Comp. ch. iv. 10. In Mark xvi. 17, 18, it is said, "These signs shall follow them that believe; *in my name* shall they cast out devils, &c.....they shall lay hands on the sick, and they shall recover." The expression means *by his authority*, or *in virtue of power derived from him.* We are here struck with a remarkable difference between the manner in which the Lord Jesus wrought miracles, and that in which it was done by his apostles. *He* did it in his *own name*, and by virtue of his own power. He claimed dominion over disease and death The apostles never attempted to perform a miracle by their *own power.* It was only in the name of Jesus; and this circumstance alone shows that there was a radical difference between Christ and all other prophets and teachers. ¶ *Of Nazareth.* This was the name by which he was commonly known. By this name he had been designated among the Jews, and on the cross. It is by no means improbable that the man had heard of him by this name; and it was important that he should understand that it was by the authority of him who had been crucified as an impostor. ¶ *Rise and walk.* To do this would be evidence of signal power. It is remarkable that in cases like this, they were commanded to do the thing at once. See similar cases in John v. 8. Matt. ix. 6; xii. 13. It would have been easy to allege that they had *no power*, that they were lame, or sick, or palsied, and could do nothing until God should give them strength. But the command was *to do the thing;* nor did the Saviour or the apostles stop to convince them that they *could* do nothing. They did not doubt that if it were done, the would ascribe the power to God. Precisely like this is the condition of the sinner. God commands him *to do the thing;* to repent, and believe, and lead a holy life. It is not merely to *attempt* to do it; to make use of means; or to wait on him: but it is *actually to repent and believe* the gospel. Where he may obtain power to do it is another question. It is easy for him to involve himself in difficulty, as it

7 And he took him by the right hand, and lifted *him* up: and immediately his feet and ankle-bones received strength.

8 And he, leaping [a] up, stood, and walked, and entered with them into the temple, walking, and leaping, and praising God.

9 And all the people saw him walking and praising God:

10 And they knew that it was he which sat for alms at the Beautiful gate of the temple: and they were filled with wonder and amazement at that which had happened unto him.

a Is.35.6

would have been in these cases. But the command of God is positive, and must be obeyed. If not obeyed, men must perish; just as this man would have been always lame if he had put forth no effort of his own. When done, a convicted sinner will do just as this man did, *instinctively give all the praise to God.* ver. 8.

7. *And he took him.* He took hold of his hand. To take hold of the hand in such a case was an offer of aid, an indication that Peter was sincere, and was an inducement to him to make an effort. This may be employed as a beautiful illustration of the manner of God when he commands men to repent and believe. He does not leave them alone; he extends help, and aids their efforts. If they tremble, and feel that they are weak, and needy, and helpless, his hand is stretched out, and his power exerted to impart strength and grace. ¶ *His feet and ankle-bones.* The fact that strength was immediately imparted; that the feet, long lame, were now made strong, was a full and clear proof of miraculous power.

8. *And he, leaping up.* This was a natural expression of joy; and it was a striking fulfilment of the prophecy in Isa. xxxv. 6: "Then shall the lame man leap as an hart." The account here given is one that is perfectly natural. The man would be filled with joy, and would express it in this manner. He had been lame from a child; he had never walked; and there was more in the miracle than merely giving *strength.* The act of *walking* is one that is acquired by long practice. Children learn slowly. *Casper Hauser*, lately discovered in one of the cities of Germany, who had been confined in prison from a child, was unable to walk in an easy way when released, but stumbled in a very awkward manner. (See his Life.) When, therefore, this man was able at once to walk, it was clear proof of a miracle. ¶ *Praising God.* This was the natural and appropriate expression of his feelings on this occasion. His heart would be full; and he could have no doubt that this blessing had come from God alone. It is remarkable that he did not even express his gratitude to Peter and John. They had not pretended to restore him in their own name; and he would feel that man could not do it. It is remarkable that he praised God without being *taught* or entreated to do it. It was instinctive—the natural feeling of the heart. So a sinner. His first feelings when renewed, will be to ascribe the praise to God. While he may and will feel regard for the ministry by whose instrumentality he has received the blessing, yet his main expression of gratitude will be to God. And this he will do instinctively; he needs no prompter; he knows that no power of man is equal to the work of converting the soul, and will rejoice, and give all the praise to the God of grace.

9, 10. *And all the people*, &c. The people who had been accustomed to see him sit in a public place. ¶ *And they knew*, &c. In this they could not be deceived; they had seen him a long time, and now they saw the same man expressing his praise to God for complete recovery. The particulars in this miracle are the following; and they are as far as possible from any appearance of imposture. 1. The man had been afflicted from a child This was known to all the people. At this time he was forty years of age. ch. iv. 22. 2. He was not an impostor. If he had *pretended* lameness, it is wonderful that he had not been detected before, and not have been suffered to occupy a place thus in the temple. 3. The apostles had no agency in placing him there. They had not seen him before. There was manifestly no *collusion* or *agreement* with him to attempt to impose on the people. 4. The man himself was convinced of the miracle; and did not doubt that the power by which he had been healed was of God 5. The *people* were convinced of the same thing. They saw the effects; they had known him well; they had had every opportunity to know that he was diseased; and they were now satisfied that he was restored. There was no possi

11 And, as the lame man which
was healed held Peter and John,
all the people ran together unto
them, in the porch [a] that is called
Solomon's, greatly wondering.
12 And when Peter saw *it*, he
answered unto the people, Ye men
of Israel, why marvel ye at this?
or why look ye so earnestly on us,
as though by our own [b] power or
holiness we had made this man to
walk?
13 The God [c] of Abraham, and
of Isaac, and of Jacob, the God of
our fathers, [d] hath glorified [e] his Son
Jesus; whom ye delivered up, and

a Jno.10.23. c.5.12. b 2Cor.3.5. c Matt.22.32. d c.5.30,31. e Jno.17.1. Ep.1.20-22. Ph.2.9-11. He.2.9. Re.1.5,18.

---

bility of deception in the case. It was not merely the *friends* of Jesus that saw this; not those who had an *interest* in the miracle, but those who had been his enemies, and who had just before been engaged in putting him to death. Let this miracle be compared, in these particulars, with those *pretended* miracles which have been affirmed to have been wrought in defence of other systems of religion, and it will be seen at once that here is every appearance of sincerity, honesty, and ruth; and in them every mark of deception, fraud, and imposition. (See Paley's Evidences of Christianity, Proposition ii. ch ii.)

11. *Held Peter and John.* The word *held* means he *adhered* to them; he joined himself to them; he was desirous of remaining with them, and participating with them. ¶ *All the people,* &c. Excited by curiosity, they came together. The fact of the cure, and the conduct of the man, would soon draw together a crowd, and thus furnish a favourable opportunity for preaching to them the gospel. ¶ *In the porch,* &c. This *porch* was a covered way or passage on the east side of the temple. It was distinguished for its magnificence. See the Plan and description of the temple, Notes on Matt. xxi. 12.

12. *When Peter saw it.* Saw the people assembling in such multitudes and wondering at the miracle. ¶ *He answered.* The word *answer,* with us, implies that a question had been asked, or that some subject had been proposed for consideration. But the word is used in a different sense in the Bible. It is often used when no question was asked, but when *an occasion* was offered for remarks, or where an opportunity was presented to make a statement. It is the same as replying *to a thing,* or making *a statement* in regard to some subject. Dan. ii. 26. Acts v. 8. ¶ *Ye men of Israel.* Jews. Comp. ch. ii. 14. ¶ *Why marvel ye at this?* The particular thing which he intended to reprove here, was not that they *wondered,* for that was proper; but that they *looked on Peter and John* as if they had been the authors of this healing. They ought to have understood it. The Jews were sufficiently acquainted with miracles to interpret them, and to know whence they proceeded; and they ought not, therefore, to ascribe them to *man,* but to inquire *why* they had been wrought *by God.* ¶ *Why look ye,* &c. Why do ye fix the eyes with amazement *on us,* as though *we* could do this? Why not look at once to God? ¶ *By our own power.* By any *art of healing,* or by any medicine, we had done this. ¶ *Or holiness.* Piety. As if God had bestowed this on us on account of our personal and eminent piety. It may be remarked, that here was ample opportunity for them to establish a reputation of their own. The people were disposed to pay them honours; they *might* at once have laid claim to vast authority over them; but they refused all such personal honours, and ascribed all to the Lord Jesus. Whatever success may attend the ministers of the gospel; or however much the world may be disposed to do them honour; they should disclaim all power in themselves, and ascribe it to the Lord Jesus Christ. It is not by the talents or personal holiness of ministers, valuable as these are, that men are saved; it is only by the power of God, designed to honour his Son. See 2 Cor. iii. 5, 6.

13. *The God of Abraham.* He is called the God of Abraham because Abraham *acknowledged* him as his God, and because God showed himself to be his friend. Comp. Matt. xxii. 32. Ex. iii. 6. 15. Gen xxviii. 13; xxvi. 24. It was important to show that it was the *same* God who had done this that had been acknowledged by their fathers; and that they were not about to introduce the worship of any other God. And it was especially important, because the promise had been made to Abraham, that in his seed should all the families of the earth be blessed. Gen. xii. 3. Comp. Gal. iii. 16. ¶ *Hath glorified.* Has honoured. *You* denied, despised, and murdered him; but God has exalted

denied [a] him in the presence of Pilate, when he [b] was determined to
let *him* go.
14 But ye denied the Holy [c] One
and the Just, [d] and desired a murderer to be granted unto you;

15 And killed the [1] Prince of life,
whom God hath raised [e] from the
dead; whereof [f] we are witnesses.
16 And his name, through faith
in his name, hath made this man
strong, whom ye see and know;

a Jno.19.15. b Matt.27.17-25. Lu.23.16-23. c Ps.16.10. Lu.1.35 d c.7.52;22.14.

1 or, *author*. Jno.1.4. 1Jno.5.11. e Matt. 28.2-6. Ep.1.20. f c.2.32.

and honoured him. This miracle was done in the *name* of Jesus. ver. 6. It was the *power of God* that had restored him; and by putting forth this power God had shown that he approved the work of his Son, and was disposed to honour him in the view of men. Comp. John xvii. 1. Eph. i. 20—22. Phil. ii. 9—11. Heb. ii. 9. Rev. i. 5—18. ¶ *Ye delivered up.* That is, you delivered him to the Romans to be put to death. See Note, ch. ii. 23. ¶ *And denied him in the presence of Pilate.* Denied that he was the Messiah. Were unwilling to own him as your long-expected King. John xix. 15. ¶ *When he was determined,* &c. Matt. xxvii. 17—25. Luke xxiii. 16—23. Pilate was satisfied of his innocence; but he was weak, and timid, and irresolute, and yielded to their wishes. The fact that *Pilate* regarded him as innocent was a strong aggravation of their crime. They should have regarded him as innocent; but they urged on his condemnation, against the deliberate judgment of him before whom they had arraigned him; and thus showed how obstinately they were resolved on his death.

14. *The holy One,* &c. See Ps. xvi. 10. Comp. Note, Acts ii. 27. ¶ *And the just.* The word *just* here denotes *innocent,* or one who was free from crime. It properly is used in reference to *law,* and denotes one who stands upright in the view of the law, or who is not chargeable with crime. In this sense the Lord Jesus was not only *personally* innocent, but even before his judges he stood unconvicted of any crime The crime charged on him at first was *blasphemy* (Matt. xxvi. 65); and on *this* charge the Sanhedrim had condemned him, without proof. But of *this* charge Pilate would not take cognizance, and hence *before him* they charged him with sedition. Luke xxiii. 2. Neither of these charges were made out; and, of course, in the eye of the law he was innocent and just. It greatly aggravated their crime that they demanded his death still, even *after* it was ascertained that they could prove nothing against him; thus showing that it was mere hatred and malice that led them to seek his death

¶ *And desired a murderer.* Matt. xxvii. 21.

15. *And killed the Prince of Life.* The word rendered *prince* denotes properly a *military leader* or commander. Hence, in Heb ii. 10, it is translated *captain;* "It became him....to make the *Captain of their salvation* perfect through sufferings.' As a captain or commander leads on to victory, and is said to obtain it, so the word comes to denote one who is the *cause,* the *author,* the *procurer,* &c. In this sense it is used, Acts v. 31, "Him hath God exalted to be a *Prince* and a Saviour, *for to give* repentance to Israel," &c. In Heb. xii. 2, it is properly rendered *author;* "Looking unto Jesus, the *author* and finisher of our faith." The word *author,* or giver, would express the meaning of the word here. It also implies that he has *dominion* over life; an idea, indeed, which is essentially connected with that of his being the author of it. The word *life* here is used in a large sense, as denoting *all* manner of life. In this sense it is used in reference to Christ in John i. 4, "In him was *life,*" &c. Comp. John v. 26. 1 John v. 11. 1 Cor. xv. 45. Jesus is here called the *Prince of life* in contrast with him whom the Jews demanded in his place, Barabbas. He was a *murderer* (Luke xxiii. 19. Mark xv. 7), one who had *destroyed life;* and yet they demanded that he whose character it was *to destroy life* should be released, and *the Author of life* to be put to death. ¶ *Whom God hath raised,* &c. ch. ii. 24. 32.

16. *And his name.* The *name* of Jesus is here put for Jesus himself; and it is the same as saying, "and *he,*" &c. In this way the word *name* is often used by the Hebrews, especially when speaking of God. Acts i. 15; iv. 12. Eph. i. 21. Rev. iii. 4. It does not mean that there was any efficacy in the mere *name* of Jesus that should heal the man, but that it was done by his authority and power. ¶ *Through faith in his name.* By means of faith in him; that is, by the faith which Peter and John had in Jesus. It does not refer to any faith that the man had himself, for there is no evidence that he believed in him. But it was by means

yea, the faith which is by him hath given him this perfect soundness in the presence of you all.

17 And now, brethren, I wot that through ignorance [a] ye did *it*, as *did* also your rulers.

a Lu.23.34. Jno.16.3. 1Cor.2.8

---

of the faith which the apostles exercised in him that the miracle was wrought, and was thus a fulfilment of the declaration in Matt. xvii. 20, "If ye have faith....ye shall say to this mountain, remove hence," &c. This truth Peter repeats two or three times in the verse to impress it more distinctly on the minds of his hearers. ¶ *Whom ye see and know.* There could therefore be no mistake. He was well known to them. There was no doubt about the truth of the miracle (ch. iv. 16), and the only inquiry was in what way it had been done. This Peter affirms to have been accomplished *only* by the power of the Lord Jesus. ¶ *Perfect soundness.* ὁλοκληρίαν. This word is not used elsewhere in the New Testament. It denotes *integrity of parts, freedom from any defect;* and it here means that the cure was perfect and entire, or that he was *completely* restored to the use of his limbs. ¶ *In the presence of you all.* You are all witnesses of it, and can judge for yourselves. This shows how confident the apostles were that a *real* miracle had been performed. They were willing that it should be examined; and this is conclusive proof that there was no attempt at imposture. A deceiver, or one who *pretended* to work miracles, would have been *cautious* of exposing the subject to the danger of detection.

17. *And now, brethren.* Though they had been guilty of a crime so enormous, yet Peter shows the tenderness of his heart in addressing them still as his *brethren.* He regarded them as of the same nation with himself, as having the same hopes, and as being entitled to the same privileges. The expression also shows that he was not disposed to exalt himself as being by nature more holy than they. This verse is a remarkable instance of *tenderness* in appealing to sinners. It would have been easy to have reproached them for their enormous crimes; but it was not the way to reach the heart. He had indeed stated and *proved* their wickedness. The object now was to bring them to repentance for it; and this was to be done by *tenderness,* and *kindness,* and *love.* Men are melted to contrition, not by *reproaches,* but by *love.* ¶ *I wot.* I know; I am well apprized of it. I know you will affirm it; and I admit that it was so. Still the enormous deed *has been done.* It cannot be recalled and it cannot be innocent. It remains, therefore, that you should repent of it, and seek for pardon. ¶ *That through ignorance,* &c. Peter does not mean to affirm that they were *innocent* in having put him to death, for he had just proved the contrary; and he immediately proceeds to exhort them to repentance. But he means to say that their offence was *mitigated* by the fact that they were ignorant that he was the Messiah. The same thing the Saviour himself affirmed when dying. Luke xxiii. 34. "Father, forgive them, for they know not what they do." Comp. Acts xiii. 27 1 Cor. ii. 8. The same thing the apostle Paul affirmed in relation to himself, as one of the reasons why he obtained pardon from the enormous crime of persecution. 1 Tim. i. 13. In cases like these, though crime might be *mitigated,* yet it was not taken entirely away. They were guilty of demanding a man to be murdered who was declared innocent; they were urged on with ungovernable fury; they did it from contempt and malice; and the crime of *murder* remained, though they were ignorant that he was the Messiah. It is plainly implied that if they had put him to death *knowing* that he was the Messiah, and *as the Messiah,* there would have been no forgiveness. Comp. Heb. x. 26—29. Ignorance, therefore, is a circumstance which must always be taken into view in an estimate of crime. It is at the same time true, that they had opportunity to know that he was the Messiah; but the *mere fact* that they were ignorant of it, was still a mitigating circumstance in the estimate of their crime. There can be no doubt that the *mass* of the people had no fixed belief that he was the Messiah. ¶ *As did also your rulers.* Comp. 1 Cor. ii. 8, where the apostle says that none of the princes of this world knew the wisdom of the gospel, for had they known it, they would not have crucified the Lord of glory. It is certain that the *leading* Scribes and Pharisees were urged on by the most ungovernable fury and rage to put Jesus to death, even when they had abundant opportunity to know his true character. This was particularly the case with the high-priest. But yet it was true that they did not *believe* that he was the Mes-

18 But those [a] things which God before had showed by the mouth of all his prophets, that Christ should suffer, he hath so fulfilled.

a Lu.24.44. c.26.22,23.

19 Repent [b] ye therefore, and be converted, [c] that your sins may be [d] blotted out, when the times of refreshing [e] shall come from the presence of the Lord;

b c.2.38. c Is.1.16-20. Joel 2.13. d Is.43.25. e Jer.31.23-25. Zep.3.14-20. Re.21.4.

siah. Their minds had been prejudiced. They had expected a prince and a conqueror. All their views of the Messiah were different from the character which Jesus manifested. And though they *might* have known that he was the Messiah; though he had given abundant proof of the fact, yet it is clear that they did not believe it. It is not credible that they *would* have put to death one whom they *really* believed to be the Christ. He was the hope, the only hope of their nation; and they would not have dared to imbrue their hands in the blood of him whom they really believed to be the illustrious personage so long promised, and expected by their fathers. It was also probably true that no small part of the Sanhedrim was urged on by the zeal and fury of the chief-priests. They had not courage to resist them; and yet they *might* not have entered heartily into this work of persecution and death. Comp. John vii. 50—53. The speech of Peter, however, is not intended to free them entirely from blame; nor should it be pressed to show that they were innocent. It is a mitigating circumstance thrown in to show them that there was still *hope of mercy*.

18. *But those things.* To wit, those things that *did* actually occur, pertaining to the life and death of the Messiah. ¶ *Had showed.* Had announced, or foretold. ¶ *By the mouth of all his prophets.* That is, by the prophets in general, without affirming that *each* individual prophet had a distinct prediction respecting this. The prophets *taken together*, or the prophecies *as a whole*, had declared this. The word *all* is not unfrequently used in this somewhat limited sense. Mark i. 37. John iii. 26. In regard to the prophecies respecting Christ, see Note, Luke xxiv. 27. ¶ *Hath so fulfilled.* He has caused to be fulfilled *in this manner;* that is, by the rejection, denial, and wickedness of the rulers. It has *turned out* to be in strict accordance with the prophecy. This fact Peter uses in exhorting them to repentance; but it is not to be regarded as an *excuse* for their sins. The mere fact that all this was foretold, that it was in accordance with the purposes and predictions of God, does not take away the *guilt* of it, or constitute an excuse for it. In regard to this, we may remark, (1.) The prediction did not change the *nature* of the act. The mere fact that it was *foretold*, or foreknown, did not change its character. See Note, ch. i 23. (2.) Peter still regarded them as guilty. He did not urge the fact that this was foreknown as an excuse for their sin, but to show them that *since* all this happened according to the prediction and the purpose of God, they had hope in his mercy. The plan was that the Messiah should die to make a way for pardon; and, therefore, they *might* have hope in his mercy. (3.) This was a signal instance of the power and mercy of God in overruling the wicked conduct of men to further his purposes and plans. (4.) All the other sins of men *may* thus be overruled, and thus the wrath of man may be made to praise him. But, (5.) This will constitute no excuse for the sinner. It is no part of his *intention* to honour God, or to advance his purposes; and there is no direct *tendency* in his crimes to advance his glory. The direct tendency of his deeds is counteracted and overruled; and God brings good out of the evil. But this surely constitutes no excuse for the sinner.

If it be asked why Peter insisted on this, if he did not mean that it should be regarded as an *excuse* for their sin; I reply, that it was his design to prove *that Jesus was the Messiah*, and having proved this, he could assure them that there was mercy. Not because they had not been guilty; not because they *deserved* favour; but because *the fact* that the Messiah had come was an argument that *any* sinners might obtain mercy, as he immediately proceeds to show them.

19. *Repent ye.* Note, Matt. iii 2. ¶ *Therefore. Because* of your sin in putting Jesus to death; and *because* he is the Messiah, and God through him is willing to show mercy to the chief of sinners. ¶ *And be converted.* This expression conveys an idea not at all to be found in the original. It conveys the idea of *passivity* BE *converted*, as if they were to yield to some foreign influence that they were now resisting. But the idea of being *passive* in this, is not conveyed by the origi-

nal word. The word means properly to *turn;* to return to a path from which one has gone astray; and then to turn away from sins, or to forsake them. It is a word used in a general sense to denote the whole *turning* to God. That the form of the word here (ἐπιστρέψατε) does not denote *passivity* may be clearly seen by referring to the following places, where the same form of the word is used. Matt. xxiv 18. Mark xiii. 16. Luke xvii. 31. 1 Thess. i. 9. The expression, therefore, would have been more appropriately rendered "*repent,* and *turn,* that your sins," &c. *To be converted* cannot be a matter of obligation; but to *turn* to God is the duty of every sinner. The crimes of which he exhorted them to repent were those pertaining to the death of the Lord Jesus, as well as all the past sins of their life. They were to turn from the course of wickedness in which they and the nation had been so long walking. ¶ *That your sins,* &c. *In order* that your sins *may be* forgiven. Sin *cannot* be pardoned *before* man repents of it. In the order of the work of grace, repentance must always precede pardon. Of course, no man can have evidence that his sin is pardoned until he repents. Comp. Isa. i. 16—20. Joel ii. 13. ¶ *May be blotted out.* May be forgiven, or pardoned. The expression, *to blot out sins,* occurs also in Isa. xliii. 25. Ps. li. 1. 9. Jer. xviii. 23. Neh. iv. 5. Isa. xliv. 22. The expression, *to blot out a name,* is applied to expunging it from a *roll,* or *catalogue,* or *list,* as of an army, &c. Ex. xxxii. 32, 33. Deut. ix. 14; xxv. 19; xxix. 20, &c. The expression, *to blot out sins,* is taken from the practice of creditors charging their debtors, and when the debt was paid, cancelling it, or wholly removing the record. The word used here *properly* refers to the practice of writing on tables covered with wax, and then by inverting the stylus, or instrument of writing, smoothing the wax again, and thus removing *every trace* of the record. This more entirely expresses the idea of *pardoning,* than *blotting* does. It means wholly *to remove* the record, the charge, and every *trace* of the account against us. In this way *God* forgives sins. ¶ *When the times,* &c. The word ὅπως, rendered "when," is commonly rendered *that,* and denotes the *final cause,* or the *reason* why a thing is done. Matt. ii. 23; v. 16. 45, &c. By many it has been supposed to have this sense here, and to mean "repent.... *in order that* the times of refreshing may come," &c. Thus Kuinoel, Grotius, Lightfoot, the Syriac version, &c. If used in this sense, it means that their repentance and forgiveness would be the *means* of introducing peace and joy. Others have rendered it in accordance with our translation, "when," meaning that they might find peace in the day when Christ should return to judgment; which return would be to them a day of *rest,* though of terror to the wicked. Thus Calvin, Beza, the Latin Vulgate, Schleusner, &c. The *grammatical* construction will admit of either, though the former is more in accordance with the usual use of the word. The objection to the former is, that it is not easy to see how their repenting, &c. should be the *means* of introducing the times of refreshing. And this, also, corresponds very little with the *design* of Peter in this discourse. That was to *encourage them* to repentance; to adduce arguments why they should repent; and why they might hope in his mercy. To do this, it was needful only to assure them that they were living under the times graciously promised by God, the times of refreshing, when pardon might be obtained. The main inquiry, therefore, is, what did Peter refer to by *the times of refreshing,* and by the *restitution of all things?* Did he refer to any particular manifestation to be made then; or to the influence of the gospel on the earth; or to the future state, when the Lord Jesus shall come to judgment? The idea which I suppose Peter intended to convey was this: 'Repent, and be converted. You have been great sinners, and are in danger. Turn from your ways, that your sins may be forgiven.' But then, what encouragement would there be for this? or why should it be done? Answer. 'You are living under the times of the gospel, the reign of the Messiah, the times of refreshing. This happy, glorious period has been long anticipated, and is to continue to the close of the world, the period *including* the restitution of all things, and the return of Christ to judgment, has come, and is, therefore, the period when you *may* find mercy, and when you *should* seek it, to be prepared for his return.' In this sense the passage refers to the fact that this time, this dispensation, this economy, *including all this,* had come, and they were living under it, and *might* and should seek for mercy. It expresses, therefore, the *common belief of the Jews* that such a time *should* come, and the comment of *Peter* about its nature and continuance. The belief of the Jews was that such times *should* come. Peter affirms that the belief of such a period was well-founded—a time when mercy may be obtained. That time *has come*

20 And he [a] shall send Jesus Christ, which before was preached unto you:

a c.1.11. He.9.28.

21 Whom the heavens must receive until the times [b] of restitution of all things, which God hath

b Matt.17.11.

The doctrine that it *should* come was *well-founded*, and has been fulfilled. This was a reason why they should repent, and hope in the mercy of God. Peter goes on, then, to state further *characteristics* of that period. It should include the restitution of all things, the return of Christ to judgment, &c. And *all this* was an additional consideration why they should repent, and turn from their sins, and seek for forgiveness. The meaning of the passage may, therefore, be thus summed up: 'Repent, *since* such times *shall* come; they are clearly predicted; they were to be expected; and you are now living under them. *In these times;* in this dispensation, also, God shall send his Son again to judge the world; and all things shall be closed and settled for ever. Since you live under this period, you may seek for mercy; and you *should* seek to avoid the vengeance due to the wicked, and to be admitted to heaven when the Lord Jesus shall return.' ¶ *Times of refreshing.* The word rendered *refreshing*, ἀνάψυξις, means properly the *breathing*, or *refreshment*, after being *heated* with *labour, running*, &c. It hence denotes any kind of refreshment, as rest, or deliverance from evils of any kind. It is used nowhere else in the New Testament, except that the *verb* is used in 2 Tim. i. 16, "Onesiphorus....oft *refreshed* me, and was not ashamed of my chain." He administered comfort to me in my trials. It is used by the LXX. in the Old Testament nine times. Ex. viii. 15, "But when Pharaoh saw that there was *respite*," i. e. cessation or rest from the plagues. Hos. xii. 8. Jer. xlix. 31, Ps. lxix. 11, &c. In no place in the Old Testament is the *word* applied to the terms of the gospel. The *idea*, however, that the times of the Messiah would be times of *rest*, and *ease*, and *prosperity*, was a favourite one among the Jews, and was countenanced in the Old Testament. See Isa. xxviii. 12, "To whom he said, This is the rest wherewith ye may cause the weary to rest; and this is the refreshing," &c. They anticipated the times of the gospel as a period when they should have rest from their enemies; a respite from the evils of oppression and war, and a period of great national prosperity and peace. Under the idea that the *happy times of the Messiah* had come, Peter now addresses them, and assures them that they might obtain pardon and peace. ¶ *Shall come.* This does not mean that this period was *still future*, for it had come; but that the expectation of the Jews that such a Messiah should come was well-founded. A remarkably similar construction we have concerning Elijah (Matt. xvii. 11), "And Jesus answered and said, Elias truly *shall first come*, and restore," &c.; that is, the doctrine that Elijah should come was true; though he immediately adds that it *had already* taken place, ver. 12. See Note on the place ¶ *From the presence of the Lord.* Greek, "from *the face* of the Lord." The expression means that God was *its author*. From the face of the Lord means from *the Lord himself*. Mark i. 2, "I send thy messenger *before thy face*," i. e. before *thee*, Comp. Mal. iii. 1. Luke i. 76; ii. 31.

20. *And he shall send*, &c. ch. i. 11. *Under this economy of things*, he shall send Jesus Christ, i. e. the Messiah, to teach men; to redeem them; to save them; to judge the world; to gather his people to himself; and to condemn the wicked. Under *this* economy they were then. *This*, therefore, was an argument why they should repent and turn to God, that they might escape in the day of judgment. ¶ *Which before was preached*, &c. Who has been proclaimed as the Messiah. The name *Jesus Christ* is equivalent here to *the Messiah*. The *Messiah* had been proclaimed to the Jews as about to come In his time was to be the period of refreshing. He *had* come; and they were under the economy in which the blessings of the Messiah were to be enjoyed. This does not refer to his personal ministry, or to the preaching of the apostles; but to the fact that the Messiah had been a long time *announced* to them by the prophets as about to come. All the prophets had *preached* him, as the hope of the nation. It may be remarked, however, that there is here a difference in the manuscripts. A large majority of them read προκεχειρισμένον, who was *designated* or *appointed* instead of who was preached. This reading is approved by Griesbach, Knapp, Bengel, &c. It was followed in the ancient Syriac, the Arabic, &c. and is undoubtedly the true reading.

21. *Whom the heaven must receive.* The common belief of the Jews was, that the Messiah would reign on the earth for

spoken [a] by the mouth of all his holy prophets since the world began.

22 For Moses truly said unto the fathers, A [b] Prophet shall the Lord

a Lu.1.70. b De.18.15–19.

ever. John xii. 34. On this account they would object that Jesus could not be the Messiah; and hence it became so important for the apostles to establish the fact that he had ascended to heaven. The evidence which they adduced was the fact that they *saw* him ascend. Acts i. 9. The meaning of the expression "whom the heaven MUST receive," is that it was *fit* or *proper* (δεῖ) that he should ascend. *One* reason of that fitness or propriety he himself stated in John xvi. 7, comp. xvii. 2. It was also *fit* or expedient that he should do it, to direct the affairs of the universe for the welfare of the church (Eph. i. 20—22), and that he should exercise there his office as a priest in interceding for his people. 1 John ii. 1, 2. Heb. vii. 25; ix. 24. Rom. viii. 34, &c. It is remarkable that Peter did not adduce any passage of Scripture on this subject; but it was one of the points on which there was no clear revelation. Obscure intimations of it might be found in Ps. cx. xvi. &c. but the fact that he should *ascend* to heaven was not made prominent in the Old Testament. The words "whom the heaven must receive," also convey the idea of *exaltation* and *power;* and Peter doubtless intended to say that he was clothed with power, and exalted to honour in the presence of God. See Ps. cxv. 3, comp. 1 Pet. iii. 22, "Who is gone into heaven, and is on the right hand of God; angels and authorities and powers being made subject unto him." Note, Acts ii. 33. ¶ *Until.* This word implies that he would then *return* to the earth; but it does not imply that he would not again ascend to heaven. ¶ *The times of the restitution of all things.* The *noun* rendered *restitution* (ἀποκαταστάσεως) does not elsewhere occur in the New Testament. The *verb* from which it is derived occurs eight times. It means properly to *restore a thing to its former situation,* as restoring a *sprained* or *dislocated* limb to its former soundness. Hence it is used to restore, or to *heal,* in the New Testament. Matt. xii. 13, "And it (the hand) was *restored whole* as the other." Mark iii. 5. Luke vi. 10. And hence it is applied to the *preparation* or *fitness* for the coming of the Messiah which was to attend the preaching of John in the character of Elias. Matt. xvii. 11. Mark ix. 12. Thus in Josephus (Antiq. ii. 3. 8), the word is used to denote the return of the Jews from the captivity of Babylon, and their restoration to their former state and privileges. The word has also the idea of *consummation, completion,* or *filling up.* Thus it is used in Philo, Hesychius, Phavorinus, and by the Greek classics. (See Lightfoot and Kuinoel.) Thus it is used here by the Syriac. "Until the *complement* or *filling up* of the times;" that is, of all the events foretold by the prophets, &c. Thus the Arabic. "Until the times which shall establish the perfection or completion of all the predictions of the prophets," &c. In this sense the passage means that the heavens must receive the Lord Jesus until all things spoken by the prophets in relation to his work, his reign, the spread of the gospel, the triumph of religion, &c. shall have been fulfilled. It also conveys the idea of the predicted recovery of the world from sin, and the restoration of peace and order; the *consummation* of the work of the Messiah, now begun, but not yet complete; slow it may be in its advances, but triumphant and certain in its progress, and its close. ¶ *All things.* All things which *have been foretold by the prophets.* The expression is limited by the connexion to this; and of course it does not mean that all men shall be saved, or that all the evils of sin can be repaired or remedied. This can never be, for the mischief is done, and cannot be undone; but every thing which the prophets have foretold shall receive their completion and fulfilment. ¶ *Which God hath spoken.* Which have been revealed, and are recorded in the Old Testament. ¶ *Of all his holy prophets.* This does not mean that *each* one of the prophets had spoken of these things; but that all which *had been spoken* should be fulfilled. ¶ *Since the world began.* This is an expression denoting the same as *from the beginning* meaning to affirm with emphasis that *all* the prophecies should be fulfilled. The apostles were desirous to show that they, as well as the Jews, held entirely to the prophets, and taught no doctrine which they had not taught before them.

22. *For Moses truly said.* The authority of Moses among the Jews was absolute and final. It was of great importance, therefore, to show not only that they were not *departing* from his law, but that he had actually *foretold* these very things. The object of the passage is not to prove that the heavens must receive him, but that he was truly the Messiah. ¶ *Unto the fathers.* To their ancestors, or the

your God raise up unto you of your brethren, like unto me; him shall ye hear in all things, whatsoever he shall say unto you.

---

founders of the nation. See Deut. xviii. 15—19 ¶ *A prophet.* Literally, one who foretels future events. But it is also used to denote a religious teacher in general. See Rom. xii. 6. In. Deut. it is evidently used in a large sense, to denote one who should infallibly guide and direct the nation in its religious affairs; one who should be commissioned by *God* to do this, in opposition to *the diviners* (ver. 14) on which other nations relied. The meaning of this passage in Deuteronomy is apparent from the connexion. Moses is stating to them (ver. 1—8) the duty and office of the priests and Levites. He then cautions them against conforming to the surrounding nations, particularly on the subject of religious instruction and guidance. They, said he, consult, in times of perplexity, with enchanters,and charmers, and necromancers, and wizards, &c. (ver. 11—14), but it shall not be so with you. You shall not be *left* to this false and uncertain guidance in times of perplexity and danger; for the Lord will raise up, from time to time, a *prophet*, a man directly commissioned in an extraordinary manner from heaven, like me, who shall direct and counsel you. The promise, therefore, pertains to *the series of prophets* which God would raise up; or it is a promise that God would send his prophets, as occasion might demand, to instruct and counsel the nation. The *design* was to keep them from consulting with diviners, &c. and to preserve them from following the pretended and false religious teachers of surrounding idolatrous people. In this interpretation most commentators agree. See particularly *Calvin* on this place. Thus explained, the prophecy had no *exclusive* or even *direct* reference to the Messiah, and there is no evidence that the Jews understood it to have any such reference, except as *one of the series* of prophets that God would raise up and send to instruct the nation. If then it be asked *on what principle* Peter appealed to this, we may reply, (1.) That the Messiah was to sustain the character of a prophet, and the prophecy had reference to him as *one* of the teachers that God would raise up to instruct the nation. (2.) It would apply to him *by way of eminence*, as *the greatest* of the messengers that God would send to instruct the people. In this sense it is probable that the Jews would understand it. (3.) This was one of those *emergencies* in the history of the nation when they might expect such an intervention. The prophecy implied that in times of perplexity and danger, God would raise up such a prophet. Such a time then existed. The nation was corrupt, distracted, subjected to a foreign power, and *needed* such a teacher and guide. If it be asked *why* Peter appealed to this, rather than to *explicit* prophecies of the Messiah, we may remark, (1.) That his main object was to show their *guilt* in having rejected him and put him to death. ver. 14, 15. (2.) That in order to do this, he sets before them clearly the *obligation* to *obey* him; and in doing this, appeals to the express command of Moses. He shows them that, according to Moses, whoever would not obey such a prophet should be cut off from among the people. In refusing, therefore, to hear this great prophet, and putting him to death, they had violated the express command of their own lawgiver. But it was possible *still* to obey him, for he still *lived* in heaven; and all the authority of *Moses*, therefore, made it a matter of obligation for them still to hear and obey him. The Jews were accustomed to apply the name *prophet* to the Messiah (John i. 21; vi. 14; vii. 40. Matt. xxi. 11. Luke iv. 24), and it has been shown from the writings of the Jewish Rabbins, that they believed the Messiah would be the greatest of the prophets, even greater than Moses. See Note, John i. 21. ¶ *The Lord your God.* In the Hebrew, "Jehovah, thy God." ¶ *Raise up unto you.* Appoint, or commission to come to you. ¶ *Of your brethren.* Among yourselves; of your own countrymen; so that you shall not be dependent on foreigners, or on teachers of other nations. All the prophets were native-born Jews. And it was particularly true of the Messiah that he was to be a Jew, descended from Abraham, and raised up from the midst of his brethren. Heb. ii. 11. 16, 17. On this account it was to be presumed that they would feel a deeper interest in him, and listen more attentively to his instructions. ¶ *Like unto me.* Not in all things, but only in the point which was under discussion He was to resemble him in being able to make known to them the will of God, and thus preventing the necessity of looking to other teachers. The idea of *resemblance* between Moses and the prophet is not very strictly expressed in the Greek except in the mere circumstance of being

23 And it shall come to pass, *that* every soul which will not hear that Prophet shall be destroyed from among the people.

24 Yea, and all the prophets from Samuel, and those that follow after, as many as have spoken, have likewise foretold of these days.

---

raised up. God shall raise up to you a prophet *as he has raised up me*—ὡς ἐμέ. The resemblance between Moses and the Messiah should not be pressed too far. The Scriptures have not traced it farther than to the fact that *both* were raised up by God to communicate his will to the Jewish people; and therefore one should be heard as well as the other. ¶ *Him shall ye hear.* That is, him shall you *obey*, or you shall receive his instructions as a communication from God. ¶ *In all things whatsoever, &c.* These words are not quoted *literally* from the Hebrew, but they express the *sense* of what is said in Deut. xviii. 15. 18.

23. *And it shall come to pass.* It shall be. or shall occur. This is not the usual word rendered "it shall come to pass." It is a word commonly expressing *futurity*, but here it conveys the notion of *obligation*. In this verse Peter has not quoted the passage in Deuteronomy *literally*, but he has given the *sense*. ¶ *Every soul.* Every *person*, or *individual*. Soul is often put for the whole man by the Hebrews. Acts vii. 14. Josh. x. 28. ¶ *Hear that prophet.* That is, *obey* his instructions. He shall have *authority* to declare the will of God; and he that does not obey him refuses to obey God. Comp. Luke x. 16. John xiii. 20. ¶ *Shall be destroyed.* This quotation is made according to the *sense*, and not *literally*. In the Hebrew the expression is (Deut. xviii. 19), "I will require it of him," i. e. I will hold him *answerable*, or *responsible* for it; I will *punish* him. This expression the LXX. have rendered by "I will take vengeance on him." The idea of the passage is, therefore, that God would *punish* the man that would not hear the prophet, without specifying the particular way in which it should be done. The *usual mode* of punishing such offences was by *cutting the offender off from among the people.* Ex. xxx. 33; xii. 15; xix. 31. Num. xv. 31; xix. 13. Lev. vii. 20, 21. 25. 27, &c The sense is, that he should be punished in the usual manner; i. e. by *excision*, or by being *destroyed* from among the people. The word translated *shall be destroyed* means properly to *exterminate*; wholly to devote to ruin, as of a wicked people, a wicked man whose life is taken, &c. To be destroyed *from among the people* means, however, to be excommunicated, or to be deprived of the *privileges* of a people. Among the Jews this was probably the most severe punishment that could be inflicted. It involved the idea of being cut off from the privileges of sacrifice and worship in the temple and in the synagogue, &c. and of being regarded as a *heathen* and an outcast. The idea which Peter expressed here was, that the Jews had exposed themselves to the severest punishment in rejecting and crucifying the Lord Jesus, and that they should, therefore, repent of this great sin, and seek for mercy. The same remark is applicable still to men. The Scriptures abundantly declare the truth, that if sinners will not hear the Lord Jesus, they shall be destroyed. And it becomes each individual to inquire with honesty whether he listens to *his* instructions, and obeys his law, or whether he is rejecting him and following the devices and desires of his own heart. It will be a solemn day when the sinner shall be called to *render a reason* why he has rejected the teachings and laws of the Son of God!

24. *All the prophets.* That is, the prophets in general. It may be said of the prophets *generally*, or of all of them, that they have foretold these things. This expression is not to be pressed as if we were to look for distinct predictions of the Messiah in *each one* of the prophets. The use of language does not require so strict an interpretation. ¶ *From Samuel.* In the previous verse (22) *Moses* was mentioned as the *first* in order. The next in order was *Samuel.* The same mention of *Moses* and *Samuel* occurs in Ps. xcix. 6. The reason why *Samuel* is mentioned here is, probably, that he was the first prophet after Moses who recorded a prediction respecting the times of the Messiah. The Jews, in their divisions of the books of the Old Testament, reckoned the book of Joshua as the first of *the prophets*. But in Joshua and Judges there does not occur any distinct prediction of the Messiah. The prophecy in Samuel, to which Peter probably had reference, is in 2 Sam. vii. 16. From the time of Moses to Samuel, also, it is probable that no prophet arose. God was consulted by *Urim* and *Thummim* (Ex. xxviii. 30. Num. xxvii. 21), and consequently no extraordinary messenger was sent to instruct the nation. ¶ *As many as have spoken.* Whosoever

25 Ye [a] are the children of the
prophets, and of the covenant which
God made with our fathers, saying
unto Abraham, And [b] in thy seed
shall all the kindreds of the earth
be blessed.
26 Unto [c] you first, God, having
raised up his Son Jesus, sent him

a Ro.9.4;15.8. b Ge.22.18.

c Matt.10.5. Lu.24.47.

has declared the will of God. This is to be taken in a *general* sense. The meaning is, that the prophets had *concurred* in foretelling these days. They not merely concurred in foretelling a happy future period, but they foretold *distinctly* the very things which had actually occurred respecting Jesus of Nazareth; and the Jews, therefore, should listen to the voice of their own prophets.

25. *Ye are the children of the prophets.* Greek, "Ye are the *sons* of the prophets." The meaning is, not that they were literally the *descendants* of the prophets, but that they were their *disciples, pupils, followers.* They professed to follow the prophets as their *teachers* and *guides.* Teachers among the Jews, were often spoken of under the appellation of *fathers*, and disciples as *sons.* Matt. xii. 27. Note, Matt. i. 1. As they were the professed disciples of the prophets, they should listen to them. As they lived among the people to whom the prophets were sent, and to whom the promises were made, they should avail themselves of the offer of mercy, and embrace the Messiah. ¶ *And of the covenant.* Ye are the *sons* of the covenant; that is, you are of the posterity of Abraham, with whom the covenant was made. The word "sons' was often thus used to denote those to whom any favour appertained, whether by inheritance or in any other way. Thus Matt. viii. 12, "the children (sons) of the kingdom." John xvii. 12, "The son of perdition." The word *covenant* denotes properly a compact or agreement between equals, or those who have a right to make such a compact and to choose or refuse the terms. When applied to God and man, it denotes a *firm promise* on the part of God; a pledge to be regarded with all the sacredness of a compact, that he will do certain things on certain conditions. It is called a *covenant* only to designate its sacredness and the certainty of its fulfilment, not that *man* had any *right to reject* any of the terms or stipulations. As man has no such right, as he is bound to receive all that his Maker proposes, so, strictly and literally, there has been no *compact* or *covenant* between God and man. The *promise* to which Peter refers in the passage before us, is in Gen. xxii. 18; xii. 3. ¶ *In thy seed.* Thy posterity See Rom. iv. 13. 16. This promise the apostle Paul affirms had express reference to the Messiah. Gal. iii. 16. The word *seed* is used sometimes to denote an individual (Gen. iv. 25); and the apostle (Gal. iii. 16) affirms that there was special reference to Christ in the promise made to Abraham. ¶ *All the kindreds.* The word translated *kindreds* (πατριαι) denotes those who have a common *father* or *ancestor* and is applied to *families.* It is also referred to those larger communities which descended from the same ancestor, and thus refers to *nations.* Eph. iii. 15 Here it evidently refers to *all nations.* ¶ *Be blessed.* Be made happy.

26. *Unto you first.* To you who are Jews. This was the direction, that the gospel should be first preached to the Jews, beginning at Jerusalem. Luke xxiv. 47. Jesus himself also confined his ministry entirely to the Jews. ¶ *Having raised up* This expression does not refer to his having raised him from the dead, but is used in the same sense as in verse 22, where God promised that he would *raise up* a prophet, and send him to teach the people. Peter means that God had *appointed* his Son Jesus, or had commissioned him to go and preach to the people to turn them away from their sins. ¶ *To bless you.* To make you happy; to fulfil the promise made to Abraham. ¶ *In turning away.* That is, by his preaching, example, death, &c. The highest blessing that can be conferred on men is to be turned from sin. It is the source of all woes, and if men are turned from that, they will be happy. Christ blesses no one *in* sin, or while *loving* sin, but by turning them *from sin.* This was the object which he had in view in coming. Isa. lix. 20. Matt. i. 21. The design of Peter in these remarks was to show them that the Messiah had come, and that now they might look for happiness, pardon, and mercy through him. As the Jews might, so may all; and as Jesus while living sought to turn away men from their sins, so he does still, and still designs to bless *all nations* by the gospel which he had himself preached, and to establish which he died. All may therefore come and be blessed; and all may rejoice in the prospect that these

to bless you, in turning away [a] every one of you from his iniquities.

CHAPTER IV.

AND as they spake unto the people, the priests, and the [1] captain of the temple, and the Sadducees, [b] came upon them,

2 Being grieved that they taught the people, and preached through Jesus the resurrection from the dead.

a Is.59.20. Matt.1.21. Tit.2.11-14. [1] or, *ruler*. b Matt. 22.23. c.23.8.

---

blessings shall yet be bestowed on all the kindreds of the earth. May the happy day soon come!

CHAPTER IV.

1. *The priests.* It is probable that these *priests* were a part of the sanhedrim, or great council of the nation. It is evident that they claimed some authority for preventing the preaching of the apostles. And the whole transaction seems to show that they did not come upon them in a tumultuous manner, but as keepers of the peace. ¶ *The captain of the temple.* See Notes, Matt. xxvi. 47. Luke xxii. 4. This was the commander of the guard stationed chiefly in the tower *Antonia*, especially during the great feasts; and it was their duty to preserve order, and prevent any tumult. The captain of the temple came at this time to prevent a tumult or suppress a riot, as it was supposed that the teaching of the apostles and the crowd collected by the healing of the lame man would lead to a tumult. ¶ *And the Sadducees.* See Note, Matt. iii. 7. One of the doctrines which the Sadducees maintained was, that there was no resurrection of the dead. Hence they were particularly opposed to the apostles for preaching it, and because they gave so clear proof that Jesus had risen, and were thus spreading the doctrine of the resurrection among the people. ¶ *Came upon them.* This expression implies that they came in a *sudden* and *violent* manner. See Luke xx. 1.

2. *Being grieved.* The word thus translated occurs but in one other place in the New Testament, Acts xvi. 18. It implies more than simple *sorrow;* it was a mingled emotion of *indignation* and *anger.* They did not *grieve* because they thought it a public *calamity*, but because it interfered with their authority, and opposed their doctrine. It means that it was *painful* to them, or they could *not bear it.* It is often the case that bigots, and men in authority, have this kind of *grief* at the zeal of men in spreading the truth, and thus undermining their influence and authority. ¶ *That they taught the people.* The ground of their grief was as much *the fact* that *they* should presume to instruct the people, as the *matter* which they taught them. They were offended that unlearned Galileans, in no way connected with the priestly office, and unauthorized by *them*, should presume to set themselves up as religious teachers. *They* claimed the right to watch over the interests of the people, and to declare who was authorized to instruct the nation. It has been no unusual thing for men in ecclesiastical stations to take exceptions to the ministry of those who have not been commissioned by themselves. Men easily fancy that all power to instruct others is lodged in their hands; and they oppose others simply from the fact that they have not derived their authority from *them.* The true question in this case was, whether these Galileans gave proof that they were sent by God. The fact of the miracle in this case should have been satisfactory. We have here, also, a striking instance of the fact that men may turn away from evidence, and from most important points, and fix on something that opposes their prejudices, and which may be a matter of very little moment. No inquiry was made whether the *miracle* had been really wrought; but the only inquiry was whether they had conformed to *their* views of doctrine and order. ¶ *And preached through Jesus, &c.* The Sadducees would be particularly opposed to this. They denied the doctrine of the resurrection, and they were troubled that the apostles adduced proof of it so strong as the resurrection of Jesus. It was perceived that this doctrine was becoming established among the people; multitudes believed that he had risen, and if he *had* been raised up, it followed also that others would rise. The Sadducees, therefore, felt that their cause was in danger; and they joined with the priests in endeavouring to arrest its spread among the people. This is the account of the first opposition that was made to the gospel as it was preached by the apostles. It is worthy of remark that it excited so much and so speedily the enmity of those in power; and that the apostles were so soon called to test the sincerity of their attachment to their Master. They who but a few days before had fled at the approach of danger, were called to meet this opposition, and to show their attachment to a risen Re-

3 And they laid hands on them, and put *them* in hold unto the next day: for it was now even-tide.
4 Howbeit many[a] of them which heard the word believed; and the number of the men was about five thousand.
5 And it came to pass on the morrow, that their rulers and elders, and scribes,
6 And Annas[b] the high-priest, and Caiaphas, and John, and Alexander, and as many as were of the kindred of the high-priest, were

a c.28.24. b Jno.18.13.

deemer; and they did it without shrinking. They showed *now* that they were indeed the true friends of the crucified Saviour: and this remarkable change in their conduct is one among the many proofs that they were influenced from above.

3. *Put them in hold.* That is, they took them into *custody*, or into safe keeping. Probably they committed them to the care of a guard. ¶ *Even-tide.* Evening. It was not convenient to assemble the council at night. This was moreover the time for the evening prayer or sacrifice, and it was not usual to assemble the sanhedrim at that hour.

4. *Howbeit.* But; notwithstanding. ¶ *Many of them*, &c. This was one of the instances which has since been so often repeated, in which *persecution* has only had a tendency to extend and establish the faith which it was designed to destroy. It finally came to be a proverb that "the blood of the martyrs is the seed of the church;" and there is no lesson which men have been so slow to learn as that to *oppose* and *persecute* men is the very way to *confirm* them in their opinions, and to spread their doctrines. It was supposed here that the disciples were few, that they were without power, wealth, and influence, and that it was easy to crush them at once. But God made their persecution the means of extending, in a signal manner, the truths of the gospel and the triumphs of his word. And so in all ages it has been, and so it ever will be. ¶ *And the number*, &c. It seems probable that in this number of five thousand ther were included the one hundred and twenty who are mentioned in ch. i. 15, and the three thousand who were converted on the day of Pentecost, ch ii. 41. It does not appear probable that five thousand should have been assembled and converted in *Solomon's porch* (ch. iii. 11), on occasion of the cure of the lame man. Luke doubtless means to say that, up to this time, the number of persons who had joined themselves to the apostles was about five thousand. On this supposition, the work of religion must have made a very rapid advance. How long this was after the day of Pentecost is not mentioned; but it is clear that it was at no very distant period; and the accession of near *two thousand* to the number of believers was a very striking proof of the power and presence of the Holy Spirit. ¶ *Of the men.* Of the *persons.* The word *men* is often used without reference to sex. Luke xi. 31. Rom. iv. 8; xi. 4.

5, 6. *Their rulers.* The rulers of the Jews; doubtless the members of the *sanhedrim*, or *great council of the nation.* Comp. v. 15. Note, Matt. ii. 4; v. 22. The expression *their* rulers, looks as if this book was written for the Gentiles, or Luke would have said *our* rulers. ¶ *Elders.* Presbyters; or those who were *chosen* from among the people to sit in the sanhedrim. It is probable that the *rulers* were those who held also some other office, but were also authorized to sit in the great council. ¶ *Scribes.* See Note, Matt. ii. 4 ¶ *And Annas*, &c. Note, John xviii. 13. It is by no means certain that *Annas* was *at that time* the high-priest, but he *had been*, and doubtless retained the *title.* He was father-in-law to Caiaphas the high-priest; and from this fact, together with his former dignity, he is mentioned first. ¶ *Caiaphas.* Son-in-law of Annas, and now exercising the office of the high-priest. John xviii. 13. ¶ *John and Alexander*, &c. Of these persons nothing more is known. It is clear that they were members of the great council, and the mention of their names shows that the men of chief authority and influence were assembled to silence the apostles. Annas and Caiaphas had been concerned in the condemnation of Jesus, and they would now feel a special interest in arresting the progress of the gospel among the people. All the success of the gospel reflected back light upon the wickedness of the act of condemning the Lord Jesus. And this fact may serve, in part, to account for their strong desire to silence the apostles. ¶ *At Jerusalem.* This was the usual place of assembling the sanhedrim. But the Jewish writers (see

gathered together at Jerusalem.
7 And when they had set them in the midst, they asked, By [a] what power, or by what name, have ye done this ?

a Matt.21.23.

8 Then Peter, filled [b] with the Holy Ghost, said unto them, Ye rulers of the people, and elders of Israel,
9 If we this day be examined of

b c.7.55.

Lightfoot on this place) say that forty years before the destruction of the city, on account of the great increase of crime, &c. the sanhedrim was removed from place to place. The declaration of Luke that they were now assembled *in Jerusalem*, seems to imply that they sometimes met in other places. It is probable that the members of the sanhedrim were not in the city at the time mentioned in ver. 3, and this was the reason why the trial was deferred to the next day.

7. *In the midst.* In the presence of the great council. ¶ *By what power,* &c. A similar question was put to Christ in the temple Matt. xxi. 23. ¶ *By what name.* That is, by whose authority. It is very probable that they expected to intimidate the apostles by this question. *They* claimed the right of regulating the religious affairs of the nation. They had vast power with the people. They assumed that all power to instruct the people should originate with them: and they expected that the apostles would be confounded, as having violated the established usage of the nation. It did not seem to occur to them to enter into an investigation of the question, whether this *acknowledged* miracle did not prove that they were sent by God; but they *assumed* that they were impostors, and attempted to silence them by authority. It has been usual with the enemies of religion to attempt to *intimidate* its friends, and when *argument* fails, to attempt to *silence* Christians by appealing to their fears.

8. *Filled with the Holy Ghost.* Note, ch. ii. 4. ¶ *Ye rulers,* &c. Peter addressed the sanhedrim with perfect respect. He did not call in question their authority to propose this question. He seemed to regard this as a favourable opportunity to declare the truth and state the evidence of the Christian religion. In this he acted on the principle of the injunction which he himself afterwards gave (1 Pet. iii 15), "Be ready always to give an answer to every man that asketh you a reason of the hope that is in you, with meekness and fear." Innocence is willing to be questioned; and a believer in the truth will rejoice in *any* opportunity to state the evidence of what is believed. It is remarkable, also, that this was before the great council of the nation; the body that was clothed with the highest authority. And Peter could not have forgotten that before this very council, and these very men, his Master had been arraigned and condemned. Nor could he have forgotten that in the very room where this same council was convened to try his Lord, *he had himself* shrunk from an honest avowal of attachment to him, and shamefully and profanely denied him. That he was now able to stand boldly before this same tribunal, evinced a remarkable *change* in his feelings, and was a most clear and impressive proof of the genuineness of his repentance when he went out and wept bitterly. Comp. Luke xxii. 54—62. And we may remark here, that one of the most clear evidences of the sincerity of repentance is when it leads to a result like this. So deeply was the heart of Peter affected by his sin (Luke xxii. 62), and so genuine was his sorrow, that he doubtless remembered his crime on this occasion; and the memory of it inspired him with boldness. It may be further remarked, that *one* evidence of the genuineness of repentance is a desire to *repair* the evil which is done by crime. Peter had done dishonour to his Master and his cause, in the presence of the great council of the nation. Nothing, on such an occasion, would be more likely to do injury to the cause, than for one of the disciples of the Saviour to deny him—one of his followers to be guilty of *profaneness* and *falsehood.* But here was an opportunity, in some degree, at least, to repair the evil. Before the same council and the same men, in the same city, and in the presence of the same people, it is not an unnatural supposition that Peter rejoiced that he might have opportunity to bear *his* testimony to the divine mission of the Saviour whom he had before denied. By using the customary language of respect applied to the great council, Peter also has shown us that it is proper to evince respect for office, and for those in power. Religion requires us to render this homage, and to treat men in office with deference. Matt. xxii 21. Rom. xiii. 7 1 Pet. ii. 13—17.

the good deed done to the impotent man, by what means he is made whole;

10 Be it known unto you all, and to all the people of Israel, that [a] by the name of Jesus Christ of Nazareth, whom ye crucified, whom God raised from the dead, *even* by him doth this man stand here before you whole.

11 This is the stone [b] which was set at nought of you builders, which is become the head of the corner.

a c.3.6,16.

b Ps.118.22. Is.28.16. Matt.21.42.

10. *Be it known*, &c. Peter might have evaded the question, or he might have resorted to many excuses and subterfuges (*Calvin*), if he had been desirous of avoiding this inquiry. But it was a noble opportunity for vindicating the honour of his Lord and master. It was a noble opportunity also for repairing the evil which he had done by his guilty denial of his Lord. Although, therefore, this frank and open avowal was attended with danger, and although it was in the presence of the great and the mighty, yet he chose to state fully and clearly his conviction of the truth. Never was there an instance of greater boldness; and never could there be a more striking illustration of the fitness of the name which the Lord Jesus gave him, that of a *rock*. John i. 42. Matt. xvi. 17, 18. The timid, trembling, yielding, and vacillating Simon, he who just before was terrified by a servant girl, and who on the lake was afraid of sinking, is now transformed into the manly, decided, and firm *Cephas*, fearless before the great council of the nation, and in an unwavering tone asserting the authority of him whom *he* had just before denied, and whom *they* had just before put to death. It is not possible to account for this change except on the supposition that this religion is true. Peter had no worldly motive to actuate him. He had no prospect of wealth or fame by this. Even the hopes of honour and preferment which they had cherished before the death of Jesus, and which *might* have been supposed to influence them then, were now abandoned by the apostles. Their Master had died; and all their hopes of human honour and power had been buried in his grave. Nothing but the conviction of the *truth* could have wrought this change, and transformed this timid disciple to a bold and uncompromising apostle. ¶ *By the name.* By the authority or power. ch. iii. 6. ¶ *Of Jesus Christ.* The union of these two names would be particularly offensive to the sanhedrim. They *denied* that Jesus was the Christ, or the Messiah; Peter, by the use of the word *Christ*, affirmed that he was. In the language then used, it would be, "By the name of Jesus, *the Messiah*." ¶ *Of Nazareth.* Lest there should be any mistake about his meaning, he specified that he referred to the despised *Nazarene;* to him who had just been put death, as they supposed, covered with infamy. Christians little regard the epithets of opprobrium which may be affixed to themselves or to their religion. ¶ *Whom ye crucified.* There is emphasis in all the expressions that Peter uses. He had before charged the *people* with the crime of having put him to death. ch. ii. 23; iii. 14, 15. But he now had the opportunity, contrary to all expectation, of urging the charge with still greater force on the *rulers themselves*, on the very council which had condemned him and delivered him to Pilate. It was a remarkable providence that an opportunity was thus afforded of urging this charge in the presence of the sanhedrim, and of proclaiming *to them* the necessity of repentance. Little did *they* imagine when they condemned the Lord Jesus, that this charge would be so soon urged. This is one of the instances in which God takes the wise in their own craftiness. Job v. 13. *They* had arraigned the apostles; they demanded their authority for what they had done; and thus they had directly opened the way, and invited them to the serious and solemn charge which Peter here urges against them.

11. *This is the stone.* This passage is found in Ps. cxviii. 22. It is quoted, also, by our Saviour as applicable to himself. See Note on Matt. xxi 42. The ancient Jews applied this to David. In the Targum on Ps. cxviii. 22, this passage is rendered, "The child who was among the sons of Jesse, and was worthy to be constituted King, the builders rejected." The New Testament writers, however, apply it without any doubt to the Messiah. Comp. Isa. xxviii. 16. Rom. ix. 33. Eph. ii. 20. And from this passage we may learn, that God will overrule the devices and plans of wicked men, to accomplish his own purposes. What men despise and set at nought, *he* esteems of

12 Neither is there salvation in any other: for [a] there is none other [b] name under heaven given among men whereby we must be saved.

a c.10.43. 1Tim.2.5,6. b Ps.45.17.

inestimable value in his kingdom. What the great and the mighty contemn, he regards as the very foundation and corner-stone of the edifice which he designs to rear. Nothing has been more remarkable than this in the history of man; and in nothing is more contempt thrown on the proud projects of men, than that what *they* have rejected he has made the very basis of his schemes.

12. *Neither is there salvation.* The word *salvation* properly denotes any *preservation*, or keeping any thing in a *safe* state; a preserving it from harm. It signifies, also, deliverance from *any* evil of body or mind; from pain, sickness, danger, &c. Acts vii. 25. But it is in the New Testament applied particularly to the work which the Messiah came to do, "to seek and to *save* those which were lost." This work refers primarily to a deliverance of the soul *from* sin. Matt. i. 21. Acts v. 31. Luke iv. 18. Rom. viii. 21. Gal. v. 1. It then denotes, *as a consequence* of freedom from sin, freedom from all the ills to which sin exposes man, and the attainment of that perfect peace and joy which shall be bestowed on the children of God in the heavens. The reasons why Peter introduces this subject here seem to be these: (1.) He was discoursing of the *deliverance* of the man that was healed, his *salvation* from a long and painful calamity. This deliverance had been accomplished by the power of Jesus. The mention of this suggested that *greater* and more important *salvation* from sin and death which it was the object of the Lord Jesus to effect. As it was by *his* power that this man had been healed, so it was by *his* power only that men could be saved from death and hell. Deliverance from any temporal calamity should lead the thoughts to that higher redemption which the Lord Jesus contemplates in regard to the soul. (2.) This was a favourable opportunity to introduce the doctrines of the gospel to the notice of the great council of the nation. The occasion invited to it; the mention of a *part* of the work of Jesus invited to a contemplation of his *whole* work. Peter would not have done justice to the character and work of Christ, if he had not introduced that great design which he had in view to save men from death and hell. It is probable, also, that he advanced a sentiment in which he expected they would immediately *concur*, and which accorded with their well-known opinions, that salvation was to be obtained only by the Messiah. Thus Paul (Acts xxvi. 22, 23) says that he taught nothing else than what was delivered by Moses and the prophets, &c. Comp. Acts xxiii. 6; xxvi. 6. The apostles did not *pretend* to proclaim any doctrine which was not delivered by Moses and the prophets, and which did not in fact constitute a part of the *creed* of the Jewish nation. ¶ *In any other.* Any other person. He does not mean to say that *God* is not able to save, but that the salvation of the human family is intrusted to the hands of Jesus the Messiah. ¶ *For there is none other name.* This is an explanation of what he had said in the previous part of the verse. The word *name* here is used to denote the person himself; there is no other *being*, or *person*. As we should say, there is *no one* who can save but Jesus Christ. The word *name* is often used in this sense. See Note on iii. 6. 16. That there is no *other* Saviour, or mediator between God and man, is abundantly taught in the New Testament; and it is indeed the main design of revelation to prove this. See 1 Tim. ii. 5, 6. Acts x. 43. ¶ *Under heaven.* This expression does not materially differ from the one immediately following, "among men." They are designed to express with emphasis the sentiment that salvation is to be obtained in *Christ alone*, and not in any patriarch, or prophet, or teacher, or king, or in any false Messiah. ¶ *Given.* In this word it is implied that *salvation* has its origin in God; that a Saviour for men must be *given* by him; and that salvation cannot be originated by any power among men. The Lord Jesus is thus uniformly represented as *given*, or *appointed* by God for this great purpose (John iii. 16; xvii. 4. 1 Cor. iii. 5. Gal. i. 4; ii. 20. Eph. i. 22; v. 25. 1 Tim. ii. 6. Rom. v. 15—18. 23); and hence Christ is called the "unspeakable gift" of God. 2 Cor. ix. 15. ¶ *Whereby we must be saved.* By which it is *fit*, or proper (δεῖ), that we should be saved. There is no other way of salvation that is *adapted* to the great object contemplated; and therefore, if saved, it must be in this way, and by this plan. All other schemes by men's own devices are *not adapted* to the purpose, and therefore cannot save. The doctrine that men can be saved *only* by Jesus Christ is abundantly taught in the

Scriptures. To show the failure of all other schemes of religion was the great design of the first part of the epistle to the Romans. By a laboured argument Paul there shows (ch. i.) that the *Gentiles* had failed in their attempt to justify themselves; and in ch. ii. iii. that the same thing was true also of the Jews. If *both* these schemes failed, then there was need of some *other* plan; and that plan was that of salvation by Jesus Christ. If it be asked, then, whether this affirmation of Peter is to be understood as having respect to *infants* and *the heathen*, we may remark, (1.) That his design was primarily to address the Jews, "Whereby *we* must be saved." But (2.) The same thing is doubtless true of others. If, as Christians generally believe, infants are saved, there is no absurdity in supposing that it is by the merits of the atonement. *But* for that, there would have been no promise of salvation. No offer *has* been made except by the Mediator; and to him doubtless is to be ascribed all the glory of raising up even those in infancy to eternal life. If any of the heathen are to be saved, as most Christians suppose, and as seems in accordance with the mercy of God, it is no less certain that it will be in consequence of the intervention of Christ. Those who will be brought to heaven will sing one song (Rev. v. 9), and will be prepared for eternal union in the service of God in the skies. Still, the Scriptures have *not* declared that *great numbers* of the heathen will be saved, who have not the gospel. The contrary is more than implied in the New Testament. Rom. ii. 12. Neither has the Scripture affirmed that *all* the heathen shall certainly be cut off. It has been discovered by missionaries among the heathen that individuals have, in a remarkable way, been convinced of the folly of idolatry, and were seeking a better religion; that their minds were in a serious, thoughtful, inquiring state, and that they *at once* embraced the gospel when it was offered to them, as *exactly* adapted to their state of mind, and meeting their inquiries. Such was extensively the case in the Sandwich Islands; and the following instance recently occurred in this country. "The Flat-head Indians, living west of the Rocky mountains, recently sent a deputation to the white settlements to inquire after the Bible. The circumstance that led to this singular movement is as follows: It appears that a white man (Mr. Catlin) had penetrated into their country, and happened to be a spectator at one of their religious ceremonies. He informed them that their mode of worshipping the Supreme Being was radically wrong, and that the people away towards the rising of the sun had been put in possession of the true mode of worshipping the Great Spirit. On receiving this information, they called a national council to take this subject into consideration. Some said, if this be true, it is certainly high time we were put in possession of this mode. They accordingly deputed four of the chiefs to proceed to St. Louis, to see their great father, general Clark, to inquire of him the truth of this matter. They were cordially received by the general, who gave them a succinct history of Revelation, and the necessary instruction relative to their important mission. Two of them sunk under the severe toils attending a journey of three thousand miles. The remaining two, after acquiring what knowledge they could of the Bible, its institutions and precepts, returned, to carry back those few rays of divine light to their benighted countrymen." In *what way* their minds were led to this state we cannot say; or how this *preparation* for the gospel was connected with the *agency* and *merits* of Christ, we perhaps cannot understand. But we know that the affairs of *this entire world* are placed under the control of Christ (John xvii. 2. Eph. i. 21, 22), and that the arrangements of events by which they were brought to this state of mind are in his hands. Another remark may here be made: it is, that it often occurs that blessings come upon us *from benefactors whom we do not see, and from sources which we cannot trace.* On this principle we receive *many* of the mercies of life; and from any thing that appears, in this way many blessings of salvation may be conferred on the world, and possibly many of the heathen be saved. Still, this view does not interfere with the command of Christ to preach the gospel. Mark xvi. 15. *The great mass of the heathen* are not in this state: and this fact, so far as it goes, is an encouragement to preach the gospel to the entire world. If *Christ* thus prepares the way; if he extensively fits the minds of the heathen for the reception of the gospel; if he shows them the evil and folly of their own system, and leads them to desire a better, then this should operate not to produce indolence, but activity, and zeal, and encouragement to enter into the field white for the harvest, and to toil that *all* who seek the truth, and are *prepared* to embrace the gospel, may be brought to the light of the Sun of righteousness.

13 Now when they saw the boldness of Peter and John, and perceived that they were unlearned [a] and ignorant men, they marvelled; and they took knowledge of them, that they had been with Jesus.

a Matt 11.25. 1Cor.1.27.

13. *Boldness.* This word properly denotes *openness* or *confidence in speaking.* It stands opposed to *hesitancy,* and to *equivocation* in declaring our sentiments. Here it means, that in spite of danger and opposition, they avowed their doctrines without any attempt to conceal or disguise them. ¶ *Peter and John.* It was they only who had been concerned in the healing of the lame man. ch. iii. 1. ¶ *And perceived.* When they knew that they were unlearned. This might have been ascertained either by report, or by the manner of their speaking. ¶ *Unlearned.* This word properly denotes those who were not acquainted with *letters,* or who had not had the benefit of an education. ¶ *Ignorant men.* ἰδιῶται. This word properly denotes those who live in private, in contradistinction from those who are engaged in *public* life, or in office. As this class of persons is commonly also supposed to be less learned, talented, and refined than those in office, it comes to denote those who are rude and illiterate. The idea intended to be conveyed here is, that these men had not had opportunities of education (comp. Matt. iv. 18—21), and had not been accustomed to public speaking, and hence they were surprised at their boldness. This same character is uniformly attributed to the early preachers of Christianity. Comp. 1 Cor. i. 27. Matt. xi. 25. The Galileans were regarded by the Jews as particularly rude and uncultivated. Matt. xxvi. 73. Mark xiv. 17. ¶ *They marvelled.* They *wondered* that men who had not been educated in the schools of the Rabbins, and accustomed to speak, should declare their sentiments with so much boldness. ¶ *And they took knowledge.* This expression means simply that *they knew,* or that they obtained evidence, or proof, that they had been with Jesus. It is not said *in what way* they obtained this evidence; but the connexion leads us to suppose it was by the *miracle* which they had wrought; by their firm and bold declaration of the doctrines of Jesus; and perhaps by the irresistible conviction that none *would* be thus bold who had not been personally with him, and who had not the firmest conviction that he was the Messiah. They had not been trained in their schools, and their boldness could not be attributed to the arts of rhetoric, but was the native, ingenuous, and manly exhibition of deep conviction of the truth of what they spoke; and that conviction could have been obtained only by their having been *with* him, and having been satisfied that he was the Messiah. Such conviction is of far more value in preaching than all the mere teachings of the schools; and *without* such a conviction, all preaching will be frigid, hypocritical, and useless. ¶ *Had been with Jesus.* Had been his followers, and had attended personally on his ministry. They gave evidence that they had *seen* him, been with him, heard him, and were convinced that he was the Messiah. We may learn here, (1.) That if men wish to be successful in preaching, it must be based on deep and thorough conviction of the truth of that which they deliver. (2.) They who preach should give evidence that they are acquainted with the Lord Jesus Christ; that they have imbibed his spirit, pondered his instructions, studied the evidences of his divine mission, and are thoroughly convinced that he was from God. (3.) Boldness and success in the ministry, as well as in every thing else, will depend far more on honest, genuine, thorough conviction of the truth, than on all the endowments of talent and learning, and all the arts and skill of eloquence No man should attempt to preach without such a thorough conviction of truth, and no man who has it will preach in vain. (4.) God often employs the ignorant and unlearned to confound the wise. 1 Cor. i. 27, 28. But it is not *by* their ignorance. It was not the ignorance of Peter and John that convinced the sanhedrim. It was done *in spite* of their ignorance. It was their *boldness,* and their honest conviction of truth. Besides, though not learned in the schools of the Jews, they had been under a far more important training, under the personal direction of Christ himself for three years; and now they were directly endowed by the Holy Ghost with the power of speaking with tongues. Though not taught in the schools, yet there was an important sense in which they were *not* unlearned and ignorant men. Their example should not, therefore, be pleaded in favour of an unlearned ministry. Christ himself expressed his opposition to an unlearned ministry by *teaching them himself,* and then by bestowing on them miraculous endowments

14 And beholding the man which was healed standing with them, they could say nothing [a] against it.

15 But when they had commanded them to go aside out of the council, they conferred among themselves,

16 Saying, What [b] shall we do to these men? for that indeed a notable miracle hath been done by them *is* manifest to all them that dwell in Jerusalem; and we cannot deny *it*.

17 But that it spread no further among the people, let us straitly threaten them, that [c] they speak henceforth to no man in this name.

18 And they called them, and

a c.19.36. b Jno.11.47 c c.5.40.

which no learning at present can furnish. It may be remarked, further, that in the single selection which *he* made of an apostle after his ascension to heaven, when he came to choose one who had *not* been under his personal teaching, he chose *a learned man*, the apostle Paul, and thus evinced his purpose that there should be *training*, or *education* in those who are invested with the sacred office. (5.) Yet in the case before us, there is a striking proof of the truth and power of religion. These men had not acquired their boldness in the schools; they were not trained for argument among the Jews; they did not meet them by cunning sophistry; but they came with the honest conviction that what they were saying was true. Were they deceived? Were they not competent to bear witness? Had they any motive to attempt to palm a falsehood on men? Infidelity must answer *many* such questions as these before the apostles can be convicted of imposture.

14. *They could say nothing*, &c. The presence of the man that was healed was an unanswerable fact in proof of the truth of what the apostles alleged. The miracle was so public, clear, and decisive; the man that was healed was so well known, that there was no evasion or subterfuge by which they could escape the conclusion to which the apostles were conducting them. It evinced no little gratitude in the man that was healed that he was present on this occasion, and showed that he was deeply interested in what befell his benefactors. The miracles of Jesus and his apostles were such that they could not be denied; and hence the Jews did not *attempt* to deny that they wrought them. Comp. Matt. xii. 24. John xi. 45, 46. Acts xix. 36.

15—18. *What shall we do to these men?* The object which they had in view was evidently to prevent their preaching. The miracle was wrought; and was believed by the people to have been wrought. This they could not expect to be able successfully to deny. Their only object, therefore, was to prevent the apostles from making the use which they saw they would, to convince the people that Jesus was the Messiah. The question therefore, was, in what way they should *prevent* this; whether by putting them to death, by imprisoning them, or by scourging them; or whether by simply exerting their *authority* and forbidding them. From the former they were deterred, doubtless by fear of the multitude. And they therefore adopted the latter, and seemed to suppose that the mere exertion of their authority would be sufficient to deter them from this in future. ¶ *The council.* Greek, The *sanhedrim.* This body was composed of seventy-one or seventy-two persons, and was intrusted with the principal affairs of the nation. It was a body of vast influence and power; and hence they supposed that their command might be sufficient to restrain ignorant Galileans from speaking. Before this same body, and probably the same men, our Saviour was arraigned; and by them condemned before he was delivered to the Roman governor. Matt. xxvi. 59, &c. And before this same body, and in the presence of the same men, Peter had just before denied his Lord. Matt. xxvi. 70, &c. The fact that the disciples had fled on a former occasion, and that Peter had denied his Saviour, may have operated to induce them to believe that they would be terrified by their threats, and deterred from preaching publicly in the name of Jesus. ¶ *A notable miracle.* A known, undeniable miracle. ¶ *That it spread.* That the *knowledge* of it may not spread among them any further ¶ *Let us straitly threaten them.* Greek, *Let us threaten them with a threat.* This is a *Hebraism*, expressing *intensity, certainty*, &c. The *threat* was a *command* (ver. 18) not to teach, implying their displeasure if they did do it. This threat, however, was not effectual. On the next occasion, which occurred soon after (ch. v. 40) they added *beating* to their threats.

commanded them not to speak at
all nor teach in the name of Jesus.
19 But Peter and John answered
and said unto them, Whether it be
right in the sight of God to [a] hearken
unto you more than unto God, judge
ye.
20 For [b] we cannot but speak the
things which [c] we have seen and
heard.

a c.5.29. b Je.20.9. c c.22.15. 1Jno.1.1,3.

in order to deter them from preaching in the name of Jesus.

19. *Whether it be right*, &c. The apostles abated nothing of their boldness when threatened. They openly appealed to their judges whether their command could be right. And in doing this, they expressed their full conviction of the truth of what they had said, and their deliberate purpose not to regard their command, but still to proclaim to the people the truth that Jesus was the Messiah. ¶ *In the sight of God.* That is, whether *God* will judge this to be right. The grand question was, how *God* would regard it. If *he* disapproved it, it was wrong. It was not merely a question pertaining to their reputation, safety, or life; but it was a question of conscience before God. And we have here a striking instance of the principle on which Christians act. It is, to lay their safety, reputation, and life out of view, and to bring every thing to this test, WHETHER IT WILL PLEASE GOD. If it will, it is right; if it will not, it is wrong. ¶ *To hearken.* To *hear* and to *hearken* are often used to denote *to obey.* John v. 24; viii. 47, &c. ¶ *Judge ye.* This was an appeal to them directly as judges, and as men. And it may be presumed that it was an appeal which they could not resist. The sanhedrim acknowledged itself to have been appointed by God; and to have no authority which was not derived from his appointment. Of course, God could modify, supersede, or repeal their authority; and the abstract principle, that it was better to obey God than man, they could not call in question. The only inquiry was, whether they had *evidence* that God had issued any command in the case. Of that, the apostles were satisfied; and that, the rulers could not deny. It may be remarked, that this is one of the first and most bold appeals on record, in favour of the right of private judgment and the liberty of conscience. That liberty was supposed in all the Jewish religion. It was admitted that the authority of God in all matters was superior to that of man. And the same spirit manifested itself thus early in the Christian church against all dominion over the conscience, and in favour of the right to follow the dictates of the conscience and the will of God. As a mere historical fact, therefore, it is interesting to contemplate this; and still more interesting in its important bearings on human liberty and human happiness. The doctrine is still more explicitly stated in ch. v. 29. "We ought to obey God rather than man."

20. *For*, &c. This is given as a reason why they should obey God rather than man. They had had so clear evidence that God had sent the Messiah; and they had received so direct and solemn a command (Mark xvi. 15) to preach the gospel that they could not be restrained. There was a necessity laid on them to preach the gospel. See 1 Cor. ix. 16, comp Jer. xx. 9. Acts xviii. 5. Job xxxii. 18, 19. Ps. xxxix. 1—3.

It has already been remarked, that these two verses contain an important *principle* in favour of religious *liberty*—the liberty of conscience, and of private judgment. They contain the *great principle* of the Christian, and of the *Protestant* religion, that the responsibility of men for their religious opinions is direct to God, and that other men have no power of control. The opposite of this is tyranny and oppression. It may be proper, in addition, to present some further remarks, involved in the principle here stated. (1.) Religion, from the commencement, has been favourable to *liberty.* There was no principle more sacred among the Jews, than that they were to be independent of other nations. Perhaps no people have ever been so restive under a foreign yoke, so prone to rebel, and so difficult to be broken down by oppression and by arms, as were the Jews. So true was this, that it appeared to other nations to be mere obstinacy. They were often subdued, but they rose against their oppressors, and threw off the yoke. No people has been found who were so difficult to be reduced to slavery. It is well known that the Romans were accustomed to subject the captives taken in war to perpetual servitude; and *commonly* the spirit of the captive was broken, and he remained quietly in bondage. But not so the Jew. Nothing ever tamed his spirit. No bribes, or threats, or chains could induce him to violate the laws of his religion. Even in captivity, we are told, that the Jewish slaves at Rome *would* observe the Sabbath, would keep the feasts of their nation, and never would conform to the customs of an idolatrous people. To the Romans this appeared to be mere obstinacy. But it was the genius of their religion. The right of liberty of thought was one which they would not surrender. The spirit of the patriarchs was favourable to liberty, and implied responsibility only to God. Familiarity with the sacred books h[illegible] taught them these lessons; and neither time nor distance could obliterate them In the time of Christ, the great mass of the nation were evidently *opposed* to the tax paid to the Roman nation, and sighed under this burden, until they rose and attempted to assert their rights; and their city, and temple, and land were sacrificed rather than *yield* this great principle. (2.) This same principle was evinced by the apostles and by the early Christians. With this doctrine fresh upon their hearts, they went forth to other lands. They maintained it at the expense of their blood; and thousands fell as martyrs in the cause of liberty and of private judgment in religion. No men ever more firmly defended liberty than the early martyrs; and each one that died, died in defence of a principle which is now the acknowledged right of all men. (3.) The designs of tyranny and superstition have been to destroy this principle. This was the aim of the sanhedrim; and yet, when Peter and John appealed to their *consciences*, they did not dare to avow their purpose. This has been the aim of all tyrants; and this the effect of all superstition. Hence the church of Rome has taken away the Scriptures from the people; and has thus furnished incontestable evidence that in its view the Bible is favourable to liberty. For centuries, tyranny reigned in one black night over Europe; nor was the darkness dispelled until the Bible, that taught men the principles of freedom, was restored to them (4.) The effect of the principle avowed by the apostles has been uniform. Luther began the Reformation by finding in a monastery a copy of the Bible, when himself more than twenty years of age—a book which till that time he had never seen. The effect on the liberties of Europe was immediately seen. Hume admitted, that whatever liberty England possessed was to be traced to the Puritans. Our own land is a striking instance of the effect of this great principle, and of its influence on the rights of man. And just in proportion as the New Testament is spread abroad, will men seek for freedom, and break the chains of oppression The best way to promote universal liberty, is to spread the Bible to the ends of the earth. There is not a precept in it that is not favourable to freedom. It tends to enlarge and liberalize the mind; to teach men their rights; to put an end to *ignorance*, the universal stronghold of superstition and tyranny; and to diffuse the love of justice, truth, and order. It shows man that he is responsible to God, and that no one has a right to ordain any thing which contravenes the liberty of his fellow.

If it be asked here what the principle is, I answer, (1.) That men have a right to their private judgment in matters of religion, subject only to God. The *only* restraint which, it is now settled, can be imposed on this, is, that no man has a right, under pretence of conscience, to injure or molest his fellow-men, or to disturb the peace and harmony of society. (2.) No magistrate, church, council, or parent has a right to *impose* a creed on others, and to demand subscription to it by mere authority. (3.) No magistrate, church, or parent has a right to *control* the free exercise of private judgment in this case. The power of a *parent* is to teach, advise, and entreat. The duty of a child is to listen with respect, to examine with candour, to pray over the subject, and to be deliberate and calm, not rash, hasty, impetuous, and self-willed. But when the child is thus convinced that his duty to God requires a particular course, then here is a *higher* obligation than any earthly law, and he must obey God rather than man, even a father or a mother. Matt. x. 37, 38. (4.) Every man *is* responsible to God for his opinions and his conduct. Man may not control him but God may and will. The great question before every man is, *What is right in the sight of God?* It is not what is expedient, or safe, or pleasurable, or honourable among men; but what is right in the sight of God. Neither in their opinions nor their conduct are men free from responsibility.—From this whole subject we see the duty of spreading the Bible. If we love liberty; if we hate tyranny and superstition; if we wish to extend the knowledge of the rights of man, and break every arm of oppression, let us spread far and wide the Book of God, and place in every palace and every cottage on the globe a copy of the sacred Scriptures.

21 So when they had further
threatened them, they let them go,
finding nothing how they might
punish them, because [a] of the people: for all *men* glorified God for
that which was done.
22 For the man was above forty
years old on whom this miracle of
healing was shewed.
23 And being let go, they went [b]
to their own company, and reported
all that the chief priests and elders
had said unto them.
24 And when they heard that,

a Matt.21.26. c.5.26.

b c.2.44–46.

---

21. *Finding nothing*, &c. That is, not being able to devise any way of punishing them, without exciting a tumult among the people, and endangering their own authority. The sanhedrim was frequently influenced by this fear; and it shows that their own authority was much dependent on the caprice of the multitude. Comp. Matt. xxi. 26. ¶ *All men.* That is, the great mass or body of the people. ¶ *Glorified God. Praised* God for the miracle. This implies, (1.) That they believed that the miracle was genuine. (2.) That they were grateful to God for so signal a mercy in conferring health and comfort on a man who had been long afflicted. We may add further, that here is the highest evidence of the reality of the miracle Even the sanhedrim, with all their prejudice and opposition, did not call it in question. And the common people, who had doubtless been acquainted with this man for years, were convinced that it was real. It would have been impossible to *impose* on keen-sighted and jealous adversaries in this manner, if this had been an imposture.

22. *For the man*, &c. The *age* of the man is mentioned to show the certainty and greatness of the miracle. If it had been a man who had been lame but a few years; or if it had been a child or a very young man; the case would not have been so remarkable. But after a continuance of forty years, all hope of healing him by any ordinary means must have been abandoned; and all pretence that this was jugglery or deception must have been absurd.

23. *Their own company.* They joined the other apostles and Christians. ch. ii. 44, 45. ¶ *And reported*, &c. It doubtless became a subject of interesting inquiry, what they should do in this case. They had been *threatened* by the highest authority of the nation, and *commanded* not to preach again in the name of Jesus. Whether they should obey them and be silent; or whether they should leave Jerusalem and preach elsewhere, could not but be an interesting subject of inquiry; and they very properly sought the counsel of their brethren, and looked to God for direction; an example which all should follow who are exposed to persecution, or who are in any perplexity about the path of duty.

24. *They lift up their voice.* To lift up the voice, among the Hebrews, was a phrase denoting either an address to the people (Judg. ix. 7), or a phrase expressive of *weeping* (Gen. xxix. 11. Judg. ii. 4. Ruth i. 9. 1 Sam. xxiv. 16), or was expressive of *prayer.* To lift up the voice *to God*, means simply they *prayed* to him. ¶ *With one accord.* Unitedly. Properly with one *mind*, or purpose. See Note, ch. i. 14. The *union* of the early Christians is often noticed in the Acts of the Apostles. Thus far there was no jar or dissension in their society, and every thing has the appearance of the most entire affection and confidence. ¶ *Lord.* Greek, Δέσποτα. From this word is derived the word *despot*. This is not the usual word employed by which to address God. The word commonly translated *Lord* is Κύριος. The word here used denotes one who rules over others, and was applied to the highest magistrate or officer. It denotes authority; power; *absoluteness* in ruling. It is a word denoting more authority in *ruling* than the other. That more commonly denotes a *property* in a thing; this denotes absolute rule. It is applied *to God*, in Luke ii. 29. Rev. vi. 10. Jude 4; *to Jesus Christ*, 2 Pet. ii. 1; *to masters*, 1 Tim. vi. 1. Titus ii. 9. 1 Pet. ii. 18; *to husbands*, 1 Pet. iii. 6; and *to a possessor*, or *owner*, 2 Tim. ii. 21. ¶ *Thou art God.* This ascription of praise seems to have been designed to denote *their* sense of his *power* to deliver them; and his *right* to dispose of them. They were employed in his service; they were encompassed with dangers; and they acknowledged him as *their* God, who had made all things, and who had an entire right to direct, and to dispose of them for his own glory. In times of danger and perplexity we should remember that God has a right to do with us as he pleases; and we should go cheerfully and commit ourselves into his hands. ¶ *Which hast made*, &c. Gen.

they lift up their voice to God with one accord, and said, Lord, [a] thou *art* God, which hast made heaven and earth, and the sea, and all that in them is;

25 Who by the mouth of thy servant David hast said, Why [b] did the heathen rage, and the people imagine vain things?

26 The kings of the earth stood

a 2Ki.19.15. b Ps.2.1,2.

This passage is taken directly from Ps. cxlvi. 6. Comp. Rev. xiv. 7.

25. *Who by the mouth,* &c. Ps. ii. 1, 2. This is a strong, solemn testimony to the inspiration of David. It is a declaration of the apostles made in solemn prayer, that *God* spake himself by the mouth of David. This is the *second* part of their prayer. In the first, they acknowledge the right of God to rule; in this, they appeal to a prophecy; they plead that this was a thing foretold; and as *God* had foreseen it and foretold it, they appealed to him to protect them. The times of tumult and opposition which had been foreseen, as about to attend the introduction of the gospel, had now come. They inferred, therefore, that Jesus was the Messiah; and as God had designed to establish *his* kingdom, they appealed to him to aid and protect them in this great work. This passage is taken from Ps. ii. 1, 2, and is an exact quotation from the Septuagint. This proves that the Psalm had reference to *the Messiah.* Thus it was manifestly understood by the Jews; and the authority of the apostles settles the question. The Psalm was composed by David; on what occasion is not known; nor is it material to our present purpose. It has been a matter of inquiry whether it referred to the Messiah *primarily,* or only in a *secondary* sense. Grotius supposes that it was composed by David when exposed to the hostility of the Assyrians, the Moabites, Philistines, Amalekites, &c.; and that in the midst of his dangers, he sought consolation in the *purpose* of God to establish him and his kingdom. But the more probable opinion is, that it referred *directly* and *solely* to the Messiah. ¶ *Why did the heathen.* The nations which were not Jews. This refers, doubtless, to the opposition which would be made to the spread of Christianity: and not *merely* to the opposition made to the Messiah himself, and to the act of putting him to death. ¶ *Rage.* This word refers to the excitement and tumult of a *multitude;* not a settled *plan,* but rather the heated and disorderly conduct of a *mob.* It means that the progress of the gospel would encounter tumultuous opposition; and that the excited nations would rush violently to put it down and destroy it. ¶ *And the people.* The expression "the people" does not refer to a class of men different essentially from the heathen. The "heathen," Heb. and Greek, "*the nations,*" refer to men as *organized* into communities; the expression *the people* is used to denote the same persons without respect to their being so organized. The Hebrews were in the habit, in their poetry, of expressing the same idea essentially in parallel members of a sentence; or the last member of a sentence or verse expressed the same idea, with some slight variation, as the former. (See Lowth on the sacred poetry of the Hebrews.) ¶ *Imagine.* The word *imagine* does not express quite the force of the original. The Hebrew and the Greek both convey the idea of *meditating, thinking, purposing.* It means that they employed *thought, plan, purpose,* in opposing the Messiah. ¶ *Vain things.* The word here used (κενά) is a literal translation of the Hebrew (ריק), and means usually *empty,* as a vessel which is not filled; then *useless,* or that which amounts to nothing, &c. Here it means that they devised a plan which *turned out* to be vain, or ineffectual. They attempted an opposition to the Messiah which could not succeed. God would establish his kingdom in spite of their plans to oppose it. *Their* efforts were vain, because they were not strong enough to oppose God; because he had purposed to establish the kingdom of his Son; and he could overrule even their opposition to advance his cause.

26. *The kings of the earth.* The Psalmist specifies more particularly that *kings* and *rulers* would be opposed to the Messiah. This had occurred already by the opposition made to the Messiah by the rulers of the Jewish people; and it would be still more evinced by princes and kings, as the gospel should spread among the nations. ¶ *Stood up.* The word here used (παρίστημι) commonly means to present one's self, or to stand forth, for the purpose of aiding, counselling, &c. But here it means that they *rose,* or *presented themselves,* to evince their opposition. They stood opposed to the Messiah, and offered resistance to him. ¶ *The rulers.* This is another instance of the Hebrew

up, and the ru.ers were gathered
together, against the Lord, and
against his Christ.
27 For of a truth against thy
holy child Jesus, whom thou hast
anointed, both Herod [a] and Pontius
Pilate with the Gentiles and the
people of Israel were gathered together,
28 For [b] to do whatsoever thy
hand and thy counsel determined [c]
before to be don

a Lu.23.1-8,&c.

b c.3.18. c Pr.21.30. Is.46.10;53.10.

parallelism. The word does not denote another class of men from kings, but expresses the same idea in another form, or in a more general manner, meaning that all classes of persons in authority would be opposed to the gospel. ¶ *Were gathered together.* Hebrew, *consulted together;* were *united* in a consultation. The Greek implies that they were *assembled* for the purpose of consultation. ¶ *Against the Lord.* In the Hebrew, "against *Jehovah.*" This is the peculiar name which is given in the Scriptures to God. They rose against his plan of appointing a Messiah, and against the Messiah whom he had chosen. ¶ *Against his Christ.* Hebrew, against his *Messiah,* or his Anointed. Note, Matt. i. 1. This is one of the places where the word *Messiah* is used in the Old Testament. The word occurs in about forty places, and is commonly translated *his anointed,* and is applied to kings. The *direct* reference of the word to the Messiah in the Old Testament is not frequent. This passage implies that opposition to the *Messiah* is opposition to *Jehovah.* And this is uniformly supposed in the sacred Scriptures. He that is opposed to Christ is opposed to God. He that neglects him neglects God. He that despises him despises God. Matt. x. 40; xviii. 5. John xii. 44, 45. Luke x. 16. "He that despiseth me, despiseth him that sent me." The reasons of this are, (1.) That the Messiah is "the brightness of the Father's glory, and the express image of his subsistence." Heb. i. 3. (2.) He is equal with the Father, possessing the same attributes, and the same power. John i. 1. Phil. ii. 6, &c. To despise him, therefore, is to despise God. (3.) He is *appointed* by God to this great work of saving men. To despise him, or to oppose him, is to despise and oppose him who appointed him to this work to contemn his counsels, and to set him at nought. (4.) His work is dear to God It has engaged his thoughts. It has been approved by him. His mission has been confirmed by the miraculous power of the Father, and by every possible manifestation of his approbation and love. To oppose the Messiah, is, therefore, to oppose that which is dear to the heart of God, and which has long been the object of his tender solicitude. It follows from this, that they who *neglect* the Christian religion are exposing themselves to the sore displeasure of God, and endangering their everlasting interests. No man is safe who opposes God; and no man can have evidence that God will approve him, who does not embrace the Messiah whom He has appointed to redeem the world.

27. *For of a truth.* Truly; reality. ¶ *Thy holy child Jesus.* The word *child* is commonly applied to *infants,* or to sons and daughters in very early life. The word which is used here (παῖς) is different from that which is commonly applied to the Lord Jesus (ιος). The latter expresses sonship without respect to age. The word which is here used also sometimes expresses sonship without any regard to age; and the word *son* would have been a more happy translation. Thus the same word is translated in Acts iii. 13. 26. In Acts xx. 12, it is translated "young man." ¶ *Both Herod, &c.* Luke xxiii. 1—12. ¶ *With the Gentiles.* The Romans, to whom he was delivered to be crucified ¶ *The people of Israel.* The Jews, who were excited to this by the rulers. Matt. xxvii. 20.

28. *For to do,* &c. See Notes, ch. ii 23; iii. 18. The *facts* which are brought to view in these verses are among the most remarkable on record. They are briefly these: (1.) That the Jewish rulers were opposed to the Messiah, and slew him. (2.) That the very people to whom he came, and for whose benefit he laboured, joined in the opposition, so that it became the act of a united people. (3.) That the Romans who were there, as a sort of representation of all pagan nations, were easily prevailed on to join in the persecution, and to become the executioners. (4.) That thus opposite factions, and dissimilar and prejudiced people, became united in opposing the Messiah. (5.) That the rulers of the Roman people, the emperors, and statesmen, and philosophers, and the rulers of other nations, united to oppose the gospel, and

brought all the power of persecution to stay its progress. (6.) That the *people* of the empire, the *mass* of men, were easily prevailed upon to join in the persecution, and endeavour to arrest its progress. And (7.) That the gospel has encountered similar difficulties and opposition wherever it has been faithfully presented to the attention of men. It has become a very serious question *why* this has been; or on what pretence this opposition has been vindicated; or how it can be accounted for. A question which it is of as much importance for the infidel as for the Christian to settle. We know that accusations of the corrupt lives of the early Christians were freely circulated, and the most gross accounts given of their scandalous conduct were propagated by those who chose to persecute them. (See Lardner's Credibility.) But such accounts are not now believed; and it is not certain that they were *ever* seriously believed by the rulers of the pagan people. It is certain that it was not on *this* account that the first opposition arose to Christ and his religion.

It is not proper here to enter into an examination of the causes of this opposition. We may state the outlines, however, in few words. (1.) The Jewish *rulers* were mortified, humbled, and moved with envy, that one so poor and despised should claim to be the Messiah. They had expected a different monarch; and all their prejudices rose at once against *his* claims to this high office. Matt. xxvii. 18. Mark xv. 10. (2.) The common people, disposed extensively to acknowledge his claims, were urged on by the enraged and vindictive priests to demand his death. Matt. xxvii. 20. (3.) Pilate was pressed on against his will by the impetuous and enraged multitude to deliver one whom he regarded as innocent. (4.) The Christian religion in its advances struck at once at the whole fabric of superstition in the Roman empire, and throughout the world. It did not, like other religions, ask a place amidst the religions already existing. It was *exclusive* in its claims. It denounced *all* other systems as idolatry or superstition, and sought to overthrow them. Those religions were interwoven with all the habits of the people; they were connected with all the departments of the state; they gave occupation to a vast number of priests and other officers, who obtained their livelihood by the existing superstitions, and who brought, of course, all the supposed sacredness of their character to support them. A religion which attempted to overthrow the whole fabric, therefore, at once excited all their malice. The monarchs, whose thrones were based on the existing state of things; and the people, who venerated the religion of their ancestors, would be opposed to the new system. (5.) Christianity was despised. It was regarded as one form of the superstition of the Jews. And there was no people who were regarded with so much contempt by all other nations as the Jews. The writings of the Romans, on this point, are full proof. (6.) The new religion was opposed to all the *crimes* of the world. It began its career in a time of eminent wickedness. It plunged at once into the midst of this wickedness; sought the great cities where crimes and pollutions were condensed; and boldly reproved every form of prevailing impiety. At Athens, at Corinth, at Ephesus, at Rome itself, it denounced the judgment of God against every form of guilt. Whatever may be charged on the apostles, it will *not* be alleged that they were *timid* in denouncing the sins of the world. From all these causes it is not wonderful that the early Christians were persecuted. If it be asked, (7.) Why the same religion meets with opposition now in lands that are nominally Christian, it may be remarked, (*a*) that the human heart is the same that it always was, opposed to truth and righteousness; (*b*) that religion encounters still a host of sins that are opposed to it—pride, envy, malice, passion, the love of the world, and shame of acknowledging God; (*c*) that there has always been a peculiar opposition in the human heart to receiving salvation as the gift of God through a crucified Redeemer; and (*d*) that all the forms of vice, and lust, and profaneness that exist in the world, are opposed, and ever will be, to a religion of purity, and self-denial, and love.

On the whole, we may remark here, (1.) That the fact that Christianity has been thus opposed, and has triumphed, is no small proof of its divine origin. It has been *fairly tried*, and still survives and flourishes. It was well to put it to the *test*, and to bring to bear on it every thing which had a tendency to crush it, and thus to furnish the highest proof that it is from God. (2.) This religion cannot be destroyed; it will triumph; opposition to it is vain; it will make its way throughout the world; and the path of safety is *not* to oppose that which God is intending to establish in the earth. Sinners who stand opposed to the gospel, should tremble and be afraid; for sooner or later they *must* fall before its triumphant advances. It is

29 And now, Lord, behold their
threatenings: and grant unto thy
servants, that with all [a] boldness
they may speak thy word,
30 By stretching forth thine hand
to heal: and that signs [b] and wonders
may be done by the name of
thy holy child Jesus.

a ver.13,31. c.14.3;28.31. Ep.6.19. b c.2.43;5.12

31 And when they had prayed, [c]
the place was shaken where they
were assembled together; and they
were all filled with the Holy Ghost,
and they [d] spake the word of God
with boldness.
32 And the multitude of them
that believed were of one [e] heart

c c.2.2,4; 16.26. d ver.29. e Ro.15.5,6. 2Co.13.11. Phil.2.2. 1Pet.3.8.

---

not SAFE to oppose that which has already been opposed by kings and rulers in every form, and yet has triumphed. It is not WISE to risk one's eternal welfare on the question of successful opposition to that which God has, in so many ages and ways, pledged himself to protect; and when God has solemnly declared that the Son, the Messiah, whom he would set on his holy hill of Zion, should "break" his enemies "with a rod of iron, and dash them in pieces like a potter's vessel." Ps. ii. 9.

29. *Behold their threatenings.* So look upon them as to grant us deliverance. They did not purpose to abandon their undertaking; they resolved to persevere; and they expected that this purpose would involve them in danger. With this purpose they implored the protection of God; they asked that he would not suffer them to be deterred from speaking boldly; and they sought that constant additional proof might be granted of the presence and power of God to confirm the truth of their message. ¶ *And grant,* &c. This is an instance of heroic boldness, and a determination to persevere in doing their duty to God. When we are assailed by those in power, when we are persecuted and in danger, we should commit our way unto God, and seek his aid, that we may not be deterred from the path of duty.

30. *By stretching forth thine hand,* &c. The apostles not only desired *boldness* to speak, but they asked that God would continue to work miracles, and thus furnish to them, and to the people, evidence of the truth of what they delivered. They did not even ask that he would preserve their lives, or keep them from danger. They were intent on their work, and they confidently committed their way to God, making it their great object to promote the knowledge of the truth, and seeking that God would glorify himself by establishing his kingdom among men. ¶ *Signs and wonders.* Miracles. Notes, ch. ii. 43

31. *And when they had prayed.* The event which followed was regarded by them as an evidence that God heard their prayer. ¶ *The place was shaken.* The word which is translated "was shaken," commonly denotes violent agitation, as the raging of the sea, the convulsion of an earthquake, or trees shaken by the wind. Matt. xi. 7. Acts xvi. 26. Heb. xii. 26. The language here is fitted to express the idea of an earthquake. Whether the motion was confined to the house where they were, is not said. They probably regarded this as an answer to their prayer, or as an evidence that God would be with them, (1.) Because it was sudden and violent, and was not produced by any natural causes; (2.) Because it occurred *immediately,* while they were seeking divine direction; (3.) Because it was an exhibition of great *power,* and was an evidence that God could protect them; and (4.) Because a convulsion so great, sudden, and mighty, was fitted at that time to awe them with a proof of the presence and power of God. A similar instance of an answer to prayer by an earthquake is recorded in Acts xvi. 25, 26. Comp. ch. ii. 1, 2. It may be added that among the Jews an *earthquake* was very properly regarded as a striking and impressive proof of the presence of Jehovah. Isa. xxix. 6. Ps. lxviii. 8. "The earth shook, the heavens also dropped at the presence of God; even Sinai itself was moved at the presence of God, the God of Israel." See also the sublime description in Habakkuk iii. particularly ver. 6—11. Comp. Matt. xxvii. 54. Among the heathen, an earthquake was regarded as proof of the presence and *favour* of the Deity. (See Virgil, Æniad iii. 89.) ¶ *They were all filled,* &c. Notes, ch. ii. 4. Their being filled with the Holy Ghost here rather denotes their being inspired with *confidence* or *boldness,* than being endowed with new powers, as in Acts ii. 4.

32. *And the multitude.* The number of believers at this time had become large. In ch. iv. 4, it is said that it was

and of one soul: neither said any
of them that aught of the things
which he possessed was his own;
but [a] they had all things common.
33 And with great power [b] gave
the apostles witness [c] of the resurrection of the Lord Jesus: and great
grace [d] was upon them all.
34 Neither was there any among
them that lacked: for as many as

a c.2.14. b c.1.8. c Lu.1.48,49. c.1.22. d Jno.1.16.

five thousand; and the number was constantly increasing. ¶ *One heart.* This expression denotes tender union. They *felt* alike, or were attached to the same things, and this preserved them from jars and dissensions. ¶ *One soul.* This phrase alse denotes close and tender union. No expression could denote it more strikingly than to say of friends they have *one soul.* Plutarch cites an ancient verse in his life of Cato of Utica, with this very expression—"Two friends, one soul." (*Grotius.*) Thus Diogenes Laertius also (5. i. 11.) says respecting Aristotle, that "being asked what was a friend; answered, that it was *one soul* dwelling in two bodies." (*Kuinöel.*) The Hebrews spake of two friends as being "one man." There can be no more striking demonstration of *union* and *love* than to say of more than five thousand suddenly drawn together, that they had one soul! And this union they evinced in every way possible; in their conduct, in their prayers, and in their property. How different would have been the aspect of the church, if the union had continued to the present time. ¶ *Neither said, &c.* That is, they did not *regard* it as their own, but to be used for the benefit of the whole society. See Notes, ch. ii. 44.

33. *And with great power.* See ch. i. 8. The word *power* here denotes *efficacy*, and means that they had *ability* given them to bear witness of the resurrection of the Saviour. It refers therefore rather to their *preaching*, than to their *miracles.* ¶ *Gave the apostles witness.* The apostles bore testimony to, ¶ *the resurrection of the Lord Jesus.* This was the main point to be established. If it was proved that the Lord Jesus *came to life again* after having been put to death, it established all that he taught, and was a demonstration that he was sent from God. They exerted, therefore, all their powers to prove this; and their success was such as might have been expected. Multitudes were converted to the Christian faith. ¶ *And great grace, &c.* The word *grace* means *favour.* Note, John i. 16. And the expression here may mean either that the favour *of God* was remarkably shown to them; or that they had great favour in the sight of the people. It does not refer as the expression now does commonly, to the internal blessings of religion on a man's own soul; to their personal advancement in the Christian *graces* of humility, &c.; but to the *favour* or success that attended their preaching The meaning probably is, that the *favour* of the *people* towards them was great; or that great success attended their ministry among them. Thus the same word *grace* (Greek) is used in ch. ii. 47. If this is its meaning, then here is an instance of the power of the testimony of the resurrection of the Lord Jesus to impress the minds of men. But this is not all, nor probably is it the main idea. It is that their union, their benevolence, their liberality in supplying the wants of the needy, was a means of opening the hearts of the people, and of winning them to the Saviour. If we wish to incline others to our opinions, or to bring them to be Christians, nothing is better adapted to it, than to show them kindness, and even to minister to their temporal wants. Benevolence towards them softens the heart, and inclines them to listen to us. It disarms their prejudices, and disposes them to the exercise of the mild and amiable feelings of religion. Hence our Saviour was engaged in healing the diseases, and supplying the wants of the people. He drew around him the poor, the needy, and the diseased, and supplied their necessities, and *thus* prepared them to receive his message of truth. Thus God is love, and is constantly doing good, that his *goodness* may lead men to repentance. Rom. ii. 4. And hence no persons have better opportunities to spread the true sentiments of religion, or are clothed with higher responsibilities, than those who have it in their *power* to do good; or than those who are habitually engaged in bestowing favours. Thus physicians have access to the hearts of men which other persons have not. Thus *parents* have an easy access to the minds of children, for they are constantly doing them good. And thus Sunday-school teachers, whose whole work is a work of benevolence, have direct and most efficient access to the hearts of the children committed to their care.

34. *That lacked,* That was in want; or whose wants were not supplied by the others. ¶ *As many as, &c.* The word

were possessors of lands or houses,
sold them, and brought the prices
of the things that were sold,
35 And [a] laid *them* down at the
apostles' feet; and [b] distribution
was made unto every man according as he had need.
36 And Joses, who by the apostles was surnamed Barnabas, (which
is, being interpreted, The son of

a ver.37. c.5.2. b c.2.45;6.1.

used here is employed in a large, indefinite sense; but it would be improper to press it so as to suppose, that every individual that became a Christian sold at once all his property. The sense doubtless is, that this was done *when it was necessary;* they parted with whatever property was needful to supply the wants of their poor brethren. That it was by no means considered a matter of *obligation,* or enjoined by the apostles, is apparent from the case of Ananias. ch. v. 4. The fact that *Joses* is particularly mentioned (ver. 36), shows that it was by no means a universal practice thus to part with all their possessions. He was *one* instance in which it was done. Perhaps there were many other similar instances; but all that the passage requires us to believe is, that they parted with whatever was *needful* to supply the wants of the poor. This was an eminent and instructive instance of Christian liberality, and of the power of the gospel in overcoming one of the strongest passions that ever exist in the human bosom—the love of money. Many of the early Christians were poor. They were collected from the lower orders of the people. But *all* were not so. Some of them, it seems, were men of affluence. The effect of religion was to bring them all, in regard to feeling at least, on a level. They felt that they were members of one family; belonging to the same Redeemer; and they therefore imparted their property cheerfully to their brethren. Besides this, they were about to go to other lands to preach the gospel. They were to leave their native country; and they cheerfully parted with their lands, that they might go and proclaim the unsearchable riches of Christ. See Notes, ch. ii. 44.

35. *And laid them down,* &c That is, they committed the money received for their property to the disposal of the apostles, to distribute it as was necessary among the poor. This soon became a burdensome and inconvenient office, and they therefore appointed men who had especial charge of it. ch. vi. 1, 2, &c.

36. *And Joses.* Many manuscripts instead of *Joses* here read *Joseph.* The reasons why this individual is selected and specified particularly were, doubtless, because he was a foreigner; because it was a remarkable instance of liberality; and because he subsequently distinguished himself in the work of the ministry He gave himself, his property, his all, to the service of the Lord Jesus, and went forth to the self-denying labours of the gospel. He is elsewhere mentioned with honour in the New Testament (Acts xi. 24. 30), and usually as the companion of the apostle Paul. The occasion on which he became connected with Paul in the ministry was, when he himself was sent forth by the church at Jerusalem to Antioch. There, it seems, he heard of the fame of Paul, and went to Tarsus to seek him, and brought him with him to Antioch. Acts xi. 22—26. Before this, he had been acquainted with him, and had introduced him to the other apostles at a time when they were afraid of Paul, and unwilling to acknowledge him as an apostle. Acts ix. 26, 27. At Antioch, Barnabas was led into dissimulation by Peter in regard to the Gentiles, and was reproved by his friend and companion, Paul. Gal. ii. 13. He and Paul continued to travel in fellowship until a dispute arose at Antioch about Mark, and they separated, Paul going with Silas through Syria and Cilicia, and Barnabas with Mark sailing for his native place, Cyprus. Acts xv. 35—41 See the following places for particulars of his history: Acts xi. 22. 25. 30; xii. 25; xiii. 1, 2. 50; xiv. 12; xv. 12. 1 Cor. ix. 6. Gal. ii. 1. 9. ¶ *Who by the apostles was surnamed,* &c. This name was doubtless given by the apostles. The practice of giving surnames, as expressive of character, was not uncommon. Thus Simon was called Peter, or Cephas, John i. 44; and thus James and John were surnamed Boanerges, Mark iii. 17. ¶ *Barnabas, which is,* &c. This word properly denotes *the son of prophecy.* It is compounded of two Syriac words, the one meaning *son,* and the other *prophecy* The Greek word which is used to interpret this (παράκλησις), translated *consolation,* means properly also. exhortation, entreaty, petition, or advocacy. It also means *consolation,* or *solace;* and from *this* meaning the interpretation has been given to the word *Barnabas,* but with evident impropriety. It does not appear

consolation,) a Levite, *and* of the country of Cyprus,

37 Having land, sold *it*, and brought the money, and laid *it* at the apostles' feet.

CHAPTER V.

BUT a certain man named Ananias, with Sapphira his wife sold a possession,

2 And kept back *part* of the price

that the name was bestowed on account of this, though it is probable that he possessed it in an eminent degree, but on account of his talent for *speaking*, or *exhorting* the people to holiness, and his success in preaching. Comp. Acts xi. 23. ¶ *A Levite.* One of the descendants of Levi employed in the lower services of the temple. The whole tribe of *Levi* was set apart to the service of religion. It was divided into Priests and Levites. The three sons of Levi were Gershon, Kohath, and Merari. Of the family of *Kohath* Aaron was descended, who was the first high-priest. His eldest son succeeded him, and the remainder of his sons were *priests.* All the others of the tribe of Levi were called *Levites*, and were employed in the work of the temple, in assisting the priests in performing sacred music, &c. Num. iii. Deut. xii. 18, 19; xviii. 6—8. 1 Chron. xxiii. 24. ¶ *Of the country of Cyprus.* Cyprus is the largest island in the Mediterranean; an island extremely fertile, abounding in wine, honey, oil, wool, &c. It is mentioned in Acts xiii. 4; xv. 39. The island is near to Cilicia, and is not far from the Jewish coast. It is mentioned by Dion Cassius (lib. 68, 69) that the Jews were very numerous in that island. (*Clark.*)

Barnabas afterwards became, with Paul, a distinguished preacher to the Gentiles. It is worthy of remark, that *both* were born in heathen countries, though by descent Jews; and as they were trained in heathen lands, they were better fitted for their peculiar work. The case of Barnabas is that of a man who had property, who entered the ministry, and gave up all for the Lord Jesus. The great mass of ministers, like very many who have been distinguished in other professions, have been taken from the poor, and from humble ranks in life. But all have not been. Many have been wealthy, and have devoted all to Christ; and in regard to others, it is to be remarked, that a very considerable proportion of them could have gained more *wealth* in some other profession than they do in the ministry. The ministry is a work of self-denial; and none should enter it who are not prepared to devote all to the service of the Lord Jesus Christ.

CHAPTER V.

1. *But a certain man.* In the previous chapter, the historian had given an account of the eminent liberality and sincerity of the mass of early Christians, in being willing to give up their property to provide for the poor, and had mentioned the case of Barnabas as worthy of special attention. In this chapter he proceeds to mention a case, quite as striking, of insincerity and hypocrisy, and of the just judgment of God on those who were guilty of it. The case is a remarkable instance of the nature of *hypocrisy*, and goes to illustrate the art and cunning of the enemy of souls in attempting to corrupt the church, and to pervert the religion of the gospel. Hypocrisy consists in an attempt to *imitate* the people of God, or to assume the *appearance* of religion, in whatever form it may be manifested. In this case religion had been manifested by great self-denial and benevolence. The hypocrisy of Ananias consisted in *attempting* to imitate this appearance, and to impose in this way on the early Christians and on God. ¶ *With Sapphira his wife.* With her concurrence, or consent. It was a matter of *agreement* between them. ver. 2. 9. ¶ *Sold a possession.* The word here used (κτῆμα) does not indicate whether this was *land* or some other property. In ver. 3, however, we learn that it was *land* that was sold; and the word here translated *possession* is translated, in the Syriac, Arabic, and the Latin Vulgate, *land.* The *pretence* for which this was sold was doubtless to have the appearance of religion. That it was *sold* could be easily known by the Christian society, but it might not be so easily known for *how much* it was sold. Hence the attempt to impose on the apostles. It is clear that they were not under obligation to sell their property. But *having* sold it for the purposes of religion, it became their duty, if they professed to devote the avails of it to God, to do it entirely, and without any reservation.

2. *And kept back.* The word here used means properly *to separate, to part;* and then it means to *separate surreptitiously or clandestinely for our own use* a part of public property, as taxes, &c. It is used but three times in the New Testament,

his wife also being privy *to it*, and
brought [a] a certain part, and laid *it*
at the apostles' feet.

3 But Peter said, Ananias, why
hath Satan [b] filled thine heart [1] to
lie to [c] the Holy Ghost, and to

a c.4.34,37. b Lu.22.3. 1 or, *to deceive*. c ver.9.

ver. 3, and in Titus ii. 10, where it is rendered *purloining*. Here it means that they *secretly* kept back a part, while *professedly* devoting all to God. ¶ *His wife being privy to it.* His wife *knowing it*, and evidently concurring in it. ¶ *And laid it at the apostles' feet.* This was evidently an act *professedly* of devoting all to God. Comp. ch. iv. 37, also ver. 8, 9. That this was his *profession*, or *pretence*, is further implied in the fact that Peter charges him with having *lied* unto God. ver. 3, 4.

3. *But Peter said*, &c. Peter could have known this only by *revelation*. It was the manifest design of Ananias to deceive; nor was there any way of detecting him but by its being revealed to him by the Spirit of God. As it was an instance of enormous wickedness, and as it was very important to detect and punish the crime, it was made known to Peter directly by God. ¶ *Why hath Satan.* Great deeds of wickedness in the Scripture are traced to the influence and temptation of Satan. Comp. Luke xxii. 3. John xiii. 27. Especially is Satan called the *father of lies*. John viii. 44. 55. Comp. Gen. iii. 1—5. As this was an act of *falsehood*, or an attempt to deceive, it is with great propriety traced to the influence of Satan. The sin of Ananias consisted in his *yielding* to the temptation. Nowhere in the Bible are men supposed to be free from guilt, from the fact that they have been *tempted* to commit it. God requires them to *resist* temptation; and if they *yield* to it, they must be punished. ¶ *Filled thine heart.* A man's *heart* or *mind* is *full* of a thing when he is *intent on it;* when he is strongly *impelled* to it; or when he is fully occupied with it. The expression here means that he was *strongly impelled* or *excited* by Satan to this crime. ¶ *To lie to.* To attempt to deceive. The deception which he meant to practise was to keep back a *part* of the price, while he *pretended* to bring the whole of it; thus *tempting* God, and supposing that he could not detect the fraud. ¶ *The Holy Ghost.* τὸ πνεῦμα τὸ ἅγιον. The main inquiry here is, whether the apostle Peter intended to designate in this place the *third person* of the Trinity; or whether he meant to speak of God *as God*, without any reference to the distinction of persons; or to the *divine influence* which inspired the apostles, without reference to the peculiar offices which are commonly ascribed to the Holy Spirit. Or, in other words, is there a *distinction* here recognised between the *Father* and the *Holy Spirit?* That there *is*, will be apparent from the following considerations: (1.) If no such distinction is *intended*, it is remarkable that Peter did not use the usual and customary *name* of God. It does not appear why he guarded it so carefully as to denote that this offence was committed against the *Holy Ghost*, and *the Spirit of the Lord.* ver. 9. (2.) The name here used is the one employed in the Scriptures to designate the third person of the Trinity, as implying a distinction from the Father. See Matt. iii. 16; i. 18. 20; iii. 11; xii.32; xxviii. 19. Mark i. 8; iii. 29; xii. 36. Luke xii. 10. John xiv. 26; vii. 39; xx. 22. Acts iv. 8, v. 32, &c. (3.) Peter intended, doubtless, to designate an offence as committed particularly against the person, or influence, by which he and the other apostles were inspired. Ananias supposed that he could escape detection: and the offence was one, therefore, against the Inspirer of the apostles. Yet that was the Holy Ghost as *distinct from the Father.* See John xiv. 16, 17. 26; xv. 26; xvi. 7—11; xx. 22. Comp. Acts v. 32. The offence, therefore, being against him who was *sent* by the Father, who was appointed to a particular work, clearly supposes that the Holy Spirit is distinct from the Father. (4.) A farther incidental proof of this may be found in the fact that the sin here committed was one of peculiar magnitude; so great as to be deemed worthy of the immediate and signal vengeance of God. Yet the sin against the Holy Ghost is uniformly represented to be of this description Comp. Matt. xii. 31, 32. Mark iii. 28, 29 As these sins evidently coincide in enormity, it is clear that the same class of sins is referred to in both places; or, in other words, the sin of Ananias was against the third person of the Trinity.—Two remarks may be made here. (1.) The Holy Ghost is a distinct person from the Father and the Son; or, in other words, there is a distinction of some kind in the Divine nature that may be denominated by the word *person.* This is clear from the fact that *sin* is said to have been committed against him; a sin which it was supposed could not be detected. *Sin*

keep [a] back *part* of the price of the land?

4 Whiles it remained, was it not thine own? and after it was sold, was it not in thine own power? Why hast thou conceived this thing in thine heart? Thou hast not lied unto men, but [b] unto God.

5 And Ananias, hearing these words, [c] fell down, and gave up the ghost: and great [d] fear came on all them that heard these things.

a Nu.30.2. De.23.21. Ec.5.4. b Ps.139.4. c ver.10,11. d Ps.64.9.

---

cannot be committed against an *attribute* of God, or an *influence* from God. We cannot *lie unto* an attribute, or against wisdom, or power, or goodness; nor can we *lie unto* an *influence*, merely, of the Most High. Sin is committed against a *Being*, not against an *attribute;* and as a sin is here charged on Ananias against *the Holy Ghost*, it follows that the Holy Ghost has a *personal* existence; or there is such a distinction in the Divine essence as that it may be proper to *specify* a sin as committed peculiarly against him. In the same way sin may be represented as committed peculiarly against the *Father*, when his *name* is blasphemed; when his *dominion* is denied; when his *mercy* in sending his Son is called in question. Sin may be represented as committed against *the Son*, when his atonement is denied, his divinity assailed, his character derided, or his invitations slighted. And thus sin may be represented as committed against *the Holy Ghost* when his office of renewing the heart, or sanctifying the soul, is called in question, or when *his* work is ascribed to some malign or other influence. See Mark iii. 22—30. And as sin against the Son proves that he is in some sense distinct from *the Father*, so does sin against the Holy Ghost prove that in some sense he is distinct from the Father and the Son. (2.) The Holy Ghost is divine. This is proved, because he is represented here as being able to search the heart, and to detect insincerity and hypocrisy. Comp. Jer. xvii. 10. 1 Chron. xxviii. 9. 1 Cor. ii. 10. "The Spirit searcheth all things, yea, the deep things of God." Rev. ii. 23. And he is expressly *called* God. See Note on ver. 4.

4. *Whiles it remained.* As long as it remained unsold. This place proves that there was no *obligation* imposed on the disciples to *sell* their property. They who did it, did it voluntarily; and it does not appear that it was done by all, or expected to be done by all. ¶ *And after it was sold,* &c. Even after the property was *sold*, and Ananias had the money, still there was no obligation on him to devote it in this way. He had the disposal of it still. The apostle mentions this to show him that his offence was peculiarly aggravated. He was not *compelled* to sell his property; and he had not even the poor pretence that he was *obliged* to dispose of it, and was *tempted* to withhold it for his own use. It was *all* his, and might have been retained if he had chosen. ¶ *Thou hast not lied unto men.* Unto men *only*, or, it is not your *main* and *chief* offence that you have attempted to deceive men. It is true that Ananias *had* attempted to deceive the apostles, and it is true also that this was a crime; but still, the principal magnitude of the offence was that he had attempted to deceive *God.* So small was his crime as committed against *men*, that it was lost sight of by the apostles; and the great, crowning sin of attempting to deceive *God* was brought fully into view. Thus David also saw his sin as committed against *God* to be so enormous, that he lost sight of it as an offence to man, and said, "Against thee, *thee* ONLY, have I sinned, and done this evil in *thy* sight." Ps. li. 4. ¶ *But unto God.* It has been *particularly* and *eminently* against God. This is true, because, (1.) He had professedly *devoted* it to God. The act, therefore, had express and direct reference to him. (2.) It was an attempt to deceive him. It implied the belief of Ananias that God would not detect the crime, or see the motives of the heart. (3.) It is the prerogative of God to judge of sincerity and hypocrisy; and this was a case, therefore, which came under his special notice. Comp. Ps. cxxxix. 1—4.—The word *God* here is evidently used in its plain and obvious sense, as denoting the *supreme divinity;* and the use of the word here shows that the Holy Ghost is *divine;* and the whole passage demonstrates, therefore, one of the important doctrines of the Christian religion, that the Holy Ghost is distinct from the Father and the Son, and yet is divine.

5. *And Ananias, hearing these words,* &c. Seeing that his guilt was known; and being charged with the enormous crime of attempting to deceive God. He had not expected to be thus exposed; and it is clear that the exposure and the charge came upon him unexpectedly and terri-

6 And the young men arose, wound [a] him up, and carried *him* out, and buried *him*.
7 And it was about the space of three hours after, when his wife, not knowing what was done, came in.
8 And Peter answered unto her, Tell me whether ye sold the land

a Jno.19.40.

bly, like a bolt of thunder. ¶ *Fell down.* Greek, Having fallen down. ¶ *Gave up the ghost.* This is an unhappy translation. The original means simply, *he expired,* or *he died.* Comp. Note, Matt. xxvii. 50. This remarkable fact may be accounted for in this way: (1.) It is evidently to be regarded as a *judgment* of God for the sin of Ananias and his wife. It was not the act of Peter, but of God; and was clearly designed to show his abhorrence of this sin. (See remarks on ver. 11. (2.) Though it was the act of God, yet it does not follow that it was not in connexion with the usual laws by which he governs men, or that he did not make use of natural means to do it. The sin was one of great aggravation. It was suddenly and unexpectedly detected. The fact that it was known; the solemn charge that he had *lied unto God;* struck him with horror. His conscience would reprove him for the enormity of his crime, and overwhelm him at the memory of his act of wickedness. These circumstances may be sufficient to account for this remarkable event. It has occurred in other cases that the consciousness of crime, or the fact of being suddenly detected, has given such a shock to the frame that it has never recovered from it. The effect *commonly* is that the memory of guilt preys secretly and silently upon the frame, until, worn out with the want of rest and peace, it sinks exhausted into the grave. But there have not been wanting instances where the shock has been so great as to destroy the vital powers at once, and plunge the wretched man, like Ananias, into eternity. It is not at all improbable that the shock in the case of Ananias was so great as at once to take his life. ¶ *Great fear came,* &c. Such a striking and awful judgment on insincerity and hypocrisy was fitted to excite awful emotions among the people. Sudden death always does it; but sudden death in immediate connexion with crime, is fitted much more deeply to affect the mind.

6. *And the young men.* The youth of the congregation; very probably young men who were in attendance as *servants,* or those whose business it was to attend on the congregation, and perform various offices when Christians celebrated their worship. (*Mosheim.*) The word used here sometimes denotes a *servant.* It is used also, ver. 10, to denote *soldiers,* as they were commonly enlisted of the vigorous and young. The fact that they took up Ananias voluntarily, implies that they were accustomed to perform offices of servitude to the congregation. ¶ *Wound him up.* It was the usual custom with the Jews to wind the body up in many folds of linen before it was buried, commonly also with spices, to preserve it from putrefaction. See Notes on John xi. 44. It may be asked *why* he was so soon buried; and especially why he was hurried away without giving information to his wife. In reply to this, it may be remarked, 1. That it does not appear from the narrative that it was *known* that Sapphira was privy to the transaction, or was near at hand, or even that he had a wife. Ananias came *himself* and offered the money; and the judgment fell at once on him. 2. It was customary among the ancient Persians to bury the body almost immediately after death (*Jahn*); and it seems probable that the Jews, when the body was not embalmed, imitated the custom. It would also appear that this was an ancient custom among the Jews. See Gen. xxiii. 19; xxv. 9; xxxv. 29; xlviii. 7. 1 Kings xiii. 30. Different nations differ in their customs in burying the dead; and there is no impropriety in committing a body soon after death to the tomb. 3. There might have been some danger of an excitement and tumult in regard to this scene, if the corpse had not soon been removed; and as no valuable purpose could be answered by delaying the burial, the body was decently committed to the dust.

7. *And it was about the space,* &c. As Sapphira had been no less guilty than her husband, so it was ordered in the providence of God, that the same judgment should come upon both.

8. *For so much.* That is, for the sum which Ananias had presented. This was true, that this sum had been received for it; but it was also true that a larger sum had been received. It is as really a falsehood to deceive in this manner, as it would have been to have affirmed that they received much *more* than they actually did for the land. Falsehood consists in making an erroneous representation of

for so much? And she said, Yea, for so much.

9 Then Peter said unto her, How is it that ye have agreed [a] together to tempt the Spirit of the Lord? Behold, the feet of them which have buried thy husband *are* at the door, and shall carry thee out.

a Ps.50.18. ver.3.

a thing in any way for the purpose of deceiving. And *this* species is much more common than an open and bold lie, declaring what is in no sense true.

9. *Agreed together*. Conspired, or laid a plan. From this it seems that Sapphira was as guilty as her husband. ¶ *To tempt*. To try; to endeavour to impose on, or to deceive; that is, to act as if the Spirit of the Lord could not detect the crime. They did this by trying to see whether the Spirit of God could detect hypocrisy. ¶ *At the door*. Are near at hand. They had not yet returned. The dead were buried without the walls of cities; and this space of three hours, it seems, had elapsed before they returned from the burial. ¶ *Shall carry thee out*. This passage shows that it was by divine interposition or judgment that their lives were taken. The judgment was in immediate connexion with their crime, and was designed as an expression of the divine displeasure.

If it be asked here, *why* Ananias and Sapphira were punished in this severe and awful manner, an answer may be found in the following considerations: (1.) This was an atrocious crime; a deep and dreadful act of iniquity. It was committed knowingly, and without excuse. ver. 4. It was important that sudden and exemplary punishment should follow it, because the society of Christians was just then organized, and it was designed that it should be a *pure* society, and be regarded as a body of holy men. Much was gained by making this *impression* on the people, that sin could not be allowed in this new community, but would be detected and punished. (2.) God has often in a most solemn manner showed his abhorrence of hypocrisy and insincerity. By awful declarations and fearful judgments he has declared his displeasure at it. In a particular manner no small part of the preaching of the Saviour was employed in detecting the hypocrisy of the scribes and Pharisees, and denouncing heavy judgments on them. See the xxiiid chapter of Matthew throughout, for the most sublime and awful denunciation of hypocrisy any where to be found. Comp. Mark xii. 15. Luke xii. 1. 1 Tim. iv. 2. Job viii. 13; xiii. 16; xv. 34; xx. 5; xxxvi. 3. Matt. vii. 5. Luke xi. 44. In the very beginning of the Christian church, therefore, it was important, by a decided and awful act, to *impress* upon the church and the world the danger and guilt of hypocrisy. Well did the Saviour know that it would be one of the most insidious and deadly foes to the purity of the church; and at its very *threshold*, therefore, he set up this solemn warning to guard it; and laid the bodies of Ananias and Sapphira in the path of every hypocrite that would enter the church. If they enter and are destroyed, they cannot plead that they were not fully warned. If they practise iniquity *in* the church, they cannot plead ignorance of the fact that God intends to detect and punish them. (3.) The apostles were just then establishing their authority. They claimed to be under the influence of inspiration. To establish that, it was necessary to show that they could know the views and motives of those who became connected with the church. If easily imposed on, it would go far to destroy their authority and their claim to infallibility. If they showed that they could detect hypocrisy, even where most artfully concealed, it would establish the divine authority of their message. At the *commencement* of their work, therefore, they gave this decisive and most awful proof that they were under the guidance of an infallible Teacher. (4.) This case does not stand alone in the New Testament. It is clear from other instances that the apostles had the power of punishing sinners, and that a violation of the commands of Christ was attended by sudden and fearful judgments. See 1 Cor. xi. 30. See the case of Elymas the sorcerer, in Acts xiii. 8—11. (5.) Neither does this event stand alone in the history of the world. Acts of judgment sometimes occur as sudden and decided, in the providence of God, as in this case. The profane man, the drunkard, the profligate is sometimes as suddenly stricken down as in this instance. Cases have not been uncommon where the blasphemer has been smitten in death with the curse on his lips; and God often thus comes forth in judgment to slay the wicked, and to show that there is a God that reigns in the earth. This narrative cannot be objected to as improbable until *all* such cases are disposed of; nor can this inflic-

10 Then [a] fell she down straightway at his feet, and yielded up the ghost: and the young men came in and found her dead, and, carrying *her* forth, buried *her* by her husband.

11 And [b] great fear came upon all the church, and upon as many as heard these things.
12 And by the hands of the apostles were [c] many signs and wonders
wrought among the people; (and

a ver.5. b c.2.43. c c.4.30. Ro.15.19. He.2.4.

tion be regarded as unjust, until all the instances where men die by remorse of conscience, or by the direct judgment of heaven, are *proved* to be unjust also.

In view of this narrative, we may remark, (1.) That God searches the heart, and knows the purposes of the soul. Comp. Ps. cxxxix. (2.) God judges the *motives* of men. It is not so much the *external* act, as it is the views and feelings by which it is prompted, that determines the character of the act. (3.) God will bring forth sin that man may not be able to detect; or that may elude human justice. The day is coming when the secrets of all hearts shall be revealed, and God will reward every man according as his works shall be. (4.) Fraud and hypocrisy will be detected. They are often revealed in this life. The providence of God often lays them open to human view, and overwhelms the soul in shame at the guilt which was long concealed. But if not in this life, yet the day is coming when they will be disclosed, and the sinner shall stand *revealed* to an assembled universe. (5.) We have here an illustration of the powers of conscience. If *such* was its overwhelming effect *here*, what will it be when *all* the crimes of the life shall be disclosed in the day of judgment, and when the soul shall sink to the woes of hell. Through *eternity* the conscience shall do its office; and these terrible inflictions shall go on from age to age, for ever and ever, in the dark world of hell. (6.) We see here the guilt of attempting to impose on God in regard to *property*. There is no subject in which men are more liable to hypocrisy; none in which they are more apt to keep back a *part*. Christians professedly devote ALL that they have, to God. They profess to believe that God has a *right* to the silver and the gold, and the cattle on a thousand hills. Ps. l. 10. Their *property*, as well as heir bodies and their spirits, they have devoted to him; and profess to desire to employ it as *he* shall direct and please. And yet, is it not clear, that the sin of Ananias has not ceased in the church? How many professing Christians there are, who give *nothing* really to God; who contribute nothing for the poor and needy; who give nothing, or next to nothing, to any purposes of benevolence; who would devote "millions" for their own gratification, and their families, "but not a cent for *tribute*" to God. The case of Ananias is, to all such, a case of most fearful warning. And on no point should Christians more faithfully examine themselves than in regard to the professed devotion of their *property* to God. If God punished this sin in the beginning of the Christian church, he will do it still in its progress, and in nothing have professed Christians more to fear the wrath of God, than on this very subject. (7.) Sinners should fear and tremble before God. He holds their breath in his hands. He can cut them down in an instant. The bold blasphemer, the unjust, the liar, the scoffer, he can destroy in a moment, and sink them in all the woes of hell. Nor have they security that he will not do it. The profane man has no evidence that he will live to finish the curse which he has begun; nor the drunkard, that he will again become sober; nor the seducer that God will not arrest him in his act of wickedness, and send him down to hell! The sinner walks over his grave, and over hell! In an instant he may die, and be summoned to the judgment-seat of God! How awful it is to sin in a world like this; and how fearful the doom which *must* soon overtake the ungodly.

12. *And by the hands*, &c. By the apostles. This verse should be read in connexion with the 15th, to which it belongs. ¶ *Signs and wonders.* Miracles. See Note, Acts ii. 43. ¶ *With one accord.* With one *mind*, or intention. Note, ch. i. 14. ¶ *In Solomon's porch.* See Notes, Matt. xxi. 12. John x. 23. They were doubtless there for the purpose of worship. It does not mean that they were there constantly but at the regular periods of worship Probably they had two designs in this one was, to join in the public worship of God in the usual manner with the people, for they did not design to leave the temple-service; the other was, that they might have opportunity to preach to the people assembled there. In the presence of the great multitudes who came up to worship, they had an opportunity of mak

they were all with one accord in Solomon's porch.

13 And [a] of the rest durst no man join himself to them, but [b] the people magnified them.

14 And believers were the more added to the Lord, multitudes [c] both of men and women;)

15 Insomuch that they brought forth the sick [1] into the streets, and laid *them* on beds and couches, that at the least the shadow of Peter

a Jno.12.42. b c.4.21. c c.2.47. 1 or, *in every street.*

ng known the doctrines of Jesus, and of confirming them by miracles, the reality of which could not be denied, and which could not be resisted, as proofs that Jesus was the Messiah.

13. *And of the rest.* Different interpretations have been given of this expression. Lightfoot supposes that by *the rest* are meant the remainder of the one hundred and twenty disciples of whom Ananias had been one; and that they feared to put themselves on an equality with the apostles. But this interpretation seems to be far-fetched. Kuinoel supposes that by *the rest* are meant those who had not already joined with the apostles, whether Christians or Jews, and that they were deterred by the fate of Ananias. Pricæus, Morus, Rosenmueller, Schleusner, &c. suppose that by *the rest* are meant the *rich* men, or the men of authority and influence among the Jews, of whom Ananias was one, and that they were deterred from it by the fate of Ananias. This is by far the most probable opinion, because, (1.) There is an evident contrast between them and the people; *the rest,* i. e. the others of the rich and great, feared to join with them; but *the people,* the common people, magnified them. (2.) The fate of Ananias was fitted to have this effect on the rich and great. (3.) Similar instances had occurred before, that the great, though they believed on Jesus, yet were afraid to come forth publicly and profess him before men. See John xii. 42, 43; v. 44. (4.) The phrase *the rest* denotes sometimes that which is more excellent, or which is superior in value or importance to something else. See Luke xii. 26. ¶ *Join himself.* Become united to, or associated with. The rich and the great then, as now, stood aloof from them, and were deterred by fear or shame from professing attachment to the Lord Jesus. ¶ *But the people.* The mass of the people; the body of the nation. ¶ *Magnified them* Honoured them; regarded them with reverence and fear.

14 *And believers.* This is the name by which Christians were designated, because one of the main things that distinguished them was that they *believed* that Jesus was the Christ. It is also an incidental proof that none should join themselves to the church who are not *believers.* i. e. who do not profess to be Christians in heart and in life. ¶ *Were the more added.* The effect of all things was to increase the number of converts. Their persecutions, their preaching, and the judgment of God, *all* tended to impress the minds of the people, and to lead them to the Lord Jesus Christ. Comp. ch. iv. 4. Though the judgment of God had the effect of deterring hypocrites from entering the church; though it produced awe and caution; yet still, the number of true converts was increased. An effort to keep the church pure by wholesome discipline. by cutting off unworthy members, however rich or honoured, so far from weakening its true strength, has a tendency greatly to increase its numbers as well as its purity. Men will not seek to enter a corrupt church; or regard it as worth any thought to be connected with a society that does not endeavour to be pure. ¶ *Multitudes.* Comp. ch. iv. 4.

15. *Insomuch.* So that. This should be connected with ver. 12. Many miracles were wrought by the apostles, *insomuch,* &c. ¶ *They brought forth.* The people, or the friends of the sick, brought them forth. ¶ *Beds.* κλινῶν. This word denotes usually the *soft* and *valuable* beds on which the rich commonly lay. And it means that the rich, as well as the poor, were laid in the path of Peter and the other apostles. ¶ *Couches.* κραββάτων. The coarse and hard couches on which the poor used to lie. Mark ii. 4. 9. 11, 12; vi. 55. John v. 8—12. Acts ix. 33. ¶ *The shadow of Peter.* That is, they were laid in the path so that the shadow of Peter, as he walked, might pass over them. Perhaps the sun was near setting, and the lengthened shadow of Peter might be thrown afar across the way. They were not able to approach him on account of the crowd; and they *imagined* that if they could *any how* come under his influence, they might be healed. The sacred writer does not say, however, that any *were* healed in this way; nor that they were commanded to do this. He simply states the *impression* which was on the minds of the people that it *might be*

passing by might overshadow some of them.

16 There came also a multitude *out* of the cities round about unto Jerusalem, bringing [a] sick folks, and them which were vexed with unclean spirits: and [b] they were healed every one.

17 Then the high-priest rose up, and all they that were with him, (which is the sect of the Sadducees,) [c] and were filled with [1] indignation,

a Mar.16.17,18. Jno.14.12. b Ja.5.16. c c.4.1,2. 1 or, *envy*.

Whether they were healed by this, it is left for us merely to conjecture. An instance somewhat similar is recorded in Acts xix. 12, where it is expressly said that the sick were healed by contact with *handkerchiefs* and *aprons* that were brought from the body of Paul. Comp. also Matt. ix. 21, 22, where the woman said respecting Jesus, "If I may but touch his garment, I shall be whole." ¶ *Might overshadow.* That his shadow might pass over them. Though there is no evidence that any were healed in this way, yet it shows the full belief of the people that Peter had the power of working miracles. *Peter* was supposed by them to be eminently endowed with this power, because it was by him that the lame man in the temple had been healed (ch. iii. 4—6), and because he had been most prominent in his addresses to the people. The persons who are specified in this verse were those who dwelt at Jerusalem.

16. *There came also, &c.* Attracted by the fame of Peter's miracles, as the people formerly had been by the miracles of the Lord Jesus. ¶ *Vexed.* Troubled, afflicted, or tormented. ¶ *Unclean spirits.* Possessed with devils; called *unclean* because they prompted to sin and impurity of life. See Notes on Matt. iv. 23, 24. ¶ *And they were healed.* Of these persons it is expressly affirmed that they were healed. Of those who were so laid as that the shadow of Peter might pass over them, there is no such affirmation.

17. *Then the high-priest.* Probably *Caiaphas.* Comp. John xi. 49. It seems from this place that he belonged to the sect of the Sadducees. It is certain that he had signalized himself by opposition to the Lord Jesus and to his cause, constantly. ¶ *Rose up.* This expression is sometimes *redundant,* and at others it means simply to *begin* to do a thing, or to resolve to do it. Comp. Luke xv. 18. ¶ *And all they that were with him.* That is, all they that coincided with him in doctrine or opinion; or in other words, that portion of the sanhedrim that was composed of *Sadducees.* There was a strong party of Sadducees in the sanhedrim; and perhaps at this time it was so strong a majority as to be able to control its decisions. Comp. Acts xxiii. 6. ¶ *Which is the sect.* The word translated *sect* here is that from which we have derived our word *heresy.* It means simply *sect,* or *party,* and is not used in a bad sense as implying reproach, or even error. The idea which *we* attach to it of error, and of denying fundamental doctrines in religion, is one that does not occur in the New Testament. ¶ *Sadducees.* See Notes, Matt. iii. 7. The main doctrine of this sect was the denial of the resurrection of the dead. The reason why *they* were particularly opposed to the apostles, rather than the Pharisees, was that the apostles dwelt much on the *resurrection of the Lord Jesus,* which, if true, completely overthrew their doctrine. All the converts, therefore, that were made to Christianity, tended to diminish their numbers and influence; and also to establish the belief of the *Pharisees* in the doctrine of the resurrection. So long, therefore, as the effect of the labours of the apostles was to establish one of the main doctrines of the *Pharisees,* and to confute the *Sadducees,* so long we may suppose that the *Pharisees* would either favour them or be silent; and so long the *Sadducees* would be opposed to them, and enraged against them. One sect will often see with composure the progress of another that it really hates, if it will humble a rival. Even opposition to the gospel will sometimes be silent, provided the spread of religion will tend to humble and mortify those against whom we may be opposed. ¶ *Were filled with indignation.* Greek, *Zeal.* The word denotes any kind of *fervour* or *warmth,* and may be applied to *any* warm or violent affection of the mind, either *envy, wrath, zeal,* or *love.* Acts xiii. 45. John ii. 17. Rom. x. 2. 2 Co vii. 7; xi. 2. Here it probably *includes envy* and *wrath.* They were *envious* at the success of the apostles; at the number of converts that were made to a doctrine that they hated; they were envious that the *Pharisees* were deriving such an accession of strength to their doctrine of the resurrection; and they were *indignant* that they regarded so little their

18 And laid their hands on the apostles, and put them in the common prison.[a]

19 But the angel of the Lord by night opened the prison doors, and brought them forth, and said,

20 Go, stand and speak in the temple to the people all[b] the words[c] of this life.

21 And when they heard *that*, they entered into the temple early in the morning, and taught. But[d] the high-priest came, and they that were with him, and called the council together, and all the senate of the children of Israel, and sent to the prison to have them brought.

22 But when the officers came, and found them not in the prison, they returned and told,

23 Saying, The prison truly found we shut with all safety, and the keepers standing without before the doors: but when we had opened, we found no man within.

24 Now when the high-priest and[e] the captain of the temple and the chief priests heard these things, they doubted of them whereunto this would grow.

a c.12.5-7;16.23-27. b Ex.24.3. c Jno.6.63,68;17.8. d c.4.5,6. e c.4.1.

authority, and disobeyed the solemn injunction of the sanhedrim. Comp. ch. iv. 18—21.

18. *The common prison.* The public prison; or the prison for the keeping of common and notorious offenders.

19. *But the angel of the Lord.* This does not denote any *particular* angel, but simply *an* angel. The *article* is not used in the original. The word *angel* denotes properly a *messenger*, and particularly it is applied to the pure spirits that are sent to this world on errands of mercy. See Note, Matt. i. 20. The case here was evidently *a miracle.* An angel was employed for this special purpose; and the design might have been, (1.) To reprove the Jewish rulers, and to convince them of their guilt in resisting the gospel of God; (2.) To convince the apostles more firmly of the protection and approbation of God; (3.) To encourage them more and more in their work, and in the faithful discharge of their high duty; and (4.) To give the people a new and impressive proof of the truth of the message which they bore. That they were *imprisoned* would be known to the people. That they were made as secure as possible, was also known. When, therefore, the next morning, before they could have been tried or acquitted, they were found again in the temple, delivering the same message still, it was a new and striking proof that they were sent by God.

20. *In the temple.* In a public and conspicuous place. In this way there would be a most striking exhibition of their boldness; a proof that *God* had delivered them: and a manifestation of their purpose to obey God rather than man. ¶ *All the words.* All the *doctrines.* Comp. John vi. 68, "Thou hast *the words* of eternal life." ¶ *Of this life.* Pertaining to life, to the eternal life which they taught through the resurrection and life of Jesus. The word *life* is used sometimes to express the whole of religion, as opposed to the spiritual *death* of sin. See John i. 4; iii. 36. Their deliverance from prison was not that they might be idle, and escape to a place of safety. Again they were to engage at once in the toils, and perils, which they had just before encountered. God delivers us from danger sometimes that we may plunge into *new* dangers; he preserves us from calamity that we may be tried in some new furnace of affliction; and he calls us to encounter trials simply *because* he demands it, and as an expression of gratitude to him for his gracious interposition.

21. *Early in the morning.* Greek, At the break of day. Comp. Luke xxiv. 1. John viii. 2. ¶ *Called the council together.* The sanhedrim, or the great council of the nation This was clearly for the purpose of *trying* the apostles for disregarding their commandments. ¶ *And all the senate.* Greek, *Eldership.* Probably these were not a part of the sanhedrim, but were men of age and experience, who in ch. iv. 8, xxv. 15, are called *elders of the Jews*, and who were present for the sake of counsel and advice in a case of emergency.

23. *Found we shut.* It had not been broken open; and there was therefore clear proof that they had been delivered by the interposition of God. Nor could they have been released by the guard, for they were keeping watch, as if unconscious that any thing had happened and the officers had the only means of entering the prison.

24. *The captain of the temple.* See

25 Then came one and told them,
saying, Behold, the men whom ye
put in prison are standing in the
temple, and teaching the people.
26 Then went the captain with
the officers, and brought them without
violence: for [a] they feared the
people, lest they should have been
stoned.
27 And when they had brought
them, they set *them* before the council:
and the high-priest asked them,
28 Saying, Did not we [b] straitly
command you, that ye should not
teach in this name? and, behold,
ye have filled Jerusalem with your
doctrine, and intend to bring this
man's blood [c] upon us.
29 Then Peter and the *other* apostles
answered and said, We [d] ought
to obey God rather than men.
30 The God of our fathers raised

a Matt.21.26. b c.4.18. c Matt.27.25. c.2.23,36; 3.15; 7.52. d c.4.19.

Notes, ch. iv. 1. ¶ *Doubted of them.* They were in *perplexity* about these things. The word rendered *doubted* denotes that state of anxiety which arises when a man *has lost his way*, or when he does not know what to do to escape from a difficulty. See Luke ix. 7. ¶ *Whereunto this would grow.* What this *would be*; or what would be the result or end of these events. For (1.) Their authority was disregarded; (2.) God had opposed them by a miracle; (3.) The doctrines of the apostles were gaining ground; (4.) Their efforts to oppose them had been in vain. They need *not* have doubted; but sinners are not disposed to be convinced of the truth of religion.

26. *Without violence.* Not by force; not by *binding* them. Comp. Matt. xxvii. 2. The command of the sanhedrim was sufficient to secure their presence, as they did not intend to refuse to answer for any alleged violation of the laws. Besides, their going before the council would give them another noble opportunity to bear witness to the truth of the gospel. Christians, when charged with a violation of the laws of the land, should not refuse to answer. Acts xxv. 11, "If I be an offender, or have committed any thing worthy of death, I refuse not to die." It is a part of our religion to yield obedience to all the just laws of the land, and to evince respect for all that are in authority. Rom. xiii. 1—7. ¶ *For they feared the people.* The people were favourable to the apostles. If violence had been attempted, or they had been taken in a cruel and forcible manner, the consequence would have been a tumult, and bloodshed. In this way, also, the apostles showed that they were not disposed to excite tumult. Opposition by them would have excited commotion; and though *they* would have been rescued, yet they resolved to show that they were not obstinate, contumacious, or rebellious, but were disposed, as far as it could be done with a clear conscience, to yield obedience to the laws of the land.

28. *Straitly command you.* Did we not command you with *a threat?* ch. iv. 17 18. 21. ¶ *In this name.* In the name of Jesus. ¶ *Ye have filled Jerusalem.* This though not so designed, was an honourable tribute to the zeal and fidelity of the apostles. When Christians are arraigned or persecuted, it is well if the only charge which their enemies can bring against them is that they have been distinguished for zeal and success in propagating their religion. See 1 Pet. iv. 16, "If any man suffer as a Christian, let him not be ashamed, but let him glorify God on this behalf." Also ver. 13—15. ¶ *Intend to bring this man's blood upon us.* To bring *one's blood* upon another is a phrase denoting to hold or to prove him guilty of murdering the innocent. The expression here charges them with designing to prove that they had put Jesus to death when he was innocent; to convince *the people* of this, and thus to enrage them against the sanhedrim; and also to prove that they were guilty, and were exposed to the divine vengeance for having put the Messiah to death. Comp. ch. ii. 23 36 iii. 15; vii. 52. That the apostles *did* intend to charge them with being guilty of murder, is clear; but it is observable that on *this occasion* they had said nothing of this; and it is further observable that they did not charge it on them *except in their presence.* See the places just referred to. They took no pains to spread this among the people, *except as the people were accessary to the crime of the rulers.* ch. ii. 23. 36. Their consciences were not at ease, and the remembrance of the death of Jesus would occur to them at once at the sight of the apostles.

29. *We ought to obey,* &c. See Note, ch. iv. 19.

30 *Raised up Jesus.* This refers to his

up Jesus, whom ye slew and hanged [a] on a tree.
31 Him hath God exalted [b] with his right hand *to be* a [c] Prince and a [d] Saviour, for to give repentance to Israel, and forgiveness of sins

a Ga.3 13. 1Pet.2.24. b Ph.2.9. c Is.9.6. d Matt.1.21.

resurrection. ¶ *Hanged on a tree.* That is, on the *cross*. Gal. iii. 13. 1 Pet. ii. 24. Acts x. 39; xiii. 29. This is the amount of Peter's defence. He begins with the great principle (ver. 29), which they could not gainsay, that God ought to be obeyed rather than man. He then proceeds to state that they were convinced that God had raised up Jesus from the dead. And as they had such decisive evidence of that, and were commanded by the authority of the Lord Jesus to be *witnesses of that*, and had constant evidence that God had done it, they were not *at liberty* to be silent. They were bound to obey God rather than the sanhedrim, and to make known every where the fact that the Lord Jesus was risen. The remark that God had raised up Jesus whom they had *slain*, does not seem to have been made to irritate or to reproach them, but mainly to *identify* the person that had been raised. It was also a confirmation of the truth and reality of the miracle. Of his *death* they had no doubt, for they had been at pains to certify it. John xix. 31—34. It is certain, however, that Peter did not shrink from charging on them their guilt; nor was he at any pains to *soften* or *mitigate* the severe charge that they had murdered their own Messiah.

31. *Him hath God exalted.* See Note, ch. ii. 33. ¶ *To be a Prince.* ἀρχηγόν. See Note, Acts iii. 15. In that place he is called *the Prince of life.* Here it means that he is actually in the *exercise* of the office of a prince or a king, at the right hand of his Father. The title *Prince*, or *King*, was one which was well known as applied to the Messiah. It denotes that he has *dominion* and *power*, especially the power which is needful to give repentance and the pardon of sins. ¶ *A Saviour.* See Note, Matt. i. 21. ¶ *To give repentance.* The word *repentance* here is equivalent to *reformation*, and a change of life. The expression here does not differ from what is said in ch. iii. 26. ¶ *To Israel.* This word properly denotes the *Jews;* but his office was not to be confined to the Jews. Other passages show that it would be also extended to the *Gentiles*. The reasons why the *Jews* are particularly specified here are, probably, (1.) Because the Messiah was long promised to the Jewish people, and his first work was there; and (2.) Because Peter was addressing Jews, and was particularly desirous of leading *them* to repentance. ¶ *Forgiveness of sins.* Pardon of sin; the act which can be performed by God only. Mark ii. 7.

If it be asked, in what sense the Lord Jesus *gives repentance*, or how his *exaltation* is connected with it, we may answer, (1.) His exaltation is evidence that his work was accepted, and thus a foundation is laid by which repentance is available, and may be connected with pardon. Unless there was some way of *forgiveness*, sorrow for sin would be of no value, even if exercised. The relentings of a culprit condemned for murder, would be of no avail unless the executive can *consistently* pardon him; nor would relentings in hell be of avail, for there is no promise of forgiveness. But Jesus Christ by his death has laid a foundation by which repentance *may be* accepted. (2.) He is intrusted with all power in heaven and earth with *reference* to this, to apply his work to men; or in other words, to bring them to repentance. See John xvii. 2. Matt. xxviii. 18. (3.) His exaltation is immediately connected with the bestowment of the Holy Spirit, by whose influence men are brought to repentance. John xvi. 7—11. The Spirit is represented as being *sent* by him as well as by the Father. John xv. 26; xvi. 7. (4.) Jesus has power in this state of exaltation over all things that can affect the mind. He sends his ministers; he directs the events of sickness or disappointment; of health or prosperity; that will influence the heart. There is no doubt that he can so recall the sins of the past life, and refresh the memory, as to overwhelm the soul in the consciousness of guilt. Thus also he can appeal to man by his *goodness*, and by a sense of his mercies; and especially he can so present a view of *his* life and death as to affect the heart, and show the evil of the past life of the sinner. Knowing the heart, he knows all the avenues by which it can be approached; and in an instant he can overwhelm the soul with the remembrance of crime.

It was *proper* that the power of *pardon* should be lodged with the same being that has the power of producing repentance. Because, 1. The one appropriately follows the other 2. They are parts of

32 And we are his witnesses [a] of
these things; and *so is* also the
Holy Ghost, [b] whom God hath
given to them that obey him.
33 When they heard *that*, they [c]
were cut *to the heart* and took counsel to slay them.
34 Then stood there up one in
the council, a Pharisee, named Gamaliel, [d] a doctor of the law, had in

a Lu.24.47. b c.2.4. c c.7.54. d c.22.3.

the same great work, the work which the Saviour came to do, *to remove sin with all its effects from the human soul.* This power of *pardon* Jesus exercised when he was on the earth; and this he can now dispense in the heavens. Mark ii. 9—11.

And from this we may learn, (1.) That Jesus Christ is *divine.* It is a dictate of natural religion that none can forgive sins against God, but God himself. None can pardon but the being who has been offended. And this is also the dictate of the Bible. The power of *pardoning* sin is one that God claims as *his* prerogative; and it is clear that it can appertain to no other. See Isa. xliii. 25. Dan. ix. 9. Ps. cxxx. 4. Yet Jesus Christ exercised this power when on earth; gave *evidence* that the exercise of that power was one that was acceptable to God by working a miracle, and removing the *consequences* of sin with which *God* had visited the sinner (Matt. ix. 6); and exercises it still in heaven. He must, therefore, be divine. (2.) The sinner is dependent on him for the exercise of repentance, and forgiveness. (3.) The proud sinner must be humbled at his feet. He must be willing to come and receive eternal life at *his* hands. No step is more humiliating than this for proud and hardened men; and there is none which they are more reluctant to do. We always shrink from coming into the presence of one whom we have offended; we are extremely reluctant to confess a fault; but it *must be done*, or the soul *must* be lost for ever. (4.) Christ has *power* to pardon the greatest offender. He is exalted for this purpose; and he is fitted to his work. Even his murderers he could pardon; and no sinner need fear that he who is *a Prince and a Saviour at the right hand of God*, is unable to pardon every sin. To him we may come with confidence; and when pressed with the consciousness of the blackest crimes, and when we must feel that we deserve eternal death, we may confidently roll all on his arm.

32. *And we are witnesses.* For this purpose they had been appointed. ch. i. 8. 21, 22; ii. 32; iii. 15. Luke xxiv. 48. ¶ *Of these things.* Particularly of the resurrection of the Lord Jesus, and of the events which had followed it. Perhaps, however, he meant to include every thing pertaining to the life, teachings, and death of the Lord Jesus. ¶ *And so is also, &c.* The descent of the Holy Ghost to endow them with remarkable gifts (ch. ii. 1—4) to awaken and convert such a multitude ch. ii. 41; iv. 4; v. 14), was an unanswerable attestation of the truth of these doctrines, and of the Christian religion. So manifest and decided was the presence of God attending them, that *they* could have no doubt that what they said was true; and so open and public was this attestation, that it was an evidence to all the people of the truth of their doctrine.

33. *When they heard that.* That which the apostle Peter had said, to wit, that they were guilty of murder; that Jesus was raised up; and that he still lived as the Messiah. ¶ *They were cut* to the heart The word used here properly denotes *to cut with a saw;* and as applied to the *mind*, it means to be agitated with *rage* and *indignation*, as if wrath should seize upon the mind as a saw does upon wood, and tear it violently, or agitate it severely. It is commonly used in connexion with *the heart*, and means that the heart is violently agitated, and rent with rage. See ch. vii. 54. It is not used elsewhere in the New Testament. The *reasons* why they were thus indignant were, doubtless, (1.) Because the apostles had disregarded their command; (2.) Because they charged them with murder; (3.) Because they affirmed the doctrine of the resurrection of Jesus, and thus tended to overthrow the sect of the Sadducees. The effect of the doctrines of the gospel is, often, to make men enraged. ¶ *Took counsel.* The word rendered *took counsel* denotes commonly *to will;* then, *to deliberate;* and sometimes, *to decree*, or *to determine.* It doubtless implies here that *their minds were made up* to do it; but probably the formal decree was not passed to put them to death.

34. *There stood up one.* He *rose*, as is usual in deliberative assemblies to speak ¶ *In the council.* In the sanhedrim. ch iv. 15. ¶ *A Pharisee.* The high-priest and those who had been most active in opposing the apostles were Sadducees. The Pharisees were opposed to them,

reputation among all the people,
and commanded to put the apostles
forth a little space:

35 And said unto them, Ye men
of Israel, take heed to yourselves
what ye intend to do as touching
these men.

36 For before these days [1] rose
up Theudas boasting himself to be
somebody; to whom a number of
men, about four hundred, joined
themselves: who was slain; and
all, as many as [2] obeyed him, were
scattered, and brought to nought.

[1] *In the 3d year before the account called A. D.*

[2] *or, believed.*

particularly on the doctrine in regard to which the apostles were so strenuous, the resurrection of the dead. See Note, Matt. iii. 7. Comp. Acts xxiii. 6. ¶ *Gamaliel.* This name was very common among the Jews. Dr. Lightfoot says that this man was the teacher of Paul (Acts xxii. 3), the son of the *Simon* who took the Saviour in his arms (Luke ii.), and the grandson of the famous *Hillel,* and was known among the Jews by the title of *Rabban Gamaliel the elder.* There were other men of this name, who were also eminent among the Jews. This man is said to have died eighteen years before the destruction of Jerusalem, and he died as he had lived, a Pharisee. There is not the least evidence that he was a friend of the Christian religion; but he was evidently a man of far more liberal views than the other members of the sanhedrim. ¶ *A doctor of the law.* That is, a *teacher* of the Jewish law; one whose province it was to *interpret* the laws of Moses, and probably to preserve and transmit the *traditional* laws of the Jews. See Note, Matt. xv. 3. So celebrated was he, that Saul of Tarsus went to Jerusalem to receive the benefit of his instructions. Acts xxii. 3. ¶ *Had in reputation among all the people. Honoured* by all the people. His advice was likely, therefore, to be respected. ¶ *To put the apostles forth.* This was done doubtless, because, if the apostles had been suffered to remain, it was apprehended that they would take fresh courage, and be confirmed in their purposes. It was customary, besides, when they deliberated, to command those accused to retire. ch. iv. 15. ¶ *A little space.* A little *time.* Luke xxii. 58.

36. *For before those days.* The *advice* of Gamaliel was to suffer these men to go on. The *arguments* by which he enforced his advice were, (1.) That there were *cases* or *precedents* in point (ver. 36, 37); and (2.) That *if* it should turn out *to be* of God, it would be a solemn affair to be involved in the consequences of opposing him. How long before *these days* this transaction occurred, cannot now be determined, as it is not certain to what case Gamaliel refers. ¶ *Rose up.* That is, commenced or excited an insurrection, ¶ *Theudas.* This was a name quite common among the Jews. Of this man nothing more is known than is here recorded. Josephus (Antiq. b. xx. ch. v.) mentions one *Theudas,* in the time of *Fadus* the procurator of Judea, in the reign of the emperor Claudius (A. D. 45 or 46), who persuaded a great part of the people to take their effects with him and follow him to the river Jordan. He told them he was a prophet, and that he would divide the river, and lead them over. Fadus, however, came suddenly upon them, and slew many of them. Theudas was taken alive and conveyed to Jerusalem, and there beheaded. But this occurred at least ten or fifteen years after this discourse of Gamaliel. Many efforts have been made to reconcile Luke and Josephus, on the supposition that they refer to the same man. Lightfoot supposed that Josephus had made an error in chronology But there is no reason to suppose that there is reference to the same event; and the fact that Josephus has not recorded the insurrection referred to by Gamaliel, does not militate at all against the account in the Acts. For, (1.) Luke, for any thing that appears to the contrary, is quite as credible an historian as Josephus. (2.) The name *Theudas* was a common name among the Jews; and there is no improbability that there were *two* leaders of an insurrection of this name. If it *is* improbable, the improbability would affect Josephus's credit as much as that of Luke. (3.) It is altogether improbable that *Gamaliel* should refer to a case which was not well authenticated; and that Luke should record a speech of this kind unless it was delivered, when it would be so easy to detect the error. (4.) Josephus has recorded many instances of insurrection and revolt. He has represented the country as in an unsettled state, and by no means professes to give an account of *all* that occurred. Thus he says (Antiq. xvii. x. § 4) that there were "at this time *ten thousand* other disorders in Judea;'

37 After this man, rose up Judas
of Galilee, in the days of the taxing, and drew away much people
after him: he [a] also perished; and
all, *even* as many as obeyed him,
were dispersed.

38 And now I say unto you, Refrain from these men, and let them

a Lu.13.1 2.

and (§ 8) that "Judea was full of robberies." When this *Theudas* lived, cannot be ascertained; but as Gamaliel mentions him before Judas of Galilee, it is probable that he lived not far from the time that our Saviour was born; at a time when many false prophets appeared, claiming to be the Messiah. ¶ *Boasting himself to be somebody.* Claiming to be an eminent prophet probably, or the Messiah. ¶ *Obeyed him.* The word used here is the one commonly used to denote *belief.* As many as *believed* on him, or gave credit to his pretensions.

37. *Judas of Galilee.* Josephus has given an account of this man (Antiq. b. xvii. ch. x. § 5), and calls him a *Galilean.* He afterwards calls him a *Gaulonite,* and says he was of the city of *Gamala* (Antiq. xviii. i. 1). In this place, he says that the revolt took place under *Cyrenius,* a Roman senator, who came into "Syria to be judge of that nation, and to take account of their substance." "Moreover," says he, "Cyrenius came himself into Judea, which was now added to the province of Syria, to take an account of their substance, and to dispose of Archelaus's money." "Yet Judas, taking with him Saddouk, a Pharisee, became zealous to draw them to a revolt, who both said that this taxation was no better than an introduction to slavery, and exhorted the nation to assert their liberty," &c. *This* revolt, he says, was the commencement of the series of revolts and calamities that terminated in the destruction of the city, temple, and nation ¶ *In the days of the taxing.* Or rather, the *enrolling,* or *the census.* Josephus says it was designed to take an account of their substance. Comp. Luke ii. 1, 2.

38. *Refrain from these men.* Cease to oppose them, or to threaten them. The *reason* why he advised this he immediately adds, that if it were of men, it would come to nought; if of God, they could not overthrow it. ¶ *This counsel.* This plan, or purpose. If the apostles had originated it for the purposes of imposture. ¶ *It will come to nought.* Gamaliel *inferred* that from the two instances which he specified. They had been suppressed without the interference of the sanhedrim; and he inferred that *this* would also die away if it was a human device. It will be remembered that this is the mere advice of Gamaliel, who was not inspired; and that this opinion should not be adduced to guide us, except as it was an instance of great shrewdness and prudence. It is doubtless right to oppose *error* in the proper way and with the proper temper, not with arms, or vituperation, or with the civil power, but with argument and kind entreaty. But the sentiment of Gamaliel is full of wisdom in regard to error. For, (1.) The very way to exalt error into notice, and to confirm men in it, is to oppose it in a harsh, authoritative, and unkind manner. (2.) Error, if left alone, will often die away itself. The interest of men in it will often cease as soon as it ceases to be opposed; and having nothing to fan the flame, it will expire. It is not so with truth. (3.) In this respect the remark may be applied to the Christian religion. It has stood too long, and in too many circumstances of prosperity and adversity, to be of men. It has been subjected to all trials from its pretended friends and real foes; and it still lives as vigorous and flourishing as ever. Other kingdoms have changed; empires have risen and fallen since Gamaliel spoke this; systems of opinion and belief have had their day, and expired; but the preservation of the Christian religion, unchanged through so many revolutions, and in so many fiery trials, shows that it is not of men, but of God. The argument for the divine origin of the Christian religion from its perpetuity, is one that can be applied to no other system that has been, or that now exists. For Christianity has been opposed in every form. It confers no temporal conquests, and appeals to no base and strong native passions. Mahometanism is supported by the sword and the state; paganism relies on the arm of the civil power and the terrors of superstition, and is sustained by all the corrupt passions of men; atheism and infidelity have been short-lived, varying in their forms, dying to-day, and to-morrow starting up in a new form; never organized, consolidated, or pure; and never tending to promote the peace or happiness of men. Christianity, without arms or human power, has lived, holding its steady and triumphant movements among men, regardless alike of the opposition of

alone: [a] for if this counsel or this work be of men, it will come to nought:

39 But if [b] it be of God, ye cannot overthrow it: lest haply ye be found even to fight [c] against God.

a Pr.21.30. Is.8.10. Matt.15.13.
b Job 34.29. 1Cor.1.25. c c.9.5; 23.9.

its foes, and of the treachery of its pretended friends. If the opinion of Gamaliel was just, it is from God; and the *Jews* particularly should regard as important, an argument derived from the opinion of one of the wisest of their ancient Rabbins.

39. *But if it be of God.* If God is the *author* of this religion. From this it seems that Gamaliel supposed that it was at least possible that this religion was divine. He evinced a far more candid mind than did the rest of the Jews; but still, it does not appear that he was entirely convinced. The arguments which could not but stagger the Jewish sanhedrim were those drawn from the resurrection of Jesus, the miracle on the day of Pentecost, the healing of the lame man in the temple, and the release of the apostles from the prison. ¶ *Ye cannot overthrow it.* Because, (1.) God has almighty power, and can execute his purposes; (2.) Because he is unchanging, and will not be diverted from his plans. Job xxiii. 13, 14. The plan which God forms *must* be accomplished. All the devices of man are feebleness when opposed to him, and he can dash them in pieces in an instant. The prediction of Gamaliel has been fulfilled. Men have opposed Christianity in every way, but in vain. They have reviled it; have persecuted it; have resorted to argument and to ridicule, to fire, and fagot, and sword; they have called in the aid of science; but all has been in vain. The more it has been crushed, the more it has risen, and still exists with as much life and power as ever. The *preservation* of this religion amidst so much and so varied opposition, proves that it is of God. No severer trial *can* await it than it has already experienced; and as it has survived so many storms and trials, we have every evidence that according to the predictions, it is destined to live, and to fill the world. See Note, Matt. xvi. 18. Isa. liv. 17; lv. 11. Dan. iv. 35. ¶ *Lest.* That is, if you continue to oppose it, you may be found to have been opposing God. ¶ *Haply.* Perhaps. In the Greek this is *lest at any time*, that is, at some *future* time, when too late to retract your doings, &c. ¶ *Ye be found.* It shall appear that you have been opposing God. ¶ *Even to fight against God.* Greek, θεομάχοι. The word occurs nowhere else in the New Testament. To fight against God is to oppose him, or to maintain an attitude of hostility against him. It is an attitude that is most fearful in its character, and will most certainly be attended with an overthrow. No condition can be more awful than such an opposition to the Almighty; no overthrow more terrible than that which must follow such opposition. Comp. Acts ix. 5; xxiii. 9. Opposition to the *gospel* in the Scriptures is uniformly regarded as opposition to God. Matt. xii. 30. Luke xi. 23. Men may be said to *fight against God* in the following ways, or on the following subjects. (1.) When they oppose his *gospel*, its preaching, its plans, its influence among men; when they endeavour to prevent its spread, or to withdraw their families and friends from its influence. (2.) When they oppose the *doctrines* of the Bible. When they become angry that the real truths of religion are preached; and suffer themselves to be irritated and excited, by an *unwillingness* that those doctrines should be true, and should be presented to men. Yet this is no uncommon thing. Men by nature do not love those doctrines, and they are often indignant that they are preached. Some of the most angry feelings which men ever have, arise from this source; and man can never find peace until he is *willing* that God's truth should exert its influence on his own soul, and rejoice that it is believed and loved by others. (3.) Men oppose the *law* of God. It seems to them too *stern* and *harsh*. It condemns them; and they are unwilling that it should be applied to them. There is nothing which a sinner likes *less* than he does the pure and holy law of God. (4.) Sinners fight against the *providence* of God. When he afflicts them, they rebel. When he takes away their health, or property, or friends, they murmur. They esteem him harsh and cruel; and instead of finding peace by *submission*, they greatly aggravate their sufferings, and infuse a mixture of wormwood and gall into the cup, by murmuring and repining. There is no peace in affliction but in the feeling that God is *right*. And until this belief is cherished, the wicked will be like the troubled sea which cannot rest, whose waters cast up mire and dirt. Isa. lvii. 20. Such opposition to God is as wicked as it is foolish

40 And to him they agreed: and when they had called the apostles, and beaten [a] *them*, they commanded [b] that they should not speak in the name of Jesus, and let them go.

41 And they departed from the

a Matt.10.17. b c.4.18.

The Lord gave, and has a right to remove our comforts; and we should be still, and know that he is God. (5.) Sinners fight against God when they resist the influences of his Spirit; when they *oppose* serious thoughts; when they seek evil, or gay companions and pleasures rather than submit to God; and when they resist all the entreaties of their friends to become Christians. All these may be the appeals which God is making to men to be prepared to meet him. And yet it is common for sinners thus to stifle conviction, and refuse even to think of their eternal welfare. Nothing can be an act of more *direct* and deliberate wickedness and folly than this. Without the aid of the Holy Spirit none can be saved; and to resist his influences is to put away the only prospect of eternal life. To do it, is to do it over the grave; not knowing that another hour or day may be granted; and not knowing that *if* life is prolonged, the Spirit will ever strive again with the heart.

In view of this verse we may remark, 1. That the path of wisdom is to submit at once to all the requirements of God. Without this, we must expect conflicts with him, and perils and ruin. No man can be *opposed* to God, without endangering himself every minute. 2. Submission to God should be entire. It should extend to every doctrine, and demand; every law, and every act of the Almighty. In all his requirements, and in all afflictions, we should submit to him, and thus only shall we find peace. 3. Infidels and scoffers will gain nothing by opposing God. They have thus far been thwarted, and unsuccessful; and they will be still. None of their plans have succeeded; and the hope of destroying the Christian religion, after the efforts of almost two thousand years, must be vain, and will recoil with tremendous vengeance on those who make them.

40. *And to him they agreed.* Greek, They *were persuaded* by him; or they *trusted* to him. They agreed only so far as their design of putting them to death was concerned. They abandoned *that* design. But they did *not* comply with his advice to let them entirely alone. ¶ *And beaten them.* The usual amount of *lashes* which were inflicted on offenders was thirty-nine. 2 Cor. xi. 24. *Beating*, or *whipping*, was a common mode of punishing minor offences among the Jews. It was expressly foretold by the Saviour that the apostles would be subjected to this. Matt. x. 17. The reason why they did not adopt the advice of Gamaliel altogether, doubtless was, that if they did, they feared that their *authority* would be despised by the people. They had commanded them not to preach, they had threatened them (ch. iv. 18; v. 28); they had imprisoned them (ch. v. 18); and now if they suffered them to go without even the *appearance* of punishment, their authority, they feared, would be despised by the nation; and it would be supposed that the apostles had triumphed over the sanhedrim. It is probable also that they were so indignant, that they could not suffer them to go without the gratification of subjecting them to the public odium of a *whipping*. Men, if they cannot accomplish their *full* purposes of malignity against the gospel, will take up with even some petty annoyance and malignity, rather than let it alone.

41. *Rejoicing.* Nothing to most men would seem more disgraceful than a public whipping. It is a punishment inflicted usually not so much because it gives *pain*, as because it is esteemed to be attended with disgrace. The Jewish rulers doubtless desired that the apostles might be so affected with the sense of this disgrace as to be unwilling to appear again in public, or to preach the gospel any more. Yet in this they were disappointed. The effect was just the reverse. If it be asked *why* they *rejoiced* in this manner, we may reply, (1.) Because they were permitted thus to *imitate* the example of the Lord Jesus. He had been scourged and reviled, and they were glad that they were permitted to be treated as he was. Comp. Phil. iii. 10. Col. i. 24. 1 Pet. iv. 13 "Rejoice inasmuch as ye are partakers of Christ's sufferings." (2.) Because, by this, they had evidence that they were the friends and followers of Christ. It was clear they were engaged in the same cause that he was; enduring the same sufferings; and striving to advance the same interests. As they loved the *cause*, therefore they would rejoice in enduring even the shame and sufferings which the cause, of necessity, involved. The kingdom of the Redeemer was an object so

presence of the council, rejoicing [a]
that they were counted worthy to
suffer shame for his name.

42 And daily [b] in the temple, and
in every house, they ceased not to
teach and preach Jesus Christ.

CHAPTER VI.

AND in those days, when the number of the disciples was multiplied, there arose a murmuring of the Grecians [c] against the Hebrews, because their widows

a Matt.5.12. 2Cor.12.10. Ph.1.29. Ja.1.2 1Pet.4.13-16. b 2Tim.4.2. c c.9.29; 11.20.

transcendantly important, that *for* it, they were willing to endure *all* the afflictions and disgrace which it might involve. (3.) They had been told to *expect* this; it was a part of their enterprise. They had been warned of these things, and they now rejoiced that they had *this* evidence that they were engaged in the cause of truth. Matt. v. 11 12; x. 17 22. 2 Cor. xii. 10. Phil. i. 29. James i. 2. (4.) Religion appears to a Christian so excellent and lovely, that he is willing, for its sake, to endure trial, and persecution and death. With *all* this, it is infinite gain; and we should be willing to endure these trials, if, by them, we may gain a crown of glory. Comp. Mark x. 30. (5.) Christians are the professed friends of Christ. We show attachment for friends, by being willing to suffer for them; to bear contempt and reproach on their account; and to share *their* persecutions, sorrows, and calamities. (6.) The apostles were engaged in a cause of innocence, truth, and benevolence. They had *done* nothing of which to be ashamed; and they rejoiced, therefore, in a conscience void of offence; and in the consciousness of integrity and benevolence. When other men *disgrace themselves* by harsh, or vile, or opprobrious language, or conduct towards *us*, we should not feel that the disgrace belongs to *us*. It is *theirs*; and we should not be ashamed or distressed, though their rage should fall on us. See 1 Pet. iv. 14—16. ¶ *Counted worthy.* Esteemed to be deserving. That is esteemed *fit* for it *by the sanhedrim*. It does not mean that *God* esteemed them worthy, but that the Jewish council judged them fit to suffer shame in this cause. They evinced so much zeal, and determination of purpose, that they were judged fit objects to be treated as the Lord Jesus had himself been. ¶ *To suffer shame.* To be *dishonoured* or *disgraced* in the estimation of the Jewish rulers. The *particular* disgrace to which reference is made here was *whipping*. To various other kinds of shame they were also exposed. They were persecuted, reviled, and finally put to death.—Here we may remark, that a profession of the Christian religion has been in all ages esteemed by many to be a *disgrace*. The *reasons* are, (1.) That Jesus is himself despised; (2.) That his precepts are opposed to the gayety and follies of the world; (3.) That it attacks that on which the men of the world pride themselves, rank, wealth, fashion; (4.) That it requires a *spirit* which the world esteems mean and grovelling—meekness, humility, self-denial, patience, forgiveness of injuries; and (5.) That it requires *duties*—prayer, praise, seriousness, benevolence—which the men of the world despise. All these things the world esteem degrading and mean; and hence they endeavour to subject those who practise them to disgrace.—The *kinds* of disgrace to which Christians have been subjected are too numerous to be mentioned here. In former times they were subjected to the loss of property, of reputation, and to all the shame of public punishment, and to the terrors of the dungeon, the stake, or the rack. One main design of persecution was, to select a kind of punishment so *disgraceful* as to deter others from professing religion. Disgrace even yet may attend it. It may subject one to the ridicule of friends—of even a father, mother, or brother. Christians hear their opinions abused; their names vilified; their Bible travestied; the name of their God profaned, and of their Redeemer blasphemed. Their feelings are often wantonly and rudely torn by the cutting sarcasm, or the bitter sneer. Books and songs revile them; their peculiarities are made the occasion of indecent merriment on the stage and in novels; and in this way they are still subjected to shame for the name of Jesus. Every one who becomes a Christian should remember that this is a part of his inheritance, and should not esteem it dishonourable to be treated as his master was before him. John xv. 18—20. Matt. x. 25. ¶ *For his name.* For attachment to him.

42. *And daily,* &c. Comp. 2 Tim. iv. 2. Notes, Acts ii. 46.

CHAPTER VI.

1. *In those days,* &c. The first part of this chapter contains an account of the appointment of *deacons*. It may be asked, perhaps, why the apostles did not appoint

were neglected in [a] the daily ministration.

a c.4.35.

2 Then the twelve called the multitude of the disciples *unto*

these officers at the first organization of the church? To this question we may reply, that it was better to defer the appointment until an occasion should occur when it should appear to be manifestly necessary and proper. When the church was small, its alms could be distributed by the apostles themselves without difficulty. But when it was greatly increased; when its charities would be multiplied; and when the distribution might give rise to contentions, it was necessary that this matter should be intrusted to the hands of *laymen*, and that the *ministry* should be freed from all embarrassment, and all suspicions of dishonesty and unfairness in regard to pecuniary matters. It has never been found to be wise that the temporal affairs of the church should be intrusted in any considerable degree to the clergy; and they should be freed from such sources of difficulty and embarrassment. ¶ *Was multiplied.* By the accession of the three thousand on the day of Pentecost, and of those who were subsequently added. ch. iv. 4; v. 14. ¶ *A murmuring.* A *complaint*—as, if there had been partiality in the distribution. ¶ *Of the Grecians.* There has been much diversity of opinion in regard to these persons, whether they were *Jews* that had lived among the Gentiles, and who spoke the Greek language, or whether they were proselytes from the Gentiles. The former is probably the correct opinion. The word here used is not that which is usually employed to designate the inhabitants of Greece, but it properly denotes those who *imitate* the customs and habits of the Greeks, who use the Greek language, &c. In the time when the gospel was first preached, there were two classes of Jews—those who remained in Palestine, who used the Hebrew language, &c. and who were appropriately called *Hebrews;* and those who were scattered among the Gentiles, who spoke the Greek language, and who used in their synagogues the Greek translation of the Old Testament called the Septuagint. These were called *Hellenists*, or as it is in our translation *Grecians.* Note, John vii. 35. These were doubtless the persons mentioned here—not those who were proselyted from Gentiles, but those who were not natives of Judea, who had come up to Jerusalem to attend the great festivals of the Jews. See ch. ii. 5. 9—11. Dissensions would be very likely to arise between these two classes of persons. The Jews of Palestine would pride themselves much on the fact that they dwelt in the land of the patriarchs, and the land of promise; that they used the language which their fathers spoke, and in which the oracles of God were given; and that they were constantly near the temple, and regularly engaged in its solemnities. On the other hand, the Jews from other parts of the world would be suspicious, jealous, and envious of their brethren, and would be likely to charge them with partiality, or of taking advantage in their intercourse with them. These occasions of strife would not be destroyed by their conversion to Christianity, and one of them is furnished on this occasion. ¶ *Because their widows,* &c. The property which had been contributed, or cast into common stock, was understood to be designed for the equal benefit of *all* the poor, and particularly it would seem for the poor widows. The distribution before this, seems to have been made by the apostles themselves—or possibly, as Mosheim conjectures (Comm. de rebus Christianorum ante Constantinum, p. 139. 118), the apostles committed the distribution of these funds to the Hebrews, and hence the Grecians are represented as murmuring against them, and not against the apostles. ¶ *In the daily ministration.* In the daily distribution which was made for their wants. Comp. ch. iv. 35. The property was contributed doubtless with an understanding that it should be *equally* and justly distributed to all classes of Christians that had need.—It is clear from the Epistles that *widows* were objects of special attention in the primitive church, and that the first Christians regarded it as a matter of indispensable obligation to provide for their wants. 1 Tim. v. 3. 9, 10. 16. James i. 27.

2. *Then the twelve.* That is, the apostles. Matthias had been added to them after the apostacy of Judas, which had completed the original number. ¶ *The multitude of the disciples.* It is not necessary to suppose that *all* the disciples were convened, which amounted to many thousands, but that the business was laid before a large number; or perhaps *the multitude* here, means those merely who were more particularly interested in the matter, and who had been engaged in the complaint. ¶ *It is not reason.* The original words used here properly de-

them, and said, It [a] is not reason that we should leave the word of God, and serve tables.

3 Wherefore, brethren, look [b] ye out among you seven men of [c] honest report, full of the Holy Ghost and wisdom, whom we may appoint over this business.

a Ex.18.17-26. b De.1.13. c c.16.2. 1Tim.3.7,8,10.

note it is not *pleasing*, or *agreeable*; but the meaning evidently is, it is not *fit*, or *proper*. It would be a departure from the design of their appointment which was to preach the gospel, and not to attend to the pecuniary affairs of the church. ¶ *Leave the word of God.* That we should neglect, or abandon the preaching of the gospel so much as would be necessary, if we attended personally to the distribution of the alms of the church.—The *gospel* is here called the *word of God*, because it is *his* message; it is that which he has *spoken;* or which he has commanded to be proclaimed to men. ¶ *Serve tables.* This expression properly denotes to take care of, or to provide for the table, or for the daily wants of the family. It is an expression that properly applies to a steward, or a servant. The word *tables* is however sometimes used with reference to *money*, as being the place where money was kept for the purpose of *exchange*, &c. Matt. xxi. 12; xxv. 27. Here the expression means, therefore, to attend to the pecuniary transactions of the church, and to make the proper distribution for the wants of the poor.

3. *Look ye out.* Select, or choose. As this was a matter pertaining to their own pecuniary affairs, it was proper that *they* should be permitted to choose such men as they could confide in. By this means the apostles would be free from all suspicions. It could not be pretended that *they* were partial, nor could it ever be charged on them that they wished to embezzle a part of the funds by managing them themselves, or by intrusting them to men of their own selection.—It follows from this also that the right of selecting *deacons* resides *in* the church, and does not pertain to the ministry. And it is evidently proper that men who are to be intrusted with the alms of the church should be selected by the church itself. ¶ *Among you.* That is, from among the Grecians and Hebrews, that there may be justice done, and no further cause of complaint. ¶ *Seven men.* Seven was a sacred number among the Hebrews, but there does not appear to have been any *mystery* in choosing this number. It was a convenient number, sufficiently numerous to secure the faithful performance of the duty, and not so numerous as to produce confusion and embarrassment. It does not follow, however, that the same number is now to be chosen as deacons in a church, for the precise number is not commanded. ¶ *Of honest report.* Of fair reputation; regarded as men of integrity. Greek, *testified of*, or *borne witness to*, i. e. whose characters were well known and fair. ¶ *Full of the Holy Ghost.* This evidently does not mean endowed with miraculous gifts, or the power of speaking foreign languages, for such gifts were not necessary to the discharge of their office, but it means men who were eminently under the influence of the Holy Ghost, or who were of distinguished piety. This was all that was necessary in the case, and this is all that the words fairly imply in this place. ¶ *And wisdom.* Prudence, or skill, to make a wise and equable distribution. The qualifications of deacons are still further stated and illustrated in 1 Tim. iii. 8—10. In this place it is seen that they must be men of eminent piety and fair character, and that they must possess *prudence*, or wisdom, to manage the affairs connected with their office These qualifications are indispensable to a faithful discharge of the duty intrusted to the officers of the church. ¶ *Whom we may appoint.* Whom we may *constitute*, or *set* over this business. The way in which this was done was, by prayer and the imposition of hands. ver. 6. Though they were *selected* by the church, yet the power of ordaining them, or setting them apart, was retained by the apostles. Thus the rights of *both* were preserved, the right of the church to designate those who should serve them in the office of deacon, and the right of the apostles to organize and establish the church with its appropriate officers; on the one hand, a due regard to the liberty and privileges of the Christian community, and on the other the security of proper respect for the office, as being of apostolic appointment and authority. ¶ *Over this business.* That is, over the distribution of the alms of the church—not to preach, or to govern the church, but solely to take care of the sacred funds of charity, and distribute them to supply the wants of the poor. The office is distinguished from that of *preaching* the gospel. To that

4 But we will [a] give ourselves
continually to prayer, and to the
ministry of the word.
5 And the saying pleased the
whole multitude: and they chose
Stephen, a man full [b] of faith and
of the Holy Ghost, and Philip,
and Prochorus, and Nicanor, and
Timon, and Parmenas, and [d] Nicolas
a proselyte of Antioch:

a 1Tim.4.15. b c.11.24. c c.8.5,26; 21.8. d Re.2.6,15.

the apostles were to attend. The deacons were expressly set apart to a different work, and to that work they should be confined. In this account of their original appointment, there is not the slightest intimation that they were to *preach*, but the contrary is supposed in the whole transaction. Nor is there here the slightest intimation that they were regarded as an order of *clergy*, or as in any way connected with the clerical office.—In the ancient synagogues of the Jews there were three men to whom was intrusted the care of the poor. They were called by the Hebrews *Parnasin* or *Pastors*. (Lightfoot, Horæ Heb. et Talm. Matt. iv. 23.) From these officers the apostles took the idea probably of appointing deacons in the Christian church, and doubtless intended that their duties should be the same.

4. *But we will give ourselves continually.* The original expression here used denotes *intense and persevering* application to a thing, or unwearied effort in it. See Note, Acts i. 14. It means that the apostles meant to make this their constant and main object, undistracted by the cares of life, and even by attention to the temporal wants of the church. ¶ *To prayer.* Whether this means *private* or *public* prayer cannot be certainly determined. The passage, however, would rather incline us to suppose that the *latter* was meant, as it is immediately connected with preaching. If so, then the phrase denotes that they would give themselves to the duties of their office, one part of which was public prayer, and another preaching. Still it is to be believed that the apostles felt the need of secret prayer, and practised it, as preparatory to their public preaching. ¶ *And to the ministry of the word.* To preaching the gospel; or communicating the message of eternal life to the world. The word ministry (διακονία) properly denotes the employment of a *servant*, and is given to the preachers of the gospel because they are employed in this *service* as the servants of God, and of the church.—We have here a view of what the apostles thought to be the proper work of the ministry. They were set apart to this work. It was their main, their only employment. To this their lives were to be devoted, and both by their example and their writings they have shown that it was on this principle they acted. Comp. 1 Tim. iv. 15, 16. 2 Tim. iv. 2. It follows also that if their time and talents were to be wholly devoted to this work, it was reasonable that they should receive competent support from the churches, and this reasonable claim is often urged by the apostle. See 1 Cor. ix. 7—14. Gal. vi. 6.

5. *And the saying.* The *word*—the counsel, or command. ¶ *And they chose Stephen, &c.* A man who soon showed (ch. vii.) that he was every way qualified for his office, and fitted to defend also the cause of the Lord Jesus. This man had the distinguished honour of being the first Christian martyr. ch. vii. ¶ *And Nicolas.* From this man some of the Fathers (Ire. lib. i. 27. Epipha. Hæres. 5.) say, that the sect of the *Nicolaitanes*, mentioned with so much disapprobation (Rev. ii. 6. 15), took their rise. But the evidence of this is not clear. ¶ *A proselyte.* A *proselyte* is one who is converted from one religion to another. See Note, Matt. xxiii. 15. The word does not mean here that he was a convert to *Christianity*—which was true—but that he had been converted at Antioch from paganism to the Jewish religion. As this is the only proselyte mentioned among the seven deacons, it is evident that the others were native-born Jews, though a part of them might have been born out of Palestine, and have been of the denomination of *Grecians*, or *Hellenists*. ¶ *Of Antioch.* This city, often mentioned in the New Testament (Acts xi. 19, 20. 26; xv. 22. 35. Gal. ii. 11, &c.), was situated in Syria on the river Orontes, and was formerly called *Riblath*. It is not mentioned in the Old Testament, but is frequently mentioned in the Apocrypha. It was built by Seleucus Nicanor, A. C. 301, and was named *Antioch*, in honour of his father Antiochus. It became the seat of empire of the Syrian kings of the Macedonian race, and afterwards of the Roman governors of the eastern provinces. In this place the disciples of Christ were first called *Christians*. Acts xi. 26. Josephus says it was the third city in size of the Roman

6 Whom they set before the apostles: and when [a] they had prayed, they [b] laid *their* hands on them.

7 And [c] the word of God increased; and the number of the disciples multiplied in Jerusalem greatly; and a great company of the priests [d] were obedient to the faith.

8 And Stephen, full of faith and power, did great wonders and miracles among the people.

a c.1.24. b c.9.17; 13.3. 1Tim.4.14; 5.22. 2Tim.1.6. c Is.55.11. c.12.24; 19.20. d Ps.132,9,16. Jno.12.42.

provinces, being inferior only to Seleucia and Alexandria. It was long, indeed, the most powerful city of the East. The city was almost square, had many gates, was adorned with fine fountains, and possessed great fertility of soil and commercial opulence. It was subject to earthquakes, and was often almost destroyed by them. In A. D. 588 above sixty thousand persons perished in it in this manner. In A. D. 970 an army of one hundred thousand Saracens besieged it, and took it. In 1268 it was taken possession of by the Sultan of Egypt, who demolished it, and placed it under the dominion of the Turk. It is now called *Antakia*, and till the year 1822 it occupied a remote corner of the ancient enclosure of its walls, its splendid buildings being reduced to hovels, and its population living in Turkish debasement. It contains now about ten thousand inhabitants. (*Robinson's Calmet.*) This city should be distinguished from Antioch in Pisidia, also mentioned in the New Testament. Acts xiii. 14.

6. *And when they had prayed.* Invoking in this manner the blessing of God on them to attend them in the discharge of the duties of their office. ¶ *They laid their hands*, &c. Among the Jews it was customary to lay hands on the head of a person who was set apart to any particular office. Num. xxvii. 18. Comp. Acts viii. 19. This was done, not to impart any power or ability, but to *designate* that they received their authority, or commission, from those who thus laid their hands on them, as the act of laying hands on the sick by the Saviour was an act signifying that the power of healing came from him. Matt. ix. 18. Comp. Mark xvi. 18. In this case the laying on of the hands conveyed of itself no healing power but was a sign or token that the power came from the Lord Jesus. Ordination has been uniformly performed in this way. See 1 Tim. v. 22. Though the seven deacons had been chosen by the the church to this work, yet they derived their immediate commission and authority from the apostles.

7. *And the word of God increased.* That is, the gospel was more and more successful, or became more mighty, and extensive in its influence. An instance of this success is immediately added. ¶ *And a great company of the priests.* A great *multitude.* This is recorded justly as a remarkable instance of the power of the gospel. How great this *company* was is not mentioned. But the number of the priests in Jerusalem was very great; and their conversion was a striking proof of the power of truth. It is probable that they had been opposed to the gospel with quite as much hostility as any other class of the Jews. And it is now mentioned, as worthy of special record, that the gospel was sufficiently mighty to humble even the proud, and haughty, and selfish, and envious priest to the foot of the cross. One design of the gospel, is to evince the power of truth in subduing all classes of men; and hence in the New Testament we have the record of its having actually subdued every class to the obedience of faith Some MSS. however here instead of *priests* read *Jews.* And this reading is followed in the Syriac version. ¶ *Were obedient to the faith.* The word *faith* here is evidently put for the *Christian religion.* Faith is one of the main requirements of the gospel (Mark xvi. 16), and by a figure of speech is put for the gospel itself. To become *obedient to the faith*, therefore, is to obey the requirements of the gospel, particularly that which requires us to *believe.* Comp. Rom. x. 16. By the accession of the *priests* also no small part of the reproach would be taken away from the gospel, that it made converts only among the lower classes of the people. Comp. John vii. 48.

8. *And Stephen.* The remarkable death of this first Christian martyr, which soon occurred, gave occasion to the sacred writer to give a detailed account of his character, and of the causes which led to his death. Hitherto the opposition of the Jews had been confined to threats and imprisonment; but it was now to burst forth with furious rage and madness, that could be satisfied only with blood. This was the first in a series of persecutions against Christians that filled the church with blood, and that closed the lives of

9 Then there arose certain of the synagogue, which is called *The synagogue* of the Libertines, and Cyrenians, and Alexandrians, and of them of Cilicia and of Asia, disputing with Stephen.

---

thousands, perhaps millions in the great work of establishing the gospel on the earth. ¶ *Full of faith.* Full of confidence in God; or trusting entirely to his promises. See Note, Mark xvi. 16. ¶ *And power.* The power which was evinced in working miracles. ¶ *Wonders.* This is one of the words commonly used in the New Testament to denote miracles.

9. *Then there arose.* That is, they stood up against him; or they opposed him. ¶ *Of the synagogue.* See Note, Matt. iv. 23. The Jews were scattered in all parts of the world. In every place they would have synagogues. But it is also probable that there would be enough foreign Jews residing at Jerusalem from each of those places to maintain the worship of the synagogue; and at the great feasts those synagogues adapted to Jewish people of different nations, would be attended by those who came up to attend the great feasts. It is certain that there was a large number of synagogues at Jerusalem. The common estimate is, that there were four hundred and eighty in the city. (*Lightfoot, Vitringa.*) ¶ *Of the Libertines.* There has been very great difference of opinion about the meaning of this word. The chief opinions may be reduced to three. 1. The word is Latin, and means properly a *freedman*, a man who had been a slave and was set at liberty. And many have supposed that these persons were manumitted slaves, of Roman origin, but which had become proselyted to the Jewish religion, and who had a synagogue in Jerusalem. This opinion is not very probable; though it is certain, from *Tacitus* (Annal. lib. ii. c. 85), that there were many persons of this description at Rome. He says that four thousand Jewish proselytes of Roman slaves made free were sent at one time to Sardinia. 2. A second opinion is, that these persons were Jews by birth, and had been taken captives by the Romans, and then set at liberty, and thus called *freedmen*, or *libertines.* That there *were* many Jews of this description there can be no doubt. Pompey the Great, when he subjugated Judea, sent large numbers of the Jews to Rome. (*Philo, in Legat. ad Caium.*) These Jews were set at liberty at Rome, and assigned a place beyond the Tiber for a residence. See Introduction to the Epistle to the Romans. These persons are by *Philo* called *libertines*, or *freedmen.* (*Kuinoel* in loco.) Many Jews were also conveyed as captives by Ptolemy I. to Egypt, and obtained a residence in that country and the vicinity. But 3. Another, and more probable opinion is, that they took their name from some *place* which they occupied. This opinion is more probable from the fact that all the *other* persons mentioned here are named from the countries which they occupied. Suidas says that this is the name of a place. And in one of the Fathers this passage occurs: "Victor, bishop of the Catholic church at *Libertina*, says, unity is there," &c. From this passage it is plain that there was a place called *Libertina.* That place was in Africa, not far from ancient Carthage. See Bishop *Pearce's* Comment. on this place. ¶ *Cyrenians.* Jews who dwelt at *Cyrene* in Africa. See Note, Matt. xxvii. 32. ¶ *Alexandrians.* Inhabitants of Alexandria in Egypt. It was founded by Alexander the Great, B. C. 332, and was peopled by colonies of Greeks and Jews. This city was much celebrated, and contained not less than three hundred thousand free citizens, and as many slaves. The city was the residence of many Jews. Josephus says that Alexander himself assigned to them a particular quarter of the city, and allowed them equal privileges with the Greeks. (Antiq. xiv. 7. 2. Against Apion, ii. 4.) Philo affirms that of five parts of the city, the Jews inhabited two. According to his statement, there dwelt in his time at Alexandria and the other Egyptian cities, not less than *ten hundred thousand Jews.* Amron, the general of Omar, when he took the city, said that it contained forty thousand tributary Jews. At this place the famous version of the Old Testament called the *Septuagint*, or the Alexandrian version, was made. See Robinson's Calmet. ¶ *Cilicia.* This was a province of Asia Minor, on the sea-coast, at the north of Cyprus. The capital of this province was Tarsus, the native place of Paul. ch. ix. 11. And as Paul was of this place, and belonged doubtless to this synagogue, it is probable that he was one who was engaged in this dispute with Stephen. Comp. ch. vii. 58. ¶ *Of Asia.* See Note, ch. ii. 9. ¶ *Disputing with Stephen.* Doubtless on the question whether Jesus was the Messiah. This word does not denote *angry disputing*, but is commonly used to denote fair and impartial inquiry; and it is probable that

10 And they were not able [a] to
resist the wisdom and the spirit by
which he spake.

11 Then they suborned [b] men,
which said, We have heard him
speak blasphemous words against
Moses, and *against* God.

12 And they stirred up the people, and the elders, and the scribes
and came upon *him*, and caught
him, and brought *him* to the council,

13 And set up false witnesses,
which said, This man ceaseth not
to speak blasphemous words against
this holy place, and the law:

a Lu.21.15. b 1Ki.21.10,13. Matt.26.59,60.

the discussion began in this way; and when they were overcome by *argument*, they resorted, as disputants are apt to do, to angry criminations and violence.

10. *To resist.* That is, they were not able to *answer* his arguments. ¶ *The wisdom.* This properly refers to his knowledge of the Scriptures; his skill in what *the Jews* esteemed to be wisdom—acquaintance with their sacred writings, opinions, &c. ¶ *And the spirit.* This has been commonly understood of the Holy Spirit, by which he was aided; but it rather means the *energy, power,* or *ardour* of Stephen. He *evinced* a spirit of zeal and sincerity which they could not withstand; which served, more than mere argument could have done, to convince them that he was right.—The evidence of sincerity, honesty, and zeal in a public speaker will often go farther to convince the great mass of mankind, than the most able argument if delivered in a cold and indifferent manner.

11. *Then they suborned men.* To *suborn* in law means to procure a person to take such a false oath as constitutes perjury. (*Webster.*) It has substantially this sense here. It means that they induced them to declare that which was false, or to bring a false accusation against him. This was done not by declaring a palpable and open falsehood, but by *perverting* his doctrines, and by stating their own *inferences* as what he had actually maintained—the common way in which men oppose doctrines from which they differ. The Syriac reads this place, "Then they sent certain men, and instructed them that they should say," &c. This was repeating an artifice which they practised so successfully in relation to the Lord Jesus Christ. See Matt. xxvi. 60, 61. ¶ *We have heard, &c.* *When* they alleged that they had heard this, is not said. Probably, however, in some of his discourses with the people, when he wrought miracles and wonders among them. ver. 8. ¶ *Blasphemous words.* See Note, Matt. ix. 3. Moses was regarded with profound reverence. His laws they regarded as unchangeable. Any intimation, therefore, that there was a greater lawgiver than he, or that his institutions were mere shadows and types, and were no longer binding, would be regarded as blasphemy, even though it should be spoken with the highest respect for Moses. That the Mosaic institutions were to be changed, and give place to another and better dispensation, all the Christian teachers would affirm; but this was not said with a design to *blaspheme* or revile Moses. *In the view of the Jews*, to say that, was to speak blasphemy; and hence, instead of reporting what he actually *did* say, they accused him of *saying* what *they* regarded as blasphemy.—If reports are made of what men say, their very *words* should be reported; and we should not report *our* inferences or *impressions* as what they actually said. ¶ *And against God.* God was justly regarded by the Jews as the Giver of their law, and the Author of their institutions. But the Jews, either wilfully or involuntarily, not knowing that they were a shadow of good things to come, and were therefore to pass away, regarded all intimations of such a change as blasphemy against God. God had a right to change or abolish those ceremonial observances; and it was *not* blasphemy in Stephen to declare it.

12. *And they stirred up the people.* They *excited* the people, or alarmed their fears, as had been done before when they sought to put the Lord Jesus to death. Matt. xxvii. 20. ¶ *The elders.* The members of the sanhedrim, or great council. ¶ *Scribes.* Note, Matt. ii. 4. ¶ *To the council.* To the sanhedrim, or the great council of the nation, which claimed jurisdiction in the matters of religion. See Note, Matt. ii. 4.

13. *And set up false witnesses.* It has been made a question why these persons are called *false* witnesses, since it is supposed by many that they reported merely the *words* of Stephen. It may be replied that *if* they did report merely his *words*, if Stephen had actually said what they affirmed yet they perverted his meaning.

14 For[a] we have heard him say, That this Jesus of Nazareth shall [b]destroy this place, and shall change the [1]customs which Moses delivered us.

15 And all that sat in the council, looking steadfastly on him, saw his [c]face as it had been the face of an angel.

a c.25.8. b Dan.9.26. 1 or, rites. c Ex.34.30,35

They accused him of *blasphemy*, that is, of calumnious and reproachful words against Moses, and against God. That Stephen had spoken in such a manner, or had designed to *reproach* Moses, there is no evidence. What was said in the mildest manner, and in the way of cool argument, might easily be perverted so as in *their view* to amount to blasphemy. But there is no evidence whatever that Stephen had ever *used* these words on any occasion. And it is altogether improbable that he ever did, for the following reasons: (1.) Jesus *himself* never affirmed that *he* would destroy that place. He uniformly taught that it would be done by the *Gentiles*. Matt. xxiv. It is altogether improbable, therefore, that Stephen should declare any such thing. (2.) It is equally improbable that he taught that Jesus would abolish the peculiar customs and rites of the Jews. It was long, and after much discussion, before the apostles themselves were convinced of it; and when those customs were changed, it was done gradually. See Acts x. 14, &c. xi. 2, &c. xv. 20; xxi. 20, &c. The probability therefore is, that the whole testimony was *false*, and was artfully invented to produce the utmost exasperation among the people, and yet was at the same time so plausible as to be easily believed. For on this point the Jews were particularly sensitive; and it is clear that they had some expectations that the Messiah *would* produce some such changes. Comp. Matt. xxvi. 61 with Dan. ix. 26, 27. The same charge was afterwards brought against Paul, which he promptly denied. See Acts xxv. 8. ¶ *This holy place.* The temple. ¶ *The law.* The law of Moses.

14. *Shall change.* Shall abolish them; or shall introduce others in their place. ¶ *The customs.* The ceremonial rites and observances of sacrifices, festivals, &c. appointed by Moses.

15. *Looking steadfastly on him.* Fixing the eyes intently on him. Probably they were attracted by the unusual appearance of the man, his meekness, and calm and collected fearlessness, and the proofs of conscious innocence and sincerity. ¶ *The face of an angel.* This expression is one evidently denoting that he manifested evidence of sincerity, gravity, fearlessness, confidence in God. It is used in the Old Testament to denote peculiar wisdom. 2 Sam. xiv. 17; xix. 27. In Gen. xxxiii. 10, it is used to denote peculiar majesty and glory, as if it were the face of God. When Moses came down from mount Sinai from communing with God, it is said that the skin of his face shone, so that the children of Israel were afraid to come nigh to him. Ex. xxxiv. 29, 30. 2 Cor. iii. 7. 13. Comp. Rev. i. 16. Matt. xvii. 2. The expression is used to denote the impression which will be produced on the countenance by communion with God; the calm serenity and composure which will follow a confident committing of all into his hands. It is not meant that there was any thing *miraculous* in the case of Stephen, but is an expression denoting his calmness, and dignity, and confidence in God; all of which were so marked on his countenance, that it impressed them with clear proofs of his innocence and piety. The expression is very common in the Jewish writings. It is common for deep feeling, sincerity, and confidence in God, to impress themselves on the countenance. Any deep emotion will do this; and it is to be expected that religious feeling, the most tender and solemn of all feeling, will diffuse seriousness, serenity, calmness, and peace, not affected sanctimoniousness, over the countenance.

In this chapter we have another specimen of the manner in which the church of the Lord Jesus was reared on earth. It was from the beginning amid scenes of persecution; and encountering opposition adapted to try the nature and power of religion. If Christianity was an imposture, it had enemies acute and malignant enough to detect the imposition. The learned, the cunning, and the mighty rose up in opposition, and by all the arts of sophistry, all the force of authority, and all the fearfulness of power, attempted to destroy it in the commencement. Yet it lived; and it gained new accessions of strength from every new form of opposition; and only evinced its genuineness more and more by showing that it was superior to the arts and malice of earth and of hell.

CHAPTER VII.

THEN said the high-priest, Are these things so?

2 And he said, Men, [a] brethren, and fathers, hearken; The God of glory appeared unto our father Abraham when he was in Mesopotamia, before he dwelt in Charran,

a c.22.1.

CHAPTER VII.

THIS chapter contains the defence of Stephen before the sanhedrim, or great council of the Jews. There has been great diversity of opinion about the *object* which Stephen had in view in this defence, and about the reason why he introduced at such length the history of the Jewish people. But a few remarks may perhaps show his design. He was accused of *blasphemy in speaking against the institutions of Moses and the temple, that is, against every thing held sacred among the Jews.* To meet this charge, he gives a statement, at length, of his belief in the Mosaic religion, in the great points of their history, and in the fact that God had interposed in a remarkable manner in defending them from dangers. By this historical statement he avows his full belief in the divine origin of the Jewish religion, and thus *indirectly* repels the charge of blasphemy. It is further to be remembered, that this was the best way of securing the *attention* of the council. Had he entered on an abstract defence, he might expect to be stopped by their cavils or their clamour. But the history of their own nation was a favourite topic among the Jews. They were always ready to listen to an account of their ancestors; and to secure their attention, nothing more was necessary than to refer to their illustrious lives and deeds. Comp. Ps. lxxviii. cv. cvi. cxxxv. Ezek. xx. In this way Stephen secured their attention, and practically repelled the charge of speaking reproachfully of Moses and the temple. He showed them that *he* had as firm a belief as *they* in the great historical facts of their nation. It is to be remembered, also, that this speech was broken off in the midst (ver. 53, 54), and it is therefore difficult to tell what the design of Stephen was. It seems clear, however, that he intended to convict *them* of guilt, by showing that *they* sustained the same character as their fathers had manifested (ver. 51, 52); and there is some probability that he intended to show that the acceptable worship of God was not to be confined to any place particularly, from the fact that the worship of Abraham, and the patriarchs, and Moses, was acceptable *before* the temple was reared (ver. 2, &c.), and from the declaration in ver. 48, that God dwells not in temples made with hands. All that can be said here is, that Stephen (1.) showed his full belief in the divine appointment of Moses, and the historical facts of their religion; (2.) That he laid *the foundation* of an argument to show that those things were not perpetually binding, and that acceptable worship *might* be offered in other places and in another manner than at the temple.

It has been asked in what way Luke became acquainted with this speech so as to repeat it. The Scripture has not informed us. But we may remark, (1.) That Stephen was the first martyr. His death, and the incidents connected with it, could not but be a matter of interest to the first Christians; and the *substance* of his defence, at least, would be familiar to them. There is no improbability in supposing that imperfect copies might be preserved by writing, and circulated among them. (2.) Luke was the companion of Paul. (See Introduction to the Gospel by Luke.) Paul was present when this defence was delivered, and was a man who would be likely to *remember* what was said on such an occasion. From him Luke might have derived the account of this defence. In regard to this discourse, it may be further remarked, that it is not necessary to suppose that *Stephen* was *inspired.* Even if there should be found inaccuracies, as some critics have pretended, in the address, it would not militate against its genuineness. It is the defence of a man on trial under a serious charge; not a man of whom there is evidence that he was *inspired,* but a pious, devoted, heavenly-minded man. All that the sacred narrative is responsible for is the *correctness of the report.* Luke alleges only that *such a speech was in fact delivered,* without affirming that every particular in it is correct.

1. *Then said the high-priest.* See Note, Matt. ii. 4. In this case the high-priest seems to have presided in the council. ¶ *Are these things so?* To wit, the charge alleged against him of blasphemy against Moses and the temple. ch. vi. 13, 14.

2. *Men, brethren, and fathers.* These were the usual titles by which the sanhedrim was addressed. In all this Stephen was perfectly respectful, and showed that he was disposed to render due

3 And said [a] unto him, Get thee out of thy country, and from thy kindred, and come into the land which I shall shew thee.

a Gen.12.1.

honour to the institutions of the nation. ¶ *The God of glory.* This is a Hebrew form of expression denoting *the glorious God.* It properly denotes his majesty, or splendour, or magnificence; and the word *glory* is often applied to the splendid appearances in which God has manifested himself to men. Deut. v. 24. Ex. xxxiii. 18; xvi. 7. 10. Lev. ix. 23. Num. xiv. 10. Perhaps Stephen meant to affirm that God appeared to Abraham in some such glorious or splendid manifestation, by which he would know that he was addressed by God. Stephen, moreover, evidently uses the word *glory* to repel the charge of *blasphemy* against God, and to show that he regarded him as worthy of honour and praise. ¶ *Appeared,* &c. In what *manner* he appeared is not said. In Gen. xii. 1, it is simply recorded that God *had said* unto Abraham, &c. ¶ *To our father.* The Jews valued themselves much on being the children of Abraham. Note, Matt. iii. 9. This expression was therefore well calculated to conciliate their minds. ¶ *When he was in Mesopotamia.* In Gen. xi. 31, it is said that Abraham dwelt *in Ur of the Chaldees.* The word Mesopotamia properly denotes the region between the two rivers, the Euphrates and the Tigris. Note, Acts ii. 9. The name is Greek, and the region had also other names before the Greek name was given to it. In Gen. xi. 31; xv. 7, it is called Ur of the Chaldees. Mesopotamia and Chaldea might not exactly coincide; but it is evident that Stephen meant to say that *Ur* was in the country afterwards called Mesopotamia. Its precise situation is unknown. A Persian fortress of this name is mentioned by Ammianus (xxv. 8), between Nesibis and the Tigris. ¶ *Before he dwelt in Charran.* From Gen. xi. 31, it would seem that Terah took his son Abraham of his own accord, and removed to Haran. But from Gen. xii. 1; xv. 7, it appears that God had commanded *Abraham* to remove, and he so ordered it in his providence that *Terah* was disposed to remove his family with an intention of going into the land of Canaan.—*Charran.* This is the Greek form of the Hebrew word *Haran.* Gen. xi. 31. This place was also in Mesopotamia, in 36° 52′ N. lat. and 39° 5′ E. lon. Here Terah died (Gen. xi. 32); and to this place Jacob retired when he fled from his brother Esau. Gen. xxvii. 43 It is situated "in a flat and sandy plain, and is inhabited by a few wandering Arabs, who select it for the delicious water which it contains." (*Robinson's Calmet.*)

3. *And said unto him.* How long this was said unto him before he went is not recorded. Moses simply says that God *had* commanded him to go. Gen. xii. 1. ¶ *Thy kindred.* Thy relatives, or family connexions. It seems that *Terah* went with him as far as to Haran; but Abraham was apprized that he was to leave his family, and to go almost alone. ¶ *Into the land,* &c. The country was yet unknown. The place was to be shown him. This is presented in the New Testament as a strong instance of faith. Heb. xi. 8, 9. It was an act of *simple confidence* in God. And to leave his country and home; to go into a land of strangers, not knowing whither he went, required strong confidence in God. It is a simple illustration of what man is always required to do, at the commands of God. Thus the gospel requires him to commit all to God; to yield body and soul to his disposal; and to be ready at his command to forsake father and mother, and friends, and houses, and lands, for the sake of the Lord Jesus. Luke xiv. 33. Matt. xix. 27. 29. The trials which Abraham might have anticipated may be readily conceived. He was going, in a rude and barbarous age of the world, into a land of strangers. He was without arms or armies, almost alone. He did not even know the nature or situation of the land, or the character of its inhabitants. He had no title to it; no claim to urge; and he went depending on the simple promise of God that he would give it to him. He went, therefore, trusting simply to the promise of God. And thus his conduct illustrated precisely what *we* are to do in all the future—in reference to all our coming life, and to the eternity before us—we are to trust simply to the promise of God, and *do* that which he requires. This is faith. In Abraham it was as simple and intelligible an operation of mind as ever occurs in any instance. Nor is faith in the Scripture regarded as more mysterious than any other mental operation. Had Abraham *seen* all that was to result from his going into that land, it would have been sufficient *reason* to induce him to do as he did. But *God* saw it; and Abraham was required to act just *as if* he had seen it all, and all the reasons why he was called. On the strength of

4 Then [a] came he out of the land of the Chaldeans, and dwelt in Charran: and from thence, when his father was dead, he removed him into this land, wherein ye now dwell.

a Gen.12.5.

5 And he gave him none inheritance in it, no not *so much as* to set his foot on: yet he promised [b] that he would give it to him for a possession, and to his seed after him, when *as yet* he had no child.

b Gen.13.15.

God's promises he was called to act. This was *faith*. It did not require him to act where there was *no reason* for his so acting, but where he did not *see* the reason. So in all cases of faith. If man could see all that God sees, he would *perceive* reasons for acting as God requires. But the reasons of things are often concealed, and man is required to act on the *belief* that *God* sees reasons why he should so act. To act under the proper impression of that truth which God presents, is faith; as simple and intelligible as any other act or operation of the mind. See Note, Mark xvi. 16.

4. *Land of the Chaldeans.* From Ur of the Chaldees. Gen. xi. 31. ¶ *When his father was dead.* This passage has given rise to no small difficulty in the interpretation. The difficulty is this: From Gen. xi. 26, it would seem that Abraham was born when Terah was seventy years of age. "And Terah lived seventy years, and begat Abram, Nahor, and Haran." From Gen. xii. 4, it seems that Abraham was seventy-five years of age when he departed from Haran to Canaan. The age of Terah was therefore but one hundred and forty-five years. Yet in Gen. xi. 32, it is said that Terah was two hundred and five years old when he died; thus leaving sixty years of Terah's life beyond the time when Abraham left Haran. Various modes have been proposed of meeting this difficulty. (1.) Errors in *numbers* are more likely to occur than any other. In the *Samaritan* copy of the Pentateuch, it is said that Terah died in Haran at the age of one hundred and five years; which would suppose that his death occurred forty years before Abraham left Haran. But the Hebrew, Latin Vulgate, Septuagint, Syriac, and Arabic read it two hundred and five years. (2.) It is not affirmed that Abraham was born just at the time when Terah was seventy years of age. All that the passage in Gen. xi. 26 proves, according to the usual meaning of similar expressions, is, that Terah was seventy years old *before* he had any sons, and that the three were born subsequently to that. But which was born first, or how long intervals intervened between their birth, does not appear. Assuredly it does not mean that all were born precisely at the time when Terah was seventy years of age. Neither does it appear that Abraham was the oldest of the three. The sons of Noah are said to have been Shem, Ham, and Japheth (Gen. v. 32); yet Japheth, though mentioned last, was the eldest. (Gen. x. 21.) As Abraham afterwards became much the most distinguished, and as he was the father of the Jewish people, of whom Moses was writing, it was natural that he should be mentioned first. If it cannot be *proved* that Abraham was the eldest, as assuredly it cannot be, then there is no improbability in supposing that his birth might have occurred many years after Terah was seventy years of age. (3.) The Jews unanimously affirm that Terah relapsed into idolatry before Abraham left Haran; and this they denominate *death*, or a moral death. (*Kuinoel.*) It is certain, therefore, that, from some cause, they were accustomed to speak of Terah as *dead*, before Abraham left him. Stephen only used language which was customary among the Jews, and would use it, doubtless, correctly, though *we* may not be able to see precisely how it can be reconciled with the account in Genesis.

5. *And he gave him none inheritance.* Abraham led a wandering life. And this passage means, that he did not himself receive a permanent possession or residence in that land. The only land which he owned was the field which he *purchased* of the children of Heth, for a burial place. Gen. xxiii. As this was obtained by *purchase*, and not by the direct gift of God, and as it was not designed for a *residence*, it is said that God gave him no *inheritance*. It is mentioned as a strong instance of his faith, that he should remain there without a permanent residence himself, with only the prospect that his children, at some distant period, would inherit it. ¶ *Not so much as to set his foot on.* This is a proverbial expression, denoting in an emphatic manner that he had *no land*. Deut. ii. 5. ¶ *Would give it to him.* Gen. xiii. 15. Abraham did not himself possess all that land; and the promise is evidently equivalent to saying

6 And God spake on this wise, That [a] his seed should sojourn in a strange land; and that they should bring them into bondage, and entreat *them* evil four [b] hundred years.

a Gen.15.13,16. b Ex.12.40,41.

that it should be conferred on the family of Abraham, or the family of which he was the father, without affirming that *he* should himself personally possess it. It is true, however, that Abraham himself afterwards dwelt many years in that land as his home. Gen. xiii. &c. ¶ *For a possession.* To be held as his own property. ¶ *When as yet he had no child.* When there was no human probability that he would have any posterity. Comp. Gen. xv. 2, 3; xviii. 11, 12. This is mentioned as a strong instance of his faith; "who against hope believed in hope." Rom. iv. 18.

6. *And God spake on this wise.* In this manner. Gen. xv. 13, 14. ¶ *His seed.* His posterity; his descendants. ¶ *Should sojourn.* This means that they should have a *temporary residence* there. The word is used in opposition to a fixed, permanent home, and is applied to travellers, or foreigners. ¶ *In a strange land.* In the Hebrew (Gen. xv. 13), "Shall be a stranger in a land that is not theirs." The land of Canaan and the land of Egypt were to them strange lands, though the obvious reference here is to the latter. ¶ *Should bring them into bondage.* Or, should make them slaves. Ex. i. 11. ¶ *And entreat* them *evil.* Should *oppress* or *afflict* them. ¶ *Four hundred years.* This is the precise time which is mentioned by Moses. Gen. xv. 13. Great perplexity has been experienced in explaining this passage, or reconciling it with other statements. In Ex. xii. 40, it is said that their sojourning in Egypt was four hundred and thirty years. Josephus (Antiq. b. ii. ch. ix. § 1) also says that the time in which they were in Egypt was four hundred years; though in another place (Antiq. b. ii. ch. xv. § 2) he says that they left Egypt four hundred and thirty years after their forefather Abraham came to *Canaan*, but two hundred and fifteen years after Jacob removed to Egypt. Paul also (Gal. iii. 17) says that it was four hundred and thirty years from the time when the promise was given to Abraham to the time when the law was given on mount Sinai. The Samaritan Pentateuch says also (Ex. xii. 40) that the "dwelling of the sons of Israel, and of their fathers, which they dwelt *in the land of Canaan*, and in the land of Egypt, was four hundred and thirty years." The same is the version of the Septuagint. A *part* of this perplexity is removed by the fact that Stephen and Moses use, in accordance with a very common custom, *round numbers* in speaking of it, and thus speak of four hundred years when the *literal* time was four hundred and thirty. The other perplexities are not so easily removed. From the account which Moses has given of the lives of certain persons, it would seem clear that the time which they spent in *Egypt* was *not* four hundred years. From Gen. xlvi. 8. 11, it appears that *Kohath* was born when Jacob went into Egypt. He lived one hundred and thirty-three years. Ex vi. 18. Amram, his son, and the father of Moses, lived one hundred and thirty-seven years. Ex. vi. 20. Moses was eighty years old when he was sent to Pharaoh. Ex. vii. 7. The *whole* time thus mentioned, including the time in which the father lived *after* his son was born, was only three hundred and fifty years. Exclusive of that, it is reasonable to suppose that the actual time of their being in Egypt could not have been but about two hundred years, according to one account of Josephus. The question then is, how can these accounts be reconciled? The only satisfactory way is by supposing that the four hundred and thirty years includes the whole time from the calling of Abraham to the departure from Egypt. And that this was the fact is probable from the following circumstances. (1.) The purpose of *all* the narratives on this subject is to trace the period *before* they became finally settled in the land of Canaan. During *all* this period from the calling of Abraham, they were in a wandering, unfixed situation. This constituted substantially *one* period, including *all* their oppressions, hardships, and dangers; and it was natural to have reference to this *entire* period in any account which was given. (2.) All this period was properly the period of *promise*, not of *possession*. In this respect the wanderings of Abraham and the oppressions of Egypt came under the same general description. (3.) Abraham was himself occasionally in Egypt. He was unsettled; and since Egypt was so *pre-eminent* in all their troubles, it was natural to speak of *all* their oppressions as having occurred in that country. The phrase "residence in Egypt," or "in a

7 And the nation to whom they
shall be in bondage will I judge,
said God: and after that shall they
come forth, and serve [a] me in this
place.
8 And [b] he gave him the covenant of circumcision. And so [c]
Abraham begat Isaac, and circum
cised him the eighth day: and Isaac
[d] begat Jacob; and Jacob [e] begat the
twelve patriarchs,
9 And the patriarchs, moved with
[f] envy, sold Joseph into Egypt; but
[g] God was with him,

a Ex.3.12. b Gen.17.9–11. c Gen.21.1–4. d Gen.25.26. e Gen.29.32,&c. f Gen.37.28. Ps.105.17. g Gen.39.2.21.

strange land," would come to be synonymous, and would denote *all* their oppressions and trials. They would speak of their sufferings as having been endured in Egypt, because their afflictions *there* were so much more prominent than before. (4.) All this receives countenance from the version of the LXX., and from the Samaritan text, showing the manner in which the ancient Jews were accustomed to understand it. (5.) It should be added, that difficulties of chronology are more likely to occur than any others; and it should not be deemed strange if there are perplexities of this kind found in ancient writings which we cannot explain. It is so in *all* ancient records; and all that is usually expected in relation to such difficulties is that we should be able to present a *probable* explanation.

7. *And the nation, &c.* Referring *particularly* to the Egyptians. ¶ *Will I judge.* The word *judge* in the Bible often means to *execute judgment,* as well as to pronounce it; that is, *to punish.* See John xviii. 31; iii. 17; viii. 50; xii. 47. Acts xxiv. 6. 1 Cor. v. 13, &c. It has this meaning here. God regarded their oppressive acts as *deserving* his indignation, and he evinced it in the *plagues* with which he visited them, and in their overthrow in the Red sea. ¶ *Shall serve me.* Shall worship me, or be regarded as my people. ¶ *In this place.* That is, in the place where God made this promise to Abraham. These words are not found in Genesis; but similar words are found in Ex. iii. 12; and it was a practice in making quotations, to quote the sense only, or to connect two or more promises having relation to the same thing.

8. *And he gave him.* That is, God appointed or commanded this. Gen. xvii. 9—13. ¶ *The covenant.* The word *covenant* denotes properly a compact or agreement between two or more persons, usually attended with seals, or pledges, or sanctions. In Gen. xvii. 7, and elsewhere, it is said that God would establish his *covenant* with Abraham; that is, he made him certain definite promises, attended with pledges and seals, &c. The idea of a strict *compact* or *agreement* between God and man, as between *equal parties,* is not found in the Bible. It is commonly used, as here, to denote a promise on the part of God, attended with pledges, and demanding, on the part of man, in order to avail himself of its benefits, a stipulated course of conduct. The *covenant* is therefore another name for denoting two things on the part of God: (1.) A *command,* which man is not at liberty to reject, as he *would be* if a literal covenant; and (2.) A *promise,* which is to be fulfilled only on the condition of obedience. The covenant with Abraham was simply a *promise* to give him the land, and to make him a great nation, &c. It was *never* proposed to Abraham with the supposition that he was at liberty to *reject* it, or to *refuse* to comply with its conditions. Circumcision was appointed as the *mark* or *indication* that Abraham and those thus designated were the persons included in the gracious purpose and promise. It served to *separate* them as a peculiar people; a people whose peculiar characteristic it was that they obeyed and served the God who had made the promise to Abraham. The phrase "covenant of circumcision" means, therefore, the covenant or promise which God made to Abraham, of which circumcision was the distinguishing *mark* or *sign.* ¶ *The twelve patriarchs.* The word *patriarch* properly denotes the father and ruler of a family. But it is commonly applied, by way of eminence, to the progenitors of the Jewish race, particularly to the twelve sons of Jacob. Note, Acts ii. 29.

9. *Moved with envy.* That is, dissatisfied with the favour which their father Jacob showed Joseph, and envious at the dreams which indicated that he was *to* be raised to remarkable honour above his parents and brethren. Gen. xxxvii. 3—11. ¶ *Sold Joseph into Egypt.* Sold him, that he might be taken to Egypt. This was done at the suggestion of *Judah,* who advised it that Joseph might not be put to death by his brethren. Gen. xxxvii

10 And delivered him out of all
his afflictions, and gave him favour
and wisdom in the sight of Pharaoh
king of Egypt; and he[a] made him
governor over Egypt and all his
house.

11 Now [b] there came a dearth
over all the land of Egypt and Chanaan,
and great affliction; and our
fathers found no sustenance.

12 But [c] when Jacob heard that
there was corn in Egypt, he sent
out our fathers first.

13 And at the second *time* Joseph
[d] was made known to his brethren;
and Joseph's kindred was
made known unto Pharaoh.

14 Then sent Joseph, and called
his father Jacob to *him*, and all [e] his
kindred, threescore and fifteen souls.

15 So Jacob went down into
Egypt, and died, he, and our fathers,

16 And were carried [f] over into
Sychem, and laid in the sepulchre
that Abraham bought for a sum of
money of the sons of Emmor *the
father* of Sychem.

a Gen.41.40. b Gen.41.54. c Gen.42.1,2. d Gen.45.4,16. e Gen.46.27. De.10.22 f Jos.24.32.

28.—It is possible that Stephen, by this fact, might have designed to prepare the way for a severe rebuke of the Jews for having dealt in a similar manner with their Messiah. ¶ *But God was with him.* God protected him, and overruled al these wicked doings, so that he was raised to extraordinary honours.

10. *And delivered him,* &c. That is, restored him to liberty from his servitude and humiliation, and raised him up to high honours and offices in Egypt. ¶ *Favour and wisdom.* The favour was the result of his wisdom. His wisdom was particularly evinced in interpreting the *dreams* of Pharaoh. Gen. xli. ¶ *And made him governor,* &c. Gen. xli. 40. ¶ *All his house.* All the family, or all the court and government, of the nation.

11. *Now there came a dearth.* A famine. Gen. xli. 54. ¶ *And Chanaan.* Jacob was living at that time in Canaan. ¶ *Found no sustenance.* No food; no means of living.

12. *Was corn in Egypt.* The word *corn* here rather denotes *wheat.* Note, Matt. xii. 1. ¶ *Our fathers.* His ten sons; all his sons except Joseph and Benjamin. Gen. xlii. Stephen here *refers* only to the history, without entering into details. By this *general* reference he sufficiently showed that he *believed* what Moses had spoken, and did not intend to show him disrespect.

13. *Joseph was made known.* Gen. xlv. 4. ¶ *Joseph's kindred,* &c. His relatives; his family. Gen. xlv. 16.

14. *All his kindred.* His father, and family. Gen. xlv. 17—28; xlvi. 1—26. ¶ *Threescore and fifteen souls.* Seventy-five persons. There has been much perplexity felt in the explanation of this passage. In Gen. xlvi. 26. Ex. i. 5. and Deut. x. 22, it is expressly said that the number which went down to Egypt consisted of but seventy persons. The question is, in what way these accounts can be reconciled? It is evident that Stephen has followed the account which is given by the Septuagint. In Gen. xlvi. 27, that version reads, "But the sons of Joseph who were with him in Egypt, were nine souls; all the souls of the house of Jacob which came with Jacob into Egypt, were seventy-five souls." This number is made out by adding these *nine* souls to the sixty-six mentioned in ver. 26. The difference between the Septuagint and Moses is, that the former mentions five descendants of Joseph who are not recorded by the latter. The *names* of the sons of Ephraim and Manasseh are recorded in 1 Chron. vii. 14—21. Their names were Ashriel, Machir, Zelophehad, Peresh, sons of Manasseh; and Shuthelah, son of Ephraim. Why the Septuagint inserted these, it may not be easy to see. But such was evidently the fact; and the fact accords accurately with the historic record, though Moses did not insert their names. The solution of difficulties in regard to chronology is always difficult; and what might be entirely apparent to a Jew in the time of Stephen, may be wholly inexplicable to us.

15, 16. *And died.* Gen. xlix. 33. ¶ *He and our fathers.* The time which the Israelites remained in Egypt was two hundred and fifteen years; so that all the sons of Jacob were deceased before the Jews went out to go to the land of Canaan. ¶ *And were carried over.* Jacob himself was buried in the field of Macpelah, by Joseph and his brethren. Gen. l. 13. It is expressly said that the bones of Joseph were carried by the Israelites when they went into the land of Canaan, and buried in Shechem. Josh xxiv. 32.

17 But when the time of the promise drew nigh, which God had sworn to Abraham, the people [a] grew and multiplied in Egypt,

18 Till another king arose, which knew not Joseph.

a Ex.1.7-9

Comp. Gen. l. 25. No mention is made in the Old Testament of their carrying the bones of any of the other patriarchs; but the thing is highly probable in itself. If the descendants of Joseph carried *his* bones, it would naturally occur to them to take also the bones of each of the patriarchs, and give them an honourable sepulchre together in the land of promise. Josephus (Antiq. b. ii. ch. viii. § 2) says that "the posterity and sons of these men (of the brethren of Joseph), after some time, carried their bodies and buried them in Hebron; but as to the bones of Joseph, they carried them into the land of Canaan afterward, when the Hebrews went out of Egypt." This is the account which Josephus gives, and it is evidently in accordance with the common opinion of the Jewish writers that they were buried in Hebron. Yet the tradition is not uniform. Some of the Jews affirm that they were buried in Sychem. (*Kuinoel.*) As the Scriptures do not any where deny that the fathers were buried in Sychem, it cannot be proved that Stephen was in error. There is one circumstance of strong probability to show that he was correct. At the time this defence was delivered, *Sychem* was in the hands of the Samaritans, between whom and the Jews there was a violent hostility. Of course the Jews would not be willing to concede that the Samaritans had the bones of their ancestors; and hence perhaps the opinion had been maintained that they were buried in Hebron. ¶ *Into Sychem.* This was a town or village near to Samaria. It was called *Sichar* (Note, John iv. 5), *Shechem*, and *Sychem.* It is now called *Naplous*, or *Napolose*, and is ten miles from Shiloh, and about forty from Jerusalem, towards the north. ¶ *That Abraham bought.* The word *Abraham* here has given rise to considerable perplexity; and it is now pretty generally conceded that it is a mistake. It is certain, from Gen. xxxiii. 19. and Josh. xxiv. 32, that this piece of land was bought, not by Abraham, but by *Jacob*, of the sons of Hamor, the father of Shechem. The land which Abraham purchased was the cave of Macpelah, of the sons of Heth, in Hebron. Gen. xxiii. Various solutions have been proposed of this difficulty, which it is not necessary to detail. It may be remarked, however, (1.) That as the text now stands, it is an evident error. This is clear from the passages cited from the Old Testament, above. (2.) It is not at all probable that either Stephen or Luke would have committed such an error. Every consideration must lead us to the conclusion that they were too well acquainted with such prominent points of the Jewish history to commit an error like this. (3.) The *probability*, therefore, is, that the error has arisen since; but *how*, is not known, nor is there any way of ascertaining. All the ancient versions agree in reading *Abraham*. One MS. only reads "*Abraham our father.*" Some have supposed, therefore, that it was written "which our father bought," and that some early transcriber inserted the name of Abraham. Others, that the name was omitted entirely by Stephen; and then the antecedent to the verb "bought" will be "Jacob," in ver 15, according with the fact. Other modes have been proposed also, but none are entirely satisfactory. If there was positive proof of Stephen's inspiration, or if it were necessary to make that out, the difficulty would be much greater. But it has already been remarked that there is no decisive evidence of that: and it is not necessary to make out that point to defend the Scriptures. All that can be demanded of the historian is, that he should give a fair account of the defence as it was delivered; and though the *probability* is that Stephen would not commit such an error, yet, admitting that *he* did, it by no means proves that *Luke* was not inspired, or that Luke has committed any error in recording *what was actually said.* ¶ *Of the sons of Emmor.* In the Hebrew, (Gen. xxxiii. 19), "the children of Hamor" —but different ways of rendering the same word.

17. *The time of the promise.* The time of the *fulfilment* of the promise. ¶ *The people grew*, &c. Ex. i. 7—9.

18. *Till another king arose.* This is quoted from Ex. i. 8. What was the *name* of this king is not certainly known. The *common* name of all the kings of Egypt was *Pharaoh*, as *Cæsar* became the common name of the emperors of Rome after the time of Julius Cæsar: thus we say, Augustus Cæsar, Tiberius Cæsar, &c. It has commonly been supposed to have been the celebrated Rameses, or Ramses Mei

19 The same dealt subtilly with
our kindred, and evil-entreated our
fathers, so[a] that they cast out their
young children, to the end they
might not live.
20 In which time Moses[b] was
born, and was[1] exceeding fair, and
nourished up in his father's house
three months:
21 And when he was cast out,
Pharaoh's daughter took him up,
and[c] nourished him for her own
son.
22 And Moses was learned in all

a Ex.1.22. b Ex.2.2,&c. 1 or, *fair to God.* c Ex.2.10.

amoun, the sixth king of the eighteenth dynasty; and the event is supposed to have occurred about 1559 years before the Christian era. But M. Champollion supposes that his name was Mandonei, whose reign commenced 1585, and ended 1565 years before Christ. (Essay on the Hieroglyphic System, pp. 94, 95.) ¶ *That knew not Joseph.* It can hardly be supposed that he would be ignorant of the name and deeds of Joseph; and this expression, therefore, probably means that he did not *favour* the designs of Joseph; he did not remember the benefits he had conferred on the nation; or furnish the patronage for the kindred of Joseph which had been secured for them by Joseph under a former reign.—National ingratitude and forgetfulness of favours have not been uncommon in the world; and a change of dynasty or succession has often obliterated all memory of former obligations and compacts.

19. *Dealt subtilly.* He acted deceitfully; he used fraud. The cunning or deceitful attempt which is referred to, is his endeavour to weaken and destroy the Jewish people by causing their male children to be put to death. Ex. i. 22. ¶ *Our kindred.* Our nation, or our ancestors. ¶ *And evil-entreated.* Was unjust and cruel towards them. ¶ *So that,* &c. For that purpose, or to *cause* them to cast them out. He dealt with them in this cruel manner, hoping that the Israelites themselves would destroy their own sons, that they might not grow up to experience the same sufferings as their fathers had. The cunning or subtilty of Pharaoh extended to every thing that he did to oppress, to keep under, and to destroy the children of Israel.

20. *In which time,* &c. During this period of oppression. See Ex. ii. 2, &c. ¶ *Was exceeding fair.* Greek, "was fair to God;" properly rendered *was very handsome.* The word *God* is used in the Greek here in accordance with the Hebrew usage, by which any thing that is very handsome, or lofty, or grand, is thus designated. Thus, Ps. xxxvi. 7, *mountains of God* mean lofty mountains; Ps. lxxx. 11, *cedars of God,* mean lofty, beautiful cedars. Thus Nineveh is called "a great city *to God*" (Jonah iii. 3, Greek), meaning a very great city. The expression here means simply that Moses was *very fair,* or handsome. Comp. Heb. xi. 23, where he is called "a *proper* child," i. e. a *handsome* child. It would seem from this, that Moses was preserved by his mother on account of his *beauty;* and this is hinted at in Ex. ii. 2. And it would also seem from this, that Pharaoh had succeeded by his oppressions in what he had attempted; and that it was not unusual for parents among the Jews to *expose* their children, or to put them to death.

21. *Was cast out.* When he was exposed on the banks of the Nile. Ex. ii. 3. ¶ *And nourished him.* Adopted him, and treated him as her son. Ex. ii. 10. It is implied in this, that he was *educated* by her. An adopted son in the family of Pharaoh would be favoured with all the advantages which the land could furnish for an education.

22. *Moses was learned.* Or, was *instructed.* It does not mean that he *had* that learning, but that he was carefully *trained* or educated in that wisdom. The passage does not express the fact that Moses was distinguished for *learning,* but that he was carefully *educated,* or that pains were taken to *make* him learned. ¶ *In all the wisdom,* &c. The learning of the Egyptians was confined chiefly to astrology, to the interpretation of dreams, to medicine, to mathematics, and to their sacred science or traditionary doctrines about religion, which were concealed chiefly under their hieroglyphics. Their learning is not unfrequently spoken of in the Scriptures. 1 Kings iv. 30. Comp. Isa. xix. 11, 12. And their knowledge is equally celebrated in the heathen world. It is known that science was carried from Egypt to Phenicia, and thence to Greece; and not a few of the Grecian philosophers travelled to Egypt in pursuit of knowledge. ¶ *And was mighty.* Was powerful, or was distinguished. This means that he was eminent *in* Egypt, before he

the wisdom of the Egyptians, and
[a] was mighty in words and in deeds.
23 And [b] when he was full forty
years old, it came into his heart to
visit his brethen the children of Israel.
24 And seeing one *of them* suffer
wrong, he defended *him*, and avenged
him that was oppressed, and
smote the Egyptian:
25 For[1] he supposed his brethren
would have understood how that
God by his hand would deliver
them: but they understood not.
26 And the next day he shewed
himself unto them as they strove,
and would have set them at one
again, saying, Sirs, ye are brethren;
why do ye wrong one to another?
27 But he that did his neighbour
wrong thrust him away, saying,
Who made thee a ruler and a judge
over us?
28 Wilt thou kill me as thou

a Lu.24.19. b Ex.2.11,&c. 1 or, *Now*.

conducted the children of Israel forth. It refers to his addresses to Pharaoh, and to the miracles which he wrought *before* their departure. ¶ *In words.* From Ex. iv. 10, it seems that Moses was "slow of speech, and of a slow tongue." When it is said that he was mighty in words, it means that he was mighty in his communications to Pharaoh, though they were spoken by his brother Aaron. Aaron was in his place, and *Moses* addressed Pharaoh through him, who was appointed to deliver the message. Ex. iv. 11—16. ¶ *Deeds.* Miracles. Ex. vii. &c.

23. *Full forty years of age.* This is not recorded in the Old Testament; but it is a constant tradition of the Jews that Moses was forty years of age when he undertook to deliver them. Thus it is said, "Moses lived in the palace of Pharaoh forty years; he was forty years in Midian; and he ministered to Israel forty years." (*Kuinoel.*) ¶ *To visit,* &c. Probably with a view of delivering them from their oppressive bondage. Comp. ver. 25.

24. *Suffer wrong.* The wrong or injury was, that the Egyptian was smiting the Hebrew. Ex. ii. 11, 12. ¶ *Smote the Egyptian.* He slew him, and buried him in the sand.

25. *For he supposed.* This is not mentioned by Moses; but it is not at all improbable. When they saw him *alone* contending with the Egyptian, when it was understood that he had come and taken vengeance on one of their oppressors, it might have been presumed that he regarded himself as directed by God to interpose, and save the people.

26. *And the next day.* Ex. ii. 13. ¶ *He shewed himself.* He appeared in a sudden and unexpected manner to them. ¶ *Unto them.* That is, to *two* of the Hebrews. Ex. ii. 13 ¶ *As they strove.* As they were engaged in a quarrel. ¶ *Have set them at one* Greek. "would have urged them to peace." This he did by remonstrating with the man that did the wrong. ¶ *Saying.* What follows is not quoted literally from the account which Moses gives, but it is substantially the same. ¶ *Sirs.* Greek, "men." ¶ *Ye are brethren.* You belong not only to the same nation, but you are brethren and companions in affliction, and should not, therefore, contend with each other.—One of the most melancholy scenes in this world is that, where those who are poor, and afflicted, and oppressed, add to all their other calamities, altercations and strifes among themselves. Yet it is from this class that contentions and lawsuits usually arise. The address which Moses here makes to the contending Jews, might be applied to the whole human family, in view of the contentions and wars of nations; 'Ye are *brethren*, members of the same great family, and why do you contend with each other?'

27. *But he that did,* &c. Intent on his purpose, filled with rage and passion, he rejected all interference, and all attempts at peace.—It is usually the man that *does* the injury that is unwilling to be reconciled; and when we find a man that regards the entreaties of his friends as improper interference, when he becomes increasingly angry when we exhort him to peace, it is usually a strong evidence that he is conscious that he has been at fault. If we wish to reconcile parties, we should go first to the man that has been injured. In the controversy between God and man, it is the *sinner* who has done the wrong, that is unwilling to be reconciled, and not God. ¶ *His neighbour.* The Jew with whom he was contending. ¶ *Who made thee,* &c. What right have you to interfere in this matter? The usual salutation with which a man is greeted who attempts to prevent quarrels.

28 *Wilt thou kill me,* &c How it was

didst the Egyptian yesterday?
29 Then fled Moses at this saying; and was a stranger in the land of Madian, where he begat two sons.

30 And [a] when forty years were
expired, there appeared to him in the wilderness of mount Sina, an angel of the Lord, in a flame of fire in a bush.

a Ex.3.2,&c.

known that he had killed the Egyptian does not appear. It was probably communicated by the man who was rescued from the hands of the Egyptian. Ex. ii. 11, 12.

29. *Then Moses fled*, &c. Moses fled because he now ascertained that it was known. He supposed that it had been unobserved. Ex. ii. 12. But he now supposed that the knowledge of it might reach Pharaoh, and that his life might thus be endangered. Nor did he judge incorrectly; for as soon as Pharaoh heard of it, he sought to take his life. Ex. ii. 15. ¶ *Was a stranger.* Or became a *sojourner* (πάροικος), one who had a temporary abode in the land. The use of this word implies that he did not expect to make that his permanent dwelling. ¶ *In the land of Madian.* This was a part of Arabia. It was situated on the east side of the Red sea. The *city* of Midian is placed there by the Arabian geographers; but the Midianites seem to have spread themselves along the desert east of mount Seir, to the vicinity of the Moabites. To the west they extended also to the neighbourhood of mount Sinai. This was extensively a desert region, an unknown land; and Moses expected there to be safe from Pharaoh. ¶ *Where he begat two sons.* He married Zipporah, the daughter of *Reuel* (Ex. ii. 18), or *Jethro* (Num. x. 29. Ex. iii. 1), a *priest* of Midian. The names of the two sons were Gershom and Eliezer. Ex. xviii. 3, 4.

30. *And when forty years*, &c. At the age of eighty years. This, however, was known by tradition. It is not expressly mentioned by Moses. It is said, however, to have been after the king of Egypt had died (Ex. ii. 23); and the tradition is not improbable. ¶ *In the wilderness of mount Sinai.* In the desert adjacent to, or that surrounded mount Sinai. In Ex. iii. 1, it is said that this occurred at mount *Horeb*. But there is no contradiction; Horeb and Sinai are different peaks or elevations of the same mountain. They are represented as springing from the same base, and branching out in different elevations. The mountains, according to Burckhardt, are a prodigious pile, comprehending many peaks, and about thirty miles in diameter. From one part of this mountain, *Sinai*, the law was given to the children of Israel. ¶ *An angel of the Lord.* The word *angel* means properly a *messenger* (Note, Matt. i. 20), and is applied to the invisible spirits in heaven, to men, to the winds, or pestilence, or to whatever is appointed as a messenger *to make known* the will of God. The mere *name*, therefore, can determine nothing about the *nature* of the messenger. That *name* might be applied to *any* messenger, even an inanimate object. The *nature* and character of this messenger are to be determined by other considerations. The word *may* denote that the *bush on fire* was the messenger. But a comparison with the other places where this occurs will show that it was a celestial messenger, and perhaps that it was the Messiah who was yet to come, appearing to take the people of Israel under his own charge and direction. Comp. John i. 11, where the Jews are called "his own." In Ex. iii. 2, it is said that the angel of the Lord appeared IN a flame of fire; in ver. 4, it is said that Jehovah spake to him out of the midst of the bush; language which implies that God was there, and which is strongly expressive of the doctrine that the angel was Jehovah. In Ex. xxiii. 20, 21, God says, "I send an angel before thee, to keep thee in the way, and to bring thee into the place which I have prepared. Beware of *him*, and obey *his* voice," &c. ver. 23; xxxii. 34; xxxiii. 2. In all these places this angel is mentioned as an extraordinary messenger to conduct them to the land of Canaan. He was to guide them, defend them, and drive out the nations before them. All these circumstances seem to point to the conclusion that this was no other than the future Deliverer of the world, who came then to take his people under his own guidance, as emblematic of the future redemption of mankind. ¶ *In a flame of fire.* That is, in what *appeared* to be a flame of fire. The *bush* or clump of trees seemed to be on fire, or to be illuminated with a peculiar splendour. God is often represented as encompassed with this splendour, or glory. Luke ii. 9. Matt. xvii. 1—5. Acts ix. 3; xii. 7. ¶ *In a bush.* In a grove, or clump of trees. Probably the light was seen issuing from the *midst* of such a grove.

31 When Moses saw *it*, he wondered at the sight: and as he drew near to behold *it*, the voice of the Lord came unto him,

32 *Saying*, I *am* the God[a] of thy fathers, the God of Abraham, and the God of Isaac, and the God of Jacob. Then Moses trembled, and durst not behold.

33 Then said the Lord to him, Put[b] off thy shoes from thy feet; for the place where thou standest is holy ground.

34 I have seen, I have seen the affliction of my people which is in Egypt, and I have heard their groaning, and am come down to deliver them. And now come, I will send thee into Egypt.

35 This Moses, whom they refused, (saying, Who made thee a ruler and a judge?) the same did God send *to be* a ruler and a deliverer, by the hand of the[c] angel which appeared to him in the bush.

36 He brought them out, after[d] that he had shewed wonders and signs in the land of Egypt, and in the Red sea, and in the wilderness, forty[e] years.

37 This is that Moses which said[f] unto the children of Israel, A

a Matt.22.32. He.11.16. b Jos.5.15. Ec.5.1. c Ex.14.19. Nu.20.16. d Ex. c.7,8,9,10,11, & 14. e Ex.16.35. f De.18.15,18. c.3.22.

31. *He wondered*, &c. What particularly attracted his attention was the fact that the bush was not consumed. Ex. iii. 2, 3. ¶ *The voice of the Lord.* Jehovah spake to him from the midst of the bush. He did not see him, but he simply heard a voice.

32. *Saying, I am the God*, &c. See this explained, Notes, Matt. xxii. 32. ¶ *Then Moses trembled.* Ex. iii. 6.

33. *Then said the Lord*, &c. In Ex. iii. this is introduced in a different order, as being spoken *before* God said "I am the God," &c. ¶ *Put off thy shoes*, &c. Ex. iii. 5. To put off the shoes, or sandals, was an act of reverence. Especially the ancients were not permitted to enter a temple or holy place with their shoes on. Indeed, it was customary for the Jews to remove their shoes whenever they entered *any* house, as a mere matter of civility. Comp. Notes, John xiii. 5. See Josh. v. 15. ¶ *Is holy ground.* Is rendered sacred by the symbol of the divine presence. We should enter the sanctuary, the place set apart for divine worship, not only with reverence in our hearts, but with every *external* indication of veneration. Solemn awe, and deep seriousness, become the place set apart to the service of God.

34. *I have seen, &c.* The repetition of this word is in accordance with the usage of the Hebrew writers when they wish to represent any thing emphatically. ¶ *Their groaning.* Under their oppressions. ¶ *Am come down.* This is spoken in accordance with human conceptions. It means that God was about to deliver them. ¶ *I will send thee*, &c. This is a mere *summary* of what is expressed at much greater length in Ex. iii. 7—10.

35. *Whom they refused.* That is, when he *first* presented himself to them. Ex. ii. 13, 14. Stephen introduces and dwells upon this refusal in order, perhaps, to remind them that this had been the character of their nation; and to prepare the way for the charge which he intended to bring against those whom he addressed, as being stiff-necked and rebellious. See ver. 51, 52, &c. ¶ *A ruler.* A military leader, or a governor in civil matters. ¶ *A deliverer* A Redeemer. λυτρωτήν. It properly means one who redeems a captive or a prisoner by paying a *price* or *ransom*. And it is applied thus to our Lord Jesus, as having redeemed or purchased sinners by his blood as a price. Titus ii. 14. 1 Pet. i. 18. Heb. ix. 12. It is used here, however, in a more *general* sense to denote *the deliverance*, without specifying the manner. Comp. Ex. vi. 6. Luke xxiv. 21; i. 68; ii. 38. ¶ *By the hand of the angel.* Under the *direction* and by the *help* of the angel. Num. xx. 16. See on ver. 30.

36. *Wonders and signs.* Miracles, and remarkable interpositions of God. See Note, Acts ii. 22. ¶ *In the land of Egypt.* By the ten plagues. Ex. iv—xii. ¶ *In the Red sea.* Dividing it, and conducting the Israelites in safety, and overthrowing the Egyptians. Ex. xiv. ¶ *In the wilderness.* During their forty years' journey to the promised land. The wonders or miracles were, providing them with manna daily; with flesh in a miraculous manner, with water from the rock, &c. Ex. xvi. xvii. &c.

37. *Which said*, &c. Deu. xviii. 15 18 See this explained Acts iii. 22. Stephen introduced this to remind them of the promise of a Messiah; to show his faith in

prophet shall the Lord your God
raise up unto you of your brethren,
[1]like unto me; him [a] shall ye hear.
38 This [b] is he that was in the
church in the wilderness, with the
angel [c] which spake to him [d] in the
mount Sina, and *with* our fathers;
who [e] received [f] the lively oracles to
give unto us:
39 To whom our fathers would
not obey, but thrust *him* from them,
and in their hearts turned back
again into Egypt,
40 Saying [g] unto Aaron, Make us
gods to go before us: for *as for* this
Moses, which brought us out of the
land of Egypt, we wot not what is
become of him.
41 And they made a calf [h] in
those days, and offered sacrifice
unto the idol, and rejoiced in the
works of their own hands.
42 Then God turned and gave [i]
them up to worship the [j] host of
heaven: as it is written [k] in the
book of the prophets, O ye house
of Israel, have ye offered to me
slain beasts, and sacrifices, *by the
space of* forty years in the wilderness?

1 or, *as myself*. *a* Matt.17.5. *b* He.2.2. *c* Is.63.9. Gal.3.19. *d* Ex.19.3,17. *e* De.5.27,31. Jno.1.17. *f* Ro.3.2. *g* Ex.32.1.

h De.9.16. Ps.106.19,20. *i* Ps.81.12. *j* De.4.19. 2Ki.17.16. Jer.19.13. *k* Am.5.25,26.

it; and *particularly*, to remind them of their obligation to hear and obey him.

38. *In the church.* The word *church* means literally *the people called out*; and is applied with great propriety to the assembly or multitude called out of Egypt, and separated from the world. It has not, however, of necessity our idea of a church; but means the *assembly*, or people called out of Egypt, and placed under the conduct of Moses. ¶ *With the angel.* In this place there is undoubted reference to the giving of the law on mount Sinai. Yet that was done by God himself. Ex. xx. It is clear, therefore, that by *the angel* nere, Stephen intends to designate him who was God. It may be observed, however, that *the law* is represented as having been given by the ministry of an angel (in this place) and by the ministry of *angels*, Acts vii. 53. Heb. ii. 2. The essential idea is, that God did it by a messenger, or by mediators. The *character* and *rank* of the messengers, or of the *principal* messenger, must be learned by looking at all the circumstances of the case. ¶ *The lively oracles.* See Rom. iii. 2. The word *oracles* here means *commands* or *laws* of God. The word *lively*, or *living* (ζῶντα), stands in opposition to that which is dead, or useless, and means that which is vigorous, efficacious; and in this place it means that the commands were of such a nature, and given in such circumstances, as to secure attention; to produce obedience; to excite them to act for God—in opposition to laws which would fall powerless, and produce no effect.

39. *Would not obey*, &c. This refers to what they said of him when he was in the mount. Ex. xxxii. 1. 23. ¶ *In their hearts turned*, &c. They wished to return to Egypt. They regretted that they had come out of Egypt, and desired again the things which they had there, as preferable to what they had in the desert. Num. xi. 5. Perhaps, however, the expression means, not that they desired literally to *return* to Egypt, but that *their hearts inclined to the habits and morals of the Egyptians.* They forsook God, and imitated the idolatries of the Egyptians.

40. *Saying unto Aaron.* Ex. xxxii. 1. ¶ *Make us gods.* That is, idols.

41. *And they made a calf.* This was made of the ear-rings and ornaments which they had brought from Egypt. Ex. xxxii. 2—4. Stephen introduces this to remind them how prone the nation had been to reject God, and walk in the ways of sin.

42. *Then God turned.* That is, turned away from them; abandoned them to their own desires. ¶ *The host of heaven.* The stars, or heavenly bodies. The word *host* means *armies*. It is applied to the heavenly bodies because they are very numerous, and appear to be *marshalled* or arrayed in military order. It is from this that God is called Jehovah *of hosts*, as being the ruler of these well-arranged heavenly bodies. Isa. i. 9. The proof that they did this, Stephen proceeds to allege by a quotation from the prophets. ¶ *In the book of the prophets.* Amos v. 25, 26. The twelve minor prophets were commonly written in one volume, and were called the Book of the Prophets; the book containing these several prophecies, Daniel, Hosea, Micah, &c. They were smal

43 Yea, ye took up the tabernacle of Moloch, and the star of your
god Remphan, figures which ye
made, to worship them: and I wil
carry you away beyond Babylon.
44 Our fathers had the tabernacle

---

tracts separately, and were bound up together to preserve them from being lost. This passage is not quoted literally; it is evidently made from memory; and though in its main spirit it coincides with the passage in Amos, yet in some important respects it varies from it. ¶ *O ye house of Israel.* Ye people of Israel. ¶ *Have ye offered,* &c. That is, ye have *not* offered. The interrogative form is often an emphatic way of saying that the thing had *not* been done. But it is certain that the Jews *did* offer sacrifices to God in the wilderness, though it is also certain that they did not do it with a pure and upright heart. They kept up the *form* of worship generally, but they frequently forsook God, and offered worship to idols. *Through* the continuous space of forty years they did *not* honour God, but often departed from him, and worshipped idols.

43. *Yea, ye took up.* That is, you *bore*, or you carried with you, for purposes of idolatrous worship. ¶ *The tabernacle.* This word properly means a *tent;* but it is also applied to the small tent or house in which was contained the image of the god; the house, box, or tent, in which the idol was placed. It is customary for idolatrous nations to bear their idols about with them, enclosed in *cases* or boxes of various sizes, usually very small, as their idols are commonly small. Probably they were made in the shape of small *temples* or tabernacles; and such appear to have been the *silver shrines* for Diana, made at Ephesus. Acts xix. 24. These shrines, or images, were borne with them as a species of *amulet*, or *charm*, or *talisman*, to defend them from evil. Such images the Jews seem to have borne with them. ¶ *Moloch.* This word comes from the Hebrew word signifying *king.* This was a god of the Ammonites, to whom human sacrifices were offered. Moses in several places forbids the Israelites, under penalty of death, to dedicate their children to Moloch, by making them pass through the fire. Lev. xviii. 21; xx. 2—5. There is great probability that the Hebrews were addicted to the worship of this deity after they entered the land of Canaan. Solomon built a temple to Moloch on the mount of Olives (1 Kings xi. 7); and Manasseh made his son pass through the fire in honour of this idol. 2 Kings xxi. 3, 6. The image of this idol was made of brass, and his arms extended so as to embrace any one; and when they offered children to him, they heated the statue, and when it was burning hot, they placed the child in his arms, where it was soon destroyed by heat. It is not certain what this god was supposed to represent. Some suppose it was in honour of the planet Saturn; others, the sun; others, Mercury, Venus, &c. What particular god it was, is not material. It was the most cutting reproof that could be made to the Jews, that their fathers had been guilty of worshipping this idol. ¶ *And the star.* The Hebrew in this place is, "Chiun your images, the star of your god." The expression here used leads us to suppose that this was a *star* which was worshipped, but *what* star it is not easy to ascertain; nor is it easy to determine why it is called both *Chiun* and *Remphan.* Stephen quotes from the LXX. They have rendered the word *Chiun* by the word *Raiphan*, or *Rephan*, easily changed into *Remphan.* Why the LXX. adopted this, is not known. It was probably, however, from one of two causes. (1.) Either because the word *Chiun* in Hebrew meant the same as *Remphan* in the language of Egypt, where the translation was made; or, (2.) Because the *object* of worship called *Chiun* in Hebrew, was called *Remphan* in the language of Egypt It is generally agreed that the *object* of their worship was the planet *Saturn*, or *Mars*, both of which planets were worshipped as gods of evil influence. In Arabic, the word *Chevân* denotes the planet Saturn. Probably *Rephan*, or *Remphan*, is the Coptic name for the same planet, and the Septuagint adopted this because their translation was made in Egypt, where the Coptic language was spoken. ¶ *Figures which ye made.* Images of the god which they made. See the article *Chiun* in Robinson's Calmet. ¶ *And I will carry you away,* &c. This is simply expressing in few words what is stated at greater length in Amos v. 27. In Hebrew it is *Damascus;* but this evidently denotes the eastern region, in which also Babylon was situated.

44. *The tabernacle of witness.* The *tent* or *tabernacle* which Moses was commanded to make. It was called a tabernacle of *witness*, or of *testimony*, because it was the visible witness or proof of God's presence with them; the evidence that he to whom it was devoted was their protector

of witness in the wilderness, as he
had appointed, [1] speaking unto Moses,
that [a] he should make it according
to the fashion that he had seen.
45 Which [b] also our fathers [2] that
came after, brought in with Jesus
into the possession of the Gentiles,
whom [c] God drave out before the
face of our fathers, unto the days
of David,
46 Who found favour [d] before
God, and desired [e] to find a tabernacle
for the God of Jacob.
47 But Solomon [f] built him an
house.
48 Howbeit, [g] the Most High

[1] or, *who spake.* a Ex.25.40; 26.30. He.8.5. b Jos.3.14. [2] or, *having received.* c Ne.9.24. Ps.44.2; 78.55.

d 1Sam.16.1. e 1Chr.22.7. f 1Ki.6.1,&c.; 8.20. g 1Ki.8.27. c.17.24.

and guide. The name is given either to the *tent*, or to the two tables of stone, or to the ark; all of which were *witnesses*, or *evidences* of God's relation to them as their lawgiver and guide. Ex. xvi. 34; xxv. 16. 21; xxvii. 21; xxx. 6. 36; xxxi. 18, &c. Num. i. 50. 53. The two charges against Stephen were that he had spoken blasphemy against Moses, or his law, and against the temple. ch. vi. 13, 14. In the previous part of this defence he had shown his respect for Moses and his law. He now proceeds to show that he did not design to speak with disrespect of the temple, or the holy places of their worship. He therefore expresses his belief in the divine appointment of both the tabernacle (ver. 44—46) and of the temple (ver. 47). ¶ *According to the fashion,* &c. According to the *pattern* that was shown to him, by which it was to be made. Ex. xxv. 9. 40; xxvi. 30. As God showed him *a pattern*, it proved that the tabernacle had his sanction. Against that Stephen did not intend to speak.

45. *Our fathers that came after.* None of the generation that came out of Egypt were permitted to enter into the land of Canaan on account of their rebellion, except Caleb and Joshua. Num. xiv. 22—24; xxxii. 11, 12. Hence it is said that their fathers *who came after*, i. e. after the generation when the tabernacle was built. The Greek, however, here means, properly, "which also our fathers, having *received*, brought," &c. The sense is not materially different. Stephen means that it was not brought in by that generation, but by the next. ¶ *With Jesus.* This should have been rendered "with *Joshua.*" *Jesus* is the Greek mode of writing the name *Joshua*. But the Hebrew name should by all means have been retained here, as also in Heb. iv 8. ¶ *Into the possession of the Gentiles.* Into the land possessed *by* the Gentiles, that is, into the promised land then occupied by the Canaanites, &c. ¶ *Whom God,* &c. That is, he continued to drive them out [illegible] time of David, when they were completely expelled. Or it may mean that the tabernacle was in the possession of the Jews, and was the appointed place of worship, until the time of David, who desired to build him a temple. The Greek is ambiguous. The *connexion* favours the latter interpretation.

46. *Who found favour,* &c. That is, God granted him great prosperity, and delivered him from his enemies. ¶ *To find a tabernacle.* To prepare a permanent dwelling-place for the *ark*, and for the visible symbols of the divine presence. Hitherto the ark had been kept in the tabernacle, and had been borne about from place to place. David sought to build an house that should be permanent, where the ark might be deposited. 2 Sam. vii. 1 Chron. xxii. 7.

47. *But Solomon,* &c. Built the temple. David was not permitted to do it because he had been a man of war. 1 Chron. xxii. 8. David prepared the principal materials for the temple, but Solomon built it. 1 Chron. xxii. Comp 1 Kings vi.

48. *Howbeit.* But. Why Stephen added this, is not very clear. He was charged with speaking against the temple. He had now shown that he had due veneration for it, by his declaring that it had been built by the command of God. But he *now* adds, that God does not need such a temple. Heaven is his throne; the universe his dwelling-place; and *therefore* this temple might be destroyed. A new, glorious truth was to be revealed to mankind, that God was not *confined* in his worship to any age, or people, or nation. In entire consistency, therefore, with all proper respect for the temple at Jerusalem, it might be maintained that the time would come when that temple would be destroyed, and when God might be worshipped by all nations. ¶ *The Most High.* God. This sentiment was expressed by Solomon when the temple was dedicated. 1 Kings viii. 27. ¶ *As saith the prophet.* Isa. lxvi. 1, 2. The place is not literally quoted but the sense is given.

dwelleth not in temples made with
hands; as saith the prophet,
49 Heaven [a] *is* my throne, and
earth *is* my footstool: what house
will ye build me? saith the Lord:
or what *is* the place of my
rest?
50 Hath not my hand made all
these things?
51 Ye stiff-necked, [b] and uncircumcised [c] in heart and ears, ye do
always resist the Holy Ghost: as
your fathers *did*, so *do* ye.
52 Which [d] of the prophets have
not your fathers persecuted? And
they have slain them which shewed
before of the coming of the Just
One, of whom ye have been now
the betrayers and murderers.
53 Who have received the law

a Is.66.1,2. b Ex.32.9. Is.48.4.
c Lev.26.41. Jer.9.26. Rom.2.28,29. d 2Chr.36.16. 1Th.2.15. e c.3.14.

---

49. *Heaven is my throne.* See Note, Matt. v. 34. ¶ *Earth is my footstool.* Note, Matt. v. 35. ¶ *What house, &c.* What house or temple can be large or magnificent enough for the dwelling of Him who made all things? ¶ *The place of my rest.* My home, my abode, my fixed seat or habitation. Comp. Ps. xcv. 11.

51. *Ye stiff-necked.* The discourse of Stephen has every appearance of having been interrupted by the clamours and opposition of the sanhedrim. This verse has no immediate connexion with that which precedes; and *appears* to have been spoken in the midst of much opposition and clamour. If we may conjecture in this case, it would seem that the Jews saw the drift of his argument; that they interrupted him; and that when the tumult had somewhat subsided, he addressed them in the language of this verse, showing them that they sustained a character precisely similar to their rebellious fathers. The word *stiff-necked* is often used in the Old Testament. Ex. xxxii. 9; xxxiii. 3. 5; xxxiv. 9. Deut. ix. 6. 13; x. 16, &c. It is a figurative expression taken from oxen that were refractory, and that would not submit to be yoked. Applied to men, it means that they were stubborn, contumacious, and unwilling to submit to the restraints of law. ¶ *Uncircumcised in heart. Circumcision* was a sign of being a Jew—of acknowledging the authority of the laws of Moses. It was also emblematic of purity, and of submission to the law of God. The expression *uncircumcised in heart* denotes those who were not willing to acknowledge that law, and submit to it. They had hearts filled with vicious and unsubdued affections and desires. ¶ *And ears.* That is, who are unwilling to *hear* what God says. Comp. Lev. xxvi. 41. Jer. ix. 26. Notes on Rom. ii. 28, 29. ¶ *Resist the Holy Ghost.* You oppose the message which is brought to you by the authority of God, and the inspiration of his Spirit. The message brought by Moses; by the prophets; by the Saviour; and by the apostles—all by the infallible direction of the Holy Ghost—they and their fathers opposed. ¶ *As your fathers did, &c.* As he had specified in ver. 27. 35. 39—43.

52. *Which of the prophets, &c.* The interrogative form here is a strong mode of saying that they had persecuted *all* the prophets. It was *the characteristic of the nation* to persecute the messengers of God. This is not to be taken as literally and universally true; but it was a general truth; it was the national characteristic. See Notes, Matt. xxi. 33—40; xxiii. 29—35. ¶ *And they have slain them, &c.* That is, they have slain the prophets, whose main message was that the Messiah was to come. It was a great aggravation of their offence, that they put to death the messengers which foretold the greatest blessing that the nation could receive. ¶ *The Just One.* The Messiah. See Note, ch. iii. 14. ¶ *Of whom ye, &c.* You thus show that you resemble those who rejected and put to death the prophets. You have even gone beyond them in guilt, because you have put the Messiah himself to death. ¶ *The betrayers.* They are called *betrayers* here because they employed Judas to betray him—agreeable to the maxim in law, *He who does any thing by another, is held to have done it himself.*

53. *Who have received the law.* The law of Moses, given on mount Sinai. ¶ *By the disposition of angels.* There has been much diversity of opinion in regard to this phrase, εἰς διαταγὰς ἀγγέλων. The word translated *disposition* does not elsewhere occur in the New Testament. It properly means the *constituting* or *arranging* of an army; disposing it into ranks and proper divisions. Hence it has been supposed to mean that the law was given *amidst* the various ranks of angels, being present to witness its promulgation. Others suppose that the angels were employed as

by [a] the disposition of angels, and have not kept *it*.

54 When they heard these things, [b] they were cut to the heart, and they gnashed on him with *their* teeth.

55 But he, being [c] full of the Holy Ghost, looked up steadfastly into heaven, and saw the glory of God, and Jesus standing on the right hand of God,

56 And said, Behold, I see the [d] heavens opened, and [e] the Son of man standing on the right hand of God.

57 Then they cried out with a loud voice, and stopped their ears, and ran upon him with one accord,

58 And cast [f] him out of the city, and stoned *him*: and the witnesses

a Gal.3.19. b c.5.33. c c.6.5. d Eze.1.1. e Dan.7.13. f Lu.4.29. He.13.12,13.

agents or instruments to communicate the law. All that the expression fairly implies is the former; that the law was given amidst the attending ranks of angels, as if they were summoned to witness the pomp and ceremony of giving *law* to an entire people, and through them to an entire world. It should be added, moreover, that the Jews applied the word *angels* to any of the messengers of God; to fire, and tempest, and wind, &c. And all that Stephen means here, may be to express the common Jewish opinion, that God was attended on this occasion by the heavenly hosts; and by the symbols of his presence, the fire, and smoke, and tempest. Comp. Ps. civ. 4; lxviii. 17. Other places declare that the law was spoken by *an angel*, one eminent above all attending angels, the peculiar messenger of God. See Note on ver. 38. It is plain that Stephen spoke only the common sentiment of the Jews. Thus Herod is introduced by Josephus (Antiq. b. xv. ch. v. § 3) as saying, "We have learned from God the most excellent of our doctrines, and the most holy part of our law *by angels*," &c. In the eyes of the Jews, it justly gave increased majesty and solemnity to the law, that it had been given in so grand and imposing circumstances. And it greatly aggravated their guilt, that notwithstanding this, they had not kept it

54. *They were cut to the heart.* They were exceedingly enraged and indignant The whole course of the speech had been such as to excite their anger, and now they could restrain themselves no longer. ¶ *They gnashed on him*, &c. Expressive of the bitterness and malignity of their feeling.

55. *Full of the Holy Ghost.* See Note, ch. ii. 4. ¶ *Looked up steadfastly.* Fixed his eyes intently on heaven. Foreseeing his danger; and the effect his speech had produced—seeing that there was no safety in the great council of the nation, and no prospect of justice at their hands, he cast his eyes to heaven and sought protection there.—When dangers threaten us, our hope of safety lies in heaven. When men threaten our persons, reputation, or lives, it becomes us to fix our eyes on the heavenly world; and we shall not look in vain. ¶ *And saw the glory of God.* This phrase is commonly used to denote the visible symbols of God. It means some magnificent representation; a splendour, or light, that is the appropriate exhibition of the presence of God. Matt. xvi. 27; xxiv. 30. Note, Luke ii. 9. In the case of Stephen there is every indication of a vision, or supernatural representation of the heavenly objects; something in advance of mere *faith*, such as dying Christians now have. What was its precise nature, we have no means of ascertaining. Objects were often represented to prophets by *visions*; and probably something similar is intended here. It was such an elevation of view, such a representation of truth, and of the glory of God, as to be denoted by the word *see*; though it is not to be maintained that Stephen really saw the Saviour with the bodily eye. ¶ *On the right hand of God.* That is, exalted to a place of honour and power in the heavens. Note, Mark xxvi. 64. Acts ii. 25.

56. *I saw the heavens opened.* A figurative expression, denoting that he was permitted to see *into* heaven, or to see what was there, *as if* the firmament was divided, and the eye was permitted to penetrate the eternal world. Comp. Ezek. i. 1.

57. *Then they cried out.* That is, probably, *the people*, not the members of the council. It is evident he was put to death in a popular tumult. They had charged him with blasphemy; and they regarded what he had now said as full proof of it. ¶ *And stopped their ears.* That they might hear no more blasphemy. ¶ *With one accord.* In a tumult; unitedly.

58. *And cast him out of the city.* This was in accordance with the usual custom. In Lev. xxiv. 14, it was directed to bring forth him that had cursed without the

[a] laid down their clothes at a young man's feet, whose name was [b] Saul.
59 And they stoned Stephen, calling upon *God*, and saying, Lord Jesus, receive [c] my spirit!
60 And he kneeled down, and

a c 6.13. b c.8.1,3; 22.20. c Ps.31.5. Lu.23.46.

camp; and it was not usual, the Jewish writers inform us, to stone in the presence of the sanhedrim. Though this was a popular tumult, and Stephen was condemned without the regular process of trial, yet some of the *forms* of law were observed, and he was stoned in the manner directed in the case of blasphemers. ¶ *And stoned him.* This was the punishment appointed in the case of blasphemy. Lev. xxiv. 16. Note, John x. 31. ¶ *And the witnesses.* That is, the false witnesses who bore testimony against him. ch. vi. 13. It was directed in the law (Deut. xvii. 7) that the *witnesses* in the case should be first in executing the sentence of the law. This was done to prevent false accusations by the prospect that *they* must be employed as executioners. After *they* had commenced the process of execution, all the people joined in it. Deut. xvii. 7. Lev. xxiv. 16. ¶ *Laid down their clothes.* Their *outer garments.* They were accustomed to lay these aside when they ran or worked. Note, Matt. v. 40. ¶ *At a young man's feet,* &c. That is, they procured him to take care of their garments. This is mentioned solely because Saul, or Paul, afterwards became so celebrated, first as a persecutor, and then an apostle. His whole heart was in this persecution of Stephen; and he himself afterwards alluded to this circumstance as an evidence of his sinfulness in persecuting the Lord Jesus. Acts xxii. 20.

59. *Calling upon* God. The word *God* is not in the original, and should not have been in the translation. It is in none of the ancient MSS. or versions. It should have been rendered, They stoned Stephen, invoking, or calling upon, and saying, Lord Jesus, &c. That is, he was engaged *in prayer* to the Lord Jesus. The word is used to express *prayer* in the following, among other places: 2 Cor. i. 23, "I call God to witness." 1 Pet. i. 17, "And if ye call on the Father," &c. Acts ii. 21, "Whosoever shall call on the name of the Lord," &c. ix. 14; xxii. 16. Rom. x. 12, 13, 14. This was, therefore, an act of worship; a solemn invocation of the Lord Jesus, in the most interesting circumstances in which a man can be placed—in his dying moments. And this shows that it is *right* to worship the Lord Jesus, and to pray to him. For if Stephen was *inspired*, it settles the question. The example of an inspired man in such circumstances, is a safe and correct example. If it should be said that the inspiration of *Stephen* cannot be made out, yet the inspiration of *Luke*, who has recorded it, will not be called in question. Then the following circumstances show that *he*, an inspired man, regarded it as right, and as a proper example to be followed. (1.) He has recorded it without the slightest expression of an opinion that it was improper. On the contrary, there is every evidence that he regarded the conduct of Stephen in this case as right and praiseworthy. There is, therefore, this attestation to its propriety. (2.) The Spirit that inspired Luke knew what use would be made of this case. He knew that it would be used as an *example*, and as an evidence that it was *right* to worship the Lord Jesus. It is one of the cases which has been used to perpetuate the worship of the Lord Jesus in every age. If it was wrong, it is inconceivable that it should be recorded without some expression of disapprobation. (3.) The case is strikingly similar to that recorded in John xx. 28, where Thomas offered worship to the Lord Jesus, *as his God*, without reproof. If Thomas did it in the presence of the Saviour without reproof, it was right. If Stephen did it without any expression of disapprobation from the inspired historian, it was right. (4.) These examples were used to encourage Christians and Christian martyrs to offer homage to Jesus Christ. Thus Pliny, writing to the emperor Trajan, and giving an account of the Christians in Bythinia, says, that they were accustomed to meet and *sing hymns to Christ as to God.* (*Lardner.*) (5.) It is worthy of remark, that Stephen in his death offered the same act of homage to Christ, that Christ himself did to the Father, when he died. Luke xxiii. 46. From all these considerations, it follows that the Lord Jesus is an object of worship; that in most solemn circumstances it is proper to call upon him, to worship him, and to commit our dearest interests to his hands. If this may be done, he is divine. ¶ *Receive my spirit.* That is, receive it to thyself; take it to thine abode in heaven.

60. *And he kneeled down.* This seems to have been a *voluntary* kneeling; a placing himself in this position for the purpose of *prayer*, choosing to die in this

cried with a loud voice, Lord, lay
a not this sin to their charge! And
when he had said this, he fell
asleep.

a Matt.5.44. Lu.23.34.

CHAPTER VIII.

AND Saul b was consenting unto
his death. And at that time
there was a great persecution against

b c.7.58.

attitude. ¶ *Lord*. That is, Lord *Jesus*. Note, ch. i. 24. ¶ *Lay not*, &c. Forgive them. This passage strikingly resembles the dying prayer of the Lord Jesus. Luke xxiii. 34. Nothing but the Christian religion will enable a man to utter this passage in his dying moments. ¶ *He fell asleep*. This is the usual mode of expressing the death of saints in the Bible. It is an expression indicating, (1.) The *peacefulness* of their death, compared with the alarm of sinners; (2.) The hope of a resurrection; as we retire to sleep with the hope of again awaking to the duties and enjoyments of life. See John xi. 11, 12. 1 Cor. xi. 30; xv. 51. 1 Thess. iv. 14; v. 10. Matt. ix. 24.

In view of the death of this first Christian martyr, we may remark,

1. That it is right to address to the Lord Jesus the language of prayer.

2. It is peculiarly proper to do it in afflictions, and in the prospect of death. Heb. iv. 15.

3. Sustaining grace will be derived in trials chiefly from a view of the Lord Jesus. If we can look to him as *our* Saviour, see him to be exalted to deliver us, and truly commit our souls to him, we shall find the grace which we shall need in our afflictions.

4. We should have such confidence in him, as to enable us to commit ourselves to him at any time. To do this, we should live a life of faith. In health, and youth, and strength, we should seek him *as our first and best friend*.

5. While we are in health, we should prepare to die. What an unfit place for preparation for death would have been the situation of Stephen! How impossible then would it have been to have made preparation! Yet the dying bed is often a place as unfit to prepare as were the circumstances of Stephen. When racked with pain when faint and feeble, when the mind is indisposed to thought, or when it raves in the wildness of delirium, what an unfit place is this to prepare to die. I have seen many dying beds; I have seen many in all stages of their last sickness; but never have I yet seen a dying bed which seemed to me to be a proper place to make preparation for eternity.

6. How peaceful and calm is a death like that of Stephen, when compared with the alarms and anguish of a sinner! One moment of such peace in that trying time, is better than all the pleasures and honours which the world can bestow. And to *obtain* such peace, the dying sinner would be willing to give all the wealth of the Indies, and all the crowns of the earth. So may I die—and so may all my readers—enabled, like this dying martyr, to commit my departing spirit to the sure keeping of the great Redeemer! When we take a parting view of the world; when our eyes shall be turned for the last time to take a look of friends and relatives; and when the darkness of death shall begin to come around us; then may we be enabled to cast the eye of faith to the heavens, and say, 'Lord Jesus, receive our spirits;' and thus fall asleep, peaceful in death, in the hope of the resurrection of the just.

CHAPTER VIII.

1. *And Saul was consenting*, &c. Was pleased with his being put to death, and approved it. Comp. ch. xxii. 20. This part of the verse should have been connected with the previous chapter. ¶ *At that time*. That is, immediately following the death of Stephen. The persecution arose on account of Stephen. ch. xi. 19. The tumult did not subside when Stephen was killed. Their anger continued to be excited against *all* Christians. They had become so imbittered by the zeal and success of the apostles, and by their frequent charges of *murder* in putting the Son of God to death, that they resolved at once to put a period to their progress and success. This was the *first* persecution against Christians; the first in a series that terminated only when the religion which they wished to destroy was fully established on the ruins of both Judaism and Paganism. ¶ *The church*. The collection of Christians which were now organized into a church. The church at Jerusalem was the *first* that was collected. ¶ *All scattered*. That is, the great mass of Christians. ¶ *The regions of Judea*, &c. See Note, Matt. ii. 22 ¶ *Except the apostles*. Probably the other Christians fled from fear. Why the apostles, who were particularly in danger, did not flee also, is not stated by the historian. Having been, however, more fully in-

the church which was at Jerusalem; and they were all scattered [a] abroad throughout the regions of Judea and Samaria, except the apostles.

2 And devout men carried Stephen *to his burial*, and made great lamentation over him.

a c.11.19.

3 As for Saul, he [b] made havoc of the church, entering into every house; and haling men and women, committed *them* to prison.

4 Therefore they that were scattered abroad, went every where preaching the word.

b c.26.10,11. Gal.1.13.

---

structed than the others, and having been taught their duty by the example and teaching of the Saviour, they resolved, it seems, to remain and brave the fury of the persecutors. For *them* to have fled then would have exposed them, as leaders and founders of the new religion, to the charge of timidity and weakness. They therefore resolved to remain in the midst of their persecutors; and a merciful Providence watched over them, and defended them from harm. The dispersion extended not only to Judea and Samaria, but those who fled carried the gospel also to Phenice, and Cyprus, and Antioch. ch. xi. 19. There was a *reason* why this was permitted. The early converts were Jews. They had strong feelings of attachment to the city of Jerusalem, to the temple, and to the land of their fathers. Yet it was the design of the Lord Jesus that the gospel should be preached every where. To accomplish this, he suffered a persecution to rage; and they were scattered abroad, and bore his gospel to other cities and lands. Good thus came out of evil; and the first persecution resulted, as all others have done, in advancing the cause which was intended to be destroyed.

2. *And devout men.* Religious men. The word used here does not imply of necessity that they were Christians. There might have been Jews who did not approve the popular tumult, and the murder of Stephen, and who gave him a decent burial. Joseph of Arimathea, and Nicodemus, both Jews, thus gave to the Lord Jesus a decent burial. John xix. 38, 39. ¶ *Carried Stephen.* The word translated *carried*, means properly to *collect*, as fruits, &c. Then it is applied to all the preparations necessary for fitting a dead body for burial, as *collecting*, or confining it by bandages, with spices, &c. ¶ *And made great lamentation.* This was usual among the Jews at a funeral. See Note, Matt. ix. 23.

3. *As for Saul.* But Saul. He had no concern in the pious attentions shown to Stephen, but engaged with zeal in the work of persecution. ¶ *He made havoc.* ἐλυμαίνετο. This word is commonly applied to wild beasts, to lions, wolves, &c and denotes the devastations which they commit. Saul raged against the church like a wild beast—a strong expression, denoting the zeal and fury with which he engaged in persecution. ¶ *Entering into every house.* To search for those who were suspected of being Christians. ¶ *Haling.* Dragging, or compelling them. ¶ *Committed* them *to prison.* The sanhedrim had not power to put them to death. John xviii. 31. But they had power to imprison; and they resolved, it seems, to exercise this power to the utmost. Paul frequently refers to his zeal in persecuting the church. Acts xxvi. 10, 11. Gal. i. 13.—It may be remarked here that there never was a persecution commenced with more flattering prospects to the persecutors. Saul, the principal agent, was young, zealous, learned, and clothed with power. He showed afterwards that he had talents fitted for any station; and zeal that tired with no exertion, and that was appalled by no obstacle. With this talent he entered on his work. Christians were few and feeble. They were scattered and unarmed. They were unprotected by any civil power, and exposed, therefore, to the full blaze and rage of persecution. That the church was not destroyed, was owing to the protection of God—a protection that not only secured its existence, but which extended its influence and power by means of this very persecution far abroad on the earth.

4. *Went every where.* That is, they travelled through the various regions where they were scattered. In all places to which they came, they preached the word. ¶ *Preaching the word.* Greek, *Evangelizing*, or announcing the good news of the message of mercy, or the word of God. It is not the usual word which is rendered *preach*, but means simply announcing the good news of salvation. There is no evidence, nor is there any probability, that all these persons were *ordained* to preach. They were manifestly common Christians who were scattered by the persecution; and the mean-

5 Then Philip [a] went down to the city of Samaria, and preached Christ unto them.

6 And the people with one accord [b] gave heed unto those things which Philip spake, hearing, [c] and

a c.6.5. b 2Chr.30.12. c Jno.4.41,42.

ing is, that they communicated to their fellow-men in conversation, wherever they met them; and probably in the synagogues, where all Jews had a right to speak, the glad tidings that the Messiah had come. It is not said that they set themselves up for public teachers; or that they administered baptism; or that they founded churches: but they proclaimed every where the news that a Saviour had come. Their hearts were full of it. Out of the abundance of the heart the mouth speaks; and they made the truth known to *all* whom they met.—We may learn from this, (1.) That persecution tends to promote the very thing which it would destroy. (2.) That one of the best means to make Christians active and zealous is to persecute them. (3.) That it is right for *all* Christians to make known the truths of the gospel. When the heart is full, the lips will speak; and there is no more impropriety in their speaking of redemption than of any thing else. (4.) It should be the great object of all Christians to make the Saviour known *every where*. By their lives, conversation, and pious exhortations and entreaties, they should beseech dying sinners to be reconciled to God. And especially should this be done when they are *travelling*. Christians when away from home seem almost to imagine that they lay aside the obligations of religion. But the example of Christ and his early disciples has taught us that this is the very time to attempt to do good.

5. *Then Philip.* One of the seven deacons. ch. vi. 5. He is afterwards called *the Evangelist.* Acts xxi. 8. ¶ *The city of Samaria.* This does not mean a city whose *name* was Samaria, for no such city at that time existed. Samaria was a *region.* Matt. ii. 22. The ancient city Samaria, the capital of that region, had been destroyed by *Hyrcanus*, so completely as to leave no vestige of it remaining; and he "took away," says Josephus, "the very marks that there had ever been such a city there." (Antiq. b. xiii. ch. x. § 3.) Herod the Great afterwards built a city on this site, and called it *Sebaste*, i. e. *Augusta*, in honour of the emperor Augustus. (Jos. Antiq. b. xv. ch. viii. § 5.) Perhaps this city is intended, as being the principal city of Samaria; or possibly *Sychar*, another city where the gospel had been before preached by the Saviour himself. John iv. ¶ *And preached Christ.* Preached that the Messiah had come, and made known his doctrines. The same truths had been before stated in Samaria by the Saviour himself (John iv.); and this was doubtless one of the reasons why they so gladly now received the word of God. The field had been prepared by the Lord Jesus; and he had said that it was white for the harvest (John iv. 35); and into that field Philip now entered, and was signally blessed. His coming was attended with a remarkable *revival of religion.* The word translated *preach* here is not that which is used in the previous verse. This denotes to *proclaim as a crier*, and is commonly employed to denote the preaching of the gospel, so called. Mark v. 20; vii. 36. Luke viii. 39. Matt. xxiv. 14. Acts x. 42. Rom. x. 15. 1 Cor. ix. 27; xv. 12. 2 Tim. iv. 2. It has been argued that because *Philip* is said thus to have preached to the Samaritans, that *therefore* all *deacons* have a right to preach or that they are, under the New Testament economy, an *order* of ministers. But this is by no means clear. For, (1.) It is not evident, nor can it be shown, that the *other* deacons (ch. vi) ever preached. There is no record of their doing so; and the narrative would lead us to suppose that they did not. (2.) They were *appointed* for a very different purpose (ch. vi. 1—5); and it is fair to suppose that *as deacons*, they confined themselves to the design of their appointment. (3.) It is not said that *Philip* preached in virtue of his being *a deacon.* From any thing in *this* place, it would seem that he preached as the other Christians did—wherever he was. (4.) But *elsewhere* an express distinction is made between Philip and the others. A new appellation is given him, and he is expressly called the *Evangelist.* Acts xxi. 8. From *this*, it seems that he preached, not *because* he was a *deacon*, but because he had received a special *appointment* to this business as an evangelist. (5.) This same office, or rank of Christian teachers, is expressly recognised elsewhere. Eph. iv. 11. All these considerations show that there is *not* in the sacred Scriptures an order of ministers appointed to preach *as deacons.*

6. *With one accord.* Unitedly, or with one mind. Great multitudes of them did it. ¶ *Gave heed* Paid attention to; em-

seeing the miracles which he did.
7 For [a] unclean spirits, crying with loud voice, came out of many that were possessed *with them:* and many taken with palsies, [b] and that were lame, [c] were healed.
8 And there was great joy in that city.
9 But there was a certain man called Simon, which beforetime in the same city used sorcery, [d] and bewitched the people of Samaria, giving out [e] that himself was some great one:
10 To whom [f] they all gave heed, from the least to the greatest, saying, This man is the great power of God.

a Mar.16.17. b Mar.2.3-11. c.9.33,34. c Matt.11.5. d c.13.6. Re.22.15. e c.5.36. 2Ti.3.2,5. f 2Cor.11.19.

braced. ¶ *Hearing.* Hearing what he said.

7. *For unclean spirits.* Note, Matt. iv. 24. ¶ *Crying with loud voice.* Note, Mark i. 26. ¶ *Palsies.* Note, Matt. iv. 24.

8. *And there was great joy.* This joy arose, (1.) From the fact that so many persons, before sick and afflicted, were restored to health. (2.) From the conversion of individuals to Christ. The tendency of religion is to produce joy. (3.) From the mutual joy of *families* and *friends*, that their friends were converted. The tendency of a revival of religion is thus to produce great joy.

9. *But there was a certain man called Simon.* The Fathers have written much respecting this man, and have given strange accounts of him; but nothing more is certainly known of him than is stated in this place. Rosenmueller and Kuinoel suppose him to have been a Simon mentioned by Josephus (Antiq. b. xx. ch. vii. § 2), who was born in Cyprus. He was a magician, and was employed by Felix to persuade Drusilla to forsake her husband Azizus, and to marry Felix. But it is not very probable that this was the same person. (See Note in Whiston's Josephus.) Simon Magus was probably a *Jew* or a *Samaritan*, who had addicted himself to the arts of magic, and who was much celebrated for it. He had studied philosophy in Alexandria in Egypt (Mosheim, i. p. 113, 114, *Murdock's translation*), and then lived at Samaria. After he was cut off from the hope of adding to his other powers the power of working miracles, the *fathers* say that he fell into many errors, and became the founder of the sect of the Simonians. They accused him of affirming that he came down as the *Father* in respect to the Samaritans; the *Son* in respect to the Jews; and the *Holy Spirit* in respect to the Gentiles. He did not acknowledge Christ to be the Son of God, but a rival, and pretended himself to be Christ. He rejected the law of Moses. Many other things are affirmed of him, which rest on doubtful authority. He seems to have become an enemy to Christianity; though he was willing *then* to avail himself of some of its doctrines in order to advance his own interests. The account that he came to a tragical death in Rome; that he was honoured as a deity by the Roman senate; and that a statue was erected to his memory in the isle of Tiber, is now generally rejected. His end is not known. (See Calmet, art. *Simon Magus*, and Mosheim, i. p. 114, Note.) ¶ *Beforetime.* The practice of magic, or sorcery, was common at that time, and in all the ancient nations. ¶ *Used sorcery.* Greek, μαγεύων. Exercising the arts of the *Magi*, or *Magicians;* hence the name Simon *Magus.* See Note, Matt. ii. 1. The ancient *Magi* had their rise in Persia, and were at first addicted to the study of philosophy, astronomy, medicine, &c. This name came afterwards to signify those who made use of the knowledge of these arts for the purpose of imposing on mankind—astrologers, soothsayers, necromancers, fortune-tellers, &c. Such persons pretended to predict future events by the positions of the stars, and to cure diseases by incantations, &c. See Isa. ii. 6. See also Dan. i. 20; ii 2. It was expressly forbidden the Jews to consult such persons on pain of death. Lev. xix. 31; xx. 6. In these arts Simon had been eminently successful. ¶ *And bewitched.* This is an unhappy translation. The Greek means merely that he *astonished* or *amazed* the people, or *confounded* their judgment. The idea of *bewitching* them is not in the original. ¶ *Giving out,* &c. *Saying,* i. e. boasting. It was in this way, partly, that he so confounded them. Jugglers generally impose on people just in proportion to the *extravagance* and *folly* of their pretensions. The same remark may be made of *quack doctors*, and of all persons who attempt to delude and impose on mankind.

10. *The great power of God.* Probably this means only that they believed that he was *invested with* the power of God

11 And to him they had regard, because that of long time he had bewitched [c] them with sorceries.
12 But when they believed [b] Philip preaching the things [c] concerning the kingdom of God, and the name of Jesus Christ, they were baptized, both men and women.
13 Then Simon himself believed also: and when he was baptized, he continued with Philip, and wondered, beholding the miracles [1] and signs which were done.
14 Now when the apostles which were at Jerusalem heard that Samaria had received the word of God, they sent unto them Peter and John:

a Gal.3.1. b ver.37. c.2.41. c c.1.3.

1 or, *signs and great miracles.*

not that they supposed he was really the Great God.

13 *Then Simon...believed also.* That is, he believed that Jesus had wrought miracles, and was raised from the dead, &c. All this he could believe in entire consistency with his own notions of the power of magic; and all that the connexion requires us to suppose is that he believed this—that Jesus had power of working miracles, &c.; and as he purposed to turn this to his own account, he was willing to profess himself to be his follower. It might have injured his popularity, moreover, if he had taken a stand when so many were professing to become Christians.—Men often profess religion because, if they do not, they fear they will lose their influence, and be left with the ungodly. That Simon was not a real Christian is apparent from the whole narrative. ver. 18. 21—23. ¶ *And when he was baptized.* He was admitted to a *profession* of religion in the same way as the others. Philip did not pretend to know the heart; and Simon was admitted because he *professed* his belief. This is all the evidence that ministers can have, and it is no wonder, that they, as well as Philip, are often deceived. The reasons which influenced Simon to make a profession of religion, seem to have been these: (1.) An impression that Christianity was *true.* He seems to have been convinced of this by the miracles of Philip. (2.) The fact that many others were becoming Christians; and *he* went in with the multitude. This is often the case in revivals of religion. (3.) He had no religion; but it is clear (ver. 20, 21) that he was willing to make use of Christianity to advance his own power, influence, and popularity—a thing which multitudes of men of the same mind with Simon Magus have been willing since to do. ¶ *And continued,* &c. It was customary and natural for the disciples to remain with their teachers. See ch. ii 42. ¶ *And wondered.* This is the same word that is translated *bewitched* in ver. 9. 11. It means that he was amazed that Philip could *really* perform so much greater miracles than *he* had even pretended to.—Hypocrites will sometimes be greatly attentive to the external duties of religion, and will be greatly surprised at what is done by God for the salvation of sinners. ¶ *Miracles and signs.* Greek, Signs and *great powers,* or great miracles. That is, so much greater than he *pretended* to be able to perform.

14. *They sent.* That is, the apostles *deputed* two of their number. This shows conclusively that there was no *chief* or *ruler* among them. They acted as being equal in authority. The reason why they sent them was, probably, that there would be a demand for more labour than Philip could render; a church was to be founded, which required their presence; and it was important that they should be present to organize it, and to build it up. The *harvest* had occurred in Samaria, of which the Saviour spoke (John iv. 35), and it was proper that they should enter into it.—In times of revival there is often more to be done than can be done by the regular pastor of a people, and it is proper that he should be aided from abroad. ¶ *Peter.* This shows that *Peter* had no such authority and primacy as the Roman Catholics claim for him. He exercised no authority of *sending* others, but was himself *sent.* He was appointed by *their* united voice, instead of claiming the power himself of directing *them.* ¶ *And John.* Peter was ardent, bold, zealous, rash; John was mild, gentle, tender, persuasive. There was wisdom in uniting them in this work, as the talents of both were needed: and the excellencies in the character of the one would compensate for the defects of the other. It is observable that the apostles sent *two* together, as the Saviour had himself done. See Note, Mark vi. 7. The *reasons* why this additional aid was sent to Samaria were probably these: (1.) To assist Philip in a great work—in the *harvest* which he was there collecting. (2.) To give the *sanction* of the authority of the apostles to

15 Who, when they were come down, prayed for them, that they might receive the Holy Ghost:

16 For as yet [a] he was fallen upon none of them; only they were [b] baptized in the name of the Lord Jesus.

17 Then laid [c] they *their* hands on them, and they received the Holy Ghost.

18 And when Simon saw, that through laying on of the apostles' hands the Holy Ghost was given, he offered them [d] money,

a c.19.2. b c.2.38; 10.48; 19.5,6. 1Cor.1.13. c c.6.6. He.6.2. d 1Tim.6.5.

what he was doing. (3.) To confer on the converts the gift of the Holy Ghost. ver. 17.

15. *Were come down.* To Samaria. Jerusalem was generally represented as *up*, or *higher* than the rest of the land. Matt. xx 18. John vii. 8. ¶ *Prayed for them.* They sought at the hand of God the extraordinary communications of the Holy Spirit. They did not even pretend to have the power of doing it without the aid of God. ¶ *That they might receive the Holy Ghost.* The main question here is, what was *meant* by the Holy Ghost? In ver. 20, it is called "the gift of God." The following remarks may make this plain. (1.) It was not that gift of the Holy Ghost by which *the soul is converted*, or *renewed*, for they had this when they believed. ver. 6. Every where the conversion of the sinner is traced to his influence. Comp. John i. 13. (2.) It was not the ordinary influences of the Spirit by which the soul is sanctified; for sanctification is a progressive work, and this was sudden: sanctification is shown by the general tenor of the life; this was sudden and striking. (3.) It was something that was discernible by *external effects;* for Simon *saw* (ver. 18), that this was done by the laying on of hands. (4.) The phrase 'the gift of the Holy Ghost,' and 'the descent of the Holy Ghost,' signified not merely his *ordinary* influences in converting sinners, but those *extraordinary* influences that attended the first preaching of the gospel—the power of speaking with new tongues (ch. ii.), the power of working miracles, &c. Acts xix. 6. (5.) This is further clear from the fact that Simon wished to *purchase* this power, evidently to keep up his influence among the people, and to retain his ascendency as a juggler and sorcerer. But surely, Simon would not wish to *purchase* the *converting* and sanctifying influences of the Holy Spirit; it was the power of working miracles. These things make it clear that by the gift of the Holy Spirit here is meant the power of speaking with new tongues (comp. 1 Cor. xiv.) and the power of miracles And it is further clear that *this* passage should not be adduced in favour of "the rite of confirmation" in the Christian church. For besides the fact that there are now no *apostles*, the thing spoken of here, is entirely different from that of the rite of confirmation. *This* was to confer the extraordinary power of working miracles; *that* is for a different purpose.

If it be asked *why* this power was conferred on the early Christians, it may be replied, that it was to furnish striking proof of the truth of the Christian religion; to impress the people, and thus to win them to embrace the gospel. The early church was thus armed with the power of the Holy Spirit; and this extra ordinary attestation of God to his message was one cause of the rapid propagation and permanent establishment of the gospel.

16. *He was fallen.* This expression is several times applied to the Holy Spirit. ch. x. 44; xi. 15. It does not differ materially from the common expression, "the Holy Ghost *descended.*" It means that he came from heaven; and the expression *to fall*, applied to his influences, denotes the *rapidity* and *suddenness* of his coming. Comp. ch. xix. 2. ¶ *In the name of the Lord Jesus.* Note, ch. ii. 38. See also ch. x. 48; xix. 5, 6.

17. *Then laid they their hands, &c.* This was an act of *prayer*, expressing an invocation to God that he would impart the blessing to *them.* On *how many* they laid their hands, is not said. It is evident that it was not on *all*, for they did not thus lay hands on Simon. Perhaps it was done on a few of the more prominent and leading persons, who were to be employed particularly in bearing witness to the truth of the gospel. It was customary to lay the hands on any person when a *favour* was to be conferred, or a blessing imparted. See Note, Matt. ix. 18.

18. *Simon saw, &c.* That is, he witnessed the extraordinary effects, the power of speaking in a miraculous manner, &c. Note, ver. 15. ¶ *He offered them money.* He had had a remarkable influence over the Samaritans, and he saw that the pos-

19 Saying, Give me also this power, that on whomsoever I lay hands, he may receive the Holy Ghost.

20 But Peter said unto him, Thy money perish with thee, because [a] thou hast thought that the gift [b] of God may be purchased with money.

21 Thou hast neither part [c] nor lot in this matter: for [d] thy heart is not right in the sight of God.

a 2Ki 6.15,16. Matt.10.8. b c.10.45; 11.17. c Jos.22.25. d Ps.78.36,37. Eze.14.3.

session of this power would perpetuate and increase his influence. Men commonly employ the tricks of legerdemain for the purpose of making money; and it seems probable that such had been the design of Simon. He saw that if he could communicate to *others* this power, if he could confer on *them* the talent of speaking other languages, it might be turned to vast account, and he sought therefore to purchase it of the apostles. From this act of Simon we have derived our word *simony*, to denote the buying and selling of ecclesiastical preferment, or church offices, where religion is supported by the state. This act of Simon shows conclusively that he was influenced by improper motives in becoming connected with the church.

20. *Thy money perish with thee.* This is an expression of the horror and indignation of Peter at the base offer of Simon. It is not to be understood as an imprecation on Simon. The main idea is the apostle's contempt for the *money*, as if he regarded it as of no value. 'Let your money go to destruction. We abhor your impious offer. We can freely see *any* amount of money destroyed before we will be tempted to *sell* the gift of the Holy Ghost.' But there was here also an expression of his belief that *Simon* also would perish. It was a declaration that he was hastening to ruin, and *as if* this was certain, Peter says, let your money *perish too.* ¶ *The gift of God.* That which he has *given*, or conferred as a favour. The idea was *absurd* that that which God himself *gives* as a sovereign, could be purchased. It was *impious* to think of attempting to buy with worthless gold that which was of so inestimable value. The *gift of God* here means the extraordinary influences of the Holy Ghost. ch. x. 45; xi. 17. How can we pay a *price* to God? All that *we* can give, the silver, and the gold, and the cattle on a thousand hills, belong to him already. We have *nothing* which we can present for his favours. And yet there are many who seek to *purchase* the favour of God. Some do it by alms and prayers; some by penance and fasting; some by attempting to make their own hearts better, and by self-righteousness; and some by penitence and tears. All these will not *purchase* his favour. Salvation, like every other blessing, will be *his gift;* and if ever received, we must be willing to accept it on his own terms; at his own time; and in his own way. We are without merit; and if saved, it will be by the sovereign grace of God.

21. *Neither part.* You have no *portion* of the grace of God; that is, you are destitute of it altogether. This word commonly denotes the *part* of an inheritance which falls to one when it is divided. ¶ *Nor lot.* This word means properly a portion which *falls* to one when an estate, or when spoil in war is divided into portions, according to the number of those who are to be partakers, and the part of each one is determined by *lot.* The two words denote *emphatically* that he was in no sense a partaker of the favour of God. ¶ *In this matter.* Greek, In this *word,* i. e. thing. That which is referred to here is the religion of Christ. He was not a Christian. It is remarkable that Peter judged him so soon, and when he had seen but *one* act of his. But it was an act which satisfied him that he was a stranger to religion. One act may sometimes bring out the *whole character;* it may evince the *governing* motives; it may show traits of character utterly *inconsistent* with true religion; and then it is as certain a criterion as any long series of acts. ¶ *Thy heart.* Your *affections,* or *governing motives;* your principle of conduct. Comp. 2 Kings x. 15. You love gold and popularity, and not the gospel for what it is. There is no evidence here that Peter saw this in a miraculous manner, or by any supernatural influence. It was apparent and plain, that Simon was not influenced by the pure, disinterested motives of the gospel, but by the love of power and of the world. ¶ *In the sight of God.* That is, God *sees* or judges that your heart is not sincere and pure.—No external profession is acceptable without the heart. Reader, is *your* heart right with God? Are your motives pure; and does *God* see there the exercise of holy, sincere, and benevolent affections towards him? God *knows* the motives; and with

22 Repent therefore of this thy wickedness; and pray God, if[a] perhaps the thought of thine heart may be forgiven thee:

a Dan.4.27. 2Tim.2.25.

23 For I perceive that thou art in the gall of bitterness, [b] and *in* the bond [c] of iniquity.

b Jer.4.18. Heb.12.15. c Ps. 116.16. Prov.5.22 Isa.28.22.

unerring certainty he will judge; and with unerring justice he will fix our doom, according to the affections of the heart

22. *Repent, therefore.* Here we may remark, (1.) That Simon was at this time an unconverted sinner. (2.) That the command was given to him *as such.* (3.) That he was required to *do* the *thing;* not to wait or seek merely, but actually to repent. (4.) That this was to be the *first step* in his conversion. He was not even directed to *pray* first, but his first indispensable work was to *repent*, that is, to exercise proper sorrow for this sin, and to *abandon* his plan or principle of action. And this shows, (1.) That *all* sinners are to be exhorted to *repent*, as their first work. They are *not* to be told to *wait*, and *read*, and *pray*, in the expectation that repentance will be *given* them. With such helps as they can obtain, they are to *do the thing.* (2.) Prayer will not be acceptable, or heard, unless the sinner comes *repenting*, that is, unless he regrets his sin, and *desires* to forsake it. Then, and then only, will he be heard. When he comes *loving* his sins, and resolving still to practise them, God will not hear him. When he comes *desirous* of forsaking them, grieved that he is guilty, and *feeling* his need of help, God will hear his prayer. See Isa. i. 15. Mic. iii. 4. Prov. i. 28. Ps. lxvi. 18. ¶ *And pray God.* Having a *desire* to forsake the sin, and to be pardoned, *then* pray to God to forgive. It would be absurd to ask forgiveness until a man felt his need of it. This shows that a sinner *ought* to pray, and *how* he ought to do it. It should be with a desire and purpose to forsake sin, and in that state of mind God will hear the prayer. Comp. Dan. iv. 27. ¶ *If perhaps.* There was no certainty that God would forgive him; nor is there any evidence either that Simon prayed, or that he was forgiven.—This direction of Peter presents *another* important principle in regard to the conduct of sinners. They are to be directed to repent, not *because* they have the promise of forgiveness, and not because they *hope* to be forgiven, but because sin *is a great evil*, and because it is *right* and *proper* that they should repent, whether they are forgiven or not. That is to be left to the sovereign mercy of God. *They* are to repent of sin, and then they are to feel, not that they have any *claim* on God, but that they are dependent on him, and must be saved or lost at his will. They are not to suppose that their tears will *purchase* forgiveness, but that they lie at the foot of mercy, and that there is *hope*—not certainty—that God will forgive. The language of the humbled sinner is.

"Perhaps he will admit my plea,
Perhaps will hear my prayer;
But if I perish I will pray,
And perish only there.

"I can but perish if I go,
I am resolv'd to try,
For if I stay away, I know
I shall for ever die."

¶ *The thought*, &c. Your *purpose*, or *wish. Thoughts* may be, therefore, evil, and need forgiveness. It is not open sin only that needs to be pardoned; it is the secret purpose of the soul.

23. *For I perceive.* That is, by the act which he had done. His offer had shown a state of mind that was wholly inconsistent with true religion. One single sin *may* as certainly show that there is no true piety as *many* acts of iniquity. It may be so decided, so malignant, so utterly inconsistent with just views, as at once to determine what the character is. The sin of Simon was of this character. Peter here does not appear to have claimed the power of judging the *heart;* but he judged, as all other men would, by the act. ¶ *In the gall.* This word denotes properly *bile*, or that bitter, yellowish-green fluid that is secreted in the liver. Hence it means any thing very bitter; and also any bad passion of the mind, as anger, malice, &c. We speak of *bitterness* of mind, &c. ¶ *Of bitterness.* This is a Hebraism; the usual mode of expressing the *superlative*, and means *excessive bitterness.* The phrase is used respecting *idolatry* (Deut. xxix. 18), "Lest there should be among you a root that beareth gall and wormwood." A similar expression occurs in Heb xii. 15, "Lest any root of bitterness springing up, trouble you," &c. *Sin* is thus represented as a *bitter* or poisonous thing; a thing not only *unpleasant* in its consequences, but ruinous in its character, as a poisonous plant would be in the midst of other plants. Jer ii. 19, "It is an

24 Then answered Simon, and said, Pray [a] ye to the Lord for me, that none of these things which ye have spoken come upon me.

25 And they, when they had testified and preached the word of the Lord, returned to Jerusalem, and preached the gospel in many villages of the Samaritans.

26 And the angel of the Lord spake unto Philip, saying, Arise, and go toward the south, unto the way that goeth down from Jerusalem unto Gaza [b] which is desert

a Ex.8.8. Nu.21.7. 1Ki.13.6. Job 42.8. Ja.5.16.

b Jos.15.47.

evil and *bitter* thing that thou hast forsaken the Lord thy God." iv. 18. Rom. iii. 14, "Whose mouth is full of cursing and bitterness." Eph. iv. 31. The meaning here is, that the heart of Simon was full of dreadful, malignant sin. ¶ *Bond of iniquity.* Or, that thou art *bound by* iniquity. That is, that it has the *rule* over you, and *binds* you as a slave. Sin is often thus represented as *bondage* and *captivity*. Sinners are represented as chained to it, and kept in hard servitude. Ps. cxvi. 16. Prov. v. 22, "He shall be holden with the cords of his sins." Rom. vii. 23, 24. These expressions prove conclusively that Simon was a stranger to religion.

24. *Pray ye,* &c. Here remark, (1.) That Simon was directed to pray for himself (ver. 22), but he had no disposition to do that. Sinners will often ask others to pray for them, when they are too proud, or too much in love with sin, to pray for themselves. (2.) The main thing that Peter wished to impress on him was a sense of his *sin*. Simon did not regard this, but looked only to the *punishment*. He was terrified and alarmed; and he sought to avoid future punishment; but he had no alarm about his *sins*. So it is often with sinners. So it was with Pharaoh (Ex. viii. 28. 32), and with Jeroboam (1 Kings xiii. 6). And so sinners often quiet their own consciences by asking ministers and Christian friends to pray for them, while *they* still purpose to persevere in iniquity. If men expect to be saved, they must pray *for themselves;* and pray not chiefly to be freed from *punishment*, but from the *sin which deserves hell.*—This is all that we hear of Simon in the New Testament; and the probability is, that, like many other sinners, he did *not* pray for himself, but continued to live in the gall of bitterness, and died in the bond of iniquity. The testimony of antiquity is decided on that point. See Note, ver. 9.

25. *In many villages,* &c. They *went* at first directly to the *city* of Samaria. On their return to Jerusalem, they travelled more at leisure, and preached in the villages also—a good example for the ministers of the gospel, and for all Christians, when travelling from place to place.—The reason why they returned to Jerusalem, and made that their permanent abode, might have been, that it was important to bear witness to the resurrection of Christ in the very city where he had been crucified, and where his resurrection had occurred. If the doctrine was established *there*, it would be more easy to establish it elsewhere.

26. *And the angel of the Lord.* The word *angel* is used in the Scriptures in a great variety of significations. See Note, Matt. i. 20. Here it has been supposed by some to mean literally a celestial messenger sent from God; others have supposed that it means *a dream*, others *a vision*, &c. The word properly means *a messenger;* and all that it can be shown to signify here is, that the Lord sent a *message* to Philip of this kind. It is most probable, I think, that the passage means that God communicated the message by his Spirit; for in ver. 29, 39, it is expressly said that *the Spirit* spake to Philip, &c. Thus in Acts xvi. 7, the *Spirit* is said to have forbidden Paul to preach in Bythinia; and in ver. 9, the message on the subject is said to have been conveyed in *a vision* There is no absurdity, however, in supposing that an *angel* literally was employed to communicate this message to Philip. See Heb. i. 14. Gen. xix. 1; xxii. 11. Judg. vi. 12. ¶ *Spake unto Philip.* Comp. Matt. ii. 13. ¶ *Arise.* See Note, Luke xv. 18. ¶ *And go,* &c. Philip had been employed in Samaria. As God now intended to send the gospel to another place, he gave a special direction to Philip to go and convey it. It is evident that God designed the *conversion* of this eunuch; and the direction to Philip shows *how* he accomplishes his designs. It is not by miracle, but by the use of means. It is not by direct power without *truth*, but it is by a message fitted to the end. The salvation of a single sinner is an object worthy the attention of God. When such a sinner is converted, it is because God forms a *plan* or *purpose* to do it. *When* it is done, he

27 And he arose and went: and, behold, a man of Ethiopia, [a] an [b] eunuch of great authority under Candace queen of the Ethiopians, who had the charge of all her treasure, and had come [c] to Jerusalem for to worship,

28 Was returning; and, sitting

a Zeph.3.10. b Isa.56.3-5. c 2Chr.6.32,33.

inclines his servants to labour; he directs their labours; he leads his ministers; and he prepares the way (ver. 28) for the reception of the truth. ¶ *Toward the south.* That is, south of Samaria, where Philip was then labouring. ¶ *Unto Gaza.* Gaza, or AZZAH (Gen. x. 19), was a city of the Philistines, given by Joshua to Judah (Josh. xv. 47. 1 Sam. vi. 17). It was one of the *five* principal cities of the Philistines. It was formerly a large place; was situated on an eminence, and commanded a beautiful prospect. It was in this place that Samson took away the gates of the city, and bore them off. Judg. xvi 2, 3. It was near Askelon, about sixty miles southwest from Jerusalem. ¶ *Which is desert.* This may refer either to the *way* or to the *place.* The natural construction is the latter. In explanation of this, it is to be observed that there were *two* towns of that name, Old and New Gaza. The prophet Zephaniah (ii. 4) said that *Gaza* should be *forsaken*, i. e. destroyed. "This was partly accomplished by Alexander the Great. (Jos. Antiq. b. xi. ch. viii. § 3, 4; b. xiii. ch. xiii. § 3.) Another town was afterwards built of the same name, but at some distance from the former; and Old Gaza was abandoned to desolation. Strabo mentions 'Gaza the desert,' and Diodorus Siculus speaks of 'Old Gaza.'" (*Robin. Calmet.*) Some have supposed, however, that Luke refers here to the *road* leading to Gaza, as being desolate and uninhabited. But I regard the former interpretation as most natural and obvious. "In this place, in 1823, the American missionaries, Messrs. Fisk and King, found Gaza, a town built of stone, making a very mean appearance, and containing about five thousand inhabitants." (*Hall on the Acts.*)

27. *A man of Ethiopia.* Gaza was near the confines between Palestine and Egypt. It was in the direct road from Jerusalem to Egypt. *Ethiopia* was one of the great kingdoms of Africa, part of which is now called Abyssinia. It is frequently mentioned in Scripture under the name of *Cush.* But *Cush* comprehended a much larger region, including the southern part of Arabia, and even sometimes the countries adjacent to the Tigris and Euphrates. Ethiopia proper lay south of Egypt, on the Nile, and was bounded north by Egypt, that is, by the cataracts near Syene; east by the Red sea, and perhaps part by the Indian Ocean; south by unknown regions in the interior of Africa; and west by Lybia and the deserts. It comprehended the modern kingdoms of Nubia or Sennaar, and Abyssinia. The chief city in it was the ancient Meroë, situated on the island or tract of the same name, between the Nile and Ashtaboras, not far from the modern Shendi. (*Robinson's Calmet.*) ¶ *An eunuch,* &c. See Note, Matt. xix. 12. Eunuchs were commonly employed in attendance on the females of the harem; but the word is often used to denote any confidential officer, or counsellor of state. It is evidently so used here. ¶ *Of great authority.* Of high rank; an officer of the court. It is clear from what follows that this man was a Jew. But it is known that *Jews* were often raised to posts of high honour and distinction in foreign courts, as in the case of Joseph in Egypt, and of Daniel in Babylon. ¶ *Under Candace,* &c. Candace is said to have been the common name of the queens of Ethiopia, as *Pharaoh* was of the sovereigns of Egypt. This is expressly stated by Pliny. (Nat. Hist. vii. 29.) His words are, "The edifices of the city were few; a woman reigned there of the name of CANDACE, which name had been transmitted to these queens for many years." Strabo mentions also a queen of Ethiopia of the name of Candace. Speaking of an insurrection against the Romans, he says, "Among these were the officers of queen CANDACE, who in our days reigned over the Ethiopians." As this could not have been the Candace mentioned here, it is plain that the name was common to these queens—a sort of royal title. She was probably queen of Meroë, an important part of Ethiopia. (Bruce's Travels, vol. ii. p. 431—*Clarke.*) ¶ *Who had the charge,* &c. The treasurer was an officer of high trust and responsibility. ¶ *And had come,* &c. This proves that he was a *Jew*, or at least a Jewish proselyte. It was customary for the Jews in foreign lands, as far as practicable, to attend the great feasts at Jerusalem. He had gone up to attend the Passover, &c See Note, ch. ii. 5.

28. *And sitting in his chariot.* His carriage; his vehicle. The form of the car

in his chariot, read Esaias the prophet.

29 Then [a] the Spirit said unto
Philip, Go near, and join thyself to this chariot.

30 And Philip ran thither to *him*

a Isa.65.24. Hos.6.3.

riage is not known. In some instances the carriages of the ancients were placed on wheels; in others, were borne on poles in the form of a *litter* or palanquin, by men, or mules, or horses. (See Calmet, art. *Chariot.*) ¶ *Reading Esaias*, &c. Isaiah. Reading doubtless the translation of Isaiah called the Septuagint. This translation was made in Egypt, for the special use of the Jews in Alexandria and throughout Egypt, and was that which was commonly used. *Why* he was reading the Scriptures, and especially this prophet, is not certainly known. It is morally certain, however, that he was in Judea at the time of the crucifixion and resurrection of Jesus; that he had heard much of him; that this would be a subject of discussion; and it was natural for him, in returning, to look at the prophecies respecting the Messiah, perhaps either to meditate on them as a suitable subject of inquiry and thought, or perhaps to examine the claims of Jesus of Nazareth to this office. The prophecy in Isa. liii. was so striking, and coincided so clearly with the character of Jesus, that it was natural for a candid mind to examine whether *he* might not be the person intended by the prophet.—On this narrative we may remark, (1.) It is a proper and profitable employment on returning from *worship* to examine the sacred Scriptures. (2.) It is well to be in the habit of reading the Scriptures when we are on a journey. It may serve to keep the heart from worldly objects, and secure the affections for God. (3.) It is well at *all* times to read the Bible. It is one of the means of grace. And it is when we are searching his will, that we obtain light and comfort. The sinner should examine with a candid mind the sacred volume. It may be the means of conducting him in the true path of salvation. (4.) God often gives us light in regard to the meaning of the Bible in unexpected modes. How little did this eunuch *expect* to be enlightened in the manner in which he actually was. Yet God, who intended to instruct and save him, sent the living teacher, and opened to him the sacred scriptures, and led him to the Saviour. It is probable (ver. 30) that he was reading it aloud.

29. *The Spirit.* See Note, ver. 26. The Holy Spirit is here evidently intended. The thought in Philip's mind is here traced to his suggestion. All good thoughts and designs have the same origin. ¶ *Join thyself.* Join him in his chariot. Go and sit with him.

30. *And Philip ran*, &c. Indicating his haste, and his desire to obey the suggestions of the Spirit. A thousand difficulties might have been started in the mind of Philip if he had reflected a little. The eunuch was a stranger; he had the appearance of a man of rank; he was engaged in reading; he might be indisposed to be interrupted or to converse, &c. But Philip obeyed without any hesitation the monitions of the Spirit, and *ran* to him.—It is well to follow the *first* suggestions of the Spirit; to yield to the clear indications of duty, and to perform it *at once.* Especially in a deed of benevolence, and in conversing with others on the subject of religion, our *first* thoughts are commonly safest and best. If we do not follow them, the calculations of avarice, or fear, or some worldly prudence, are very apt to come in. We become alarmed, we are afraid of the rich and the great; and we suppose that our conversation and admonitions will be unacceptable.—We may learn from this case, (1.) To do our duty at once, without hesitation or debate. (2.) We shall often be disappointed in regard to subjects of this kind. We shall find candid, humble, Christian conversation far more acceptable to strangers, to the rich, and to the great, than we commonly suppose. If, as in this case, they are *alone;* if we approach them kindly; if we do not rudely and harshly address them, we shall find most men willing to talk on the subject of religion. I have conversed with some hundreds of persons on the subject of religion, and do not now recollect but *two* instances in which I was rudely treated, and in which it was not easy to gain a respectful and kind attention to Christian conversation. ¶ *And heard him read.* He was reading *loud*—sometimes the best way of impressing truth on the mind in our private reading the Scriptures. ¶ *And said*, &c. This question, there might have been reason to fear, would not be kindly received. But the eunuch's mind was in such a state that he took no offence from such an inquiry, though made by a footman, and a stranger. He doubtless recognised him as a brother Jew.—It is an important

and heard him read the prophet
Esaias, and said, Understandest [a]
thou what thou readest?
31 And he said, How [b] can I, except some man should guide [c] me?
And he desired Philip that he would
come up and sit with him.
32 The place of the scripture
which he read was this, [d] He was
led as a sheep to the slaughter;
and like a lamb dumb before his
shearer, so opened he not his mouth:
33 In his humiliation his judgment was taken away: and who
shall declare his generation? for
his life is taken from the earth.

a Matt.13.23,51. Ep.5.17. b Ro.10.14. c Ps.25.9. d Isa.53.7,8.

---

question to ask ourselves when we read the sacred Scriptures.

31. *And he said, &c.* This was a *general* acknowledgment of his need of direction. It evinced a humble state of mind. It was an acknowledgment, also, originating probably from this particular passage which he was reading. He did not understand how it could be applied to the Messiah; how the description of his humiliation and condemnation (ver. 33) could be reconciled to the prevalent ideas of his being a prince and a conqueror. The same sentiment is expressed by Paul in Rom. x. 14. The circumstances, the state of mind in the eunuch, and the result, strongly remind one of the declaration in Ps. xxv. 9, "The meek will he guide in judgment, and the meek will he teach his way." ¶ *And he desired, &c.* He was willing to receive instruction even from a stranger.—The rich and the great may often receive valuable instruction from a stranger, and from a poor, unknown man.

32. *The place, &c.* Isa. liii. 7, 8. ¶ *He was led, &c.* This quotation is taken literally from the Septuagint. It varies very little from the Hebrew. It has been almost universally understood that this place refers to the Messiah; and Philip expressly applies it to him. The word "was led" (ἤχθη) implies that he was conducted by others; that he was led as a sheep is led to be killed. The general idea is that of *meekness* and *submission* when he was led to be put to death; a description that applies in a very striking manner to the Lord Jesus. ¶ *To the slaughter.* To be killed. The characteristic here recorded is more remarkable in the sheep than in any other animals. ¶ *And like a lamb dumb, &c.* Still patient, unresisting. ¶ *So he opened not his mouth.* He did not *complain*, or murmur; he offered no resistance, but yielded patiently to what was done by others.

33 *In his humiliation.* This varies from the Hebrew, but is copied exactly from the Septuagint, showing that he was reading the Septuagint. The Hebrew is "he was taken from prison, and from judgment." The word rendered "prison" denotes any kind of *detention*, or even oppression. It does not mean, as with us, to be confined *in* a prison or jail, but may mean *custody*, and be applied to the detention or custody of the Saviour when his hands were bound, and he was led to be tried. Note, Matt. xxvii. 2. It is not known why the LXX. thus translated the expression "he was taken from prison," &c. by "in his humiliation," &c. The word "from prison" may mean, as has been remarked, however, from *oppression*, and this does not differ materially from *humiliation;* and in this sense the LXX. understood it. The *meaning* of the expression in the Septuagint and the Acts is clear. It denotes that in his state of oppression and calamity, when he was destitute of protectors and friends, when at the *lowest* state of his humiliation, and, therefore, most the object of pity, that *in addition to that*, justice was denied him, his judgment—a just sentence—was taken away, or withheld, and he was delivered to be put to death. His deep humiliation and friendless state was followed by an unjust and cruel condemnation, when no one would stand forth to plead his cause. Every circumstance thus goes to deepen the view of his sufferings. ¶ *His judgment.* Justice, a just sentence, was denied him, and he was cruelly condemned. ¶ *And who shall declare his generation?* The word *generation* used here, properly denotes *posterity;* then *an age* of mankind, comprehending about thirty years, as we speak of this and the next generation; then it denotes *the men* of a particular age or time. Very various interpretations have been given of this expression. Lowth translates it, "his manner of life who would declare?" referring, as he supposes, to the fact that when a prisoner was condemned and led to execution, it was customary for a proclamation to be made by a crier in these words, "Whoever knows any thing about his innocence, let him come and declare it. This passage is taken from the Gemara

34 And the eunuch answered Philip, and said, I pray thee, of whom speaketh the prophet this? of himself, or of some other man?

---

of Babylon. (*Kennicott, as quoted by Lowth.*) The same Gemara of Babylon on this passage adds, "that before the death of Jesus, this proclamation was made forty days; but no defence could be found"—a manifest falsehood; and a story strikingly illustrative of the character of the Jewish writings. The Gemara was written sometime after Christ, perhaps not far from the year 180 (*Lardner*), and is a collection of commentaries on the traditional laws of the Jews. That this custom existed is very probable; but it is certain that no such thing was done on the trial of the Saviour. But instances are wanting where the word "generation" has this meaning. The Chaldee paraphrase translates the passage in Isaiah, "He shall collect our captivity from infirmities and vengeance; and who can declare what wonderful things shall be done for us in his days?" Others have referred this question to his Deity, or divine *generation;* intimating that no one could explain the mystery of his eternal generation. But the word in the Scriptures has no such signification; and such a sense would not suit the connexion. (See Calvin in loco.) Others have referred it to *his own spiritual posterity*, his disciples, his family; 'the number of his friends and followers who could enumerate?' (*Calvin, Beza, &c.*) But this as little suits the connexion. Another sense which the word has, is to denote *the men* of any particular age or time. Matt. xi. 16; xxiii. 36. Luke xvi. 8, &c. And it has been supposed that the question here means, 'Who can describe the character and wickedness of the generation when he shall live—the enormous crime of that age, in putting him to death?' This, perhaps, is the most probable interpretation of the question, for these reasons: (1) It is the most *usual* signification of the word (see Schleusner), and would be its obvious meaning in any other connexion. (2.) It suits the connexion here. For the prophet *immediately* adds as a *reason* for the fact that no one can describe that generation, that he was *put to death*—a deed so enormous, as to make it *impossible to describe* the wickedness of the generation that would do it. This was the sum, the crowning act of human guilt—a deed so enormous as to defy all attempt at description. The murder of the Messiah; the crucifixion of the Son of God; the killing of the highest messenger that heaven could send, was the consummation of all earthly wickedness. There was no other deed so enormous that could be performed; and there were no words to describe this. The same thing is implied in what the Saviour himself said (Matt. xxiii. 37, 38, and Luke xiii. 34, 35; xix. 42), "O Jerusalem, Jerusalem," &c. The idea in these places is, that notwithstanding their sin in killing the prophets, and stoning those that had been sent to them, he would *still* have been willing to receive and pardon them, but for this enormous act of wickedness in putting the Messiah to death—a deed which they were *about* to accomplish, and which should be attended with the destruction of their state and nation. The Hebrew word "*declare*" (Isa. liii. 8), means properly to *meditate*, to *think of*, and then, to *speak*, to *declare*. It means probably in that place, 'Who can think of, who can conceive the enormity of the crimes of that age, so as fully to publish or declare them.' ¶ *For his life*, &c. This is the *act* of wickedness just referred to—putting the Messiah to death. The Hebrew is, "For he was cut off from the land of the living," i. e. he was put to death. The expression used in the Acts was taken from the Septuagint, and means substantially the same as the Hebrew.

34. *Answered Philip.* That is, *addressed* Philip. The Hebrews often use the word *answer* as synonymous with addressing one, whether he had spoken or not. ¶ *Of himself*, &c. This was a natural inquiry for there was nothing in the text itself that would determine expressly to whom the reference was. The ancient Jews expressly applied the passage to the Messiah. Thus the Targum of Jonathan on Isa. lii. 13, "Behold, my servant shall deal prudently," &c., renders it, "Behold, my servant, *the Messiah*, shall be prospered," &c. But we should remember that the eunuch was probably not deeply versed in the Scriptures. We should remember, further, that he had just been at Jerusalem, and that the public mind was agitated about the proceedings of the sanhedrim in putting Jesus of Nazareth, who claimed to be the Messiah, to death. It is by no means improbable that *this* passage had been urged as a proof that he was the Messiah; and that the Jews, to evade the force of it, had maintained that it referred to Isaiah or Jeremiah—as they have since done. Yet the subject was so

35 Then Philip opened his
mouth, and began [a] at the same
scripture, and [b] preached unto him
Jesus.
36 And as they went on *their*
way, they came unto a certain water: and the eunuch said, See, *here*
is water; what doth [c] hinder me to
be baptized?
37 And Philip said, If [d] thou believest with all thine heart, thou
mayest. And he answered and
said, I [e] believe that Jesus Christ
is the Son of God.

a Lu.24.27. *b* c.18.28. *c* c.10.47. *d* Mar.16.16.c.8.12. *e* Jno.11.27. 1Cor 12.3. 1Jno.4.15.

important and so difficult, that it had occupied the attention of the traveller during his journey; and his question shows that he had been deeply pondering the inquiry whether it *could* refer to Isaiah, or whether it must have reference to the Messiah. In this state of suspense and agitation, when his mind was just fitted to receive instruction, God sent a messenger to guide him.—He often thus prepares, by his providence, or by a train of affecting and solemn events, the minds of men for a reception of the truth; and *then* he sends his messengers to guide the mind thoughtful and anxious, in the way of peace and salvation.

35. *Opened his mouth.* See Matthew. v. 2. ¶ *At the same scripture.* Taking this as a *text* to be illustrated. ¶ *Preached unto him Jesus.* Showed him that Jesus of Nazareth exactly answered to the description of the prophet; and that therefore the prophet referred to the Messiah, and that that Messiah was Jesus of Nazareth. How far Philip detailed the circumstances of the life and death of Christ is unknown. What follows shows also that he stated the design of baptism, and the duty of being baptized.

36. *As they went on their way.* In their journey. ¶ *A certain water.* The expression used here does not determine whether this was a river, a brook, or a pond or standing pool. And there are no circumstances to determine that. It is well known, however, that there is no large river, or very considerable stream in this vicinity. All that is intimated is, that there was water enough to perform the rite of baptism, whether that was by sprinkling, pouring, or immersion. It must be admitted, I think, that there might have been water enough for either. Grotius says they came "*to a fountain* which was in the neighbourhood of *Bethsora*, in the tribe of Juda, at the twentieth milestone from Ælia (*Jerusalem*) to Hebron." This is, however, a tradition taken from *Eusebius*. The place is still shown. (*Pococke.*) ¶ *What doth hinder me,* &c. This shows that he had been instructed by Philip in the nature and design of baptism. It evinces also a purpose *at once* to give himself to Christ, to profess his name, and to be dedicated to his service. ¶ *To be baptized.* On the meaning of the word *baptize*, see Note, Matt. iii. 6.

37. *And Philip said,* &c. This was then stated to be the proper qualification for making a profession of religion. The terms are, (1.) *Faith,* that is, a reception of Jesus as a Saviour; yielding the mind to the proper influences of the truths of redemption. See Note, Mark xvi. 16. (2.) There is required not merely the assent of the understanding, but a surrender of *the heart, the will, the affections,* to the truth of the gospel. As these were the proper qualifications then, so they are now. Nothing less is required; and nothing but this can constitute a proper qualification for the Lord's supper. ¶ *I believe,* &c. This profession is more than a professed belief that Jesus was *the Messiah.* The name *Christ* implies that. 'I believe that *Jesus the Messiah*' is, &c. In addition to this, he professed his belief that he was *the Son of God*—showing either that he had before supposed that the Messiah *would be* the Son of God, or that Philip had instructed him on that point. It was natural for Philip in discoursing on the humiliation and poverty of Jesus, to add also that he sustained a higher rank of being than a man, and was the Son of God. What precise ideas the eunuch attached to this expression cannot be now determined. This verse is wanting in a very large number of manuscripts (*Mill*), and has been rejected by many of the ablest critics. It is also omitted in the Syriac and Ethiopic versions. It is not easy to conceive why it has been omitted in almost all the Greek MSS. unless it is spurious. If it was not in the original copy of the Acts, it was probably inserted by some early transcriber, and was deemed so important to the connexion, to show that the eunuch was not admitted hastily to baptism, that it was afterwards retained. It contains, however, an important truth, elsewhere abundantly taught in the Scriptures, that *faith* is ne-

38 And he commanded the chariot to stand still: and they went down both into the water, both Philip and the eunuch; and he baptized him.

39 And when they were come up out of the water, the Spirit of the Lord [a] caught away Philip, that the eunuch saw him no more: and he went on his way rejoicing.[b]

a 1Ki.18.12. Eze.3.12,14. b Ps.119.14,111.

cessary to a proper profession of religion.

38. *And they went down both into the water.* This passage has been made the subject of much discussion on the subject of baptism. It has been adduced in proof of the necessity of immersion. It is not proposed to enter into that subject here. See Note, Matt. iii. 6. It may be remarked here that the preposition εἰς, translated here "into," does not of necessity mean that. Its meaning would be as well expressed by "to" or "unto," or as we should say, 'they went to the water,' without meaning to determine whether they went *into* it or not. Out of *twenty-six* significations which Schleusner has given the word, this is one. John xi. 38, "Jesus therefore groaning in himself cometh *to* (εἰς) the grave"—assuredly not *into* the grave. Luke xi. 49, "I send them prophets." Greek, 'I send *to* (εἰς) them prophets'—*to* them, not *into* them. Comp. Rom. ii. 4. I Cor. xiv. 36. Matt. xii. 41, "They repented *at* (εἰς) the preaching of Jonas"—not *into* his preaching. John iv. 5, "Then cometh he *to* (εἰς) a city of Samaria," that is, *near to it*, for the context shows that he had not yet entered *into* it. Comp. ver. 6. 8. John xxi. 4, "Jesus stood *on* (εἰς) the shore," that is, not *in*, but *near* the shore. These passages show that the word does not necessarily mean that they entered *into* the water. But (2.) If it did, it does not necessarily follow that the eunuch was immersed. There might be various ways of baptizing, even after they were *in* the water, besides immersing. Sprinkling or pouring might be performed there as well as elsewhere. (3.) It is incumbent on those who maintain that *immersion* is the *only* valid mode of baptism, to prove that this passage cannot *possibly* mean any thing else, and that there *was* no other mode practised by the apostles. (4.) It would be still incumbent to show that *if* this were the common and even the only mode then, in a warm climate, &c. that it is indispensable that this mode should be practised every where else. No such positive command can be adduced. And it follows, therefore, that it cannot be proved that immersion is the only lawful mode of baptism. See Note, Matt. iii. 6.

39. *Out of the water*, (ἐκ.) This preposition stands opposed to εἰς, "into;" and as that may mean *to*, so this may mean *from*, if that means *into*, this means here *out of*. ¶ *The Spirit of the Lord.* See ver. 29 The *Spirit* had suggested to Philip to go to meet the eunuch and the same Spirit, now that he had fulfilled the design of his going there, directed his departure. ¶ *Caught away.* This phrase has been usually understood of a *forcible* or *miraculous* removal of Philip to some other place. Some have even supposed that he was borne through the air by an angel. (See even Doddridge.) To such foolish interpretations have many expositors been led. The meaning is, clearly, that the Spirit, who had directed Philip to go near the eunuch, now removed him in a similar manner. That this is the meaning is clear, (1.) Because it accounts for all that occurred. It is not wise to suppose the existence of a miracle, except where the effect cannot otherwise be accounted for, and except where there is a plain statement that there was a miracle. (2.) The word "caught away" (ἥρπασε) does not imply that there was a miracle. The word properly means to seize and bear away any thing violently, without the consent of the owner, as robbers and plunderers do. Then it signifies to remove any thing in a *forcible* manner; to make use of strength or power to remove it. Acts xxiii. 10. Matt. xiii. 19. John x. 28. 2 Cor. xii. 2, 4, &c. In *no case* does it ever denote that a *miracle* is performed. And all that can be signified here is, that the Spirit *strongly admonished* Philip to go to some other place; that he so *forcibly* or *vividly suggested* the duty to his mind, as to *tear him away*, as it were, from the society of the eunuch. He had been deeply interested in the case. He would have found pleasure in continuing the journey with him. But the strong convictions of duty urged by the Holy Spirit, impelled him, as it were, to break off this new and interesting acquaintanceship, and to go to some other place. The purpose for which he was sent, to instruct and baptize the eunuch, was accomplished, and now he was called to some other field of labour.—A similar instance of interpretation has been considered in the Notes on Matt.

40 But Philip was found at Azotus: and passing through, he preached in all the cities, till he came to Cesarea.

iv. 5. ¶ *And he went on his way rejoicing.* His mind was enlightened on a perplexing passage of Scripture. He was satisfied respecting the Messiah. He was baptized; and he experienced that which all feel who embrace the Saviour and are baptized, *joy.* It was joy resulting from the fact that he was reconciled to God; and a joy, the natural effect of having done his duty *promptly,* in making a profession of religion.—If we wish happiness, if we would avoid clouds and gloom, we shall *do our duty at once.* If we delay till to-morrow what we *ought* to do today, we may expect to be troubled with melancholy thoughts. If we find peace, it will be in doing promptly *just that* which God requires at our hands.—This is the last that we hear of this man. Some have supposed that this eunuch carried the gospel to Ethiopia, and preached it there. But there is strong evidence to believe that the gospel was not preached there successfully until about the year 330, when it was introduced by *Frumentius,* sent to Abyssinia for that purpose by Athanasius, bishop of Alexandria.—From this narrative we may learn, (1.) That God often prepares the mind to receive the truth. (2.) That this takes place sometimes with the great and the noble, as well as the poor and obscure. (3.) We should study the Scriptures. It is the way in which God usually directs the mind in the truths of religion. (4.) They who read the Bible with candour and care, may expect that God will, in some mode, guide them into the truth. It will often be in a way which they least expect; but they need not be afraid of being left to darkness or error. (5.) We should be ready at all times to speak to sinners. God often prepares their minds, as he did that of the eunuch, to receive the truth. (6.) We should not be afraid of the great, the rich, or of strangers. God often prepares *their* minds to receive the truth; and we may find a man willing to hear of the Saviour where we least expected it. (7.) We should do our duty in this respect, as Philip did, promptly. We should not delay or hesitate; but should *at once* do that which we believe is in accordance with the will of God. See Ps. cxix. 60.

40. *But Philip was found.* That is, he came to Azotus, or he was not heard of until he reached Azotus. The word is often used in this sense. See 1 Chron. xxix. 17, *margin.* 2 Chron. xxix. 29, *margin.* Gen. ii 20. See also Luke xvii. 18. Rom. vii. 10. In all these places the word is used in the sense of *to be,* or *to be present.* It does not mean here that there was any *miracle* in the case, but that Philip, after leaving the eunuch *came to* or was *in* Azotus. ¶ *Azotus.* This is the Greek name of the city which by the Hebrews was called *Ashdod.* It was one of the cities which were *not* taken by Joshua, and which remained in the possession of the Philistines. It was to this place that the ark of God was sent when it was taken by the Philistines from the Israelites; and here Dagon was cast down before it. 1 Sam. v. 2, 3. Uzziah, king of Judah, broke down its wall, and built cities or watch-towers around it. 2 Chron. xxvi. 6. It was a place of great strength and consequence. It was distant about thirty miles from Gaza. It was situated on the coast of the Mediterranean, and was a seaport. The distance which Philip had to travel, therefore, was not very great, and as Azotus lay almost directly *north* of Gaza, it shows that in order to reach it, he must have parted from the eunuch, whose route was almost directly *south* of Gaza. It is at present inhabited by Arabs chiefly, and is by them called *Mezdel.* Dr. Wittman describes it at present as being entered by two small gates. In passing through it, he saw several fragments of columns, capitals, &c. In the centre of the town is a handsome mosque with a minaret. The surrounding country is represented as remarkably verdant and beautiful. In the neighbourhood there stands an abundance of fine old olive-trees, and the region around it is fertile. ¶ *He preached in all the cities.* Joppa, Lydda, Askalon, Arimathea, &c. lying along the coast of the Mediterranean. ¶ *Cesarea.* This city was formerly called *Strato's Tower.* It is situated on the coast of the Mediterranean, at the mouth of a small river, and has a fine harbour. It is thirty-six miles south of Acre, and about sixty-two northwest of Jerusalem, and about the same distance northeast of Azotus. This city is supposed by some to be the Hazor mentioned in Josh. xi. 1. It was rebuilt by Herod the Great, and named *Cæsarea* in honour of Augustus Cæsar. The city was dedicated to him: the seaport was called *Sebaste,* the Greek word for Augustus. It was adorned with most splendid houses; and the temple of

CHAPTER IX.

AND Saul, yet [a] breathing out threatenings and slaughter against the disciples of the Lord, went unto the high-priest,
2 And desired of him letters to

a c.8.3. Ga.1.13.

Cæsar was erected by Herod over-against the mouth of the haven, in which was placed the statue of the Roman emperor. It became the seat of the Roman governor while Judea was a Roman province. Acts xxiii. 33; xxv. 6. 13. Philip afterwards resided at this place. See Acts xxi. 8, 9. Cesarea at present is inhabited only by jackals and beasts of prey. "Perhaps," says Dr. Clarke, "there has not been in the history of the world an example of any city that in so short a space of time rose to such an extraordinary height of splendour as did this of Cesarea; or that exhibits a more awful contrast to its former magnificence, by the present desolate appearance of its ruins. Not a single inhabitant remains. Of its gorgeous palaces and temples, enriched with the choicest works of art, scarcely a trace can be discerned. Within the space of ten years after laying the foundation, from an obscure fortress, it became the most flourishing and celebrated city of all Syria." Now it is in utter desolation. (See Robinson's Calmet, Art. *Cæsarea.*)

CHAPTER IX.

THIS chapter commences a very important part of the Acts of the Apostles—the conversion and labours of Saul of Tarsus. The remainder of the book is chiefly occupied with an account of his labours and trials in the establishment of churches, and in spreading the gospel through the Gentile world. As the fact that the gospel was to be thus preached to the Gentiles was a very important fact, and as the toils of the apostle Paul and his fellow-labourers for this purpose were of an exceedingly interesting character, it was desirable to preserve an authentic record of those labours; and that record we have in the remainder of this book.

1. *And Saul.* Note, ch. vii. 58; viii. 3. He had been engaged before in persecuting the Christians, but he now sought opportunity to gratify his insatiable desire on a larger scale. ¶ *Yet breathing.* Not satisfied with what he had done, ch. viii. 3. The word *breathing out* is expressive often of *any* deep, agitating emotion, as we then *breathe* rapidly and violently. It is thus expressive of violent *anger.* The emotion is absorbing, agitating, exhausting, and demands a more rapid circulation of blood to supply the exhausted vitality, and this demands an increased supply of oxygen, or vital air, which leads to the increased action of the lungs. The word is often used in this sense in the classics. (*Schleusner.*) It is a favourite expression with Homer. Euripides has the same expression; "Breathing out fire and slaughter." So Theocritus; "They came unto the assembly breathing mutual slaughter." Idyll. xxii. 82. ¶ *Threatening.* Denunciation; threatening them with every breath—the action of a man violently enraged, and who was bent on vengeance. It denotes also intense activity and energy in persecution. ¶ *Slaughter.* Murder. Intensely desiring to put to death as many Christians as possible. He rejoiced in their death, and joined in condemning them. Acts xxvi. 10, 11. From this latter place it seems that he had been concerned in putting many of them to death. ¶ *The disciples of the Lord.* Against Christians. ¶ *Went unto the high-priest.* Note, Matt. ii. 4. The letters were written and signed in the name, and by the authority of the sanhedrim, or great council of the nation. The high priest did it as president of that council. See ver. 14, and ch. xxii. 5. The high-priest of that time was Theophilus, son of Ananus, who had been appointed at the feast of Pentecost, A. D. 37, by Vitellius, the Roman governor. His brother Jonathan had been removed from that office the same year. (*Kuinoel.*)

2. *And desired of him.* This shows the intensity of his wish to persecute the Christians, that he was willing to *ask* for such an employment. ¶ *Letters.* Epistles, implying a *commission* to bring them to Jerusalem for trial and punishment. From this it seems that the sanhedrim at Jerusalem claimed jurisdiction over *all* synagogues every where. They claimed the authority of regulating every where the Jewish religion. ¶ *To Damascus.* This was a celebrated city of Syria, and long the capital of a kingdom of that name. It is situated in a delightful region about one hundred and twenty miles northeast of Jerusalem, and about one hundred and ninety miles southeast of Antioch. It is in the midst of an extensive plain, abounding with cypress and palm-trees, and extremely fertile. It is watered by the river Barrady, anciently called *Abana.* 2 Kings v. 12. About five miles from the city is a place called the "meeting of the wa-

Damascus to the synagogues, that, if he found any of [1] this way, whether they were men or women, he might bring them bound unto Jerusalem.

3 And [a] as he journeyed, he came

[1] or, *the way.*

[a] 1 Cor. 15.8.

ters," where the Barrady is joined by another river, and thence is divided by art into several streams that flow through the plain. These streams, six or seven in number, are conveyed to water the orchards, farms, &c. and give to the whole scene a very picturesque appearance. The city, situated in a delightful climate, in a fertile country, is perhaps among the most pleasant in the world. It is called by the Orientals themselves the *paradise on earth.* This city is mentioned often in the Old Testament. It was a city in the time of Abraham. Gen. xv. 2. By whom it was founded is unknown. It was taken and garrisoned by David, A. M. 2992. 2 Sam. viii. 6. 1 Chron. xviii. 6. It is subsequently mentioned as sustaining very important parts in the conflicts of the Jews with Syria. 2 Kings xiv. 25; xvi. 5. Isa. ix. 11. It was taken by the Romans, A. M. 3939, or about sixty years before Christ; in whose possession it was when Saul went there. It was conquered by the Saracens, A. D. 713. About the year 1250 it was taken by the Christians in the crusades, and was captured A. D. 1517, by Selim, and has been since under the Ottoman emperors.

The Arabians call this city *Damasch,* or *Demesch,* or *Schams.* It is one of the most commercial cities in the Ottoman empire, and is distinguished also for manufactures, particularly for *steel,* hence called Damascus steel. The population is estimated by Ali Bey at two hundred thousand; Volney states it at eighty thousand; Hassel, at one hundred thousand. About twenty thousand are Maronites of the Catholic church, five thousand Greeks, and one thousand are Jews. The road from Jerusalem to Damascus lies between two mountains, not above a hundred paces distant from each other; both are round at the bottom, and terminate in a point. Tha nearest the great road is called *Cocab the star,* in memory of the dazzling light which is here said to have appeared to Saul. ¶ *To the synagogues.* Note, Matt. iv. 23. The Jews were scattered into nearly all the regions surrounding Judea; and it is natural to suppose that many of them would be found in Damascus. Josephus assures us that ten thousand were massacred there in one hour; and at another time eighteen thousand, with their wives and children. (*Jewish War,* b. ii. ch. xx. § 2; b. vii ch. viii. § 7.) See Notes, Acts ii. 9—11. By whom the gospel was preached there, or how they had been converted to Christianity, is unknown. The presumption is, that some of those who had been converted on the day of Pentecost, had carried the gospel to Syria. ¶ *That if,* &c. It would seem that it was not certainly *known* that there were any Christians there. It was presumed that there were; and probably there was a report of that kind. ¶ *Of this way.* Of this *way* or *mode* of life; of this kind of opinions and conduct; that is, any Christians. ¶ *He might bring them,* &c. To be tried. The sanhedrim at Jerusalem claimed jurisdiction over religious opinions; and their authority would naturally be respected by foreign Jews.

3. *And as he journeyed.* On his way, or while he was travelling. The *place* where this occurred is not known. Tradition has fixed it at the mountain now called *Cocab.* See Note, on ver. 2. All that we know of it is that it was near to Damascus. ¶ *And suddenly.* Like a flash of lightning. ¶ *There shined round about him,* &c. The *language* which is expressed here would be used in describing a flash of lightning. Many critics have supposed that God made use of a sudden flash to arrest Paul, and that he was thus alarmed and brought to reflection. That God *might* make use of such a means cannot be denied. But to this supposition in this case there are some unanswerable objections. (1.) It was declared to be the appearance of the Lord Jesus; ver. 27, "Barnabas declared unto them how that he had *seen the Lord in the way.*" 1 Cor. xv. 8, "And last of all he was seen of me also." 1 Cor. ix. 1, "Have I not seen Jesus Christ our Lord?" (2.) Those who were *with* Saul saw the light, but did not hear the voice. Acts xxii. 9. See Note. This is incredible on the supposition that it was a flash of light ning near them. (3.) It was manifestly regarded as a message to *Saul.* The light appeared, and the voice spake to him. The others did not even *hear* the address. Besides, (4.) It was as easy for Jesus to appear in a supernatural manner, as to appear amidst thunder and lightning. That the Lord Jesus appeared, is distinctly affirmed. And we shall see that it is probable that he would appear in a supernatural manner.

near Damascus: and suddenly there shined round about him a light from heaven:

4 And he fell to the earth, and heard a voice saying unto him, Saul, Saul, why persecutest thou me?[a]

5 And he said, Who art thou,

[a] Matt.25.40,45.

In order to understand this, it may be necessary to make the following remarks: (1.) God was accustomed to appear to the Jews in a cloud; in a pillar of smoke, or of fire; in that peculiar splendour which they denominated the *Shechinah*. In this way he went before them into the land of Canaan Ex. xiii. 21, 22. Comp. Isa. iv. 5, 6. This appearance or visible manifestation they called the *glory of* JEHOVAH. Isa. vi. 1—4. Ex. xvi. 7, "In the morning ye shall see the glory of the Lord." 10. Lev. ix. 23. Num. xiv. 10; xvi. 19. 42; xxiv. 16. 1 Kings viii. 11. Ezek. x. 4. Note, Luke ii. 9, "The glory of the Lord shone round about them." (2.) The Lord Jesus, in his transfiguration on the mount, had been encompassed with that glory. Notes, Matt. xvii. 1—5. (3.) He had spoken of similar glory as pertaining to him; as that which he had been invested with before his incarnation; and to which he would return. John xvii. 5, "And now, Father, glorify thou me, &c. with the glory which I had with thee before the world was." Matt. xxv. 31, "The Son of man shall come in his glory." Comp. Matt. xvi. 27; xix. 28. To *this glory* he had returned *when* he left the earth. (4.) It is a sentiment which cannot be shown to be incorrect, that the various appearances of "the angel of Jehovah," and of Jehovah, mentioned in the Old Testament, were appearances of the Messiah; the God who should be incarnate; the peculiar protector of his people. See Isa. vi. comp. with John xii. 41. (5.) *If* the Lord Jesus appeared to Saul, it would be in this manner. It would be in his appropriate glory and honour, as the ascended Messiah. That he *did* appear is expressly affirmed. (6.) This was *an occasion* when, if ever, such an appearance was proper. The design was to convert an infuriated persecutor, and to make him an *apostle*. To do this it was necessary that he should *see* the Lord Jesus. 1 Cor. ix. 1, 2. The design was further to make him an eminent instrument in carrying the gospel to the Gentiles. A signal miracle; a demonstration that he was invested with his appropriate glory (John xvii. 5); a calling up a new *witness* to the fact of his resurrection, and his solemn investment with glory in the heavens, seemed to be required in thus calling a violent persecutor to be an apostle and friend. (7.) We are to regard this appearance, therefore, as the reappearance of the Shechinah, the Son of God invested with appropriate glory, appearing to convince an enemy of his ascension, and to change him from a foe to a friend.

It has been objected that as the Lord Jesus had ascended to heaven, that it cannot be presumed that his body would return to the earth again. To this we may reply, that the New Testament has thrown no light on this. Perhaps it is not necessary to suppose that his body returned, but that he made such a visible manifestation of himself as to convince Saul that he was the Messiah. ¶ *From heaven*. From above; from the sky. In Acts xxvi. 13, Paul says that the light was above the brightness of the sun at midday.

4. *And he fell to the earth*. He was astonished and overcome by the sudden flash of light. There is a remarkable similarity between what occurred here, and what is recorded of *Daniel* in regard to the visions which he saw. Dan. viii. 17. Also Dan. x. 8, "Therefore I was left alone, and saw this great vision; and there remained no strength in me, for my comeliness (vigour) was turned into corruption, and I retained no strength." The effect was such as to overpower the body. ¶ *And heard a voice*. The whole company heard a voice (ver. 7), but did not distinguish it as addressed particularly to Saul. *He* heard it speaking to himself. ¶ *Saying unto him*, &c. This shows that it was not *thunder*, as many have supposed. It was a distinct articulation or utterance, addressing him by name. ¶ *Saul, Saul*. A mode of address that is emphatic. The repetition of the name would fix his attention. Thus Jesus addresses Martha (Luke x. 41), and Simon (Luke xxii. 31), and Jerusalem (Matt. xxiii. 37). ¶ *Why* For what reason. Jesus had done him no injury; had given him no provocation. All the opposition of sinners to the Lord Jesus and his church, is without cause. See Note, John xv. 25, "They hated me without a cause." ¶ *Persecutest*. Note, Matt. v. 11. ¶ *Thou me?* Christ and his people are one. John xv. 1—6. To persecute *them*, therefore, was to persecute *him*. Matt. xxv. 40. 45.

5. ***And he said, who art thou, Lord?***

Lord? And the Lord said, I am
Jesus, whom thou persecutest: *it is*
hard for thee to kick [a] against the
pricks.

a c.5.39.

6 And he, trembling and astonished, said, Lord, what [b] wilt thou
have me to do? And the Lord *said*
unto him, Arise, and go into the

b c.16.30.

The word *Lord* here, as is frequently the case in the New Testament, means no more than *sir.* John iv. 19. It is evident that Saul did not as yet know that this was the Lord Jesus. He heard the voice as of a *man;* he heard himself addressed; but by whom the words were spoken, was to him unknown. In his amazement and confusion, he naturally asked who it was that was thus addressing him. ¶ *And the Lord said.* In this place the word *Lord* is used in a higher sense, to denote the Saviour. It is his usual appellation. See Note, Acts i. 24. ¶ *I am Jesus.* It is clear from this, that there was a personal appearance of the Saviour; that he was present to Saul; but in what particular *form*—whether *seen* as a man, or only appearing by the manifestation of his glory, is not affirmed. It was a personal appearance, however, of the Lord Jesus, designed to take the work of converting such a persecutor into his own hands, without the ordinary means. Yet he designed to convert him in a natural way. He *arrested* his attention; filled him with alarm at his guilt; and then presented the *truth* respecting himself. In ch. xxii. 8, the expression is thus recorded: "I am Jesus of Nazareth," &c. There is no contradiction, as Luke here records only a *part* of what was said; Paul afterwards stated the whole. This declaration was fitted peculiarly to humble and mortify Saul. There can be no doubt that he had often blasphemed his name, and profanely derided the notion that the Messiah could come out of Nazareth. Jesus here uses, however, that very designation. 'I am Jesus *the Nazarene,* the object of your contempt and scorn.' Yet Saul saw him now invested with peculiar glory. ¶ *It is hard,* &c. This is evidently a proverbial expression. Kuinoel has quoted numerous places in which a similar mode of expression occurs in Greek writers. Thus Euripides, Bacch. 791, "I, who am a frail mortal, should rather sacrifice to him who is a God, than by giving place to anger, *kick against the goads.*" So Pindar, Pyth. ii. 173, "It is profitable to bear willingly the assumed yoke. To kick against the goad is pernicious conduct." So Terence, Phorm. 1. 2. 27, "It is foolishness for thee to kick against a goad." Ovid has the same idea, Trist. b. ii 15. The word translated "pricks" here (κέντρα), means properly any sharp point which will pierce or perforate, as the sting of a bee, &c. But it commonly means an ox-goad, a sharp piece of iron stuck into the end of a stick, with which the ox is urged on. These goads among the Hebrews were made very large. Thus Shamgar slew six hundred men with one of them. Judg iii. 31. Comp. 1 Sam. xiii. 21. The expression To kick against the prick, or the goad, is derived from the action of a stubborn and unyielding ox, kicking against the goad. And as the ox would injure no one by it but himself; as he would gain nothing; it comes to denote an obstinate and refractory disposition and course of conduct, opposing motives to good conduct; resisting the authority of him who has a right to command; and opposing the leadings of Providence, to the injury of him who makes the resistance. It denotes rebellion against lawful authority, and thus getting into greater difficulty by attempting to oppose the commands to duty. This is the condition of every sinner. If men wish to be happy, they should cheerfully submit to the authority of God. They should not rebel against the dealings of Providence. They should not murmur against their Creator. They should not resist the claims of their consciences. By all this they would only injure themselves. No man can resist God or his own conscience and be happy. And nothing is more difficult than for a man to pursue a course of pleasure and sin against the admonitions of God and the reproofs of his own conscience. Men evince this temper in the following ways: (1.) By violating plain laws of God. (2.) By attempting to resist his claims. (3.) By refusing to do what their conscience requires. (4.) By grieving the Holy Spirit, by attempting to free themselves from serious impressions and alarms. They will return with redoubled frequency and power. (5.) By pursuing a course of vice and wickedness against what they know to be right. (6.) By refusing to submit to the dealings of Providence. And (7.) In any way by opposing God, and refusing to submit to his authority, and to do what is right.

6. *And he trembling.* Alarmed at what he saw and heard, and at the conscious

city, and it shall be told thee what thou must do.

7 And the men which journeyed with him stood speechless, hear-

ness of his own evil course. It is not remarkable that a sinner trembles when he sees his guilt and danger. ¶ *And astonished.* At what he saw. ¶ *Lord, what wilt thou have me to do?* This indicates a subdued soul; a humbled spirit. Just before, he had sought only to do his *own* will; now he inquired what was the will of the Saviour. Just before he was acting under a commission from the Sanhedrim; now he renounced their supreme authority, and asked what the Lord Jesus would have him to do. Just before he had been engaged in a career of *opposition* to the Lord Jesus; now he sought at once to do his will. This indicates the usual change in the sinner. The great controversy between him and God is, *whose will* shall be followed. The sinner follows his own; the first act of the Christian is to surrender his own will to that of God, and to resolve to do that which he requires. We may further remark here, that this indicates the true nature of conversion. It is decided, prompt, immediate. Paul did not *debate* the matter (Gal. i. 16); he did not inquire what the scribes and Pharisees would say; he did not consult his own reputation; he did not ask what the world would think. With characteristic promptness; with a readiness which showed what he *would* yet be; he gave himself up *at once*, and *entirely*, to the Lord Jesus; evidently with a purpose to do *his* will alone. This was the case also with the jailer at Philippi. Acts xvi 30. Nor can there be any real conversion where the *heart* and *will* are not given to the Lord Jesus, to be directed and moulded by him at his pleasure. We may test our conversion then by the example of the apostle Paul. If our hearts have been given up as his was, we are true friends of Christ. ¶ *Go into the city.* Damascus. They were near it. ver. 3. ¶ *And it shall be told thee.* It is remarkable that he was thus directed. But we may learn from it, (1.) That even in the most striking and remarkable cases of conversion, there is not *at once* a clear view of duty. What course of life should be followed; what should be done; nay, what should be *believed*, is not at once apparent. (2.) The aid of others, and especially of ministers, and of experienced Christians, is often very desirable to aid even those who are converted in the most remarkable manner. Saul was converted by a miracle: the Saviour appeared to him in his glory; of the truth of his Messiahship he had no doubt, but still he was dependent on an humble disciple in Damascus to be instructed in what he should do. (3.) Those who are converted, in however striking a manner it may be, should be *willing* to seek the counsel of those who are in the church and in the ministry before them. The most striking evidence of their conversion will not prevent their deriving important direction and benefit from the aged, the experienced, and the wise in the Christian church. (4.) Such remarkable conversions are fitted to *induce* the subjects of the change to seek counsel and direction. They produce humility, a deep sense of sin and of unworthiness; and a willingness to be taught and directed by any one who *can* point out the way of duty and of life.

7. *And the men which journeyed with him.* *Why* these men attended him is unknown. They might have been appointed to aid him, or they may have been travellers with whom Saul had accidentally fallen in. ¶ *Stood speechless.* In Acts xxvi. 14, it is said that they all fell to the earth at the appearance of the light. But there is no contradiction. The narrative in that place refers to the *immediate* effect of the appearance of the light. They were *immediately* smitten to the ground together. This was *before* the voice spake to Saul. Acts xxvi. 14. In *this* place (ix. 7) the historian is speaking of what occurred *after* the first alarm. There is no improbability that they rose from the ground immediately, and surveyed the scene with silent amazement and alarm. The word *speechless* (ἐννεοὶ) properly denotes those who are so astonished or stupified as to be unable to speak. In the Greek writers it means those who are deaf and dumb. ¶ *Hearing a voice.* Hearing a *sound* or *noise*. The word here rendered voice is thus frequently used, as in Gen. iii. 8 1 Sam. xii. 18. Ps. xxix. 3, 4. Matt. xxiv. 31. (Greek.) 1 Thess. iv. 16. In Acts xxii. 9, it is said, "They which were with me (Paul) saw indeed the light, and were afraid, but they *heard not the voice* of him that spake to me." In this place, the words, "heard not the voice," must be understood in the sense of *understanding the words*, of hearing the address, the distinct articulation, which Paul heard They heard a *noise*, they were amazed

ing a voice, but [a] seeing no man.
8 And Saul arose from the earth; and when his eyes were opened, he saw no man: but they led him by the hand, and brought *him* into Damascus.
9 And he was three days without sight, and neither did eat nor drink.
10 And there was a certain disciple at Damascus, named Ananias;[b] and to him said the Lord in a

a Da.10.7.
b c. 22.12.

and alarmed, but they did not hear the distinct words addressed to Saul. A similar instance we have in John xii. 28, 29, when the voice of God came from heaven to Jesus. "The people who stood by and heard it said it thundered." They heard the *sound*, the *noise;* they did *not* distinguish the *words* addressed to him. See also Dan. x. 7, and 1 Kings xix. 11—13.

8. *When his eyes were opened.* He naturally closed them at the appearance of the light; and in his fright kept them closed for some time. ¶ *He saw no man.* This darkness continued three days. ver. 9. There is no reason to suppose that there was a *miracle* in this blindness, for in ch. xxii. 11, it is expressly said to have been caused by the intense light. "And when I could not see for the glory of that light," &c. The intense, sudden light had so affected the optic nerve of the eye as to cause a temporary blindness. This effect is not uncommon. The disease of the eye which is thus produced is called *amaurosis*, or more commonly *gutta serena.* It consists in a loss of sight without any apparent defect of the eye. Sometimes the disease is periodical, coming on suddenly, continuing for three or four days, and then disappearing. (*Webster*) A disease of this kind is often caused by excessive light. When we look at the sun, or into a furnace, or into a crucible, with fused metal, we are conscious of a temporary pain in the eye, and of a momentary blindness. "In northern and tropical climates, from the glare of the sun or snow, a variety of amaurosis (gutta serena) occurs, which, if it produces blindness during the day, is named nyctalopia, if during the night, hemeralopia. Another variety exists in which the individual is blind all day, until a certain hour, when he sees distinctly, or he sees and is blind every alternate day, or is only blind one day in the week, fortnight, or month." (Edin. Encyc. Art. *Surgery.*) A total loss of sight has been the consequence of looking at the sun during an eclipse, or of watching it as it sets in the west. This effect is caused by the intense action of the light on the optic nerve, or sometimes from a disorder of the brain. A case is mentioned by Michaelis (*Kuinoel in loco*) of a man who was made blind by a bright flash of lightning, and who continued so for four weeks, who was again restored to sight in a tempest by a similar flash of lightning. Electricity has been found one of the best remedies for restoring sight in such cases.

9. *And neither did eat nor drink.* Probably because he was overwhelmed with a view of his sins, and was thus indisposed to eat. All the circumstances would contribute to this. His past life; his great sins; the sudden change in his views; his total absorption in the vision; perhaps also his grief at the loss of his sight, would all fill his mind, and indispose him to partake of food. Great grief always produces this effect. And it is not uncommon now for an awakened and convicted sinner, in view of his past sins and danger, to be so pained, as to destroy his inclination for food, and to produce in voluntary fasting. We are to remember also that Paul had yet no assurance of forgiveness. He was arrested; alarmed; convinced that Jesus was the Messiah; and humbled, but he had not comfort. He was brought to the dust, and left to three painful days of darkness and suspense, before it was told him what he was to do. In this painful and perplexing state, it was natural that he should abstain from food. This case should not be brought now, however, to prove, that convicted sinners *must* remain in darkness and under conviction. Saul's case was extraordinary. His blindness was literal. This state of darkness was necessary to humble him and fit him for his work. But the moment a sinner will give his heart to Christ, he may find peace. If he resists, and rebels longer, it will be his own fault. By the nature of the case, as well as by the promises of the Bible, if a sinner will yield himself at once to the Lord Jesus, he may obtain peace. That sinners do not sooner obtain peace, is because they do not sooner submit themselves to God.

10. *A certain disciple.* A Christian. Many have supposed that he was one of the seventy disciples. But nothing more

vision, Ananias. And he said, Behold, I *am here*, Lord.
11 And the Lord *said* unto him,
Arise, and go into the street which
is called Straight, and inquire in
the house of Judas for *one* called
Saul of Tarsus: for behold, he
prayeth,

is certainly known of him than is related here. He had very probably been some time a Christian (ver. 13), and had heard of Saul, but was personally a stranger to him. In ch. xxii. 12, it is said that he was a devout man according to the law, having a good report of all the Jews which dwelt there. There was wisdom in sending such a Christian to Saul, as it might do much to conciliate the minds of the Jews there towards him. ¶ *Said the Lord.* The Lord *Jesus* is alone mentioned in all this transaction. And as he had commenced the work of converting Saul, it is evident that he is intended here. See Note, ch. i. 24. ¶ *In a vision.* Perhaps by a dream. The main idea is, that he *revealed* his will to him in the case. The word *vision* is often used in speaking of the communications made to the prophets, and commonly means that future events were made to pass in review before the mind, as we look upon a landscape. See Isa. i. 1. Gen. xv. 1. Num. xii. 6. Ezek. xi. 24. Acts x. 3; xi. 5; xvi. 9. Dan. ii. 19; vii. 2; viii. 1, 2. 26; x. 7. Note, Matt. xvii. 9.

11. *Into the street which is called Straight.* This street extends now from the eastern to the western gate, about three miles, crossing the whole city and suburbs in a direct line. Near the eastern gate is a house, said to be that of Judah, in which Paul lodged. There is in it a very small closet, where tradition reports that the apostle passed three days without food, till Ananias restored him to sight. Tradition also says that he had here the vision recorded in 2 Cor. xii. 2. There is also in this street a fountain whose water is drunk by Christians, in remembrance of that which, they suppose, the same fountain produced for the baptism of Paul. (*Rob Calmet.*) ¶ *Of Tarsus.* This city was the capital of Cilicia, a province of Asia Minor. It was situated on the banks of the river Cydnus. It was distinguished for the culture of Greek philosophy and literature, so that at one time in its schools, and in the number of its learned men, it was the rival of Athens and Alexandria. In allusion to this, perhaps, Paul says that he was "born in Tarsus, a citizen of no mean city." Acts xxi. 39. In reward for its exertions and sacrifices during the civil wars of Rome, Tarsus was made a free city by Augustus. See Note, Acts xxii. 28. 24; xxi. 39; xvi. 37. ¶ *Behold he prayeth.* This gives us a full indication of the manner in which Saul passed the three days mentioned in ver 9. It is plain from what follows, that Ananias regarded Saul as a foe to Christianity, and that he would have been apprehensive of danger if he were with him. ver. 13, 14. This remark, "behold he prayeth," is made to him to silence his fears, and to indicate the change in the feelings and views of Saul. Before, he was a persecutor; now his change is indicated by his giving himself to prayer. That Saul did not *pray* before, is not implied by this; for he fully accorded with the customs of the Jews. Phil. iii. 4—6. But his prayers then were not the prayers of a saint. They were then the prayers of a Pharisee (comp. Luke xviii. 10, &c.); now they were the prayers of a broken-hearted sinner; then he prayed depending on his own righteousness; now, depending on the mercy of God in the Messiah.—We may learn here, (1.) That one indication of conversion to God is real prayer. A Christian may as well be characterized by that as by any single appellation—'a man of prayer.' (2.) It is always the attendant of true conviction for sin, that we pray. The convicted sinner feels his danger, and his need of forgiveness. Conscious that he has no righteousness himself, he now seeks that of another, and depends on the mercy of God. Before, he was too proud to pray; now, he is willing to humble himself through Jesus Christ, and ask for mercy. (3.) It is a sufficient indication of the character of *any* man to say, 'behold, he prays.' It at once tells us, better than volumes would without this, his *real* character. Knowing this, we know all about him. We at once confide in his piety, his honesty, his humility, his willingness to do good. It is at once the indication of his state with God, and the pledge that he will do his duty to men. We mean, of course, *real* prayer. Knowing that a man is sincere, and humble, and faithful in his private devotions, and in the devotions of his family, we confide in him, and are willing at once to trust to his readiness to do all that he is convinced that he *ought* to do. Ananias, apprized of this in Saul, had full evidence of the change of his character, and was convinced that he ought to

12 And hath seen in a vision a
man named Ananias coming in, and
putting *his* hand on him, that he
might receive his sight.
13 Then Ananias answered, Lord,
I have heard by many of this man [a]
how much evil he hath done to thy
saints at Jerusalem:
14 And here he [b] hath authority
from the chief priests to bind all
that call [c] on thy name.
15 But the Lord said unto him,
Go thy way: for [d] he is a chosen
vessel unto me, to bear my name
before [e] the Gentiles, and kings, [f]
and the [g] children of Israel.
16 For I will shew him how
great things he must suffer [h] for my
name's sake.
17 And Ananias went his way,
and entered into the house; and
putting [i] his hands on him, said,

a 1Tim.1.13. b ver.21. c 1Cor.1.2. 2Tim.2.22. d c.13.2. Ro.1.1. 1Cor.15.10. Gal.1.15. Eph.3.7,8. e Ro.11.13. Gal.2.7,8. f c.25.23 &c. g c.26,17,&c. h c.20.23. 2Cor.11.23-27. 2Tim.1.11,12. i c.8.17.

lay aside all his former views, and at once to seek him, and to acknowledge him as a brother.

12. *And he hath seen in a vision,* &c. *When* this was shown to Saul, or how, is not recorded. The vision was shown to Saul to assure him when he came that he was no impostor. He was thus *prepared* to receive consolation from this disciple. He was even apprized of his *name,* that he might be more confirmed.

13, 14. *I have heard by many,* &c. This was in the *vision.* ver. 10. The passage of such a train of thoughts through the mind was perfectly natural at the command to go and search out Saul. There would instantly occur all that had been heard of his fury in persecution; and the expression here may indicate the state of a mind *amazed* that such an one should need his counsel, and *afraid,* perhaps, of intrusting himself to one thus bent on persecution. All this evidently passed in the *dream or vision* of Ananias; and perhaps cannot be considered as any *deliberate* unwillingness to go to him. It is clear, however, that *such* thoughts should have been banished, and that he should have gone *at once* to the praying Saul. When Christ commands, we should suffer no suggestion of our own thoughts, and no apprehension of our own danger, to interfere. ¶ *By many* Probably many who had fled from persecution, and had taken refuge in Damascus. It is also evident (ver. 14), that Ananias had been *apprized,* perhaps by letters from the Christians at Jerusalem, of the purpose which Saul had in view in now going to Damascus. ¶ *To thy saints* Christians; called saints (ἅγιοι) because they are holy, or consecrated to God.

15. *Go thy way.* This is often the only answer that we obtain to the suggestion of our doubts and hesitations about duty. God tells us still to *do* what he requires, with an assurance only that his commands are just, and that there are good reasons for them. ¶ *A chosen vessel.* The usual meaning of the word *vessel* is well known. It usually denotes a *cup* or *basin,* such as is used in a house. It then denotes *any* instrument which may be used to accomplish a purpose, perhaps particularly with the notion of *conveying* or communicating. In the Scriptures it is used to denote the *instrument* or *agent* which God employs to convey his favours to mankind; and is thus employed to represent the ministers of the gospel, or the *body* of the minister. 2 Cor. iv. 7. 1 Thess. iv. 4. Comp. Isa. x. 5. Paul is called *chosen* because Christ had *selected* him, as he did his other apostles, for this service. Note, John xv. 16. ¶ *To bear my name.* To communicate the knowledge of me. ¶ *Before the Gentiles.* The nations; all who were not Jews. This was the *principal* employment of Paul. He spent his life in this, and regarded himself as peculiarly called to be the apostle of the Gentiles. Rom. xi. 13; xv. 16. Gal. ii. 8. ¶ *And kings.* This was fulfilled, Acts xxv. 23, &c. xxvi. 32; xxvii. 24. ¶ *And the children of Israel.* The Jews. This was done. He *immediately* began to preach to them, ver. 20—22. Wherever he went, he preached the gospel first to them, and then to the Gentiles. Acts xiii. 46; xxviii 17.

16. *For I will shew him,* &c. This seems to be added to encourage Ananias He had feared Saul. The Lord now informs him that Saul, hitherto his enemy would ever after be his friend. He would not merely *profess* repentance, but would *manifest* the sincerity of it by encountering trials and reproaches for his sake. The prediction here was fully accomplished, ch. xx. 23. 2 Cor. xi. 23—27 2 Tim. i. 11, 12.

17. *Putting his hands on him.* This was not *ordination,* but was the usual mode of imparting or communicating

Brother Saul, the Lord, *even* Jesus,
that appeared unto thee in the way
as thou camest, hath sent me, that
thou mightest receive thy sight,
and [a] be filled with the Holy Ghost.

18 And immediately there fell
from his eyes as it had been scales;
and he received sight forthwith
and arose, and was baptized.
19 And when he had received

a c.2.4

blessings. See Note Matt. xix. 13; ix. 18. ¶ *Brother Saul.* An expression recognising him as a fellow-christian. ¶ *Be filled with the Holy Ghost.* Note, Acts ii. 4.

18. *As it had been scales.* ὡσεὶ λεπίδες. The word ὡσεὶ, "as it had been," is designed to *qualify* the following word. It is not said that scales *literally* fell from his eyes; but that an effect followed *as if* scales had been suddenly taken off. Evidently the whole expression is designed to mean no more than this. The effect was such as would take place if some dark, impervious substance had been placed before the eyes, and had been suddenly removed. The cure was as sudden, the sight was as immediate, *as if* such an interposing substance had been suddenly removed. This is all that the expression fairly implies, and this is all that the nature of the case demands. As the blindness had been caused by the natural effect of the light, probably on the optic nerve (ver. 8, 9, *Note*), it is manifest that no *literal* removing of scales would restore the vision. We are therefore to lay aside the idea of *literal* scales falling to the earth; no such thing is affirmed, and no such thing would have met the case. The word translated *scales* is used nowhere else in the New Testament. It means properly the small crust or layer which composes a part of the covering of a fish, and also any thin layer or leaf exfoliated or separated; as scales of iron, bone, or a piece of bark, &c. (*Webster.*) An effect similar to this is described in Tobit xi. 8. 13. It is evident that there was a miracle in the *healing* of Saul. The *blindness* was the natural effect of the light. The *cure* was by miraculous power. This is evident, (1.) Because there were no means used that would naturally restore the sight. It may be remarked here that *gutta serena* has been regarded by physicians as one of the most incurable of diseases. Few cases are restored; and few remedies are efficacious. (See Ed. Encyc. Art. *Surgery*, on *Amaurosis*.) (2.) Ananias was *sent* for this very purpose to heal him. ver. 17. (3.) The *immediate* effect shows that this was miraculous. Had it been a *slow* recovery, it might have been doubtful. but here it was instantaneous, and thus put beyond a question that it was a miracle. ¶ *And was baptized.* In this he followed the example of all the early converts to Christianity. They were baptized immediately. See Acts ii. 41; viii. 12. 36—39

19. *Had received meat.* Food. The word *meat* has undergone a change since our translation was made. It then meant, as the original does, food of all kinds. ¶ *With the disciples.* With Christians. Comp. Acts ii. 42. ¶ *Certain days.* How long is not known. It was long enough, however, to preach the gospel. ver. 22. ch. xxvi. 20. It might have been for some months, as he did not go to Jerusalem under three years from that time. He remained some time at Damascus, and then went to Arabia, and returned again to Damascus, and then went to Jerusalem. Gal. i. 17. This visit to *Arabia* Luke has omitted, but there is no contradiction. He does not affirm that he did *not go* to Arabia.

We have now passed through the account of one of the most remarkable conversions to Christianity that has ever occurred—that of the apostle Paul. This conversion has always been justly considered as a strong proof of the Christian religion. For, (1.) This change could not have occurred by any want of fair prospects of honour. He was distinguished already as a Jew. He had had the best opportunities for education that the nation afforded. He had every prospect of rising to distinction and office. (2.) It could not have been produced by any prospect of wealth or fame, by becoming a Christian. Christians were poor; and to be a Christian then was to be exposed to contempt, persecution, and death. Saul had no reason to suppose that *he* would escape the common lot of Christians. (3.) He was as firmly opposed to Christianity before his conversion as possible. He had already distinguished himself for his hostility. Infidels often say that Christians are prejudiced in favour of their religion. But here was a man, at first, a bitter infidel, and foe to Christianity. All the prejudices of his education, and his prospects, all his former views and feelings, were opposed to the gospel of Christ. He became however, one of its most firm advocates

meat, he was strengthened. Then
was Saul certain days with the
disciples which were at Damascus.[a]
20 And straightway he preached Christ in the synagogues, that
he is the Son of God.
21 But all that heard *him* were [b]
amazed, and said, Is not this he [c]
that destroyed them which called
on this name in Jerusalem, and
came hither for that intent, that he
might bring them bound unto the
chief priests?
22 But Saul increased the more
in strength, [d] and confounded the
[e] Jews, which dwelt at Damascus,
proving that this is very Christ.

a c.26.20 Ga.1.17. b Ga.1.13,23. c c.8.3. d Ps.84.7. e c.18.28.

and friends; and it is for infidels to account for this change. There must have been *some* cause, some motive for it; and is there any thing more rational than the supposition, that Saul was convinced in a most striking and wonderful manner of the truth of Christianity? (4.) His subsequent life showed that his change was sincere and real. He encountered danger and persecution to evince his attachment to Christ; he went from land to land, and exposed himself to every danger, and every mode of obloquy and scorn, always rejoicing that he was a Christian, and was permitted to suffer *as* a Christian; and has thus given the highest proofs of his sincerity. If *these* sufferings, and if the life of Paul were not evidences of sincerity, then it would be impossible to fix on any circumstances of a man's life that would furnish proof that he was not a deceiver. (5.) If Paul was sincere; if this conversion was genuine, the Christian religion is true. Nothing else *but* a religion from heaven could produce this change. There is here, therefore, the independent testimony of a man, who was once a persecutor; converted, not by the preaching of the apostles; changed in a wonderful manner; his whole life, views, and feelings revolutionized, and all his subsequent days evincing the sincerity of his feelings, and the reality of the change. He is just such a *witness* as infidels ought to be satisfied with; whose testimony cannot be impeached; who had no interested motives, and who was willing to stand forth any where, and avow his change of feeling and purpose. We adduce him as such a witness; and infidels are *bound* to dispose of his testimony, or to embrace the religion which *he* embraced. (6.) The example of Saul does not stand alone. Hundreds and thousands of enemies, persecutors, and slanderers have been changed, and each one becomes a living witness of the power and truth of the Christian religion. The scoffer becomes reverent; the profane man learns to speak the praise of God; the sullen, bitter foe of Christ becomes his friend, and lives and dies under the influence of his religion. Could better proof be asked that this religion is from God?

20. *And straightway.* Immediately This was an evidence of the genuineness of his conversion, that he was willing at once to avow himself to be the friend of the Lord Jesus. ¶ *He preached Christ.* He proclaimed and proved that Jesus was the Christ. See ver. 22. Many manuscripts read here *Jesus* instead of *Christ.* Griesbach has adopted this reading. Such is also the Syriac, the Vulgate, and the Ethiopic. This reading accords much better with the subject than the common reading. That *Christ*, or the *Messiah*, was the son of God, all admitted. In the New Testament the names *Christ* and *Son of God* are used as synonymous. But the question was, whether *Jesus* was the Christ, or the Son of God, and this Paul showed to the Jews Paul continued the practice of attending the synagogues; and in the synagogues any one had a right to speak, who was invited by the officiating minister. See ch. xiii. 15 ¶ *That he is the Son of God.* That he is the Messiah.

21. *Were amazed.* Amazed at his sudden and remarkable change. ¶ *That destroyed.* That opposed; laid waste; or persecuted. Comp. Gal. i. 13. ¶ *For that intent.* With that design, that he might destroy the church at Damascus.

22. *Increased the more in strength.* His conviction of the truth of the Christian religion became stronger every day. Hence his *moral* strength or boldness increased. ¶ *And confounded.* See Acts ii. 6 The word here means *confuted.* It means also occasionally to produce a *tumult*, or *excitement.* Acts xix. 32; xxi. 31. Perhaps the idea of producing such a tumult is intended to be conveyed here. Paul confuted the Jews, and by so doing he was the occasion of their tumultuous proceedings, or he so enraged them as to lead to great agitation and excitement

23 And after that many days were fulfilled, the Jews took counsel [a] to kill him.

a c.23.12; 25.3.

24 But their laying await was known of Saul. And they watched [b] the gates day and night, to kill him.

b 2Cor.11.26,&c. Ps.21.11; 37.32,33.

A very common effect of close and conclusive argumentation. ¶ *Proving that this.* This Jesus. ¶ *Is very Christ.* Greek. That this is *the* Christ. The word *very* means here simply *the.* Greek, ὁ Χριστός. It means that Paul showed by strong and satisfactory arguments, that Jesus of Nazareth was the true Messiah. The arguments which he would use may be easily conceived; but the evangelist has not seen fit to record them.

23. *And after that many days,* &c. How long a time elapsed before this, is not recorded in this place; but it is evident that the writer means to signify that a *considerable* time intervened. There is, therefore, an *interval* here which Luke has not filled up; and if this were the only narrative which we had, we should be at a loss how to understand this. From all that we know now of the usual conduct of the Jews towards the apostles, and especially towards Paul, it would seem highly improbable that this interval would be passed peaceably or quietly. Nay, it would be highly improbable that he would be allowed to remain in Damascus *many days* without violent persecution. Now it so happens that by turning to another part of the New Testament, we are enabled to ascertain the manner in which this interval was filled up. Turn then to Gal. i 17, and we learn from Paul himself that he went into Arabia, and spent some time there, and then returned again to Damascus. The precise *time* which would be occupied in such a journey is not specified; but it would not be performed under a period of some months. In Gal. i. 18, we are informed that he did not go to Jerusalem until *three years* after his conversion; and as there is reason to believe that he went up to Jerusalem *directly* after escaping from Damascus the second time (Acts ix. 25, 26), it seems probable that the three years were spent chiefly in Arabia. We have thus an account of the "*many days*" here referred to by Luke. And in this instance we have a striking example of the truth and honesty of the sacred writers. By comparing these *two* accounts together, we arrive at the whole state of the case. Neither seems to be complete without the other. Luke has left a chasm which he has nowhere else supplied. But that chasm we are enabled to fill up from the apostle himself, in a letter written long after, and without any *design* to amend or complete the history of Luke: for the introduction of this history into the epistle to the Galatians was for a very different purpose—to show that he received his commission directly from the Lord Jesus, and in a manner independent of the other apostles. The two accounts, therefore, are like the two parts of a *tally;* neither is complete without the other; and yet being brought together, they so exactly fit as to show that the one is precisely adjusted to the other. And as the two parts were made by different individuals, and without design of adapting them to each other, they show that the writers had formed no collusion or agreement to impose on the world; that they are separate and independent witnesses; that they are honest men; that their narratives are true records of what actually occurred; and the two narratives constitute, therefore, a strong and very valuable proof of the correctness of the sacred narrative. If asked why *Luke* has omitted this in the Acts, it may be replied, that there are many circumstances and facts omitted in all histories from the necessity of the case. Comp. John xxi. 25. It is remarkable here, not that he has *omitted* this, but that he has left a *chasm* in his own history which can be so readily filled up. ¶ *Were fulfilled.* Had elapsed. ¶ *Took counsel,* &c. Laid a scheme; or designed to kill him. Comp. ch. xxiii. 12; xxv. 3. His zeal and success would enrage them, and they knew of no other way in which they could free themselves from the effects of his arguments and influence.

24. *But their laying await.* Their counsel; their design. ¶ *Was known of Saul.* Was made known to him. In what way this was communicated, we do not know. This design of the Jews against Saul is referred to in 2 Cor. xi. 32, 33, where it is said, "In Damascus, the governor under Aretas the king kept the Damascenes with a garrison, desirous to apprehend me; and through a window in a basket was I let down by the wall, and escaped their hands." ¶ *And they watched the gates.* Cities were surrounded by high walls; and of course the *gates* were presumed to be the only places of escape. As they supposed that Saul, apprized of their designs would make an attempt to

25 Then the disciples took him
by night, and let [a] *him* down by the
wall, in a basket.
26 And when Saul was come [b] to
Jerusalem, he assayed to join himself to the disciples: but they were
all afraid of him, and believed not
that he was a disciple.
27 But Barnabas [c] took him, and
brought *him* to the apostles, and declared unto them how he had seen
the Lord in the way, and that he

a Jos.2.15. b Gal.1.18 c c.4.36.

escape, they stationed guards at the gates to intercept him. In 2 Cor. xi. 32, it is said that the *governor* kept the city for the purpose of apprehending him. It is possible that the governor might have been a Jew, and one, therefore, who would enter into their views. Or if not a Jew, the Jews who were there might easily represent Saul as an offender, and demand his being secured; and thus a garrison or guard might be furnished them for their purpose. See a similar attempt made by the Jews recorded in Matt. xxviii. 14.

25. *Took him by night*, &c. This was done through a window in the wall. 2 Cor. xi. 33. ¶ *In a basket.* This word is used to denote commonly the basket in which food was carried. Matt. xv. 37. Mark viii. 8. 20. This conduct of Saul was in accordance with the direction of the Lord Jesus (Matt. x. 23), "When they persecute you in one city, flee ye into another," &c. Saul was certain of death if he remained; and as he could secure his life by flight without abandoning any principle of religion, or denying his Lord, it was his duty to do so. Christianity requires us to sacrifice our lives only when we cannot avoid it without denying the Saviour, or abandoning the principles of our holy religion.

26. *Was come to Jerusalem*, It is probable that he then went immediately to Jerusalem. Gal. i. 18. This was three years after his conversion. ¶ *He assayed.* He attempted; he endeavoured. ¶ *To join himself.* To become connected with them as their fellow-christian. ¶ *But they were all afraid of him.* Their fear, or suspicion, was excited probably on these grounds: (1.) They remembered his former violence against Christians. They had an instinctive shrinking from him, and suspicion of the man that had been so violent a persecutor. (2.) He had been absent three years. If they had *not* heard of him during that time, they would naturally retain much of their old feelings towards him. If they *had*, they might suspect the man who had not returned to Jerusalem; who had not before sought the society of other Christians; and who had spent that time in a distant country, and among strangers. It would seem remarkable that he had not at once returned to Jerusalem and connected himself with the apostles. But the sacred writer does not justify the fears of the apostles. He simply records the *fact* of their apprehension. It is not unnatural, however, to have doubts respecting an open and virulent enemy of the gospel who suddenly professes a change in favour of it. The human mind does not easily cast off suspicion of some unworthy motive, and open itself at once to entire confidence. When great and notorious sinners profess to be converted—men who have been violent, or artful, or malignant—it is natural to ask whether they have not some unworthy motive still in their professed change. Confidence is a plant of slow growth, and starts up not by a sudden profession, but by a course of life which is *worthy* of affection and of trust. ¶ *A disciple.* A sincere Christian.

27. *But Barnabas.* See Note, ch. iv. 36. Barnabas was of Cyprus, not far from Tarsus, and it is not improbable that he had been before acquainted with Saul. ¶ *To the apostles.* To Peter and James. Gal. i. 18, 19. Probably the other apostles were at that time absent from Jerusalem. ¶ *And declared unto them*, &c. It may seem remarkable that the apostles at Jerusalem had not before heard of the conversion of Saul. The following considerations may serve in some degree to explain this. (1.) It is certain that intercourse between different countries was then much more difficult than it is now. There were no posts; no public conveyances; nothing that corrresponded with our modes of intercourse between one part of the world and another. (2.) There was at this time a state of animosity amounting to hostility subsisting between Herod and Aretas. Herod the tetrarch had married the daughter of Aretas king of Arabia, and had put her away. (Josephus, Antiq. b. xviii. ch. v. § 1, 2.) The result of this was a long misunderstanding between them, and a war; and the effects of that war might have been to interrupt the communication very much throughout all that country. (3.) Though the *Jews* at

had spoken to him, and how he had preached boldly[a] at Damascus in the name of Jesus.

28 And he was with them coming in and going out at Jerusalem.

29 And he spake boldly in the name of the Lord Jesus, and disputed against the Grecians: but[b] they went about to slay him.

30 *Which* when the brethren knew, they brought him down to Cesarea, and sent him forth to Tarsus.

31 Then[c] had the churches rest[d]

a ver.20.22. b ver.23. c Zec.9.1, c.8.1 d Ps.94.13

Jerusalem *might* have heard of the conversion of Saul, yet it was for their interest to keep it a secret, and not to mention it to Christians. But, (4.) Though the Christians who were there *had* heard of it, yet it is probable that they were not fully informed on the subject; that they had not had all the evidence of his conversion which they desired; and that they looked with suspicion on him. It was therefore proper that they should have a *full* statement of the evidence of his conversion; and this was made by Barnabas

28. *And he was with them, &c.* That is, he was admitted to their friendship, and recognised as a Christian and an apostle. The *time* during which he then remained at Jerusalem was, however, only fifteen days. Gal. i. 18.

29 *And spake boldly.* He openly defended the doctrine that Jesus was the Messiah. ¶ *In the name, &c.* By the authority of the Lord Jesus. ¶ *Against the Grecians.* See the word *Grecians* explained in the note on Acts vi. 1. It means that he not only maintained that Jesus was the Christ in the presence of those Jews who resided at Jerusalem, and who spoke the Hebrew language, but also before those *foreign* Jews, who spoke the Greek language, and who had come up to Jerusalem. They would be as much opposed to the doctrine that Jesus was the Christ, as those who resided in Jerusalem. ¶ *They went about.* They *sought* to slay him; or they formed a purpose or plan to put him to death as an apostate. See ver. 23.

30. *To Cesarea.* Note ch. viii. 40. ¶ *And sent him forth to Tarsus.* This was his native city. Note ver. 11. It was in Cilicia, where Paul doubtless preached the gospel. Gal. i. 21, "Afterwards I came into the regions of Syria and Cilicia."

31. *Then had the churches rest.* That is, the persecutions against Christians ceased. Those persecutions had been excited by the opposition made to Stephen (Acts xi. 19); they had been greatly promoted by Saul (Acts viii. 3); and had extended doubtless throughout the whole land of Palestine. The precise causes of this cessation of the persecution are not known. Probably they were the following. (1.) It is not improbable that the great mass of Christians had been driven into other regions by these persecutions. (2.) He who had been most active in exciting the persecution who was, in a sort, its leader, and who was best adapted to carry it on, had been converted. He had ceased his opposition; and even he now was removed from Judea. All this would have some effect in causing the persecution to subside. (3.) But it is not improbable that the civil state of things in Judea contributed much to turn the attention of the Jews to other matters. Dr. Lardner accounts for this in the following manner "Soon after Caligula's accession, the Jews at Alexandria suffered very much from the Egyptians in that city, and at length their oratories there were all destroyed. In the third year of Caligula, A. D. 39, Petronius was sent into Syria, with orders to set up the emperor's statue in the temple at Jerusalem. This order from Caligula was, to the Jews, a thunder-stroke. The Jews must have been too much engaged after this to mind any thing else, as may appear from the accounts which Philo and Josephus have given us of this affair. Josephus says, 'That Caligula ordered Petronius to go with an army to Jerusalem, to set up his statue in the temple there: enjoining him if the Jews opposed it to put to death all who made any resistance, and to make all the rest of the nation slaves. Petronius, therefore marched from Antioch into Judea, with three legions and a large body of auxiliaries raised in Syria. *All were hereupon filled with consternation*, the army being come as far as Ptolemais.'" See Lardner's Works, vol. i. p. 101, 102. Lond. Ed 1829. Philo gives the same account of the consternation as Josephus. Philo de legat. ad Cai. p. 1024, 1025. He describes the Jews "as abandoning their cities, villages, and open country, as going to Petronius in Phenicia, both men

throughout all Judea and Galilee
and Samaria, and were edified; [a]
and walking [b] in the fear of the
Lord, and in the comfort [c] of the
Holy Ghost, were multiplied.[d]
32 And it came to pass, as Peter
passed throughout all *quarters*, he
came down also to the saints which
dwelt at Lydda.
33 And there he found a certain
man named Eneas, which had kept
his bed eight years, and was sick
of the palsy.
34 And Peter said unto him,
Eneas, Jesus Christ maketh thee [e]
whole; arise, and make thy bed.
And he arose immediately.
35 And all that dwelt in Lydda [g]
and [f] Saron saw him, and turned
to the Lord

a Ro.14.19. *b* Ps. 86.11 Col.1.10. *c* Jno.14. 16,17. *d* Zec.8.20.22.

e c.3.6,16;4.10. *f* 1 Ch.5.16. *g* c.11.21. 2Cor.3.16

and women, the old, the young, the middle aged; as throwing themselves on the ground before Petronius with weeping and lamentation," &c. The effect of this consternation in diverting their minds from the Christians can be easily conceived. The prospect that the images of the Roman emperor were about to be set up by violence in the temple, or, that in case of resistance, death or slavery was to be their portion; the advance of a large army to execute that purpose; all tended to throw the nation into alarm. By the providence of God, therefore, this event was permitted to occur to divert the attention of bloody-minded persecutors from a feeble and a bleeding church. Anxious for their own safety, the Jews would cease to persecute the Christians, and thus by the conversion of the main instrument in persecution, and by the universal alarm for the welfare of the nation, the trembling and enfeebled church was permitted to obtain repose. Thus ended the *first* general persecution against Christians, and thus effectually did God show that he had power to guard and protect his chosen people. ¶ *All Judea*, &c. These three places included the land of Palestine. See Note on Matt. ii. 22. The formation of churches in Galilee is not expressly mentioned before this; but there is no improbability in supposing that Christians had travelled there, and had preached the gospel. Comp. Acts xi. 19. The formation of churches in Samaria is expressly mentioned. ch. viii. ¶ *Were edified.* Were built up, increased, and strengthened. See Rom. xiv. 19; xv. 2. 1 Cor. viii. 1. ¶ *And walking.* Proceeding. Living. The word is often used to denote Christian conduct, or manner of life. Col. i. 10. Luke i. 6. 1 Thess. iv. 1. 1 John ii. 6 The idea is, that of *travellers* who are going to any place, and who walk in the right path. Christians are thus travellers to another country, an heavenly. ¶ *In the fear of the Lord.* Fearing the Lord; with reverence for him and his commandments. This expression is often used to denote piety in general. 2 Chron. xix. 7. Job xxviii. 28. Ps. xix. 9; cxi. 10; Prov. i. 7; ix. 10; xiii. 13. ¶ *In the comfort of the Holy Ghost.* In the consolations which the Holy Ghost produced. John xiv. 16, 17. Rom. v. 1—5. ¶ *Were multiplied.* Were increased.

32. *To the saints.* To the Christians. ¶ *Which dwelt at Lydda.* This town was situated on the road from Jerusalem to Cesarea Philippi. It was about fifteen miles east of Joppa, and belonged to the tribe of Ephraim. It was called by the Greeks Diospolis, or city of Jupiter, probably because a temple was at some period erected to Jupiter in that city. It is now so entirely ruined as to be a miserable village. Since the crusades, it has been called by the Christians St. George, on account of its having been the scene of the martyrdom of a saint of that name. Tradition says that in this city the emperor Justinian erected a church.

33. *Eneas.* This is a Greek name; and probably he was a Hellenist. Note ch. vi. 1. ¶ *Sick of the palsy.* See Note. Matt. iv. 24.

34. *Maketh thee whole.* Cures thee. Peter claimed no power to do it himself. Comp. ch. iii. 6. 16; iv. 10. ¶ *Make thy bed.* This would show that he was truly healed. Comp. Matt. ix. 6. Mark. ii. 9. 11. John v 11, 12.

35. *And all.* The mass, or body of the people. The affliction of the man had been long, and was probably well known: the miracle would be celebrated, and the effect was an extensive revival of religion. ¶ *Saron.* This was the *champaign*, or open country, usually mentioned by the name of *Sharon* in the Old Testament. 1 Chron. v. 16; xxvii. 29. Cant. ii. 1. Isa. xxxiii. 9. It was a region of extraordinary fertility, and the name was almost proverbial to denote

36 Now there was at Joppa a
certain disciple named Tabitha,
which by interpretation is called
[1] Dorcas: this woman was full [a] of
good works and almsdeeds which
she did.
37 And it came to pass in those
days, that she was sick, and died:
whom, when they had washed, they
laid *her* in an upper chamber.
38 And forasmuch as Lydda was
nigh to Joppa, and the disciples had
heard that Peter was there, they
sent unto him two men, desiring
him that he would not [2] delay to
come to them.
39 Then Peter arose, and went
with them. When he was come,
they brought him into the upper
chamber: and all the widows stood
by him weeping, and shewing the
coats and garments which Dorcas
made while [b] she was with them.
40 But Peter put [c] them all forth,
and kneeled down, and prayed: and
turning *him* to the body, said, Ta-

1 or, *Doe*, or, *Roe*. *a* 1Tim.2.10. Tit.2.7.
2 or, *be grieved*. *b* Ec.9.11. *c* Mat.9.25.

any country of great beauty and fertility. Comp. Isa. xxxiii. 9; xxxv. 2; lxv. 10. It was situated south of mount Carmel, along the coast of the Mediterranean, extending to Cesarea and Joppa. Lydda was situated in this region. ¶ *Turned to the Lord.* Were converted; or received the Lord Jesus as the Messiah. ch. xi. 21. 2 Cor. iii. 16.

36. *At Joppa.* This was a seaport town situated on the Mediterranean, in the tribe of Dan, about thirty miles south of Cesarea, and forty-five northwest of Jerusalem. It was the principal seaport of Palestine; and hence, though the harbour was poor, it had considerable celebrity. It was occupied by Solomon to receive the timber brought for the building of the temple from Tyre (2 Chron. ii. 16), and was used for a similar purpose in the time of Ezra. Ezra iii. 7. The present name of the town is *Jaffa.* It is situated on a promontory jutting out into the sea, rising to the height of about one hundred and fifty feet above its level, and offering on all sides picturesque and varied prospects. The streets are narrow, uneven, and dirty. The inhabitants are estimated at between four and five thousand, of whom the greater part are Turks and Arabs. The Christians are stated to be about six hundred, consisting of Roman Catholics, Greeks, Maronites, and Arminians. It is several times mentioned in the New Testament. Acts x. 5. 23; xi. 5. ¶ *Tabitha.* This word is properly Syriac, and means literally the *gazelle* or *antelope.* The name became an appellation of a female probably on account of the beauty of its form. "It is not unusual in the East to give the names of beautiful animals to young women." (*Clark.*) Comp. Cant. ii. 9; iv. 5. ¶ *Dorcas.* A Greek word signifying the same as Tabitha. Our word *doe* or *roe* answers to it in signification. ¶ *Full of good works.* Distinguished for good works. Comp. 1 Tim. ii. 10. Titus ii. 7. ¶ *And almsdeeds.* Acts of kindness to the poor.

37. *Whom, when they had washed.* Among most people it has been customary to wash the body before it is buried or burned. They prepared her in the usual manner for interment. ¶ *In an upper chamber.* See Note, Acts i. 13. There is no evidence that they expected that Peter would raise her up to life.

38. *Was nigh unto Joppa.* It was about six miles. ¶ *They sent unto him,* &c Why they sent is not affirmed. It is probable that they desired his presence to comfort and sustain them in their affliction. It is certainly *possible* that they expected he would restore her to life; but as this is not mentioned; as the apostles had as yet raised up no one from the dead; as even Stephen had not been restored to life; we have no authority for assuming, or supposing, that they had formed any such expectation.

39. *Then Peter arose.* See Note on Luke xv. 18. ¶ *And all the widows.* Whom Dorcas had benefited by her kindness. They had lost a benefactress; and it was natural that they should recall her kindness, and express their gratitude by enumerating the proofs of her beneficence. Each one would therefore naturally dwell on the kindness which had been shown to herself.

40. *But Peter put them all forth.* From the room. See a similar case in Matt. ix. 25. *Why* this was done is not said. Perhaps because he did not wish to appear as if seeking publicity. If done in the presence of many persons, it might seem like ostentation. Others suppose it was that he might offer more fervent and agonizing prayer to God than he would be willing they should witness Compare 2 Kings iv. 33. ¶ *Tabitha, arise.* Comp. Mark v. 41, 42.

bitha, [a] arise. And she opened her eyes: and when she saw Peter, she sat up.

41 And he gave her *his* hand, and lift her up: and when he had called the saints and widows, he [b] presented her alive.

42 And it was known throughout all Joppa; and [c] many believed in the Lord.

43 And it came to pass, that he tarried many days in Joppa, with one Simon a tanner.

CHAPTER X.

THERE was a certain man in Cesarea, called Cornelius a

a Mar.5.41,42. Jno.11.43. b 1Ki.17.23. c Jno.12.11.

41. *He presented her alive.* He exhibited, or showed her to them alive. Comp. 1 Kings xvii. 23.

42. *And many believed, &c.* A similar effect followed when Jesus raised up Lazarus. See John xii. 11.

This was the first miracle of this kind that was performed by the apostles. The effect was that many believed. It was not merely a work of benevolence, in restoring to life one who contributed largely to the comfort of the poor, but it was used as a means of extending and establishing, as it was designed doubtless to do, the kingdom of the Saviour.

CHAPTER X.

THIS chapter commences a very important part of the history of the transactions of the apostles. Before this, they had preached the gospel to the Jews only. They seemed to have retained the feelings of their countrymen on this subject, that the Jews were to be regarded as the peculiarly favoured people, and that salvation was not to be offered beyond the limits of their nation. It was important, indeed, that the gospel should be offered to them first; but the whole tendency of the Christian religion was to enlarge and liberalize the mind; to overcome the narrow policy and prejudices of the Jewish people; and to diffuse itself over all the nations of the earth. In various ways, and by various parables, the Saviour had taught the apostles, indeed, that his gospel should be spread among the Gentiles. He had commanded them to go and preach it to every creature. Mark xvi. 15. But he had told them to tarry in Jerusalem until they were endued with power from on high. Luke xxiv. 49. It was natural, therefore, that they should receive *special* instructions and divine revelation on a point so important as this; and God selected the case of Cornelius as the instance by which he would fully establish his purpose of conveying the gospel to the Gentile world. It is worthy of observation, also, that he selected *Peter* for the purpose of conveying the gospel first to the Gentiles. The Saviour had told him that on him he would build his church; that he would give to him first the key of the kingdom of heaven; that is, that he should be the agent in opening the doors of the church to both Jews and Gentiles. See Notes on Matt. xvi. 18, 19. Peter had, in accordance with these predictions, been the agent in first presenting the gospel to the Jews (Acts ii.); and the prediction was now to be *completely* fulfilled in extending the same gospel to the Gentile world. The transaction recorded in this chapter, is one, therefore, that is exceedingly important in the history of the church; and we are not to be surprised that it is recorded at length. It should be remembered, also, that this point became afterwards the source of incessant controversy in the early church. The converts from Judaism insisted on the observance of the whole of the rites of their religion; the converts from among the Gentiles claimed exemption from them all. To settle these disputes, and to secure the reception of the gospel among the Gentiles, and to introduce them to the church with all the privileges of the Jews, required all the wisdom, talent, and address of the apostles. See Acts xi. 1—18; xv. Rom. xiv. xv. Gal. ii. 11—16.

1. *In Cesarea.* Note, ch. viii. 40. ¶ *Cornelius.* This is a Latin name, and shows that the man was doubtless a Roman. It has been supposed by many interpreters that this man was "a proselyte of the gate;" that is, one who had renounced idolatry, and who observed some of the Jewish rites, though not circumcised, and not called a Jew. But there is no sufficient evidence of this. The reception of the narrative of Peter (ch. xi. 1—3), shows that the other apostles regarded him as a Gentile. In ch. x. 28, Peter evidently regards him as a foreigner; one who did not in any sense esteem himself to be a Jew In ch. xi. 1, it is expressly said that "*the Gentiles*" had received the word of God; evidently alluding to Cornelius and those who were with him. ¶ *A centurion.* One who was the commander of a division in the Roman army, consisting of a hundred men. A captain of a hundred. Note, Matt. viii. 5. ¶ *Of the band.* A division

centurion of the band called the
Italian *band*,
2 *A* devout [a] *man*, and one that
feared [b] God with all [c] his house,
which gave much alms to [d] the
people, and prayed [e] to God alway.
3 He saw in a vision evidently,
about the ninth hour of the day, an
angel [f] of God coming in to him,
and saying unto him, Cornelius.
4 And when he looked on him,
he was afraid, and said, What is it,

a c.8.2; 22.12. b Zc.7.18. c Gen.18.19 Ps.101.2-7. c.18.8. d Ps.41.1. e Ps.119.2. Pr.2.3-5. f Heb.1.14.

of the Roman army, consisting of from four hundred to six hundred men. Note, Matt. xxvii. 27. ¶ *The Italian* band. Probably a band or regiment that was composed of soldiers from *Italy*, in distinction from those which were composed of soldiers born in provinces. It is evident that many of the soldiers in the Roman army would be those who were born in other parts of the world; and it is altogether probable that those who were born in Rome or Italy would claim pre-eminence over those enlisted in other places.

2. A *devout* man. Pious; or one who maintained the worship of God. See Note, Luke ii. 25. Comp. Acts ii. 5; viii. 2. ¶ *And one that feared God.* This is often a designation of piety. Note, ch. ix. 31. It has been supposed by many that the expressions here used denote that Cornelius was a Jew, or was instructed in the Jewish religion, and was a proselyte. But this by no means follows. It is probable that there might have been among the Gentiles a few at least who were fearers of God, and who maintained his worship according to the light which they had. So there may be now persons found in pagan lands, who, in some unknown way, have been taught the evils of idolatry; the necessity of a purer religion; and who may be *prepared* to receive the gospel. The Sandwich Islands were very much in this state when the American missionaries first visited them. They had thrown away their idols, and seemed to be *waiting* for the message of mercy and the word of eternal life, as Cornelius was. A few other instances have been found by missionaries in heathen lands, who have thus been prepared by a train of providential events, or by the teaching of the Spirit, for the gospel of Christ. ¶ *With all his house.* With all his family. It is evident here that Cornelius instructed his family, and exerted his influence to train them in the fear of God. True piety will always lead a man to seek the salvation of his family. ¶ *Much alms.* Large and liberal charity. This is always an effect of piety. See James i. 27. Ps. xli. 1. ¶ *Prayed to God alway.* Constantly; meaning that he was in the regular habit of praying to God. Comp. Rom. xii. 12. Luke xviii. 1. Ps. cxix. 2. Prov. ii. 2—5. As no particular *kind* of prayer is mentioned except secret prayer, we are not authorized to affirm that he offered prayer in any other manner. It may be observed, however, that he who prays in secret will usually pray in his family; and as the *family* of Cornelius is mentioned as being also under the influence of religion, it is perhaps not a forced inference that he observed family worship.

3. *He saw in a vision.* See Note, ch ix. 10. ¶ *Evidently.* Openly; manifestly ¶ *About the ninth hour.* About three o'clock, P. M. This was the usual hour of evening worship among the Jews. ¶ *An angel of God.* Note, Matt. i. 20. Comp. Heb. i. 14. This angel was sent to signify to Cornelius that his alms were accepted by God as an evidence of his piety, and to direct him to send for Peter to instruct him in the way of salvation. The importance of the occasion—the introduction of the gospel to a *Gentile*, and hence to the entire Gentile world—was probably the chief reason why an angel was commissioned to visit the Roman centurion. Comp. ch. xvi. 9, 10.

4. *And when he looked on him.* Greek, Having fixed his eyes attentively on him. ¶ *He was afraid.* At the suddenness and unexpected character of the vision. ¶ *What is it, Lord?* This is the expression of surprise and alarm. The word *Lord* should have been translated *sir*, as there is no evidence that this is an address to *God*, and still less that he regarded the personage present as *the Lord.* It is such language as a man would naturally use who was suddenly surprised; who should witness a strange form appearing unexpectedly before him; and who should exclaim, 'Sir, what is the matter?' ¶ *Are come up for a memorial.* Are remembered before God. Comp. Isa. xlv. 19. They were an evidence of piety towards God, and were accepted as such Though he had not offered sacrifice according to the Jewish laws; though he had not been circumcised; yet, having acted according to the light which he had, his prayers were heard, and his alms

Lord? And he said unto him, Thy
prayers and thine alms are come up
for a memorial [a] before God.
5 And now send men to Joppa,
and call for *one* Simon, whose surname is Peter.
6 He lodgeth with one Simon [b] a
tanner, whose house is by the seaside: he shall tell thee [c] what thou
oughtest to do.
7 And when the angel which
spake unto Cornelius was departed, he called two of his household
servants, and a devout soldier of
them that waited on him continually:
8 And when he had declared all
these things unto them, he sent
them to Joppa.
9 On the morrow, as they went
on their journey, and drew nigh
unto the city, Peter went [d] up upon
the house-top to pray, about the
sixth hour:

a Isa.45.19. b c.9.43. c c.11.14. d c.11.5,&c.

---

accepted. This was done in accordance with the general principle of the divine administration, that God prefers the offering of the *heart* to external forms; the expressions of love, to sacrifice without it. This he had often declared. Isa. i. 11—15. Amos v. 21, 22. 1 Sam. xv. 22, "To obey is better than sacrifice, and to hearken, than the fat of rams." Hos. vi. 6. Eccl. v. 1. It should be remembered, however, that Cornelius was not depending on external morality. His *heart* was in the work of *religion.* It should be remembered, further, that he was ready to receive *the gospel* when it was offered to him, and to become a Christian. In this there was an important difference between him and those who are depending for salvation on their morality in Christian lands. Such men are apt to defend themselves by the example of Cornelius, and to suppose that as *he* was accepted *before* he embraced the gospel, so they may be *without* embracing it. But there is an important difference in the two cases. For, (1.) There is no evidence that Cornelius was depending on *external morality* for salvation. His offering was that of the *heart,* and not merely an external offering. Moral men in Christian lands depend on their *external morality* in the sight of men. But God looks upon the heart. (2.) Cornelius did not rely on his *morality* at all. His was a work of *religion.* He feared God; he prayed to him; he exerted his influence to bring his *family* to the same state. Moral men do neither. "All their works they do to be seen of men;" and in their heart there is 'no good thing towards the Lord God of Israel." Comp. 1 Kings xiv. 13. 2 Chron. xix. 3. Who hears of a man that "fears God" and that prays, and that instructs his household in *religion,* that *depends* on his *morality* for salvation? (3.) Cornelius was disposed to do the will of God as far as it was made known to him. Where this exists there is religion. The moral man is not. (4.) Cornelius was willing to embrace a Saviour when he was made known to him. The moral man is not. He hears of a Saviour with unconcern; he listens to the message of God's mercy from year to year without embracing it. In all this there is an important difference between him and the Roman centurion; and while we hope there may be many in pagan lands who are in the same state of mind that he was—disposed to do the will of God as far as made known, and therefore accepted and saved by his mercy in the Lord Jesus—yet this cannot be adduced to encourage the hope of salvation in those who *do* know his will, and yet will not do it.

6. *He lodgeth.* He remains as a guest at his house. See ch. ix. 43. ¶ *By the seaside.* Joppa was a seaport on the Mediterranean. Tanneries are erected on the margin of streams, or of any body of water, to convey away the filth produced in the operation of dressing skins.

7. *A devout soldier.* A pious man. This is an instance of the effect of piety in a military officer. Few men have more influence; and in this case the effect was seen not only in the piety of his family, but of this attending soldier. Such men have usually been supposed to be far from the influence of religion; but this instance shows that even the labours and disadvantages of a camp are not necessarily hostile to the existence of piety Comp. Luke iii. 14.

8. *And when,* &c. "It has been remarked that from Joppa, Jonah was sent to preach to the Gentiles at Nineveh, and that from the same place Peter was sent to preach to the Gentiles at Cesarea' (*Clark.*)

9. *Peter went up,* &c. The small room in the second story, or on the roof of the

10 And he became very hungry,
and would have eaten; but while
they made ready, he fell into a
trance,
11 And saw [a] heaven opened,
and a certain vessel descending unto
him, as it had been a great sheet,
knit at the four corners, and let
down to the earth;
12 Wherein were all manner of
four-footed beasts of the earth, and
wild beasts, and creeping things,
and fowls of the air.
13 And there came a voice to

a c.7.56. Re.19.11.

house, was the usual place for retirement and prayer. See Note, Matt. vi. 6; ix. 2. ¶ *About the sixth hour.* About twelve o'clock at noon. The Jews had two stated seasons of prayer—morning, and evening. But it is evident that the more pious of the Jews frequently added a *third* season of devotion probably at noon. Thus David says (Ps. lv. 17), "Evening and morning, and *at noon*, will I pray, and cry aloud." Thus Daniel "kneeled upon his knees three times a day and prayed." Dan. vi. 10. 13. It was also customary in the early Christian church to offer prayer at the third, sixth, and ninth hours. (Clem. Alex. as quoted by Doddridge.) Christians will, however, have not merely *stated* seasons for prayer, but they will seize upon moments of leisure, and when their feelings strongly incline them to it, to pray.

10. *And he became very hungry.* From the connexion, where it is said, that they were making ready, that is, preparing a meal, it would seem that this was the customary hour of dining. The Hebrews, Greeks, and Romans, however, had but two meals, and the first was usually taken about ten or eleven o'clock. This meal usually consisted of fruit, milk, cheese, &c. Their principal meal was about six or seven in the afternoon; at which time they observed their feasts. See Jahn's Bib. Archæ. § 145. ¶ *He fell into a trance.* Greek, An ecstasy, ἔκστασις, fell upon him. In ch. xi 5, Peter says that *in* a trance he saw a vision. The word *trance*, or *ecstasy*, denotes a state of mind when the attention is absorbed in a particular train of thought, so that the external senses are partially or entirely suspended. It is a high species of abstraction from external objects; when the mind becomes forgetful of surrounding things, and is fixed solely on its own thoughts, so that appeals to the external senses do not readily rouse it. The soul seems to have passed out of the body, and to be conversant only with spiritual essences. Thus Balaam is said to have seen the vision of the Almighty, falling into a trance (Num. xxiv 4. 16); thus Paul, in praying in the temple, fell into a trance (Acts xxii. 17); and perhaps a similar state is described in 2 Cor. xii. 2. This effect seems to be caused by so intense and absorbing a train of thought, as to overcome the senses of the body; or wholly to withdraw the mind from their influence, and to fix it on the unseen object that engrosses it. It is often a high state of *revery*, or absence of mind, which Dr. Rush describes as "induced by the stimulus of ideas of absent subjects, being so powerful as to destroy the perception of present objects." (Diseases of the Mind, p. 310, Ed. Phila. 1812.) In the case of Peter, however, there was a supernatural influence that drew his attention away from present objects.

11. *And saw heaven opened.* ch. vii. 56. Note, Matt. iii. 16. This *language* is derived from a common mode of speaking in the Hebrew scriptures, as if the sky above us was a solid, vast expanse, and if it were *opened* to present an opportunity for any thing to descend. It is language that is highly figurative. ¶ *And a certain vessel.* See Note on ch. ix. 15. ¶ *As it had been.* It is important to mark this expression. The sacred writer does not say that Peter literally saw such an object descending; but he uses this as an imperfect description of the vision. It was not a literal descent of a vessel, but it was such a kind of representation to him, producing the same impression, and the same effect, *as if* such a vessel had descended. ¶ *Knit at the four corners.* Bound, united, or *tied*. The corners were collected, as would be natural in putting any thing into a great sheet.

12. *Wherein, &c.* This particular vision was suggested by Peter's hunger. ver. 10. It was designed, however, to teach him an important lesson in regard to the introduction of all nations to the gospel. Its descending from heaven may have been an intimation, that that religion which was about to abolish the distinction between the Jews and other nations was of divine origin. See Rev. xxi. 2.

him, Rise, Peter; kill, and eat.
14 But Peter said, Not so, Lord;
for I have never eaten any thing
that is [a] common or unclean.
15 And the voice *spake* unto him
again the second time, What God
hath cleansed, [b] *that* call not thou
common.
16 This was done thrice: and
the vessel was received up again
into heaven.
17 Now while Peter doubted in

a Le.11.2,&c. 20.25. De.14.3,&c. Ez.4.14.

b Matt.15.11. ver.28. Ro.14.14,&c. 1Cor.10.25. 1Ti.4.4.

---

14. *I have never eaten, &c.* In the Old Testament God had made a distinction between clean and unclean animals. See Lev. xi. 2—27. Deut. xiv. 3—20. This law remained in the Scriptures, and Peter plead that he *had* never violated it, implying that he could not now violate it, as it was a law of God, and as it was unrepealed, he did not dare to act in a different manner from what it required. Between that law, and the command which he now received in the vision, there was an apparent variation, and Peter naturally referred to the well-known and admitted written law. One design of the vision was to show him that that law was now to pass away. ¶ *That is common.* This word properly denotes *that which pertains to all*, but among the Jews, who were bound by special laws, and who were prohibited from many things that were freely indulged in by other nations, the word *common* came to be opposed to the word *sacred*, and to denote that which was in common use among the heathens, hence that which was *profane*, or *polluted*. Here it means the same as *profane*, or *forbidden*. ¶ *Unclean.* Ceremonially unclean; i. e. that which is forbidden by the ceremonial law of Moses.

15. *What God hath cleansed.* What God hath pronounced or declared pure. If God has commanded you to do a thing, it is not impure or wrong. Its use is lawful if he has commanded it. Perhaps Peter would have supposed that the design of this vision was to instruct him, that the distinction between clean and unclean food, as recognised by the Jews, was about to be abolished, ver. 17. But the result showed that it had a higher, and more important design. It was to show him, that they who had been esteemed by the Jews as unclean or profane—the entire Gentile world—might now be admitted to similar privileges with the Jews. That barrier was to be broken down, and the whole world was to be admitted to the same fellowship and privileges in the gospel. See Eph. ii. 14. Gal. iii. 28. It was also true that the ceremonial laws of the Jews in regard to clean and unclean beasts was to pass away, though this was not directly taught in this vision. But when once the barrier was removed that separated the Jews and Gentiles, all the laws which *supposed* such a distinction, and which were framed to *keep up* such a distinction, passed away of course. The ceremonial laws of the Jews were designed *solely* to keep up the distinction between them and other nations. When the distinction was abolished; when other nations were to be admitted to the same privileges, the laws which were made to keep up such a difference received their death-blow, and expired of course. For it is a maxim of all law, that when the *reason* why a law was made ceases to exist, the law becomes obsolete. Yet it was not easy to convince the Jews that their laws ceased to be binding. This point the apostles laboured to establish; and from this point arose most of the difficulties between the Jewish and Gentile converts to Christianity. See Acts xv. and Rom. xiv. xv.

16. *This was done thrice.* Three times, doubtless to impress the mind of Peter with the certainty and importance of the vision. Comp. Gen. xli. 32.

17. *Doubted in himself.* Doubted in his own mind. He was perplexed to understand it. ¶ *Behold the men, &c.* We see here an admirable arrangement of the events of Providence to fit each other. Every part of this transaction is made to harmonize with every other part; and it was so arranged, that just in the moment when the mind of Peter was filled with perplexity, that the very event should occur which should relieve him of his embarrassment. Such a coincidence is not uncommon. An event of divine Providence may be as clear an expression of his will, and may as certainly serve to indicate our duty, as the most manifest revelation would do, and a state of mind may, by an arrangement of circumstances, be produced, that shall be extremely perplexing until some event shall occur, or some field of usefulness shall open, that shall exactly correspond to it, and shall indicate to us the will of God. We

himself what this vision which he
had seen should mean, behold, the
men which were sent from Cornelius had made inquiry [a] for Simon's
house, and stood before the gate.
18 And called, and asked whether Simon, which was surnamed
Peter, were lodged there.
19 While Peter thought on the
vision, the Spirit [b] said unto him,
Behold, three men seek thee.
20 Arise, [c] therefore, and get thee
down, and go with them, doubting
nothing: for I have sent them.
21 Then Peter went down to the
men which were sent unto him
from Cornelius; and said, Behold,
I am he whom ye seek: what *is*
the cause wherefore ye are come?
22 And they said, Cornelius, [d]
the centurion, a just man, and
one that feareth God, and of good
report [e] among all the nation of
the Jews, was warned from God
by an holy angel, to send for thee
into his house, and to hear words
of thee.
23 Then called he them in, and
lodged *them*. And on the morrow
Peter went away with them, and
certain [f] brethren from Joppa accompanied him.
24 And the morrow after they
entered into Cesarea. And Cornelius waited for them, and had called together his kinsmen and near
friends.
25 And as Peter was coming in
Cornelius met him, and fell down
at his feet, and worshipped *him*.
26 But Peter took him up, saying, [g] Stand up; I myself also am
a man.
27 And as he talked with him,
he went in, and found many that
were come together.

a 9.43. b c.11.12. c c.15.7. d ver.1,&c. e c.22.12. He.11.2. f ver.45. g c.14.14,15. Re.19.10;22.9.

should observe then the events of God's providence. We should mark and record the train of our own thoughts, and we should watch with interest any event that occurs, when we are perplexed and embarrassed, to obtain, if possible, an expression of the will of God. ¶ *Before the gate.* The word here rendered "gate," πυλῶνος, refers properly to *the porch* or principal entrance to an eastern house. See Note, Matt. ix. 2; xxvi. 71. It does not mean, as with us, a *gate*, but rather a *door*. See Acts xii. 13.

19. *The Spirit.* See Note, Acts viii. 29. Comp. Isa. lxv. 24. "And it shall come to pass, that before they call I will answer," &c.

22. *To hear words of thee.* To be instructed by thee.

23. *And lodged them.* They remained with him through the night. Four days were occupied before Peter met Cornelius at Cesarea. On the first the angel appeared to Cornelius. On the second the messengers arrived at Joppa, ver. 9. On the third, Peter returned with them, ver. 23; and on the fourth they arrived at Cesarea, ver. 24. 30. ¶ *And certain brethren.* Some Christians. They were six in number, ch. xi. 12. It was usual for the early Christians to accompany the apostles in their journeys. See Rom. xv. 24. Acts xv. 3. 3 John 6. 1 Cor. xvi. 6. 11. As this was an important event in the history of the church—the bearing of the gospel to a Gentile—it was more natural and proper that Peter should be attended with others.

24. *His kinsmen.* His relatives, or the connexions of his family. A man may often do vast good by calling his kindred and friends to hear the gospel.

25. *Fell down at his feet.* This was an act of profound regard for him as an ambassador of God. In oriental countries it was usual to prostrate themselves at length on the ground before men of rank and honour. ¶ *Worshipped him.* This does not mean religious *homage*, but civil respect, the homage, or profound regard which was due to one in honour See Note, Matt. ii. 2.

26. *Stand up.* &c. This does not imply that Peter supposed that Cornelius intended to do him *religious* reverence It was practically saying to him, "I am nothing more than a man as thou art, and pretend to no right to such profound respects as these, but am ready in civil life to show thee all the respect that is due." (*Doddridge.*)

27. *And as he talked with him.* He probably met him at the door or at a small distance from the house. It was

28 And he said unto them, Ye
know how that it is an unlawful
thing [a] for a man that is a Jew to
keep company, or come unto one
of another nation; but God hath
shewed me [b] that I should not call
any man common or unclean.

29 Therefore came I *unto you*
without gainsaying, as soon as I
was sent for. I ask, therefore, for
what intent ye have sent for me?

30 And Cornelius said, Four
days ago I was fasting until this
hour; and at the ninth hour I prayed in my house; and, behold, a
man stood before me [c] in bright
clothing.

31 And said, Cornelius, thy [d]
prayer is heard, and thine alms are
had in remembrance in the sight
of God.

32 Send therefore to Joppa, and
call hither Simon, whose surname
is Peter: he is lodged in the house
of *one* Simon a tanner, by the seaside; who, when he cometh, shall
speak unto thee.

33 Immediately therefore I sent
to thee: and thou hast well done
that thou art come. Now [e] therefore are we all here present before
God, to hear all things that are
commanded thee of God.

34 Then Peter opened *his* mouth,
and said, Of a truth, perceive that
God [f] is no respecter of persons:

a Jno.4.9. b c.15.8.9. Ep.3.6. c Matt.28.3. c.1.10. d ver.4,&c. Da.10.12. He.6 10. e De.5.27. f De.10.17. Ch.19.7. Job 34—19. Ro.2.11. Ga.2.6. 1Pe.1.17.

an expression of joy thus to go out to meet him.

28. *It is an unlawful thing.* This was not explicitly enjoined by Moses, but it seemed to be implied in his institutions, and was at any rate the common understanding of the Jews. The design was to keep them a separate people. To do this Moses forbid alliances by contract, or marriage, with the surrounding nations, which were idolatrous. See Lev. xviii. 24—30. Deut. vii. 3—12. Comp. Ezra ix. 11, 12. This command the Jews perverted; and explained as referring to intercourse of all kinds, even to the exercise of friendly offices and commercial transactions. Comp. John iv. 9. ¶ *Of another nation.* Greek, Another *tribe.* It refers here to all who were not Jews. ¶ *God hath shewed me* Comp. ch. xv. 8, 9. He had showed him by the vision, ver. 11, 12. ¶ *Any man common or unclean.* See Note, ver. 14. That no man was to be regarded as excluded from the opportunity of salvation; or be despised and abhorred. The gospel was to be preached to all; the barrier between Jews and Gentiles to be broken down; and all were to be regarded as capable of being saved.

29. *Without gainsaying.* Without *saying any thing against it*; without hesitation or reluctance. ¶ *I ask, therefore, &c.* The main design for which Cornelius had sent for him had been mentioned to Peter by the messenger, ver. 22. But Peter now desired from his own lips a more particular statement of the considerations which had induced him to send for him. ¶ *For what intent.* For what purpose or design.

30. *Four days ago.* See Note, on ver. 23. ¶ *Until this hour* The ninth hour, or three o'clock, P. M. See ver. 3. ¶ *A man.* Called, in ver. 3, an angel. He had the *appearance* of a man. Comp. Mark xvi. 5. ¶ *In bright clothing.* See Note, Matt. xxviii. 3.

33. *Thou hast well done.* This is an expression of grateful feeling. ¶ *Before God.* In the presence of God. It is implied, that they believed that God saw them, and that they were assembled at his command, and that they were disposed to listen to his instructions.

34. *Then Peter opened his mouth.* Began to speak. Matt. v. 2. ¶ *Of a truth.* Truly, evidently. That is, I have *evidence here* that God is no respecter of persons. ¶ *Is no respecter of persons.* The word used here denotes the act of showing favour to one on account of rank, family, wealth, or partiality, arising from any cause. It is explained in James ii. 1—4. A judge is a respecter of persons when he favours one of the parties on account of private friendship; or because he is a man of rank, influence, or power; or because he belongs to the same political party, &c. The Jews supposed that they were peculiarly favoured by God, and that salvation was not extended to other nations, and that the fact of *being a Jew* entitled them to this favour. Peter here says that he has learned the error of this doctrine. That a

35 But in [a] every nation he that feareth him, and worketh righteousness, is accepted with him.

a Rom.2.13,27;3.22,29;10.12,13. Eph.2.13-18.

man is not to be *accepted* because he is a *Jew*, nor is he to be *excluded* because he is a *Gentile*. The barrier is broken down; the offer is made to all; and God will save all on the same principle; not by external privileges, or rank, but according to their character. The same doctrine is elsewhere explicitly stated in the New Testament. Rom. ii. 11, Eph. vi. 9. Col. iii. 25. It may be observed here that this does not refer to the doctrine of divine sovereignty or election. It simply affirms that God will not save a man because he is a Jew; nor because he is rich, or learned, or of elevated rank; nor by any external privileges. Nor will he exclude a man because he is destitute of these privileges But this does not affirm that he will not make a difference *in their character*, and then treat them *according* to their character; nor that he will not pardon whom he pleases, which is a different question. The interpretation of this passage should be limited strictly to the case in hand—to mean that God will not accept and save a man on account of external national rank and privileges. That by receiving some, and leaving others, *on other grounds*, he will not make *a difference*, is not any where denied. Comp. 1 Cor. iv. 7. Rom. xii. 6. It is worthy of remark further, that the most strenuous advocate for the doctrines of sovereignty and election in the New Testament—the apostle Paul—is also the one that laboured most to establish the doctrine that God was no respecter of persons, that is, that there was no difference between the Jews and Gentiles in regard to the way of salvation; that God would not *save* a man because he was a Jew, nor *destroy* a man because he was a Gentile. Yet in regard to *the whole race viewed as lying on a level*, he maintained that God had a right to exercise the prerogatives of a sovereign, and to have mercy on whom he would have mercy. The doctrine may be thus stated. (1.) The barrier between the Jews and Gentiles was broken down. (2.) All men thus were placed on a level—none to be saved by external privileges, none to be lost by the want of them. (3.) *All* were guilty (Rom. i. ii. iii.), and none had a claim on God. (4.) If any were saved, it would be by God's showing mercy on such of this *common mass* as he chose. See Rom. iii. 22; x. 12; ii. 11. Gal. i 6. Compared with Rom. ix and Eph. i.

35. *But in every nation, &c.* This is given as a reason for what Peter had just said, that God was no respecter of persons. The sense is, that he now perceived that the favours of God were not confined to the *Jew*, but might be extended to all others on the same principle. The remarkable circumstances here, the vision to him, and to Cornelius, and the declaration that the alms of Cornelius were accepted, now convinced Peter that the favours of God were no longer to be confined to the Jewish people, but might be extended to all. This was what the vision was designed to teach; and to communicate this to the apostles was an important step in their work of spreading the gospel. ¶ *In every nation.* Among all people. Jews or Gentiles. Acceptance with God does not depend on the fact of being descended from Abraham, or of possessing external privileges, but on the state of the heart. ¶ *He that feareth him.* This is put for piety towards God in general. See Note, ch. ix. 31. It means that he that honours God, and keeps his law; that is a true worshipper of God, according to the light and privileges which he has, is approved by him, as giving evidence that he is his friend. ¶ *And worketh righteousness.* Does that which is right and just. This refers to his conduct towards man. He that discharges conscientiously his duty to his fellow-men, and evinces by his conduct that he is a righteous man. These *two* things comprehend the whole of religion, the sum of all the requirements of God—piety towards God, and justice towards all men; and as Cornelius had showed these, he showed that, though a Gentile, he was actuated by true piety. We may observe here, (1.) That it is not said that Cornelius was accepted *on account* of his good works Those works were simply an evidence of true piety in the heart; a proof that he feared and loved God, and not a meritorious ground of acceptance. (2.) He improved the light which he had. (3.) *He embraced the Saviour when he was offered to him.* This circumstance makes an essential difference between the case of Cornelius, and those who depend on their morality in Christian lands. They do *not* embrace the Lord Jesus, and they

36 The word which *God* sent
unto the children of Israel, preaching peace [a] by Jesus Christ; (he
is [b] Lord of all;)
37 That word, *I say*, ye know,
which was published throughout
all Judea, and began from Galilee, after the baptism which John
preached:
38 How God anointed [c] Jesus of
Nazareth with the Holy Ghost and
with power, who [d] went about doing

a Isa.57 19. Col.1.20. b Ps.24.1-10. Matt.28.18. Ro.14.9. 1Cor.15.27. Eph.1.20-22. 1Pet.3.22. Rev 17.14. c Lu.14.18. Heb.1.9. d Matt.12.15.

are, therefore, totally unlike the Roman centurion. His example should not be plead, therefore, by those who *neglect* the Saviour, for it furnishes no evidence that *they* will be accepted, when they are totally unlike him.

36. *The word.* That is, this is the word, or the doctrine. Few passages in the New Testament have perplexed critics more than this. It has been difficult to ascertain to what the term "word" in the accusative case (τὸν λόγον) here refers. Our translation would lead us to suppose that it is synonymous with what is said in the following verse. But it should be remarked that the term used there, and translated "word," as if it were a repetition of what is said here, is a different term. It is not λόγον, but ῥῆμα—a word, a thing; not a doctrine. I understand the first term "word" to be an introduction of the doctrine which Peter set forth, and to be governed by a preposition understood. The whole passage may be thus expressed: Peter had been asked to *teach* Cornelius and his assembled friends. It was expected, of course, that he would instruct him in regard to the true doctrines of religion—the doctrine which had been communicated to the Jews. He commences, therefore, with a statement respecting the true doctrine of the Messiah, or the way of salvation which was now made known to the Jews. 'In regard to the *word*, or the doctrine which God sent to the children of Israel, proclaiming peace through Jesus Christ (who is Lord of all) you know already that which was done, or the transactions which occurred throughout all Judea, from Galilee, where he commenced after John had preached, that this was by Jesus Christ since God had anointed him,' &c. Peter here assumes that Cornelius had *some* knowledge of the principal events of the life of the Saviour, though it was obscure and imperfect; and his discourse professes only to state this more *fully and clearly*. He commences his discourse with stating the true doctrine on the subject: and explaining more perfectly that of which Cornelius had been only imperfectly informed ¶ *Unto the children of Israel.* To the *Jews* The Messiah was promised to them, and spent his life among them. ¶ *Preaching.* That is, proclaiming, or announcing. God did this by Jesus Christ. ¶ *Peace.* This word sometimes refers to the *peace* or union which was made between Jews and Gentiles, by breaking down the wall of division between them. But it is here used in a wider sense, to denote peace or reconciliation with God. He announced the way by which man might be reconciled to God, and might find peace. ¶ *He is Lord of all.* That is, Jesus Christ. He is Sovereign, or Ruler of both Jews and Gentiles; he is their proprietor; and hence Peter saw the propriety of preaching the gospel to the Gentiles as well as Jews. See John xvii. 2. Matt. xxviii. 18. Eph. i. 20—22. This does not necessarily imply divinity; but only that the Lord Jesus, as Mediator, had been constituted or appointed Lord over all nations. It is true, however, that this is a power which we cannot conceive to have been delegated to one that was not divine. Comp. Rom. ix. 5.

37. *That word.* Greek, ῥῆμα—a different word from that in the previous verse. It may be translated *thing* as well as *word*. ¶ *Which was published.* Greek, Which was *done*. 'You know, though it may be imperfectly, what was *done* or accomplished in Judea,' &c. ¶ *Throughout all Judea.* The miracles of Christ were not confined to any place, but were wrought in every part of the land. For an account of the divisions of Palestine, see Notes, Matt. ii. 22. ¶ *And began*, &c Greek, Having been begun in Galilee. Galilee was not far from Cesarea There was, therefore, the more probability that Cornelius had heard of what had occurred there. Indeed, the Gospels themselves furnish the highest evidence that the fame of the miracles of Christ spread into all the surrounding regions.

38. *How God anointed*, &c. That is, set him apart to this work, and was with him, acknowledging him as the Messiah See Note, Matt. i. 1. ¶ *With the Holy*

good, and healing all that were oppressed [a] of the devil: for [b] God
was with him.
39 And we [c] are witnesses of all
things which he did, both in the
land of the Jews and in Jerusalem;
whom they slew and hanged on a
tree.
40 Him God raised up [d] the third
day, and shewed him openly;
41 Not [e] to all the people, but
unto witnesses chosen before [f] of
God, *even* to us, who did eat and
drink with him after he rose from
the dead.
42 And he commanded us [g] to
preach unto the people, and to testify that [h] it is he which was ordained of God *to be* the Judge of quick
and dead.
43 To him [i] give all the prophets
witness, that through his name
whosoever [j] believeth in him shall
receive remission of sins.

a 1 Jno.3.8. b Jno.3.2. c Lu.24.48. c.3.32. d Matt.28.1,2. e Jno.14.22. Jno.c.20 & 21. f Jno. 15.16

g Matt.28.19,20. h Jno.5.22,27. c.17.31. 2Cor.5.10 1Pet.4.5. i Lu.24.27,44. Jno.5.39. j Jno.3.14 17. Rom.10 11.

Ghost. See Note, Luke iv. 19. The act of anointing the kings and priests seems to have been emblematic of the influences of the Holy Ghost. Here it means that God communicated to him the influences of the Holy Spirit, thus setting him apart for the work of the Messiah. See Matt. iii. 16, 17. John iii. 34, "God giveth not the Spirit by measure unto him." ¶ *And with power.* The power of healing the sick, raising the dead, &c. ¶ *Who went about doing good.* Whose main business it was to travel from place to place to do good. He did not go for applause, or wealth, or comfort, or ease, but to diffuse happiness as far as possible. This is the simple but sublime record of his life. This, in few, but most affecting words, tells us all about the Saviour. It gives us a distinct portrait of his character, as he is distinguished from conquerors and kings, and false prophets and the mass of men. ¶ *And healing,* &c. Restoring to health. ¶ *All that were oppressed of the devil.* All that were possessed by him. See Note, Matt. iv. 23, 24. ¶ *God was with him.* God appointed him, and furnished by his miracles the highest evidence that *he* had sent him. His miracles were such that they could be wrought only by God.

39. *And we are witnesses.* We who are apostles. See Note, Luke xxiv. 48. ¶ *In the land of the Jews.* In the country of Judea. ¶ *Whom they slew,* &c. Our translation would seem to imply that there were two separate acts—first slaying him, and *then* suspending him. But this is neither according to truth nor to the Greek text. The original is simply, whom they put to death, *suspending him on a tree.*' ¶ *On a tree.* On a cross. See Note, ch. v. 30.

40 *Shewed him openly.* Manifestly; so that there could be no deception, no doubt of his resurrection.

41. *Not to all the people.* Not to the nation at large; for this was not necessary in order to establish the truth of his resurrection. He however showed himself to *many* persons. See the Harmony of the accounts of the resurrection of Jesus at the close of the Notes on Matthew. ¶ *Chosen of God.* Appointed *by* God, or set apart by his authority through Jesus Christ. ¶ *Who did eat and drink,* &c. And by doing this he furnished the clearest possible proof that he was truly risen; and that they were not deceived by an illusion of the imagination, or by a phantasm. Comp. John xxi. 12, 13.

42. *And he commanded us,* &c. Matt. xxviii. 19, 20. Mark xvi. 15, 16. ¶ *And to testify.* To bear witness. ¶ *That it is he,* &c. See Notes, John v. 22—27. Comp the references in the margin. ¶ *Of quick.* The *living.* The doctrine of the New Testament is, that those which are alive when the Lord Jesus shall return to judge the world, shall be caught up in vast numbers like clouds, to meet him in the air, without seeing death. 1 Thess. iv. 16, 17. Yet before this, they shall experience such a *change* in their bodies as shall fit them for the judgment and for their eternal residence—a change which shall liken them to those who have died, and have been raised from the dead. What this change will be, speculation may fancy, but the Bible has not revealed. See 1 Cor. xv. 52. "The dead shall be raised, and we shall be changed."

43. *To him give,* &c. See Note, Luke xxiv. 27. 44. ¶ *That through his name,* &c. This was *implied* in what the prophets said. See Rom. x. 11 It was not, indeed, expressly affirmed that they who believed in him should be pardoned; but

44 While Peter yet spake these
words, the Holy Ghost [a] fell on all
them which heard the word.
45 And they [b] of the circumcision which believed were astonished, as many as came with Peter,
because that on the Gentiles also
was poured out the gift of the Holy
Ghost:
46 For they heard them speak [c]
with tongues, and magnify God.
Then answered Peter,
47 Can [d] any man forbid water,
that these should not be baptized
which have received the Holy Ghost
as well as we?
48 And he commanded them to
be baptized in the name of the Lord.
Then prayed they him to tarry certain days.

CHAPTER XI.

AND the apostles and brethren
that were in Judea heard that
the Gentiles had also received the
word of God.
2 And when Peter was come up
to Jerusalem, they [e] that were of
the circumcision contended with
him,
3 Saying, Thou wentest in to
men uncircumcised, and didst eat
with them.

a c.4.31. b ver.23. c c.2.4. d c.8.12. e c.10.23,28. Gal.2.12. c.10.9,&c.

---

this was *implied* in what they said. They promised a Messiah; and their religion consisted mainly in believing in a Messiah to come. See the reasoning of the apostle Paul in Rom. iv.

44. *The Holy Ghost fell*, &c. Endowing them with the power of speaking with other tongues. ver. 46. Of this the apostle Peter makes much in his argument in ch. xi. 17. By this, God showed that the *Gentiles* were to be admitted to the same privileges with the Jews, and to the blessings of salvation in the same manner. Comp. ch. ii. 1—4. ¶ *Which heard the word.* The word of God; the message of the gospel.

45. *And they of the circumcision.* Who had been Jews. ¶ Were *astonished.* Were amazed that *Gentiles* should be admitted to the same favour as themselves.

46. *Speak with tongues.* In other languages than their native language. ch. ii. 4. ¶ *And magnify God.* And praise God.

47. *Can any man forbid water*, &c. They have shown that they are favoured in the same way as the Jewish converts. God has manifested himself to them, as he did to the Jews on the day of Pentecost. Is it not clear, therefore, that they are entitled to the privilege of Christian baptism? The expression here used is one that would *naturally* refer to water's being *brought*; that is, to a small quantity; and would seem to imply that they were baptized, not by immersion, but by pouring or sprinkling.

48. *And he commanded them*, &c. Why Peter did not himself baptize them is unknown. But it *might* be, perhaps, because he chose to make use of the ministry of the brethren who were with him, to prevent the possibility of future cavil. If *they* did it themselves, they could not so easily be led by the Jews to find fault with it. It may be added, also, that it seems not to have been the practice of the apostles themselves to baptize very extensively. This was left to be performed by others. See 1 Cor. i. 14—17, "Christ sent me not to baptize, but to preach the gospel."

CHAPTER XI.

1. *And the apostles and brethren.* The Christians who were in Judea. ¶ *Heard*, &c. So extraordinary an occurrence as that at Cesarea, the descent of the Holy Spirit on the Gentiles, and their reception into the church, would excite attention, and be likely to produce much sensibility in regard to the conduct of Peter and those with him. It was so contrary to all the ideas of the Jews, that it is not to be wondered at that it led to contention.

2. *They that were of the circumcision* The Christians who had been converted from among the Jews. ¶ *Contended with him.* Disputed; or reproved him; charged him with being in fault. This is one of the circumstances which show conclusively that the apostles and early Christians did not regard Peter as having any particular *supremacy* over the church, or as being in any peculiar sense the *vicar* of Christ upon earth. If Peter had been regarded as having the authority which the Roman Catholics claim for him, they would have submitted at once to what he had thought proper to do. But the primitive Christians had no such idea of his authority. This claim for Peter is not only opposed to this place, but to every part of the New Testament.

3. *And didst eat with them.* See Note, ch. x. 13, 14.

4 But Peter rehearsed *the matter*
from the beginning, and expounded
it by order unto them, saying,
5 I was in the city of Joppa,
praying: and in a trance I saw a
vision, A certain vessel descend, as
it had been a great sheet let down
from heaven by four corners; and
it came even to me:
6 Upon the which when I had
fastened mine eyes, I considered,
and saw four-footed beasts of the
earth, and wild beasts, and creeping
things, and fowls of the air.
7 And I heard a voice saying
unto me, Arise, Peter; slay, and
eat.
8 But I said, Not so, Lord: for
nothing common or unclean hath
at any time entered into my mouth.
9 But the voice answered me
again from heaven, What God hath
cleansed, *that* call not thou common.
10 And this was done three
times: and all were drawn up
again into heaven.
11 And, behold, immediately
there were three men already come
unto the house where I was, sent
from Cesarea unto me.
12 And the Spirit [a] bade me go
with them, nothing doubting.
Moreover, these six brethren accompanied
me; and we entered
into the man's house:
13 And he shewed us how he had
seen an angel in his house, which
stood and said unto him, Send men
to Joppa, and call for Simon, whose
surname is Peter;
14 Who shall tell thee words [b]
whereby thou and all thy house
shall be saved.
15 And as I began to speak, the
Holy Ghost fell on them, as [c] on
us at the beginning.
16 Then remembered I the word
of the Lord, how that he said, John
[d] indeed baptized with water; but
[e] ye shall be baptized with the Holy
Ghost.
17 Forasmuch then as God gave
[f] them the like gift as *he did* unto

a Jno.16.13. b Ps.19.7-11. Jno.6.63,68 c c.2.4. d Matt.3.11. Jno.1.26,33. c.1.5. e Isa.44.3. Jo. 2.28. f c.15.8,9.

4. *But Peter rehearsed.* Greek, Peter beginning, explained it to them in order. That is, he began with the vision which he saw, and gave a narrative of the various events in order, as they actually occurred. A simple and unvarnished statement of *facts* is usually the best way of disarming prejudice and silencing opposition. In revivals of true religion, the best way of silencing opposition, and especially among Christians, is to make a plain statement of things as they actually occurred. Opposition most commonly arises from prejudice, or from false and exaggerated statements; and those can be best removed, not by angry contention, but by an unvarnished relation of the facts. In most cases prejudice will thus be disarmed, and opposition will die away, as was the case in regard to the admission of the Gentiles to the church. ¶ *And expounded it.* Explained it; stated it as it actually occurred. ¶ *In order.* One event after another, as they happened. He thus showed that *his own mind* had been as much biassed as theirs, and stated in what manner his prejudices had been removed. It often happens that those who become most zealous and devoted in and new plans for the advancement of religion, were as much opposed to them a first as others. They are led from one circumstance to another, until their prejudices die away, and the providence and Spirit of God indicate clearly their duty.

5—14. See ch. x. 9—33.

14. *And all thy house.* Thy family. This is a circumstance which is omitted in the account in ch. x. It is said, however, in ch. x. 2, that Cornelius feared God *with all his house.* And it is evident from ch. x. 48, that the family also received the ordinance of baptism, and was received into the church.

15. *And as I began to speak.* Or, while I was speaking. ¶ *The Holy Ghost, &c.* x. 44.

16. *The word of the Lord* See Note, ch. i. 5.

17. *What was I.* What power or right had I to oppose the manifest will of God that the Gentiles should be received into the Christian church. ¶ *Withstand God.* Oppose or resist God? He had indicated his will; he had showed his intention to save the Gentiles; and the prejudices of

us who believed on the Lord Jesus
Christ, what [a] was I, that I could
withstand God?
18 When they heard these things,
they held their peace, and glorified
God, saying, Then hath God also
to the Gentiles [b] granted repentance
unto life.
19 Now they [c] which were scattered abroad upon the persecution
that arose about Stephen, travelled
as far as Phenice, and Cyprus, and

a Rom.9.21-26. b Rom.10.12,13; 15.9,16. c c.8.1.

Peter were all overcome. One of the best means of destroying prejudice and false opinions, is a powerful revival of religion. More erroneous doctrines and unholy feelings are overcome in such scenes, than in all the angry controversies, and bigoted and fierce contentions that have ever taken place. If men wish to root error out of the church, they should strive by all means to promote every where, revivals of pure and undefiled religion. The Holy Spirit more easily and effectually silences false doctrine, and destroys heresy, than all the denunciations of fierce theologians; all the alarms of professed zeal for truth; and all the anathemas which professed orthodoxy and love for the purity of the church ever uttered from the icebergs on which such champions usually seek their repose and their home.

18. *They held their peace.* They were convinced, as Peter had been, by the manifest indications of the will of God. ¶ *Then hath God,* &c. The great truth is in this manner established, that the doors of the church are opened to the entire Gentile world—a great and glorious truth, that was worthy of this remarkable interposition. It at once changed the views of the apostles and of the early Christians; gave them new, large, and liberal conceptions of the gospel; broke down all their long-cherished prejudices; taught them to look upon all men as their brethren; and impressed their hearts with the truth, never after to be eradicated, that the Christian church was founded for the wide world, and opened the same glorious pathway to life wherever man might be found, whether with the narrow prejudice of the Jew, or amidst the degradations of the pagan world. To this truth we owe our hopes; for this, we should thank the God of heaven; and impressed with it, we should seek to invite the entire world to partake with us of the rich provisions of the gospel of the blessed God.

19. *Now they,* &c. This verse introduces a new train of historical remark; and from this point the course of the history of the Acts of the Apostles takes a new direction. Thus far, the history had recorded chiefly the preaching of the gospel to the Jews only. From this point the history records the efforts made to convert the Gentiles. It begins with the labours put forth in the important city of Antioch (ver. 19, 20); and, as during the work of grace that occurred in that city, the labours of the apostle Paul were especially sought (ver. 25, 26), the sacred writer thenceforward confines the history mainly to his travels and labours. ¶ *Which were scattered abroad.* See ch. viii. 1. ¶ *As far as Phenice.* Phœnice, or Phœnicia, was a province of Syria, which in its largest sense comprehended a narrow strip of country lying on the eastern coast of the Mediterranean, and extending from Antioch to the borders of Egypt. But Phœnice Proper extended only from the cities of Laodicea to Tyre, and included only the territories of Tyre and Sidon. This country was called sometimes simply *Canaan.* See Note, Matt. xv. 22. ¶ *And Cyprus.* An island off the coast of Asia Minor, in the Mediterranean sea. See Note, Acts iv. 36. ¶ *And Antioch.* There were two cities of this name, one situated in Pisidia in Asia Minor (see ch. xiii. 14); the other, referred to here, was situated on the river Orontes, and was long the capital of Syria. It was built by Seleucus Nicanor, and was called Antioch in honour of his father Antiochus. It was founded three hundred and one years before Christ. It is not mentioned in the Old Testament, but is several times mentioned in the Apocrypha, and in the New Testament. It was long the most powerful city of the East, and was inferior only to Seleucia and Alexandria. It was famous for the fact that the right of citizenship was conferred by Seleucus on the Jews as well as the Greeks and Macedonians, so that here they had the privilege of worship in their own way without molestation. It is probable that the Christians would be regarded merely as a sect of Jews, and would be here suffered to celebrate their worship without interruption. On this account it may have been, that the early Christians regarded this city as of such particular importance, because here they could find a refuge from persecution, and be permitted to worship

Antioch, preaching the word to none
but [a] unto the Jews only.
20 And some of them were men
of Cyprus and Cyrene, which,
when they were come to Antioch,
spake unto the Grecians, [b] preaching
the Lord Jesus.
21 And the [c] hand of the Lord
was with them: and a great number believed, and turned [d] unto the
Lord.
22 Then tidings of these things
came unto the ears of the church
which was in Jerusalem: and they
sent forth Barnabas, [e] that he
should go as far as Antioch.
23 Who, when he came, and
had seen the grace of God, was

a Matt.10.6. b c.6.1;9.29. c Lu.1.66. d c.15.19. 1Th.1.9. e c.9.27.

God without molestation. This city was honoured as a Roman colony, a metropolis, and an asylum. It was large; was almost square; had many gates; was adorned with fine fountains; and was a city of great opulence. It was however subject to earthquakes, and was several times nearly destroyed. In the year 588 it experienced an earthquake in which 60,000 persons were destroyed. It was taken by the Saracens in A. D. 638, and after some changes and revolutions, it was taken during the crusades, after a long and bloody siege, by Godfrey of Bouillon, June 3, A. D. 1098. In 1268 it was taken by the sultan of Egypt, who demolished it, and placed it under the dominion of the Turk. Antioch is now called Antakia, and contains about 10,000 inhabitants. (*Robinson's Calmet.*) ¶ *Preaching the word.* The word of God, the gospel. ¶ *To none but unto the Jews only.* They had the common prejudices of the Jews, that the offers of salvation were to be made only to Jews.

20. *Were men of Cyprus and Cyrene.* Were natives of Cyprus and Cyrene. Cyrene was a province and city of Lybia in Africa. It is at present called Cairoan, and is situated in the kingdom of Barca. In Cyprus the Greek language was spoken; and from the vicinity of Cyrene to Alexandria, it is probable that the Greek language was spoken there also. From this circumstance it might have happened that they were led more particularly to address the *Grecians* who were in Antioch. It is possible, however, that they might have heard of the vision which Peter saw, and felt themselves called on to preach the gospel to the Gentiles. ¶ *Spake unto the Grecians,* πρὸς τοὺς Ἑλληνιστάς. To the Hellenists. This word usually denotes in the New Testament those Jews residing in foreign lands, who spoke the Greek language. See Note, ch. vi. 1. But to them the gospel had been already preached and yet in this place it is evidently the intention of Luke to affirm, that the men of Cyprus and Cyrene preached to those who were *not* Jews, and that thus their conduct was distinguished from those (ver. 19) who preached to the Jews only. It is thus manifest that we are here required to understand the *Gentiles,* as those who were addressed by the men of Cyprus and Cyrene. In many MSS. the word used here is Ἕλληνας, *Greeks,* instead of *Hellenists.* This reading has been adopted by Griesbach, and is found in the Syriac, the Arabic, the Vulgate, and in many of the fathers. The Æthiopic version reads 'to the Gentiles.' There is no doubt that this is the true reading; and that the sacred writer means to say that the gospel was here preached to those who were not Jews, for all were called *Greeks* by them who were not Jews. Rom. i. 16. The connexion would lead us to suppose that they had heard of what had been done by Peter, and that, imitating his example, they preached the gospel now to the Gentiles also.

21. *And the hand of the Lord.* See Note, Luke i. 66. Comp. Ps. lxxx. 17. The meaning is, that God showed them favour, and evinced his power in the conversion of their hearers.

22. *Then tidings, &c.* The church at Jerusalem heard of this. It was natural that so remarkable an occurrence as the conversion of the Gentiles, and the extraordinary success of the gospel in a splendid and mighty city, should be reported at Jerusalem, and excite deep interest there. ¶ *And they sent forth.* To aid the disciples there, and to give them their sanction. They had done a similar thing in the revival which occurred in Samaria. Note, ch. viii. 14. ¶ *Barnabas.* See ch. iv. 36, 37. He was a native of Cyprus, and was probably well acquainted with Antioch. He was, therefore, peculiarly qualified for the work on which they sent him.

23. *Had seen the grace of God.* The *favour,* or *mercy* of God, in converting sinners to himself. ¶ *Was glad.* Approved of what had been done in preach-

glad [a] and exhorted [b] them all, that with purpose [c] of [d] heart they would cleave unto the Lord

24 For he was a good man, and full [e] of the Holy Ghost, and of faith; and [f] much people was added unto the Lord.

25 Then [g] departed Barnabas

a 3Jno.4. b c.13.43;14.22. c Ps.17.2. 2Cor.1.17. d Pr.23 ,26. e c.6.5. f ver.21. g c.9.27,30.

ing the gospel to the Gentiles, and rejoiced that God had poured down his Spirit on them. The effect of a revival is to produce joy in the hearts of all those who love the Saviour. ¶ *And exhorted them all.* Entreated them. They would be exposed to many trials and temptations, and he sought to secure their affections in the cause of religion. ¶ *That with purpose of heart.* With a firm mind; with a fixed, settled resolution; that they would make this their settled plan of life, their main object. A *purpose*, πρόθεσις, is a resolution of the mind, a plan, or intention. Rom. viii. 28. Eph. i. 11; iii. 11. 2 Tim. i. 9; iii. 10. It is a resolution of the mind in regard to future conduct, and the doctrine of Barnabas here was, undoubtedly, that it should be a regular, fixed, determined *plan*, or *design*, in their minds, that they *would* henceforward adhere to God. This plan must be formed by all Christians in the beginning of their Christian life, and without such a plan there can be no evidence of piety. We may also remark that such a plan is one of the *heart*. It is not simply of the *understanding*, but is of the entire mind, including the will and affections. It is the leading principle; the strongest affection; the guiding purpose of the *will* to adhere to God. And unless this is the prevalent, governing desire of the heart, there can be no evidence of conversion. ¶ *That they would cleave.* Greek, That they would *remain*, i. e. that they would *adhere* constantly and faithfully attached to the Lord.

24. *For he was a good man.* This is given as a reason why he was so eminently successful. It is not said that he was a man of distinguished talents, or learning; that he was a splendid or an imposing preacher; but simply that he was a pious, humble man of God. He was honest, and devoted to his master's work. We should not undervalue talent, eloquence, or learning in the ministry; but we may remark, that humble piety will often do more in the conversion of souls than the most splendid talents. No endowments can be a substitute for this. The real power of a minister is concentrated in this; and without this his ministry will be barrenness and a curse. There is nothing on this earth so mighty as *goodness*. If a man wished to make the most of his powers, the true secret would be found in employing them for a good object, and suffering them to be wholly under the direction of benevolence. John Howard's purpose *to do good* has made a more permanent impression on the interests of the world than the mad ambition of Alexander or Cæsar. Perhaps the expression, "he was a good man," means that he was a man of a kind, amiable, and sweet disposition. ¶ *Full of the Holy Ghost.* Was entirely under the influence of the Holy Spirit. He was eminently a pious man. This is the *second* qualification here mentioned of a good minister. He was not merely exemplary for mildness and kindness of temper, but he was eminently a man of God. He was filled with the influences of the sacred Spirit, producing zeal, love, peace, joy, &c. See Gal. v. 22, 23. Comp. Acts ii. 4, Note. ¶ *And of faith.* Confidence in the truth and promises of God. This is the *third* qualification mentioned; and this was another cause of his success. He confided in God. He trusted to his promises. He depended, not on his own strength, but on the strength of the arm of God. With these qualifications he engaged in his work, and he was successful. These qualifications should be sought by the ministry of the gospel. Others should not indeed be neglected, but a man's ministry will usually be successful only as he seeks to possess those endowments which distinguished Barnabas—a kind, tender, benevolent heart; devoted piety; the fulness of the Spirit's influence; and strong, unwavering confidence in the promises and power of God. ¶ *And much people.* Many people. ¶ *Was added unto the Lord.* Became Christians.

25. *Then departed*, &c. *Why* Barnabas sought Saul is not known. It is probable, however, that it was owing to the remarkable success which he had in Antioch. There was a great revival of religion; and there was need of additional labour. In such scenes the ministers of the gospel need additional help

to Tarsus, for to seek Saul:
26 And when he had found him,
he brought him unto Antioch. And
it came to pass, that a whole year
they assembled themselves [1] with
the church, and taught [a] much people.
And the disciples were called
Christians first in Antioch.

[1] or, in. [a] Matt.28.19.

as men in harvest-time seek the aid of others. Saul was in this vicinity (ch. ix. 30), and he was eminently fitted to aid in this work. With him Barnabas was well acquainted (Act. ix. 27), and probably there was no other one in that vicinity whom he could obtain. ¶ *To Tarsus.* Note, Acts ix. 11.

26. *That a whole year.* Antioch was a city exceedingly important in its numbers, wealth, and influence. It was for this reason, probably, that they spent so long a time there, instead of travelling in other places. The attention of the apostles was early and chiefly directed to *cities*, as being places of influence and centres of power. Thus Paul passed three years in the city of Ephesus. Acts xx. 31. And thus he continued a year and a half at Corinth. Acts xviii. 11. It may be added that the first churches were founded in cities; and the most remarkable success attended the preaching of the gospel in large towns. ¶ *They assembled themselves,* &c They came together for worship. ¶ *With the church.* Marg. *in* the church. The Greek (ἐν) will bear this construction; but there is no instance in the New Testament where the word *church* refers to the *edifice* in which a congregation worships. It evidently here means that Barnabas and Saul convened *with* the Christian assembly at proper times, through the space of a year, for the purposes of public worship. ¶ *And the disciples were called Christians,* &c. As this became the distinguishing name of the followers of Christ, it was worthy of record. The name was evidently given because they were the followers of *Christ.* But by *whom,* or with what views, it was given, is not certainly known. Whether it was given by their enemies in *derision,* as the names *Puritan, Quaker, Methodist,* &c. have been; or whether the disciples assumed it themselves: or whether it was given by divine intimation, has been a matter of debate. That it was given in derision is not probable. For in the name *Christian* there was nothing dishonourable. To be the professed friends of *the Messiah,* or *the Christ,* was not with Jews a matter of reproach, for they *all* professed to be the friends of the Messiah. The cause of reproach with the disciples was that they regarded *Jesus of Nazareth* as the Messiah; and hence, when they wished to speak of them with contempt, they would speak of them as *Galileans* (Acts ii. 7), or as *Nazarenes* (Acts xxiv. 5), "And a ring-leader of the sect *of the Nazarenes.*" It is possible that the name might have been given to them as a mere *appellation,* without intending to convey by it any reproach. The *Gentiles* would probably use this name to distinguish them; and it might have become thus the common appellation. It is evident from the New Testament, I think, that it was not designed as a term of reproach. It is but twice used besides this place: Acts xxvi. 28, "Agrippa said unto Paul, Almost thou persuadest me to be *a Christian.*" 1 Pet. iv. 16, "Yet if any man suffer as *a Christian,* let him not be ashamed." No certain argument can be drawn in regard to the source of the name from the word which is used here. The word Χρηματίζω used here, means, (1.) To transact any business; to be employed in accomplishing any thing, &c. This is its usual signification in the Greek writers. It means, (2.) To be divinely admonished, to be instructed by a divine communication, &c. Matt. ii. 12. Luke ii. 26. Acts x. 22. Heb. viii. 5; xi. 7; xii. 25. It also means, (3.) To be named, or called, in any way, without a divine communication. Rom. vii. 3, "She shall be *called* an adulteress." It cannot be denied, however, that the most usual signification in the New Testament is that of a *divine monition,* or *communication;* and it is certainly *possible* that the name was given by Barnabas and Saul. I incline to the opinion, however, that it was given to them by the Gentiles who were there, simply as an appellation, without intending it as a name of reproach, and that it was readily assumed by the disciples as a name that would fitly designate them. If it had been assumed by them, or if Barnabas and Saul had conferred the name, the record would probably have been to that effect; not simply that they "*were called*" but that they took this name, or that it was given by the apostles. It is, however, of little consequence whence the name originated. It soon became a name of reproach and has usually been in all ages since, by the wicked, the gay, the licentious, and

27 And in these days came[a] prophets from Jerusalem unto Antioch.

28 And there stood up one of them, named Agabus, [b] and signified by the Spirit that there should

a c.2.17; 13.1. Eph.4.11.

b c.21.10.

the ungodly. It is, however, an honoured name; the *most* honourable appellation that can be conferred on a mortal. It suggests at once to a Christian the name of his great Redeemer; the idea of our intimate relation to him; and the thought that we receive him as our chosen Leader, the source of our blessings, the author of our salvation, the fountain of our joys. It is the *distinguishing* name of all the redeemed. It is not that we belong to this or that denomination; it is not that our names are connected with high and illustrious ancestors; it is not that they are recorded in the books of heralds; it is not that they stand high in courts, and among the gay, and the fashionable, and the rich, that true honour is conferred on men. These are not the things that give *distinction* and *peculiarity* to the followers of the Redeemer. It is that they are *Christians;* that this is their peculiar name; that by this they are known; that this at once suggests their character, their feelings, their doctrines, their hopes, their joys. This binds them all together—a name which rises above every other appellation; which unites in one the inhabitants of distant nations and tribes of men; which connects the extremes of society, and places them in most important respects on a common level; and which is a bond to unite in one family all those who love the Lord Jesus, though dwelling in different climes, speaking different languages, engaged in different pursuits in life, and occupying distant graves at death. He who lives according to the import of this name is the most blessed and eminent of mortals. The name shall be had in remembrance when the names of royalty shall be remembered no more, and when the appellations of nobility shall cease to amuse or to dazzle the world.

27. *And in those days.* While Barnabas and Saul were at Antioch. ¶ *Came prophets.* The word prophet denotes properly one who foretells future events. See Note, Matt. vii. 15. It is sometimes used in the New Testament to denote simply *religious teachers, instructors sent from God,* without particular reference to future events. To teach the people in the doctrines of religion was a part of the prophetic office; and this idea only was sometimes denoted by the use of the word. See Rom. xii. 6. 1 Cor. xii. 10. 28; xiii. 2. 8; xiv. 3. 5. 24. These *prophets* seem to have been endowed in a remarkable manner with the knowledge of future events; with the power of explaining mysteries; and in some cases with the power of speaking foreign languages. In this case, it seems that one of them at least had the power of foretelling future events.

28. *Named Agabus.* This man is mentioned but in one other place in the New Testament. In Acts xxi. 10, 11, he is mentioned as having foretold that Paul would be delivered into the hands of the Gentiles. It is not expressly said that he was a Christian, but the connexion seems to imply that he was. ¶ *And signified.* See John xii. 33. The word usually denotes *to indicate by signs,* or with a degree of obscurity and uncertainty, not to declare in explicit language. But here it seems to denote simply to foretell, to predict. ¶ *By the Spirit.* Under the influence of the Spirit. He was inspired. ¶ *A great dearth.* A great famine. ¶ *Throughout all the world.* The word here used (οἰκουμένην), usually denotes the inhabitable world, the parts of the earth which are cultivated and occupied. It is sometimes limited, however, to denote an *entire land* or *country,* in contradistinction from *the parts* of it: thus, to denote *the whole* of the land of Palestine in distinction from its parts; or to denote that an event would have reference to *all* the land, and not be confined to one or more parts, as Galilee, Samaria, &c. See Note. Luke ii. 1. The meaning of this prophecy evidently is, that the famine would be extensive; that it would not be confined to a single province or region, but that it would extend so far as that it might be called *general.* In fact, though the famine was particularly severe in Judea, yet it extended much farther. This prediction was uttered not long after the conversion of Saul, and probably therefore, about the year A. D. 38, or A. D. 40. Dr Lardner has attempted to show that the prophecy had reference *only* to the land of Judea, though in fact there were famines in other places (*Lardner's Works,* vol. i pp. 253, 254. Ed. Lond. 1829.) ¶ *Which came to pass, &c.* This is one of the few instances in which the sacred writers in the New Testament affirm the fulfilment

be great dearth throughout all the
world: which came to pass in the
days of Claudius Cesar.
29 Then the disciples, every
man according to his ability, determined to send [a] relief unto the
brethren which dwelt in Judea:
30 Which also they did, and [b]
sent it to the elders by the hands
of Barnabas and Saul.

a Rom.15.26. 1Cor.16.1. 2Cor.9.1,2. b c.12.25.

of a prophecy. The history having been written after the event, it was natural to give a passing notice of the fulfilment. ¶ *In the days of Claudius Cæsar.* The Roman emperor. He began his reign A. D. 41, and reigned thirteen years. He was at last poisoned by one of his wives, Agrippina, who wished to raise her son Nero to the throne. During his reign no less than *four* different famines are mentioned by ancient writers, one of which was particularly severe in Judea, and was the one doubtless to which the sacred writer here refers. (1.) The first happened at Rome, and occurred in the first or second year of the reign of Claudius. It arose from the difficulties of importing provisions from abroad. It is mentioned by Dio, whose words are these: "There being a great famine, he (Claudius) not only took care for a present supply, but provided also for the time to come." He then proceeds to state the great expense which Claudius was at in making a good port at the mouth of the Tiber, and a convenient passage from thence up to the city. Dio, lib. lx. p. 671, 672. See also Suetonius, Claud. cap. 20. (2.) A second famine is mentioned as having been particularly severe in Greece. Of this famine Eusebius speaks in his Chronicon, p. 204. "There was a great famine in Greece, in which a modius of wheat (about half a bushel) was sold for six drachms." This famine is said by Eusebius to have occurred in the ninth year of the reign of Claudius. (3.) In the latter part of his reign, A. D. 51, there was another famine at Rome, mentioned by Suetonius (Claud. cap. 18), and by Tacitus (Ann. xii. 43). Of this Tacitus says that it was so severe, that it was deemed to be a divine judgment. (4.) A *fourth* famine is mentioned as having occurred particularly in Judea. This is described by Josephus (Ant. b. xx. ch. 2, § 5). "A famine," says he, "did oppress them at that time (in the time of Claudius); and many people died for the want of what was necessary to procure food withal. Queen Helena sent some of her servants to Alexandria with money to buy a great quantity of corn, and others of them to Cyprus to bring a cargo of dried figs." This famine is described as having continued under the two procurators of Judea, Tiberias Alexander and Cassius Fadus. Fadus was sent into Judea, on the death of Agrippa, about the fourth year of the reign of Claudius, and the famine, therefore, continued probably during the fifth, sixth, and seventh years of the reign of Claudius. See Note in Whiston's Josephus, Ant. b. xx. ch. 2. § 5; also Lardner as quoted above. Of this famine, or of the want consequent on the famine, repeated mention is made in the New Testament.

29. *Then the disciples.* The Christians at Antioch. ¶ *According to his ability* According as they had prospered. It does not imply that they were rich, but that they rendered aid as they could afford it. ¶ *Determined to send relief* This arose not merely from their general sense of their obligation to aid the poor, but they felt themselves particularly bound to aid their Jewish brethren. The obligation to aid the *temporal* wants of those from whom they had received so important spiritual mercies, is repeatedly enforced in the New Testament. Comp. Rom. xv. 25—27. 1 Cor. xvi. 1, 2. 2 Cor ix. 1, 2. Gal. ii. 10.

30 *Sent it to the elders.* Greek, To the presbyters. This is the first mention which we have in the New Testament of *elders*, or *presbyters*, in the Christian church. The word literally denotes *aged men*, but it was a name of office only in the Jewish synagogue. It is clear, however, I think, that the elders of the Jewish synagogue here are not included, for the relief was intended for the "brethren, ver. 29, that is, the Christians who were at Jerusalem, and it is not probable that a charity like this would have been intrusted to the hands of Jewish elders. The connexion here does not enable us to determine any thing about the sense in which the word was used. I think it probable that it does not refer to *officers* in the church but that it means simply that the charity was intrusted to the *aged*, prudent, and experienced men in the church, for distribution among the members. Calvin supposes that the apostles were particularly intended But this is not probable. It

CHAPTER XII.

NOW about that time, Herod the king stretched [1] forth *his* hands to vex certain of the church.

2 And he killed James [a] the brother of John with the sword.

3 And because he saw it pleased [b] the Jews, he proceeded further to

[1] or, *began*.

[a] Matt.4.21;20.23. [b] c.24.27.

is possible that the *deacons*, who were probably aged men, may be here particularly referred to, but I am rather inclined to think that the charity was sent to the aged members of the church without respect to their office, to be distributed according to their discretion.

CHAPTER XII.

1. *Now about that time.* That is, during the time that the famine existed; or the time when Barnabas and Saul went up to Jerusalem. This was probably about the fifth or sixth year of the reign of Claudius, not far from A. D. 47. ¶ *Herod the king.* This was Herod Agrippa. The Syriac so renders it expressly, and the chronology requires us so to understand it. He was a grandson of Herod the Great, and one of the sons of Aristobulus, whom Herod put to death. Josephus, Antiquities, b. xviii. 5. Herod the Great left three sons, between whom his kingdom was divided—Archelaus, Philip, and Antipas. Note, Matt. ii. 19. To Philip was left Ituroa and Trachonitis. See Luke iii. 1. To Antipas, Galilee and Perea; and to Archelaus, Judea, Idumea, and Samaria. Archelaus, being accused of cruelty, was banished by Augustus to Vienna in Gaul, and Judea was reduced to a province, and united with Syria. When Philip died, this region was granted by the emperor Caligula to Herod Agrippa. Herod Antipas was driven as an exile also into Gaul, and then into Spain, and Herod Agrippa received also *his* tetrarchy. In the reign of Claudius also, the dominions of Herod Agrippa were still farther enlarged. When Caligula was slain, he was at Rome, and having ingratiated himself into the favour of Claudius, he conferred on him also Judea and Samaria, so that his dominions were equal in extent to those of his grandfather, Herod the Great. See Josephus, Antiquities, b. xix. ch. 5, § 1. ¶ *Stretched forth his hands.* A figurative expression, denoting that he laid his hands on them, or that he endeavoured violently to oppress the church. ¶ *To vex.* To injure, to do *evil to.* κακῶσαι. ¶ *Certain.* Some of the church. Who they were the writer immediately specifies.

2. *And he killed,* &c. He caused to be put to death with a sword, either by beheading, or piercing him through. The Roman procurators were intrusted with authority over life, though in the time of Pilate the Jews had not this authority. ¶ *James the brother of John.* This was the son of Zebedee. Matt. iv. 21. He is commonly called James the Greater, in contradistinction from James the son of Alpheus, who is called James the Less. Matt. x. 3. In this manner were the predictions of our Saviour respecting him fulfilled. Matt. xx. 23, "Ye shall indeed drink of my cup, and be baptized with the baptism that I am baptized with."

3. *And because he saw that it pleased the Jews.* This was the principle on which he acted. It was not from a sense of right; it was not to do justice, and protect the innocent; it was not to discharge the appropriate duties of a magistrate, and a king; but it was to promote his own popularity. It is probable that Agrippa would have acted in this way in any circumstances. He was ambitious, vain, and fawning; he sought, as his great principle, popularity. And he was willing to sacrifice, like many others, truth and justice to obtain this end. But there was also a particular reason for this in his case. He held his appointment under the Roman emperor. This foreign rule was always unpopular among the Jews. In order, therefore, to secure a peaceful reign, and to prevent insurrection, and tumult, it was necessary for him to court their favour; to indulge their wishes, and to fall in with their prejudices. Alas! how many monarchs and rulers there have been, who were governed by no better principle, and whose sole aim has been to secure popularity, even at the expense of law, and truth, and justice. That this was the character of Herod, is attested by Josephus, Ant. xix. ch. 8, § 3. "This king (Herod Agrippa) was by nature very beneficent, and liberal in his gifts *and very ambitious to please the people* with such large donations; and he made himself very illustrious by the many expensive presents he made them. He took delight in giving, and rejoiced in living *with good reputation.*" ¶ *To take Peter also.* Peter was one of the most consti

take Peter [a] also. Then were the
days [b] of unleavened bread.
4 And when he had apprehended
him, he put *him* in prison, and delivered *him* to four quaternions of
soldiers, to keep him; intending
after Easter to bring him forth to
the people.
5 Peter therefore was kept in
prison; but [1] prayer was made without ceasing of the church unto God
for him.

a Jno.21.18. b Ex.12.14,15.

1 or, *instant and earnest prayer was made.* 2Cor.1 11. Eph.6.18,19. 1Thess.5.17. Jas.5.16.

cuous men in the church. He had made himself particularly obnoxious by his severe and pungent discourses, and by his success in winning men to Christ. It was natural therefore that he should be the next object of attack. ¶ *The days of unleavened bread.* The Passover, or the seven days immediately succeeding the Passover, during which they were required to eat bread without leaven. Ex. xii. 15—18. It was sometime during this period that Herod chose to apprehend Peter. *Why* this season was selected is not known. As it was, however, a season of religious solemnity, and as Herod was desirous of showing his attachment to the *religious* rites of the nation (Jos. Antiq. xix. 7. 3), it is probable that he chose *this* period to show to them more impressively his purpose to oppose all false religions, and to maintain the existing establishments of the nation.

4. *And when he had apprehended him.* When he had *taken* or *arrested* him. ¶ *He put him in prison.* During the solemnities of this religious festival, it would have been deemed improper to have engaged in the trial of a supposed criminal. The minds of the people were expected to be devoted solely to the solemnities of religion; and hence Herod chose to retain him in custody until the Passover had ended. ¶ *To four quaternions of soldiers.* A *quaternion* was a company of *four;* consequently the whole number employed here was sixteen. The Romans divided the night into four watches, so that the guards could be relieved; those who were on guard occupying three hours, and being then relieved. Of the *four* who were on guard, *two* were with Peter in the prison (ver. 6), and two kept watch before the door of the prison. The utmost precaution was thus taken that he should not escape; and Herod thus gave the most ample assurance to the Jews of his intention to secure Peter, and to bring him to trial. ¶ *Intending after Easter.* There never was a more absurd or unhappy translation than this. The original is simply *after the Passover* (μετὰ τὸ πάσχα). The word *Easter* now denotes the festival observed by many Christian churches in honour of the resurrection of the Saviour. But the original has no reference to that; nor is there the slightest evidence that any such festival was observed at the time when this book was written. The translation is not only unhappy, as it does not convey at all the meaning of the original, but because it may contribute to foster an opinion that such a festival was observed in the times of the apostles The word *Easter* is of Saxon origin, and is supposed to be derived from *Eostre,* the goddess of love, or the Venus of the North, in honour of whom a festival was celebrated by our pagan ancestors in the month of April. (*Webster.*) As this festival coincided with the Passover of the Jews, and with the feast observed by Christians in honour of the resurrection of Christ, the name came to be used to denote the latter. In the old Anglo-Saxon service-books the term *Easter* is used frequently to translate the word Passover. In the translation by Wiclif, the word *paske,* i. e. passover, is used. But Tindal and Coverdale used the word *Easter,* and hence it has very improperly crept into our translation. (*Clark.*) ¶ *To bring him forth to the people.* That is, evidently, to put him publicly to death to gratify them The providence of God in regard to Peter is thus remarkable. Instead of his being put suddenly to death, as was James, he was reserved for *future* trial; and thus an abundant opportunity was given for the prayers of the church, and for his consequent release.

5. *But prayer was made.* The church was apprized of his imprisonment and danger; and had no resource but to apply to God by prayer. In scenes of danger there is no other refuge; and the result shows that even in most discouraging circumstances, God can hear prayer Nothing scarcely could appear more hopeless than the idea of rescuing Peter out of the hands of Herod, and out of the prison, and out of the custody of sixteen men, by prayer. But the prayer of faith was prevalent with God. ¶ *Without ceasing.* Intense, steady, ardent prayer. The word here used (ἐκτενὴς) is found in but one other place in the New Testament

6 And when Herod would have
brought him forth, the same night
Peter was sleeping between two
soldiers, bound with two chains;
and the keepers before the door
kept the prison
7 And, behold, the [a] angel of
the Lord came upon *him*, and a
light shined in the prison: and he
smote Peter on the side, and raised
him up, saying, Arise up quickly.
And [b] his chains fell off from *his*
hands.
8 And the angel said unto him,
Gird thyself, and bind on thy sandals: and so he did. And he saith
unto him, Cast thy garment about
thee, and follow me.

[a] Ps.37.32,33. c.5.19. [b] c.16.26.

1 Pet. iv. 8, "Have *fervent* charity among yourselves." The word has rather the idea that their prayer was *earnest* and *fervent*, than that it was constant. ¶ *Of the church.* By the church.

6. *And when Herod would have brought him forth.* When he was about to bring him to be put to death. ¶ *The same night.* That is, the night *preceding.* The intention of Herod was to bring him out as soon as the Passover was over; but during the night which immediately *preceded* the day in which Herod intended to bring him to punishment, Peter was rescued. ¶ *Peter was sleeping.* Here is an instance of remarkable composure, and one of the effects of peace of conscience and of confidence in God. It was doubtless known to Peter what the intention of Herod was. James had just been put to death; and Peter had no reason to expect a better fate. And yet in this state, he slept as quietly as if there had been no danger, and was roused even by an *angel* to contemplate his condition, and to make his escape.—There is nothing that will give quiet rest and gentle sleep so certainly as a conscience void of offence; and in the midst of imminent dangers, he who confides in God may rest securely and calmly. ¶ *Between two soldiers.* Note, ver. 4. Peter was bound to the two. His left hand was chained to the right hand of one of the soldiers, and his right hand to the left hand of the other. This was a common mode of securing prisoners among the Romans. See abundant authorities for this quoted in Lardner's Credibility, part i. ch. x. § 9. Lond. ed. 1829. vol. i. pp. 242, 243, &c. ¶ *And the keeper, &c.* See ver. 4. Two soldiers were stationed at the door. We may see now that every possible precaution was used to ensure the safe custody of Peter. (1.) He was in prison. (2.) He was in the charge of sixteen men, who could relieve each other when weary, and thus every security was given that he could not escape by inattention or weariness on their part. (3.) He was bound fast between two men. And (4.) He was further guarded by two others, whose business it was to watch the door of the prison. It is to be remembered, also, that it was death for a Roman soldier to be found sleeping at his post. And in this way every possible security was given for the safe keeping of Peter. But God can deliver in spite of all the precautions of men; and it is easy for him to overcome the most cunning devices of his enemies.

7. *And behold the angel of the Lord.* See Note, ch. v. 19. ¶ *Came upon him.* Greek, Was present with him; stood near him (ἐπέστη). ¶ *And a light shined in the prison.* Many have supposed that this was lightning. But *light*, and *splendour*, and shining apparel are commonly represented as the accompaniments of the heavenly beings when they visit the earth Luke ii. 9; xxiv. 4. Comp. Mark ix. 3. It is highly probable that this light was discerned only by Peter; and it would be to him an undoubted proof of the divine interposition in his behalf. ¶ *And he smote Peter on the side.* This was doubtless a gentle blow or stroke to arouse him from sleep. ¶ *And his chains, &c.* This could have been only by divine power. No natural means were used, or could have been used without arousing the guard. It is a sublime expression of the *ease* with which God can deliver from danger, and rescue his friends. Comp. ch xvi. 26.

8. *Gird thyself.* When they slept, the outer garment was thrown off, and the *girdle* with which they bound their inner garment, or tunic, was loosed. He was directed now to gird up that inner garment as they usually wore it; that is, to *dress himself*, and prepare to follow him. ¶ *Bind on thy sandals.* Put on thy sandals—prepared to walk. Note, Matt. iii. 11. ¶ *Cast thy garment about thee* The *outer* garment, that was thrown loosely around the shoulders. It was nearly square, and was laid aside when they slept, or worked, or ran. The direction was that he should dress himself in his

9 And he went out, and followed him; and wist not [a] that it was true which was done by the angel; but thought he saw a vision.[b]

10 When they were past the first and the second ward, they came unto the iron gate that leadeth unto the city, which opened to them of his own accord; and they went out, and passed on through one street; and forthwith the angel departed from him.

a Ps.126.1. b c.10.3,17.

11 And when Peter was come to himself, he said, Now I know of a surety that the Lord hath sent [c] his angel, and hath [d] delivered me out of the hand of Herod, and *from* all the expectation of the people of the Jews.

12 And when he had considered *the thing*, he came to the house of Mary the mother of John, whose surname was Mark; where many [e] were gathered together, praying.

c 2Ch.16.9. Ps.34.7. Da.3.28;6.22. Heb.1.14. d Ps 33.18,19;97.10. 2Cor.1.10. 2Pet.2.9. e ver. 5.

usual apparel. See Note, Matt. v. 38—42.

9. *And wist not.* Knew not. ¶ *That it was true.* That it was real. ¶ *Saw a vision.* That is, was a representation made to his mind. similar to that which he had seen before. Comp. ch. x. 11, 12. It was so astonishing, so unexpected, so wonderful, that he could not realize that it was true.

10. *The first and second ward.* The word which is here rendered *ward* (φυλακὴν), properly denotes the act of guarding; but it is most commonly used to denote a prison, or place of confinement. In this place it seems to denote the *guard* itself—the soldiers stationed at intervals in the entrance into the prison. These were passed silently, probably a deep sleep having been sent on them to facilitate the escape of Peter. ¶ *The iron gate.* The outer gate, secured with iron, as the doors of prisons are now. ¶ *That leadeth unto the city.* Or rather *into* (εἰς) the city. Jerusalem was surrounded by three walls. (See Lightfoot on this place.) The prison is supposed to have been situated between two of these walls. And it is probable that the *entrance* to the prison was immediately from the inner wall, so that this gate opened directly into the city. ¶ *Of his own accord.* Itself. It opened spontaneously, without the application of any force, or key, thus showing conclusively that Peter was delivered by miraculous interposition. ¶ *And passed on through one street.* Till Peter was entirely safe from any danger of pursuit, and then the angel left him. God had effected his complete rescue, and now left him to his own efforts as usual.

11. *And when Peter was come to himself.* This expression naturally means when he had overcome his amazement, and astonishment at the unexpected deliverance, so as to be capable of reflection. He had been amazed by the whole transaction. He thought it was a vision; and in the suddenness and rapidity with which it was done, he had no time for cool reflection. The events of divine providence often overwhelm and amaze us; and such are their suddenness, and rapidity, and unexpected character in their development, as to confound us, and prevent calm and collected reflection. ¶ *Of a surety.* Certainly, surely. He considered all the circumstances, he saw that he was actually at liberty, and that it could have been effected only by divine interposition. ¶ *The expectation of the people.* From this it appears that the people earnestly desired his death; and it was to gratify that desire that Herod had imprisoned him.

12. *And when he had considered, &c.* Thinking on the subject; considering what he should do in these circumstances. ¶ *He came to the house of Mary, &c.* Probably this house was near him; and he would naturally seek the dwelling of a Christian friend. ¶ *The mother of John, &c.* Probably this was the John *Mark* who wrote the gospel. But this is not certain. ¶ *Whose surname.* Greek, Who was *called* Mark. It does not mean that he had two names conferred, as with us, *both* of which were used at the same time. But he was called by either, the Greeks probably using the name *Mark*, and the Jews the name *John.* He is frequently mentioned afterwards, as having been the attendant of Paul and Barnabas in their travels. ver. 25; xv. 39. 2 Tim. iv. 11. He was a nephew of Barnabas. Col. iv. 10. ¶ *Where many were gathered together, praying.* This was in the *night*, and it shows the propriety of observing extraordinary seasons of prayer, even in the night. Peter was to have been put to death the next

13 And as Peter knocked at the door of the gate, a damsel came[1] to hearken, named Rhoda.

14 And when she knew Peter's voice, she opened not the gate for gladness, but ran in, and told how Peter stood before the gate.

15 And they said unto her,

[1] or, *to ask who was there.*

day; and they assembled to pray for his release, and did not intermit their prayers. When dangers increase around us and our friends, we should become more fervent in prayer. While life remains we may pray; and even when there is no human hope and we may have no power to heal or deliver, still God may interpose, as he did here, in answer to prayer.

13. *At the door of the gate.* Rather the door of the *vestibule*, or principal entrance into the house. The house was entered through such a *porch* or *vestibule*, and it was the *door* opening into this which is here intended See Note, Matt. ix. 2. ¶ *A damsel.* A girl. ¶ *Came to hearken.* To hear who was there. ¶ *Named Rhoda.* This is a Greek name signifying *a rose.* It was not unusual for the Hebrews to give the names of flowers, &c. to their daughters. Thus *Susanna*, a lily; *Hadessa*, a myrtle; *Tamar*, a palm-tree, &c. (*Grotius.*)

14. *She opened not the gate.* At this time of night, and in these circumstances, the door would be fastened. Christians were doubtless alarmed by the death of James, and the imprisonment of Peter, and they would take all possible precautions for their own safety. ¶ *For gladness.* In her joy she hastened to inform those who were assembled of the safety of Peter.

15. *Thou art mad.* Thou art insane. They seemed to have regarded his rescue as so difficult and so hopeless, that they deemed it proof of derangement that she now affirmed it. And yet this was the very thing for which they had been so earnestly praying. When it was now announced to them that the object of their prayers was granted, they deemed the messenger that announced it insane. Christians are often surprised even when their prayers are answered. They are overwhelmed and amazed at the success of their own petitions, and are slow to believe that the very thing for which they have sought could be granted. It shows perhaps with how *little faith*, after all, they pray; and how slow they are to believe that God can hear and answer prayer. In a revival of religion, in answer to prayer, Christians are often overwhelmed, and astonished when even their own petitions are granted, and when God manifests his own power in his own way and time Prayer should be persevered in, and we should place ourselves in a waiting posture to catch the first indications that God has heard us with joy. ¶ *But she constantly affirmed it.* She insisted on it. How much better it would have been to have hastened at once to the gate, than thus to have engaged in a controversy on the subject. Peter was suffered to remain knocking, while they debated the matter. Christians are often engaged in some unprofitable controversy, when they should hasten to catch the first tokens of divine favour, and open their arms to welcome the proofs that God has heard their prayers. ¶ *Then said they.* Still resolved not to be convinced. ¶ *It is his angel.* Any way of accounting for it rather than to admit the simple fact, or to ascertain the simple truth. All this was produced by the *little hope* which they had of his release, and their earnest desire that it should be so. It was just such a state of mind as is indicated when we say 'the news is too good to be believed.' The expression *it is his angel* may mean, that they supposed the *tutelary guardian*, or angel appointed to attend Peter, had come to announce something respecting him, and that he had assumed the voice and form of Peter, in order to render them certain that he came from him. This notion arose from the common belief of the Jews, that each individual had assigned to him, at birth, a celestial spirit, whose office it was to guard and defend him through life. Note, Matt. xviii. 10. That the Jews entertained this opinion is clear from their writings. (See *Kuinoel.*) Lightfoot thinks that they who were assembled supposed that this angel had assumed the voice and manner of Peter, in order to intimate to them that he was about to die, and to excite them to earnest prayer that he might die with constancy and firmness. Whatever their opinions were, however, it *proves* nothing on these points. There is no evidence that they were inspired in these opinions, nor are their notions countenanced by the Scriptures They were the mere common traditions of the Jews, and prove nothing in regard

Thou art mad. But she constantly
affirmed that it was even so. Then
said they, It is his [a] angel.
16 But Peter continued knocking: and when they had opened
the door, and saw him, they were
astonished.
17 But he beckoning [b] unto them
with the hand, to hold their peace,
declared [c] unto them how the Lord
had brought him out of the prison.
And he said, Go, shew these things
unto James, and to the brethren
And he departed, and went into another place.
18 Now as soon as it was day,
there was no small stir among the
soldiers, what was become of Peter.
19 And when Herod had sought
for him, and found him not, he examined the keepers, and command-

a Matt.18.10. b c.13.16. c Ps.66.16

to the truth of the opinion one way or the other.

16. *Were astonished.* They were now convinced that it was Peter, and they were amazed that he had been rescued. As yet they were of course ignorant of the manner in which it was done.

17. *But he beckoning,* &c. To prevent the noise, and tumult, and transport which was likely to be produced. His wish was, not that there should be clamorous joy, but that they should listen in silence to what God had done. It was sufficient to awe the soul, and produce deep, grateful feeling. A noise might excite the neighbouring Jews, and produce danger. But religion is calm and peaceful; and its great scenes and surprising deliverances are rather fitted to awe the soul, to produce calm, sober, and grateful contemplation, than the noise of rejoicing, and the shoutings of exultation. The consciousness of the presence of God, and of his mighty power, does not produce rapturous disorder and tumult, but holy, solemn, calm, grateful emotion. ¶ *Go, shew these things,* &c. Acquaint them that their prayer is heard, and that they may rejoice also at the mercy of God. ¶ *Unto James.* James the son of Alpheus, commonly called the Less. Note, ver. 2. Acts i. 13. Matt. x. 2. ¶ *And to the brethren.* Particularly to the other apostles. ¶ *And went into another place.* Probably a place of greater safety. Where he went is not known. The papists pretend that he went to Rome. But of this there is no evidence. He is mentioned as in Jerusalem again in ch. xv. The meaning is evidently that he went into some place of retirement till the danger was passed.

18. *No small stir.* Amazement that he had escaped, and apprehension of the consequences. The punishment which they had reason to expect, for having suffered his escape, was death.

19. *He examined the keepers.* The soldiers who were intrusted with his custody. Probably only those who had the special care of him at that watch of the night. The word *examine* here means to inquire diligently, to make investigation. He subjected them to a rigid scrutiny to ascertain the manner of his escape; for it is evident that Herod did not mean to admit the possibility of a miraculous interposition. ¶ *Should be put to death.* For having failed to keep Peter. This punishment they had a right to expect for having suffered his escape. ¶ *And he went down,* &c. How soon after the escape of Peter he went down to Cæsarea, or how long he abode there, is not known. Cæsarea was rising into magnificence, and the Roman governors made it often their abode. Note, Acts viii. 40. Comp. Acts xxv. 1. 4. This journey of Herod is related by Josephus, Antiq. b. xix. ch. viii § 2. He says that it was after he had reigned over all Judea three years. ¶ *And there abode.* That is, till his death, which occurred shortly after. We do not learn that he made any further inquiry after Peter, or that he attempted any further persecutions of the Christians. The guard was undoubtedly put to death; and thus Herod used all his power to create the impression that Peter had escaped by their negligence; and this would undoubtedly be believed by the Jews. See Matt. xxviii. 15. He might *himself* perhaps be convinced, however, that the escape was by miracle, and be afraid to attempt any further persecutions; or the affairs of his government might have called off his attention to other things; and thus, as in the case of the "persecution that arose about Stephen," the political changes and dangers might divert the attention from putting Christians to death. Note, ch. ix. 31. Thus by the providence of God *this* persecution, that had been commenced, not by popular tumult but by royal authority

ed that *they* should be put to death.
And he went down from Judea to
Cesarea, and *there* abode.
20 And Herod [1] was highly displeased with them of Tyre and Sidon: but they came with one accord to him, and, having made
Blastus [2] the king's chamberlain
their friend, desired peace; because
their [a] country was nourished by
the king's *country*.
21 And upon a set day, Herod,
arrayed in royal apparel, sat upon
his throne, and made an oration unto
them.
22 And the people gave a shout,
saying, *It is* [b] the voice of a god, and
not of a man.

1 or, *bare an hostile mind, intending war.*
2 *That was over the king's bed-chamber.*

a Ezek.27.17. b Jude 16.

and power, and that was aimed at the very pillars of the church, ceased. The prayers of the church prevailed; and the monarch was overcome, disappointed, humbled, and by divine judgment soon put to death.

20 *And Herod was highly displeased*, &c. Greek, *Bare an hostile mind, intending war.* See the margin. The Greek word (θυμομαχῶν) does not occur elsewhere in the New Testament. It means to meditate war; to purpose war in the mind; or here probably, to be *enraged* or *angry* at them. What was the cause of this hostility to the people of Tyre and Sidon is not mentioned, and conjecture is useless. It is not at all inconsistent, however, with the well known character of Herod. It was probably from some cause relating to commerce. Tyre and Sidon were under the Roman power, and had some shadow of liberty (*Grotius*); and it is probable that they might have embarrassed Herod in some of his regulations respecting commerce. ¶ *Tyre and Sidon.* Note, Matt. xi. 21. They were *north* of Cæsarea. ¶ *They came with one accord.* Fearing the effects of his anger, they united in sending an embassage to him to make peace. ¶ *Blastus the king's chamberlain.* See Rom. xvi. 23. The word *chamberlain* denotes an officer who is charged with the direction and management of a chamber, or chambers, particularly a bed-chamber. It denotes here a man who had charge of the bed-chamber of Herod. ¶ *Because their country was nourished*, &c. Was supplied by the territories of Herod. The country of Tyre and Sidon included a narrow strip of land on the coast of the Mediterranean. Of course they were dependent for provisions, and for articles of commerce, on the interior country; but this belonged to the kingdom of Herod; and as they were entirely dependent on his country, as he had power to dry up the sources of their support and commerce, they were the more urgent to secure his favour.

21. *And upon a set day.* An *appointed, public* day. This was the second day of the sports and games which Herod celebrated in Cæsarea in honour of Claudius Cæsar. Josephus has given an account of this occurrence, which coincides remarkably with the narrative here. The account is contained in his Antiquities of the Jews, b. xix. ch. viii. § 2, and is as follows: "Now when Agrippa had reigned three years over all Judea, he came to the city Cæsarea, which was formerly called Strato's Tower; and there he exhibited shows in honour of Cæsar, upon his being informed that there was a certain festival celebrated to make vows for his safety. At which festival a great multitude was gotten together of the principal persons, and such as were of dignity throughout his province. On the second day of which shows, he put on a garment made wholly of silver," &c. ¶ *Arrayed in royal apparel.* In the apparel of a king. Josephus thus describes the dress which Herod wore on that occasion. "He put on a garment made wholly of silver, and of wonderful contexture, and early in the morning came into the theatre [place of the shows and games], at which time the silver of his garment, being illuminated by the first reflection of the sun's rays upon it, shone after a surprising manner, and was so resplendent as to spread a horror over those that looked intently on him." ¶ *Sat upon his throne.* This does not denote a *throne* in the usual sense of that word, but a high seat in the theatre, where he sat, and from whence he could have a full view of the games and sports. From this place he made his speech. ¶ *Made an oration.* Addressed the people. What was the subject of this speech is not intimated by Luke or Josephus.

22. *And the people gave a shout.* A loud applause. ¶ It is *the voice of a god*, &c. It is not probable that the *Jews* joined in this acclamation, but that it was made by the idolatrous Gentiles. Josephus gives

23 And immediately the angel of
the Lord smote him, because he gave
not God the glory: and he was eaten
of worms, and gave up the ghost.
24 But the word of God grew[a]
and multiplied.

a Col.1.6.

a similar account of their feelings and conduct. He says, "And presently his flatterers cried out, one from one place, and another from another (though not for his good), that he was a god; and they added, Be thou merciful unto us, for although we have hitherto reverenced thee only as a king, yet shall we henceforth own thee as a superior to mortal nature.'" It is true that Josephus says that this was done when they saw his splendid apparel, and that he gives no account of his addressing the people; while Luke describes it as the effect of his speech. But the discrepancy is of no consequence. Luke is as credible an historian as Josephus; and his account is more consistent than that of the Jewish historian. It is far more probable that this applause and adoration would be excited by a speech, than simply by beholding his apparel.

23. *And immediately the angel of the Lord.* Diseases and death are in the Scriptures often attributed to an angel. See 2 Sam. xxiv. 16. 1 Chron. xxi. 12. 15. 20. 27. 2 Chron. xxxii. 21. It is not intended that there was a *miracle* in this case, but it certainly *is* intended by the sacred writer, that his death was a divine judgment on him for his receiving homage as a god. Josephus says of him that he "did neither rebuke them [the people], nor reject their impious flattery. A severe pain arose in his belly, and began in a most violent manner. And when he was quite worn out by the pain in his belly for five days, he departed this life, in the fifty-fourth year of his age, and the seventh of his reign." Josephus does not mention that it was done by *an angel*, but says that when he looked up, he saw an owl sitting on a rope over his head, and judging it to be an evil omen, he immediately became melancholy, and was seized with the pain. ¶ *Because he gave not God the glory.* Because he was willing himself to receive the worship due to God. It was the more sinful in him as he was a Jew, and was acquainted with the true God, and with the evils of idolatry. He was proud, and willing to be flattered, and even adored. He had *sought* their applause; he had arrayed himself in this splendid manner to excite their admiration; and when they carried it even so far as to offer *divine homage*, he did not reject the impious flattery, but listened still to their praises. Hence he was judged; and God vindicated his own insulted honour by inflicting severe pains on him, and by his most awful death ¶ *And he was eaten of worms.* The word used here is not elsewhere found in the New Testament. A similar disease is recorded of Antiochus Epiphanes, in the Apocrypha. 2 Mac. ix. 5, "But the Lord Almighty, the God of Israel smote him with an invisible and incurable plague, for a pain in the bowels that was remediless, came upon him, and sore torments of the inner parts (ver. 9), so that worms rose up out of the body of this wicked man," &c. Probably this was the disease known as *morbus pedicularis.* It is loathsome, offensive, and most painful. See the death of Antiochus Epiphanes, described in 2 Mac. ix. With this disease also Herod the Great, grandfather of Herod Agrippa, died. Josephus, Antiquities, b. xvii. ch. 6, § 5. Such a death, so painful, sudden, and loathsome was an appropriate judgment on the pride of Herod. We may here learn, (1.) That sudden and violent deaths are often an act of direct divine judgment on wicked men. (2.) That men, when they seek praise and flattery, expose themselves to the displeasure of God. His glory he will not give to another. (3.) That the most proud, and mighty, and magnificent princes have no security of their lives. God can in a moment—even when they are surrounded by their worshippers and flatterers—touch the seat of life, and turn them to loathsomeness and putrefaction. What a pitiable being is a man of pride receiving from his fellow-men that homage which is due to God alone! See Isa. xiv. (4.) Pride and vanity, in any station of life, are hateful in the sight of God. Nothing is more inappropriate to our situation as lost, dying sinners. and nothing will more certainly meet the wrath of heaven. (5.) We have here a strong confirmation of the truth of the sacred narrative. In all essential particulars, Luke coincides in his account of the death of Herod with Josephus. This is one of the many circumstances which go to show that the sacred Scriptures were written at the time when they professed to be; and that they accord with the truth. See Lardner's Credibility, part i. ch. 1, § 6.

25 And Barnabas and Saul returned from Jerusalem when they had fulfilled *their* [1] ministry, and took with them John, whose surname was Mark.

[1] or, *charge*. c.11.29,30.

CHAPTER XIII.

NOW there were in the church that was at Antioch, certain prophets and teachers; as Barnabas, and Simeon that was called

24. *But the word of God grew*, &c. Great success attended it. The persecutions had now ceased; and notwithstanding all the attempts which had been made to crush it, still the church increased and flourished. The liberation of Peter and the death of Herod would contribute to extend it. It was a new evidence of divine interposition in behalf of the church; it would augment the zeal of Christians; it would humble their enemies; and fill those with fear who had attempted to oppose and crush the church of God.

25. *Returned from Jerusalem.* They had gone to Jerusalem to carry alms, and they now returned to Antioch. ch. xi. 30. ¶ *When they had fulfilled their ministry.* When they had accomplished the purpose for which they had been sent there; that is, to deposite the alms of the church at Antioch, in the hands of the elders of the churches. ch. xi. 30. ¶ *John, whose surname was Mark.* Note, ver. 12. From this period the sacred historian records chiefly the labours of Paul. The labours of the other apostles are, after this, seldom referred to in this book; and the attention is fixed almost entirely on the trials and travels of the great apostle of the Gentiles. His important labours, his unwearied efforts, his eminent success, and the fact that *Luke* was his companion, may be the reasons why *his* labours are made so prominent in the history. Through the previous chapters we have seen the church rise from small beginnings, until it was even now spreading into surrounding regions. We have seen it survive two persecutions, commenced and conducted with all the power and malice of Jewish rulers. We have seen the most zealous of the persecutors converted to the faith which he once destroyed; and the royal persecutor put to death by the divine judgment. And we have thus seen that God was the protector of the church; that no weapon formed against it could prosper; and that, according to the promise of the Redeemer, the gates of hell could not prevail against it. In that God and Saviour, who *then* defended the church, we may still confide, and may be assured that He who was then its friend has it still "engraved on the palms of his hands," and intends that it shall extend until it fills the earth with light and salvation.

CHAPTER XIII.

1. *The church that was at Antioch.* Note, ch. xi. 20. ¶ *Certain prophets.* Note, ch. xi. 27. ¶ *And teachers.* Teachers are several times mentioned in the New Testament as an order of ministers, 1 Cor. xii. 28, 29. Eph. iv. 11. 2 Pet. ii. 1. Their precise rank and duty are not known. It is probable that those here mentioned as prophets were the same persons as the teachers. They might discharge *both* offices, predicting future events, and instructing the people. ¶ *As Barnabas.* Barnabas was a *preacher* (ch. iv. 35, 36; ix. 27; xi. 22. 26); and it is not improbable that the names "prophets and teachers" here simply designate the preachers of the gospel. ¶ *Simeon that was called Niger.* *Niger* is a Latin name meaning black. Why the name was given is not known. Nothing more is known of him than is here mentioned. ¶ *Lucius of Cyrene.* Cyrene was in Africa. Note, Matt. xxvii. 32. He is afterwards mentioned as with the apostle Paul when he wrote the epistle to the Romans. Rom. xvi. 21. ¶ *And Manaen.* He is not elsewhere mentioned in the New Testament. ¶ *Which had been brought up with Herod the tetrarch.* Herod Antipas, not Herod Agrippa. Herod was *tetrarch* of Galilee. Luke iii. 1. The word here translated "which had been brought up," σύντροφος, denotes one who is educated or, nourished at the same time with another. It is not elsewhere used in the New Testament. He might have been connected with the royal family, and being nearly of the same age, was educated by the father of Herod Antipas with him. He was therefore a man of rank and education, and his conversion shows that the gospel was not confined entirely in its influence to the poor. ¶ *And Saul.* Saul was an apostle; and yet he is here mentioned among the "prophets and teachers." Showing that these words denote ministers of the gospel in general, without reference to any particular order or rank.

Niger, and Lucius of Cyrene, and Manaen, [1] which had been brought up with Herod the tetrarch, and Saul.

2 As they ministered to the Lord, and fasted, the Holy Ghost said, Separate [a] me Barnabas and Saul for the work [b] whereunto I have called them.

3 And when they had fasted and prayed, and laid *their* hands on them, they sent *them* away.

1 or, *Herod's foster-brother.*

a Gal.1.15. b 1Tim.2.7.

2. *As they ministered to the Lord.* It is probable that this took place on some day set apart for fasting and prayer. The expression "ministered to the Lord," denotes as they were engaged in prayer to the Lord, or as they were engaged in divine service. The Syriac thus renders the passage. ¶ *The Holy Ghost said.* Evidently by direct revelation. ¶ *Separate me.* Set apart to me, or for my service. It does not mean to *ordain*, but simply to designate, or appoint to this specific work. ¶ *For the work whereunto I have called them.* Not the apostolic office, for Saul was called to that by the express revelation of Jesus Christ (Gal. i. 12), and Barnabas was not an apostle. The "work" to which they were now set apart was that of preaching the gospel in the regions round about Antioch. It was not any *permanent* office in the church, but was a temporary designation to a *missionary enterprise* in extending the gospel especially through Asia Minor and the adjacent regions. Accordingly, when, in the fulfilment of this appointment, they had travelled through Seleucia, Cyprus, Paphos, Pamphylia, Pisidia, &c. they returned to Antioch, having fulfilled the work to which they were separated. See Acts xiv. 26, 27. ¶ *Whereunto I have called them.* This proves that they received their commission to this work directly from God the Holy Spirit. It is possible that Paul and Barnabas had been influenced by the Spirit to engage in this work, but they were to be sent forth by the concurrence and designation of the church.

3. *And when they had fasted.* They were *fasting* when they were commanded to set them apart. Yet this probably refers to an appointed day of prayer, with reference to this very purpose. The first formal *mission* to the Gentiles was an important event in the church; and they engaged in this appointment with deep solemnity, and with humbling themselves before God. ¶ *And prayed.* This enterprise was a new one. The gospel had been preached to the Jews, to Cornelius, and to the Gentiles at Antioch. But there had been no solemn, and public, and concerted plan of sending it to the Gentiles, or of appointing a mission to the heathen. It was a new event, and was full of danger and hardships. The primitive church felt the need of divine direction and aid in the great work. Two missionaries were to be sent forth among strangers, to be exposed to perils by sea and land; and the commencement of the enterprise demanded *prayer.* The church humbled itself, and this primitive missionary society sought, as all others should do, the divine blessing, to attend the labours of those employed in this work. The result showed that the prayer was heard. ¶ *And laid their hands on them.* That is, those who are mentioned in ver. 1. This was not to set them apart to the apostolic office. Saul was chosen by Christ himself, and there is no evidence that any of the apostles were ordained by the imposition of hands. Note, Acts i. 26. Matt. x. 1—5 Luke vi. 12—16. And Barnabas was not an apostle in the original and peculiar sense of the word. Nor is it meant that this was an *ordination* to the *ministry*, to the office of preaching the gospel. For both had been engaged in this before. Saul received his commission directly from the Saviour, and began at once to preach. Acts ix. 20. Gal. i. 11—17. Barnabas had preached at Antioch, and was evidently recognised as a preacher by the apostles. Acts ix. 27; xi. 22, 23. It follows, therefore, that this was not an *ordination* in the doctrinal sense of this term, either Episcopal, or Presbyterian, but was a designation to a particular work—a work of vast importance; strictly a *missionary appointment* by the church, under the authority of the Holy Ghost. The act of laying hands on any person was practised, not only in ordination, but in conferring a favour; and in setting apart *for any purpose.* See Lev iii. 2. 8. 13; iv. 4. 29; xvi. 21. Num. viii. 12. Mark v 23; xvi. 18. Matt. xxi. 46. It means in this case that they appointed *them* to a particular field of labour, and by laying hands on them they implored the blessing of God to attend them. ¶ *They sent them away.* The church by

4 So they, being sent forth by
the Holy Ghost, departed unto Seleucia; and from thence they sailed
to Cyprus.
5 And when they were at Salamis, they preached the word of God
in the synagogues of the Jews: and
they had also John to *their* minister.
6 And when they had gone
through the isle unto Paphos, they
found a certain sorcerer, a false
prophet, a Jew, whose name *was*
Bar-jesus:
7 Which was with the deputy
of the country, Sergius Paulus, a
prudent man; who called for Barnabas and Saul, and desired to hear
the word of God.

---

its teachers sent them forth under the direction of the Holy Ghost. All missionaries are thus sent by the church; and the church should not forget its ambassadors in their great and perilous work.

4. *Being sent forth by the Holy Ghost.* Having been called to this work by the Holy Spirit, and being under his direction. ¶ *Departed unto Seleucia.* This city was situated at the mouth of the river Orontes, where it falls into the Mediterranean. Antioch was also built on this river, some distance from its mouth. ¶ *They sailed to Cyprus.* An island in the Mediterranean, not far from Seleucia. Note, ch. iv. 36.

5. *And when they were at Salamis.* This was the principal city and seaport of Cyprus. It was situated on the southeast part of the island, and was afterwards called Constantia. ¶ *In the synagogues of the Jews.* Jews were living in all the countries adjacent to Judea; and in those countries they had synagogues. The apostles uniformly preached *first* to them. ¶ *And they had also John to their minister.* John Mark. ch. xii. 12. He was their *attendant;* he was with them as a companion, yet not pretending to be equal to them in office. They had been specifically designated to this work. He was with them as their friend and travelling companion; perhaps also employed in making the needful arrangements for their comfort, and for the supply of their wants in their travels.

6. *And when they had gone through the isle.* The length of the island, according to Strabo, was one thousand and four hundred stadia, or nearly one hundred and seventy miles. ¶ *Unto Paphos.* Paphos was a city at the western extremity of the island. It was the residence of the proconsul, and was distinguished for a splendid temple erected to *Venus,* who was worshipped throughout the island. Cyprus was fabled to be the place of the birth of this goddess. It had, besides Paphos and Salamis, several towns of note—Citium, the birth-place of Zeno; Amathus, sacred to Venus, &c. Its present capital is Nicosia. Whether Paul preached at any of these places is not recorded. The island is supposed formerly to have had a million of inhabitants. ¶ *A certain sorcerer.* Greek, Magus, or magician. See Note, ch. viii. 9. ¶ *A false prophet.* Pretending to be endowed with the gift of prophecy; or a man, probably, who pretended to be inspired. ¶ *Bar-jesus.* The word *Bar* is Syriac, and means *son.* Jesus, or Joshua, was not an uncommon name among the Jews. The name was given from his father—son of Jesus, or Joshua; as Bar-jonas, son of Jonas.

7. *Which was with the deputy.* Or with the proconsul. Cyprus was at this time subject to the Roman empire, and was governed by a proconsul appointed by the emperor. The provinces subject to Rome were governed by persons who held their office originally from the *consul,* or chief magistrate of the Roman republic. Men of the rank of senators were usually appointed to these offices. See on this subject Lardner's Credibility, part i. ch. i. § 11, where he has fully vindicated the accuracy of the appellation which is here given to Sergius by Luke. ¶ *Sergius Paulus, a prudent man.* The word here rendered *prudent* means *intelligent, wise, learned.* It also may have the sense of *candid,* and may have been given to this man because he was of large and liberal views, of a philosophic and inquiring turn of mind, and was willing to obtain knowledge from any source. Hence he had entertained the Jews; and hence he was willing also to listen to Barnabas and Saul. It is not often that men in office, and men of rank, are thus willing to listen to the instructions of the professed ministers of God. ¶ *Who called for Barnabas and Saul.* It is probable that they had preached in Paphos, and Sergius was desirous himself of hearing the import of their new doctrine. ¶ *And desired to hear,* &c There is no evidence that he then wished to listen to this as divine truth, or that he was anxious about his own salvation, but rather as a speculative inquiry. It was a

8 But Elymas the sorcerer (for
so is his name by interpretation)
[a] withstood them, seeking to turn
away the deputy from the faith.
9 Then Saul (who also *is called*
Paul), filled with the Holy Ghost
set his eyes on him,
10 And said, O full of all subtilty
and all mischief, *thou* child of the
devil, *thou* enemy of all righteous-

a 2Tim.3.8.

professed characteristic of many ancient philosophers to be willing to receive instruction from any quarter. Comp. Acts xvii 19, 20.

8. *But Elymas the sorcerer, for so is his name by interpretation.* Elymas the magician. Elymas is the interpretation, not of the name Bar-jesus, but of the word rendered *the sorcerer.* It is an Arabic word, and means the same as *Magus.* It seems that he was better known by this foreign name than by his own. ¶ *Withstood them.* Resisted them. He was sensible that if the influence of Saul and Barnabas should be extended over the proconsul, that *he* would be seen to be an impostor, and his power be at an end. His *interest,* therefore, led him to oppose the gospel. His own popularity was at stake; and being governed by this, he opposed the gospel of God. The love of popularity and power, the desire of retaining some *political* influence, is often a strong reason why men oppose the gospel. ¶ *To turn away the deputy from the faith.* To prevent the influence of the truth on his mind; or to prevent his becoming the friend and patron of the Christians.

9. *Then Saul (who is also called Paul).* This is the last time that this apostle is called *Saul.* Henceforward he is designated by the title by which he is usually known, as *Paul.* When, or why, this change occurred in the name, has been a subject on which commentators are not agreed. From the fact that the change in the name is here first intimated, it would seem probable that it was first used in relation to him at this time. *By whom* the name was given him—whether he assumed it himself, or whether it was first given him by Christians or by Romans—is not intimated. The name is of Roman origin. In the Latin language the name *Paulus* signifies *little, dwarfish;* and some have conjectured that it was given by his parents to denote that he was small when born; others, that it was assumed or conferred in subsequent years because he was little in stature. The name is not of the same signification as the name *Saul.* This signifies one that is asked, or desired. After all the conjectures on this subject, it is probable, (1.) That this name was first used here; for before this, even after his conversion, he is uniformly called *Saul.* (2.) That it was given by the Romans, as being a name with which they were more familiar, and one that was more consonant with their language and pronunciation. It was made by the change of a single letter; and probably because the name Paul was common among them, and pronounced perhaps with greater facility. (3.) Paul suffered himself to be called by this name, as he was employed chiefly among the Gentiles. It was common for names to undergo changes quite as great as this, without our being able to specify any particular cause, in passing from one language to another. Thus the Hebrew name Jochanan among the Greeks and Latins was Johannes, with the French it is Jean, with the Dutch Hans, and with us John. (*Doddridge.*) Thus Onias becomes Menelaus; Hillel, Pollio; Jakim, Alcimus; Silas, Silvanus, &c. (*Grotius.*) ¶ *Filled with the Holy Ghost.* Inspired to detect his sin; to denounce divine judgment; and to inflict punishment on him. Note, ch. ii. 4. ¶ *Set his eyes on him.* Looked at him intently.

10. *O full of all subtilty and mischief.* The word *subtilty* denotes deceit and fraud; and implies that he was practising an imposition, and that he knew it. The word rendered *mischief* (ῥᾳδιουργίας) denotes properly *facility of acting,* and then *slight of hand;* sly, cunning arts, by which one imposes on another, and deceives him with a fraudulent intention. It is not elsewhere used in the New Testament. The art of Elymas consisted probably in slight of hand, legerdemain, or trick, aided by skill in the abstruse sciences, by which the ignorant might be easily imposed on. See Note, ch. viii. 9. ¶ *Child of the devil.* Being under his influence; practising his arts; promoting his designs by deceit and imposture, so that *he* may be called your father. Note, John viii. 44. Satan is here represented as the author of deceit, and the father of lies. ¶ *Enemy of all righteousness.* Practising deceit and iniquity, and thus opposed to righteousness and honesty. A man who lives by wickedness will, of course, be the foe of every form of integrity. A man who lives by fraud will be opposed to the truth; a pander to the vices of men will

ness, wilt thou not cease to pervert
the right ways of the Lord?
11 And now, behold, the hand of
the Lord *is* upon thee, and thou
shalt be blind, not seeing the sun
for a season. And immediately
there fell on him a mist and a
darkness; and he went about, seeking some to lead him by the hand.
12 Then the deputy, when he

---

hate the rules of chastity and purity; a manufacturer or vender of ardent spirits will be the enemy of temperance societies. ¶ *Wilt thou not cease to pervert.* In what way he had opposed Paul and Barnabas is not known. Probably it might be by misrepresenting their doctrines; by representing them as apostate Jews; and thus by retarding or hindering the progress of the gospel. The expression "wilt thou *not cease*" implies that he had been engaged sedulously in doing this, probably from the commencement of their work in the city. ¶ *The right ways of the Lord.* The straight paths, or doctrines of the Christian religion, in opposition to the *crooked* and *perverse* arts of deceivers and impostors. Straight paths denote integrity, sincerity, truth. Jer. xxxi. 9. Heb. xii. 13. Comp. Isa. xl. 3, 4; xlii. 16. Luke iii. 5. *Crooked* ways denote the ways of the sinner, the deceiver, the impostor. Deut. xxxii. 5. Ps. cxxv. 5. Prov. ii. 15. Isa. lix. 8. Phil. ii. 15.

11. *The hand of the Lord is upon thee.* God shall punish thee. By this sudden and miraculous punishment, he would be awed and humbled; and the proconsul and others would be convinced that he was an impostor, and that the gospel was true. His *wickedness* deserved such a punishment; and at the same time that due punishment was inflicted, it was designed that the gospel should be extended by this means. In all this there was the highest evidence that Paul was under the inspiration of God. He was full of the Holy Ghost; he detected the secret feelings and desires of the heart of Elymas: and he inflicted on him a punishment that could have proceeded from none but God. That the apostles had the power of inflicting *punishment* in many cases, is apparent from various places in the New Testament. 1 Cor. v. 5. 1 Tim. i. 20. The punishment inflicted on Elymas, also, would be highly emblematic of the *darkness* and *perverseness* of his conduct. ¶ *Not seeing the sun for a season.* For how long a time this blindness was to continue, is nowhere specified. It was however in mercy ordained that the blindness should not be permanent and final. Nothing would be more likely to lead him to reflection and repentance than such a state of blindness. It was such a manifest proof that God was opposed to him; it was such a sudden divine judgment; and it so completely cut him off from all possibility of practising his arts of deception, that it was adapted to bring him to repentance. Accordingly there is a tradition in the early church that he became a Christian. Origen says, that "Paul, by a word striking him blind, by anguish converted him to godliness." (*Clark.*) ¶ *A mist.* The word here used properly denotes a darkness or obscurity of the air; a cloud, &c. But it also denotes an extinction of sight by the drying up or disturbance of the humours of the eye. (*Hippocrates, as quoted by Schleusner.*) ¶ *And darkness.* Blindness; night. What was the precise cause or character of this miracle is not specified. ¶ *And he went about, &c.* This is a striking account of the effect of the miracle. The change was so sudden that he knew not where to go. He sought some one to guide him in the ways in which he had before been familiar.—How soon can God bring down the pride of man, and make him helpless as an infant! How easily can he touch our senses, the organs of our most exquisite pleasures, and wither all our enjoyments! How dependent are we on him for the inestimable blessings of vision! And how easily can he annihilate all the sinner's pleasures, break up all his plans, and humble him in the dust! Sight is his gift; and it is a mercy unspeakably great that he does not whelm us in thick darkness, and destroy for ever all the pleasure that through this organ is conveyed to the soul.

12. *Then the deputy....believed.* Was convinced that Elymas was an impostor, and that the doctrine of Paul was true. There seems no reason to doubt that his faith was that which is connected with eternal life; and if so, it is an evidence that the gospel was not always confined to the poor, and to the obscure ranks of life. ¶ *At the doctrine of the Lord* The word *doctrine* here seems to denote, not the *teaching* or *instruction*, but the wonderful effects which were connected with the doctrine. It was particularly *the miracle* with which he was astonished; but he might have been also deeply impressed and amazed at the purity and sublimity of the truths which were now expanded

saw what was done, believed, being astonished at the doctrine of the Lord.

13 Now when Paul and his company loosed from Paphos, they came to Perga in Pamphylia; and John departing [a] from them, returned to Jerusalem.

14 But when they departed from Perga, they came to Antioch in Pisidia, and went into the synagogue [b] on the Sabbath-day, and sat down.

15 And after the reading [c] of the law and the prophets, the rulers of the synagogue sent unto them, saying, *Ye* men *and* brethren, if ye have any word [d] of exhortation for the people, say on.

16 Then Paul stood up, and beckoning with *his* hand, said, Men of Israel, and ye that fear God, give audience.

17 The God of this people of

a c.15.38. b c.18.4. c ver.27. d Heb.13.22.

to his view. We learn nothing further respecting him in the New Testament.

13. *Paul and his company.* Those with him—Barnabas and John—and perhaps others who had been converted at Paphos; for it was common for many of the converts to Christianity to attend on the apostles in their travels. See, ch. ix. 30. ¶ *Loosed from Paphos.* Departed from Paphos. ¶ *They came to Perga and Pamphylia.* Pamphylia was a province of Asia Minor, lying over-against Cyprus, having Cilicia east, Lycia west, Pisidia north, and the Mediterranean south. Perga was the metropolis of Pamphylia, and was situated, not on the seacoast, but on the river Cestus, at some distance from its mouth. There was on a mountain near it a celebrated temple of Diana. ¶ *And John departing from them,* &c. Why he departed from them is unknown. It might have been from fear of danger; or from alarm in travelling so far into unknown regions. But it is plain from ch. xv. 38, that it was from some cause which was deemed blameworthy, and that his conduct now was such as to make Paul unwilling again to have him as a companion.

14. *They came to Antioch in Pisidia.* Pisidia was a province of Asia Minor, and was situated north of Pamphylia. Antioch was not *in* Pisidia, but within the limits of Phrygia; but it belonged to Pisidia, and was called Antioch of Pisidia to distinguish it from Antioch in Syria. Pliny, Nat. Hist. 5. 27. Strabo, 12. p. 577. (*Kuinoel. Robinson's Calmet.*) ¶ *Went into the synagogue.* Though Paul and Barnabas were on a special mission to the Gentiles, yet they availed themselves of every opportunity to offer the gospel to the Jews first.

15. *And after the reading of the law and the prophets.* See Note, Luke iv. 16. ¶ *The rulers of the synagogue.* These were persons who had the general charge of the synagogue and its service, to keep every thing in order, and to direct the affairs of public worship. They designated the individuals who were to read the law; and called on those whom they pleased to address the people, and had the power also of inflicting punishment, and of excommunicating, &c. (*Schleusner.*) Mark v. 22. 35, 36. 38. Luke viii. 49; xiii. 14. Acts xviii. 8. 17. Seeing that Paul and Barnabas were Jews, though strangers, they sent to them, supposing it probable that they would wish to address their brethren. ¶ *Men and brethren.* An affectionate manner of commencing a discourse, recognising them as their own countrymen, and as originally of the same religion. ¶ *Say on.* Greek, Speak.

16. *Men of Israel.* Jews. The design of this discourse of Paul was to introduce to them the doctrine that Jesus was the Messiah. To do this, he evinced his usual wisdom and address. To have commenced at once on this would have probably excited their prejudice and rage. He, therefore, pursued a train of argument which showed that he was a firm believer in the Scriptures; that he was acquainted with the history and promises of the Old Testament; and that he was not disposed to call in question the doctrines of their fathers. The passage which had been read, perhaps Deut. i. had probably given occasion for him to pursue this train of thought. By going over, in a summary way, their history, and recounting the former dealings of God with them, he showed them that he believed the Scriptures; that a promise had been given of a Messiah; and that he had actually come according to the promise. ¶ *Ye that fear God.* Probably *proselytes of the gate,* who had not yet been circumcised, but who had renounced idolatry, and were accustomed to worship with them in their synagogues. ¶ *Give audience.* Hear.

17. *The God of this people.* Who has manifested himself as the peculiar friend

Israel chose our fathers, [a] and exalted the people when they dwelt [b]
as strangers in the land of Egypt,
and with an high [c] arm brought he
them out of it.

18 And about the time of forty
[d] years suffered [1] he their manners
in the wilderness.

19 And when he had destroyed
seven nations in the land of Chanaan [f] he divided their land to
them by lot.

a De.7.6,7. b Ps.105.23. c Ex.13.14,16. d Ex.16.35. 1 ἐτροποφόρησεν, perhaps for ἐτροφοφόρησεν, *bore, or, fed them, as a nurse beareth, or feedeth her child.* De.1.31, according to the LXX; and so Chrysostom. e De.7.1. f Jos.14,&c.

and protector of this nation. This implied a belief that he had been particularly *their* God; a favourite doctrine of the Jews, and one that would conciliate their favour towards Paul. ¶ *Of Israel.* The Jews. ¶ *Chose our fathers.* Selected the nation to be a chosen and peculiar people to himself. Deut. vii. 6, 7. ¶ *And exalted the people.* Raised them up from a low and depressed state of bondage. He elevated them from a prostrate state of slavery to freedom, and to peculiar privileges as a nation. ¶ *When they dwelt as strangers in Egypt.* ἐν τῇ παροικίᾳ. This properly refers to their dwelling there as foreigners. They were always strangers there in a strange land. It was not their home. They never mingled with the people; never became constituent parts of the government; never united with their usages and laws. They were a strange, separate, depressed people there; not less so than Africans are strangers, and foreigners, and a depressed and degraded people in this land. Gen. xxxvi. 7. Ex. vi. 4; xxii. 21; xxiii. 9. Lev. xix. 34. Deut. x. 19. ¶ *And with an high arm.* This expression denotes great power. The *arm* denotes strength, as that by which we perform any thing. A *high* arm, an arm lifted up, or stretched out, denotes that strength exerted to the utmost. The children of Israel are represented as having been delivered with an "outstretched arm." Deut. xxvi. 8. Ex. vi. 6. "With a strong hand." Ex. vi. 1. Reference is made in these places to the plagues inflicted on Egypt, by which the Israelites were delivered; to their passage through the Red Sea; to their victories over their enemies, &c.

18. *And about the time of forty years.* They were this time going from Egypt to the land of Canaan. Ex. xvi. 35. Num xxxiii. 38. ¶ *Suffered he their manners.* This passage has been very variously rendered. See the margin. Syriac, "He *nourished* them," &c. Arabic, "He blessed them, and nourished them," &c. The word is not elsewhere used in the New Testament. The word properly means to *tolerate*, or *endure the conduct* of any one, implying that that conduct is evil, and tends to provoke to punishment. This is doubtless its meaning here. Probably Paul referred to the passage in Deut. i. 31, "The Lord thy God bare thee." But instead of this word, ἐτροποφόρησεν many MSS. read ἐτροφοφόρησεν, he sustained or nourished. This reading was followed by the Syriac, Arabic, and has been admitted by Griesbach into the text. This is also found in the Septuagint, in Deut. i. 31, which place Paul doubtless referred to. This would well suit the connexion of the passage; and a change of a single letter might easily have occurred in a MS. It adds to the probability that this is the true reading, that it accords with Deut. i. 31. Num. xi. 12. Deut. xxxii. 10. It is furthermore not probable that Paul would have commenced a discourse by reminding them of the obstinacy and wickedness of the nation. Such a course would rather tend to exasperate than to conciliate; but by reminding them of the *mercies* of God to them, and showing them that God had been their protector, he was better fitting them for his main purpose—that of showing them the kindness of the God of their fathers, in sending to them a Saviour. ¶ *In the wilderness.* The desert through which they passed in going from Egypt to Canaan.

19. *And when he had destroyed.* Subdued; cast out; or extirpated *as nations.* It does not mean that all were put to death, for many of them were left in the land; but that they were subdued as nations, they were broken up and overcome. Deut. vii. 1, "And hath *cast out* many nations before them," &c. ¶ *Seven nations.* The Hittites, the Girgashites, the Amorites, the Canaanites, the Perrizites, the Hivites, and the Jebusites Deut. vii. 1. Josh. iii. 10. Neh. ix. 8 ¶ *In the land of Canaan.* The whole land was called by the name of one of the principal nations. This was the promised land; the holy land, &c. ¶ *He*

20 And after that, he gave *unto them* judges, [a] about the space of four hundred and fifty years, until Samuel the prophet.

21 And afterward they [b] desired a king; and God gave unto them Saul [c] the son of Cis, a man of the tribe of Benjamin, by the space of forty years.

a Judg.2.16. *b* 1Sam.8.5. *c* 1Sam.10.1.

divided, &c. See an account of this in Josh. xiv. xv. The *lot* was often used among the Jews to determine important questions. Note, ch. i. 26.

20. *He gave unto them judges.* Men who were raised up in an extraordinary manner to administer the affairs of the nation, to defend it from enemies, &c. See Judg ii. 16. ¶ *About the space of four hundred and fifty years.* This is a most difficult passage, and has exercised all the ingenuity of chronologists. The ancient versions agree with the present Greek text. The *difficulty* has been to reconcile it with what is said in 1 Kings vi. 1, "And it came to pass in the four hundred and eightieth year after the children of Israel were come out of the land of Egypt, in the fourth year of Solomon's reign over Israel....he began to build the house of the Lord." Now if to the forty years that the children of Israel were in the wilderness, there be added the four hundred and fifty said in Acts to have been passed under the administration of the judges, and about seventeen years of the time of Joshua, forty for Samuel and the reign of Saul together, and forty for the reign of David, and three of Solomon before he began to build the temple, the sum will be five hundred and ninety years, a period greater by one hundred and ten years than that mentioned in 1 Kings vi. 1. Various ways have been proposed to meet the difficulty. Doddridge renders it, "After these transactions,[which lasted] four hundred and fifty years, he gave them a series of judges," &c., reckoning from the birth of Isaac, and supposing that Paul meant to refer to this whole time. But to this there are serious objections. (1.) It is a forced and constrained interpretation, and one manifestly made to meet a difficulty. (2.) There is no propriety in commencing this period at the birth of *Isaac.* That was in no manner remarkable, so far as Paul's narrative was concerned; and Paul had not even referred to it. This same solution is offered also by Calovius, Mill, and Lud De Dieu. Luther and Beza think it should be read *three* hundred, instead of *four* hundred. But this is a mere conjecture, without any authority from MSS. Vitringa and some others suppose that the text has been corrupted by some transcriber, who has inserted this without authority. But there is no evidence of this; and the MSS. and ancient versions are uniform None of these explanations are satisfactory. In the solution of the difficulty we may remark, (1.) That nothing is more perplexing than the chronology of ancient facts. The difficulty is found in all writings; in profane as well as sacred. Mistakes are so easily made in transcribing numbers where *letters* are used instead of writing the words at length, that we are not to wonder at such errors. (2.) Paul would naturally use the chronology which was in current, common use among the Jews. It was not his business to *settle* such points; but he would speak of them as they were usually spoken of, and refer to them as others did (3.) There is reason to believe that that which is here mentioned was the *common* chronology of his time It accords remarkably with that which is used by Josephus. Thus, Antiq. b. vii. ch. iii. § 1, Josephus says expressly that Solomon "began to build the temple in the fourth year of his reign, *five hundred and ninety-two years* after the Exodus out of Egypt," &c. This would allow forty years for their being in the wilderness, seventeen for Joshua, forty for Samuel and Saul, forty for the reign of David, and *four hundred and fifty-two* years for the time of the judges and the times of anarchy that intervened. This remarkable coincidence shows that this was the chronology which was then used and which Paul had in view (4.) This chronology has the authority, also, of many eminent names. See Lightfoot, and Boyle's Lectures, ch. xx. In what way this computation of Josephus and the Jews originated, it is not necessary here to inquire. It is a sufficient solution of the difficulty that *Paul spoke in their usual manner*, without departing from his regular object by settling a point of chronology.

21. *And afterward they desired a king.* See 1 Sam. viii. 5. Hos. xiii. 10. It was predicted that they would have a king. Deut. xvii. 14, 13. ¶ *Saul the son of Cis. Cis* is the Greek mode of writing the Hebrew name *Kish.* In the Old Testament it is uniformly written *Kish*, and it is to be regretted that this has not been retained in the New Testament. See 1 Sam

22 And when [a] he had removed
him, he raised up unto them David
[b] to be their king; to whom also he
gave testimony, and said, I have
found David the *son* of Jesse, a man
[c] after mine own heart, which shall
fulfil all my will.
23 Of this man's seed hath God,
according to *his* promise, [d] raised
unto Israel [e] a Saviour, Jesus:
24 When John [f] had first preached, before his coming, the baptism
of repentance to all the people of
Israel.
25 And as John fulfilled his
course, he said, Whom think ye
that I am? I am not *he*: but, behold, there cometh one after me,
whose shoes of *his* feet I am not
worthy to loose.
26 Men *and* brethren, children
of the stock of Abraham, and who-

a 1Sam.31.6. b 2Sam.5.3. c 1Sam.13.14. d Ps.132.11. e Matt.1.21. f Matt.3.1-11

ix. 1. ¶ *By the space of forty years.* During forty years. The Old Testament has not mentioned the time during which Saul reigned. Josephus says (Antiq. b. vi. ch. xiv. § 9) that he reigned eighteen years while Samuel was alive, and twenty-two years after his death. But Dr. Doddridge (Note in loco) has shown that this cannot be correct, and that he probably reigned, as some copies of Josephus have it, but two years after the death of Samuel. Many critics suppose that the term of forty years here mentioned includes also the time in which Samuel judged the people. This supposition does not violate the text in this place, and may be probable. See Doddridge and Grotius on the place.

22. *And when he had removed him.* This was done because he rebelled against God in sparing the sheep and oxen and valuable property of Amalek, together with Agag the king, when he was commanded to destroy all. 1 Sam. xv. 8—23. He was put to death in a battle with the Philistines. 1 Sam. xxxi. 1—6. The phrase "when he removed him" refers probably to his *rejection* as a king, and not to his death; for David was anointed king before the death of Saul, and almost immediately after the rejection of Saul on account of his rebellion in the business of Amalek. See 1 Sam. xvi. 12, 13. ¶ *He gave testimony.* He bore witness 1 Sam. xiii. 14. ¶ *I have found David,* &c. This is not quoted *literally*, but contains the *substance* of what is expressed in various places. Compare 1 Sam. xiii. 14, with Ps. lxxxix. 20, and 1 Sam. xvi. 1. 12. ¶ *A man after mine own heart.* This expression is found in 1 Sam. xiii. 14. The connexion shows that it means simply a man who would not be rebellious and disobedient as Saul was, but would do his will, and keep his commandments. This refers, doubtless, rather to the public than to the private character of David; or to his character *as a king*. It means that he would make the will of God the great rule and law of his reign, in contradistinction from Saul, who, *as a king*, had disobeyed God. At the same time it is true that the *prevailing* character of David, as a pious, humble, devoted man, was, that he was a man after God's own heart, and was beloved by him as a saint and a holy man. He had faults; he committed sin, but who is free from it? He was guilty of great offences; but he also evinced, in a degree equally eminent, *repentance* (see Ps. li.); and not less in his private than his public character did he evince those traits which were *prevailingly* such as accorded with *the heart*, i. e. the earnest desires of God. ¶ *Which shall fulfill all my will.* Saul had not done it. He had disobeyed God in a case where he had received an express command. The characteristic of David would be that he would *obey* the commands of God. That David *did* this—that he maintained the worship of God, opposed idolatry, and sought to promote universal obedience to God among the people—is expressly recorded of him. 1 Kings xiv. 8, 9, "And thou [Jeroboam] hast not been as my servant David, *who kept my commandments and who followed me with all his heart, to do that only which was right in mine eyes*," &c. 1 Kings xv. 3. 5.

23. *Of this man's seed.* Of his posterity. ¶ *According to his promise.* Note, Acts ii. 30. ¶ *Raised unto Israel.* Note, Acts ii. 30. ¶ *A Saviour, Jesus.* Note, Matt. i. 21.

24. *When John had first preached,* &c. After John had preached, and prepared the way. Matt. iii.

25. *And as John fulfilled his course.* As he was engaged in completing his work. His ministry is called a *course* or *race*, that which was to be *run*, or completed. ¶ *He said,* &c. These are not the precise words which the evangelists have recorded, but the sense is the same. Note, John i. 20 Matt. iii. 11.

26. *Men* and *brethren.* Paul now ex

soever among you feareth God, to
you [a] is the word of this salvation
sent.
27 For they that dwell at Jerusalem, and their rulers, because
they knew him not, nor yet the
voices of the prophets which are
read every Sabbath-day, they [b]
have fulfilled *them* in condemning
him.
28 And though they found no
cause of death in *him*, yet desired
they Pilate that he should be slain
29 And when they had fulfilled
all that was written of him, they
took *him* down from the tree, and
laid *him* in a sepulchre.
30 But God raised him from
the dead:
31 And he was seen [c] many days
of them which came up with him
from Galilee to Jerusalem, who
are his witnesses unto the people.

a Matt.10.6. b Luke 24.20,44. c c.1.3.

horts them to embrace the Lord Jesus as the Messiah. He uses therefore the most respectful and fraternal language. ¶ *Children of the stock of Abraham.* Descendants of Abraham; who regard Abraham as your ancestor. He means here to address particularly the native-born Jews; and this appellation is used because they valued themselves highly on account of their descent from Abraham (Note, Matt. iii. 9); and because the promise of the Messiah had been specially given to him. ¶ *And whosoever, &c.* Proselytes. Note, ver. 16. ¶ *Is the word of this salvation sent.* This message of salvation. It was sent *particularly* to the Jewish people. The Saviour was sent to that nation (Matt. xv. 24); and the design was to offer to them first the message of life. See Note, ver. 46.

27. *Because they knew him not.* The statement in this verse is designed, not to reproach the Jews at Jerusalem, but to introduce the fact that Jesus had died, and had risen again. With great wisdom and tenderness, he speaks of his murderers in such a manner as not to exasperate, but as far as possible to mitigate their crime. There was sufficient guilt in the murder of the Son of God to overwhelm the nation with alarm, even after all that could be said to mitigate the deed. See Acts ii. 23. 36, 37. When Paul says, "They knew him not," he means that they did not know him to be the Messiah (see 1 Cor. ii. 8); they were ignorant of the true meaning of the prophecies of the Old Testament; they regarded him as an impostor. (See Note, Acts iii. 17.) ¶ *Nor yet the voices of the prophets.* Neither the meaning of the predictions in the Old Testament, respecting the Messiah. They expected a prince, and a conqueror, but did not expect a Messiah poor and despised, and a man of sorrows, and that was to die on a cross. ¶ *Which are read every Sabbath-day.* In the synagogues. Though the Scriptures were read so constantly, yet they were ignorant of their true meaning. They were blinded by pride, and prejudice, and preconceived opinions. Men may often in this way read the Bible a good part of their lives, and for want of attention, or of a humble mind, never understand it. ¶ *They have fulfilled them, &c.* By putting him to death they have accomplished what was foretold.

28. *And though they found, &c.* They found no crime which deserved death. This is conclusively shown by the trial itself. After all their efforts; after the treason of Judas; after their employing false witnesses; still no crime was laid to his charge. The sanhedrim condemned him for blasphemy; and yet they knew that they could not substantiate this charge before Pilate, and they therefore endeavoured to procure his condemnation on the ground of sedition. Comp. Luke xxii. 70, 71, with xxiii. 1, 2 ¶ *Yet desired they Pilate, &c.* Matt. xxvii. 1, 2. Luke xxiii. 4, 5.

29. *They took him down, &c.* That is, it was done by the Jews. Not that it was done by those who put him to death, but by Joseph of Arimathea, a Jew, and by Nicodemus, and their companions. Paul is speaking of what was done to Jesus by *the Jews* at Jerusalem; and he does not affirm that the *same* persons put him to death and laid him in a tomb, but that all this was done *by Jews.* See John xix. 38, 39.

30. *But God raised him, &c.* Note, ch. ii. 23, 24.

31. *And he was seen.* See Note at the end of Matthew. ¶ *Many days.* Forty days. ch. i. 3. ¶ *Of them which came up.* By the apostles particularly. He was seen by others; but they are especially mentioned as having been chosen for

32 And we declare unto you glad tidings, how that the promise [a] which was made unto the fathers,
33 God hath fulfilled the same unto us their children, in that he hath raised up Jesus again; as it is also written in the second psalm, Thou [b] art my Son, this day have I begotten thee.

a Rom.4.13. b Ps.2.7.

this object, to bear witness to him, and as having been particularly qualified for it.

32. *And we.* We who are here present. Paul and Barnabas. ¶ *Declare unto you glad tidings.* We preach the gospel—the good news. To a Jew, nothing could be more grateful intelligence than that the Messiah had come; to a sinner convinced of his sins nothing can be more cheering than to hear of a Saviour. ¶ *The promise, &c.* The *promise* here refers to *all* that had been spoken in the Old Testament respecting the advent, sufferings, death, and resurrection of Christ.

33. *God hath fulfilled.* God has *completed* or carried into effect by the resurrection of Jesus. He does not say that all the promise had reference to *his resurrection;* but his being raised up *completed* or *perfected* the fulfilment of the promises which had been made respecting him. ¶ *In the second psalm.* ver. 7. ¶ *Thou art my Son.* This psalm has been usually understood as referring to the Messiah. See Note, ch. iv. 25. ¶ *This day have I begotten thee.* It is evident that Paul uses the expression here as implying that the Lord Jesus is called the Son of God because he raised him up from the dead; and that he means to imply that it was for *this* reason that he is so called in the psalm. This interpretation of an inspired apostle fixes the meaning of this passage in the psalm; and proves that it is not there used with reference to the doctrine of eternal generation, or to his incarnation, but that he is here called his Son because he was raised from the dead. And this interpretation accords with the scope of the psalm. In ver. 1—3 the psalmist records the combination of the rulers of the earth against the Messiah, and their efforts to cast off his reign. This was done, and the Messiah was rejected. All this pertains, not to his previous existence, but to the Messiah on the earth. In ver. 4, 5, the psalmist shows that their efforts should not be successful; that God would laugh at their designs, that is, that their plans should not succeed. In ver. 6, 7, he shows that the Messiah would be established as a king; that this was the fixed decree, that he had *begotten* him for this. All this is represented as *subsequent* to the raging of the heathen, and to the counsel of the kings against him, and *must,* therefore, refer. not to his eternal generation, or his incarnation, but to something succeeding his death; that is, to his resurrection, and establishment as king at the right hand of God. This interpretation by the apostle Paul proves therefore that this passage is not to be used to establish the doctrine of the eternal generation of Christ Christ is called the Son of God from various reasons In Luke i. 35, because he was begotten by the Holy Ghost. In this place, on account of his resurrection. In Rom. i. 4, it is also said, that he was declared to be the Son of God by the resurrection from the dead. See Note on that place. The resurrection from the dead is represented as in some sense *the beginning* of life, and it is with reference to this that the terms Son, and *begotten from the dead,* are used, as the birth of a child is the beginning of life. Thus Christ is said, Col. i. 18, to be "the *first-born* from the dead," and thus in Rev. i. 5, he is called "the *first-begotten* of the dead," and with reference to this *renewal* or beginning of life he is called *a Son.* In whatever other senses he is called *a Son* in the New Testament, yet it is here proved, (1.) That he is called a Son from his resurrection; and (2.) That this is the sense in which the expression in the psalm is to be used. ¶ *This day.* The day in the mind of the psalmist, and of Paul, of his resurrection. Many efforts have been made, and much learned criticism has been expended, to prove that this refers to eternity, or to his pre-existence. But the signification of the word, which never refers to eternity, and the connexion, and the obvious intention of the speaker, is against this. Paul understood this manifestly of the resurrection. This settles the inquiry, and this is the *indispensable* interpretation in the psalm itself. ¶ *Have I begotten thee.* This evidently cannot be understood in a *literal* sense. It *literally* refers to the relation of an earthly father to his children: but in no

34 And as concerning that he raised him up from the dead, *now* no more to return to corruption, he said on this wise, I will give you the sure [1] mercies of David.

35 Wherefore he saith also in [a] another *psalm*, Thou shalt not suffer thine Holy One to see corruption.

1 τα οσια, *holy*, or, *just things*; which word the LXX, both in the place of Isa.55.3, and in many others, use for that which is in the Hebrew, *mercies*.

a Ps.16.10.

such sense can it be applied to the relation of God the Father to the Son. It *must* therefore be figurative. The word sometimes figuratively means to produce, to cause to exist in any way. 2 Tim. ii. 23, "Unlearned questions avoid, knowing that they do *gender* [beget] strifes." It refers also to the labours of the apostles in securing the conversion of sinners to the gospel. 1 Cor. iv. 15, "In Christ Jesus I have *begotten* you through the gospel." Phil. ver. 10, "Whom [Onesimus] I have *begotten* in my bonds." It is applied to Christians (John i. 13). "Which were born [begotten] not of blood, &c. but of God." iii. 3, "Except a man be born [begotten] again," &c. In all these places it is used in a figurative sense to denote the commencement of spiritual life by the power of God attending the truth; raising up sinners from the death of sin; or so producing spiritual life as that they should sustain to God the relation of sons. Thus he raised up Christ from the dead; imparted life to his body; by his own power restored him; and hence is said figuratively to have *begotten* him from the dead, and hence sustains towards the risen Saviour the relation of Father. Comp. Col. i. 18. Rev. i. 5. Heb. i. 5.

34. *And as concerning.* In further proof of that. To show that he actually did it, he proceeds to quote another passage of Scripture. ¶ *No more to return to corruption.* The word *corruption* is usually employed to denote putrefaction, or the mouldering away of a body in the grave; its returning to its native dust. But it is certain (ver. 35. Note, ch. ii. 27) that the body of Christ never in this sense saw corruption. The word is therefore used to denote *death*, or *the grave*, the cause and place of corruption. The word is thus used in the Septuagint. It means here simply that he should not again *die.* ¶ *He said on this wise.* He said thus. (ὁυτως.) ¶ *I will give you.* This quotation is made from Isa. lv. 3. It is quoted from the Septuagint, with a change of but one word, not affecting the sense. In Isaiah the passage does not refer particularly to the *resurrection* of the Messiah: nor is it the design of Paul to affirm that it does. His object in this verse is not to prove that he would *rise from the dead*; but that *being* risen, he would *not again die.* That the passage in Isaiah refers to the Messiah there can be no doubt. ver. 1. 4. The passage here quoted is an address to the people, an assurance to them that the promise made to David should be performed, a solemn declaration that he would make an everlasting covenant with them through the Messiah, the promised descendant of David. ¶ *The sure mercies of David.* The word *mercies* here refers to the *promise* made to David; the *mercy* or *favour* shown to him by promising to him a successor that should not fail to sit on his throne. 2 Sam. vii. 16. Ps. lxxxix. 4, 5; cxxxii. 11, 12. These mercies and these promises are called "sure," as being true, or unfailing; they should certainly be accomplished. Comp. 2 Cor. i. 20. The word *David* here does not refer, as many have supposed, to the Messiah, but to the king of Israel. God made to David a promise, a certain pledge; he bestowed on him this special *mercy*, in promising that he should have a successor who should sit for ever on his throne. This promise was understood by the Jews, and is often referred to in the New Testament, as relating to the Messiah. And Paul here says that that promise here is fulfilled. The only question is, how it refers to the subject on which Paul was immediately discoursing. That point was not mainly to prove his *resurrection*, but to show particularly that he would *never die* again, or that he would for ever live and reign. And the argument is, that as God had promised that David should have a successor who should sit for ever on his throne; and as this prediction now terminated in the Messiah, the Lord Jesus, it followed, that, as that promise was sure and certain, he would never die again. He must live, if the sure promise was fulfilled. And though he had been put to death, yet under that general promise was the certainty that he would live again. It was impossible, the meaning is, that the Messiah, the promised successor of David, the perpetual occupier of his throne, should remain under the power of death. Under this assurance the church now reposes its hopes. Zion's King now lives, ever able to vindicate and save his people.

35. *Wherefore.* Διο. To the same in

36 For David, [1] after he had served his own generation by the will
of God, [a] fell on sleep, and was laid
unto his fathers, and saw corruption:
37 But he, whom God [b] raised
again, saw no corruption.
38 Be it known unto you, therefore, men *and* brethren, that through
[c] this man is preached unto you the
forgiveness of sins:
39 And by him, [d] all that believe
are justified from all things, from
which ye could not be justified by
the law of Moses.
40 Beware, therefore, lest that
come upon you which is spoken of
in [e] the prophets;

1 or, *after he had in his own age served the will of God.* a 1Ki.2.10. b c.2.24.

c Dan.9.24. Lu.24.47. 1Jno.2.12. d Isa.53.11. Hab 2.4.Rom.3.28; 8.3. e Isa.29.14. Hab.1.5.

tent, or end. In the proof of the same thing—that he must rise and live for ever. ¶ *He saith.* God says by David; or David declares the promises made by God. ¶ *In another* psalm. Ps. xvi. 10. ¶ *Thou wilt not suffer,* &c. See this explained in Notes, ch. ii. 27.

36. *For David,* &c. This verse is designed to show that the passage in Ps. xvi. could not refer to David, and must therefore relate to some other person. In ver. 37, it is affirmed that this *could* refer to no one, in fact, but to the Lord Jesus. ¶ *After he had served his generation.* See the margin. Syriac, 'David in his own generation having served the will of God, and slept,' &c. Arabic, 'David served in his own age, and saw God.' The margin probably most correctly expresses the sense of the passage. To serve a generation, or an age, is an unusual and almost unintelligible expression. ¶ *Fell on sleep.* Greek, Slept; that is, *died.* This is the usual word to denote the death of saints. It is used of David in 1 Kings ii. 10. Note, Matt. xxvii. 52. ¶ *And was laid unto,* &c. And was buried with his fathers, &c. 1 Kings ii. 10. ¶ *And saw corruption.* Remained in the grave, and returned to his native dust. See this point argued more at length by Peter, in Acts ii. 29—31, and explained in the Notes on that place.

37. *But he, whom God raised again.* The Lord Jesus. ¶ *Saw no corruption.* Was raised without undergoing the usual change that succeeds death. As David *had* returned to corruption, and the Lord Jesus had *not,* it followed that this passage in Ps. xvi. referred to the Messiah.

38. *Be it known,* &c. Paul, having proved his resurrection, and shown that he was the Messiah, now states the *benefits* that were to be derived from his death. ¶ *Through this man.* See Note, Luke xxiv. 47.

39. *And by him.* By means of him; by his sufferings and death. ¶ *All that believe.* Note, Mark xvi. 16 ¶ *Are justified.* Are regarded and treated as if they were righteous. They are pardoned, and admitted to the favour of God, and treated as pardoned sinners, and as if they had not offended. See this point explained in the Notes on Rom. i. 17; iii. 24, 25; iv. 1—8. ¶ *From all things.* From the guilt of all offences. All will be pardoned. ¶ *From which ye could not,* &c. The law of Moses commanded what was to be done. It appointed sacrifices and offerings, as typical of a greater sacrifice. But the same apostle has fully shown in the epistle to the Hebrews that those sacrifices could not take away sin. ch. ix. 7—14; x. 1—4. 11. The design of the *law* was not to reveal a way of pardon. That was reserved to be the peculiar purpose of the gospel. ¶ *The law of Moses.* The commands and institutions which he, under the direction of God, established.

40. *Beware, therefore.* Avoid that which is threatened. It will come on *some;* and Paul exhorted his hearers to beware lest it should come on them. It was the more important to caution them against this danger, as the Jews held that *they* were safe. ¶ *Lest that come.* That calamity, that threatened punishment. ¶ *In the prophets.* In that part of the Scriptures called "the prophets." The Jews divided the Old Testament into three parts, of which "the book of the prophets" was one. Note, Luke xxiv. 44. The place where this is recorded is Hab. i. 5. It is not taken from the Hebrew, but substantially from the Septuagint. The original design of the threatening was to announce the destruction that would come upon the nation by the Chaldeans. The original threatening was fulfilled. But it was as *applicable* to the Jews in the time of Paul as in the time of Habakkuk. The *principle* of the passage is, that if they held in contempt the doings of God, they would perish. The work which God was to do by means of the Chaldeans was so fearful, so unusual, and so remarkable, that they would not believe it in time to

41 Behold, ye despisers, and wonder, and perish: for I work a work in your days, a work which you shall in no wise believe, though a man declare it unto you.

42 And when the Jews were gone out of the synagogue, the Gentiles besought that these words might be preached to them the [1] next Sabbath.

[1] *in the week between, or, in the Sabbath between.*

avoid the calamity. In the same way, that which God did in giving a Messiah so little in accordance with their expectation, the manner of the introduction of his kingdom by miracles; and the gift of his Spirit, was so much at variance with their expectations, that they might see it, yet disbelieve it; they might have the fullest proof, and yet despise it; they might wonder, and be amazed and astonished, and unable to account for it, and yet refuse to believe it, and be destroyed. ¶ *Behold, ye despisers.* Heb. "Behold, ye among the heathen." The change from this expression to "ye despisers," was made by the Septuagint translators, by a very slight change in the Hebrew word—probably from a variation in the copy which they used. It arose from reading בוגרים instead of בגוים, *Bogedim* instead of *Baggoim.* The Syriac, the Arabic, as well as the LXX. follow this reading. ¶ *And wonder.* Heb. "and regard, and wonder marvellously." ¶ *And perish.* This is not in the Hebrew, but is in the Septuagint and the Arabic. The word means literally to be removed from the sight, to disappear, and then to corrupt, defile, destroy. Matt. vi. 16. 19. The word, however, may mean *to be suffused with shame;* to be overwhelmed, and confounded (*Schleusner*), and it may perhaps have this meaning here, answering to the Hebrew. The word used here is not that which is commonly employed to denote eternal perdition; though Paul seems to use it with reference to their destruction for rejecting the gospel. ¶ *For I work a work.* I do a thing. The thing to which the prophet Habakkuk referred was, that God would bring upon them the Chaldeans, that would destroy the temple and nation. In like manner Paul says, that God in *that* time might bring upon the nation similar calamities. By rejecting the Messiah and his gospel, and by persevering in wickedness, they would bring upon themselves the destruction of the temple, and city, and nation. It was this threatened destruction doubtless to which the apostle referred. ¶ *Which ye shall in no wise believe.* Which you will not believe. So remarkable, so unusual, so surpassing any thing which had occurred. The original reference in Habakkuk is to the destruction of the temple by the Chaldeans; a thing which the Jews would not suppose *could* happen. The temple was so splendid; it had been built by the direction of God; it had been so long under his protection; that they would suppose that it *could not* be given into the hands of their enemies to be demolished. And even though it were predicted by a prophet of God, still they would not believe it. The same feelings the Jews would have respecting the temple and city in the time of Paul. Though it was foretold by the Messiah, yet they were so confident that it was protected by God, that they would not believe that it could *possibly* be destroyed. The same infatuation seems to have possessed them during the siege of the city by the Romans. ¶ *Though a man,* &c. Though it be plainly predicted. We may learn, (1.) That men may see, and be amazed at the works of God, and yet be destroyed. (2.) There may be a prejudice so obstinate that even a divine revelation will not remove it. (3.) The fancied security of sinners will not save them. (4.) There are men who will not believe in the possibility of their being lost, though it be declared by the prophets, by apostles, by the Saviour, and by God. They will still remain in fancied security, and suffer nothing to alarm or rouse them. But (5.) The fancied security of the Jews furnished no safety against the Babylonians or the Romans. Nor will the indifference and unconcern of sinners furnish any security against the dreadful wrath of God. Yet there are multitudes who live amidst the displays of God's power and mercy in the redemption of sinners who witness the effects of his goodness and truth in revivals of religion, who live to *despise* it all; who are amazed and confounded by it; and who shall yet perish.

42. *And when the Jews,* &c There is a great variety in the MSS. on this verse; and in the ancient versions. Griesbach and Knapp read it, "And when they were gone out, they besought them that these words might be spoken," &c. The Syriac reads it, "When they departed from them, they sought from them that these words might be spoken to them on

43 Now when the congregation
was broken up, many of the Jews
and religious proselytes followed
Paul and Barnabas: who speaking
to them, persuaded them to continue [a] in the grace of God.
44 And the next Sabbath-day
came almost the whole city together, to hear the word of God.
45 But when the Jews saw the
multitudes, they were filled with
envy, and spake against those
things which were spoken by Paul,
contradicting [b] and blaspheming.

a c.14.22. Heb.6.11,12;12.15.

b c.18.6.

another Sabbath." The Arabic, "Some of the synagogue of the Jews asked of them that they would exhort the Gentiles with them," &c. If these readings be correct, then the meaning is, that some of the Jews exhorted the apostles to proclaim these truths at some other time; particularly to the Gentiles. The MSS. greatly vary in regard to the passage, and it is perhaps impossible to determine the true reading. If the present reading in the English translation is to be regarded as genuine—of which, however, there is very little evidence—the meaning is, that a *part* of the Jews, perhaps a majority of them, rejected the message, and went out, though many of them followed Paul and Barnabas. ver. 43. ¶ *The Gentiles besought.* This expression is wanting in the Vulgate, Coptic, Arabic, and Syriac versions, and in a great many MSS. (*Mill.*) It is omitted by Griesbach, Knapp, &c. and is probably spurious. Among other reasons which may be suggested why it is not genuine, this is one, that it is not evident or probable that the *Gentiles* were in the habit of attending the synagogue. Those who attended there were called *proselytes*. The expression, if genuine, might mean, either that the *Gentiles* besought, or that *they* besought the Gentiles. The latter would be the more probable meaning. ¶ *The next Sabbath.* The *margin* has probably the correct rendering of the passage. The meaning of the verse is, that a wish was expressed that these doctrines might be repeated to them in the intermediate time before the next Sabbath.

43. *When the congregation.* Greek, When *the synagogue* was dissolved. ¶ *Broken up.* Dismissed. It does not mean that it was broken up by violence or disorder. It was dismissed in the usual way. ¶ *Many of the Jews.* Probably the majority of them rejected the message. See ver. 45. Still a deep impression was made on many of them. ¶ *And religious proselytes.* See ver. 16. Comp. Note, Matt. xxiii. 15. Greek, *Proselytes worshipping.* ¶ *Persuaded them to continue,* &c It would appear from this, that they professedly received the truth and embraced the Lord Jesus. This success was remarkable, and shows the power of the gospel when it is preached faithfully to men. ¶ *In the grace of God.* In *his favour*—in the faith, and prayer, and obedience, which would be connected with his favour. The *gospel* is called the *grace* or *favour* of God, and they were exhorted to persevere in their attachment to it.

44. *And the next Sabbath-day.* This was the *regular* day for worship, and it was natural that a greater multitude should convene on that day than on the other days of the week. ¶ *Came almost the whole city.* Whether this was in the synagogue is not affirmed; but it is probable that that was the place where the multitude convened. The news of the presence of the apostles, and of their doctrines, had been circulated doubtless by the Gentiles who had heard them, and curiosity attracted the multitude to hear them. Comp. Note, ver. 7.

45. *They were filled with envy.* Greek, *Zeal.* The word here denotes *wrath, indignation,* that such multitudes should be disposed to hear a message which they rejected, and which threatened to overthrow their religion. ¶ *Spake against.* Opposed the doctrine that Jesus was the Messiah; that the Messiah would be humble, lowly, despised, and put to death, &c. ¶ *Contradicting.* Contradicting the apostles. This was evidently done in their presence, ver. 46, and would cause great tumult and disorder. ¶ *And blaspheming.* Note, Matt. ix. 3. The sense evidently is, that they *reproached* and *vilified* Jesus of Nazareth; they spake of him with contempt and scorn. To speak thus of him is denominated *blasphemy.* Luke xxii. 65. When men are enraged, they little regard the words which they utter, and little care how they may be estimated by God. When men attached to sect and party, in religion or politics, have no good *arguments* to employ, they attempt to overwhelm their adversaries by bitter and reproachful words. Men in the heat of strife, and in

46 Then Paul and Barnabas waxed bold, and said, It was necessary
that the word of God should first [a]
have been spoken to you: but seeing ye put it from you, and judge
yourselves unworthy of everlasting
life, lo, we [b] turn to the Gentiles.

47 For so hath the Lord commanded us, *saying*, [c] I have set
thee to be a light of the Gentiles,
that thou shouldest be for salvation
unto the ends of the earth.
48 And when the Gentiles heard
this, they were glad and glorified

a Mat.10.6. Lu.24.47. Rom.1.16. b Deut.32.21. Matt.21.43. Rom.10.19. c Isa.49.6.

professed zeal for peculiar doctrines, and for sect and party, more frequently utter *blasphemy* than they are aware. Precious and pure doctrines are often thus vilified, because *we* do not believe them; and the heart of the Saviour is pierced anew, and his cause bleeds by the wrath and wickedness of his professed friends. Comp. ch. xviii. 6.

46. *Waxed bold.* Became bold; spake boldly and openly. They were not terrified by their strife, or alarmed by their opposition. The contradictions and blasphemies of sinners often show that their consciences are alarmed; that the truth has taken effect; and then is not the time to shrink, but to declare more fearlessly the truth. ¶ *It was necessary.* It was so designed; so commanded. They regarded it as their duty to offer the gospel *first* to their own countrymen. Note, Luke xxiv. 47. ¶ *Ye put it from you.* Ye reject it. ¶ *And judge yourselves.* By your conduct, by your rejecting it, you declare this. The word *judge* here does not mean *they expressed such an opinion*, or that *they regarded themselves* as unworthy of eternal life; for they thought just the reverse; but that by their conduct they CONDEMNED *themselves.* By such conduct they did in fact *pass sentence* on themselves, and show that they were unworthy of eternal life, and of having the offer any farther made to them.—Sinners by their conduct do in fact condemn themselves, and show that they are not only unfit to be saved, but that they have advanced so far in wickedness that there is no *hope* of their salvation, and no propriety in offering them, any farther, eternal life. Note, Matt. vii. 6. ¶ *Unworthy*, &c. Unfit to be saved. They had *deliberately* and *solemnly* rejected the gospel, and thus shown that they were not fitted to enter into everlasting life.—When men, even but *once*, deliberately and solemnly *reject* the offers of God's mercy, it greatly endangers their salvation. The *probability* is, that they then put the cup of salvation for ever away from themselves. The gospel produces an effect wherever it is preached. And when sinners are hardened, and spurn the gospel, it may often be the duty of ministers to turn their efforts towards others, where they may have more prospect of success. A man will not long labour on a rocky, barren, sterile soil, when there is near him a rich and fertile valley that will abundantly reward the pains of cultivation. ¶ *Lo, we turn*, &c. We shall offer salvation to them and devote ourselves to seeking their salvation.

47. *For so*, &c. Paul, as usual, appeals to the Scriptures in order to justify his course. He here appeals to the *Old Testament*, rather than to the command of the Saviour, because the Jews recognised the authority of their own Scriptures, while they would have turned in scorn from the command of Jesus of Nazareth. ¶ *I have set thee*, &c. I have constituted or appointed thee. This passage is found in Isa. xlix. 6. That it refers to the Messiah there can be no doubt. From the xlth chapter of Isaiah to the end of the prophecies, Isaiah had a primary and main reference to the times of the Messiah. ¶ *To be a light.* Note, John i. 4. ¶ *To the Gentiles* This was in accordance with the uniform doctrines of Isaiah. Isa. xlii. 1; liv. 3; lx. 3. 5. 16; lxi. 6. 9; lxii. 2; lxvi. 12. Comp. Rom. xv. 9—12. ¶ *For salvation.* To save sinners. ¶ *Unto the ends of the earth.* To all lands; in all nations. Note, ch. i. 8.

48. *When the Gentiles heard this.* Heard that the gospel was to be preached to them. The doctrine of the Jews had been that salvation was confined to themselves. The Gentiles rejoiced that from the mouths of Jews they now heard a different doctrine. ¶ *They glorified the word of the Lord.* They honoured it as a message from God; they recognised and received it as the word of God. The expression conveys the idea of *praise* on account of it, and of *reverence* for the message as the word of God ¶ *And as many as were ordained.* ὅσοι ἦσαν τεταγμένοι. Syriac, "Who were *destined*," or constituted. Vulgate, "As many as were foreordained (quotquot erant præordinati) to eternal life believed." There has been

the word of the Lord: and [a] as
many as were ordained to eternal
life, believed.
49 And the word of the Lord was
published throughout all the region.
50 But the Jews stirred up the
devout and honourable women, and
the chief men of the city, and [b] rais
ed persecution against Paul and
Barnabas, and expelled them out
of their coasts.
51 But they shook [c] off the dust
of their feet against them, and came
unto Iconium.

a c.2.47. Rom.8.30. b 2Tim.3.11. c Mar.6.11. Lu.9.5. c.18.6.

much difference of opinion in regard to this expression. One class of commentators have supposed that it refers to the doctrine of election—to *God's ordaining* men to eternal life; and another class, to their being *disposed themselves* to embrace the gospel—to those among them who did not reject and despise the gospel, but who were *disposed* and *inclined* to embrace it. The main inquiry is, what is the meaning of the word rendered *ordained?* The word is used but eight times in the New Testament. Matt. xxviii. 16, "Into a mountain where Jesus *had appointed* them," i. e. *previously* appointed, or commanded them—before his death. Luke vii. 8, "For I also am a man *set under authority;*" appointed, or designated, as a soldier, to be under the authority of another. Acts xv. 2, "They *determined* that Paul and Barnabas, &c. should go to Jerusalem." Acts xxii. 10, "It shall be told thee of all things which *are appointed* for thee to do." xxviii. 23, "And when they *had appointed* him a day," &c. Rom. xiii. 1, "The powers that be, *are ordained* of God." 1 Cor. xvi. 15, "They *have addicted* themselves to the ministry of saints." The word Τάσσω or Τάττω properly means *to place; to place in a certain rank or order.* Its meaning is derived from arranging or disposing a body of soldiers in regular order; to arrange in military order. In the places which have been mentioned above, the word is used to denote the following things: (1.) *To command,* or to designate. Matt. xxviii. 16. Acts xxii. 10; xxviii. 23. (2.) To institute, constitute, or appoint. Rom. xiii. 1. Comp. 2 Sam. vii. 11. 1 Sam. xxii. 7. (3.) To determine, to take counsel, to resolve. Acts xv. 2. (4.) To subject to the authority of another. Luke vii. 8. (5.) To addict to; to devote to. 1 Cor. xvi. 15. The meaning may be thus expressed: (1.) The word is *never* used to denote an internal *disposition* or *inclination* arising from one's own self. It does *not* mean that they *disposed themselves* to embrace eternal life. (2.) It has uniformly the notion of an *ordering, disposing,* or *arranging from without,* i. e. from some other source than the individual himself; as of a soldier, who is arranged or classified according to the will of the proper officer In relation to these persons it means therefore, that they were *disposed* or inclined to this from some other source than themselves. (3.) It does not properly refer to an eternal decree, or directly to the doctrine of election; though that may be *inferred* from it; but it refers to their being THEN IN FACT *disposed* to embrace eternal life. They were *then inclined* by an influence from without themselves, or so *disposed* as to embrace eternal life. It refers not to an eternal decree, but that *then* there was such an influence as to dispose them, or incline them, to lay hold on salvation. That this was done by the influence of the Holy Spirit, is clear from all parts of the New Testament. Titus iii. 5, 6. John i. 13. It was not a disposition or *arrangement* originating with themselves, but with God. (4.) This *implies* the doctrine of election. It was *in fact* that doctrine expressed. It was nothing but God's disposing them to embrace eternal life. And that he does this according to a plan in his own mind —a plan which is unchangeable as God himself is unchangeable—is clear from the Scriptures. Comp. Acts xviii. 10. Rom. viii. 28—30; ix. 15, 16. 21. 23. Eph. i. 4, 5. 11. The meaning may be expressed in few words—*who were* THEN *disposed, and in good earnest determined, to embrace eternal life, by the operation of the grace of God on their hearts* ¶ *Eternal life.* Salvation. Note, John iii. 36.

50. *But the Jews stirred up.* Excited opposition. ¶ *Honourable women.* Note, Mark xv. 43. Women of influence, and connected with families of rank. Perhaps they were proselytes, and were connected with the magistrates of the city. ¶ *And raised persecution* Probably on the ground that they produced disorder and excitement. The aid of "*chief men*" has often been called in to oppose revivals of religion, and to put a period, if possible, to the spread of the gospel. ¶ *Out of their coasts.* Out of the regions of their country; out of their province.

51 *But they shook off the dust,* &c. See Note, Matt. x. 14 ¶ *And came into Ico*

51 And the disciples were filled
with joy, [a] and with the Holy
Ghost.

CHAPTER XIV.

AND it came to pass in Iconium, that they went both together into the synagogue of the
Jews, and so spake, that a great
multitude, both of the Jews and
also of the Greeks, believed.
2 But the unbelieving Jews stirred up the Gentiles, and made
their minds evil-affected against
the brethren.
3 Long time therefore abode
they speaking boldly in the Lord,
which [b] gave testimony unto the
word of his grace, and granted
signs and wonders to be done by
their hands.
4 But the multitude of the city
was divided; and [c] part held with
the Jews, and part with the apostles.
5 And when there was an assault made, both of the Gentiles
and also of the Jews, with their
rulers, to use *them* despitefully,
and to stone them,
6 They were ware of *it*, and
fled [d] unto Lystra, and Derbe, cities

a Matt.5.12. 1Thess.1.6. *b* Mark 16.20. Heb.2.4. *c* c.28.24. *d* Matt.10.23.

---

nium. This was the capital of Lycaonia. It is now called Cogni, or Konieh, and is the capital of Caramania.

52. *And the disciples.* The disciples in Antioch. ¶ *Were filled with joy.* This happened even in the midst of persecution, and is one of the many evidences that the gospel is able to fill the soul with joy even in the severest trials.

CHAPTER XIV.

1. *In Iconium.* Note, ch. xiii. 51. In this place it appears that Timothy became acquainted with Paul and his manner of life. 2 Tim. iii. 10, 11. ¶ *So spake.* Spake with such power—their preaching was attended so much with the influence of the Spirit. ¶ *And of the Greeks.* Probably *proselytes* from the Greeks, who were in the habit of attending the synagogue.

2. *But the unbelieving Jews,* &c. Note, ch. xiii. 50. ¶ *And made their minds evil-affected.* Irritated, or exasperated them. ¶ *Against the brethren.* One of the common appellations by which Christians were known.

3. *Long time therefore.* In this city they were not daunted by persecution. It seems probable that there were here no forcible or public measures to expel them, as there had been at Antioch (ch. xiii. 50), and they therefore regarded it as their duty to remain. God granted them here also great success, which was the main reason for their continuing a long time. Persecution and opposition may be attended often with signal success to the gospel. ¶ *Spake boldly in the Lord.* In the *cause* of the Lord Jesus; or in his name and authority. Perhaps also the expression includes the idea of their *trusting* in the Lord. ¶ *Which gave testimony.* Bore witness to the truth of their message by working miracles, &c Comp. Mark xvi. 20. This was evidently *the Lord Jesus* to whom reference is here made, and it shows that he was still, though bodily absent from them, clothed with power, and still displayed that power in the advancement of his cause. The conversion of sinners accomplished by him is always a *testimony* as decided as it is cheering to the labours and messages of his servants. ¶ *Unto the word of his grace.* His gracious word, or message. ¶ *And granted signs,* &c. Miracles. See Note, Acts ii. 22.

4. *Was divided.* Into parties. Greek, There was a schism, Εσχίσθη. ¶ *A part held with the Jews.* Held to the doctrines of the Jews, in opposition to the apostles. A revival of religion may produce excitement by the bad passions of opposers The enemies of the truth may form parties, and organize opposition. It is no uncommon thing even now for such parties to be formed; but the fault is not in Christianity. It lies with those who form a party *against* religion, and who confederate themselves, as was done here, to oppose it.

5. *An assault made.* Greek, A *rush*, ὁρμή. It denotes an impetuous excitement, and aggression; a *rush* to put them to death. It rather describes a popular tumult than a calm and deliberate purpose. There was a violent, tumultuous excitement. ¶ *Both of the Gentiles* &c. Of that part of them which was opposed to the apostles. ¶ *To use them despitefully.* Note, Matt. v. 44. To *reproach* them; to bring contempt upon them; to injure them. ¶ *To stone them.* To put them to death by stoning; probably as blasphemers. Acts vii. 57—59.

6. *They were ware of it.* They were

of Lycaonia and unto the region
that lieth round about:
7 And there they preached the
gospel.
8 And there sat a certain man at
Lystra, impotent in his feet, being
a [a] cripple from his mother's womb,
who never had walked.
9 The same heard Paul speak;
who steadfastly beholding him,
and perceiving that he had faith [b]
to be healed,
10 Said with a loud voice, Stand
upright on thy feet. And he leaped [c] and walked.
11 And when the people saw
what Paul had done, they lift up
their voices, saying in the speech
of Lycaonia, The [d] gods are come
down to us, in the likeness of men.

a c.3.2. b Matt.9.28,29. c Isa.35.36. d c.28.6.

in some way informed of the excitement and of their danger. ¶ *And fled unto Lystra* This was a city of Lycaonia, and was a few miles south of Iconium. It is now called *Latik.* ¶ *And Derbe.* Derbe was a short distance east of Lystra. ¶ *Cities of Lycaonia.* Lycaonia was one of the provinces of Asia Minor. It had Galatia north, Pisidia south, Cappadocia east, and Phrygia west. It was formerly within the limits of Phrygia, but was erected into a separate province by Augustus. ¶ *And unto the region.* &c. The adjacent country. Though persecuted, they still preached; and though driven from one city, they fled into another. This was the direction of the Saviour. Matt. x. 23.

8. *And there sat.* There dwelt. Matt. ix. 16. Acts xviii. 11. *Margin.* The word *sat*, however, indicates his usual posture; his helpless condition. Such persons commonly sat at the way side, or in some public place to ask for alms. Mark x. 46. ¶ *Impotent in his feet.* ἀδύνατος. Without any power. Entirely deprived of the use of his feet. ¶ *Being a cripple.* Lame. ¶ *Who never had walked.* The miracle therefore would be more remarkable, as the man would be well known, and there could be no plea that there was an imposition. As they were persecuted from place to place, and opposed in every manner, it was desirable that a signal miracle should be performed to carry forward and establish the work of the gospel

9. *Who steadfastly beholding him.* Fixing his eyes intently on him. Note, Acts i. 10. ¶ *And perceiving.* How he perceived this is not said. Perhaps it was indicated by the ardour, humility, and strong desire depicted in his countenance. He had heard Paul, and perhaps the apostle had dwelt particularly on the *miracles* with which the gospel had been attested. The miracles wrought also in Iconium had doubtless also been heard of in Lystra. ¶ *Had faith to be healed.* Compare, Matt. ix. 21, 22. 28, 29. Luke vii. 50; xvii. 19; xviii. 42.

10. *Said with a loud voice.* Note John xi. 43. ¶ *And he leaped.* Note, Acts iii. 8. Comp. Isa. xxxv. 6.

11. *They lift up their voices.* They spoke with astonishment, such as might be expected when it was supposed that the gods had come down. ¶ *In the speech of Lycaonia.* What this language was has much puzzled commentators. It was probably a mixture of the Greek and Syriac. In that region generally the Greek was usually spoken with more or less purity; and from the fact that it was not far from the regions of Syria, it is probable that the Greek language was corrupted with this foreign admixture. ¶ *The gods, &c.* All the region was idolatrous. The gods which were worshipped there were those which were worshipped throughout Greece. ¶ *Are come down.* The miracle which Paul had wrought led them to suppose this. It was evidently beyond human ability, and they had no other way of accounting for it than by supposing that their gods had personally appeared. ¶ *In the likeness of men.* Many of their gods were heroes, whom they worshipped after they were dead. It was common among them to suppose that the gods appeared to men in human form. The poems of Homer, of Virgil, &c. are filled with accounts of such appearances, and the only way in which they supposed the gods to take knowledge of human affairs, and to aid men, was by their personally appearing in this form. See Homer's Odyssey, xvii 485. Catullus, 64. 384 Ovid's Metamorphosis, i. 212. (*Kuinoel.*) Thus Homer says:

For in similitude of strangers oft
The gods who can with ease all shapes assume,
Repair to populous cities, where they mark
Th' outrageous and the righteous deeds of men.
COWPER.

Among the Hindoos, the opinion has

12 And they called Barnabas,
Jupiter; and Paul, Mercurius, because he was the chief speaker.
13 Then the priest of Jupiter,
which was before their city, brought
oxen and garlands unto the gates,
and [a] would have done sacrifice
with the people.
14 *Which*, when the apostles,
Barnabas and Paul, heard *of*, they
[b] rent their clothes, and ran in
among the people, crying out,
15 And saying, Sirs, why do ye
these things? We [c] also are men
of like passions with you, and
preach unto you, that ye should
turn from these vanities [d] unto [e] the
living God, which made [f] heaven
and earth, and the sea, and all
things that are therein:

a Dan.2.46. b Matt.26.65. c c.10.26. James 5.17. Rev.19.10. d 1Sam.12.21. 1Ki.16.13. Jer.14.22. Jno.2.8. 1Cor.8.4 e 1Thess.1.9. f Gen.1.1. Ps.33.6; 146.6. Rev.14.7.

---

been prevalent that there have been many incarnations of their gods.

12. *And they called Barnabas, Jupiter.* Jupiter was represented as the most powerful of all the gods of the ancients. He was represented as the son of Saturn and Ops, and was educated in a cave on mount Ida, in the island of Crete. The worship of Jupiter was almost universal. He was the Ammon of Africa, the Belus of Babylon, the Osiris of Egypt. His common appellation was, the father of gods and men. He was usually represented as sitting upon a golden or an ivory throne, holding in one hand a thunderbolt, and in the other a sceptre of cypress. His power was supposed to extend over other gods; and every thing was subservient to his will, except the fates. There is the most abundant proof that he was worshipped in the region of Lycaonia, and throughout Asia Minor. There was besides a fable among the inhabitants of Lycaonia that Jupiter and Mercury had once visited that place, and had been received by Philemon. The whole fable is related by Ovid. Metam. 8. 611, &c. ¶ *And Paul, Mercurius.* Mercury, called by the Greeks *Hermes*, was a celebrated god of antiquity. No less than five of this name are mentioned by Cicero. The most celebrated was the son of Jupiter and Maia. He was the messenger of the gods, and of Jupiter in particular; he was the patron of travellers and shepherds; he conducted the souls of the dead into the infernal regions; and he *presided over orators, and declaimers*, and merchants; and he was also the god of thieves, pickpockets, and all dishonest persons. He was regarded as *the god of eloquence;* and as light, rapid, and quick in his movements. The conjecture of Chrysostom is, that Barnabas was a large, athletic man, and was hence taken for Jupiter; and that Paul was small in his person, and was hence supposed to be Mercury ¶ *Because he was the chief speaker.* The office of Mercury was to deliver the messages of the gods; and as Paul only had been discoursing, he was supposed to be Mercury

13. *Then the priest of Jupiter.* He whose office it was to conduct the worship of Jupiter, by offering sacrifices, &c. ¶ *Which was before their city.* The word "which" here refers not to *the priest*, but to *Jupiter*. The temple or image of Jupiter was in front of their city, or near the gates. Ancient cities were supposed to be under the protection of particular gods; and their *image*, or a temple for their worship, was placed commonly in a conspicuous place at the entrance of the city. ¶ *Brought oxen.* Probably brought two—one to be sacrificed to each. It was common to sacrifice bullocks to Jupiter. ¶ *And garlands.* The victims of sacrifice were usually decorated with ribands and chaplets of flowers. See *Kuinoel.* ¶ *Unto the gates.* The gates of the city where were the images or temple of the gods. ¶ *Would have done sacrifice.* Would have offered sacrifice to Barnabas and Paul. This the priest deemed a part of his office. And here we have a remarkable and most affecting instance of the folly and stupidity of idolatry.

14. *Which, when the apostles.* Barnabas is called an apostle because he was *sent forth* by the church on a particular message (ch. xiii. 3. Comp. ch. xiv. 26); not because he had been chosen to the peculiar work of the apostleship—to bear witness to the life and resurrection of Christ See Note, ch. i. 22. ¶ *They rent their clothes.* As an expression of their abhorrence of what they were doing, and of their deep grief that they should thus debase themselves by offering worship to men. See Note, Matt. xxvi. 65.

15. *And saying, Sirs.* Greek, *Men.* ¶ *Why do ye these things?* This is an expression of solemn remonstrance at the folly of their conduct in worshipping those who were *men*. The *abhorrence* which

16 Who [a] in times past suffered all nations to walk in their own ways.
17 Nevertheless, [b] he left not himself without witness, in that he did good, and gave us rain [c] from heaven, and fruitful seasons, filling our hearts with food and gladness.

a Ps.81.12. c.17.30. b Rom.1.20. c Job 5.10. Ps.147.8. Matt.5.45.

they evinced at this, may throw strong light on the rank and character of the Lord Jesus Christ. When an offer was made to worship Paul and Barnabas, they shrank from it with strong expressions of indignation and abhorrence. Yet when similar worship was offered to the Lord Jesus, when he was addressed by Thomas in the language of worship, "My Lord and my God" (John xx. 28), he commended the disciple. For this act he uttered not the slightest reproof. Nay, he approved it; and expressed his approbation of others who should also do it. ver. 29. Comp. John v. 23. How can this difference be accounted for, except on the supposition that the Lord Jesus was divine? Would he, if a mere man, receive homage as God, when his disciples rejected it with horror? ¶ *Of like passions with you.* We are *men* like yourselves. We have no claim, no pretensions to any thing more. The word "passions" here means simply that they had the common feelings and propensities of men; we have the *nature* of men; the affections of men. It does not mean that they were subject to any improper *passions*, to ill temper, &c. as some have supposed; but that they did not pretend to be gods. 'We need food and drink; we are exposed to pain and sickness, and death.' The Latin Vulgate renders it, 'We are *mortal* like yourselves.' The expression stands opposed to the proper conception of God. who is not subject to these affections, who is most blessed and immortal. Such a Being *only* is to be worshipped; and the apostles remonstrated strongly with them on the folly of paying religious homage to beings like themselves. Comp. James v. 17, "Elias [Elijah] was a man subject to like passions as we are," &c. ¶ *That ye should turn from these vanities.* That you should cease to worship idols. Idols are often called vanities, or vain things. Deut. xxxii. 21. 2 Kings xvii. 15. 1 Kings xvi. 13. 26. Jer. ii. 5; viii 19; x. 8. Jonah ii. 8. They are called *vanities*, and often a *lie*, or lying vanities, as opposed to the living and true God, because they are *unreal*, because they have no power to help, because confidence in them is vain. ¶ *Unto the living God.* 1 Thess. i. 9. He is called the *living* God to distinguish him from idols. See Note, Matt. xvi. 16. ¶ *Which made heaven,* &c. Whe thus showed that he was the only proper object of worship. This doctrine, that there was *one* God, who had made all things, was new to them. They worshipped multitudes of divinities; and though they regarded Jupiter as the father of gods and men, yet they had no conception tha all things had been formed from nothing by the will of one Infinite Being.

16. *Who in times past.* Previous to the gospel; in past ages. ¶ *Suffered all nations.* Permitted all nations; that is, all Gentiles. Acts xvii. 30, "And the times of this ignorance God winked at." ¶ *To walk in their own ways.* To conduct themselves without the restraints and instructions of a written law. They were permitted to follow their own reason and passions, and their own system of religion. He gave them no written laws, and sent to them no messengers. *Why* he did this we cannot determine. It might have been, among other reasons, to show to the world conclusively, (1.) The insufficiency of *reason* to guide men in the matters of religion. The experiment was made under the most favourable circumstances. The most enlightened nations, the Greeks and Romans, were left to pursue the inquiry, and failed no less than the most degraded tribes of men. The trial was made for four thousand years, and attended with the same results every where. (2.) It showed the need of revelation to guide man. (3.) It evinced, beyond the possibility of mistake, the depravity of man. In all nations, in all circumstances, men had shown the same alienation from God. By suffering them to walk in their *own* ways, it was seen that those ways were sin, and that some power more than human wasnecessary to bring men back to God.

17. *Nevertheless.* Though he gave them no revelation. ¶ *He left not himself without witness.* He gave demonstration of his existence, and of his moral character. ¶ *In that he did good.* By doing good. The manner in which he did it, he immediately specifies. Idols did *not* do good or confer favours, and were therefore unworthy of their confidence. ¶ *And gave us rain from heaven.* Rain from above from the clouds. Mark viii. 11. Luke ix 54; xvii. 29; xxi. 11 John vi. 31, 32

18 And with these sayings
scarce restrained they the people,
that they had not done sacrifice
unto them.
19 And there came thither *cer-*
tain Jews from Antioch and Iconium, who persuaded the people, and
having [a] stoned Paul, drew *him* out
of the city, supposing he had been
dead.

a 2Cor.11.25.

Rain is one of the evidences of *his* goodness. Man could not cause it; and without it, regulated at proper intervals of time, and in proper quantities, the earth would soon be one wide scene of desolation. There is scarcely any thing that more certainly indicates unceasing care and wisdom than the needful and refreshing showers of rain. The sun and stars move by fixed laws, whose operation we can see and anticipate. The falling of rain and dew is regulated by laws which we cannot trace, and *seems* therefore to be poured, as it were, directly from God's hollow hand. Ps. cxlvii. 8, "Who covereth the heaven with clouds; who prepareth rain for the earth."

'He sends his show'rs of blessings down,
To cheer the plains below;
He makes the grass the mountains crown,
And corn in valleys grow.

"The cheering wind, the flying cloud,
Obey his mighty word;
With songs and honours sounding loud,
Praise ye the sovereign Lord."—WATTS.

¶ *And fruitful seasons.* Seasons when the earth produces abundance. It is remarkable, and a shining proof of the divine goodness, that so few seasons are unfruitful. The earth yields her increase; and the labours of the husbandman are crowned with success: and the goodness of God demands the expressions of praise. His ancient covenant God does not forget (Gen. viii. 22), though *man* forgets it, and disregards his great Benefactor. ¶ *Filling our hearts with food.* The word *hearts* is here used as a Hebraism, to denote *persons themselves;* filling *us* with food, &c. Comp. Matt. xii. 40. ¶ *Gladness.* Joy; comfort—the comfort arising from the supply of our constantly returning wants. This is proof of ever watchful goodness. It is demonstration at once that there *is* a God, and that he is good. It would be easy for God to withdraw these blessings, and leave us to want. A single word, or a single deviation from the fulness of benevolence, would blast all these comforts, and leave us to lamentation, wo, and death. Ps. cxlv. 15, 16.

'The eyes of all wait upon thee,
And thou givest them their food in due season.
Thou openest thine hand,
And satisfiest the desire of all the living."

18. *And with these sayings.* With these arguments. ¶ *Scarce restrained they the people.* They were so fully satisfied that the gods had appeared, and were so full of zeal to do them honour.

19. *And there came thither certain Jews.* Not satisfied with having expelled them from Antioch and Iconium, they still pursued them.—Persecutors often exhibit a zeal and perseverance in a bad cause, which it would be well if Christians evinced in a holy cause. Men will often travel farther to do evil than they will to do good; and many men show more zeal in opposing the gospel than professed Christians do in advancing it. ¶ *Antioch and Iconium.* Note, ch. xiii. 14. 51. ¶ *Who persuaded the people.* That they were impostors; and who excited their rage against them. ¶ *And having stoned Paul.* Whom they were just before ready to worship as a god! What a striking instance of the fickleness and instability of idolaters! and what a striking instance of the instability and uselessness of mere *popularity.* Just before, they were ready to adore him; now, they sought to put him to death. Nothing is more fickle than mere popular favour. The unbounded admiration of a man may soon be changed into unbounded indignation and contempt! It was well for Paul that he was not *seeking* this popularity, and that he did not depend on it for happiness. He had a good conscience; he was engaged in a good cause; he was under the protection of God; and his happiness was to be sought from a higher source than the applause of men, fluctuating and uncertain as the waves of the sea. To this transaction Paul referred when he enumerated his trials, in 2 Cor. xi. 25, "Once was I stoned." ¶ *Drew him out of the city.* Probably in haste, and in popular rage, as if he was unfit to be *in* the city, and was unworthy of a decent burial; for it does not appear that they contemplated an interment, but indignantly dragged him beyond the walls of the city to leave him there. Such sufferings and trials it cost to establish that religion in the world which has shed so many blessings on man, and which now crowns us with comfort, and saves us from the abominations and degradations of idolatry

20 Howbeit, as the disciples stood round about him, he rose up, and came into the city: and the next day he departed with Barnabas to Derbe.

21 And when they had preached the gospel to that city, and [1] had taught many, they returned again to Lystra, and *to* Iconium, and Antioch,

22 Confirming the souls of the disciples, *and* exhorting them to

[1] *Had made many disciples.*

here, and from the pains of hell hereafter. ¶ *Supposing he had been dead.* The next verse shows that he was really *not* dead, though many commentators, as well as the Jews, have supposed that he was, and was miraculously restored to life. It is remarkable that Barnabas was not exposed to this popular fury. But it is to be remembered that Paul was the chief speaker, and it was his peculiar zeal that exposed him to this tumult.

20. *Howbeit.* But. Notwithstanding the supposition that he was dead. ¶ *As the disciples stood round about him.* It would seem that *they* did not suppose that he was dead; but might be expecting that he would revive. ¶ *He rose up,* &c. Most commentators have supposed that this was the effect of a miracle. They have maintained that he could not have risen so soon, and entered into the city, without the interposition of miraculous power. (Calvin, Doddridge, Clark, &c.) But the commentators have asserted that which is not intimated by the sacred penman. Nor is there propriety in supposing the intervention of miraculous agency where it is not necessary. The probability is, that he was *stunned* by a blow—perhaps a single blow—and after a short time recovered from it. Nothing is more common than thus by a violent blow on the head to be rendered apparently lifeless, the effect of which soon is over, and the person restored to strength. Pricæus and Wetstein suppose that Paul *feigned* himself to be dead, and when out of danger rose and returned to the city. But this is wholly improbable. ¶ *And came into the city.* It is remarkable that he should have returned again into the same city. But probably it was only among the new converts that he showed himself. The Jews supposed that he was dead; and it does not appear that he again exposed himself to their rage. ¶ *And the next day,* &c. The opposition here was such that it was vain to attempt to preach there any longer. Having been seen by the disciples after his supposed death, their faith was confirmed, and he departed to preach in another place. ¶ *To Derbe.* ver. 6.

21. *Had taught many.* Or rather, had made many disciples (*margin*). ¶ *To Lystra.* ver. 6. ¶ *And to Iconium.* ver. 1. We have here a remarkable instance of the *courage* of the apostles. In these very places they had been persecuted and stoned, and yet in the face of danger they ventured to return. The welfare of the infant churches they deemed of more consequence than their own safety; and they threw themselves again into the midst of danger, to comfort and strengthen those just converted to God. There are times when ministers should not count their own lives dear to them (Acts xx. 24), but when they should fearlessly throw themselves into the midst of danger, confiding only in the protecting care of their God and Saviour.

22. *Confirming. Strengthening.* Ἐπιστηρίζοντες. The expression "to confirm" has in some churches a technical signification, denoting "to admit to the full privileges of a Christian, by the imposition of hands." (*Johnson.*) It is scarcely necessary to say that the word here refers to no such rite. It has no reference to any imposition of hands, nor to the thing which is usually supposed to be denoted by the rite of "confirmation." It means simply, that they *established, strengthened,* made firm, or encouraged by the presentation of truth, and by the motives of the gospel. Whether the rite of confirmation, as practised by some churches, be founded on the authority of the New Testament or not, it is certain that it can receive no support from this passage. The truth was, that these were young converts; that they were surrounded by enemies, exposed to temptations, and to dangers; that they had as yet but a slight acquaintance with the truths of the gospel, and that it was therefore important that they should be further instructed in the truth, and established in the faith of the gospel. This was what Paul and Barnabas returned to accomplish. There is not the slightest evidence that they had not been admitted to the full privileges of the church before, or that any *ceremony* was now performed in confirming or strengthening them. ¶ *The souls.* The minds, the hearts; or *the disciples themselves.* ¶ *Disciples.* They were as yet *scholars,* or *learners.*

continue [a] in the faith, and that [b]
we must through much tribulation
enter into the kingdom of God.
23 And when they had ordained
them elders in every church, and
had prayed with fasting, they commended them to the Lord, on whom
they believed.

a c.13.43. b Rom.8.17. 2Tim.3.12.

and the apostles returned to instruct them further in the doctrines of Christ. ¶ *And exhorting them*, &c. ch. xiii. 43. ¶ *In the faith*. In the belief of the gospel. ¶ *And that we must*. καὶ ὅτι δεῖ. That it is fit or proper that we should, &c. Not that it is in itself fixed by any fatal necessity; but that such is the nature of religion, and such the wickedness and opposition of the world, *that it will happen*. We are not to expect that it will be otherwise. We are to calculate on it when we become Christians. *Why* it is proper, or fit, the apostle did not state. But we may remark that it is proper, (1.) Because such is the opposition of the world to pure religion, that it cannot be avoided. Of this they had had striking demonstration in Lystra and Iconium. (2.) It is necessary to reclaim us from wandering, and to keep us in the path of duty. Ps. cxix. 67. 71. (3.) It is necessary to wean us from the world, to keep before one's mind the great truth, that we have here "no continuing city, and no abiding place." Trial here, makes us pant for a world of rest. The opposition of sinners makes us desire that world where "the wicked shall cease from troubling," and where there shall be eternal friendship and peace. (4.) When we are persecuted and afflicted, we may remember that it has been the lot of Christians from the beginning. We tread a path that has been watered by the tears of the saints, and rendered sacred by the shedding of the best blood on the earth. The Saviour trod that path; and it is enough that the "disciple be as his master, and the servant as his lord." Matt. x. 24, 25. ¶ *Through much tribulation*. Through many afflictions. ¶ *Enter into the kingdom of God*. Be saved. Enter into heaven. Note, Matt. iii. 2.

23. *And when they had ordained*. Χειροτονήσαντες. The word *ordain* we now use in an ecclesiastical sense, to denote a setting apart to an office by the imposition of hands. But it is evident that the word here is not employed in that sense. That imposition of hands *might* have occurred in setting apart afterwards to this office is certainly possible, but it is not implied in the word employed here, and did not take place in the transaction to which this word refers. The word occurs but in one other place in the New Testament, 2 Cor. viii 19, where it is applied to Luke, and translated, "who was also chosen of the church (i. e. appointed or elected by suffrage by the churches), to travel with us" &c. The verb properly denotes *to stretch out the hand*; and as it was customary to elect to office, or to vote, by stretching out or elevating the hand, so the word simply means to elect, appoint, or designate to any office. The word here refers simply to an *election* or *appointment* of the elders. It is said indeed that Paul and Barnabas did this. But probably all that is meant by it is, that they presided in the assembly when the choice was made. It does not mean that they appointed them without consulting the church; but it evidently means that they appointed them in the usual way of appointing officers, by the suffrages of the people. See *Schleusner*, and the notes of Doddridge and Calvin. ¶ *Ordained them*. Appointed for *the disciples*, or for the church. It is not meant that the elders were ordained for the apostles. ¶ *Elders*. Greek, Presbyters. Literally this word refers to the aged. Note, ch. xi. 30. But it may also be a word relating to office, denoting those who were more experienced than others, to preside over and to instruct the rest. What was the nature of this office, and what was the design of the appointment, is not intimated in this word. All that seems to be implied is, that they were to take the charge of the churches during the absence of the apostles. The apostles were about to leave them. They were just organized into churches; were inexperienced; needed counsel and direction; were exposed to dangers; and it was necessary, therefore, that persons should be designated to watch over the spiritual interests of the brethren. The probability is, that they performed all the functions that were required in the infant and feeble churches; in exhorting, instructing, governing, &c. The more experienced and able would be most likely to be active in exhorting and instructing the brethren; and all would be useful in counselling and guiding the flock. The same thing occurred in the church at Ephesus. See Notes on Acts xx. 17 -28. It is not improbable

24 And after they had passed throughout Pisidia, they came to Pamphylia.

25 And when they had preached the word in Perga, they went down into Attalia:

26 And thence sailed to Antioch, [a] from whence they had been recommended to [b] the grace of God for the work which they fulfilled.

27 And when they were come, and had gathered the church together they rehearsed [c] all that God had done with them, and how he

a c.13.1,3. b c.15.40. c c.15.4.

that the business of instructing, or teaching, would be gradually confined to the more talented and able of the elders, and that the others would be concerned mainly in governing and directing the general affairs of the church. ¶ *In every church.* It is implied here that there were *elders in each church;* that is, that in each church there was more than one. See ch. xv. 21, where a similar phraseology occurs, and where it is evident that there was more than one reader of the law of Moses in each city. Titus i. 5, "I left thee in Crete, that thou shouldst .... ordain *elders in every city.*" Acts xx. 17, "And from Miletus he sent to Ephesus, and called *the elders of the church.*" It could not mean, therefore, that they appointed a *single* minister or pastor to each church. but they committed the whole affairs of the church to a bench of elders. ¶ *And had prayed with fasting.* With the church. They were about to leave them. They had intrusted the interests of the church to a body of men chosen for this purpose; and they now commended the church and its elders together to God. Probably they had no prospect of seeing them again; and they parted as ministers and people should part, and as Christian friends should part, with humble prayer, commending themselves to the protecting care of God. ¶ *They commended them,* &c. They *committed* the infant church to the guardianship of the Lord. They were feeble, inexperienced, and exposed to dangers; but in his hands they were safe. ¶ *To the Lord,* &c. The Lord Jesus. The connexion shows that he is particularly referred to. In his hands, the redeemed are secure. When we part with Christian friends, we may, with confidence, leave them in his holy care and keeping.

24 *Throughout Pisidia.* Note ch. xiii. 14. ¶ *They came to Pamphylia.* Note, ch. xiii. 13. These places they had visited before.

25. *In Perga.* Note, ch. xiii. 13. ¶ *They went down into Attalia.* This was a city of Pamphylia, situated on the sea-shore. It was built by Attalus Philadelphus, king of Pergamus who gave it his own name. It is now called *Antali.* (*Rob. Cal.*)

26. *And thence sailed to Antioch.* Note, ch. xi. 19. ¶ *From whence they had been recommended,* &c. Where they had been appointed to this missionary tour by the church. ch. xiii. 1—4. ¶ *To the grace of God.* His favour and protection had been implored for them in their perilous undertaking. ¶ *For the work which they fulfilled.* This shows conclusively, (1.) That they had accomplished fully the work which was originally contemplated. It was strictly a *missionary tour* among the Gentiles. It was an important and hazardous enterprise; and was the first in which the church formally engaged. Hence so much importance is attached to it, and so faithful a record of it is preserved. (2.) It shows that the act by which they were set apart to this (Acts xiii. 1—3) was not an ordination to the ministerial office. It was an appointment to a missionary tour. (3.) It shows that the act was not an appointment to *the apostleship.* Paul was an apostle before by the express appointment of the Saviour; and Barnabas was never an apostle in the original and proper sense of the term. It was a designation to a temporary work, which was now fulfilled.

We may remark, also, in regard to this *missionary tour* (1.) That the work of *missions* is one which early engaged the attention of Christians. (2.) It entered into their *plans,* and was one in which the church was deeply interested. (3.) The work of missions is attended with danger. Men are now no less hostile to the gospel than they were in Lystra and Iconium. (4.) Missionaries should be sustained by the prayers of the church. And, (5.) In the conduct of Paul and Barnabas, missionaries have an example in founding churches, and in regard to their own trials and persecutions. If Paul and Barnabas were persecuted, missionaries may be now. And if the grace of Christ was sufficient to sustain them, it is not the less sufficient to sustain those of our own times amidst all the dangers attending the preaching of the cross in pagan lands.

27. *They rehearsed,* &c. ch. xi. 4. They

had opened [a] the door of faith unto the Gentiles.

28 And there they abode long time with the disciples.

a 1Cor.16.9. 2Cor.2.12. Rev.3.8.

CHAPTER XV.

AND [b] certain men which came down from Judea, taught the brethren, *and said*, Except [c] ye be

b Gal.2.12. c Jno.7.22.

related what had happened; their dangers and their success. This they did because they had been sent out by the church, and it was proper that they should give an account of their work; and because it furnished a suitable occasion of gratitude to God for his mercy. ¶ *All that God had done*, &c. In protecting, guarding them, &c. All was traced to God. ¶ *Had opened the door of faith.* Had furnished an opportunity of preaching the gospel to the Gentiles. 1 Cor. xvi. 9. 2 Cor. ii. 12.

28. *And there they abode.* At Antioch. ¶ *Long time.* How long is not intimated; but we hear no more of them until the council at Jerusalem, mentioned in the next chapter. If the transactions recorded in this chapter occurred, as is supposed, about A. D. 45 or 46, and the council at Jerusalem assembled A. D. 51 or 53, as is supposed, then here is an interval of from five to eight years in which we have no account of them. Where they were, or what was their employment in this interval, the sacred historian has not informed us. It is certain, however, that Paul made several journeys of which we have no particular record in the New Testament; and it is possible that some of those journeys occurred during this interval. Thus he preached the gospel as far as Illyricum. Rom. xv. 19. And in 2 Cor. xi. 23—27, there is an account of trials and persecutions, of many of which we have no distinct record, and which might have occurred during this interval. We may be certain that these holy men were not idle. And we may learn from their example to fill up our time with usefulness; to bear all persecutions and trials without a murmur; and to acknowledge the good hand of God in our preservation in our travels; in our defence when we are persecuted; in all the opportunities which may be open before us to do good; and in all the success which may attend our efforts. Christians should remember that it is *God* who opens doors of usefulness; and they should regard it as a matter of thanksgiving that such doors *are* opened, and that they are permitted to spread the gospel, whatever toil it may cost, whatever persecution they may endure, whatever perils they may encounter.

CHAPTER XV.

1. *And certain men.* These were men undoubtedly who had been Jews, but who were now converted to Christianity. The fact that they were willing to refer the matter in dispute to the apostles and elders (ver. 2), shows that they had professedly embraced the Christian religion. The account which follows is a record of the first internal dissension which occurred in the Christian church. Hitherto they had been struggling against external foes. Violent persecutions had raged, and had fully occupied the attention of Christians. But now the churches were at peace. They enjoyed great external prosperity in Antioch. And the great enemy of souls took occasion then, as he has often done in similar circumstances since, to excite contentions in the church itself; so that when external violence could not destroy it, an effort was made to secure the same object by internal dissension and strife. The history, therefore, is particularly important, as it is the record of the first unhappy debate which arose in the bosom of the church. It is further important, as it shows the manner in which such controversies were settled in apostolic times; and as it established some very important principles respecting the perpetuity of the religious rites of the Jews. ¶ *Came down from Judea.* To Antioch, and to the regions adjacent which had been visited by the apostles. ver. 23. Judea was a high and hilly region, and going from that toward the level countries adjacent to the sea, was represented to be descending or going down. ¶ *Taught the brethren.* That is, Christians. They endeavoured to *convince* them of the necessity of keeping the laws of Moses. ¶ *Except ye be circumcised.* This was the leading or principal rite of the Jewish religion. It was indispensable to the name and privileges of a Jew. Proselytes to their religion were circumcised as well as native-born Jews, and they held it to be indispensable to salvation.—It is evident from this, that Paul and Barnabas had dispensed with this rite in regard to the Gentile converts, and that they intended to found the Christian church on the principle that the Jewish ceremonies were to cease. When however, it was necessary to conciliate

circumcised after [a] the manner of
Moses, ye cannot be saved.

2 When therefore Paul and Barnabas had no small dissension and disputation with them, they determined that [b] Paul and Barnabas, and certain other of them, should go up to Jerusalem, unto the apostles and elders, about this question.

a Lev.12.3.

b Gal.2.1.

the minds of the Jews and to prevent contention, Paul did not hesitate to practise circumcision. ch. xvi. 3. ¶ *After the manner of Moses.* According to the custom which Moses commanded; according to the Mosaic ritual. ¶ *Ye cannot be saved.* The Jews regarded this as indispensable to salvation. The grounds on which they would press it on the attention of Gentile converts would be very plausible, and such as would produce much embarrassment. For, (1.) It would be maintained that the laws of Moses were the laws of God, and were therefore unchangeable; and, (2.) It would doubtless be maintained that the religion of the Messiah was only a completing and perfecting of the Jewish religion;—that it was designed simply to carry out its principles according to the promises, and not to subvert and destroy any thing that had been established by divine authority.—It is usually not difficult to perplex and embarrass young converts with questions of modes, and rites, and forms of religion; and it is not uncommon that a revival is followed by some contention just like this. Opposing sects urge the claims of their peculiar rites, and seek to make proselytes, and introduce contention and strife into an otherwise peaceful and happy Christian community.

2. *Had no small dissension and disputation.* The word rendered *dissension* (στάσις) denotes sometimes sedition or intestine war, and sometimes earnest and violent disputation or controversy. Acts xxiii. 7. 10. In this place it clearly denotes that there was earnest and warm discussion; but it is *not* implied that there was any improper heat or temper on the part of Paul and Barnabas. Important principles were to be settled in regard to the organization of the church. Doctrines were advanced by the Judaizing teachers which were false, and which tended to great strife and disorder in the church. Those doctrines were urged with great zeal, were declared to be essential to salvation, and would therefore tend greatly to distract the minds of Christians, and to produce great anxiety. It became therefore necessary to meet them with a determined purpose, and to establish the truth on an immoveable basis.—And the case shows that it is right to "contend earnestly for the faith" (Jude 3); and when similar cases occur it is proper to resist the approach of error with all the arguments which may be at our command, and with all the weapons which truth can furnish. It is further implied here, that it is the duty of the ministers of the gospel to defend the truth and to oppose error. Paul and Barnabas regarded themselves as set for this purpose (comp. Phil. i. 17, "Knowing that I am set for the *defence* of the gospel"); and Christian ministers should be *qualified* to defend the truth; and should be willing with a proper spirit and with great earnestness to maintain the doctrines revealed. ¶ *They determined.* There was no prospect that the controversy would be settled by contention and argument. It would seem, from this statement, that those who came down from Judea were also willing that the whole matter should be referred to the apostles at Jerusalem. The reason for this may have been, (1.) That Jerusalem would be regarded by them as the source of authority in the Christian church, as it had been among the Jews. (2.) Most of the apostles and the most experienced Christians were there. They had listened to the instructions of Christ himself; had been long in the church; and were supposed to be better acquainted with its design and its laws. (3.) Those who came from Judea would not be likely to acknowledge the authority of Paul as an apostle: the authority of those at Jerusalem they would recognise. (4.) They might have had a very confident expectation that the decision there would be in their favour. The question had not been agitated there. They had all been Jews. And it is certain that they continued as yet to attend in the temple service, and to conform to the Jewish customs. They might have expected therefore, with great confidence, that the decision would be in their favour, and they were willing to refer it to those at Jerusalem. ¶ *Certain other of them* Of the brethren; probably of each party They did not go to debate; or to give their opinion; or to vote in the case themselves; but to lay the question fairly before the apostles and elders. ¶ *Unto the*

3 And being [a] brought on their way by the church, they passed through Phenice and Samaria, declaring the conversion [b] of the Gentiles: and they caused great joy [c] unto all the brethren.

4 And when they were come to Jerusalem, they were received of the church, and *of* the apostles and elders; and they [d] declared all things that God had done with them.

5 But [1] there rose up certain of the sect of the Pharisees which believed, saying, [e] That it was needful to circumcise them, and to command *them* to keep the law of Moses.

a Rom.15.24. 1Cor.16.6,11.3 Jno.6. b c.14,27. c Luke 15.7,10. d c.21.19. 1 or, rose up, said they, certain. e ver.1.

apostles. The authority of the apostles in such a case would be acknowledged by all. They had been immediately instructed by the Saviour, and had the promise of infallible guidance in the organization of the church. Notes, Matt. xvi. 19; xviii. 18. ¶ *And elders.* Note, ch. xi. 30. *Gr.* Presbyters. See Note, ch. xiv. 23. Who these were, or what was their office and authority, it is not easy now to determine. It may refer to the *aged* men in the church at Jerusalem, or to those who were appointed to rule and to preach in connexion with the apostles. As in the synagogue it was customary to determine questions by the advice of a bench of elders, there is no improbability in the supposition that the apostles would imitate that custom, and appoint a similar arrangement in the Christian church. (*Grotius.*) It is generally agreed that this is the journey to which Paul refers in Gal. ii. 1—10. If so, it happened fourteen years after his conversion. Gal. ii. 1. It was done in accordance with the divine command, "by revelation." Gal. ii. 2. And among those who went with him was Titus, who was afterwards so much distinguished as his companion. Gal. ii. 3. ¶ *About this question* The question whether the ceremonial laws of Moses were binding on Christian converts. In regard to the nature and design of this council at Jerusalem, see Note on ver. 30, 31.

3. *And being brought on their way by the church.* Being attended and conducted by the Christian brethren. See Note, Rom. xv 24. It was customary for the Christians to attend the apostles in their travels. Comp. 1 Cor. xvi. 6.11. 3 John 6. ¶ *Through Phenice.* Note, ch. xi. 19. ¶ *And Samaria.* These places were directly on their route to Jerusalem. ¶ *Declaring the conversion, &c.* Of the Gentiles in Antioch, and in the regions in Asia Minor through which they had travelled. These remarkable events they would naturally communicate with joy to the Christians with whom they would have intercourse in their journey. ¶ *Caused great joy.* At the news of the extensive spread of the gospel. It was an indication of their deep feeling in the interests of religion, that they thus rejoiced. Where Christians are themselves awake, and engaged in the service of Christ, they rejoice at the news of the conversion of sinners. Where they are cold, they hear such news with indifference, or with the utmost unconcern. One way of testing our feelings on the subject of religion is, by the emotions which we have when we hear of extensive and glorious revivals of religion. Comp. Note, Acts viii. 8.

4. *They were received of the church.* By the church, in a hospitable and friendly manner. They were acknowledged as Christian brethren, and received with Christian kindness. See Gal. ii. 9. ¶ *And they declared.* Paul and Barnabas, and those with them. That is, they stated the case; the remarkable conversion of the Gentiles, the evidence of their piety, and the origin of the present dispute.

5. *But there rose up, &c.* It has been doubted whether these are the words of Paul and Barnabas, relating what occurred at Antioch; or whether they are the words of Luke, recording what took place at Jerusalem. The correct exposition is probably that which refers it to the latter. For, (1.) This seems to be the most obvious interpretation. (2.) The use of the words "rose up" implies that. Those who disturbed the church at Antioch are said to have come down from Judea (ver 1); and if this place referred to that occurrence, the same words would have been retained. (3.) The particular specification here of "the sect of the Pharisees," looks as if this was an occurrence taking place at Jerusalem. No such specification exists respecting those who came down to Antioch; but it would seem here, as if this party in Jerusalem resolved still to abide by the law, and to impose those rites on the Christian converts. However, this interpretation is

6 And the apostles and elders came together, [a] for to consider of this matter.

7 And when there had been much disputing, Peter rose up and said unto them, Men *and* brethren, ye know [b] how that a good while ago God made choice among us, that the Gentiles by my mouth should hear the word of the gospel, and believe.

8 And God, which [c] knoweth the hearts, bare them witness, giving them the Holy Ghost, even as *he did* unto us;

9 And put no difference between us and them, purifying [d] their hearts by faith.

10 Now therefore why tempt ye God, to put a yoke [e] upon the neck of the disciples, which neither our fathers nor we were able to bear?

a Matt.18.20. b Matt.16.18,19. c.10.20. c c.1.24. d Heb.9.13,14. 1Pet.1.22. e Gal.5.1.

by no means certain. ¶ *Which believed.* Who maintained, or taught. ¶ *That it was needful,* &c. Note, ver. 1.

6. *And the apostles and elders,* &c. They came together in accordance with the authority in Matt. xviii. 19, 20. It would seem, also, that the whole church was convened on this occasion; and that they concurred, at least, in the judgment expressed in this case. See ver. 12. 22, 23. ¶ *For to consider this matter.* Not to decide it arbitrarily, or even by authority, without deliberation; but to compare their views, and to express the result of the whole to the church at Antioch. It was a grave and difficult question, deeply affecting the entire constitution of the Christian church, and they therefore solemnly engaged in deliberation on the subject.

7. *Much disputing.* Or rather, much *inquiry,* or *deliberation.* With our word *disputing* we commonly connect the idea of heat and anger. This is not necessarily implied in the word used here. It might have been calm, solemn, deliberate inquiry; and there is no evidence that it was conducted with undue warmth or anger. ¶ *Peter rose up and said.* Peter was probably the most aged, and was most accustomed to speak. ch. ii. 14, &c. iii. 6. 12. Besides, there was a particular reason for his speaking here, as he had been engaged in similar scenes, and understood the case, and had had evidence that God had converted sinners *without* the Mosaic rites, and knew that it would have been inexpedient to have imposed these rites on those who had thus been converted. ¶ *A good while ago.* See ch. x. Some time since. So long since that there had been opportunity to ascertain whether it was necessary to observe the laws of Moses in order to the edification of the church. ¶ *God made choice,* &c. That is, of all the apostles, he designated me to engage in this work. Comp. Note, Matt. xvi. 18, with Acts x ¶ *That the Gentiles.* Cornelius, and those who were assembled with him at Cæsarea. This was the first case that had occurred, and therefore it was important to appeal to it

8. *And God, which knoweth the hearts* ch. i. 24. God thus knew whether they were *true* converts or not, and gave a demonstration that he acknowledged them as his. ¶ *Giving them the Holy Ghost,* &c. ch. x. 45, 46.

9. *And put no difference,* &c. Though they had not been circumcised, and though they did not conform to the law of Moses. Thus God showed that the observance of these rites was not necessary in order to the true conversion of men, and to acceptance with him. He did not give us, who are Jews, any advantage over them, but justified and purified all in the same manner. ¶ *Purifying their hearts.* Thus giving the best evidence that he had renewed them, and admitted them to favour with him. ¶ *By faith.* By believing on the Lord Jesus Christ. This showed that the plan on which God was now about to show favour to men, was not by external rites and ceremonies, but by a scheme which required faith as the only condition of acceptance. It is further implied here, that there is no true faith which does not purify the heart.

10. *Why tempt ye God?* Why provoke him to displeasure? Why, since he has shown his determination to accept them *without* such rites, do you provoke him by attempting to impose on his own people rites without his authority, and against his manifest will? The *argument* is, that God had already accepted them. To attempt to impose these rites would be to provoke him to anger; to introduce observances which he had shown it was his purpose should now be abolished. ¶ *To put a yoke.* That which would be burdensome and oppressive, or which would infringe on their just freedom, as the children of God. It is called in Gal. v. 1 "a yoke of bondage." Note, Matt. xxiii. 4

11 But we believe that through [a] the grace of the Lord Jesus Christ we shall be saved, even as they.

12 Then all the multitude kept silence, and gave audience to Barnabas and Paul, declaring what miracles and wonders God had wrought [b] among the Gentiles by them.

13 And after they had held their peace, James answered, saying, Men *and* brethren, hearken unto me:

14 Simeon hath declared [c] how God at the first did visit the Gentiles, to take out of them a people for his name.

15 And to this agree the words of the prophets; as it is written,[d]

a Rom.3.24. Eph.2.8. Tit.3.4,5. *b* c.14.27. *c* Lu.2.31,32. *d* Am.9.11,12.

A *yoke* is an emblem of slavery or bondage (1 Tim. vi. 1); or of affliction (Lam. iii. 27); or of punishment (Lam. i. 14); or of oppressive and burdensome ceremonies, as in this place; or of the restraints of Christianity. Matt. xi. 29, 30. In this place they are called *a yoke* because, (1.) They were burdensome and oppressive; and, (2.) Because they would be an infringement of Christian freedom. One design of the gospel was to set men free from such rites and ceremonies. The yoke here referred to is not the moral law, and the just restraints of religion; but the ceremonial laws and customs of the Jews. ¶ *Which neither our fathers*, &c. Which have been found burdensome at all times. They were expensive, and painful, and oppressive: and as they had been found to be so, it was not proper to impose them on the Gentile converts, but should rather rejoice at any evidence that the people of God might be delivered from them. ¶ *Were able to bear.* Which are found to be oppressive and burdensome. They were attended with great inconvenience, and many transgressions, as the consequence.

11. *But we believe.* We apostles, who have been with them, and have seen the evidences of their acceptance with God. ¶ *Through the grace*, &c. By the grace or mercy of Christ alone, without any of the rites and ceremonies of the Jews. ¶ *We shall be saved, even as they.* In the same manner, by the mere grace of Christ. So far from being necessary to *their* salvation, they are really of no use in *ours*. We are to be saved not by these ceremonies, but by the mere mercy of God in the Redeemer They should not, therefore, be imposed on others.

12. *Then all the multitude.* Evidently the multitude of private Christians who were assembled on this occasion. That it does not refer to a synod of ministers and elders merely, is apparent, (1.) Because the church, the brethren, are represented as having been present, and concurring in the final opinion (ver. 22, 23); and, (2.) Because the word *multitude* (τὸ πλῆθος) would not have been used in describing the collection of apostles and elders merely. Comp. Luke i. 10, 11. 13; v. 6; vi. 17; xix. 37. John v. 3; xxi. 6. Acts iv. 32; vi. 2. Matt. iii. 7. ¶ *Gave audience.* Heard, listened attentively to. ¶ *Barnabas and Paul.* They were deeply interested in it; and they were qualified to give a fair statement of the facts as they had occurred. ¶ *Declaring what miracles and wonders*, &c. The argument here evidently is, that God had approved their work by miracles; that he gave evidence that what they did had his approbation; and that as all this was done without imposing on them the rites of the Jews, so it would follow that those were not now to be commanded.

13. *James answered.* James the Less, son of Alpheus. See Note, ch. xii. 1. ¶ *Hearken unto me.* This whole transaction shows that *Peter* had no such authority in the church as the Papists pretend, for otherwise his opinion would have been followed without debate. James had an authority not less than that of Peter. It is possible that he might have been next in age (comp. 1 Cor. xv. 7); and it seems morally certain that he remained for a considerable part of his life in Jerusalem. Acts xii. 17; xxi. 18. Gal i. 19; ii. 9. 12.

14. *Simeon.* This a Hebrew name. The Greek mode of writing it commonly was *Simon*. It was one of the names of Peter. Matt. iv. 18. ¶ *To take out of them a people.* To choose from among the Gentiles those who should be his friends.

15. *The words of the prophets.* Amos ix. 11, 12. It was a very material point with them, as Jews, to inquire whether this was in accordance with the predictions of the Scriptures. The most powerful revivals of religion, and the most striking demonstrations of the divine presence, will be in accordance with the Bible; and should be tested by them. This habit was always manifested by the apostles and early Christians, and should

16 After this I will return, and will build again the tabernacle of David, which is fallen down; and I will build again the ruins thereof, and I will set it up:

17 That the residue of men might seek after the Lord, and all the Gentiles, upon whom my name is called, saith the Lord, who doeth all these things.

---

be followed by Christians at all times. Unless a supposed work of grace accords with the Bible, and can be defended by it, it must be false, and should be opposed. Comp. Isa. viii. 20.

16. *After this.* This quotation is not made literally either from the Hebrew, or the Septuagint, which differs also from the Hebrew. The 17th verse is quoted literally from the Septuagint; but in the 16th the general sense only of the passage is retained. The *main point* of the quotation, as made by James, was, to show that according to the prophets it was contemplated that *the Gentiles* should be introduced to the privileges of the children of God; and on this point the passage has a direct bearing. The prophet Amos (ix. 8—10) had described the calamities that should come upon the nation of the Jews, by their being scattered and driven away. This implied that the city of Jerusalem, and the temple, and the walls of the city should be destroyed. But *after that* (Heb. "on that day," ver. 11, that is, the day when he should revisit them, and recover them), he would restore them to their former privileges; would rebuild their temple, their city, and their walls. ver. 11. And not only so, not only should the blessing descend on the Jews, but it should also be extended to others. The "remnant of Edom," "the heathen upon whom" his "name would be called" (Amos ix. 12), should also partake of the mercy of God, and be subject to the Jewish people; and a time of general prosperity and of permanent blessings should follow. Amos ix. 13—15. James understands this as referring to the times of the Messiah, and to the introduction of the gospel to the Gentiles. And so the passage (Amos ix. 12) is rendered in the Septuagint. See ver. 17. ¶ *I will return.* When the people of God are subjected to calamities and trials, it is often represented as if God had *departed* from them. This *returning*, therefore, is an image of their restoration to his favour, and to prosperity. This is not, however, in the Hebrew, in Amos ix. 11. ¶ *I will build again.* In the calamities that should come upon the nation (Amos ix. 8), it is implied that the temple and the city should be destroyed. To build them again would be a proof of his returning favour. ¶ *The tabernacle of David.* The *tent* of David. Here it means the house, or royal residence of David, and the kings of Israel. That is, he would restore them to their former glory and splendour, as his people. The reference here is not to the *temple*, which was the work of Solomon; but to the magnificence and splendour of the dwelling place of David; that is, to the full enjoyment of their former high privileges and blessings. ¶ *Which is fallen down.* Which would be destroyed by the captivity under the king of Babylon, and by the long neglect and decay resulting from their being carried to a distant land. ¶ *The ruins thereof.* Heb. "close up the breaches thereof." That is, it should be restored to its former prosperity and magnificence; an emblem of the favour of God, and of the spiritual blessings that should in future times descend on the Jewish people.

17. *That the residue of men.* This verse is quoted literally from the Septuagint, and differs in some respects from the Hebrew. The phrase "the residue of men" here, is evidently understood, both by the LXX. and by James, as referring to others than Jews, to the Gentiles. The *rest* of the world—implying that many of them would be admitted to the friendship and favour of God. The Hebrew is, "that they may possess the remnant of Edom." This change is made in the Septuagint by a slight difference in the reading of two Hebrew words. The LXX., instead of the Hebrew יירשו, *shall inherit*, read ידרשך, *shall seek of thee;* and instead of אדום, *Edom*, they read אדם, *Man*, or *mankind*, i. e. men. Why this variation occurred; cannot be explained; but the *sense* is not materially different. In the Hebrew, the word *Edom* has undoubted reference to another nation than the Jewish; and the expression means, that in the great prosperity of the Jews, after their return, they should extend the influence of their religion to other nations; that is, as James applies it, the *Gentiles* might be brought to the privileges of the children of God. ¶ *And also the Gentiles*, Heb. All the heathen; i. e. all who were not Jews. This was a clear prediction that other nations were to be favoured with the light of the true religion, and that without any mention of their con

18 Known[a] unto God are all his
works, from the beginning of the
world.
19 Wherefore my sentence is,
that we trouble not them, which
from among the Gentiles are turned
to God :
20 But that we write unto them,
that they abstain from pollutions
of [c] idols, and *from* fornication,[d]

a Num.23.19. Isa.46.10.

b 1Thess.1.9. c Ex.20.4,5. 1Cor.8.1,&c. 10.28. Rev. 2.14,20; 9.20. d 1Cor.6.9,18. Col.3.5 1Thess.4.3.

forming to the rites of the Jewish people. ¶ *Upon whom my name is called.* Who are called by my name, or who are regarded by me as my people. ¶ *Who doeth all these things.* That is, who will certainly accomplish this in its time.

18. *Known unto God*, &c. Note, ch. i. 24. The meaning of this verse, in this connexion, is this. God sees every thing future ; he knows what he will accomplish ; he has a plan ; and all his works are so arranged in his mind, that he sees all things distinctly and clearly. As he foretold these, it was a part of his plan ; and as it was a part of his plan long since foretold, it should not be opposed and resisted by us.

19. *My sentence.* Gr. I judge (κρίνω); that is, I give my opinion. It is the usual language in which a judge delivers his opinion ; but it does not imply here that James assumed authority to settle the case, but merely that he gave his opinion, or counsel. ¶ *That we trouble not them.* That we do not molest, disturb, or oppress them, by imposing on them unnecessary and burdensome rites and ceremonies.

20. *That we write unto them.* Expressing our judgment, or our views of the case. This verse has greatly perplexed commentators. The main grounds of difficulty have been, (1.) Why fornication—an offence against the moral law, and about which there could be no dispute—should have been included, and, (2.) Whether the prohibition to abstain from blood is still binding. ¶ *That they abstain.* That they refrain from these things, or wholly avoid them. ¶ *Pollutions of idols.* The word rendered *pollutions* means any kind of defilement. But here it is evidently used to denote the flesh of those animals that were offered in sacrifice to idols. See ver. 29. That flesh, after being offered in sacrifice, was often exposed for sale in the markets, or was served up at feasts. 1 Cor. x. 25—29. It became a very important question whether it was *right* for Christians to partake of it. The Jews would contend that it was, in fact, partaking of idolatry. The Gentile converts would allege that they did not eat it *as a sacrifice* to idols, or lend their countenance in any way to the idolatrous worship where it had been offered. See this subject discussed at length in 1 Cor. viii. 4—13. As idolatry was forbidden to the Jews in every form, and as partaking even of the sacrifices to idols, in their feasts, might seem to countenance idolatry, the Jews would be utterly opposed to it ; and for the sake of peace, James advised that they be recommended to abstain from this. To partake of that food might not be *morally* wrong (1 Cor. viii. 4), but it would give occasion for scandal and offence ; and, therefore, as a matter of *expediency*, it was advised that they should abstain from it. ¶ *And from fornication.* The word used here (πορνεία) is applicable to all illicit intercourse ; and may refer to adultery, incest and licentiousness in any form. There has been much diversity of opinion in regard to this expression. Interpreters have been greatly perplexed to understand why this violation of the *moral* law has been introduced amidst the violations of the *ceremonial* law ; and the question is naturally asked, whether this was a sin about which there could be any debate between the Jewish and Gentile converts ? Were there any who would practise it, or plead that it was lawful ? If not, why is it prohibited here ? Various interpretations have been proposed. Some have supposed that James refers here to the *offerings* which harlots would make of their gains to the service of religion, and that James would prohibit the reception of it. Beza, Selden, and Schleusner suppose the word is taken for *idolatry*, as it is often represented in the Scriptures as consisting in unfaithfulness to God, and as it is often called adultery. Heringius supposes that marriage between idolaters and Christians is here intended. But, after all, the usual interpretation of the word, as referring to illicit intercourse of the sexes of any kind, is undoubtedly here to be retained. There is no reason for departing from the ordinary and usual meaning of the word. If it be asked, then, why *this* was particularly forbidden, and was introduced in this connexion, we may reply, (1.) That this vice prevailed every where among the Gentiles, and

and *from* things strangled, and *from* [a] blood.

21 For Moses of old time hath in every city them that preach him being [b] read in the synagogues every sabbath-day:

a Lev.17.14. Deut.12.16,23. b c.13.15,27.

was that to which all were particularly exposed. (2.) That it was not deemed by the Gentiles disgraceful. It was practised without shame, and without remorse. Terence, Adelph. 1, 2. 21. See Grotius. It was important, therefore, that the pure laws of Christianity on this subject should be known, and that special pains should be taken to instruct the early converts from paganism in those laws. The same thing is necessary still in heathen lands. (3.) This crime was connected with religion. It was the practice not only to introduce indecent pictures and emblems into their worship, but also for females to devote themselves to the service of particular temples, and to devote the avails of indiscriminate prostitution to the service of the god, or the goddess. The vice was connected with no small part of the pagan worship; and the images, the emblems, and the customs of idolatry every where tended to sanction and promote it. A mass of evidence on this subject, which sickens the heart—but which would be too long and too indelicate to introduce here—may be seen in Tholuck's Nature and Moral Influence of Heathenism, in the Biblical Repository, for July, 1832, pp. 441—464. As this vice was almost universal; as it was practised without shame or disgrace; as there were no laws among the heathen to prevent it; as it was connected with all their views of idol worship, and of religion; it was important for the early Christians to frown upon and to oppose it, and to set a peculiar guard against it in all the churches. It was the sin to which, of all others, they were the most exposed, and which was most likely to bring scandal on the Christian religion. It is for this cause that it is so often and so pointedly forbidden in the New Testament. Rom. i. 29. 1 Cor. vi. 13. 18. Gal. v. 19. Eph. v. 3. 1 Thess. iv. 3. ¶ *And from things strangled.* That is, from animals or birds that were killed without shedding their blood. The reason why these were considered by the Jews unlawful to be eaten was, that thus they would be under a necessity of eating blood, which was positively forbidden by the law. Hence it was commanded in the law, that when any beast or fowl was taken in a snare, the blood should be poured out before it was lawful to be eaten. Lev. xvii. 13. ¶ *And from blood.* The eating of blood was strictly forbidden to the Jews. The reason of this was that it contained *the life*. Lev. xvii. 11. 14. See Note on Rom. iii. 25. The use of *blood* was common among the Gentiles. They *drank* it often at their sacrifices, and in making covenants or compacts. To separate the Jews from them in this respect was one design of the prohibition. See Spencer, De Leg. Hebræ. pp. 144, 145. 169. 235. 377. 381. 594. Ed. 1732. See also this whole passage examined at length in Spencer. pp. 588—626. The primary reason of the prohibition was, that it was thus used in the feasts and compacts of idolaters. That blood was thus drank by the heathens, particularly by the Sabians, in their sacrifices, is fully proved by Spencer, De Leg. pp. 377—380. But the prohibition specifies a *higher* reason, that the *life* is in the blood, and that *therefore* it should not be eaten. On this opinion see Note, Rom. iii. 25. This reason existed before any ceremonial law; is founded in the nature of things; has no particular reference to any custom of the Jews; and therefore is as forcible in any other circumstances as in theirs. It was proper, therefore, to forbid it to the early Christian converts; and for the same reason its use should be abstained from every where. It adds to the force of these remarks, when we remember that the same principle was settled before the laws of Moses were given; and that God regarded the fact that the life was in the blood as of so much importance as to make the shedding of it worthy of death. Gen. ix. 4—6. It is supposed, therefore, that this law is still obligatory. Perhaps also there is no food more unwholesome than blood; and it is a further circumstance of some moment that all men naturally revolt from it as an article of food.

21. *For Moses.* The meaning of this verse is, that the law of Moses, prohibiting these things, was read in the synagogues constantly. As these commands were constantly read, and as the Jewish converts would not soon learn that their ceremonial law had ceased to be binding, it was deemed to be a matter of expediency that no needless offence should be given to them. For the sake of peace, it was better that they should abstain from meat offered to idols than to give offence

22 Then pleased it the apostles
and elders, with the whole church,
to send chosen men of their own
company to Antioch, with Paul and
Barnabas; *namely*, Judas surnamed
Barsabas, [a] and Silas, chief men
among the brethren:
23 And wrote *letters* by them
after this manner: The apostles
and elders, and brethren, *send* greeting unto the brethren which are of
the Gentiles in Antioch, and Syria,
and Cilicia:
24 Forasmuch as we have heard,
that certain [b] which went out from
us have troubled [c] you with words,
[d] subverting your souls, saying, *Ye
must* be circumcised, and keep the
law: to whom [e] we gave no such
commandment:
25 It seemed good unto us, being
assembled with one accord, to send

a c.1.23. b ver.1. c Gal.5.12. d Gal.5.4. e Gal.2.4.

to the Jewish converts. Comp. 1 Cor. viii. 10—13. ¶ *Of old time.* Greek, From ancient generations. It is an established custom; and therefore his laws are well known, and have, in their view, not only the authority of revelation, but the venerableness of antiquity. ¶ *In every city.* Where there were Jews. This was the case in all the cities to which the discussion here had reference. ¶ *Them that preach him.* That is, by reading the law of Moses But in addition to *reading* the law, it was customary also to offer an *explanation* of its meaning. See Notes on Luke iv. 16—22.

22. *Then it pleased.* It seemed fit and proper to them. ¶ *The apostles and elders.* To whom the business had been particularly referred. ver. 2. Comp. ch xvi. 4. ¶ *With the whole church.* All the Christians who were there assembled together. They *concurred* in the sentiment, and expressed their approbation in the letter that was sent. ver. 23. Whether they were *consulted*, does not particularly appear. But as it is not probable that they would volunteer an opinion unless they were consulted, it seems most reasonable to suppose that the apostles and elders submitted the case to them for their approbation. It would seem that the apostles and elders deliberated on it, and decided it; but still, for the sake of peace and unity, they also took measures to ascertain that their decision agreed with the unanimous sentiment of the church. ¶ *Chosen men.* Men chosen for this purpose. ¶ *Of their own company.* From among themselves. Greater weight and authority would thus be attached to their message. ¶ *Judas, surnamed Barsabas.* Possibly the same who was nominated to the vacant place in the apostleship. ch. i. 23. But Grotius supposes that it was his brother. ¶ *And Silas.* He was afterwards the travelling companion of Paul. ver. 40. ch. xvi. 25. 29; xvii. 4. 10. 15. He is also the same person, probably, who is mentioned by the name of *Silvanus.* 2 Cor. i. 19. 1 Thess. i. 1. 2 Thess. i. 1. 1 Pet. v. 12. ¶ *Chief men among the brethren.* Greek, *Leaders.* Comp. Luke xxii. 26. Men of influence, experience, and authority in the church. Judas and Silas are said to have been *prophets.* ver. 32. They had, therefore, been engaged as preachers and rulers in the church at Jerusalem.

23. *And wrote* letters. Greek, *Having written.* It does not mean that they wrote more than one epistle. ¶ *By them.* Greek, By their hand. ¶ *After this manner.* Greek, These things. ¶ Send *greeting.* A word of salutation, expressing their desire of the happiness (χαίρειν) of the persons addressed. Comp. Matt. xxvi. 49; xxvii. 29. Luke i. 28. John xix. 3. ¶ *In Antioch.* Where the difficulty first arose. ¶ *And Syria.* Antioch was the capital of Syria, and it is probable that the dispute was not confined to the capital. ¶ *And Cilicia.* Note, Acts vi. 9. Cilicia was adjacent to Syria. Paul and Barnabas had travelled through it; and it is probable that the same difficulty would exist there which had disturbed the churches in Syria.

24. *Forasmuch.* Since we have heard ¶ *That certain.* That some. ver. 1. ¶ *Have troubled you with words.* With doctrines They have disturbed your minds, and produced contentions. ¶ *Subverting your souls.* The word here used occurs nowhere else in the New Testament (ἀνασκευάζοντες). It properly means to collect together the vessels used in a house—the household furniture—for the purpose of removing it. It is applied to marauders, robbers, and enemies, who remove and bear off property; thus producing distress, confusion, and disorder. It is thus used in the sense of disturbing, or destroying; and here denotes that they unsettled their minds; that they produced anxiety, disturbance, and distress, by these doctrines about Moses. ¶ *To whom we gave no such commandment.* They went, therefore,

chosen men unto you, with our beloved Barnabas and Paul,

26 Men that have hazarded [a] their lives for the name of our Lord Jesus Christ.

27 We have sent therefore Judas and Silas, who shall also tell *you* the same things by [1] mouth.

28 For it seemed good to the Holy Ghost, and to us, to lay upon you no greater burthen [b] than these necessary things;

29 That ye abstain [c] from meats offered to idols, and from blood, and from things strangled, and from fornication: from which if ye keep [d] yourselves, ye shall do well. Fare ye well.

30 So when they were dismissed, they came to Antioch; and when they had gathered the multitude together, they delivered the epistle:

31 *Which*, when they had read, they rejoiced for the [2] consolation.

a c.13.50; 14.19. [1] *word.* *b* Rev.2.24.

c ver.20. *d* 2Cor.11.9. Jam.1.27. 1Jno.5.21. Jude 20,21. [2] or, *exhortation.*

without authority. Self-constituted and self-sent teachers not unfrequently produce disturbance and distress. Had the apostles been consulted on this subject, the difficulty would have been avoided. By thus saying that they had not given them a command to teach these things, they practically assured the Gentile converts that they did not approve of the course which those who went from Judea had taken.

26. *Men that have hazarded their lives,* &c. See ch. xiv. This was a noble testimony to the character of Barnabas and Paul. It was a commendation of them to the confidence of the churches, and an implied expression that they wished their authority to be regarded in the establishment and organization of the church. ¶ *For the name.* In the cause of the Lord Jesus.

27. *The same things.* The same things that we wrote to you. They shall confirm all by their own statements.

28. *For it seemed good to the Holy Ghost.* This is a strong and undoubted claim to inspiration. It was with special reference to the organization of the church, that the Holy Spirit had been promised to them by the Lord Jesus. Matt. xviii. 18—20. John xiv. 26. ¶ *No greater burthen.* To impose no greater restraints; to enjoin no other observances. See Note, ver. 10. ¶ *Than these necessary things.* Necessary, (1.) In order to preserve the peace of the church. (2.) To conciliate the minds of the Jewish converts. ver. 21. (3.) Necessary in their circumstances, particularly, because the crime which is specified—licentiousness—was one to which all early converts were particularly exposed. Note, ver. 20.

29. *From meats offered to idols.* This explains what is meant by "pollutions of idols." ver. 20. ¶ *Ye shall do well.* You will do what ought to be done in regard to the subjects of dispute.

31. *They rejoiced for the consolation.* They acquiesced in the decision of the apostles and elders, and rejoiced that they were not to be subjected to the burdensome rites and ceremonies of the Jewish religion. This closes the account of the first Christian council. It was conducted throughout on Christian principles, in a mild, kind, conciliatory spirit; and is a model for all similar assemblages. It came together, not to promote, but to silence disputation; not to persecute the people of God, but to promote their peace; not to be a scene of harsh and angry recrimination, but to be an example of all that was mild, and tender, and kind. Those who composed it came together, not to carry a point, not to overreach their adversaries, not to be party men, but to mingle their sober counsels, to inquire what was right, and to express, in a Christian manner, that which was proper to be done. Great and important principles were to be established, in regard to the Christian church; and they engaged in their work evidently with a deep sense of their responsibility, and with a just view of their dependence on the aid of the Holy Spirit. How happy would it have been if this spirit had been possessed by all professedly Christian councils! How happy, if all had really sought the peace and harmony of the churches; and if none had ever been convened to kindle the fires of persecution, to evince the spirit of party, or to rend and destroy the church of God!

This council has been usually appealed to as the authority for councils in the church, as a permanent arrangement; and especially as an authority for courts of appeal and control. But it establishes neither, and should be brought as an au-

32 And Judas and Silas, being prophets also themselves, exhorted the brethren with many words, and confirmed [a] *them*.

33 And after they had tarried *there* a space, they were let go [b] in peace from the brethren unto the apostles.

34 Notwithstanding, it pleased Silas to abide there still.

a c.14.22. b 1Cor.16.11. 2Jno.10.

thority for neither. For, (1.) It was *not* a court of appeal in any intelligible sense. It was an assembly convened for a special purpose; designed to settle an inquiry which arose in a particular part of the church, and which required the collected wisdom of the apostles and elders to settle. (2.) It had none of the marks or appendages of a *court*. The term court, or judicature, is nowhere applied to it; nor to any assembly of Christian men, in the New Testament. Nor should these terms be used now in the churches. Courts of judicature imply a degree of authority, which cannot be proved from the New Testament to have been conceded to any ecclesiastical body of men. (3.) There is not the slightest intimation that any thing like permanency was to be attached to this council; or that it would be periodically or regularly repeated. It will prove, indeed, that when cases of difficulty occur; when Christians are perplexed and embarrassed; or when contentions arise, it will be proper to refer to Christian men for advice and direction. Such was the case here; and such a course is obviously proper. If it should be maintained that it is well that Christian ministers and laymen should assemble periodically, at stated intervals, on the supposition that such cases may arise, this is conceded; but the example of the apostles and elders should not be pleaded as making such assemblies of divine right and authority, or as being essential to the existence of a church of God. Such an arrangement has been deemed to be so desirable by Christians, that it has been adopted by Episcopalians in their regular annual and triennial conventions; by Methodists in their conferences; by Presbyterians in their general assembly; by Friends in their yearly meetings; by Baptists and Congregationalists in their associations, &c. But the example of the council *summoned on a special emergency* at Jerusalem, should not be pleaded as giving divine authority to all, or to any of these periodical assemblages. They are wise and prudent arrangements, contributing to the peace of the church; and the example of the council at Jerusalem can be adduced as furnishing *as much* divine authority for one as for another; that is, it does not make all or either of them of divine authority, or as obligatory on the church of God. (4.) It should be added, that a degree of authority (comp. ch. xvi. 4) would, of course, be attached to the decision of the apostles and elders at that time, which cannot be to any body of ministers and laymen now. Besides it should never be forgotten—what, alas, it seems to have been the pleasure and the interest of ecclesiastics to forget—that neither the apostles nor elders *asserted* any jurisdiction over the churches of Antioch, Syria, and Cilicia; that they did not claim a *right* to have these cases referred to them; that they did not attempt "to lord it" over their faith or their consciences. The case was a single, specific, definite question, *referred to them;* and they decided it as such. They asserted no abstract right of such jurisdiction; they sought not to intermeddle with it; they enjoined no future reference to them, to their successors, or to any ecclesiastical tribunal. They evidently regarded the churches as blessed with the most ample freedom; and evidently contemplated no arrangement of a permanent character, asserting a right to legislate on articles of faith, or to make laws for the direction of the Lord's freemen.

32. *Being prophets.* See Note, ch. xi. 27. This evidently implies that they had been preachers before they went to Antioch. What was the precise nature of the office of a *prophet* in the Christian church, it is not easy to ascertain. Possibly it may imply that they were *teachers* of unusual or remarkable ability. ¶ *Confirmed them.* Strengthened them; that is, by their instructions and exhortations. Note, ch. xiv. 22.

33. *A space.* For some time. ¶ *They were let go in peace.* An expression implying that they departed with the affectionate regard of the Christians to whom they had ministered, and with their highest wishes for their prosperity. 1 Cor. xvi. 11. 2 John 10. Silas, however, it seems chose to remain. ¶ *Unto the apostles.* At Jerusalem. Many MSS. however, instead of "unto the *apostles*," read, "unto those who had sent them." The sense is not materially different.

34. *Notwithstanding*, &c. This whole

35 Paul also and Barnabas continued in Antioch, teaching and preaching the word of the Lord, with many others also.

36 And some days after, Paul said unto Barnabas, Let us go again and visit our brethren in [a] every city where we have preached the word of the Lord, *and see* how they do.

37 And Barnabas determined to take with them John [b] whose surname was Mark.

38 But Paul thought not good to take him with them, who departed from them from Pamphylia, and went not with them to the work.

39 And the contention was so sharp between them, that they departed asunder one from the other: and so Barnabas took Mark, and sailed unto Cyprus:

40 And Paul chose Silas, and departed, being recommended [d] by the brethren unto the grace of God.

41 And he went through Syria and Cilicia, confirming [e] the churches.

a c.13.4,&c. b c.12.12,25. Col.4.10. c c.13.13. d c.14.26; 20.32. e c.16.5

verse is wanting in many MSS. in the Syriac, Arabic, and Coptic versions; and is regarded as spurious by Mill, Griesbach, and by other critics. It was probably introduced by some early transcriber, who judged it necessary to complete the narrative. The Latin Vulgate reads, "It seemed good to Silas to remain, but Judas went alone to Jerusalem."

35. *Paul also, and Barnabas continued in Antioch.* How long a time is unknown. It is probable that at this time the unhappy incident occurred between Paul and Peter, which is recorded in Gal. ii. 11—14.

36. *Let us go again and visit our brethren.* That is, in the churches which they had established in Asia Minor. ch. xiii. xiv. This was a natural wish; and was an enterprise that might be attended with important advantages to those feeble churches.

37. *But Barnabas determined.* Greek, Willed, or was disposed to (ἐβουλεύσατο). ¶ *John, &c.* Note, ch. xii. 12. He had been with them before as a travelling companion. ch. xii. 25; xiii. 5. He was the son of a sister of Barnabas (Col. iv. 10), and it is probable that Barnabas' affection for his nephew was the main reason for inducing him to wish to take him with him in the journey.

38. *But Paul thought not good.* Did not think it proper. Because he could not confide in his perseverance with them in the toils and perils of their journey. ¶ *Who departed from them, &c.* ch. xiii. 13. Why he did this is not known. It was evidently, however, for some cause which Paul did not consider satisfactory, and which in his view disqualified him from being their attendant again. ¶ *To the work.* Of preaching the gospel.

39. *And the contention was so sharp.* The word used here (παροξυσμὸς) is that from which our word *paroxysm* is derived It may denote any excitement of mind, and is used in a good sense in Heb. x. 24. It here means evidently a violent altercation that resulted in their separation for a time, and in their engaging in different spheres of labour. ¶ *And sailed unto Cyprus.* This was the native place of Barnabas. Note, ch. iv. 36.

40. *Being recommended.* Being commended by prayer to God. Note, ch. xiv.26

41. *Syria and Cilicia.* These were countries lying near to each other, which Paul, in company with Barnabas, had before visited. ¶ *Confirming the churches.* Strengthening them by instruction and exhortation. It has no reference to the rite of confirmation. See Note, Acts xiv. 22.

In regard to this unhappy contention between Paul and Barnabas, and their separation from each other, we may make the following remarks. (1.) That no apology or vindication of it is offered by the sacred writer. It was undoubtedly improper and evil. It was a melancholy instance in which even apostles evinced an improper spirit, and engaged in improper strife. (2.) In this contention it is probable that Paul was, in the main, right. Barnabas seems to have been influenced by attachment to a relative; Paul sought a helper who would not shrink from duty and danger. It is clear that Paul had the sympathies and prayers of the church in his favour (ver. 40), and it is more than probable that Barnabas departed without any such sympathy. ver. 39. (3.) There is reason to think that this contention was overruled for the furtherance of the gospel. They went to different places, and preached to different people. It often happens that the unhappy and wicked strifes of Christians

CHAPTER XVI.

THEN came he to Derbe [a] and
Lystra: and behold, a certain
disciple was there, named Timotheus, [b] the son of a [c] certain woman, which was a Jewess, and believed; but his father *was* a Greek:
2 Which was well [d] reported of
by the brethren that were at Lystra
and Iconium.
3 Him would Paul have to go
forth with him; and took and circumcised him, [e] because of the
Jews [f] which were in those quarters; for they knew all that his
father was a Greek.

a c.14.6. b c.19.22. Rom.16.21. 1Cor.4.17. 2Tim.1.5. d c.6.3. 1Tim.5.10. Heb.11.2.

e Gal.2.3–8; 5.1–3. f 1Cor.9.20.

are the means of exciting their zeal, and of extending the gospel, and of establishing churches. But no thanks to their contention; nor is the guilt of their anger and strife mitigated by this. (4.) This difference was afterwards reconciled, and Paul and Barnabas again became travelling companions. 1 Cor. ix. 6. Gal. ii. 9. (5.) There is evidence that Paul also became reconciled to John Mark. Col. iv. 10. Philem. 24. 2 Tim. iv. 11. How long this separation continued is not known; but perhaps in this journey with Barnabas, John gave such evidence of his courage and zeal as induced Paul again to admit him to his confidence as a travelling companion, and as to become a profitable fellow-labourer. See 2 Tim. iv. 11, "Take Mark, and bring him with thee; for he is profitable to me for the ministry." (6.) This account proves that there was no *collusion* or *agreement* among the apostles to impose upon mankind. Had there been such an agreement, and had the books of the New Testament been an imposture, the apostles would have been represented as *perfectly harmonious*, and as united in all their views and efforts. What impostor would have thought of the device of representing the early friends of the Christian religion as *divided*, and *contending*, and *separating* from each other? Such a statement has an air of candour and honesty, and at the same time is apparently so much *against* the truth of the system, that no impostor would have thought of resorting to it.

CHAPTER XVI.

1. *Then came he.* That is, Paul, in company with Silas. Luke does not give us the history of Barnabas, but confines his narrative to the journey of Paul. ¶ *To Derbe and Lystra.* Note, ch. xiv. 6 ¶ *And behold a certain disciple named Timotheus.* It was to this disciple that Paul afterwards addressed the two epistles which bear his name. It is evident that he was a native of one of these places, but whether of Derbe or Lystra it is impossible to determine. ¶ *The son of a certain woman*, &c. Her name was Eunice. 2 Tim. i. 5. ¶ *And believed.* And was a Christian. It is evident also that *her* mother was a woman of distinguished Christian piety. 2 Tim. i. 5. It was not lawful for a Jew to marry a woman of another nation, or to give his daughter in marriage to a Gentile. Ezra ix. 12. But it is probable that this law was not regarded very strictly by the Jews who lived in the midst of heathen nations. It is evident that Timothy, at this time, was very young; for when Paul besought him to abide at Ephesus, to take charge of the church there (1 Tim. i. 3), he addressed him then as a young man. 1 Tim. iv. 12, "Let no man despise thy youth." ¶ *But his father was a Greek.* Evidently a man who had not been circumcised, for had he been, Timothy would have been also.

2. *Which.* That is, *Timothy.* The connexion requires us to understand this of him. Of the character of his father nothing is known. ¶ *Was well reported of* Was esteemed highly as a young man of piety and promise. Note, ch. vi. 3. Comp. 1 Tim. v. 10. Timothy had been religiously educated. He was carefully trained in the knowledge of the Holy Scriptures, and was therefore the better qualified for his work. 2 Tim. iii. 15.

3. *Him would Paul have*, &c. This was an instance of Paul's selecting young men of piety for the holy ministry. It shows (1.) That he was disposed to look up and call forth the talent that might be in the church, that might be usefully employed. It is quite evident that Timothy would not have thought of this, had it not been suggested by Paul. The same thing, Education societies are attempting now to accomplish. (2.) That Paul sought proper qualifications, and valued them. Those were, (*a*) That he had a good reputation for piety, &c. ver. 2. This he demanded as an indispensable qualification for a minister of the gospel. 1 Tim. iii. 7 "Moreover he (a bishop) must have a good report of them which are without'

4 And as they went through the
cities, they delivered them the decrees for to keep, that were ordained [a] of the apostles and elders
which were at Jerusalem.
5 And so were the churches [b] established in the faith, and increased
in number daily.

6 Now when they had gone
throughout Phrygia and the region
of [c] Galatia, and were forbidden of
[d] the Holy Ghost to preach the
word in [e] Asia,
7 After they were come to Mysia,
they assayed to go into Bythinia:
but the Spirit suffered them not.

a c.15.28,29. b c.15.41.

c Gal.1.2. 1Pet.1.1. d Amos 8.11,12. 1Cor.12.11. e Rev.1.4,11.

Comp. Acts xxii. 12. (*b*) Paul esteemed him to be a young man of talents and prudence. His admitting him to a partnership in his labours, and his intrusting to him the affairs of the church at Ephesus, prove this. (*c*) He had been carefully trained in the Holy Scriptures. A foundation was thus laid for usefulness. And this qualification seems to have been deemed by Paul of indispensable value for the right discharge of his duties in this holy office. ¶ *And he took and circumcised him.* This was evidently done to avoid the opposition and reproaches of the Jews. It was a measure not binding in itself (comp. ch. xv. 1. 28, 29); but the neglect of which would expose to contention and opposition among the Jews, and greatly retard or destroy his usefulness. It was an act of expediency for the sake of peace, and was in accordance with Paul's uniform and avowed principle of conduct. 1 Cor. ix. 20, "And unto the Jews I became as a Jew, that I might gain the Jews." Comp. Acts xxi. 23—26.

4. *And as they went through the cities.* The cities of Syria, Cilicia, &c. ¶ *They delivered them.* Paul and Silas delivered to the Christians in those cities. ¶ *The decrees.* Τὰ δόγματα. The decrees in regard to the four things specified in ch. xv. 20. 29. The word translated *decrees* occurs in Luke ii. 1, "*A decree* from Cæsar Augustus;" in Acts xvii. 7, "The *decrees* of Cæsar;" in Eph. ii. 15, and in Col. ii. 14. It properly means a law or edict of a king, or legislature. In this instance it was the decision of the council in a case submitted to it; and implied an obligation on the Christians to submit to that decision. The laws of the apostles would, and ought to be, in such cases, esteemed to be binding. It is probable that a correct and attested copy of the letter (ch. xv. 23—29) would be sent to the various churches of the Gentiles. ¶ *To keep.* To obey, or to observe. ¶ *That were ordained.* Gr. That were adjudged, or determined.

5. *Established in the faith.* Confirmed in the belief of the gospel. The effect of the wise and conciliatory measure was to increase and strengthen the churches.

6. *Throughout Phrygia.* This was the largest province of Asia Minor. It had Bythinia north; Pisidia and Lycia south; Galatia and Cappadocia east; and Lydia and Mysia west. ¶ *And the region of Galatia.* This province was directly east of Phrygia. The region was formerly conquered by the Gauls. They settled in it, and called it, after their own name, *Galatia.* The Gauls invaded the country at different times, and no less than three tribes or bodies of Gauls had possession of it. Many Jews were also settled there. It was from this cause that so many parties could be formed there, and that so much controversy would arise between the Jewish and Gentile converts. See the Epistle to the Galatians. ¶ *And were forbidden.* Probably by a direct revelation. The reason of this was, doubtless, that it was the intention of God to extend the gospel farther into the regions of Greece than would have been done if they had remained in Asia Minor. This prohibition was the means of the first introduction of the gospel into Europe. ¶ *In Asia.* See Note, ch. ii. 9. This was doubtless the region of proconsular Asia. This region was also called *Ionia.* Of this region Ephesus was the capital; and here were situated also the cities of Smyrna, Thyatira, Philadelphia, &c., within which the seven churches mentioned in Rev. i. ii. iii. were established. Cicero speaks of proconsular Asia as containing the provinces of Phrygia, Mysia, Caria, and Lydia. In all this region the gospel was afterwards preached with great success. But now a more important and a wider field was opened before Paul and Barnabas, in the extensive country of Macedonia.

7. *Mysia.* This was a province of Asia Minor, having Propontis on the north, Bythinia on the east, Lydia on the south, and the Ægean sea on the west. ¶ *They assayed.* They endeavoured; they at-

8 And they passing by Mysia, came down to [a] Troas.

9 And a vision appeared to Paul in the night; There stood a man [b] of Macedonia, and prayed him, saying, Come over into Macedonia, and help us.

10 And after he had seen the vision, immediately we endeavoured to go [c] into Macedonia, assuredly gathering that the Lord had called us for to preach the gospel unto them.

11 Therefore loosing from Troas, we came with a straight course to Samothracia, and the next *day* to Neapolis;

12 And from thence to Philippi,[d] which is the [1] chief city of that part of Macedonia, *and* a colony. And we were in that city abiding certain days.

a 2Cor.2.12. 2Tim.4.13. b c.19.30. c 2Cor.2.13. d Phil.1.1. 1 or, *the first.*

tempted. ¶ *Into Bythinia.* A province of Asia Minor, lying east of Mysia.

8. *Came down to Troas.* This was a city of Phrygia or Mysia, on the Hellespont, between Troy north, and Assos south. Sometimes the name *Troas*, or *Troad*, is used to denote the whole country of the Trojans, the province where the ancient city of Troy had stood. This region was much celebrated in the early periods of Grecian history. It was here that the events recorded in the Iliad of Homer are supposed to have occurred. The city of Troy has long since been completely destroyed. *Troas* is several times mentioned in the New Testament. 2 Cor. ii. 12. 2 Tim. iv. 13. Acts xx. 5.

9. *And a vision.* Note, ch. ix. 10. ¶ *There stood a man, &c.* The appearance of a man, who was known to be of Macedonia, probably, by his dress and language. Whether this was in a dream, or whether it was a representation made to the senses while awake, it is impossible to tell. The will of God was at different times made known in both these ways. Comp. Matt. ii. 12. Note, Acts x. 3. Grotius supposes that this was the guardian angel of Macedonia, and refers for illustration to Dan. x. 12, 13. 20, 21. But there seems to be no foundation for this opinion. ¶ *Of Macedonia.* This was an extensive country of Greece, having Thrace on the north, Thessaly south, Epirus west, and the Ægean sea east. It is supposed that it was peopled by Kittim, son of Javan. Gen. x. 4. The kingdom rose into celebrity chiefly under the reign of Philip and his son Alexander the Great. It was the first region in Europe in which we have any record that the gospel was preached. ¶ *And help us.* That is, by preaching the gospel. This was a call to preach the gospel in an extensive heathen land, amidst many trials and dangers. To this call, notwithstanding all this prospect of danger, they cheerfully responded, and gave themselves to the work. Their conduct was thus an example to the church. From all portions of the earth a similar call is now coming to the churches. Openings of a similar character, for the introduction of the gospel, are presented in all lands. Appeals are coming from every quarter; and all that seems now necessary for the speedy conversion of the world is, for the church to enter into these vast fields with the self-denial, spirit, and zeal which characterized the apostle Paul.

10. *We endeavoured.* This is the first instance in which Luke refers to himself as being in company with Paul. It is hence probable that he joined Paul and Silas about this time; and it is evident that he attended him in his travels, as recorded throughout the remainder of the Acts. ¶ *Assuredly gathering.* Being certainly convinced.

11. *Loosing from Troas.* Setting sail from this place. ¶ *To Samothracia.* This was an island in the Ægean sea, not far from Thrace. It was peopled by inhabitants from Samos and from Thrace, and hence called *Samothracia.* It was about twenty miles in circumference; and was an asylum for fugitives and criminals. ¶ *And the next day to Neapolis.* This was a maritime city of Macedonia, near the borders of Thrace. It is now called *Napoli.*

12. *And from thence to Philippi.* The former name of this city was Dathos. It was repaired and adorned by Philip, the father of Alexander the Great, and after him was called Philippi. It was famous for having been the place where several battles were fought in the civil wars of the Romans, and among others, for the decisive battle between Brutus and Antony. At this place Brutus killed himself. To the church in this place Paul afterwards wrote the epistle which bears its name. ¶ *Which is the chief city of that part of Macedonia.* This whole region

13 And on the [1] sabbath we went
out of the city by a river side, where
prayer [a] was wont to be made: and
we sat down, and spake unto the
women which resorted *thither.*
14 And a certain woman named
Lydia, a seller of purple, of the city
of Thyatira, which worshipped God,
heard *us:* whose heart [b] the Lord
opened, that she attended unto the
things which were spoken of Paul.
15 And when she was baptized,
and her household, she besought [c]
us, saying, If ye have judged me
to be faithful to the Lord, come into
my house, and abide *there.* And she
constrained us.
16 And it came to pass, as we

[1] *sabbath-day* [a] c.21.5. [b] Luke 24.45. [c] Heb.13.2.

had been conquered by the Romans under Paulus Emilius. By him it was divided into four parts or provinces. (*Livy.*) The Syriac version renders it, "a city of the *first* part of Macedonia;" and there is a medal extant which also describes this region by this name. It has been proposed, therefore, to alter the Greek text in accordance with this, since it is known that Amphipolis was made the chief city by Paulus Emilius. But it may be remarked, that although Amphipolis was the chief city in the time of Paulus Emilius, it may have happened that in the lapse of two hundred and twenty years from that time, Philippi might have become the most extensive and splendid city. The Greek here may also mean simply that this was the *first* city to which they arrived in their travels. ¶ And *a colony.* This is a Latin word, and means that this was a Roman colony. The word denotes a city or province which was planted or occupied by Roman citizens. On one of the coins now extant, it is recorded that Julius Cæsar bestowed the advantages and dignity of a colony on Philippi, which Augustus afterwards confirmed and augmented. See *Rob. Cal.* Art. Philippi. ¶ *Certain days.* Some days.

13. *And on the Sabbath.* There is no doubt that in this city there were Jews. In the time of the apostles they were scattered extensively throughout the known world. ¶ *By a river side.* What river this was, is not known. It is known, however, that the Jews were accustomed to provide water, or to build their synagogues and oratories near water, for the convenience of the numerous washings before and during their religious services. ¶ *Where prayer.* Where there was a *proseuchæ*, or place of prayer; or where prayer was commonly offered. The Greek will bear either; but the sense is the same. Places for prayer were erected by the Jews in the vicinity of cities and towns, and particularly where there were not Jewish families enough, or where they were forbidden by the magistrate to erect a synagogue. These *proseuchæ*, or places of prayer, were simple enclosures made of stones in a grove, or under a tree, where there would be a retired and convenient place for worship. ¶ *Was wont.* Was accustomed to be offered; or where it was established by custom. ¶ *And spake unto the women*, &c. This was probably before the regular service of the place commenced.

14. *A seller of purple.* Purple was a most valuable colour, obtained usually from shell-fish. It was chiefly worn by princes and by the rich; and the traffic in it might be very profitable. ¶ *The city of Thyatira.* This was a city of Lydia in Asia Minor, now called *Ak-hisar.* The art of dying was particularly cultivated, as appears from an inscription found there. (See *Kuinoel.*) ¶ *Which worshipped God.* A religious woman, a proselyte. Note, ch. xiii. 16. ¶ *Whose heart the Lord opened.* See Note, Luke xxiv. 45.

15. *And when she was baptized.* Apparently without any delay. Comp. Acts ii. 41; viii. 38. It was usual to be baptized immediately on believing. ¶ *And her household.* Greek, Her house (ὁ οἶκος αὐτῆς). Her family. No mention is made of *their* having believed. And the case is one that affords a strong presumptive proof that this was an instance of *household* or infant baptism. For, (1.) *Her* believing is particularly mentioned. (2.) It is not intimated that *they* believed. On the contrary, it is strongly implied that they did not. (3.) It is manifestly implied that *they* were baptized because *she* believed. It was the offering of her family to the Lord It is just such an account as would now be given of a household or family that were baptized on the faith of the parent. ¶ *If ye have judged me to be faithful.* If you deem me a Christian, or a believer. ¶ *And she constrained us.* She urged us. This was an instance of great hospitality and also an evidence of her desire for further instruction in the doctrines of religion.

16. *As we went to prayer* Greek, A

went to prayer, a certain damsel possessed [a] with a spirit of [1] divination met us, which brought her masters much gain [b] by soothsaying:

17 The same followed Paul and us, and cried, saying, These men are the servants of the most high [c] God, which shew unto us the way of [d] salvation.

18 And this she did many days. But Paul, being grieved, turned and said [e] to the spirit, I command thee in the name of Jesus Christ, to come out of her. And [f] he came out the same hour.

a 1Sam.28.7. 1 or, *Python.* b c.19.24. c Gen.14.18–22. d c.18.26. Heb.10.20. e Mark 1.25,34. f Mark 16.17.

we were going to the *proseuchæ*, the place of prayer. ver. 13. Whether this was on the same day in which the conversion of Lydia occurred, or at another time, is not mentioned by the historian. ¶ *A certain damsel.* A maid, a young woman. ¶ *Possessed with a spirit of divination.* Gr. *Python.* See the margin. Python, or Pythios, was one of the names of Apollo, the Grecian god of the fine arts, of music, poetry, medicine, and eloquence. Of these he was esteemed to have been the inventor. He was reputed to be the third son of Jupiter and Latona. He had a celebrated temple and oracle at Delphi, which was resorted to from all parts of the world, and which was perhaps the only oracle that was in universal repute. The name *Python* is said to have been given him because, as soon as he was born, he destroyed with arrows a serpent of that name, that had been sent by Juno to persecute Latona; hence his common name was *the Pythian Apollo.* He had temples on mount Parnassus, at Delphi, Delos, Claros, Tenedos, &c., and his worship was almost universal. In the celebrated oracle at Delphi, the priestess of Apollo pretended to be inspired; became violently agitated during the periods of pretended inspiration, and during those periods gave such responses to inquirers as were regarded as the oracles of the god. Others would also make pretensions to such inspiration; and the art of fortune-telling, or of jugglery, was extensively practised, and was the source of much gain. See Note, ch viii. 8—10. What was the cause of this extensive delusion in regard to the oracle at Delphi, it is not necessary now to inquire. It is plain that Paul regarded this as a case of demoniacal possession and treated it accordingly. ¶ *Her masters.* Those in whose employ she was. ¶ *By soothsaying.* Pretending to foretell future events.

17. *The same followed Paul,* &c. Why she did this, or under what pretence, the sacred writer has not informed us. Various conjectures have been formed of the reason why this was done. It *may* have been, (1.) That as she prophesied for gain, she supposed that Paul and Silas would reward her if she publicly proclaimed that they were the servants of God. Or, (2.) Because she was conscious that an evil spirit possessed her, and that she feared that Paul and Silas would expel that spirit; and that, by proclaiming them to be the servants of God, she hoped to conciliate their favour. Or, (3.) More probably, it was because she saw evident tokens of their being sent from God, and that their doctrine would prevail; and by proclaiming this she hoped to acquire more authority, and a higher reputation for being herself inspired. Comp. Mark v. 7.

18. *But Paul, being grieved.* Being molested, troubled, offended. Paul was grieved, probably, (1.) Because her presence was troublesome to him; (2.) Because it might be said that he was in alliance with her, and that his pretensions were just like hers; (3.) Because what she did was for the sake of gain, and was a base imposition; (4.) Because her state was one of bondage and delusion, and it was proper to free her from this demoniacal possession; and, (5.) Because the system under which she was acting was a part of a vast scheme of delusion and imposture, which had spread over a large portion of the pagan world, and which was then holding it in bondage. Throughout the Roman empire, the inspiration of the priestesses of Apollo was believed in, and temples were every where reared to perpetuate and celebrate the delusion. Against this extensive system of imposture and fraud, Christianity must oppose itself; and this was a favourable instance to expose the delusion, and to show the power of the Christian religion over all the arts and powers of imposture. The mere fact that in a *very few* instances—of which this was one—they spoke the truth, did not make it improper for Paul to interpose. That fact would only tend to perpetuate the delusion, and to make his interposition more proper and neces

19 And when her masters saw
that the hope of their gains [a] was
gone, they caught Paul and Silas,
and drew *them* into [1] the market-
place, unto [b] the rulers,
20 And brought them to the magistrates, saying, These men, being
Jews, do exceedingly trouble [c] our
city,
21 And teach customs which are
not lawful for us to receive, neither
to observe, being Romans.

a Mark c.19.24,27. 1 or, *court*. b Matt.10.18. c 1Kings 18.17. c.17.6.

sary. The expulsion of the evil spirit would also afford a signal proof of the fact that the apostles were *really* from God. A far better proof than her noisy and troublesome proclamation of it would furnish. ¶ *In the name of Jesus Christ.* Or, by the authority of Jesus Christ. See Note, ch. iii. 6.

19. *The hope of their gains was gone.* It was this that troubled and enraged them. And this is as likely to enrage men as any thing. Instead of regarding the act as proof of divine power, they were intent only on their profits. And their indignation furnishes a remarkable illustration of the fixedness with which men will regard wealth; of the fact that the love of it will blind them to all the truths of religion, and all the proofs of the power and presence of God; and of the fact that *any* interposition of divine power that destroys their hopes of gain, fills them with wrath and hatred and murmuring. Many a man has been opposed to God and his gospel, because, if religion should be extensively prevalent, the hopes of gain would be gone. Many a slave-dealer, and many a trafficker in ardent spirits, and many a man engaged in other unlawful modes of gain, have been unwilling to abandon their employments, simply because the hopes of their gain would be destroyed. No small part of the opposition to the gospel arises from the fact, that if embraced, it would strike at so much of the dishonourable employments of men, and make them honest and conscientious. ¶ *The market-place.* The court or forum. The market-place was a place of concourse; and the courts were often held in or near those places. ¶ *The rulers.* The term used here refers commonly to *civil magistrates.*

20. *And brought them to the magistrates.* To the *military rulers* (στρατηγοῖς) or pretors. Phillippi was a Roman colony; and it is probable that the officers of the army exercised the double function of civil and military rulers. ¶ *Do exceedingly trouble our city.* In what way they did it they specify in the next verse. The charge which they wished to substantiate was, that of being disturbers of the public peace. All at once they became conscientious. They forgot the subject of their gains, and were greatly distressed about the violation of the laws. There is nothing that will make men more hypocritically conscientious, than to denounce, and detect, and destroy their unlawful and dishonest practices. Men who are thus exposed, become suddenly filled with reverence for the law or for religion; and they, who have heretofore cared nothing for either, become greatly alarmed lest the public peace should be disturbed. Men slumber quietly in sin, and pursue their wicked gains; they hate or despise all law and all forms of religion; but the moment their course of life is attacked and exposed, they become full of zeal for laws that they would not themselves hesitate to violate, and for the customs of religion, which in their hearts they thoroughly despise. Worldly-minded men often thus complain that their towns, and cities, and villages are disturbed by revivals of religion; and the preaching of the truth and attacking vice often arouses this hypocritical conscientiousness, and makes them alarmed for the laws, and for religion, and for order, which they at other times are the first to disturb and disregard.

21. *And teach customs.* The word *customs* here (ἔθη) refers to religious *rites* or forms of worship. See Note, ch. vi. 14. They meant to charge the apostles with introducing a new mode of worship and a new religion, which was unauthorized by the Roman laws. This was a cunning and artful accusation. It is perfectly evident that they cared nothing either for the religion of the Romans or of the Jews. Nor were they really concerned about any change of religion. Paul had destroyed their hopes of gain; and as they could not prevent that except by securing his punishment or expulsion, and as they had no way of revenge except by endeavouring to excite indignation against him and Silas for violating the laws, they endeavoured to convict them of such violation. This is one, among many instances, where wicked and unprincipled men will endeavour to make religion the

22 And the multitude rose up together against them: and the magistrates rent off their clothes, and commanded to beat *them*.

23 And when they had laid many [a] stripes upon them, they cast *them* into prison, charging the jailer to keep them safely:

24 Who having received such a charge, thrust them into the inner prison, and made their feet fast in the stocks.

a 2Cor.6.5; 11.23,25. 1Thess.2.22.

means of promoting their own interest. If they can make money by it, they will become its professed friends; or if they can annoy Christians, they will at once have remarkable zeal for the laws and for the purity of religion. Many a man opposes revivals of religion and the real progress of evangelical piety, from professed zeal for truth and order. ¶ *Which are not lawful for us to receive.* There were *laws* of the Roman empire under which they might shield themselves in this charge, though it is evident that their zeal was, not because they loved the laws *more*, but because they loved Christianity *less*. Thus Servius on Virgil, Æneid, viii. 187, says, "Care was taken among the Athenians and the Romans, that no one should introduce new religions. It was on this account that Socrates was condemned, and the Chaldeans or Jews were banished from the city." Cicero (de Legibus ii. 8) says, "No person shall have any separate gods, or new ones; nor shall he privately worship any strange gods, unless they be publicly allowed." Wetstein (in loco) says, "The Romans would indeed allow foreigners to worship their own gods, but not unless it were done secretly, so that the worship of foreign gods would not interfere with the allowed worship of the Romans, and so that occasion for dissension and controversy might be avoided. Neither was it lawful among the Romans to recommend a new religion to the citizens, contrary to that which was confirmed and established by the public authority, and to call off the people from that. It was on this account that there was such a hatred of the Romans against the Jews." (*Kuinoel.*) Tertullian says, that "there was a decree that no god should be consecrated, unless approved by the senate." (*Grotius.*) See many other authorities quoted in bishop Watson's "Apology for Christianity." ¶ *To observe.* To do. ¶ *Being Romans.* Having the privileges of Roman citizens. Note, ver. 12.

22. *And the multitude*, &c. It is evident that this was done in a popular tumult, and without even the form of law. Of this, Paul afterwards justly complained, as it was a violation of the privileges of a Roman citizen, and contrary to the laws. See Note, ver. 37. It was one instance in which men affect great zeal for the honour of the law, and yet are among the first to disregard it. ¶ *And the magistrates.* ver. 20. They who should have been their protectors until they had had a fair trial according to law. ¶ *Rent off their clothes.* This was always done when one was to be scourged or whipped. The criminal was usually stripped entirely naked. Livy says (ii. 5), "The lictors, being sent to inflict punishment, beat them with rods, *being naked.*" Cicero against Verres says, "He commanded the man to be seized, and to be stripped naked in the midst of the forum, and to be bound, and rods to be brought." ¶ *And commanded to beat them.* Ῥαβδίζειν. To beat them with rods. This was done by *lictors*, whose office it was, and was a common mode of punishment among the Romans. Probably Paul alludes to this when he says (2 Cor. xi. 25), "Thrice was I beaten with rods."

23. *And when they had laid many stripes on them.* The Jews were by law prohibited from inflicting more than forty stripes, and usually inflicted but thirty-nine. 2 Cor. xi. 24. But there was no such law among the Romans. They were unrestricted in regard to the number of lashes; and probably inflicted many more. Perhaps Paul refers to this when he says (2 Cor. xi. 23), "In stripes above measure," i. e. beyond the usual measure among the Jews, or beyond moderation. ¶ *They cast them into prison.* The magistrates (ver. 36, 37), as a punishment; and probably with a view hereafter of taking vengeance on them, more according to the forms of law.

24. *Thrust them into the inner prison.* Into the most retired and secure part of the prison. The cells in the interior of the prison would be regarded as more safe, being doubtless more protected, and the difficulty of escape would be greater. ¶ *And made their feet fast in the stocks.* Greek, And made their feet secure to wood. The word *stocks*, with us, denotes a machine made of two pieces of timber

25 And at midnight Paul and Silas prayed[a] and sang[b] praises unto God: and the prisoners heard them

26 And suddenly there was a great earthquake, so[c] that the foundations of the prison were shaken: and immediately[d] all the doors were opened, and every one's bands were loosed.

a Jam.5.13. b Ps.34.1. c c.4.31. d Isa.42.7. c.5.19; 12.7,10.

between which the feet of the criminals are placed, and in which they are thus made secure. The account here does not imply necessarily that they were secured precisely in this way, but that they were fastened or secured by the feet, probably by cords, to a piece or beam of wood, so that they could not escape. It is supposed that the legs of the prisoners were bound to large pieces of wood, which not only encumbered them, but which often were so placed as to extend their feet to a considerable distance. In this condition it might be necessary for them to lie on their backs; and if this, as is probable, was on the cold ground, after their severe scourging, their sufferings must have been very great. Yet in the midst of this they sang praises to God.

25. *And at midnight.* Probably their painful posture, the sufferings of their recent scourging, prevented their sleeping. Yet though they had no repose, they had a quiet conscience, and the supports of religion. ¶ *Prayed.* Though they had suffered much, yet they had reason to apprehend more. They sought, therefore, the sustaining grace of God. ¶ *And sang praises.* Nothing but religion would have enabled them to do this. They had endured much, but they had cause still for gratitude. A Christian may find more true joy in a prison, than the monarch on his throne. ¶ *And the prisoners heard them.* And doubtless with astonishment. Prayer and praise were not common in a prison. The song of rejoicing and the language of praise is not usual among men lying bound in a dungeon. From this narrative we may learn, (1.) That the Christian has the sources of his happiness within him. External circumstances cannot destroy his peace and joy. In a dungeon he may find as real happiness as on a throne. On the cold earth, beaten and bruised, he may be as truly happy as on a bed of down. (2.) The enemies of Christians cannot destroy their peace. They may incarcerate the body, but they cannot bind the spirit. They may exclude from earthly comforts, but they cannot shut them out from the presence and sustaining grace of God. (3.) We see the value of a good conscience. Nothing else can give peace; and amidst the wakeful hours of the night, whether in a dungeon or on a bed of sickness, it is of more value than all the wealth of the world. (4.) We see the inestimable worth of the religion of Christ. It fits for all scenes; supports in all trials; upholds by day or by night; inspires the soul with confidence in God; and puts into the lips the songs of praise and thanksgiving. (5.) We have here a sublime and holy scene, which sin and infidelity could never furnish. What more sublime spectacle has the earth witnessed than that of scourged and incarcerated men, suffering from unjust and cruel inflictions, and anticipating still greater sorrows; yet, with a calm mind, a pure conscience, a holy joy, pouring forth their desires and praises at midnight, into the ear of the God who always hears prayer! The darkness, the stillness, the loneliness, all give sublimity to the scene, and teach us how invaluable is the privilege of access to the throne of mercy in this suffering world.

26. *And suddenly.* While they were praying and singing. ¶ *A great earthquake.* Matt. xxviii. 2. An earthquake, in such circumstances, was regarded as a symbol of the presence of God, and as an answer to prayer. See Note, ch. iv. 31. The *design* of this was, doubtless, to furnish them proof of the presence and protection of God, and to provide a way for them to escape. It was one among the series of wonders by which the gospel was established, and the early Christians protected amidst their dangers. ¶ *And immediately all the doors were opened.* An effect that would naturally follow from the violent concussion of the earthquake. Comp. ch. v. 19. ¶ *Every one's bands were loosed.* This was evidently a miracle. Some have supposed that their chains were dissolved by electric fluid; but the narrative gives no account of any such fluid, even supposing such an effect to be possible. It was evidently a direct interposition of divine power. But for what purpose it was done is not recorded. Grotius supposes that it was that they might know that the apostles might be useful to them and to others, and that by them their spiritual bonds might be loosed Probably the design was to impress all the

27 And the keeper of the prison
awaking out of his sleep, and seeing the prison doors open, he drew
out his sword, and would have killed himself, supposing that the prisoners had been fled.
28 But [a] Paul cried with a loud
voice, saying, Do thyself [b] no harm;
for we are all here.
29 Then he called for a light,
and sprang in, and came trembling, [c] and fell down before Paul
and Silas:
30 And brought them out, and

a Prov.24.11,12. 1Thess.5.15. b Eccl.5.17. c Jer.5.22.

prisoners with the conviction of the presence and power of God, and thus to prepare them to receive the message of life from the lips of his servants Paul and Silas. They had just before heard them singing and praying; they were aware, doubtless, of the cause for which they were imprisoned; they saw evident tokens that they were the servants of the Most High, and under his protection; and their own minds were impressed and awed by the terrors of the earthquake, and by the fact of their own liberation. It renders this scene the more remarkable, that though the doors were opened, and the prisoners loosed, yet no one made any attempt to escape.

27. *Would have killed himself.* This was all done in the midst of agitation and alarm. He supposed that the prisoners had fled. He presumed that their escape would be charged on him. It was customary to hold a jailer responsible for the safe keeping of prisoners, and to subject him to the punishment due them, if he suffered them to escape. See ch. xii. 19. It should be added, that it was common and approved among the Greeks and Romans for a man to commit suicide when he was encompassed with dangers from which he could not escape. Thus Cato was guilty of self-murder in Utica; and thus, at this very place—at Philippi—Brutus and Cassius, and many of their friends, fell on their own swords, and ended their lives by suicide. The custom was thus sanctioned by the authority and example of the great; and we are not to wonder that the jailer, in a moment of alarm, should also attempt to destroy his own life. It is not one of the least benefits of Christianity, that it has proclaimed the evil of self-murder, and that it has done so much to drive it from the world.

28. *Do thyself no harm.* This is the solemn command of religion in his case, and in all others. It enjoins on men to do themselves no harm—by self-murder, whether by the sword, the pistol, the halter or by intemperance, and lust, and dissipation. In all cases, Christianity seeks the true welfare of man. In all cases, if it were obeyed, men would do themselves no harm. They would promote their own best interests here, and their eternal welfare hereafter.

29. *Then he called for a light.* Greek, *Lights*, in the plural. Probably several torches were brought by his attendants. ¶ *And came trembling.* Alarmed at the earthquake, and amazed that the prisoners were still there, and probably not a little confounded at the calmness of Paul and Silas, and overwhelmed at the proof of the presence of God. Comp. Jer. v. 22, "Fear ye not me, saith the Lord? will ye not tremble at my presence?" &c. ¶ *And fell down*, &c. This was an act of profound reverence. See Note, Matt. ii. 11. It is evident that he regarded them as the favourites of God, and was constrained to recognise them in their character as religious teachers.

30. *And brought them out.* From the prison. ¶ *Sirs.* Greek, κύριοι, lords—an address of respect; a title usually given to masters, or owners of slaves. ¶ *What must I do to be saved?* Never was a more important question asked than this. It is evident that by this question he did not refer to any danger to which he might be exposed from what had happened. For (1.) The apostles evidently understood him as referring to his eternal salvation, as is manifest from their answer; since to believe on the Lord Jesus would have no effect in saving him from any danger of punishment to which he might be exposed from what had occurred. (2.) He could scarcely consider himself as exposed to punishment by the Romans. The prisoners were all safe; none had escaped, or showed any disposition to escape: and besides, for the earthquake and its effects he could not be held responsible. It is not improbable that there was much confusion in his mind. There would be a *rush* of many thoughts; a state of agitation and alarm, and fear; and in view of all he would naturally ask those whom he now saw to be men sent by God, and under his protection, what he should do to obtain the favour of that great Being under whose protection he saw that they manifestly were Perhaps the following thoughts might have gone to produce this

said, Sirs, what [a] must I do to be saved?

31 And they said, Believe [b] on the Lord Jesus Christ, and thou

a c.2.37; 9.6.

b Hab.2.4. Jno.3.16,36; 6.47. c.13.39.

state of agitation and alarm. (1.) They had been designated by the Pythoness (ver. 17) as religious teachers sent from God, and appointed to "show *the way of salvation*," and in her testimony he might have been disposed to put confidence, or it might now be brought fresh to his recollection. (2.) He manifestly saw that they were under the protection of God. A remarkable interposition—an earthquake—an event which all the heathen regarded as ominous of the presence of the divinity—had showed this. (3.) The guilt of their imprisonment might rush upon his mind; and he might suppose that he, the agent of the imprisonment of the servants of God, would be exposed to his displeasure. (4.) His own guilt in attempting his own life might overwhelm him with alarm. (5.) The whole scene was fitted to show him the need of the protection and friendship of the God that had thus interposed. In this state of agitation and alarm, the apostles directed him to the only source of peace and safety—the blood of the atonement. The feelings of an awakened sinner are often strikingly similar to those of this jailer. He is agitated, alarmed, and fearful; he sees that he is a sinner, and trembles; the sins of his life rush over his memory, and fill him with deep anxiety, and he inquires what he must do to be saved. Often too, as here, the providence of God is the means of awakening the sinner, and of leading to this inquiry. Some alarming dispensation convinces him that God is near, and that the soul is in danger. The loss of health, or property, or of a friend, may thus alarm the soul; or the presence of the pestilence, or any fearful judgment, may arrest the attention, and lead to the inquiry, "What must I do to be saved?" Reader, have you ever made this inquiry? Have you ever, like the heathen jailer at Philippi, seen yourself to be a lost sinner, and been willing to ask the way to life?

In this narrative we see the *contrast* which exists in periods of distress and alarm between Christians and sinners. The guilty jailer was all agitation, fear, distress, and terror; the apostles, all peace, calmness, joy. The one was filled with thoughts of self-murder; the others, intent on saving life and doing good. This difference is to be traced to religion. It was confidence in God that gave peace to *them*; it was the want of that, which led to agitation and alarm in *him*. It is so still. In the trying scenes of this life, the same difference is still seen. In bereavements, in sickness, in times of pestilence, in death, it is still so. The Christian is calm; the sinner is agitated and alarmed. The Christian can pass through such scenes with peace and joy; to the sinner, they are scenes of terror and of dread. And thus it will be beyond the grave. In the morning of the resurrection, the Christian will rise with joy and triumph; the sinner, with fear and horror. And thus at the judgment-seat. Calm and serene, the saint shall witness the solemnities of that day, and triumphantly hail the Judge as his friend: fearful and trembling, the sinner shall regard these solemnities, and with a soul filled with horror, shall listen to the sentence that consigns him to eternal wo! With what solicitude, then, should we seek, without delay, an interest in that religion which alone can give peace to the soul!

31. *Believe on the Lord Jesus Christ.* This was a simple, a plain, and an effectual direction. They did not direct him to use the means of grace, to pray, or to continue to seek for salvation. They did not advise him to delay, or to wait for the mercy of God. They told him to believe at once; to commit his agitated, and guilty, and troubled spirit to the Saviour, with the assurance that he should find peace. They presumed that he would understand what it was to believe; and they commanded him *to do the thing.* And this was the uniform direction which the early preachers gave to those inquiring the way to life. See Note, Matt. xvi. 16. Comp. Note, Acts viii. 22. ¶ *And thy house.* And thy family. That is, the same salvation is equally adapted to, and offered to your family. It does not mean that his family would be saved simply by *his* believing; but that the offers had reference to them as well as to himself; that they might be saved as well as he. His attention was thus called at once, as every man's should be, to his family. He was reminded that they needed salvation; and he was presented with the assurance that they might unite with him in the peace and joy of redeeming mercy. Comp. Note, ch. ii. 39. It *may be* implied here that the faith of a father may be expected to be the means of the salvation of his family. It often is so in fact: but the direct meaning of this is, that salvation was offered to his family as well as

shalt be saved, and thy [a] house.
32 And they spake unto him the
word of the Lord, and [b] to all that
were in his house.
33 And he took them the same
hour of the night, and washed *their*
stripes; and was baptized, he, and
all his, straightway.
34 And when he had brought
them into his house, he set meat [c]
before them, and rejoiced, [d] believing in God with all his house.
35 And when it was day, the
magistrates sent the serjeants, saying, Let those men go.
36 And the keeper of the prison
told this saying to Paul, The magistrates have sent to let you go:
now therefore depart, and go in
peace.

a c.2.39. b Rom.1.14,16. Luke 5.29. d Rom.5.11.

himself; implying that if they believed, they should also be saved.

32. *To all that were in his house.* Old and young. They instructed them in the doctrines of religion. and doubtless in the nature of the ordinances of the gospel, and then baptized the entire family.

33. *And he took them.* To a convenient place for washing. It is evident from this, that though the apostles had the gift of miracles, that they did not exercise it in regard to their own sufferings, or to heal their own wounds. They restored others to health; not themselves. ¶ *And washed their stripes.* The wounds which had been inflicted by the severe scourging which they had received the night before. We have here a remarkable instance of the effect of religion in producing humanity and tenderness. This same man, a few hours before, had thrust them into the inner prison, and made them fast in the stocks. He evidently had then no concern about their stripes or their wounds. But no sooner was he converted, and his heart changed, than one of his first acts was an act of humanity. He saw them suffering; he pitied them, and hastened to minister to them and to heal their wounds. Till the time of Christianity, there never had been a hospital or an almshouse. Nearly all the hospitals for the sick since, have been reared by Christians. They who are most ready to minister to the sick and dying are Christians. They who are willing to encounter the pestilential damps of dungeons to aid the prisoner, are, like Howard, Christians. Who ever saw an infidel attending a dying bed, if he could help it? and where has infidelity ever reared a hospital or an almshouse, or made provision for the widow and the fatherless? Often one of the most striking changes that occurs in conversion is seen in the disposition to be kind and humane to the suffering. Comp. James i. 27. ¶ *And was baptized.* This was done *straightway;* that is immediately. As it is altogether improbable that either in his house or in the prison there would be water sufficient for *immersing* them, there is every reason to suppose that this was performed in some other mode. All the circumstances lead us to suppose that it was not by immersion. It was at the dead of night; in a prison; amidst much agitation; and evidently performed in haste.

34. *He set meat before them.* Food. Gr. He placed a *table.* The word *meat* formerly meant food of all kinds. ¶ *And rejoiced.* This was the effect of believing. Religion produces joy. See Note, ch. viii. 8. He was free from danger and alarm; he had evidence that his sins were forgiven, and that he was the friend of God. The agitating and alarming scenes of the night had passed away; the prisoners were safe; and religion, with its peace, and pardon, and rejoicings, had visited his family. What a change to be produced in one night! What a difference between the family, when Paul was thrust into prison, and when he was brought out and received as an honoured guest at the very table of the renovated jailer! Such a change would Christianity produce in every family, and such joy would it diffuse through every household. ¶ *With all his house.* With all his family. Whether they believed *before* they were baptized, or *after,* is not declared. But the whole narrative would lead us to suppose, that as soon as the jailer believed, he and all his family were baptized. It is subsequently added, that they believed also. The *joy* arose from the fact, that they all believed the gospel; the *baptism* appears to have been performed on account of the faith of the head of the family.

35. *And when it was day,* &c. It is evident from the narrative that it was not contemplated at first to release them so soon. ver. 22—24 But it is not known what produced this change of purpose in the magistrates. It is probable, however that they had been brought to reflection,

37 But Paul said unto them, They have beaten us openly uncondemned, [a] being Romans, and have cast *us* into prison; and now do they thrust us out privily? Nay, verily; but let them come them-

a c.22.25.

somewhat as the jailer had, by the earthquake; and that their consciences had been troubled by the fact, that in order to please the multitude, they had caused strangers to be beaten and imprisoned without trial, and contrary to the Roman laws. An earthquake is always fitted to alarm the guilty; and among the Romans it was regarded as an omen of the anger of the gods, and was therefore fitted to produce agitation and remorse. Their agitation and alarm were shown by the fact that they sent the officers *as soon* as it was day. The judgments of God are eminently adapted to alarm sinners. Two ancient MSS. read this, "The magistrates, *who were alarmed by the earthquake,* sent," &c. (*Doddridge.*) Whether this reading be genuine or not, it doubtless expresses the true cause of their sending to release the apostles. ¶ *The sergeants.* ῥαβδούχους. Literally, those having rods; the lictors. These were public officers, who went before magistrates with the emblems of authority. In Rome, they bore before the senators the *fasces;* that is, a bundle of rods with an axe in its centre, as a symbol of office. They performed somewhat the same office as a beadle in England, or as a constable in our courts.

37. *They have beaten us openly uncondemned.* There are three aggravating circumstances mentioned, of which Paul complains. (1.) That they had been *beaten,* contrary to the Roman laws. (2.) That it had been *public;* the disgrace had been in the presence of the people, and the reparation ought to be as public; and, (3.) That it had been done without a trial, and while they were uncondemned; and therefore the magistrates ought themselves to come and release them, and thus publicly acknowledge their error. Paul knew the privileges of a Roman citizen; and at proper times, when the interests of justice and religion required it, he did not hesitate to assert them. In all this, he understood and accorded with the Roman laws. The Valerian law declared, that if a citizen appealed from the magistrate to the people, it should not be lawful for the magistrate to beat him with rods, or to behead him. Plutarch, Life of P. Valerius Publicola. Livy, ii. 8. By the Porcian law, it was expressly forbidden that a citizen should be beaten. Livy, iv. 9 Cicero (Pro. Rabir ch. 4) says, that the body of every Roman citizen was inviolable. "The Porcian law," he adds, "has removed the rod from the body of every Roman citizen." And in his celebrated oration against Verres, he says, "A Roman citizen was beaten with rods in the forum, O judges; where, in the mean time, no groan, no other voice of this unhappy man was heard, except the cry, 'I am a Roman citizen!' Take away this hope," he says, "take away this defence from the Roman citizens, let there be no protection in the cry *I am a Roman citizen,* and the prætor can with impunity inflict any punishment on him who declares himself a citizen of Rome," &c. ¶ *Being Romans.* Being Romans, or having the privilege of Roman citizens. They were born Jews, but they claimed that they were Roman citizens, and had a right to the privileges of citizenship. On the ground of this claim, and the reason why Paul claimed to be a Roman citizen, see Notes, ch. xxii. 28. ¶ *Privily.* Privately. The release should be as public as the unjust act of imprisonment. As they have publicly attempted to disgrace us, so they should as publicly acquit us. This was a matter of mere justice; and as it was of great importance to their character and success, they insisted on it. ¶ *Nay, verily; but let them come,* &c. It was proper that they should be required to do this, (1.) Because they had been illegally imprisoned, and the injustice of the magistrates should be acknowledged. (2.) Because the Roman laws had been violated, and the majesty of the Roman people thus insulted, and honour should be done to the laws. (3.) Injustice had been done to Paul and Silas, and they had a right to demand just treatment and protection. (4.) Such a public act on the part of the magistrates would strengthen the young converts, and show them that the apostles were not guilty of a violation of the laws. (5.) It would tend to the honour and to the furtherance of religion. It would be a public acknowledgment of their innocence; and would go far towards lending to them the sanction of the laws as religious teachers. We may learn from this also, (1.) That though Christianity requires meekness in the reception of injuries, yet that there are occasions where Christians may insist on their rights according to the laws. Comp. John xviii. 23. (2.) That

selves,[a] and fetch us out.
38 And the serjeants told these
words unto the magistrates; and
they feared, when they heard that
they were Romans.
39 And they came and besought[b]
them, and brought *them* out, and
desired[c] *them* to depart out of the
city.
40 And they went out of the
prison, and entered into *the house
of* Lydia:[d] and when they had seen
the brethren, they comforted them,
and departed.

a Dan.6.18,19. Matt.10.16. b Ex.11.8. Rev.3.9. c Matt.8.34. d ver.14.

this is to be done, particularly where the honour of religion is concerned, and where by it the gospel will be promoted. A Christian may bear much as a man in a private capacity, and may submit, without any effort to seek reparation; but where the honour of the gospel is concerned; where submission, without any effort to obtain justice, might be followed by disgrace to the cause of religion, a higher obligation may require him to seek a vindication of his character, and to claim the protection of the laws. His name, and character, and influence belong to the church. The laws are designed as a protection to an injured name, or of violated property and rights, and of an endangered life. And when that protection can be had only by an appeal to the laws, such an appeal, as in the case of Paul and Silas, is neither vindictive nor improper. My private interests I may sacrifice, if I choose; my public name, and character, and principles belong to the church and the world; and the laws, if necessary, may be called in for their protection.

38. *They feared when they heard, &c.* They were apprehensive of punishment for having imprisoned them in violation of the laws of the empire. To punish unjustly a Roman citizen was deemed an offence to the majesty of the Roman people, and was severely punished by the laws. Dionysius Hali. (Ant. Rom. ii.) says, that "The punishment appointed for those who abrogated or transgressed the Valerian law was death, and the confiscation of his property." The emperor Claudius deprived the inhabitants of Rhodes of freedom for having crucified some Roman citizens. Dio. Cass. lib. 60. (See *Kuinöel* and *Grotius*.)

39. *And they came and besought them.* A most humiliating act for Roman magistrates, but in this case it was unavoidable. The apostles had them completely in their power, and could easily effect their disgrace and ruin. Probably they *besought* them by declaring them innocent; by affirming that they were ignorant that they were Roman citizens, &c. ¶ *And desired them to depart, &c.* Probably, (1.) To save their own character, and be secure from their taking any further steps to convict the magistrates of violating the laws; and, (2.) To evade any further popular tumult on their account. This advice they saw fit to comply with, after they had seen and comforted the brethren. ver. 40. They had accomplished their main purpose in going to Philippi; they had preached the gospel; had laid the foundation of a flourishing church (comp. the Epistle to the Philippians); and they were now prepared to prosecute the purpose of their agency into surrounding regions. Thus, the opposition of the people and the magistrates at Philippi was the occasion of the founding of the church there; and thus their unkind and inhospitable request that they should leave them, was the means of the extension of the gospel into adjacent regions.

40. *They comforted them.* They exhorted them, and encouraged them to persevere, notwithstanding the opposition and persecution which they might meet with. ¶ *And departed.* That is, Paul and Silas departed. It would appear probable that Luke and Timothy remained in Philippi, or, at least, did not attend Paul and Silas. For Luke, who, in ch. xvi. 10, uses the first person, and speaks of himself as with Paul and Silas, speaks of them now in the third person, implying that he was not with them until Paul had arrived at Troas, where Luke joined him from Philippi. ch. xx. 5, 6. In ch. xvii. 14, also, Timothy is mentioned as being at Berea in company with Silas, from which it appears that he did not accompany Paul and Silas to Thessalonica. Comp. ch. xvii. 1. 4. Paul and Silas, when they departed from Philippi, went to Thessalonica. ch. xvii. 1.

CHAPTER XVII.

NOW when they had passed
through Amphipolis and Apollonia, they came to Thessalonica,
where was a synagogue of the
Jews:
2 And Paul, as his manner was,[a]
went in unto them, and three sab
bath-days reasoned with them out
of the Scriptures,
3 Opening and alleging, that
Christ must[b] needs have suffered,
and risen again from the dead; and
that this[1] Jesus, whom I preach

a Luke 4.16 c.9.20; 13.5,14.

b Luke 24.26,46. c.18.28. Gal.3.1. 1Thess.1.5,6.
1 or, *whom, said he, I preach.*

CHAPTER XVII.

1. *Amphipolis.* This was the capital of the eastern province of Macedonia. It was originally a colony of the Athenians; but under the Romans it was made the capital of that part of Macedonia. It was near to Thrace, and was situated not far from the mouth of the river Strymon, which flowed *around the city*, and thus occasioned its name, *around the city*. In the middle ages it was called Chrysopolis. The village which now stands upon the site of the ancient city, is called *Empoli* or *Yamboli*, a corruption of Amphipolis. (*Rob. Cal.*) ¶ *And Apollonia.* This city was situated between Amphipolis and Thessalonica, and was formerly much celebrated for its trade. ¶ *They came to Thessalonica.* This was a seaport of the second part of Macedonia. It is situated at the head of the bay Thermaicus. It was made the capital of the second division of Macedonia by Æmilius Paulus, when he divided the country into four districts. It was formerly called Therma, but afterwards received the name of Thessalonica, either from Cassander, in honour of his wife Thessalonica, the daughter of Philip, or in honour of a victory which Philip obtained over the armies of Thessaly. It was inhabited by Greeks, Romans, and Jews. It is now called *Saloniki*, and is a wretched place, though it has a population of near sixty thousand. In this place a church was collected, to which Paul afterwards addressed the two epistles to the Thessalonians. ¶ *Where was a synagogue.* Gr. Where was THE synagogue (ἡ συναγωγὴ) of the Jews. It has been remarked by Grotius and Kuinoel, that the article used here is emphatic, and denotes that there was probably no synagogue at Amphipolis and Apollonia. This was the reason why they passed through those places without making any delay.

2. *His manner was.* His custom was to attend on the worship of the synagogue, and to preach the gospel to his countrymen first. ch. ix. 20; xiii. 5. 14. ¶ *Reasoned with them.* Discoursed to them, or attempted to prove that Jesus was the Messiah. The word used here (διελέγετο) means often no more than to make a public address or discourse. Note, ch. xxiv. 25. ¶ *Out of the Scriptures.* By many critics this is connected with the following verse, 'Opening and alleging from the Scriptures, that Christ must needs have suffered,' &c. The sense is not varied materially by the change.

3. *Opening.* Διανοίγων. See Luke, xxiv. 32. The word means, to explain, or to unfold. It is usually applied to that which is *shut*, as to the eyes, &c. Then it means to explain that which is concealed or obscure. It means here, that he *explained* the Scriptures in their true sense. ¶ *And alleging.* Παρατιθέμενος. Laying down the proposition; that is, maintaining that it must be so. ¶ *That Christ must needs have suffered.* That there was a fitness and necessity in his dying, as Jesus of Nazareth had done. The sense of this will be better seen by retaining the word Messiah. 'That there was a fitness or necessity that the *Messiah* expected by the Jews and predicted in their Scriptures, should suffer.' This point the Jews were unwilling to admit; but it was essential to his argument in proving that Jesus was the Messiah, to show that it was foretold that he should die for the sins of men. On the *necessity* of this, see Note, Luke xxiv. 26, 27 ¶ *Have suffered.* That he should die. ¶ *And that this Jesus.* And that this Jesus of Nazareth, who has thus suffered and risen, whom, said he, I preach to you, is the Messiah.

The arguments by which Paul probably proved that Jesus was the Messiah, were, (1.) That he corresponded with the *prophecies* respecting him, in the following particulars. (*a*) He was born at Bethlehem Micah v. 2. (*b*) He was of the tribe of Judah. Gen. xlix. 10. (*c*) He was descended from Jesse, and of the royal line of David. Isa. xi. 1. 10. (*d*) He came at the *time* predicted. Dan. ix. 24—27. (*e*) His appearance, character, work, &c. corresponded with the predictions. Isa. liii (2.) His miracles proved that he was the Messiah, for he *professed* to be, and God

unto you, is Christ.
4 And some [a] of them believed,
and [b] consorted with Paul and Silas; and of the devout Greeks a
great multitude, and of the chief
women not a few.
5 But the Jews which believed not,
moved with envy, took unto them
certain lewd fellows of the baser
sort, and gathered a company, and set
all the city on an uproar, and assault-
ed the house of Jason, [c] and sought
to bring them out to the people.
6 And when they found them
not, they drew Jason and certain
brethren unto the rulers of the city,
crying, These [d] that have turned
the world upside down, are come
hither also;
7 Whom Jason hath received:
and these all do contrary [e] to the
decrees of Cesar, saying that there
is another king, *one* Jesus.
8 And they troubled [f] the people.

a c.28.24. b 2Cor.8.5. c Rom.16.21. d Luke 23.5. c.16.20. e Luke 23.2. Jno.19.12. f Matt.2.3. Jno.11.48.

would not work a miracle to confirm the claims of an impostor. (3.) For the same reason, his resurrection from the dead proved that he was the Messiah.

4. *And consorted.* Literally, had their lot with Paul and Silas; that is, they united themselves to them, and became their disciples. The word is commonly applied to those who are partakers of an inheritance. ¶ *And of the devout Greeks. Religious* Greeks; or, of those who worshipped God. Those are denoted who had renounced the worship of idols, and who attended on the worship of the synagogue, but who were not fully admitted to the privileges of Jewish proselytes. They were called, by the Jews, proselytes of the gate. ¶ *And of the chief women.* Note, ch. xiii. 50.

5. *Moved with envy.* That they made so many converts and met with such success. ¶ *Certain lewd fellows of the baser sort.* This is an unhappy translation. The word *lewd* is not in the original. The Greek is, 'And having taken certain wicked men of those who were about the forum,' or market-place. The forum, or market-place, was the place where the idle assembled, and where those were gathered together that wished to be employed. Matt. xx. 3. Many of these would be of abandoned character,—the idle, the dissipated, and the worthless; and, therefore, just the materials for a mob. It does not appear that they felt any particular interest in the subject; but they were, like other mobs, easily excited, and urged on to any acts of violence. The pretence on which the mob was excited was, that they had every where produced disturbance, and that they violated the laws of the Roman emperor. ver. 6, 7. It may be observed, however, that a mob usually regards very little the cause in which they are engaged. They may be roused either for or against religion, and become as full of zeal *for* the *insulted* honour of religion as *against* it. The profane, the worthless, and the abandoned thus often become violently enraged for the *honour* of religion, and full of indignation and tumult against those who are accused of violating public peace and order. ¶ *The house of Jason.* Where Paul and Silas were. ver. 7. Jason appears to have been a relative of Paul, and for this reason it was probably that he lodged with him. Rom. xvi. 21.

6. *These that have turned the world upside down.* That have excited commotion and disturbance in other places. The charge has been often brought against the gospel, that it has been the occasion of confusion and disorder.

7. *Whom Jason hath received.* Has received into his house, and entertained kindly. ¶ *These all do contrary to the decrees of Cesar.* The charge against them was that of sedition and rebellion against the Roman emperor. Grotius on this verse remarks, that the Roman people, and after them the emperors, would not permit the name of king to be mentioned in any of the vanquished provinces, except by their permission. ¶ *Saying that there is another king.* This was probably a charge of mere malignity. They probably understood, that when the apostles spoke of Jesus as a king, they did not do it as of a temporal prince. But it was easy to pervert their words, and to give plausibility to the accusation. The same thing had occurred in regard to the Lord Jesus himself. Luke xxiii. 2.

8. *And they troubled the people.* They excited the people to commotion and alarm. The rulers feared the tumult that was excited, and the people feared the Romans, when they heard the charge that there were rebels against the govern

and the rulers of the city, when they heard these things.

9 And when they had taken security of Jason, and of the other, they let them go.

10 And the brethren immediately sent away [a] Paul and Silas by night unto Berea: who coming *thither*, went into the synagogue of the Jews.

11 These were more [b] noble than those in Thessalonica, in that they received the word with all readiness [c] of mind, and searched the Scriptures [d] daily, whether those things were so.

a c.9.25. ver.14.

b Ps.119.99,100. c Jam.1.21. 1Pet.2.2. d Isa. 34.16. Luke 16.29; 24.44. Jno.5.39.

---

ment in their city. It does not appear that there was a disposition in the rulers or the people to persecute the apostles; but they were excited and alarmed by the representations of the Jews, and by the mob that they had collected.

9. *And when they had taken security of Jason.* This is an expression taken from courts, and means that Jason and the other gave satisfaction to the magistrates for the good conduct of Paul and Silas, or became responsible for it. Whether it was by depositing a sum of money, and by thus giving bail, is not quite clear. The sense is, that they did it in accordance with the Roman usages, and gave sufficient security for the good conduct of Paul and Silas. Heuman supposes that the pledge given was, that they should leave the city. Michaelis thinks that they gave a pledge that they would no more harbour them; but that if they returned again to them, they would deliver them to the magistrates. ¶ *And of the other.* The other brethren (ver. 6) who had been drawn to the rulers of the city.

10. *And the brethren immediately sent away Paul and Silas.* Comp. ch. ix. 25. They did this for their safety. Yet this was not done until the gospel had taken deep root in Thessalonica. Having preached there, and laid the foundation of a church; having thus accomplished the purpose for which they went there, they were prepared to leave the city. To the church in this city Paul afterwards addressed two epistles. ¶ *Unto Berea.* This was a city of Macedonia, near Mount Cithanes. There is a medal of Berea extant, remarkable for being inscribed, "of the second Macedonia."

11. *These were more noble.* Εὐγενέστεροι. This literally means more noble by birth; descended from more illustrious ancestors. But here the word is used to denote a quality of mind and heart; they were more generous, liberal, and noble in their feelings; more disposed to inquire candidly into the truth of the doctrines advanced by Paul and Silas. It is always proof of a noble, liberal, and ingenuous disposition, to be willing to examine into the truth of any doctrine presented. The writer refers here particularly to the Jews. ¶ *In that.* Because. ¶ *They received the word,* &c. They listened attentively and respectfully to the gospel They did not reject and spurn it, as unworthy of examination. This is the first particular in which they were more noble than those in Thessalonica. ¶ *And searched the Scriptures.* That is, the Old Testament. Note, John v. 39. The apostles always affirmed that the doctrines which they maintained respecting the Messiah were in accordance with the Jewish Scriptures. The Bereans made diligent and earnest inquiry in respect to this, and were willing to ascertain the truth. ¶ *Daily.* Not only on the Sabbath, and in the synagogue; but they made it a daily employment. It is evident from this, that they *had* the Scriptures; and this is one proof that Jewish families would, if possible, obtain the oracles of God. ¶ *Whether these things were so.* Whether the doctrines stated by Paul and Silas were in accordance with the Scriptures. The Old Testament they received as the standard of truth, and whatever could be shown to be in accordance with that they received. On this verse we may remark, (1.) That it is proof of true nobleness and liberality of mind to be willing to examine the proofs of the truth of religion. What the friends of Christianity have had most cause to lament and regret is, that so many are unwilling to examine its claims; that they spurn it as unworthy of serious thought, and condemn it without hearing. (2.) The Scriptures should be examined *daily.* If we wish to arrive at the truth, they should be the object of constant study. That man has very little reason to expect that he will grow in knowledge and grace who does not peruse, with candour and with prayer, a portion of the Bible every day. (3.) The constant searching of the Scriptures is the best way to keep the

12 Therefore many of them believed: also of honourable women which were Greeks, and of men, not a few.

13 But when the Jews of Thessalonica had knowledge that the word of God was preached of Paul at Berea, they came thither also, and stirred up [a] the people.

14 And then immediately the brethren sent away [b] Paul, to go as it were to the sea: but Silas and Timotheus abode there still.

15 And they that conducted Paul

a Luke 12.51. b Matt.10.23

mind from error. He who does not do it daily may expect to "be carried about with every wind of doctrine," and to have no settled opinions. (4.) The preaching of ministers should be examined by the Scriptures. Their doctrines are of no value unless they accord with the Bible. Every preacher should expect his doctrines to be examined in this way, and to be rejected if they are not in accordance with the word of God. The church, in proportion to its increase in purity and knowledge, will feel this more and more; and it is an indication of advance in piety when men are increasingly disposed to examine every thing by the Bible. How immensely important then is it, that the young should be trained up to diligent habits of searching the word of God. And how momentous is the duty of parents, and of Sabbath-school teachers, to inculcate just views of the interpretation of the Bible, and to form the habits of the rising generation so that they shall be disposed and enabled to examine every doctrine by the sacred oracles. The purity of the church depends on the extension of the spirit of the noble-minded Bereans; and that spirit is to be extended mainly by the instrumentality of Sabbath-schools.

12. *Therefore.* As the result of their examination. They found that the doctrines of Paul and Silas accorded with the Old Testament. This result will commonly follow when people search the Scriptures. Much is gained when men can be induced to examine the Bible. We may commonly take it for granted that such an examination will result in their conviction of the truth. The most prominent and invariable cause of infidelity is found in the fact that men will not investigate the Scriptures. Many infidels have confessed that they had never carefully read the New Testament. Thomas Paine confessed that he wrote the first part of the "Age of Reason" without having a Bible at hand; and without its being possible to procure one where he then was (in Paris). "I had," says he, "neither Bible nor Testament to refer to, though I was writing against both; nor could I procure any." *Age of Reason,* p. 65. Ed. 1831. Also p. 33. None have ever read the Scriptures with candour, and with the true spirit of prayer, who have not been convinced of the truth of Christianity, and been brought to submit their souls to its influence and its consolations. The great thing which Christians desire their fellow men to do is, candidly to search the Bible; and when this is done, they confidently expect that they will be truly converted to God. ¶ *Of honourable women.* Note, ch. xiii. 50.

13. *Stirred up the people.* The word used here (σαλεύειν) denotes properly *to agitate,* or *excite,* as the waves of the sea are agitated by the wind. It is with great beauty used to denote the agitation and excitement of a popular tumult, from its resemblance to the troubled waves of the ocean. The figure is often employed by the classic writers, and also occurs in the Scriptures. See Ps. lxv. 7. Isa. xvii. 12, 13. Jer. xlvi. 7, 8.

14. *The brethren.* Those who were Christians. ¶ *Sent away Paul.* In order to secure his safety. A similar thing had been done in Thessalonica. ver. 10. The tumult was great; and there was no doubt, such was the hostility of the Jews, that the life of Paul would be endangered, and they therefore resolved to secure his safety. ¶ *As it were.* Rather, 'even to the sea,' for that is its signification. It does not imply that there was any feint or sleight in the case, *as if* they intended to deceive their pursuers. They took him to the sea-coast, not far from Berea, and from that place he probably went by sea to Athens.

15. *Unto Athens.* This was the first visit of Paul to this celebrated city; and perhaps the first visit of a Christian minister. His success in this city, for some cause, was not great. But his preaching was attended with the conversion of some individuals. See ver. 34. Athens was the most celebrated city of Greece, and was distinguished for the military talents, learning, eloquence, and politeness of its inhabitants. It was

brought him unto Athens: and receiving a commandment unto Silas and Timotheus [a] for to come to him with all speed, they departed.

a c.18.5.

16 Now while Paul waited for them at Athens, [b] his spirit was stirred in him, when he saw the city [1] wholly given to idolatry.

b Ps.119.136. 2Pe. 2.8 1 or, *full of idols*.

founded by Cecrops and an Egyptian colony, about 1556 years before the Christian era. It was called *Athens* in honour of Minerva, who was chiefly worshipped there, and to whom the city was dedicated. The city, at first, was built on a rock in the midst of a spacious plain; but in process of time the whole plain was covered with buildings, which were called the lower city. No city of Greece, or of the ancient world, was so much distinguished for philosophy, learning, and the arts. The most celebrated warriors, poets, statesmen, and philosophers were either born or flourished there. The most celebrated models of architecture and statuary were there; and for ages it held its pre-eminence in civilization, arts, and arms. The city still exists, though it has been often subject to the calamities of war, to a change of masters, and to the mouldering hand of time. It was twice burnt by the Persians; destroyed by Philip II. of Macedon; again by Sylla; was plundered by Tiberius; desolated by the Goths in the reign of Claudius; and the whole territory ravaged and ruined by Alaric. From the reign of Justinian to the thirteenth century, the city remained in obscurity, though it continued to be a town at the head of a small state. It was seized by Omar, general of Mahomet the Great, in 1455; was sacked by the Venetians in 1464; and was taken by the Turks again in 1688. In 1812, the population was 12,000; but it has since been desolated by the sanguinary contests between the Turks and the Greeks, and left almost a mass of ruins. It is now free; and efforts are making by Christians to restore it to its former elevation in learning and importance, and to impart to it the blessings of the Christian religion. Two American missionaries are labouring in the place where Paul preached almost two thousand years ago; and schools under their immediate superintendence and care, are established by American Christian missionaries, in the place that was once regarded as "the eye of Greece," and the light of the civilized world. In the revolutions of ages it has been ordered that men should bear the torch of learning to Athens from a land unknown to its ancient philosophers, and convey the blessings of civilization to them by that gospel which in the time of Paul they rejected and despised. ¶ *And receiving a commandment.* They who accompanied Paul received his commands to Silas and Timothy. ¶ *With all speed.* As soon as possible. Perhaps Paul expected much labour and success in Athens, and was therefore desirous of securing their aid with him in his work.

16. *Now while Paul waited.* How long he was there is not intimated; but doubtless some time would elapse before they could arrive. In the mean time, Paul had ample opportunity to observe the state of the city. ¶ *His spirit was stirred within him.* His mind was greatly excited. The word used here (παρωξύνετο) denotes any excitement, agitation, or *paroxysm* of mind. 1 Cor. xiii. 5. It here means that the mind of Paul was greatly *concerned*, or agitated, doubtless with pity and distress, at their folly and danger. ¶ *The city wholly given to idolatry.* Gr. κατείδωλον. It is well translated in the margin, "or full of idols." The word is not elsewhere used in the New Testament. That this was the condition of the city is abundantly testified by profane writers. Thus Pausanias (in Attic. i. 24, says, "the Athenians greatly surpassed others in their zeal for religion." Lucian (T. i. Prometh. p. 180) says of the city of Athens, "On every side there are altars, victims, temples, and festivals." Livy (45. 27) says, that Athens "was full of the images of gods and men, adorned with every variety of material, and with all the skill of art." And Petronius (Sat. xvii.) says humorously of the city, that "it was easier to find a god than a man there." See *Kuinoel.* In this verse we may see how a splendid, idolatrous city will strike a pious mind. Athens then had more that was splendid in architecture, more that was brilliant in science, and more that was beautiful in the arts, than any other city of the world; perhaps more than all the rest of the world united Yet there is no account that the mind of Paul was filled with admiration; there is no record that he spent his time in examining the works of art; there is no evidence that he forgot his high purpose in an idle and useless contemplation of temples and statuary. His was a Christian mind; and he contemplated all

17 Therefore disputed he in the synagogue with the Jews, and with the devout [a] persons, and in the market daily with them that met with him.

a c.8.2.

18 Then certain philosophers [b] of the Epicureans, and of the Stoics, encountered him. And some said, What will this [1] babbler say? Other some, He seemeth to be a

b Col.2.8. 1 or, *base fellow*.

this with a Christian heart. That heart was deeply affected in view of the amazing guilt of a people that were ignorant of the true God, and that had filled their city with idols reared to the honour of imaginary divinities; and who, in the midst of all this splendour and luxury, were going down to the gates of death. So should every pious man feel who treads the streets of a splendid and guilty city The Christian will not despise the productions of art; but he will feel, deeply feel, for the unhappy condition of those who, amidst wealth and splendour and adorning, are withholding their affections from the living God, bestowing them on the works of their own hands, or on objects degraded and polluting; and who are going unredeemed to eternal wo. Happy would it be if every Christian traveller who visits cities of wealth and splendour, would, like Paul, be affected in view of their crimes and dangers, and happy if, like him, men could cease their unbounded admiration of magnificence and splendour in temples and palaces and statuary, to regard the condition of *mind*, not perishable like marble; and of *the soul*, more magnificent even in its ruins than all the works of Phidias or Praxiteles.

17. *Therefore disputed he.* Or reasoned. He engaged in an argument with them. ¶ *With the devout persons.* Those worshipping God after the manner of the Jews. They were Jewish proselytes, who had renounced idolatry, but who had not been fully admitted to the privileges of the Jews. See Note, ch. x. 2. ¶ *And in the market.* In the forum. It was not only the place where provisions were sold, but was also a place of great public concourse. In this place the philosophers were not unfrequently found engaged in public discussion.

18. *Then certain philosophers.* Athens was distinguished, among all the cities of Greece and the world, for the cultivation of a subtle and refined philosophy. This was their boast, and the object of their constant search and study. 1 Cor. i. 22. ¶ *Of the Epicureans.* This sect of philosophers was so named from Epicurus, who lived about 300 years before the Christian era. They denied that the world was created by God, and that the gods exercised any care or providence over human affairs, and also the immortality of the soul. Against these positions of the sect, Paul directed his main argument, in proving that the world was created and governed by God. One of the distinguishing doctrines of Epicurus was, that pleasure was the *summum bonum*, or chief good, and that virtue was to be practised only as it contributed to pleasure. By pleasure, however, Epicurus did not mean sensual and grovelling appetites, and degraded vices, but rational pleasure, properly regulated and governed. See Good's Book of Nature. But whatever *his* views were, it is certain that his followers had embraced the doctrine that voluptuousness and the pleasures of sense were to be practised without restraint. Both in principle and practice, therefore, they devoted themselves to a life of gayety and sensuality, and sought happiness only in indolence, effeminacy, and voluptuousness. Confident in the belief that the world was not under the administration of a God of justice, they gave themselves up to the indulgence of every passion; the infidels of their time, and the exact example of the gay and fashionable multitudes of all times, that live without God, and that seek *pleasure* as their chief good. ¶ *And of the Stoics.* These were a sect of philosophers, so named from the Greek στοά, *Stoa*, a porch, or portico, because Zeno, the founder of the sect, held his school and taught in a *porch*, in the city of Athens. Zeno was born in the island of Cyprus, but the greater part of his life was spent at Athens in teaching philosophy. After having taught publicly 48 years, he died at the age of 96, two hundred and sixty-four years before Christ. The doctrines of the sect were, that the universe was created by God; that all things were fixed by fate; that even God was under the dominion of fatal necessity; that the fates were to be submitted to; that the passions and affections were to be suppressed and restrained, that happiness consisted in the insensibility of the soul to pain. and that a man should gain an absolute mastery over all the passions and affections of his nature

setter forth of strange gods: because he preached unto them Jesus, and the resurrection.

19 And they took him, and
brought him unto [1] Areopagus,
saying, May we know what this

[1] or, *Mars' hill*. It was the highest court in Athens.

They were stern in their views of virtue, and, like the Pharisees, prided themselves on their own righteousness. They supposed that matter was eternal, and that God was either the animating principle or soul of the world, or that all things were a part of God. They fluctuated much in their views of a future state; some of them holding that the soul would exist only until the destruction of the universe, and others that it would finally be absorbed into the divine essence, and become a part of God. It will be readily seen, therefore, with what pertinency and address Paul discoursed to them. The leading doctrines of both sects were met by him. ¶ *Encountered him.* Contended with him; opposed themselves to him. ¶ *And some said.* This was said in scorn and contempt. He had excited attention; but they scorned the doctrines that should be delivered by an unknown foreigner from Judea. ¶ *What will this babbler say?* Margin, *base fellow.* Greek, σπερμολογος. The word occurs nowhere else in the New Testament. It properly means *one who collects seeds,* and was applied by the Greeks to the poor persons who collected the scattered grain in the fields after harvest, or to gleaners; and also to the poor, who obtained a precarious subsistence around the markets and in the streets. It was also applied to birds that picked up the scattered seeds of grain in the field, or in the markets. The word came hence to have a two-fold signification. (1.) It denoted the poor, needy, and vile; the refuse and off-scouring of society; and, (2.) From the birds which were thus employed, and which were troublesome by their continual unmusical sounds, it came to denote those who were talkative, garrulous, and opinionated; those who collected the opinions of others, or scraps of knowledge, and retailed them fluently, without order or method. It was a word, therefore, expressive of their contempt for an unknown foreigner who should pretend to instruct the learned men and philosophers of Greece. Doddridge renders it, "retailer of scraps." Syriac, "collector of words." ¶ *Other some.* Others. ¶ *He seemeth to be a setter forth.* He announces or declares the existence of strange gods. The reason why they supposed this, was, that he made the capital points of his preaching to be Jesus and the resurrection, which they mistook for the names of divinities. ¶ *Of strange gods.* Of *foreign* gods, or demons. They worshipped many gods themselves, and as they believed that every country had its own peculiar divinities, they supposed that Paul had come to announce the existence of some such foreign, and to them unknown divinities. The word translated *gods* (δαιμονίων) denotes properly the genii, or spirits who were superior to men, but inferior to the gods. It is, however, often employed to denote the gods themselves; and is evidently so used here. The *gods* among the Greeks were such as were supposed to have that rank by nature. The *demons* were such as had been exalted to divinity from being heroes and distinguished men. ¶ *He preached unto them Jesus.* He proclaimed him as the Messiah. The mistake which they made, by supposing that he was a foreign divinity, was one which was perfectly natural for minds degraded like theirs by idolatry. They had no idea of a pure God; they knew nothing of the doctrine of the Messiah; and they naturally supposed, therefore, that he of whom Paul spoke so much must be a god of some other nation, of a rank similar to their own divinities. ¶ *And the resurrection.* The resurrection of Jesus, and through him the resurrection of the dead. It is evident, I think, that by the resurrection (τὴν ἀνάστασιν) they understood him to refer to the name of some goddess. Such was the interpretation of Chrysostom. The Greeks had erected altars to Shame, and Famine, and Desire (Paus. i. 17), and it is probable that they supposed 'the resurrection,' or *the Anastasis,* to be the name also of some unknown goddess who presided over the resurrection. Thus they regarded him as a setter forth of *two* foreign or strange gods—Jesus, and the Anastasis, or resurrection.

19. *And brought him unto Areopagus.* Margin, or Mars' hill. This was the place or court in which the Areopagites, the celebrated supreme judges of Athens, assembled. It was on a hill almost in the middle of the city; but nothing now remains by which we can determine the form or construction of the tribunal. The hill is almost entirely a mass of stone, and is not easily accessible, its sides being steep and abrupt. On many accounts this was the most celebrated tribunal in the world. Its decisions were distin

new [a] doctrine, whereof thou speak-
est, *is?*
20 For thou bringest certain [b]
strange things to our ears: we
would know therefore what these
things mean.

21 (For all the Athenians, and
strangers which were there, spent
their time in nothing else, but either
to tell or to hear some new thing.)
22 Then Paul stood in the midst
of Mars' [1] Hill, and said, *Ye* men

a Jno.13.34. 1Jno.2.7,8. *b* Hos.8.12.

1 or, *the court of the Areopagites.*

guished for justice and correctness; nor was there any court in Greece in which so much confidence was placed. This court took cognizance of murders, impieties, and immoralities; they punished vices of all kinds, including idleness; they rewarded the virtuous; they were peculiarly attentive to blasphemies against the gods, and to the performance of the sacred mysteries of religion. It was, therefore, with the greatest propriety that Paul was questioned before this tribunal, as being regarded as a setter forth of strange gods, and as being supposed to wish to introduce a new mode of worship. See Potter's Antiquities of Greece, b. i. ch. 19; and Travels of Anacharsis, vol. i. 136. 185; ii. 292—295. ¶ *May we know.* We would know. This seems to have been a respectful inquiry; and it does not appear that Paul was brought there for the sake of *trial.* There are no accusations; no witnesses; none of the forms of trial. They seem to have resorted thither because it was the place where the subject of religion was usually discussed, and because it was a place of confluence for the citizens and judges and wise men of Athens, and of foreigners. The design seems to have been, not to *try* him, but fairly to canvass the claims of his doctrines. See ver. 21. It was just an instance of the inquisitive spirit of the people of Athens, willing to hear before they condemned, and to examine before they approved.

20. *Certain strange things.* Literally, something pertaining to a *foreign* country, or people. Here it means something unusual, remarkable, to which we are not accustomed. It was something different from what they had been accustomed to hear from their philosophers and religious teachers. ¶ *What these things mean.* We would understand more clearly what is affirmed respecting Jesus and the resurrection.

21. *For all the Athenians.* This was their *general* character. ¶ *And strangers which were there.* Athens was greatly distinguished for the celebrity of its schools of philosophy. It was at that time at the head of the literary world. Its arts and its learning were celebrated in all lands. It is known, therefore, that it was the favourite resort of men of other nations, who came there to become acquainted with its institutions, and to listen to its sages. ¶ *Spent their time in nothing else.* The learned and subtle Athenians gave themselves much to speculation, and employed themselves in examining the various new systems of philosophy that were proposed. Strangers and foreigners who were there, having much leisure, would also give themselves to the same inquiries. ¶ *But either to tell or to hear some new thing.* Greek, *something newer.* Καινότερον. The latest news; or the latest subject of inquiry proposed. This is well known to have been the character of the people of Athens at all times. "Many of the ancient writers bear witness to the garrulity, and curiosity, and intemperate desire of novelty, among the Athenians, by which they inquired respecting all things, even those in which they had no interest, whether of a public or private nature." (*Kuinoel.*) Thus Thucyd. (3. 38) says of them, "you excel in suffering yourselves to be deceived with *novelty of speech.*" On which the old Scholiast makes this remark, almost in the words of Luke: "He (Thucydides) here blames the Athenians, who care for nothing else but to tell or to hear something new." Thus Ælian (5. 13) says of the Athenians, that they are versatile in novelties. Thus Demosthenes represents the Athenians "as inquiring in the place of public resort if there were any NEWS?" Τί καινότερον. Meursius has shown, also, that there were more than three hundred public places in Athens of public resort, where the principal youth and reputable citizens were accustomed to meet for the purpose of conversation and inquiry.

22. *Then Paul.* This commences Paul's explanation of the doctrines which he had stated. It is evident that Luke has recorded but a mere summary or outline of the discourse; but it is such as to enable us to see clearly his course of thought, and the manner in which he met the two principal sects of their philosophers. ¶ *In the midst of Mars' hill.* Greek, Areopagus

of Athens, I perceive that in all
things ye are too superstitious. [a]
23 For as I passed by, and beheld your devotions, [1] I found an altar with this inscription, TO THE
UNKNOWN GOD. Whom there-

a Jer.50.38.

1 or, *gods that ye worship*. Gal.4.8.

This should have been retained in the translation. ¶ Ye *men of Athens*. This language was perfectly respectful, notwithstanding his heart had been deeply affected by their idolatry. Every thing about this discourse is calm, grave, cool, and argumentative. Paul understood the character of his auditors, and did not commence his discourse by denouncing them, or suppose that they would be convinced by mere dogmatical assertion. No happier instance can be found, of cool, collected argumentation, than is furnished in this discourse. ¶ *I perceive*. He perceived this by his observations of their forms of worship, in passing through their city. ver. 23. ¶ *In all things*. In respect to all events. ¶ *Ye are too superstitious*. Δεισιδαιμονεστέρους. This is a most unhappy translation. We use the word *superstitious* always in a bad sense, to denote being over-scrupulous and rigid in religious observances, particularly in smaller matters; or to a zealous devotion to rites and observances which are not commanded. But the word here is designed to convey no such idea. It properly means reverence for the gods or demons. It is used in the classic writers in a *good* sense, to denote piety towards the gods, or suitable *fear* and reverence for them; and also in a *bad* sense, to denote improper fear or excessive dread of their anger; and in this sense it accords with our word superstitious. But it is altogether improbable that Paul should have used it in a bad sense. For, (1.) It was not his custom needlessly to blame or offend his auditors. (2.) It is not probable that he would commence his discourse in a manner that would only excite their prejudice and opposition. (3.) In the thing which he specifies (ver. 23) as proof on the subject, he does not introduce it as a matter of blame, but rather as a proof of their devotedness to the cause of religion, and of their regard for God. (4.) The whole speech is calm, dignified, and argumentative—such as became such a place, such a speaker, and such an audience. The meaning of the expression is, therefore, 'I perceive that you are greatly devoted to reverence for religion; that it is a characteristic of the people to honour the gods, to rear altars to them, and to recognise the divine agency in times of trial.' The *proof* of this was the altar reared to the unknown God; its *bearing* on his purpose was, that such a state of public sentiment must be favourable to an inquiry into the truth of what he was about to state.

23. *For as I passed by*. Greek, 'For I, coming through, and seeing,' &c. ¶ *And beheld*. Diligently contemplated; attentively considered (ἀναθεωρῶν). The worship of an idolatrous people will be an object of intense and painful interest to a Christian. ¶ *Your devotions*. Τὰ σεβάσματα. Our word *devotions* refers to the *act of worship*—to prayers, praises, &c. The Greek word here used means properly any sacred *thing*; any *object* which is worshipped, or which is connected with the place or rites of worship. Thus it is applied either to the gods themselves, or to the temples, altars, shrines, sacrifices, statues, &c., connected with the worship of the gods. This is its meaning here. It does not denote that Paul saw them engaged in the *act* of worship, but that he was struck with the numerous temples, altars, statues, &c., which were reared to the gods, and which indicated the state of the people. Syriac, "The temple of your gods." Vulgate, "your images." Margin, "gods that ye worship." ¶ *I found an altar*. An altar usually denotes a place for sacrifice. Here, however, it does not appear that any sacrifice was offered; but it was probably a monument of stone, reared to commemorate a certain event, and dedicated to the unknown God. ¶ *To the unknown God*. Ἀγνώστῳ Θεῷ. Where this altar was reared, or on what occasion, has been a subject of much debate with expositors. That there was such an altar in Athens, though it may not have been specifically mentioned by the Greek writers, is rendered probable by the following circumstances. (1.) It was customary to rear such altars. Minutius Felix says of the Romans, "they build altars to unknown divinities." (2.) The term *unknown God* was used in relation to the worship of the Athenians. Lucian, in his Philopatris, uses this form of an oath: "I swear by the *unknown God* at Athens," the very expression used by the apostle. And again he says (ch. xxix. 180), "We have found out the *unknown God* at Athens, and worshipped him with our hands stretched up to heaven," &c.

fore ye ignorantly worship, him declare I unto you.

24 God [a] that made the world, and all things therein, seeing that he is [b] Lord of heaven and earth, dwelleth [c] not in temples made with hands;

25 Neither is worshipped with

a c.14.15. b Matt.11.25. c c.7.48.

(3.) There were altars at Athens inscribed *to the unknown gods.* Philostratus says (in Vita. Apollo. vi. 3), "And this at Athens, where there are even altars to the *unknown gods.*" Thus Pausanius (in Attic. ch. 1) says, that "at Athens there are altars of gods which are called the UNKNOWN ones." Jerome, in his commentary (Epistle to Titus i. 12), says that the whole inscription was, "to the gods of Asia, Europe, and Africa; to *the unknown and strange gods.*" (4.) There was a remarkable altar reared in Athens in a time of pestilence, in honour of the unknown god which had granted them deliverance. Diogenes Laertius says that Epimenides restrained the pestilence in the following manner: "Taking white and black sheep, he led them to the Areopagus, and there permitted them to go where they would, commanding those who followed them to sacrifice (τῷ προσήκοντι θεῷ) to the god to whom these things pertained [or who had the power of averting the plague, whoever he might be, without adding the name], and thus to allay the pestilence. From which it has arisen, that at this day, through the villages of the Athenians, altars are found without any name." Dioge. Laer. b. i. § 10. This took place about 600 years before Christ, and it is not improbable that one or more of those altars remained until the time of Paul. It should be added that the natural inscription on those altars would be, "to the unknown god." None of the gods to whom they usually sacrificed could deliver them from the pestilence. They therefore reared them to some unknown Being who had the power to free them from the plague. ¶ *Whom therefore.* The true God, who had really delivered them from the plague. ¶ *Ye ignorantly worship.* Or worship without knowing his name. You have expressed your homage for him by rearing to him an altar. ¶ *Him declare I unto you.* I make known to you his name, attributes, &c. There is remarkable address and *tact* in Paul's seizing on this circumstance; and yet it was perfectly fair and honest. God only could deliver in the time of the pestilence. This altar had, therefore, been really reared to him, though his name was unknown. The same Being who had interposed at that time, and whose interposition was recorded by the building of this altar, was He who had made the heavens; who ruled over all; and whom Paul was now about to make known to them. There is another feature of skill in the allusion to this altar. In other circumstances it might seem to be presumptuous for an unknown Jew to attempt to instruct the sages of Athens. But here they had confessed and proclaimed their ignorance. By rearing this altar they acknowledged their need of instruction. The way was, therefore, fairly open for Paul to address even these philosophers, and to discourse to them on a point on which they acknowledged their ignorance.

24. *God that made the world.* The main object of this discourse of Paul is, to convince them of the folly of idolatry (ver. 29), and thus to lead them to repentance. For this purpose he commences with a statement of the true doctrine respecting God as the Creator of all things. We may observe here, (1.) That he speaks here of *God* as the Creator of the world—thus opposing *indirectly* their opinions that there were *many* gods. (2.) He speaks of him as the *Creator* of the world, and thus opposes the opinion that matter was eternal; that all things were controlled by fate; and that he could be confined to temples. The Epicureans held that matter was eternal, and that the world was formed by a fortuitous concourse of atoms. To this opinion Paul opposed the doctrine that all things were *made* by one God. Comp. ch. xiv. 15 ¶ *Seeing that,* &c. Gr. "He being Lord of heaven and earth." ¶ *Lord of heaven and earth.* Proprietor and Ruler of heaven and earth. It is highly absurd, therefore, to suppose that he who is present in heaven and in earth at the same time, and who rules over all, should be confined to a temple of an earthly structure, or dependent on man for any thing. ¶ *Dwelleth not,* &c. See Note, ch. vii. 48.

25. *Neither is worshipped with men's hands.* The word here rendered *worshipped* (θεραπεύεται) denotes to *serve;* to wait upon; and then to render religious service or homage. There is reference here, undoubtedly, to a notion pre-

men's hands, as though he [a] needed
any thing; seeing he [b] giveth to
all, life, and breath, and [c] all
things;

26 And hath made of one [d] blood
all nations of men, for to dwell on
all the face of the earth; and hath
determined the times [e] before ap-

a Ps.50.8. b Job 12.10. Zech.12.1. c Rom.11.36. d Mal.2.10. e Ps.31.15.

valent among the heathen, that the gods were fed or nourished by the offerings made to them. The idea is prevalent among the Hindoos, that the sacrifices which are made, and which are offered in the temples, are consumed by the gods themselves. Perhaps, also, Paul had reference to the fact that so many persons were employed in their temples in serving them *with their hands;* that is, in preparing sacrifices and feasts in their honour. Paul affirms that the great Creator of all things cannot be thus dependent on his creatures for happiness; and consequently that that mode of worship must be highly absurd. The same idea occurs in Ps. l. 10, 11, 12:

For every beast of the forest is mine;
And the cattle upon a thousand hills.
I know all the fowls of the mountain;
And the wild beasts of the field are mine.
If I were hungry, I would not tell thee;
For the world is mine, and the fulness thereof.

¶ *Seeing he giveth.* Gr. He having given to all, &c. ¶ *Life.* He is the source of life; and therefore he cannot be dependent on that life which he has himself imparted. ¶ *And breath.* The power of breathing, by which life is sustained. He not only originally gave life, but he gives it at each moment; he gives the power of drawing each breath by which life is supported. It is possible that the phrase "life and breath" may be the figure *hendyades,* by which one thing is expressed by two words. And it is highly probable that Paul here had reference to Gen. ii. 7: "And the LORD God breathed into his nostrils the breath of life." The same idea occurs in Job xii. 10:

In whose hand is the life (*margin*) of every living thing;
And the breath of all mankind.

¶ *And all things.* All things necessary to sustain life. We may see here how dependent man is on God. There can be no more absolute dependence than that for every *breath.* How easy it would be for God to suspend our breathing! How incessant the care, how unceasing the Providence by which, whether we sleep or wake—whether we remember or forget him, he heaves our chest; fills our lungs; restores the vitality of our blood; and infuses vigour into our frame! Comp. Note, Rom. xi. 36

26. *And hath made of one blood.* All the families of men are descended from one origin, or stock. However different their complexion, features, language, &c., yet they are derived from a common parent. The word *blood* is often used to denote *race, stock, kindred.* This passage completely proves that all the human family are descended from the same ancestor; and that, consequently, all the variety of complexion, &c., is to be traced to some other cause than that there were originally different races created. See Gen. i. Comp. Mal. ii. 10. The *design* of the apostle in this affirmation was, probably, to convince the Greeks that he regarded them all as brethren; and that, although he was a Jew, yet he was not enslaved to any narrow notions or prejudices in reference to other men. It follows also from this, that no one nation, and no individual, can claim any pre-eminence over others in virtue of birth or blood. All are in this respect equal; and the whole human family, however they may differ in complexion, customs, and laws, are to be regarded and treated as brethren. It follows, also, that no one part of the race has a right to enslave or oppress any other part, on account of difference of complexion. Nor has man a right because

He finds his fellow guilty of a skin
Not coloured like his own; and having power
T' enforce the wrong, for such a worthy cause
to
Doom and devote him as his lawful prey.

¶ *For to dwell,* &c. To cultivate and til the earth. This was the original command (Gen. i. 28); and God, by his providence, has so ordered it that the descendants of one family have found their way to all lands, and have become adapted to the climate where he has placed them. ¶ *And hath determined.* Gr. ὁρίσας. Having fixed, or marked out a boundary. Note, Rom i. 4. The word is usually applied to a *field,* which is designated by a boundary. It means here that God hath marked out, or designated in his purpose, their future abodes. ¶ *The times before appointed.* This evidently refers to the dispersion and migration of nations. And it means that God had, in his plan, fixed the times when each country should be

pointed, and the bounds [a] of their habitation:
27 That they should seek the Lord, if haply they might feel after
him, and find him, though [b] he be not far from every one of us:
28 For in [c] him we live, and move, and have our being; as [d] cer-

a Isa.45.21 b c.14.17. c Col.1.17. d Tit.1.12.

settled; the time of the location, the rise, the prosperity, and the fall of each nation. It implies, (1.) That these *times* had been before appointed; and, (2.) That it was done in wisdom. It was his plan; and the different continents and islands had not, therefore, been settled by chance, but by a wise rule, and in accordance with his arrangement and design. ¶ *And the bounds of their habitation.* Their limits, and boundaries as a people. He has designated the black man to Africa; the white man to northern regions; the American savage he fixed in the wilds of the western continent, &c. By customs, laws, inclinations, and habits, he fixed the boundaries of their habitations, and disposed them to dwell there. We may learn, (1.) That the revolutions and changes of nations are under the direction of infinite wisdom; (2.) That men should not be restless, and dissatisfied with the place where God has located them; (3.) That God has given sufficient limits to all, so that it is not needful to invade others; and, (4.) That wars of conquest are evil. God has given to men their places of abode, and we have no right to disturb those abodes, or to attempt to displace them in a violent manner This strain of remark by the apostle was also opposed to all the notions of the Epicurean philosophers, and yet so obviously true and just, that they could not gainsay or resist it.

27. *That they should seek the Lord.* Gr. To seek the Lord. The design of thus placing them on the earth—of giving them their habitation among his works—was, that they should contemplate his wisdom in his works, and thus come to a knowledge of his existence and character. All nations, though living in different regions and climates, have thus the opportunity of becoming acquainted with God. Rom. i. 19, 20. The fact, that the nations did *not* thus learn the character of the true God, shows their great stupidity and wickedness. The design of Paul in this was, doubtless, to reprove the idolatry of the Athenians. The argument is this: 'God has given to each nation its proper opportunity to learn his character. Idolatry, therefore, is folly and wickedness; since it is possible to find out the existence of the *one* God from his works.' ¶ *If haply.* εἰ ἄραγε. If perhaps—implying that it was *possible* to find God, though it might be attended with some difficulty. God has placed us here that we may make the trial; and has made it possible thus to find him. ¶ *They might feel after him.* The word used here (ψηλαφήσειαν) means properly *to touch, to handle* (Luke xxiv. 39. Heb. xii. 18), and then to ascertain the qualities of an object by the sense of touch. And as the sense of touch is regarded as a certain way of ascertaining the existence and qualities of an object, the word means to search diligently, that we may know distinctly and certainly. The word has this sense here. It means to search diligently and accurately for God, to learn his existence and perfections. The Syriac renders it, "that they may seek for God, and find him from his creatures." ¶ *And find him.* Find the proofs of his existence. Become acquainted with his perfections and laws. ¶ *Though he be not far, &c.* This seems to be stated by the apostle to show that it was *possible* to find him; and that even those who were without a revelation, need not despair of becoming acquainted with his existence and perfections. He is near to us, (1.) Because the proofs of his existence and power are round about us every where. Ps. xix. 1—6. (2.) Because he fills all things in heaven and earth by his essential presence. Ps. cxxxix. 7—10. Jer. xxiii. 23, 24. Amos ix. 2—4. 1 Kings viii. 27. We should learn then, (1.) To be afraid to sin. God is present with us, and sees all. (2.) He can protect the righteous. He is ever with them. (3.) He can detect and punish the wicked. He sees all their plans and thoughts, and records all their doings. (4.) We should seek him continually. It is the design for which he has made us; and he has given us abundant opportunities to learn his existence and perfections.

28. *For in him we live.* The expression "*in* him" evidently means *by* him; by his originally forming us, and continually sustaining us. No words can better express our constant dependence on him He is the original fountain of life; and he upholds us each moment. A similar sentiment is found in Plautus (5. 4. 14) "O Jupiter, who dost cherish and nourish the race of man; by whom we live

tain also of your own poets have
said, For we are also his offspring.
29 Forasmuch then as we are
the offspring of God, we ought not
[a] to think that the Godhead is like
unto gold, or silver, or stone, graven by art and man's device.
30 And the times of this igno-

a Isa.40.18,&c.

---

and with whom is the hope of the life of all men." (*Kuinoel.*) It does not appear however that Paul intended this as a quotation; yet he doubtless intended to state a sentiment with which they were familiar, and with which they would agree. ¶ *And move.* Κινούμεθα. Doddridge translates this, "And are moved." It may however be in the middle voice, and be correctly rendered as in our version. It means that we derive strength to move from him; an expression denoting constant and absolute dependence. There is no idea of dependence more striking than that we owe to him the ability to perform the slightest motion. ¶ *And have our being.* Καὶ ἐσμέν. And *are.* This denotes that our *continued* existence is owing to him. That we live at all is his gift; that we have power to move is his gift; and our *continued* and *prolonged* existence is his gift also. Thus Paul traces our dependence on Him from the lowest pulsation of life to the highest powers of action and of continued existence. It would be impossible to express in more emphatic language our entire dependence on God. ¶ *As certain also.* As some. The sentiment which he quotes was found substantially in several Greek poets. ¶ *Of your own poets.* He does not refer particularly here to poets of Athens, but to Greek poets—poets who had written in their language. ¶ *For we are also his offspring.* This precise expression is found in Aratus (Phænom. v. 5), and in Cleanthus in a hymn to Jupiter. Substantially the same sentiment is found in several other Greek poets. Aratus was a Greek poet of Cilicia, the native place of Paul, and flourished about 277 years before Christ. As Paul was a native of the same country, it is highly probable he was acquainted with his writings. Aratus passed much of his time at the court of Antigonus Gonatas, king of Macedonia. His principal work was the Phænomena, which is here quoted, and was so highly esteemed in Greece that many learned men wrote commentaries on it. The sentiment here quoted was directly at variance with the views of the Epicureans; and it is proof of Paul's address and skill, as well as his acquaintance with his auditors, and with the Greek poets, that he was able to adduce a sentiment so directly in point, and that had the concurrent testimony of so many of the Greeks themselves. It is *one* instance among thousands where an acquaintance with profane learning may be of use to a minister of the gospel.

29. *Forasmuch then.* Admitting or assuming this to be true. The argument which follows is drawn from the concessions of their own writers. ¶ *We ought not to think.* It is absurd to suppose. The argument of the apostle is this: 'Since we are formed by God; since we are like him, living and intelligent beings; since we are more excellent in our nature than the most precious and ingenious works of art; it is absurd to suppose that the original source of our existence can be like gold, and silver, and stone. Man himself is far more excellent than an image of wood and stone; how much more excellent still must be the great Fountain and Source of all our wisdom and intelligence.' See this thought pursued at length in Isa. xl. 18—23. ¶ *The Godhead.* The divinity (τὸ Θεῖον), the divine nature, or essence. The word used here is an adjective employed as a noun, and does not occur elsewhere in the New Testament. ¶ *Is like unto gold, &c.* All these things were used in making images, or statues of the gods. It is absurd to think that the source of all life and intelligence resembles a lifeless block of wood or stone. Even degraded heathen, one would think, might see the force of an argument like this. ¶ *Graven.* Sculptured; wrought into an image.

30. *And the times of this ignorance.* The long period when men were ignorant of the true God, and when they worshipped stocks and stones. Paul here refers to the times preceding the gospel. ¶ *God winked at.* Ὑπεριδών. Overlooked, connived at; did not come forth to punish. In ch. xiv. 16, it is expressed thus, "Who in times past suffered all nations to walk in their own ways." The sense is, he passed over those times without punishing them, as if he did not see them. For wise purposes he suffered them to walk in ignorance, and to make the fair experiment to show what men would do; and how much necessity there was for a revelation to instruct them in the true knowledge of God. We are not to sup-

rance God winked [a] at, but now
[b] commandeth all men every where
to repent:
31 Because he hath appointed
[c] a day, in the which he will judge
the world in righteousness, by *that*
man whom he hath ordained; *where-*
of he hath given assurance [1] unto
all *men*, in that he hath raised him
from the dead.
32 And when they heard of the
resurrection of the dead, [d] some
mocked: and others said, We will
hear thee again [e] of this *matter*.
33 So Paul departed from among
them.

a Rom.3.23. b Luke 24.47. Tit.2.11,12. c Rom.2.16. 1 or, *offered faith*. d c.26.8. e Luke 14.18. c 24.25.

pose that God regarded idolatry as innocent, or the crimes and vices to which idolatry led as of no importance; but their ignorance was a mitigating circumstance, and he suffered the nations to live without coming forth in direct judgment against them. Comp. Notes on ch. iii. 17; xiv. 16. ¶ *But now commandeth.* By the gospel. Luke xxiv. 47. ¶ *All men.* Not Jews only, who had been favoured with peculiar privileges, but all nations. The barrier was broken down, and the call to repentance was sent abroad into all the earth. ¶ *To repent.* To exercise sorrow for their sins, and to forsake them. If God *commands* all men to repent, we may observe, (1.) That it is their *duty* to do it. There is no higher obligation than to obey the command of God. (2.) It *can* be done. God would not command an impossibility. (3.) It is binding on *all*. The rich, the learned, the great, the gay, are as much bound as the beggar and the slave. There is no distinction made. It pertains to all people, in all lands. (4.) It *must* be done, or the soul lost. It is not wise, and it is not safe, to neglect a plain law of God. It will not be well to die reflecting that we have all our life neglected and despised his plain commands. (5.) We should send the gospel to the heathen. God calls on the *nations* to repent, and to be saved. It is the duty of Christians to make known to them the command, and to invite them to the blessings of pardon and heaven.

31. *Because he hath appointed a day.* This is given as a reason why God commands men to repent. They must be judged; and if they are not penitent and pardoned, they must be condemned. See Note, Rom. ii. 16. ¶ *Judge the world.* The whole world—Jews and Gentiles. ¶ *In righteousness.* According to the principles of strict justice. See Matt. xxv. ¶ *Whom he hath ordained.* Or whom he has constituted or appointed as judge. See Note, ch. x. 42. John v. 25. ¶ *Hath given assurance.* Has afforded evidence of this. That evidence consists, (1.) In the fact that Jesus *declared* that he would judge the nations (John v. 25, 26. Matt. xxv.); and, (2.) God confirmed the truth of his declarations by raising him from the dead, or gave his sanction to what the Lord Jesus had said, for God would not work a miracle in favour of an impostor.

32. *Some mocked.* Some of the philosophers derided him. It was believed by none of the Greeks; it seemed incredible; and they regarded it as so absurd as not to admit of an argument. It has not been uncommon for even professed philosophers to mock at the doctrines of religion, and to meet the arguments of Christianity with a sneer. The Epicureans particularly would be likely to deride this, as they denied altogether any future state. It is not improbable that this derision by the Epicureans produced such a disturbance as to break off Paul's discourse, as that of Stephen had been by the clamour of the Jews. ch. vii. 54. ¶ *And others said.* Probably some of the Stoics. The doctrine of a future state was not denied by them; and the fact, affirmed by Paul, that one had been raised up from the dead, would appear more plausible to them, and it *might* be a matter worth inquiry to ascertain whether the alleged fact did not furnish a new argument for their views. They, therefore, proposed to examine this further at some future time. That the inquiry was prosecuted any further does not appear probable, for. (1.) No church was organized at Athens. (2.) There is no account of any future interview with Paul. (3.) He departed almost immediately from them. ch. xviii. 1. Men who defer inquiry on the subject of religion, seldom find the favourable period arrive. Those who propose to examine its doctrines at a future time, often do it to avoid the *inconvenience* of becoming Christians now; and as a plausible and easy way of rejecting the gospel altogether, without appearing to be rude, or to give offence.

34 Howbeit certain men clave unto him, and believed: among the which *was* Dionysius the Areopagite, and a woman named Damaris, and others with them.

CHAPTER XVIII.

AFTER these things, Paul departed from Athens, and came to Corinth:

2 And found a certain Jew named

---

33. *So Paul departed.* Seeing there was little hope of saving them. It was not his custom to labour long in a barren field, or to preach where there was no prospect of success

34. *Clave unto him.* Adhered to him firmly; embraced the Christian religion. ¶ *Dionysius.* Nothing more is certainly known of this man than is here stated. ¶ *The Areopagite.* Connected with the court of Areopagus, but in what way is not known. It is probable that he was one of the judges. The conversion of *one* man was worth the labour of Paul. And the secret influence of that conversion might have had an extensive influence on others.

In regard to this interesting account of the visit of Paul to Athens—probably the only one which he made to that splendid capital—we may remark, (1.) That he was indefatigable and constant in his great work. (2.) Christians, amidst the splendour and gayeties of such cities, should have their hearts deeply affected in view of the moral desolations of the people. (3.) They should be willing to do their duty, and to bear witness to the pure and simple gospel in the presence of the great and the noble. (4.) They should not consider it their main business to admire splendid temples, and statues, and paintings—the works of art; but their main business should be, to do good as they may have opportunity. (5.) A discourse, even in the midst of much wickedness, and idolatry, may be calm and dignified; not an appeal merely to the passions, but to the understanding. Paul *reasoned* with the philosophers of Athens; he did not denounce them; he endeavoured calmly to convince them, not harshly to censure them. (6.) The example of Paul is a good one for all Christians. In all places—cities, towns, or country; amidst all people—philosophers, and the rich, and the poor; among friends and countrymen, or among strangers and foreigners, the great object should be to do good, to instruct mankind, and to seek to elevate the human character, and promote human happiness, by diffusing the mild and pure precepts of the gospel of Christ.

CHAPTER XVIII

1. *After these things.* After what occurred at Athens, as recorded in the previous chapter. ¶ *Came to Corinth.* Corinth was the capital of Achaia, called anciently Ephyra, and was seated on the isthmus which divides the Peloponnesus from Attica. The city itself stood on a little island; it had two ports, Lechæum on the west, and Cenchrea on the east. It was one of the most populous and wealthy cities of Greece; and, at the same time, one of the most luxurious, effeminate, proud, ostentatious, and dissolute. Lasciviousness here was not only practised and allowed, but was consecrated by the worship of Venus; and no small part of the wealth and splendour of the city arose from the offerings made by licentious passion in the very temples of this goddess. No city of ancient times was more profligate. It was the *Paris* of antiquity; the seat of splendour, and show, and corruption. Yet even here, notwithstanding all the disadvantages of splendour, gayety, and dissoluteness, Paul entered on the work of rearing a church, and here he was eminently successful. The two epistles which he afterwards wrote to this church show the extent of his success; and the well-known character and propensities of the people will account for the general drift of the admonitions and arguments in those epistles. Corinth was destroyed by the Romans 146 years before Christ; and during the conflagration, several metals in a fused state, running together, produced the composition known as Corinthian brass. It was afterwards restored by Julius Cæsar, who planted in it a Roman colony. It soon regained its ancient splendour, and soon relapsed into its former dissipation and licentiousness. Paul arrived there A. D 52 or 53.

2. *And found a certain Jew.* Aquila is elsewhere mentioned as the friend of Paul. Rom. xvi. 3. 2 Tim. iv. 19. 1 Cor. xvi. 19. Though a Jew by birth, yet it is evident that he became a convert to the Christian faith. ¶ *Born in Pontus.* Note, ch. ii. 9. ¶ *Lately come from Italy* Though the command of Claudius extended only to Rome, yet it was probably

[a] Aquila, born in Pontus, lately
come from Italy, with his wife
Priscilla; (because that Claudius
had commanded all Jews to depart
from Rome;) and came unto them.
3 And because he was of the
same craft, he abode with them,
and [b] wrought: for by their occu
pation they were tent-makers.
4 And he reasoned in the [c] synagogue every sabbath, and persuaded
the Jews and the Greeks.
5 And when [d] Silas and Timotheus were come from Macedonia,

a Rom.16.3. b c.20.34. c c.17.2. d c.17.14,15.

deemed not safe to remain, or it might have been difficult to procure occupation in any part of Italy. ¶ *Because that Claudius.* Claudius was the Roman emperor. He commenced his reign A. D. 41, and was poisoned A. D. 54. At what time in his reign this command was issued is not certainly known. ¶ *Had commanded,* &c. This command is not mentioned by Josephus; but it is recorded by Suetonius, a Roman historian (Life of Claudius, ch. 25), who says, that "he expelled the Jews from Rome, who were constantly exciting tumults under their leader, Chrestus." Who this *Chrestus* was is not known. It *might* have been a foreign Jew, who raised tumults on some occasion of which we have no knowledge; as the Jews in all heathen cities were greatly prone to excitements and insurrections. Or it *may* be that Suetonius, little acquainted with Jewish affairs, mistook this for the name *Christ,* and supposed that he was the leader of the Jews. This explanation has much plausibility; for, (1.) Suetonius could scarcely be supposed to be intimately acquainted with the affairs of the Jews. (2.) There is every reason to believe, that before this, the Christian religion was preached at Rome (3.) It would produce there, as every where else, great tumult and contention among the Jews. (4.) Claudius, the emperor, might suppose that such tumults endangered the peace of the city, and resolve to remove the cause at once by the dispersion of all the Jews. (5.) A Roman historian might easily mistake the true state of the case; and while they were contending *about* Christ, he might suppose that it was *under* him, as a leader, that these tumults were excited. All that is material, however, here, is *the fact,* in which Luke and Suetonius agree, that the Jews were expelled from Rome during his reign.

3. *The same craft.* Of the same *trade,* or *occupation.* ¶ *And wrought.* And worked at that occupation. *Why* he did it, the historian does not affirm; but it seems pretty evident that it was because he had no other means of maintenance. He also laboured for his own support in Ephesus (Acts xx. 34), and also at Thessalonica. 2 Thess. iii. 9, 10. The apostle was not ashamed of honest industry for a livelihood; nor did he deem it any disparagement that a minister of the gospel should labour with his own hands. ¶ *For by their occupation.* By their trade; that is, they had been brought up to this business. Paul had been designed originally for a lawyer, and had been brought up at the feet of Gamaliel. But it was a regular custom among the Jews to train up their sons to some useful employment, that they might have the means of an honest livelihood. Even though they were trained up to the liberal sciences, yet they deemed a handicraft trade, or some honourable occupation, an indispensable part of education. Thus Maimonides (in the Tract Talmud. Tora, c. i. § 9) says, that "the wise generally practise some of the arts, lest they should be dependent on the charity of others." See Grotius. The wisdom of this is obvious; and it is equally plain that a custom of this kind now might preserve the health and lives of many professional men, and save from ignoble dependence or vice, in future years, many who are trained up in the lap of indulgence and wealth. ¶ *They were tent-makers.* Σκηνοποιοί. There have been various opinions about the meaning of this word. Many have supposed that it denotes a weaver of tapestry. Luther thus translated it. But it is probable that it denotes, as in our translation, a manufacturer of tents, made of skin, or cloth. In eastern countries, where there was much travel; where there were no inns; and where many were shepherds, such a business might be useful, and a profitable source of living. It was an honourable occupation, and Paul was not ashamed to be employed in it.

4. *And he reasoned,* &c. Note, ch xvii. 2.

5. *And when Silas and Timotheus,* &c They came to Paul according to his re quest, which he had sent by the brethren who accompanied him from Thessalo-

Paul was pressed in spirit, and testified to the Jews *that* Jesus [1] *was* Christ.

6 And when they opposed [a] themselves, and blasphemed, he shook [b] *his* raiment, and said unto them, Your [c] blood *be* upon your own heads: I *am* clean: from henceforth I will go unto the Gentiles.

7 And he departed thence, and entered into a certain *man's* house, named Justus, *one* that worshipped God, whose house joined hard to the synagogue.

8 And [d] Crispus, the chief ruler of the synagogue, believed on the Lord, with all his house: and many of the Corinthians hearing, believed, and were baptized.

9 Then spake the Lord to Paul in the night by a vision, Be not afraid, but speak, and hold not thy peace:

10 For I [e] am with thee, and no

1 or, *is the Christ*. a 2Tim.2.25. b Neh.5.13. c Ezek.33.4.

d 1Cor.1.14. e Matt.28.20.

nica. ch. xvii. 15. ¶ *Paul was pressed*. Was urged; was borne away by an unusual impulse. It was deeply impressed on him as his duty. ¶ *In spirit*. In his mind, in his feelings. His love to Christ was so great, and his conviction of the truth so strong, that he laboured to make known to them the truth that Jesus was the Messiah ¶ That *Jesus* was *Christ*. That Jesus of Nazareth was the Messiah. Comp. ch. xvii. 16. The presence of Silas and Timothy animated him; and the certainty of aid in his work urged him to zeal in making known the Saviour.

6. *And when they opposed themselves*. To him and his message. ¶ *And blasphemed*. Note, ch. xiii. 45. ¶ *He shook his raiment*. As an expressive act of shaking off the guilt of their condemnation. Comp. ch. xiii. 45. He shook his raiment to show that he was resolved henceforward to have nothing to do with them; perhaps, also, to express the fact that God would soon shake them off, or reject them. (*Doddridge*.) ¶ *Your blood*, &c. The guilt of your destruction is your own. You only are the cause of the destruction that is coming upon you. See Note on Matt. xxvii. 25. ¶ *I am clean*. I am not to blame for your destruction. I have done my duty. The gospel had been fairly offered, and deliberately rejected; and Paul was not to blame for their ruin, which he saw was coming upon them. ¶ *I will go*, &c. See ch. xiii. 46.

7. *A certain man's house*. Probably he had become a convert to the Christian faith. ¶ *Joined hard*. Was near to the synagogue

8. *And Crispus*. He is mentioned in 1 Cor. i. 14. as having been one of the few whom Paul baptized with his own hands. The conversion of such a man must have tended greatly to exasperate the other Jews, and to further the progress of the Christian faith among the Corinthians. ¶ *With all his house*. With all his family. ch. x. 2. ¶ *And many of the Corinthians*. Many even in this voluptuous and wicked city. Perhaps the power of the gospel was never more signal than in converting sinners in Corinth, and rearing a Christian church in a place so dissolute and abandoned. If it was adapted to such a place as *Corinth*; if a church, under the power of Christian truth, could be organized *there*; it is adapted to any city; and there is none so corrupt that the gospel cannot change and purify it.

9. *By a vision*. Comp. Note, ch. ix. 10; xvi. 9. ¶ *Be not afraid*. *Perhaps*, Paul might have been intimidated by the learning, refinement, and splendour of Corinth; *perhaps*, embarrassed in view of his duty of addressing the rich, the polite, and the great. To this he may allude in 1 Cor. ii. 3: "And I was with you in weakness, and in fear, and in much trembling." In such circumstances it pleased God to meet him, and disarm his fears. This he did by assuring him of success. The fact that God had much people in that city (ver. 10), was employed to remove his apprehensions. The fact of success in the ministry, and certainty of the presence of God, will take away the fear of the rich, the learned, and the great.

10. *For I am with thee*. I will attend, bless, and protect you. See Note, Matt. xxviii. 20. ¶ *No man shall set on thee*. No one who shall rise up against thee shall be able to hurt thee. His life was in God's hands, and he would preserve him, in order that his people might be collected into the church. ¶ *For I have*. Gr. There is to me; i. e. I possess, or there belongs to me. ¶ *Much people*.

man shall set on thee, to hurt thee: for I have much people in this city.
11 And he [1] continued *there* a year and six months, teaching the word of God among them.
12 And when Gallio was t... nuty of Achaia, the Jews made ...
surrection with one accord against Paul, and brought him to the judgment-seat, [a]
13 Saying, This *fellow* persuadeth men to worship God contrary to the law.
14 And when Paul was now

[1] or, *sat* there.

[a] Jam.2.6.

Many who should be regarded as his true friends, and who should be saved. ¶ *In this city.* In that very city that was so voluptuous; so rich; so effeminate; and where there had been already so decided opposition shown to the gospel. This passage evidently means that God had a design or purpose to save many of that people. For it was given to Paul as an encouragement to him to labour there, evidently meaning that God *would* grant him success in his work. It cannot mean that the Lord meant to say that the great mass of the people, or that the moral and virtuous part, if there were any such, was *then* regarded as *his* people; but that he *intended* to convert many of those guilty and profligate Corinthians to himself, and to gather a people for his own service there. We may learn from this, (1.) That God has a *purpose* in regard to the salvation of sinners. (2.) That that purpose is so fixed in the mind of God that *he* can say that those in relation to whom it is formed are *his*. There is no chance; no hap-hazard; no doubt in regard to his gathering them to himself. (3.) This is the ground of encouragement to the ministers of the gospel. Had God no purpose to save sinners, they could have no hope in their work. (4.) This plan may have reference to the most gay, and guilty, and abandoned population; and ministers should not be deterred by the amount or the degree of wickedness from attempting to save them. (5.) There may be more hope of success among a dissolute and profligate populatio[illegible] among proud, and cold, and si[illegible] philosophers. Paul had little su[illegible] in philosophic Athens; he had great u[illegible]ccess in dissolute Corinth. There is often more hope of converting a man openly dissolute and abandoned, than one who prides himself on his philosophy, and is confident in his own wisdom.

11. *And he continued*, &c. Paul was not accustomed to remain long in a place. At Ephesus, indeed, he remained three years (Acts xx. 31); and his stay at Corinth was caused by his success, and by the necessity of placing a church, coll-ed out of such corrupt, and dissolute materials, on a firm foundation.

12. *And Gallio.* After the Romans had conquered Greece, they reduced it to two provinces, Macedonia and Achaia, which were each governed by a proconsul. Gallio was the brother of the celebrated philosopher Seneca, and was made proconsul of Achaia A. D. 53. His proper name was Marcus Annæus Novatus, but having been adopted into the family of Gallio, a rhetorician, he took his name. He is described by ancient writers as having been of a remarkably mild and amiable disposition. His brother Seneca (Præf. Quest. Natu. 4) describes him as being of the most lovely temper: "No mortal," says he, "was ever so mild to any one, as he was to all; and in him there was such a natural power of goodness, that there was no semblance of art or dissimulation." ¶ *Was deputy.* See this word explained in Acts xiii. 7. It means here proconsul. ¶ *Of Achaia.* This word, in its largest sense, comprehended the whole of Greece. Achaia proper, however, was a province of which Corinth was the capital. It embraced that part of Greece lying between Thessaly and the southern part of the Peloponnesus. ¶ *The Jews made insurrection.* Excited a tumult, as they had in Philippi, Antioch, &c. ¶ *And brought him to the judgment-seat.* The tribunal of Gallio; probably intending to arraign him as a disturber of the peace.

13. *Contrary to the law.* Evidently intending contrary to *all* law—the laws of the Romans and of the Jews. It was permitted to the Jews to worship God according to their own views in Greece; but they could easily pretend that Paul had departed from *that* mode of worshipping God. It was easy for them to maintain that he taught contrary to the laws of the Romans, and their acknowledged religion; and their design seems to have been to accuse him of teaching men to worship God in an unlawful and irregular way, a way unknown to *any* of the laws of the empire.

¶ [illegible] *to open his mouth.* In self-

about to open *his* mouth, Gallio said unto the Jews, If it were a matter of wrong, or wicked lewdness, O *ye* Jews, [a] reason would that I should bear with you:

15 But if it be a question of words and names, and *of* your law, [b] look ye *to it;* for I will be no judge of such *matters.*

16 And he drave them from the judgment-seat.

17 Then all the Greeks took

a Rom.13.3.

b Jno. 18.31. c.23.29; 25.11,19.

defence, ever ready to vindicate his conduct. ¶ *A matter of wrong.* Injustice, or crime, such as could be properly brought before a court of justice. ¶ *Or wicked lewdness.* Any flagrant and gross offence. The word used here occurs nowhere else in the New Testament. It denotes properly an act committed by him who is skilled, facile, or an adept in iniquity—an act of a veteran offender. Such crimes Gallio was willing to take cognizance of. ¶ *Reason would,* &c. Greek, 'I would bear with you according to reason.' There would be propriety or fitness in my hearing and trying the case. That is, it would fall within the sphere of my duty, as appointed to guard the peace, and to punish crimes.

15. *Of words.* A dispute about *words,* for such he would regard all their controversies about religion to be. ¶ *And names.* Probably he had heard something of the nature of the controversy, and understood it to be a dispute about *names,* i. e. whether Jesus was to be called the Messiah or not. To him this would appear as a matter pertaining to the Jews alone, and to be ranked with their other disputes arising from the difference of sect and name. ¶ *Of your law.* A question respecting the proper interpretation of the law, or the rites and ceremonies which it commanded. The Jews had many such disputes, and Gallio did not regard them as coming under his cognizance as a magistrate. ¶ *Look ye to it.* Judge this among yourselves; settle the difficulty as you can. Comp. John xviii. 31. ¶ *For I will be no judge* &c. I do not regard such questions as pertaining to my office, or deem myself called on to settle them.

16. *And he drave them,* &c. He refused to hear and decide the controversy. He commanded them to depart from the court. The word used here does not denote that there was any violence used by Gallio, but merely that he dismissed them in an authoritative manner.

17. *Then all the Greeks.* The Greeks who had witnessed the persecution of Paul by the Jews, and who had seen the tumult which they had excited. ¶ *Took Sosthenes,* &c. As he was the chief ruler of the synagogue, he had probably been a leader in the opposition to Paul, and in the prosecution. Indignant at the Jews at their bringing such questions before the tribunal; at their bigotry, and rage and contentious spirit, they probably fell upon him in a tumultuous and disorderly manner as he was leaving the tribunal. The Greeks would feel no small measure of indignation at these disturbers of the public peace, and they took this opportunity to express their rage. ¶ *And beat him.* ἔτυπτον. This word is not that which is commonly used to denote a judicial act of scourging. It probably means that they fell upon him, and beat him with their fists, or with whatever was at hand. ¶ *Before the judgment-seat.* Probably while leaving the tribunal. Instead of "Greeks" in this verse, some MSS. read "Jews," but the former is probably the true reading. The Syriac, Arabic, and Coptic read it "the Gentiles." It is probable that this Sosthenes afterwards became a convert to the Christian faith, and a preacher of the gospel. See 1 Cor. i. 1, 2, "Paul, and *Sosthenes our brother,* unto the church of God which is at Corinth." ¶ *And Gallio cared,* &c. This has been usually charged on Gallio as a matter of reproach, as if he were wholly indifferent to religion. But the charge is unjustly made; and his name is often most improperly used to represent the indifferent, the worldly, the careless, and the skeptical. But by the testimony of ancient writers, he was a most mild and amiable man; and an upright and just judge. Nor is there the least evidence that he was indifferent to the religion of his country, or that he was of a thoughtless and skeptical turn of mind. All that this passage implies is, (1.) That he did not deem it to be his duty, or a part of his office, to settle questions of a theological nature that were started among the Jews. (2.) That he was unwilling to make this subject a matter of legal discussion and investigation. (3.) That he would not interfere, either on one side or the other, in the question about making proselytes either to or from Judaism. So far certainly his conduct was exemplary and proper.

[a] Sosthenes, the chief ruler of the synagogue, and beat *him* before the judgment-seat. And Gallio cared for none of those things.

a 1Cor.1.1.

18 And Paul *after this* tarried *there* yet a good while, and then took his leave of the brethren, and sailed thence into Syria, and with

(4.) That he did not choose to interpose, and rescue Sosthenes from the hands of the mob. From *some* cause he was willing that *he* should feel the effects of the public indignation. Perhaps it was not easy to quell the riot; perhaps, he was not unwilling that he who had joined in a furious and unprovoked persecution, should feel the effect of it in the excited passions of the people. At all events, he was but following the common practice among the Romans, which was to regard the Jews with contempt, and to care little how much they were exposed to popular fury and rage. In this he was wrong; and it is certain also that he was indifferent to the disputes between Jews and Christians; but there is no propriety in defaming his name, and making him the type and representative of all the thoughtless and indifferent men on the subject of religion in subsequent times. Nor is there propriety in using this passage as a text as applicable to this class of men.

18. *And sailed thence into Syria.* Or set sail for Syria. His design was to go to Jerusalem to the festival which was soon to occur. ver. 21. ¶ *Having shorn his head.* Many interpreters have supposed that this refers to Aquila, and not to Paul. But the connexion evidently requires us to understand it of Paul, though the Greek construction does not with certainty determine to which it refers. The Vulgate refers it to Aquila, the Syriac to Paul. ¶ *In Cenchrea.* Cenchrea was the eastern port of Corinth. A church was formed in that place. Rom. xvi. 1. ¶ *For he had a vow.* A *vow* is a solemn promise made to God respecting any thing. The use of vows is observable throughout the Scripture. Jacob going into Mesopotamia, vowed the tenth of his estate, and promised to offer it at Bethel to the honour of God. Gen. xxviii. 22. Moses made many regulations in regard to vows. A man might devote himself or his children to the Lord. He might devote any part of his time or property to his service. The vow they were required sacredly to observe (Deut. xxiii. 21, 22), except in certain specified cases they were permitted to redeem that which had been thus devoted. The most remarkable vow among the Jews was that of the Nazarite; by which a man made a solemn promise to God to abstain from wine, and all intoxicating liquors, to let the hair grow, and not to enter any house polluted by having a dead body in it, or to attend any funeral. This vow generally lasted eight days, sometimes a month, sometimes during a definite period fixed by themselves, and sometimes during their whole lives. When the vow expired, the priest made an offering of a he-lamb for a burnt-offering, a she-lamb for an expiatory sacrifice, and a ram for a peace-offering. The priest then, or some other person, shaved the head of the Nazarite at the door of the tabernacle, and burnt the hair on the fire of the altar. Those who made the vow out of Palestine, and who could not come to the temple when the vow was expired, contented themselves with observing the abstinence required by the law, and cutting off the hair where they were. This I suppose to have been the case with Paul. His hair he cut off at the expiration of the vow at Cenchrea, though he delayed to perfect the vow by the proper ceremonies until he reached Jerusalem. Acts xxi. 23. 24. *Why* Paul made this vow, or on what occasion, the sacred historian has not informed us, and conjecture perhaps is useless. We may observe, however, (1.) That it was common for the Jews to make such vows to God, as an expression of gratitude or of devotedness to his service, when they had been raised up from sickness, or delivered from danger or calamity. See Josephus b. i. 2. 15. Vows of this nature were also made by the Gentiles on occasions of deliverance from any signal calamity. Juvenal Sat. 12. 81. It is *possible* that Paul may have made such a vow in consequence of signal deliverance from some of the numerous perils to which he was exposed. But, (2.) There is reason to think that it was mainly with a design to convince the Jews, that he did not despise their law, and was not its enemy See ch. xxi. 22, 23, 24. In accordance with the custom of the nation, and in compliance with a law which was not wrong in itself, he might have made this vow, not for a time-serving purpose, but in order to conciliate them, and to mitigate their anger against the gospel But where

him Priscilla and Aquila; having
shorn [a] *his* head in Cenchrea: [b] for
he had a vow.

19 And he came to Ephesus, and
left them there: but he himself entered into the synagogue, and reasoned [c] with the Jews.

20 When they desired *him* to
tarry longer time with them, he
consented not;

21 But bade them farewell, saying, I must by all means keep this
feast that cometh in Jerusalem:
[d] but I will return again unto you,
if [e] God will. And he sailed from
Ephesus.

22 And when he had landed at
Cesarea, and gone up, and saluted
the church, he went down to Antioch.

23 And after he had spent some
time *there*, he departed, and went
over *all* the country of Galatia [f] and
Phrygia in order, strengthening
[g] all the disciples.

24 And a certain Jew named
[h] Apollos, born at Alexandria, an
eloquent man, *and* mighty in the
Scriptures, came to Ephesus.

25 This man was instructed in
the way of the Lord; and being
fervent [i] in the spirit, he spake and

a Num.6.18. c.21.24. b Rom.16.1. c c.17.2. d c.19.21; 20.16. e 1Cor.4.19. Jam.4.15.

f Gal.1.2. g c.14.22; 15.32,41. h 1Cor.1.12; 3.5,6. Tit.3.13. i Rom.12.11. Jam.5.16.

nothing is recorded, conjecture is useless. Those who wish to see the subject discussed, may consult Grotius and Kuinöel in loco, and Spencer de Legibus Hebræ. p. 862, and Calmet's Dic. art. *Nazarite.*

19. *And he came to Ephesus.* This was a celebrated city in Ionia, in Asia Minor, about forty miles south of Smyrna. It was chiefly famous for the temple of Diana, usually reckoned one of the seven wonders of the world. Pliny styles this city the ornament of Asia. In the times of the Romans it was the metropolis of Asia. This city is now under the dominion of the Turks, and is almost in a state of ruin. Dr. Chandler, in his travels in Asia Minor, says—"The inhabitants are a few Greek peasants, living in extreme wretchedness, dependence, and insensibility; the representatives of an illustrious people, and inhabiting the wreck of their greatness; some in the substructions of the glorious edifices which they raised; some beneath the vaults of the stadium, once the crowded scene of their diversions; and some in the sepulchres which received their ashes." Travels, p. 131, Oxford, 1775. The Jews, according to Josephus, were very numerous in Ephesus, and had obtained the privilege of citizenship. ¶ *Left them there.* That is, Aquila and Priscilla. ver. 24—26. ¶ *Reasoned with the Jews.* Note, ch. xvii. 2.

21. *Keep this feast.* Probably the Passover is here referred to. *Why* he was so anxious to celebrate that feast at Jerusalem, the historian has not informed us. It is probable, however, that he wished to meet as many of his countrymen as possible, and to remove, if practicable, the prejudices which had every where been raised against him. ch. xxi. 20, 21. Perhas, also, he supposed that there would be many Christian converts present, whom he might meet also. ¶ *But I will return,* &c. This he did (ch. xix. 1), and remained there three years. ch. xx. 31.

22. *At Cesarea.* Note, ch. viii. 40. ¶ *And gone up.* From the ship. ¶ *And saluted the church.* Having expressed for them his tender regard and affection. ¶ *To Antioch.* In Syria. Note, ch. xi. 19.

23. *The country of Galatia and Phrygia.* He had been over these regions before, preaching the gospel. ch. xvi. 6. ¶ *Strengthening.* Establishing them by exhortation and counsel. Note, ch. xiv. 22.

24. *And a certain Jew named Apollos.* Apollos afterwards became a distinguished and successful preacher of the gospel. 1 Cor. i. 12; iii. 5, 6; iv. 6. Titus iii. 13. Nothing more is known of him than is stated in these passages. ¶ *Born at Alexandria.* Alexandria was a celebrated city in Egypt, founded by Alexander the Great. There were large numbers of Jews resident there. Note, ch. vi. 9. ¶ *An eloquent man.* Alexandria was famous for its schools, and it is probable that Apollos, in addition to his natural endowments, had enjoyed the benefit of these schools. ¶ *Mighty in the Scriptures.* Well instructed, or able in the Old Testament. The foundation was thus laid for future usefulness in the Christian church. Note, Luke xxiv. 19.

25. *This man was instructed.* Greek, was *catechised.* He was instructed, in some degree into the knowledge of the

taught diligently the things of the Lord, knowing [a] only the baptism of John.

26 And he began to speak boldly in the synagogue: whom when Aquila and Priscilla had heard, they took him unto *them*, and expounded unto him the way of God more [b] perfectly.

27 And when he was disposed to pass into Achaia, the brethren wrote, exhorting the disciples to receive him: who, when he was come, helped [c] them much which had believed [d] through grace:

28 For he mightily convinced

a c.19.3. b Heb.6.1. 2Pet.3.18. c 1Cor.3.6. d Eph.2.8.

Christian religion. By whom this was done, we have no information. See Note, ch. ii. 9—11. ¶ *In the right way of the Lord.* The word *way* often refers to doctrine. Matt. xxi. 32. It means here that he had been correctly taught in regard to the Messiah; yet his knowledge was imperfect. ver. 26. The amount of his knowledge seems to have been,—(1.) He had correct views of the Messiah to come—views which he had derived from the study of the Old Testament. He was expecting a Saviour that should be humble, obscure, and a sacrifice, in opposition to the prevailing notions of the Jews. (2.) He had heard of John; had embraced his doctrine; and probably had been baptized with reference to him that was to come. Comp. Matt. iii. 2. Acts xix. 4. But it is clear that he had not heard that Jesus was the Messiah. With his correct views in regard to the coming of the Messiah, he was endeavouring to instruct and reform his countrymen. He was just in the state of mind to welcome the announcement that the Messiah had come, and to embrace Jesus of Nazareth as the hope of the nation. ¶ *Being fervent in the spirit.* Being zealous and ardent. See Note, Rom. xii. 11. ¶ *Taught diligently.* Defended with zeal and earnestness his views of the Messiah. ¶ *The things of the Lord.* The doctrines pertaining to the Messiah as far as he understood them. ¶ *Knowing only the baptism of John.* Whether he had heard John, and been baptized by him, has been made a question, and cannot now be decided. It is not necessary, however, to suppose this, as it seems that the knowledge of John's preaching and baptism had been propagated extensively into other nations besides Judea. ch. xix. 1—3. The Messiah was expected about that time. The foreign Jews would be waiting for him; and the news of John's ministry, doctrine, and success would be rapidly propagated from synagogue to synagogue into the surrounding nations. John preached repentance, and baptized with reference to him that was to come after him. (ch. xix. 4), and this doctrine Apollos seems to have embraced.

26. *And expounded.* Explained. ¶ *The way of God.* Gave him full and ample instructions respecting the Messiah as having already come, and respecting the nature of his work.

27. *Into Achaia.* Note, ch. xviii. 12. ¶ *The brethren wrote.* The brethren at Ephesus. *Why* he went, the historian does not inform us. But he had heard of the success of Paul there; of the church which he had established; of the opposition of the Jews; and it was doubtless with a desire to establish that church, and with a wish to convince his unbelieving countrymen that their views of the Messiah were erroneous, and that Jesus of Nazareth corresponded with the predictions of the prophets. Many of the Greeks at Corinth were greatly captivated with his winning eloquence (1 Cor. i. 12; iii. 4, 5), and his going there was the occasion of some unhappy divisions that sprung up in the church. But in all this he retained the confidence and love of Paul. 1 Cor. i. iii. It was thus shown that Paul was superior to envy, and that great success by one minister need not excite the envy, or alienate the confidence and good will of another. ¶ *Helped them much.* Strengthened them, and aided them in their controversies with the unbelieving Jews. ¶ *Which had believed through grace.* The words "through grace" may either refer to Apollos, or to the Christians who had believed. If to *him*, it means that he was enabled by grace to strengthen the brethren there, if to *them*, it means that they had been led to believe by the grace or favour of God. Either interpretation makes good sense. Our translation has adopted that which is most natural and obvious.

28. *For he mightily convinced the Jews.* He did it by strong arguments; he bore down all opposition, and effectually silenced them. ¶ *And that publicly.* In his public preaching in the synagogue and elsewhere. ¶ *Showing by the Scriptures.* Proving from the Old Testament. Show-

the Jews, *and that* publicly, showing by [a] the Scriptures that Jesus [1] was Christ.

CHAPTER XIX.

AND it came to pass, that while Apollos [b] was at Corinth, Paul having passed through the upper coasts, came to Ephesus; and finding certain disciples,

2 He said unto them, have ye received the Holy Ghost since ye believed? And they said unto him, We have not [c] so much as heard whether there be any Holy Ghost.

3 And he said unto them, Unto what then were ye baptized? And they said, Unto [d] John's baptism.

4 Then said Paul, John [e] verily baptized with the baptism of repentance, [f] saying unto the people,

a Jno.5.39. 1 or, *is the Christ*, ver.5. b 1Cor. 3.5,6. c c.8.16. 1Sam 3.7. d c.18.25. e Matt.3.11 f Jno.1.15,27,30.

ing that Jesus of Nazareth corresponded with the account of the Messiah given by the prophets. See Note, John v. 39. ¶ *That Jesus was Christ.* See the margin. That Jesus of Nazareth was the Messiah.

CHAPTER XIX.

1. *While Apollos was at Corinth.* It is probable that he remained there a considerable time. ¶ *Paul having passed through the upper coasts.* The upper, or more elevated regions of Asia Minor. The writer refers here particularly to the provinces of Phrygia and Galatia. ch. xviii. 23. These regions were called *upper*, because they were situated on the high table-land in the interior of Asia Minor, while Ephesus was in the low maritime regions, and called the *low* country. ¶ *Came to Ephesus.* Agreeably to his promise. ch. xviii. 21. ¶ *And finding certain disciples.* Certain persons who had been baptized into John's baptism, and who had embraced John's doctrine, that the Messiah was soon to appear. ver. 3, 4. It is very clear that they had not yet heard that he had come, or that the Holy Ghost was given. They were evidently in the same situation as Apollos. Notes, ch. xviii. 25.

2. *Have ye received the Holy Ghost?* Have ye received the extraordinary effusions and miraculous influences of the Holy Ghost? Paul would not doubt that, if they had "believed," they had received the ordinary converting influences of the Holy Spirit—for it was one of his favourite doctrines, that the Holy Spirit renews the heart. But, besides this, the miraculous influences of the Spirit were conferred on most societies of believers. The power of speaking with tongues, or of working miracles, was imparted as an evidence of the presence of God, and of their acceptance with him. ch. x. 45, 46. 1 Cor. xiv. It was natural for Paul to ask whether *this* evidence of the divine favour had been granted to them. ¶ *Since ye believed.* Since you embraced the doctrine of John, that the Messiah was soon to come. ¶ *We have not so much as heard*, &c. This seems to be a very remarkable and strange answer. Yet we are to remember, (1.) That these were mere disciples of *John's* doctrine, and that *his* preaching related particularly to the Messiah, and not to the Holy Ghost. (2.) It does not even appear that they had heard that the Messiah *had* come, or had heard of Jesus of Nazareth ver. 4, 5. (3.) It is not remarkable, therefore, that they had no clear conceptions of the character and operations of the Holy Ghost. Yet, (4.) They were just in that state of mind, that they were willing to embrace the doctrine when it was proclaimed to them; thus showing that they were *really* under the influence of the Holy Spirit. God may often produce important changes in the hearts and lives of sinners, even where they have no clear and systematic views of religious doctrines. In all such cases, however, as in this, there will be a readiness of heart to embrace the truth where it is made known.

3. *Unto what.* Unto what faith, or doctrine. What did you profess to believe when you were baptized. ¶ *Unto John's baptism.* Note, ch. xviii. 25.

4. *John verily baptized.* John did indeed baptize. ¶ *With the baptism of repentance.* Having special relation to repentance, or as a profession that they *did* repent of their sins. Note, Matt. iii. 6 ¶ *Saying unto the people.* The design of his coming was, to turn the people from their sins, and to prepare them for the coming of the Messiah. He therefore directed their attention principally to him that was to come. John i. 15. 22—27. ¶ *That is on Christ Jesus.* These are the words of Paul, explaining what John taught. He taught them to believe in the Messiah, and that the Messiah was Jesus of Nazareth. The argument of Paul is,

that they should believe on him which should come after him, that is, on Christ Jesus.

5 When they heard *this*, they were baptized in the name [a] of the Lord Jesus.

6 And when Paul had laid [b] *his* hands upon them, the Holy Ghost came on them; [c] and they spake with tongues, [d] and prophesied.

7 And all the men were about twelve.

8 And he went into the synagogue, and spake boldly for the space of three months, disputing, [e] and persuading [f] the things concerning the kingdom of God.

9 But when divers were hardened, [g] and believed not, but spake evil [h] of that [i] way before the mul-

a c.8.16. 1Cor.1.13. b c.8.17. c c.2.4;10.46. d 1Cor.14.1,&c.

e c.18.19. f c.28.23. g Rom.11.7. Heb.3 13. h 2Tim.1.15. 2Pet.2.2. Jude 10. i ver.23.

---

that it was highly proper for them now to profess publicly that Saviour to whom John had borne such explicit testimony. 'Jesus is the Messiah for whom John came to prepare the way; and as you have embraced John's doctrine, you ought now publicly to acknowledge that Redeemer by baptism in his name.'

5. *When they heard this.* When they heard what Paul had said respecting the nature of John's baptism. ¶ *They were baptized, &c.* As there is no other instance in the New Testament of any persons having been rebaptized, it has been made a question by some critics, whether it was done here; and they have supposed that all this is the narrative of Luke respecting what took place under the ministry of John, to wit: that he told them to believe on Christ Jesus, and then baptized them in his name. But this is a most forced construction; and it is evident that these persons were *rebaptized* by the direction of Paul. For, (1.) This is the *obvious* interpretation of the passage—that which would strike all persons as correct, unless there were some previous theory to support. (2.) It was not a matter of fact that John baptized in the name of Christ Jesus. His was the baptism of repentance; and there is not the slightest evidence that he ever used the name of Jesus in the form of baptism. (3.) If this be the sense of the passage, that John baptized them in the name of Jesus, then this verse is a mere repetition of ver. 4; a tautology of which the sacred writers would not be guilty. (4.) It is evident, that the persons on whom Paul laid his hands (ver. 6), and those who were baptized, were the same But these were the persons who *heard* (ver. 5) what was said. The narrative is *continuous*, all barts of it cohering together as relating to a transaction that occurred at the same time. If the *obvious* interpretation of the passage be the true one, it follows, that the baptism of John was not strictly Christian baptism. It was the baptism of repentance; a baptism designed to prepare the way for the introduction of the kingdom of the Messiah. It will *not* follow, however, from this that Christian baptism is now ever to be repeated. For this, there is no warrant, no example in the New Testament. There is no command to repeat it, as in the case of the Lord's supper; and the nature and design of the ordinance evidently supposes that it is to be performed but once. The disciples of John were rebaptized, not because baptism is designed to be repeated, but because they never had been, in fact, baptized in the manner prescribed by the Lord Jesus. ¶ *In the name of the Lord Jesus.* Note, ch. ii. 38.

6. *And when Paul laid his hands, &c.* Note, ch. viii. 17. ¶ *And they spake with tongues.* Notes, ch. ii. 4; x. 46. ¶ *And prophesied.* Notes, ch. ii. 17; xi. 27.

7. *And all the men.* The whole number.

8. *Persuading the things.* Endeavouring to persuade them of the truth of what was affirmed respecting the kingdom of God

9. *But when divers.* When *some* were hardened. ¶ *Were hardened.* When their hearts were hardened, and they became violently opposed to the gospel. When the truth made no *impression* on them. The word *harden*, as applied to the heart, is often used to denote insensibility, and opposition to the gospel. ¶ *But spake evil of that way.* Of the gospel—the *way*, path, or manner in which God saves men. See Acts xvi. 17; xviii. 26. Matt. vii. 13, 14. ¶ *Separated the disciples.* Removed them from the influence and society of those who were seeking to draw them away from the faith. This is often the best way to prevent the evil influence of others. Christians, if they wish to preserve their minds calm and peaceful; if they wish to avoid the agitations of conflict, and the temptations of those who

titude, he departed [a] from them,
and separated the disciples, disputing daily in the school of one
Tyrannus.
10 And this continued by the
space [b] of two years; so that all
they which dwelt in Asia [c] heard
the word of the Lord Jesus, both
Jews and Greeks.
11 And God wrought special [d]
miracles by the hands of Paul:
12 So that from his body were
brought unto the sick handkerchiefs
[e] or aprons, and the diseases departed from them, and the evil spi
rits went out of them.

a 1Tim.6.5. b c.20.31. c c.20.18. d Mark 16.20. e c.5.15.

would lead them astray, may often find it necessary to withdraw from their society, and should seek the fellowship of their Christian brethren. ¶ *Disputing daily.* This is not a happy translation. The word used here (διαλεγόμενος) does not of necessity denote *disputation* or *contention*, but is often used in a good sense of reasoning (Acts xvii. 2; xviii. 4. 19; xxiv. 25), or of public *preaching.* Acts xx. 7. 9. It is used in this sense here, and denotes that Paul taught publicly, or reasoned on the subject of religion in this place. ¶ *In the school of one Tyrannus.* Who this Tyrannus was, is not known. It is probable that he was a Jew, who was engaged in this employment, and who might not be unfavourable to Christians. In his school, or in the room which he occupied for teaching, Paul instructed the people when he was driven from the synagogue. Christians at that time had no churches, and they were obliged to assemble in any place where it might be convenient to conduct public worship.

10. *This continued.* This public instruction. ¶ *By the space,* &c. For two whole years. ¶ *So that all.* That is, the great mass of the people. ¶ *That dwelt in Asia.* In that province of Asia Minor of which Ephesus was the principal city. The name *Asia* was used sometimes to denote that single province. See Note, Acts ii. 9. Ephesus was the capital; and there was, of course, a constant and large influx of people there for the purposes of commerce and worship. ¶ *Heard the word of the Lord Jesus.* Heard the doctrine respecting the Lord Jesus.

11. *Special miracles.* Miracles that were remarkable; that were not common, or that were very unusual (οὐ τὰς τυχούσας). This expression is classic Greek. Thus Longinus says of Moses, that he was no common man. Οὐχ' ὁ τυχὼν ἀνήρ.

12. *So that from his body.* That is, those handkerchiefs which had been applied to his body, which he had used, or which he had touched. An instance somewhat similar to this occurs in the case of the woman who was healed by touching the hem of the Saviour's garment. Matt. ix. 20—22. ¶ *Unto the sick.* The sick who were at a distance, and who were unable to go where he was. If it be asked *why* this was done, it may be observed, (1.) That the working of miracles in that region would greatly contribute to the spread of the gospel. (2.) We are not to suppose that there was any *efficacy* in the aprons thus brought, or in the mere fact that they had touched the body of Paul, any more than there was in the hem of the Saviour's garment which the woman touched, or in the clay which he made use of to open the eyes of the blind man. John viii. 6. (3.) In this instance, the fact, that the miracles were wrought in this manner by garments which had touched his body, was *a mere sign*, or *an evidence* to the persons concerned, that it was done by the instrumentality of Paul, as the fact that the Saviour put his fingers into the ears of a deaf man, and spit and touched his tongue (Mark vii. 33), was an evidence to those who saw it, that the power of healing came from him. The bearing of these aprons to the sick was, therefore, a mere *sign*, or *evidence* to all concerned, that miraculou power was given to *Paul.* ¶ *Handkerchiefs.* The word used here (σουδάρια) is of Latin origin, and properly denotes a piece of linen with which *sweat* was wiped from the face; and then any piece of linen used for tying up, or containing any thing. In Luke xix. 20, it denotes the "napkin" in which the talent of the unprofitable servant was concealed; in John xi. 44; xx. 7, the "napkin" which was used to bind up the face of the dead, applied to Lazarus and to our Saviour. ¶ *Or aprons.* Σιμικίνθια. This is also a Latin word, and means literally a *half-girdle*—a piece of cloth which was girded round the waist to preserve the clothes of those who were engaged in any kind of work. The word *aprons* expresses the idea. ¶ *And the diseases departed.* The sick were healed. ¶ *And the evil spirits.* See Notes, Matt. iv. 24. It is evident that this power of working miracles would

13 Then certain of the vagabond Jews, exorcists, took upon them [a] to call over them which had evil spirits the name of the Lord Jesus, saying, We adjure [b] you by Jesus, whom Paul preacheth.

14 And there were seven sons of *one* Sceva, a Jew, *and* chief of the priests, which did so.

15 And the evil spirit answered and said, Jesus I know, and Paul I know; but who are ye?

16 And the man in whom the evil spirit was, leapt [c] on them, and overcame them, and prevailed against them, so that they fled out of that house naked and wounded.

17 And this was known to all the Jews and Greeks also dwelling at Ephesus; and fear [d] fell on them

a Mark 9.38. Luke 9.49. *b* Josh.6.26.

c Luke 8.29. *d* Luke 1.65. c.2. 43; 5.5,11.

contribute greatly to Paul's success among the people.

13. *The vagabond Jews.* Gr. *Jews going about.* Περιερχομένων. The word *vagabond* with us is now commonly used in a bad sense, to denote a vagrant; a man who has no home; an idle, worthless fellow. The word, however, properly means one wandering from place to place, without any settled habitation, from whatever cause it may be. Here it denotes those Jews who wandered from place to place, practising exorcism. ¶ *Exorcists.* Ἐξορκιστῶν. This word properly denotes those who went about pretending to be able to expel evil spirits, or to cure diseases by charms, incantations, &c. The word is derived from ὅρκος, *orkos, an oath,* and from ὁρκίζω, to bind with an oath. It was applied in this sense, because those who pretended to be able to expel demons used the formula of an oath, or adjured them, to compel them to leave the possessed persons. Comp. Matt. xii. 27. They commonly used the name of God, or called on the demons in the name of God to leave the person. Here they used the name Jesus to command them to come out. ¶ *To call over them.* To name, or to use his name as sufficient to expel the evil spirit. ¶ *The name of the Lord Jesus.* The reasons why they attempted this were, (1.) That Jesus had expelled many evil spirits; and, (2.) That it was in his name that Paul had wrought his miracles. Perhaps they supposed there was some *charm* in this name to expel them. ¶ *We adjure you.* We bind you by an oath; we command you as under the solemnity of an oath. Mark v. 7. 1 Thess. v. 27. It is a form of putting one under oath. 1 Kings ii. 43. Gen. xxiv. 37. 2 Kings xi. 4. Neh. xiii. 25. (Septuagint.) That this art was practised then, or attempted, is abundantly proved from Irænaeus, Origen, and Josephus. (Ant. b. viii. ch. 2. § 5.) See Doddridge. The common name which was used, was the incommunicable name of God, JEHOVAH, by pronouncing which, in a peculiar way, it was pretended they had the power of expelling demons.

14. *One Sceva.* Sceva is a Greek name, but nothing more is known of him. ¶ *Chief of the priests.* Ἀρχιερέως. This cannot mean that he was high-priest among the Jews, as it is wholly improbable that his sons would be wandering exorcists. But it denotes that he was of the sacerdotal order. He was a Jewish chief priest; a priest of distinction, and that had held the office of a ruler. The word *chief priest,* in the New Testament, usually refers to men of the sacerdotal order who were also rulers in the sanhedrim.

15. *Jesus I know.* His power to cast out devils I know. Comp. Matt. viii. 29 ¶ *Paul I know.* Paul's power to cast out devils. ver. 12. ¶ *But who are ye?* What power have you over evil spirits? By what right do you attempt to expel them? The meaning is, 'you belong neither to Jesus nor Paul; you are not of their party; and you have no right or authority to attempt to work miracles in the name of either.'

16. *Leapt on them.* Several such instances are recorded of the extraordinary power and rage of those who were possessed with evil spirits. Mark v. 3; ix 29. Luke ix. 42.

17. *The name of the Lord Jesus was magnified.* Acquired increasing honour. The transaction showed that the miracles performed in the name of the Lord Jesus, by Paul, were real, and were wrought in attestation of the truth of the doctrine which he taught. Impostors could not work such miracles; and they who pretended to be able to do it only exposed themselves to the rage of the evil spirits. It was thus shown that there was a real, vital difference between Paul and these impostors; and their failure only served to extend his

all, and the name of the Lord Jesus was magnified.

18 And many that believed, came, and confessed, [a] and shewed their deeds.

19 Many also of them which

a Matt.3.6. Rom.10.10.

reputation and the power of the gospel.

18 *Their deeds.* Their actions; their evil course of life. Their deeds of iniquity in their former state. The direct reference here is to the magical arts which had been used, but the word may also be designed to denote iniquity in general. They who make a profession of religion will be willing to confess their transgressions. And no man can have evidence that he is truly renewed who is not willing to *confess* as well as to *forsake* his sins. Rom. x. 10. Prov. xxviii. 13. "He that covereth his sins shall not prosper; but whoso confesseth and forsaketh them shall find mercy."

19. *Curious arts.* Arts or practices requiring *skill, address, cunning.* The word used here (περίεργα) denotes properly those things that require care, or skill; and was thus applied to the arts of magic, and jugglery, and sleight of hand, that were practised so extensively in eastern countries. That such arts were practised at Ephesus is well known. The *Ephesian letters,* by which incantations and charms were supposed to be produced, were much celebrated. They seem to have consisted of certain combinations of letters or words, which, by being pronounced with certain intonations of voice, were believed to be effectual in expelling diseases, or evil spirits; or which, by being written on parchment and worn, were supposed to operate as *amulets,* or charms, to guard from evil spirits, or from danger. Thus Plutarch (Sympos. 7) says, "the magicians compel those who are possessed with a demon to recite and pronounce *the Ephesian letters,* in a certain order, by themselves." Thus Clemens Alex. (Strom. ii.) says, "Androcydes, a Pythagorean, says that the letters which are called Ephesian, and which are so celebrated, are symbols," &c. Erasmus says (Adagg. Cent. 2), that there were certain marks and magical words among the Ephesians, by using which they succeeded in every undertaking. Eustha. ad Homer Odys. τ says, "that those letters were incantations which Crœsus used when on the funeral pile, and which greatly befriended him." He adds, that in the war between the Milesians and Ephesians, the latter were thirteen times saved from ruin by the use of these letters. See Grotius and Kuinoel *in loco.* ¶ *Brought their books.* Books which explained the arts; or which contained the magical forms and incantations—perhaps pieces of parchment, on which were written the letters which were to be used in the incantations and charms. ¶ *And burned them before all men.* Publicly. Their arts and offences had been public, and they sought now to *undo* the evil, as much as lay in their power, as extensively as they had done it. ¶ *And they counted.* The price was estimated. By whom this was done does not appear. Probably it was not done by those who had been engaged in this business, and who had suffered the loss, but by the people, who were amazed at the sacrifice, and who were astonished at their folly in thus destroying their own property. ¶ *Fifty thousand pieces of silver.* What coin the word (ἀργυρίου) here translated *silver* denotes, it is impossible to tell; and consequently the precise value of this sacrifice cannot be ascertained. If it refers to the Jewish *shekel,* the sum would be $25,000, as the shekel was worth about half a dollar. If it refers to Grecian or Roman coin—which is much more probable, as this was a heathen country, where the Jewish coin would not probably be much used—the value would be much less. Probably, however, it refers to the Attic *drachm,* which was a silver coin worth about 9d. sterling, or not far from 17 cents; and then the value would be about $8,500. The precise value is not material. It was a large sum; and it is recorded to show that Christianity had power to induce men to forsake arts that were most lucrative, and to destroy the means of extending and perpetuating those arts, however valuable in a pecuniary point of view they might be. We are to remember, however, that this was not the *intrinsic* value of these books, but only their value *as* books of incantation. In themselves they might have been of very little worth. *The universal prevalence of Christianity would make much that is now esteemed valuable property utterly worthless*—as, e. g. all that is used in gambling; in fraud; in counterfeiting; in distilling ardent spirits for drink; in the slave-trade; and in at-

used curious arts, brought their books together, and burned them before all *men*: and they counted the price of them, and found *it* fifty thousand *pieces* of silver.

20 So mightily grew[a] the word of God, and prevailed.

21 After[b] these things were ended. Paul purposed in the spirit, when he had passed through Macedonia and Achaia, to go to Jerusalem, saying, After I have been there, I must also see Rome.[c]

22 So he sent into Macedonia

a c.12.24

b Gal.2.1. c Rom.15.23-28.

tempts to impose on and defraud mankind.

20. *So mightily.* So powerfully. It had such efficacy and power in this wicked city. The power *must* have been mighty that would thus make them willing, not only to cease to practise imposition, but to give up all hopes of future gains, and to destroy their property. On this instructive narrative, we may remark, (1.) That religion has power to break the hold of sinners on unjust and dishonest means of living. (2.) That those who have been engaged in an unchristian and dishonourable practice, will abandon it when they become Christians. (3.) That their abhorrence of their former course will be, and ought to be, expressed as publicly as was the offence. (4.) That the evil practice will be abandoned at any sacrifice, however great. The only question will be, *what is right;* not, *what will it cost.* Property, in the view of a converted man, is nothing when compared with a good conscience. (5.) This conduct of those who had used curious arts shows us what ought to be done by those who have been engaged in any evil course of life, and who are then converted. If their conduct was right—and who can doubt it?—it settles a great principle on which young converts should act. If a man has been engaged in the slave-trade, he will abandon it; and his duty will *not* be to sell his ship to one who he knows will continue the traffic. His property should be withdrawn from the business publicly, either by being destroyed, or by being converted to a useful purpose. If a man has been a distiller of ardent spirits as a drink, his duty will be to forsake his evil course. Nor will it be his duty to sell his distillery to one who will continue the business; but to withdraw his property from it *publicly,* either by destroying it, or converting it to some useful purpose. If a man has been engaged in the *traffic* in ardent spirits, his duty is not to sell his stock to those who will continue the sale of the poison, but to withdraw it from public use; converting it to some useful purpose, if he can; if not, by destroying it. All that has ever been said by money-loving distillers, or venders of ardent spirits, about the loss which they would sustain by abandoning the business, might have been said by these practitioners of curious arts in Ephesus. And if the excuses of rum-selling men are valid, *their* conduct was folly: and they should either have continued the business of practising "curious arts" after they were converted, or have sold their "books" to those who would have continued it. For assuredly it was not worse to practise jugglery and fortune-telling than it is to destroy the bodies and souls of men by the traffic in ardent spirits. And yet, how few men there are in Christian lands who practise on the principle of these honest, but comparatively unenlightened men at Ephesus!

21. *After these things were ended.* After the gospel was firmly established at Ephesus, so that his presence was no longer necessary. ¶ *Purposed in the spirit.* Resolved in his mind. ¶ *When he had passed through Macedonia and Achaia.* In these places he had founded flourishing churches. It is probable that his main object in this visit was to take up a collection for the poor saints at Jerusalem. See Note, Rom. xv. 25, 26. ¶ *To go to Jerusalem.* To bear the contribution of the Gentile churches to the poor and oppressed Christians in Judea. ¶ *I must also see Rome.* See Note, Rom xv. 24. He did go to Rome, but he went in chains, as a prisoner.

22. *Timotheus.* Timothy. He was a proper person to send there to visit the churches, as he had been there before with Paul, when they were established. ch. xvi. 3; xvii. 14. ¶ *And Erastus.* Erastus was chamberlain of Corinth (Rom. xvi. 23), or more properly the *treasurer* of the city (see Note on that place); and he was, therefore, a very proper person to be sent with Timothy, for the purpose of making the collection for the poor at Jerusalem. Paul had wisdom enough to employ a man accustomed to moneyed transactions in making a collection. On

two of them that ministered unto
him, Timotheus and Erastus ; [a] but
he himself stayed in Asia for a
season.
23 And the same time there arose
no small stir [b] about that way.
24 For a certain *man* named Demetrius, a silversmith, which made
silver shrines for Diana, brought no
small [c] gain unto the craftsmen ;
25 Whom he called [d] together
with the workmen of like occupation, and said, Sirs, ye know that
by this craft we have our wealth.
26 Moreover, ye see and hear,
that not alone at Ephesus, but al-

a Rom.16.23. 2Tim.4.20. b 2Cor.1.8; 6.9 c c.16.16.19. d Rev.18.11.

this collection his heart was intent, and he afterwards went up with it to Jerusalem. See 2 Cor. viii. ix., and Notes, Rom. xv. 25, 26. ¶ *Stayed in Asia.* At Ephesus. ¶ *For a season.* How long is uncertain. He waited for a convenient opportunity to follow them; probably intending to do it as soon as they had fully prepared the way for the collection. See Paley's Horæ Paulinæ, p. i. ch. ii.

23. *No small stir.* No little excitement, disturbance, or tumult (τάραχος). Comp. ch. xvii. 4, 5. ¶ *About that way.* Respecting the doctrines of Christianity which Paul preached. Note, ch. ix. 2; xviii. 26; xix. 9

24. *A silversmith.* The word used here denotes one who works in silver in any way, either in making money, in stamping silver, or in forming utensils of it. It is probable that the employment of this man was confined to the business here specified, that of making shrines ; as his complaint (ver. 26, 27) implied, that destroying this would be sufficient to throw them all out of employment ¶ *Silver shrines.* Ναούς. Temples. The word *shrine* properly means a case, small chest, or box ; particularly applied to a box in which sacred things are deposited. Hence we hear of the *shrines* for relics. (*Webster.*) The word *shrines* here denotes small portable temples, or edifices, made of silver, so as to resemble the temple of Diana, and probably containing a silver image of the goddess. Such shrines would be purchased by devotees and by worshippers of the goddess, and by strangers, who would be desirous of possessing a representation of one of the seven wonders of the world. See Note on ver. 27. The great number of persons that came to Ephesus for her worship would constitute an ample sale for productions of this kind, and make the manufacture a profitable employment. It is well known that pagans every where are accustomed to carry with them small images, or representations of their gods, as an amulet, or charm. The Romans had such images in all their houses, called *Penates*, or household gods. A similar thing is mentioned as early as the time of Laban (Gen. xxxi. 19), whose *images* Rachel had stolen and taken with her. Comp. Judg. xvii. 5. "The man Micah had an house of gods." 1 Sam. xix. 13. Hos. iii. 4. These images were usually enclosed in a box, case, or chest, made of wood, iron, or silver; and probably, as here, usually made to resemble the temple where the idol was worshipped. ¶ *Diana.* This was a celebrated goddess of the heathen, and one of the twelve superior deities. In the heavens she was Luna, or Meni (the moon); on earth Diana; and in hell Hecate. She was sometimes represented with a crescent on her head, a bow in her hand, and dressed in a hunting-habit, at other times with a triple face, and with instruments of torture. She was commonly regarded as the goddess of hunting. She was also worshipped under the various names of Lucina, Proserpine, Trivia, &c. She was also represented with a great number of breasts, to denote her being the fountain of blessings, or as distributing her benefits to each in their proper station. She was worshipped in Egypt, Athens, Cilicia, and among heathen nations generally; but the most celebrated place of her worship was Ephesus—a city peculiarly dedicated to her. ¶ *To the craftsmen.* To the labourers employed under Demetrius in the manufacture of shrines.

25. *With the workmen of like occupation.* Those who were in his employ, and all others engaged in the same business. As they would be all affected in the same way, it was easy to produce an excitement among them all. ¶ *Sirs.* Gr. Men. ¶ *By this craft.* By this business, or occupation. This is our *trade.* ¶ *Our wealth.* Gr. Our acquisition ; our property. We are dependent on it for a living. It does not mean that they were *rich*, but that they relied on this for a subsistence. That it was a lucrative business is apparent; but it is not affirmed that they were in fact rich.

26. *Ye see and hear.* You see at Ephesus; and you hear the same of other places. ¶ *Throughout all Asia.* All Asia

most throughout all Asia, this Paul
hath persuaded and turned away
much people, saying that [a] they be
no gods which are made with
hands:

27 So that not only this our craft
is in danger to be set at nought;
but also that the temple of the great
goddess Diana should be despised, [b]
and her magnificence should be de-

a Ps.115.4. Isa.44.10-20.

b Zeph.2.11.

Minor; or perhaps the province of which Ephesus was the capital. Note, ch. ii. 9. ¶ *This Paul hath persuaded.* We have here the noble testimony of a heathen to the zeal and success of the ministry of Paul. It is an acknowledgment that his labours had been most strikingly successful in turning the people from idolatry. ¶ *Saying that they be no gods*, &c. Note, ch. xiv. 14, 15.

27. *So that not only*, &c. The grounds of the charge which Demetrius made against Paul were two;—first, that the business of the craftsmen would be destroyed—usually the first thing that strikes the mind of a sinner who is influenced by self-interest alone; and second, that the worship of Diana would cease if Paul and his fellow-labourers were suffered to continue their efforts. ¶ *This our craft.* This business in which we are engaged, and on which we are dependent. Gr. This part (τὸ μέρος) which pertains to us. ¶ *To be set at nought.* To be brought into contempt. It will become so much an object of ridicule and contempt that we shall have no further employment. Gr. '*Is in danger of coming into refutation.*' Εἰς ἀπελεγμόν. As that which is *refuted* by argument is deemed *useless*, so the word comes also to signify that which is useless, or which is an object of contempt or ridicule. We may here remark, (1.) That the extensive prevalence of the Christian religion would *destroy* many kinds of business in which men now engage. It would put an end to all that now ministers to the pride, vanity, luxury, vice, and ambition of men. Let religion prevail, and wars would cease, and all the preparations for war which now employ so many hearts and hands would be useless. Let religion prevail, and *temperance* would prevail also; and consequently all the capital and labour now employed in distilling and vending ardent spirits would be withdrawn, and the business be broken up. Let religion prevail, and luxury ceases, and the arts which minister to licentiousness would be useless. Let Christianity prevail, and all that goes now to minister to idolatry, and the corrupt passions of men, would be destroyed. No small part of the talent, also, that is now worse than wasted in corrupting others by ballads and songs, by fiction and licentious tales, would be withdrawn. A vast amount of capital and talent would thus be at once set at liberty, to be employed in nobler and better purposes. (2.) The effect of religion is often to bring the employments of men into shame and contempt. A revival of religion often makes the business of distilling an object of abhorrence. It pours shame on those who are engaged in ministering to the vices and luxuries of the world. Religion reveals the evil of such a course of life, and those vices are banished by the mere prevalence of better principles. Yet, (3.) The talent and capital thus disengaged is not rendered useless. It may be directed to other channels and other employments. Religion does not make men idle. It devotes talents to useful employments, and opens fields in which all may toil usefully to themselves and to their fellow-men. If all the capital, and genius, and learning which are now wasted, and worse than wasted, were to be at once withdrawn from their present pursuits, they might be profitably employed. There is not now a useless man who might not be useful; there is not a cent wasted which might not be employed to advantage in the great work of making the world better and happier. ¶ *But also that the temple of the great goddess Diana should be despised.* This temple, so celebrated, was regarded as one of the seven wonders of the world. It was two hundred and twenty years in building, before it was brought to perfection. It was built at the expense of all Asia Minor. The original object of worship among the Ephesians was a small statue of Diana, of elm, or ebony, made by one Canitias, though commonly believed in those days to have been sent down from heaven by Jupiter. It was merely an Egyptian hieroglyphic, with many breasts, representing the goddess of Nature—under which idea Diana was probably worshipped at Ephesus. As the original figure became decayed by age, it was propped up by two rods of iron like spits, which were carefully copied in the image which was afterwards made in imitation of the first. A temple, most magnificent in structure

stroyed, whom all Asia and the
world [a] worshippeth.
28 And when they heard *these*
sayings, they were full of wrath, [b]
and cried out, saying, Great *is* Diana
of the Ephesians!
29 And the whole city was filled
with confusion: and having caught
Gaius [c] and Aristarchus, [d] men of
Macedonia, Paul's companions in
travel, they rushed with one accord
into the theatre.
30 And when Paul would have
entered in unto the people, the disciples
suffered him not.
31 And certain of the chief of

a 1Jno.5.19. Rev.13.8. b Jer.50.38. c Rom.16.23. 1Cor.1.14. d c.4.10.

was built to contain the image of Diana, which appears to have been several times built and rebuilt. The first is said to have been completed in the reign of Servius Tullius, at least 570 years before Christ. Another temple is mentioned as having been designed by Ctesiphon, 540 years before the Christian era, and which was completed by Daphnis of Miletus, and a citizen of Ephesus. This temple was partially destroyed by fire on the very day on which Socrates was poisoned, 400 years B. C., and again 356 years B. C., by the philosopher Herostratus, on the day on which Alexander the Great was born. He confessed, on being put to the torture, that the only motive which he had was to immortalize his name. The four walls, and a few columns only, escaped the flames. The temple was repaired, and restored to more than its former magnificence, in which, says Pliny (Lib. xxxvi. c. 14), 220 years were required to bring it to completion. It was four hundred and twenty-five feet in length, two hundred and twenty in breadth, and was supported by one hundred and twenty-seven pillars of Parian marble, each of which was sixty feet high. These pillars were furnished by as many princes, and thirty-six of them were curiously carved, and the rest were finely polished. Each pillar, it is supposed, with its base, contained one hundred and fifty tons of marble. The doors and panneling were made of cypress wood, the roof of cedar, and the interior was rendered splendid by decorations of gold, and by the finest productions of ancient artists. This celebrated edifice, after suffering various partial demolitions, was finally burnt by the Goths, in their third naval invasion, in A. D. 260. Travellers are now left to conjecture where its site was. Amidst the confused ruins of ancient Ephesus, it is now impossible to tell where was this celebrated temple, once one of the wonders of the world. "So passes away the glory of this world." See Edinburgh Ency. art. Ephesus; also Anacharsis' Travels, vol. vi. 188. Ancient Universal History, vol. vii. 416; and Pococke's Travels. ¶ *And her magnificence.* Her majesty and glory; i. e. the splendour of her temple and her worship. ¶ *Whom all Asia.* All Asia Minor. ¶ *And the world.* Other parts of the world. The temple had been built by contributions from a great number of princes; and doubtless multitudes from all parts of the earth came to Ephesus to pay their homage to Diana.

28. *Were full of wrath.* Were greatly enraged—probably at the prospect of losing their gains. ¶ *Great is Diana, &c.* The term *great* was often applied by the Greeks to Diana. Thus in *Xenophon* (Ephes. i.) he says, "I adjure you by your own goddess, the great (τὴν μεγάλην) Diana of the Ephesians." The *design* of this clamour was doubtless to produce a persecution against Paul; and thus to secure a continuance of their employment. Often, when men have no arguments, they raise a clamour; when their employments are in danger of being ruined, they are filled with rage. We may learn, also, that when men's pecuniary interests are affected, they often show great zeal for religion, and expect by clamour in behalf of some doctrine, to maintain their own interest, and to secure their own gains.

29. *Confusion.* Tumult; disorder. ¶ *Gaius.* He had lived at Corinth, and had kindly entertained Paul at his house 1 Cor. i. 14. Rom. xvi. 23. ¶ *Aristarchus* He attended Paul to Rome, and was there a prisoner with him. Col. iv. 10. ¶ *With one accord.* Tumultuously; or with one mind, or purpose. ¶ *Into the theatre.* The *theatres* of the Greeks were not only places for public exhibitions, but also for holding assemblies, and often for courts elections, &c. The people, therefore, naturally rushed there, as being a suitable place to decide this matter.

30. *Would have entered in unto the people.* Probably to have addressed them, and to defend his own cause.

31. *Certain of the chief of Asia.* Τῶν Ἀσιαρχῶν. Of the *Asiarchs.* These

Asia, which were his friends, sent
unto him, desiring [a] him that he
would not adventure himself into
the theatre.
32 Some [b] therefore cried one
thing, and some another; for the
assembly was confused: and the
more part knew not wherefore they
were come together.
33 And they drew Alexander out
of the multitude, the Jews putting
him forward. And Alexander [c]
beckoned with the hand, and
would have made his defence unto
the people.
34 But when they knew that he
was a Jew, all with one voice,
about the space of two hours, cried
out, Great *is* Diana of the Ephesians!

a c.21.12 *b* c.21.34. *c* 1Ti.1.20. 2Ti.4.14.

were persons who presided over sacred things, and over the public games. It was their business to see that the proper services of religion were observed, and that proper honour was rendered to the Roman emperor in the public festivals, at the games, &c. They were annually elected, and their election was confirmed at Rome before it was valid. They held a common council at the principal city within their province, as at Ephesus, Smyrna, Sardis, &c., to consult and deliberate about the interests committed to their charge in their various provinces. (*Kuinoel* and *Schleusner*.) Probably they were assembled on such an occasion now; and during their remaining there they had heard Paul preach, and were friendly to his views and doctrines. ¶ *Which were his friends.* It does not appear from this that they were Christian converts; but they probably had feelings of respect towards him, and were disposed to defend him and his cause. Perhaps, also there might have existed a present acquaintance and attachment. ¶ *Would not adventure.* Would not risk his life in the tumult, and under the excited feelings of the multitude.

32. *Some therefore cried one thing, &c.* This is an admirable description of a mob, assembled for what purpose they knew not; but agitated by passions, and strifes, and tumults. ¶ *And the most part knew not, &c.* The greater part did not know. They had been drawn together by the noise and excitement; but a small part would know the real cause of the commotion. This is usually the case in tumultuous meetings.

33. *And they drew Alexander.* Who this Alexander was, is not known. Grotius supposes that it was "Alexander the coppersmith," who had in some way done Paul much harm (2 Tim. iv. 14); and whom, with Philetus, Paul had excommunicated. He supposes that it was a device of the Jews to put forward one who had been of the Christian party, in order to accuse Paul, and to attempt to cast the odium of the tumult on him. But it is not clear that the Alexander whom Paul had excommunicated was the person concerned in this transaction. All that appears in this narrative is, that Alexander was one who was known to be a Jew; and who wished to defend the Jews from being regarded as the authors of this tumult. It would be supposed by the heathen that the Christians were only a sect of the Jews, and the Jews wished doubtless to show that *they* had not been concerned in giving occasion to this tumult, but that it was to be traced wholly to Paul and his friends. ¶ *The Jews putting him forward.* That he might have a convenient opportunity to speak to the people. ¶ *Would have made his defence.* Our translation, by the phrase "*his* defence," would seem to imply that he was personally accused. But it was not so. The Greek is simply, 'was about to apologize to the people;' that is, to make a defence, not of himself particularly, but of the Jews in general. The translation should have been '*a defence*.'

34. *But when they knew.* When they perceived or ascertained. ¶ *That he was a Jew.* There was a general prejudice against the Jews They were disposed to charge the whole difficulty on Jews—esteeming Christians to be but a sect of the Jews. They were, therefore, indignant and excited, and indiscriminate in their wrath, and unwilling to listen to any defence. ¶ *With one voice.* Unitedly in one continued shout and clamour ¶ *About the space of two hours.* The day from sunrise to sunset, among the Greeks and Romans, was divided into twelve equal parts. John xi. 9. An *hour*, therefore, did not differ materially from an hour with us. It is not at all improbable that the tumult would continue for so long a time, before it would be possible to allay the excitement. ¶ *Cried out, &c.* This they at first did to silence Alexander. The excitement, however, was con-

35 And when the town-clerk had
appeased the people, he said, *Ye*
men [a] of Ephesus, what man is
there that knoweth not how that
the city of the Ephesians is a
[1] worshipper of the great goddess
Diana, and of the *image* which fell
down from Jupiter?
36 Seeing then that these things
cannot be spoken against, ye ought

a Eph.2.12.

1 *The temple-keeper.*

tinued in order to evince their attachment to Diana, as would be natural in an excited and tumultuous mob of debased heathen worshippers.

35. *And when the town-clerk.* Ὁ γραμματεύς. The scribe; the secretary. The word is often used in the New Testament, and is commonly translated *scribe,* and is applied to public notaries in the synagogues; to clerks, and to those who transcribed books, and hence to men skilled in the law or in any kind of learning. Comp. 2 Sam. viii. 17. 2 Kings xii. 11. Ezra vii. 6. 11, 12. Matt. v. 20; xii. 38; xiii. 52; xv. 1; xxiii. 34. 1 Cor. i. 20. It is, however, nowhere else applied to a heathen magistrate. It probably denoted a recorder; or a transcriber of the laws; or a chancellor. (*Kuinoel, Doddridge.*) This officer had a seat in their deliberative assemblies; and on him it seems to have devolved to keep the peace. The Syriac, 'Prince of the city.' The Vulgate and Arabic, 'Scribe.' ¶ *Had appeased the people.* Καταστείλας. Having restrained, quieted, tranquillized, so as to be able to address them. ¶ *What man is there.* Who is there that can deny this? It is universally known and admitted. This is the language of strong confidence, of reproof, and of indignation. It implied, that the worship of Diana was so well established, that there was no danger that it could be destroyed by a few Jews; and he therefore reproved them for what he deemed their unreasonable alarms. But he little knew the power of that religion which had been the innocent cause of all this tumult; nor that, at no very distant period, this then despised religion would overturn, not only the worship of Diana at Ephesus, but the splendid idolatry of the mighty Roman empire. ¶ *Is a worshipper.* Νεωκόρον. Margin. Temple-keeper. The word here used does not occur elsewhere in the New Testament. It is derived from νεὼς for ναὸς a temple, and κορέω, to sweep, to cleanse. But among the ancients, the office of keeping their temples was by no means as humble as that of sexton is with us. It was esteemed to be an office of honour and dignity to have charge of the temples of the gods, and to keep them in order. The name was also given to the cities that were regarded as the peculiar patrons or worshippers of certain gods and goddesses. They esteemed it an honour to be regarded as the peculiar *keepers* of their temples and images; and as having adopted them as their tutelar divinities. Such was Ephesus in regard to Diana. It was esteemed a high honour that the city was known, and every where regarded as being *intrusted* with the worship of Diana, or with keeping the temple regarded by the whole world as peculiarly her own. See *Schleusner* on this word. ¶ *And of the image.* A special guardian of the image, or statue of Diana. ¶ *Which fell down,* &c. Which was feigned or believed to have been sent down from heaven. Of what this image was made is not known. Pliny says (Hist. Nat. xvi. 79) that it was made of a vine. Mucian (on Pliny) says, that the image was never changed, though the temple had been seven times rebuilt. It is probable that the image was so ancient that the maker of it was unknown, and it was therefore feigned to have fallen from heaven. It was for the interest of the priests to keep up this impression. Many cities pretended to have been favoured in a similar manner with images or statues of the gods, sent directly from heaven. The safety of Troy was supposed to depend on the *Palladium,* or image of Pallas Minerva, which was believed to have fallen from heaven. Numa pretended that the *ancilia,* or sacred shields, had descended from heaven. Thus Herodian expressly affirms, that "the Phenicians had no statue of the sun polished by the hand, but only a certain large stone, circular below, and terminated acutely above in the figure of a cone, of a black colour, and that they believe it to have fallen from heaven." It has been supposed that this image at Ephesus was merely a conical or pyramidal stone which fell from the clouds—*a meteorite*—and that it was regarded with superstitious reverence, as having been sent from heaven. See the Edinburgh Ency. art. *Meteorites.* ¶ *From Jupiter.* See Note, ch. xiv. 12.

36. *Seeing then,* &c. Since this is established and admitted. Since no one can call in question the zeal of the Ephesians on this subject, or doubt the sin

to be quiet, and to do [a] nothing
rashly.
37 For ye have brought hither
these men, which are neither [b] robbers of churches, nor yet blasphemers of your goddess.
38 Wherefore if Demetrius, and
the craftsmen which are with him,
have a matter against any man,
[1] the law is open, and there are
deputies: let them implead one
another.
39 But if ye inquire any thing
concerning other matters, it shall

a Prov.14.29. b c.25.8.

1 or, *the court-days are kept.*

---

cerity of their belief. And since there can be no danger that this well-established worship is to be destroyed by the efforts of a few evil-disposed Jews, there is no occasion for this tumult. ¶ *Be quiet.* Be appeased. The same Greek word which is used in ver. 35, "had *appeased* the people." ¶ *To do nothing rashly.* To do nothing in a heated, inconsiderate manner. There is no occasion for tumult and riot. The whole difficulty can be settled in perfect consistency with the maintenance of order.

37. *For ye,* &c. Demetrius and his friends. The blame was to be traced to them. ¶ *Which are neither robbers of churches.* The word *churches* we now apply to edifices reared for purposes of Christian worship. As no such churches had then been built, this translation is unhappy, and is not at all demanded by the original. The Greek word (ἱεροσύλους) is applied properly to those who *commit sacrilege,* who plunder temples of their sacred things. The meaning here is, that Paul and his companions had not been guilty of robbing the temple of Diana, or any other temple. The charge of *sacrilege* could not be brought against them. Though they had preached against idols and idol worship, yet they had offered no violence to the temples of idolaters, nor had they attempted to strip them of the sacred utensils employed in their service. What they had done, they had done peaceably. ¶ *Nor yet blasphemers of your goddess.* They had not used harsh or reproachful language of Diana. This had not been charged on them, nor is there the least evidence that they had done it. They had opposed idolatry; had reasoned against it; and had endeavoured to turn the people from it. But there is not the least evidence that they had ever done it in harsh or reproachful language. And it shows that men should employ *reason,* and not harsh or reproachful language against any pervading evil; and that the way to remove it, is, to *enlighten* the minds of men, and to *convince* them of the error of their ways. Men gain nothing by bitter and reviling words; and it is much to obtain the testimony of even the enemies of religion—as Paul did of the chancellor of Ephesus—that no such words had been used in describing their crimes and follies.

38. *Have a matter against any man.* Have a complaint of injury; if injustice has been done them by any one. ¶ *The law is open.* See the margin. Ἀγοραῖοι ἄγονται, i. e. ἡμέραι. There are *court days;* days which are open, or appointed for judicial trials, where such matters can be determined in a proper manner. Perhaps the courts were then held, and the matter might be immediately determined. ¶ *And there are deputies.* Roman proconsuls. Note, ch. xiii. 7. The cause might be brought before them with the certainty that it might be heard and decided. The Syriac reads this in the singular number—'Lo, the proconsul is in the city.' ¶ *Let them implead one another.* Let them *accuse* each other in the court; i. e. let them defend their own cause, and arraign one another. The laws are equal, and impartial justice will be done.

39. *But if ye inquire.* If you seek to determine any other matters than that pertaining to the alleged wrong which Demetrius has suffered in his business. ¶ *Other matters.* Any thing respecting public affairs; any thing pertaining to the government and the worship of Diana. ¶ *In a lawful assembly.* In an assembly convened, not by tumult and riot, but in conformity to law. This was a tumultuous assemblage, and it was proper in the public officer to demand that they should disperse; and that, if there were any public grievances to be remedied, it should be done in an assembly properly convened. It may be remarked here that the original word rendered *assembly,* is that which is usually in the New Testament rendered *church.* Ἐκκλησία. It is properly rendered by the word *assembly*—not denoting here a *mixed* or *tumultuous* assemblage, but one convened in the legal manner. The proper meaning of the word is, *that which is called out.* The *church,* the Christian *assembly* of the

be determined in a ¹lawful assembly
40 For we are in danger to be
called in question for this day's
uproar, there being no cause whereby we may give an account of this
concourse.
41 And when he had thus spoken,
he dismissed the assembly. [a]

CHAPTER XX.

AND after the uproar [b] was ceased, Paul called unto *him* the
disciples, and embraced *them*, and
departed, for to go [c] into Macedonia.
2 And when he had gone over
those parts, and had given them
much [d] exhortation, he came into
Greece,
3 And *there* abode three months.
And when the Jews laid wait [e] for
him, as he was about to sail into
Syria, he purposed to return through
Macedonia.
4 And there accompanied him
into Asia, Sopater of Berea; and

¹ or, *ordinary*. a 2Cor.1.8–10. b c.19.40. c 1Cor.16.5 1Tim.1.3. d 1Thess.2.3,11. e c.23.12;25.3. 2Cor.11.26.

faithful, is made up of those who are *called out* from the world.

40. *To be called in question.* By the government; by the Roman authority. Such a tumult, continued for so long a time, would be likely to attract the attention of the magistrates, and expose them to their displeasure. Popular commotions were justly dreaded by the Roman government; and such an assembly as this, convened without any good cause, would not escape their notice. There was a Roman law which made it capital for any one to be engaged in promoting a riot. *Sui cœtum, et concursum fecerit, capite puniatur:* 'He who raises a mob, let him be punished with death.'

41 *Dismissed the assembly.* τὴν ἐκκλησίαν. The word usually translated *church.* Here it is applied to the irregular and tumultuous assemblage which had convened in a riotous manner.

CHAPTER XX.

1. *The uproar.* The tumult excited by Demetrius and the workmen. After it had been quieted by the town-clerk ch. xix. 40, 41. ¶ *Embraced them.* Saluted them; gave them parting expressions of kindness. Comp. Note, Luke vii. 45. Rom. xvi. 16. 1 Cor. xvi. 20 2 Cor. xiii. 12. 1 Thess. v. 26. 1 Peter v. 14. The Syriac translates this, 'Paul called the disciples, and consoled them, and kissed them.' ¶ *To go to Macedonia.* On his way to Jerusalem, agreeably to his purpose, recorded ch. xix. 21.

2. *Over those parts.* The parts of country in and near Macedonia. He probably went to Macedonia by *Troas*, where he expected to find Titus (2 Cor. ii. 12); but not finding him there, he went by himself to Philippi, Thessalonica, &c., and then returned to Greece proper. ¶ *Into Greece.* Into Greece proper, of which Athens was the capital. While in Macedonia, he had great anxiety and trouble, but was at length comforted by the coming of Titus, who brought him intelligence of the liberal disposition of the churches of Greece in regard to the collection for the poor saints at Jerusalem. 2 Cor. vii. 5—7. It is probable that the second epistle to the Corinthians was written during this time in Macedonia, and sent to them by Titus. See Note of Doddridge.

3. *And there abode.* Why he remained here is unknown. It is probable, that while in Greece, he wrote the epistle to the Romans. Comp. Rom. xv. 25—27. ¶ *Laid wait.* There was a design formed against him by the Jews, which they sought to execute. Why they formed this purpose, the historian has not informed us. ¶ *As he was about to sail.* It would seem from this, that the design of the Jews was to attack the ship in which he was about to sail, or to arrest him on ship-board. This fact determined him to take a much more circuitous route by land, so that the churches of Macedonia were favoured with another visit from him. ¶ *Into Syria.* On his way to Jerusalem. ¶ *He purposed,* &c. He resolved to avoid the snare which they had laid for him, and to return by the same way in which he had come into Greece.

4. *And there accompanied him.* It was usual for some of the disciples to attend the apostles in their journeys. ¶ *Into Asia.* It is not meant that they attended him from Greece through Macedonia; but that they went with him to Asia, having gone before him, and joined him at Troas. ¶ *Sopater of Berea.* Perhaps the same person who, in Rom. xvi. 21, is called *Sosipater,* and who is there said to have been a kinsman of Paul ¶ *Aristarchus,*

of the Thessalonians, Aristarchus [a]
and Secundus; and Gaius of Derbe, and [b] Timotheus; and of Asia,
Tychicus [c] and [d] Trophimus.
5 These going before, tarried for
us at Troas.
6 And we sailed away from Philippi after the days of [e] unleavened
bread, and came unto them at Troas
[f] in five days; where we abode
seven days.
7 And upon the first [g] day of the
week, when the disciples came together to break [h] bread, Paul
preached unto them, ready to depart on the morrow; and continued
his speech until midnight.
8 And there were many lights in
the upper [i] chamber, where they
were gathered together.
9 And there sat in a window a
certain young man named Euty-

a c.19.29. b c.16.1. c Eph.6.21. Col.4.7. 2Tim. 4.12. Tit.3.12. d c.21.29. 2Tim.4.20. e Ex.23.15. f 2Tim. 4.13.

g 1Cor.16.2. Rev.1.10. h c.2.42.46. 1Cor.10.16. 5 1.20-34. i c.1.13.

ch. xix. 29. ¶ *Gaius of Derbe* Note, ch. xix. 29. ¶ *Tychicus* This man was high in the confidence and affection of Paul. In Eph. vi. 21, 22, he styles him "a beloved brother, and faithful minister in the Lord." ¶ *And Trophimus.* Trophimus was from Ephesus. ch. xx. 29. When Paul wrote his second epistle to Timothy, he was at Miletum, sick. 2 Tim. iv. 20.

5. *These going before.* Going before Paul and Luke. Dr. Doddridge supposes that only Tychicus and Trophimus went before the others. Perhaps the Greek most naturally demands this interpretation. ¶ *Tarried for us.* The word "us" here, shows that Luke had again joined Paul as his companion. In ch. xvi. 12, it appears that Luke was in Philippi, in the house of Lydia. Why he remained there, or why he did not attend Paul in his journey to Athens, Corinth, Ephesus, &c. is not known. It is evident, however, that he here joined him again. ¶ *At Troas.* Note, ch. xvi. 8.

6. *After the days of unleavened bread.* After the seven days of the passover, during which they ate only unleavened bread. See Ex. xii. ¶ *In five days.* They crossed the Ægean sea. Paul, when he crossed it on a former occasion, did it in two days (ch. xvi. 11, 12); but the navigation of the sea is uncertain, and they were now probably hindered by contrary winds.

7. *And upon the first day of the week.* Showing thus, that this day was then observed by Christians as holy time. Comp. 1 Cor. xvi. 2. Rev. i. 10. ¶ *To break bread.* Evidently to celebrate the Lord's supper Comp. ch. ii. 46. So the Syriac understands it, by translating it, 'to break the eucharist,' i. e. the eucharistic bread. It is probable that the apostles and early Christians celebrated the Lord's supper on every Lord's-day. ¶ *And continued his speech until midnight.* The discourse of Paul continued until the breaking of day. ver. 11. But it was interrupted about midnight by the accident that occurred to Eutychus. The fact that Paul was about to leave them on the next day, probably to see them no more, was the principal reason why his discourse was so long continued. We are not to suppose, however, that it was one continued or set discourse. No small part of the time might have been passed in hearing and answering questions, though Paul was the chief speaker. The case proves that such seasons of extraordinary devotion may, in peculiar circumstances, be proper. Occasions may arise where it will be proper for Christians to spend a much longer time than usual in public worship. It is evident, however, that such seasons do not often occur.

8. *And there were many lights.* Why this circumstance is mentioned is not apparent. It, however, meets one of the slanders of the early enemies of Christianity, that Christians in their assemblies were accustomed to extinguish all the lights, and to commit every kind of abomination. Perhaps the mention of many lights here is designed to intimate that it was a place of public worship, as not only the Jews, but the Gentiles were accustomed to have many lights burning in such places. ¶ *In the upper chamber.* Note, ch. i. 13.

9. *And there sat in a window.* The window was left open, probably to avoid the malice of their enemies, who might be disposed otherwise to charge them with holding their assemblies in darkness for purposes of iniquity. The window was a mere opening in the wall to let in light, as there was no *glass* known at that time; and as the shutters of the window were not closed, there was nothing to prevent Eutychus from falling down. ¶ *The*

chus, being fallen into a deep
sleep: and as Paul was long
preaching, he sunk down with
sleep, and fell down from the third
loft, and was taken up dead.
10 And Paul went down, and
fell [a] on him, and embracing *him*,
said, [b] Trouble not yourselves; for
his life is in him.
11 When he therefore was come
up again, and had broken bread, and
eaten, and talked a long while, even
till break of day, so he departed.
12 And they brought the young
man alive, and were not a little
comforted.
13 And he went before to ship,
and sailed unto Assos, there intending to take in Paul: for so had he
appointed, minding himself to go
afoot.
14 And when he met with us at
Assos, we took him in, and came to
Mitylene.
15 And we sailed thence, and
came the next *day* over against
Chios; and the next *day* we arrived
at Samos, and tarried at Trogyl-

a 1Kings 17.21. 2Kings 4.34. b Matt.9.24.

third loft. The third story. ¶ *And was taken up dead.* Some have supposed that he was merely stunned with the fall, and that he was still alive. But the obvious, and therefore the safest interpretation is, that he was actually killed by the fall, and was miraculously restored to life. This is an instance of sleeping in public worship that has some apology. The late hour of the night, and the length of the services, were the excuse. But, though the thing is often done now, yet how seldom is a sleeper in a church furnished with an excuse for it. No practice is more shameful, disrespectful, and abominable, than that so common of sleeping in the house of God.

10. *And fell on him*, &c. Probably stretching himself on him as Elisha did on the Shunammite's son. 2 Kings iv. 33—35. It was an act of tenderness and compassion, evincing a strong desire to restore him to life. ¶ *Trouble not yourselves.* They would doubtless be thrown into great consternation by such an event. Paul therefore endeavoured to compose their minds by the assurance that he would live. ¶ *For his life is in him.* He is restored to life. This has all the appearance of having been a miracle. Life was restored to him as Paul spoke.

11. *Come up again.* To the upper room. ver. 8. ¶ *And had broken bread, and eaten.* Had taken refreshment. As this is spoken of Paul only, it is evidently distinguished from the celebration of the Lord's supper.

12. *Not a little comforted.* By the fact that he was alive; perhaps also strengthened by the evidence that a miracle had been wrought.

13. *Sailed unto Assos.* There were several cities of this name. One was in Lydia: one in the territory of Eolis; one in Mysia; one in Lydia; and another in Epirus. The latter is the one intended here. It was between Troas and Mitylene. The distance to it from Troas by sea was much greater than by land, and accordingly Paul chose to go to it on foot. ¶ *Minding himself.* Choosing or preferring to go on foot. Most of his journeys were probably performed in this way.

14. *Came to Mitylene.* This was the capital of the island of Lesbos. It was distinguished by the beauty of its situation, and the splendour and magnificence of its edifices. The island on which it stood, Lesbos, was one of the largest in the Ægean sea, and the seventh in the Mediterranean. It is a few miles distant from the coast of Aeolia, and is about one hundred and sixty-eight miles in circumference. The name of the city now is *Castro.*

15. *Over-against.* Opposite to. Into the neighbourhood of; or near to it. ¶ *Chios*, called also *Coos*, an island in the Archipelago, between Lesbos and Samos. It is on the coast of Asia Minor, and is now called *Scio.* It will long be remembered as the seat of a dreadful massacre of almost all its inhabitants by the Turks in 1823. ¶ *At Samos.* This was also an island of the Archipelago, lying off the coast of Lydia, from which it is separated by a narrow strait. These islands were celebrated among the ancients for their extraordinary wines. ¶ *Trogyllium.* This was the name of a town and promontory of Ionia in Asia Minor, between Ephesus and the mouth of the river Meander, opposite to Samos. The promontory is a spur of mount Mycale. ¶ *Miletus.* Called also Miletum. It was a city and seaport, and the ancient capital of Ionia. It was originally composed of a

lium; and the next *day* we came to
Miletus.
16 For Paul had determined to
sail by Ephesus, because he would
not spend the time in Asia; for he
hasted, if it were possible for him,
to be [a] at Jerusalem the day of
[b] Pentecost.
17 And from Miletus he sent to
Ephesus, and called the elders of
the church.
18 And when they were come to
him, he said unto them, Ye know,
from the first day [c] that I came into
Asia, after what manner I have been
with you at all seasons,
19 Serving the Lord with all
[d] humility of mind, and with many

a c.19.21; 24.17 b c.2.1. 1Cor.16.8. c c.19.1,10. d 1Cor.15.9,10.

colony of Cretans. It became extremely powerful, and sent out colonies to a great number of cities on the Euxine sea. It was distinguished for a magnificent temple dedicated to Apollo. It is now called by the Turks *Melas*. It was the birthplace of Thales, one of the seven wise men of Greece. It was about forty or fifty miles from Ephesus.

16. *To sail by Ephesus.* The word *by* in our translation is ambiguous. We say to go *by* a place, meaning either to take it in our way, to go *to* it, or to go *past* it. Here it means the latter. He intended to sail *past* Ephesus without going *to* it. ¶ *For he hasted, &c.* Had he gone *to* Ephesus, he would probably have been so delayed in his journey that he could not reach Jerusalem at the time of Pentecost. ¶ *The day of Pentecost.* Note, ch. ii. 1.

17 *He sent to Ephesus.* Perhaps a distance of forty miles. ¶ *The elders of the church.* Who had been appointed while he was there to take charge of the church. Note, ch. xv. 2.

18. *And when they were come unto him.* The discourse which follows is one of the most tender, affectionate, and eloquent which is any where to be found. It is strikingly descriptive of the apostle's manner of life while with them; evinces his deep concern for their welfare; is full of tender and kind admonition; expresses the firm purpose of his soul to live to the glory of God, and his expectation to be persecuted still; and is a most affectionate and solemn farewell. No man can read it without being convinced that it came from a heart full of love and kindness; and that it evinces a great and noble purpose to be entirely employed in one great aim and object—the promotion of the glory of God, in the face of danger and of death. ¶ *Ye know.* From your own observation. He had been with them three years, and could make this solemn appeal to themselves, that he had led a faithful and devoted life. How happy is it, when a minister can thus appeal to those with whom he has laboured, in proof of his own sincerity and fidelity! How comforting to himself, and how full of demonstration to a surrounding world, of the truth and power of the gospel which is preached. We may further remark, that this appeal furnishes strong proof of the purity and holiness of Paul's life. The elders at Ephesus must have had abundant opportunity to know him. They had seen him, and heard him publicly, and in their private dwellings. A man does not make such an appeal unless he has a consciousness of integrity, nor unless there is conclusive *proof* of his integrity. It is strong evidence of the holiness of the character of the apostles, and proof that they were not impostors, that they could thus appeal with the utmost assurance to those who had every opportunity of knowing them. ¶ *From the first day.* He was with *them* three years. ver. 31. ¶ *Into Asia.* Asia Minor. They would probably know not only how he had demeaned himself while with them, but also how he had conducted in other places near them. ¶ *After what manner I have been with you.* How I have lived and acted. What has been my manner of life. What *had* been his mode of life. he specifies in the following verses. ¶ *At all seasons.* At all times.

19. *Serving the Lord.* In the discharge of the appropriate duties of his apostolic office, and in private life. To discharge aright our duties in any vocation, is serving the Lord. Religion is often represented in the Bible as a *service* rendered to the Lord. ¶ *With all humility.* Without arrogance, pride, or a spirit of dictation; without a desire to "lord it over God's heritage," without being elated with the authority of the apostolic office, the variety of the miracles which he was enabled to perform, or the success which attended his labours. What an admirable model for all who are in the ministry, for all who are endowed with talents and learning, and for all who meet with remarkable success in their work. The

tears, [a] and temptations, [b] which befell me by [c] the lying in wait of the Jews:

20 *And* how [d] I kept back nothing that was profitable *unto you*, but have shewed you, and have

a Phil.3.18. b 2Cor.4.8–11. c ver.3. d ver.27.

proper effect of such success, and of such talent, will be to produce true humility. Eminent success in the work of the ministry tends to produce lowliness and humbleness of mind; and the greatest endowments are usually connected with the most simple and childlike humility. ¶ *And with many tears.* Paul, not unfrequently, gives evidence of the tenderness of his heart, and his regard for the souls of men, and his deep solicitude for the salvation of sinners. ver. 31. Phil. iii. 18. 2 Cor. ii. 4. The *particular* thing, however, here specified as producing weeping, was the opposition of the Jews. But it cannot be supposed that those tears were shed from an apprehension of personal danger. It was rather because the opposition of the Jews impeded his work, and retarded his progress in winning souls to Christ. A minister of the gospel will, (1.) Feel, and deeply feel for the salvation of his people. He will weep over their condition when he sees them going astray, and in danger of perishing. He will, (2.) Be especially affected with opposition, because it will retard his work, and prevent the progress and the triumph of the gospel. It is not because it is a *personal* concern, but because it is the cause of his Master. ¶ *And temptations.* Trials, arising from their opposition. We use the word *temptation* in a more limited sense, to denote inducements offered to one to lead him into sin. The word in the Scriptures most commonly denotes *trials* of any kind. ¶ *Which befell me.* Which happened to me; which I encountered. ¶ *By the lying in wait,* &c. By their snares and plots against my life. Comp. ver. 3. Those snares and plans were designed to blast his reputation, and to destroy his usefulness.

20. *I kept back nothing,* &c. No doctrine, no admonition, no labour. Whatever he judged would promote their salvation, he had faithfully and fearlessly delivered. A minister of the gospel must be the judge of what will be profitable to the people of his charge. His aim should be to promote their real welfare—to preach that which will be *profitable.* His object will not be to please their fancy; to gratify their taste; to flatter their pride; or to promote his own popularity. "All Scripture is *profitable*" (2 Ti. iii. 16); and it will be his aim to declare that only which will tend to promote their real welfare. Even if it be unpalatable; if it be the language of reproof and admonition; if it be doctrine to which the heart is by nature opposed; if it run counter to the native prejudices and passions of men; yet, by the grace of God, it should be, and will be delivered. No doctrine that will be profitable should be kept back; no plan, no labour, that may promote the welfare of the flock, should be withheld. ¶ *But have shewed you.* Have announced or declared to you. The word here used (ἀναγγεῖλαι) is most commonly applied to preaching in public assemblies, or in a public manner. ¶ *Have taught you publicly.* In the public assembly; by public preaching. ¶ *And from house to house.* Though Paul preached in public, and though his time was much occupied in manual labour for his own support (ver. 34), yet he did not esteem his *public* preaching to be all that was required of him; nor his daily occupation to be an excuse for not visiting from house to house. We may observe here, (1.) That Paul's example is a warrant and an implied injunction for family visitation by a pastor. If proper in Ephesus, it is proper still. If practicable in that city, it is in other cities. If it was useful there, it will be elsewhere. If it furnished to him consolation in the retrospect when he came to look over his ministry, and if it was *one* of the things which enabled *him* to say "I am pure from the blood of all men," it will be so in other cases. (2.) The design for which ministers should visit should be a *religious* design. Paul did not visit for mere ceremony, nor for idle gossip, or chit-chat; nor to converse on the mere news or politics of the day. His aim was, to show the way of salvation, and to teach in private what he taught in public. (3.) How much of this is to be done is, of course, to be left to the discretion of every minister. Paul, in private visiting, did not neglect public instruction. The latter he evidently considered to be his main or chief business. His high views of the ministry are evinced in his life, and in his letters to Timothy and Titus. Yet, while public preaching is the main, the prime, the leading business of a minister, and while his first efforts should be directed to pre

taught you publicly, and [a] from
house to house,
21 Testifying both to the Jews
and also to the Greeks, repentance
[b] toward God, and faith toward our
Lord Jesus Christ.
22 And now, behold, I go [c] bound
in the spirit unto Jerusalem, not
knowing [d] the things that shall befall me there:
23 Save that the Holy Ghost
witnesseth in every city, say

a 2Tim.4.2. b Mark 1.15. Luke 24.47. c c.19.21. d Jam.4.14.

paration for that, he may and should find time to enforce his public instructions by going from house to house; and often he will find that his most *immediate* and *apparent* success will result from such family instructions. (4.) If it is his duty to visit, it is the duty of his people to receive him as becomes an ambassador of Christ. They should be willing to listen to his instructions; to treat him with kindness, and to aid his endeavours in bringing a family under the influence of religion.

21. *Testifying.* Bearing witness to the necessity of repentance towards God. Or *teaching* them the nature of repentance, &c., and exhorting them to repent and believe. Perhaps the word *testifying* includes both ideas of giving evidence, and of urging with great earnestness and affection that repentance and faith were necessary. See 1 Tim. v. 21. 2 Tim. ii. 14; where the word here used, and here translated *testify*, is there translated, correctly, *charge*, in the sense of strongly *urging*, or entreating with great earnestness. ¶ *And to the Greeks.* To all who were not Jews. The *Greeks* properly denoted those who lived in Greece, and who spoke the Greek language. But the phrase, 'Jews and Greeks,' among the Hebrews, denoted the whole human race. He urged the necessity of repentance and faith in all. Religion makes no distinction, but regards all as sinners, and as needing salvation by the blood of the Redeemer. ¶ *Repentance toward God.* Note, Matt. iii. 2. Repentance is to be exercised "toward God," because, (1.) Sin has been committed *against* him, and it is proper that we express our sorrow to the Being whom we have offended; and, (2.) Because God only can pardon. Sincere repentance exists only where there is a willingness to make acknowledgment to the very Being whom we have offended, or injured. ¶ *And faith.* Note, Mark xvi. 16. ¶ *Toward.* Εἰς. In regard to; in; confidence *in* the work and merits of the Lord Jesus. This is required, because there is no other one who can save from sin. Note, ch. iv. 12.

22. *Bound in the spirit.* Strongly urged or constrained by the influences of the Holy Spirit on my mind. Not by any desire to see the place where my fathers worshipped, and not urged merely by reason, but by the convictions and mighty promptings of the Holy Spirit to do my duty in this case. The expression "bound in the spirit" (δεδεμένος τῷ Πνεύματι) is one of great strength and emphasis. The word Δέω, *to bind*, is usually applied to confinement by cords, fetters, or bands (Matt. xiii. 30; xiv. 3; xxi. 2); and then denotes any strong obligation (Rom. vii. 2), or any thing that strongly urges, or impels. Matt. xxi. 2. When we are strongly urged by the convictions of duty, by the influences of the Holy Spirit, we should not shrink from danger or from death. Duty is to be done at all hazards. It is ours to follow the directions of God; *results* we may safely and confidently leave with him. ¶ *Not knowing the things that shall befall me there.* He knew that calamities and trials of some kind awaited him (ver. 23), but he did not know, (1.) Of what particular kind they would be; nor, (2.) Their issue, whether it should be life or death. We should commit our way unto God, not knowing what trials may be before us in life; but knowing that, if we are found faithful at the post of duty, we have nothing to fear in the issue.

23. *Save that.* Except that. This was all that he knew, that bonds and afflictions were to be his portion. ¶ *The Holy Ghost witnesseth.* Either by direct revelation to him, or by the predictions of inspired men whom Paul might meet. An instance of the latter mode occurs in ch. xxi. 11. It is probable that the meaning here is, that the Holy Ghost had deeply impressed the mind of Paul by his direct influences, and by his experience in every city, that bonds and trials were to be his portion. Such had been his experience in every city where he had preached the gospel by the direction of the Holy Ghost, that he regarded it as his certain portion that he was thus to be afflicted. ¶ *In every city.* In almost every city where Paul had been, he had been subjected to these trials. He had been persecuted,

ing [a] that bonds and afflictions [1]
abide me.
24 But none [b] of these things
move me, neither count I my life
dear unto myself, so that I might [c]
finish my course with joy, and the

a c.9.16; 21.11. [1] or *wait for me.* *b* c.21.13. Rom.8.35,37. 2Cor.4.16.

c 2Tim.4.7.

stoned, and scourged. So uniform was this, so constant had been his experience in this way, that he regarded it as his certain portion to be thus afflicted; and he approached Jerusalem, and every other city, with a confident expectation that such trials awaited him there. ¶ *Saying.* In his experience; by direct revelation; and by the mouth of prophets. ch. xxi. 11. When Paul was called to the apostleship, it was predicted that he would suffer much. ch. ix. 16. ¶ *Bonds.* Chains. That I would be bound, as prisoners are who are confined. ¶ *Abide me.* See the margin. They remain or wait for me; i. e. I must expect to suffer them.

24. *Move me.* Alarm me; or deter me from my purpose. Gr. 'I make an account of none of them.' I do not regard them as of any moment, or as worth consideration, in the great purpose to which I have devoted my life. ¶ *Neither count I my life.* I do not consider my life as so valuable as to be retained by turning away from bonds and persecutions. I am *certain* of bonds and afflictions; I am willing also, if it be necessary, to lay down my life in the prosecution of the same purpose. ¶ *Dear unto myself.* So precious or valuable as to be retained at the sacrifice of duty. I am willing to sacrifice it if it be necessary. This was the spirit of the Saviour, and of all the early Christians. Duty is of more importance than life; and when either duty or life is to be sacrificed, life is to be cheerfully surrendered. ¶ *So that.* This is my main object, to finish my course with joy. It is implied here, (1.) That this was the great purpose which Paul had in view. (2.) That if he should even lay down his life in this cause, it *would* be a finishing his course with joy. In the faithful discharge of duty, he had nothing to fear. Life would be ended with peace whenever God should require him to finish his course. ¶ *Finish my course.* Close my career as an apostle and a Christian. Life is thus represented as a *course*, or *race* that is to be run. 2 Tim. iv. 7. Heb. xii. 1. 1 Cor. ix. 24. Acts xiii. 25. ¶ *With joy.* With the approbation of conscience and of God; with peace in the recollection of the past. Man should strive so to live that he will have nothing to regret when he lies on a bed of death. It is a glorious privilege to finish life with joy. It is most sad and awful when the last hours are imbittered with the reflection that life has been wasted, or that the course has been evil. The only way in which the course of life may be finished with joy, is by meeting faithfully every duty, and encountering, as Paul did, every trial with a constant desire to glorify God. ¶ *And the ministry.* That I may fully discharge the duty of the apostolic office, the preaching of the gospel. In 2 Tim. iv. 5, he charges Timothy to *make full proof of his ministry.* He here shows that this was the ruling principle of his own life. ¶ *Which I have received of the Lord Jesus.* Which the Lord Jesus has committed to me. Acts ix. 15—17. Paul regarded his ministry as an office intrusted to him by the Lord Jesus himself. On this account he deemed it to be peculiarly sacred, and of high authority. Gal. i. 12. Every minister has been intrusted with an office by the Lord Jesus. He is not his own; and his great aim should be, to discharge fully and entirely the duties of that office. ¶ *To testify the gospel.* To bear witness to the good news of the favour of God. This is the great design of the ministry. It is to bear witness to a dying world of the good news that God is merciful, and that his favour may be made manifest to sinners. From this verse we may learn, (1.) That we all have a course to run; a duty to perform. Ministers have an allotted duty; and so have men in all ranks and professions. (2.) We should not be deterred by danger, or the fear of death, from the discharge of that duty. We are safe only when we are doing the will of God. We are really in danger only when we neglect our duty, and make the great God our enemy. (3.) We should so live as that the end of our course may be joy. It is, at best, a solemn thing to die; but death may be a scene of triumph and of joy. (4.) It matters little when, or where, or how we die, if we die in the discharge of our duty to God. He will order the circumstances of our departure; and he can sustain us in the last conflict. Happy is that life which is spent in doing the will of God, and peaceful that death which

ministry [a] which I have received [b]
of the Lord Jesus, to testify the
gospel of the grace of God.
25 And now, behold, I know
that ye all among whom I have
gone preaching the kingdom of
God, shall see my face no more.
26 Wherefore I take you to record this day that I *am* pure [c] from
the blood of all *men*.
27 For I have not shunned to declare unto you all the counsel [d] of God.

a 2Cor.4.1. b Gal.1.1. c 2Cor.7.2. d Eph.1.11.

closes a life of toil and trial in the service of the Lord Jesus.

25. *I know that ye all.* Perhaps this means simply, 'I have no expectation of seeing you again; I have every reason to suppose that this is my final interview with you.' He expected to visit Ephesus no more. The journey to Jerusalem was dangerous. Trials and persecutions he knew awaited him. Besides, it is evident that he designed to turn his attention to other countries, and to visit Rome; and probably had already formed the purpose of going into Spain. See Acts xix. 21. Comp. Rom. xv. 23—28. From all these considerations it is evident that he had no expectation of being again at Ephesus; it is probable, however, that he did again return to that city. See Note, ch xxviii. 31. ¶ *Among whom I have gone preaching.* Among whom I have preached. The parting of a minister and people is among the most tender and affecting of the separations that occur on earth. ¶ *The kingdom of God.* Making known the nature of the reign of God on earth by the Messiah. See Note, Matt. iii. 2

26. *Wherefore.* Διό. In view of the past, of my ministry and labours among you, I appeal to your own selves to testify that I have been faithful. ¶ *I take you to record.* Gr. I call you to witness; I appeal to you to testify. If any of you are lost if you prove unfaithful to God, I appeal to yourselves that the fault is not mine. It is well when a minister can make this appeal, and call his hearers to bear testimony to his own faithfulness. Ministers who preach the gospel with fidelity *may* thus appeal to their hearers; and in the day of judgment may call on them to witness that the fault of the ruin of the soul is not to be charged to them. ¶ *That I am pure.* I am not to be charged with the guilt of your condemnation, as owing to my unfaithfulness. This does not mean that he set up a claim to absolute perfection; but that, in the matter under consideration, he had a conscience void of offence. ¶ *The blood of all men.* The word *blood* is used often in the sense of *death*, or blood *shed*; and hence of the guilt or crime of putting one to death, or condemnation for it. Matt. xxiii. 35; xxvii. 25. Acts v. 28; xviii. 6. It here means, that if they should die the second death, if they should be lost for ever, *he* would not be to blame. He had discharged his duty, in faithfully warning and teaching them; and now if they were lost, the fault would be their own, not his. ¶ *All men.* All classes of men—Jews and Gentiles. He had warned and instructed all alike. Ministers may have many fears that their hearers will be lost. Their aim, however, should be, (1.) To save them, if possible; and, (2.) If they *are* lost, that it should be by no neglect or fault of theirs.

27. *For.* This verse contains a reason for what had been said in the previous verse. It shows *why* Paul regarded himself as innocent if they should be lost. ¶ *I have not shunned.* I have not kept back; I have not been deterred by fear, by the desire of popularity, by the fact that the doctrines of the gospel are unpalatable to men, from declaring them fully. The proper meaning of the word translated here, "I have not shunned" (ὑπεστειλάμην), is to *disguise* any important truth; to *withdraw* it from public view; to *decline* publishing it from fear, or an apprehension of the consequences. Paul means that he had not *disguised* any truth; he had not *withdrawn* or kept it from open view, by any apprehension of the effect which it might have on their minds. Truth may be disguised or kept back. (1.) By avoiding the subject altogether from timidity, or an apprehension of giving offence if it is openly proclaimed; or, (2.) By giving it too little prominency, so that it shall be lost in the multitude of other truths; or, (3.) By presenting it amidst a web of metaphysical speculations, by entangling it with other subjects; or, (4.) By making use of other terms than the Bible does, for the purpose of involving it in a mist, so that it cannot be understood. Men may resort to this course, (1.) Because the truth itself will be unpalatable; (2.) Because they may apprehend the loss of reputation or support; (3.) Because they may not love the truth

28 Take heed [a] therefore unto yourselves, and to all the flock, over the which the Holy Ghost hath made you [b] overseers, to feed

a Col.4.17. 1Tim.4.16.

b Heb.13.17.

---

themselves, and choose to conceal its prominent and offensive points; (4.) Because they may be afraid of the rich, the great, and the gay, and apprehend that they shall excite their indignation; and, (5.) By a love of metaphysical philosophy, and a constant effort to bring every thing to the test of their own reason. Men often preach a *philosophical explanation* of a doctrine instead of the *doctrine itself*. They deserve the credit of ingenuity, but not that of being open and bold proclaimers of the truth of God. ¶ *The whole counsel.* Πᾶσαν τὴν βουλήν. The word counsel (βουλή) denotes properly consultation, deliberation; and then will or purpose. Luke xxiii. 51. Acts ii. 23. It means here the will or purpose of God, as revealed in regard to the salvation of men. Paul had made a full statement of that plan—of the guilt of men, of the claims of the law, of the need of a Saviour, of the provisions of mercy, and of the state of future rewards and punishments. Ministers ought to declare *all* that counsel, because God commands it; because it is needful for the salvation of men; and, because the message is not theirs, but God's, and they have no right to change, to disguise, or to withhold it. And if it is the duty of ministers to *declare* that counsel, it is the duty of a people to *listen* to it with respect and candour, and with a desire to know the truth, and to be saved by it. *Declaring* the counsel of God will do no good, unless it is *received* into honest and humble hearts, and with a disposition to know what God has revealed for salvation.

28. *Take heed therefore.* Attend to; be on your guard against the dangers which beset you, and seek to discharge your duty with fidelity. ¶ *To yourselves.* To your own piety, opinions, and mode of life. This is the first duty of a minister; for, without this, all his preaching will be vain. Comp. Col. iv. 17. 1 Tim. iv. 14. Ministers are beset with peculiar dangers and temptations, and against them they should be on their guard. In addition to the temptations which they have in common with other men, they are exposed to those peculiar to their office—arising from flattery, and ambition, and despondency, and worldly-mindedness. And just in proportion to the importance of their office, is the importance of the injunction of Paul, to take heed to themselves. ¶ *And to all the flock.* The church; the charge intrusted to them. The church of Christ is often compared *to a flock*. See Notes on John x 1—20; also John xxi. 15—17. The word *flock* here refers particularly to *the church*, and not to the congregation in general, for it is represented to be that which was purchased with the blood of the atonement. The command here is, (1.) To *take heed* to the church: i. e. to instruct, teach, and guide it; to guard it from enemies (ver. 29), and to make it their special object to promote its welfare. (2.) To take heed to ALL the flock—the rich and the poor, the bond and the free, the old and the young. It is the duty of ministers to seek to promote the welfare of each individual of their charge—not to pass by the poor because they are poor; and not to be afraid of the rich because they are rich. A shepherd regards the interest of the tenderest of the fold as much as the strongest; and a faithful minister will seek to advance the interest of *all*. To do this, he should *know all* his people; should be acquainted, as far as possible, with their peculiar wants, character, and dangers, and should devote himself to their welfare as his first and main employment. ¶ *Over the which the Holy Ghost.* Though they had been appointed, doubtless, by the church, or by the apostles, yet it is here represented as having been done by the Holy Ghost. It was by him, (1.) Because he had called and qualified them for their work; and, (2.) Because they had been set apart in accordance with his direction and will. ¶ *Overseers.* Ἐπισκόπους. Bishops. The word properly denotes those who are appointed to oversee, or inspect any thing. This passage proves that the name was applicable to elders; and that in the time of the apostles, the name *bishop* and *presbyter*, or *elder*, was given to the same class of officers, and, of course, that there was no distinction between them. One term was originally used to denote *office*, the other *age*, and both were applied to the same persons in the church. The same thing occurs in Titus i. 5—7, where those who in ver. 5 are called elders, are in ver. 7 called bishops. See also 1 Tim. iii. 1—10. Phil. i. 1. ¶ *To feed.* Ποιμαίνειν. This word is properly applied to the care which a shepherd exercises over his flock. See Notes John xxi. 15

[a] the church of God, which he hath purchased [b] with his own blood.
29 For I know this, that after my departing shall grievous wolves [c] enter in among you, not sparing [d] the flock.

a Prov.10.21. Jer.3.15. Jno.21.15-17. 1Pet.5.2,3. b Eph.1.14. Col.1.14. Heb.9.12,14. 1Pet.1.18,19. Rev. 5.9.

c Matt.7.15. 2Pet.2.1. d Jer.13.20;23.1. Ezek.34. 2,3. Zech.11.17.

16. It applies not only to the act of *feeding* a flock, but also to that of protecting, guiding, and guarding it. It here denotes not merely the duty of properly *instructing* the church, but also of *governing* it; of securing it from enemies (ver. 29), and of directing its affairs so as to promote its edification and peace. ¶ *The church of God.* This is one of the three passages in the New Testament in regard to which there has been a long controversy among critics, which is not yet determined. The controversy is, whether this is the correct and genuine reading. The other two passages are, 1 Tim. iii. 16; and 1 John v. 7. The MSS. and versions exhibit three readings: *the church* OF GOD (τοῦ Θεοῦ); *the church* OF THE LORD (τοῦ Κυρίου); and *the church of* THE LORD *and* GOD (Κυρίου καὶ Θεοῦ). The Latin vulgate reads it *God.* The Syriac, *the Lord.* The Arabic, *the Lord God.* The Ethiopic, *the Christian family of God.* The reading which now occurs in our text is found in no ancient MSS., except the Vatican codex; and occurs nowhere among the writings of the fathers, except in Athanasius, in regard to whom also there is a various reading. It is retained, however, by Beza, Mill, and Whitby, as the genuine reading. The most ancient MSS and the best, read *the church of the Lord,* and this probably was the genuine text. It has been adopted by Griesbach and Wetstein; and many important reasons may be given why it should be retained. See those reasons stated at length in Kuinöel in loco; see also Griesbach and Wetstein. It may be remarked, that a change from Lord to God might easily be made in the transcribing, for in ancient MSS. the words are not written at length, but are abbreviated. Thus, the name *Christ* (Χριστος) is written ΧΟΣ; the name God (Θεος) is written ΘΟΣ; the name Lord (Κυριος) is written ΚΟΣ; and a mistake, therefore, of a single letter would lead to the variations observable in the manuscripts. Comp. in this place the Note of Mill in his Greek Testament, who thinks that the name God should be retained. The authority however is so doubtful, that it should not be used as a proof text on the divinity of Christ; and is not necessary, as there are so many undisputed passages on that subject. ¶ *Which he hath purchased.* The word here used (περιεποιήσατο) occurs but in one other place in the New Testament. 1 Tim. iii. 13, "For they that have used the office of deacon well,*purchase* to themselves a good degree and great boldness in the faith." The word properly means to *acquire* or *gain* any thing; or to *make it ours.* This may be done by a price, or by labour, &c. The noun (περιποίησις) derived from this verb is several times used in the New Testament, and denotes *acquisition.* 1 Thess. v. 9, "God hath appointed us *to obtain* [unto the obtaining or acquisition of] salvation." 2 Thess. ii. 14, "Whereunto he called you by our gospel, to the *obtaining* of the glory of our Lord Jesus Christ." 1 Pet. ii. 9. Tit. ii. 14. Eph. i. 14. In this place, it means that Christ had *acquired, gained,* or *procured* the church for himself by paying his own life as the price. The church is often represented as having thus been bought with a *price.* 1 Cor. vi. 20; vii. 23. 2 Pet. ii. 1. ¶ *With his own blood.* With the sacrifice of his own life; for blood is often put for life, and to shed the blood is equivalent to taking the life. See Note, Rom. iii. 25. The doctrines taught here are, (1.) That the death of Christ was an atoning-sacrifice; that he offered himself to purchase a people to his own service. (2.) That the church is, therefore, of peculiar value—a value to be estimated by the worth of the price paid for it. Comp. 1 Pet. i. 18, 19. (3.) That this fact should make the purity and salvation of the church an object of special solicitude with the ministers of the gospel. They should be deeply affected in view of that blood which has been shed for the church; and they should guard and defend it as having been bought with the highest price in the universe. The chief consideration that will make ministers faithful and self-denying is, that the church has been bought with a price If the Lord Jesus so loved it; if he gave himself for it, they should be willing to deny themselves, to watch, and toil, and pray, that the great object of his death—the purity and the salvation of that church—may be obtained.

29. *For I know this.* By what he had

30 Also of [a] your own selves
shall men arise, speaking perverse
things, to draw away disciples
after them.
31 Therefore watch, [b] and remember that by the space of three
years I ceased not to warn [c] every
one night and day with tears.
32 And now, brethren, I commend you to God, and to the word

a 1Jno.2.19. Jude 4,&c. b 2Tim.4.5. c Col.1.28.

seen in other places; by his knowledge of human nature, and of the dangers to which they were exposed; and by the guidance of inspiration. ¶ *After my departure.* His presence had been the means of guarding the church, and preserving it from these dangers. Now that the founder and guide of the church was to be removed, they would be exposed to dissensions and dangers. ¶ *Grievous wolves.* Heavy (βαρεῖς), strong, mighty, dangerous wolves—so strong that the feeble flock would not be able to resist them. The term *wolves* is used to denote the enemies of the flock—false, and hypocritical, and dangerous teachers. Comp. Matt. x. 16. Note, vii. 15. ¶ *Enter in among you.* From abroad; doubtless referring particularly to the *Jews*, who might be expected to distract and divide them. ¶ *Not sparing the flock.* Seeking to destroy the church. The Jews would regard it with peculiar hostility, and would seek to destroy it in every way. Probably they would approach them with great professed friendship for them, and expressing a desire only to defend the laws of Moses.

30. *Also of your own selves.* From your own church; from those who profess to be Christians. ¶ *Speaking perverse things.* Crooked, perverted, distracting doctrines (διεστραμμένα). Comp. Note, Acts xiii. 10. They would proclaim doctrines tending to distract and divide the church. The most dangerous enemies which the church has had, have been nurtured in its own bosom, and have consisted of those who have perverted the true doctrines of the gospel. Among the Ephesians, as among the Corinthians (Cor. i. 11—13), there might be parties formed; there might be men influenced by ambition, like Diotrephes (3 John 9), or like Phygellus or Hermogenes (2 Tim. i. 15), or like Hymeneus and Alexander. 1 Tim. i. 20. Men under the influence of ambition, or from the love of power or popularity, form parties in the church, produce divisions and distractions, and greatly retard its internal prosperity, and mar its peace. The church of Christ would have little to fear from external enemies if it nurtured no foes in its own bosom; and all the power of persecutors is not so much to be dreaded as the counsels and plans, the parties, strifes, heart-burnings, and contentions which are produced by those who have power, among the professed friends of Christ.

31. *Therefore watch.* Matt. xxiv. 42. In view of the dangers which beset yourselves (ver. 28), the danger from men not connected with the church (ver. 29), and the danger that shall arise from the lovers of power among yourselves (ver. 30), be on your guard. Observe the approach of danger, and set yourselves against it. ¶ *Remember.* Recall my counsels and admonitions in reference to these dangers. ¶ *By the space of three years.* In ch. xix. 10, we are told that Paul spent two years in the school of Tyrannus. In ch. xix. 8, it is said that he was teaching in the synagogue at Ephesus three months. In addition to this, it is not improbable that he spent some months more in Ephesus in instructing the church in other places. Perhaps, however, by the phrase three years, he meant to use merely a round number, denoting *about* three years; or, in accordance with the Jewish customs, part of each of the three years—one whole year, and a considerable portion of the two others. Comp. Note, Matt. xii. 40. ¶ *I ceased not.* I continued to do it. ¶ *To warn.* To admonish; to place before the mind (νουθετῶν); setting the danger and duty of each individual before him. ¶ *Every one.* He had thus set them an example of what he had enjoined. ver. 28. He had admonished each individual, whatever was his rank or standing. It is well when a minister can refer to his own example as an illustration of what he meant by his precepts. ¶ *Night and day.* Continually; by every opportunity. ¶ *With tears.* Expressive of his deep feeling and his deep interest in their welfare. Note on ver. 19.

32. *And now, brethren.* About to leave them, probably to see them no more, he committed them to the faithful care and keeping of God. Amidst all the dangers of the church, when human strength fails or is withdrawn, we may commit that church to the safe keeping and tender care of God. ¶ *I commend you.* I commit you; I *place you* (παρατίθεμαι) in

of his grace, which [a] is able to
build you up, and to give you an
inheritance [b] among all them which
are sanctified.

a Jno.17.17. b c.26.18. Col.1.12. Heb.9.15. 1Pet.1.4.

33 I [c] have coveted no man's silver, or gold, or apparel.
34 Yea, ye yourselves [d] know,
that these hands have ministered

c 1Sam.12.3. 1Cor.9.12. 2Cor.7.2. d c.18.3.1Cor. 4.12. 1Thess.2.9. 2Thess. 3.8.

---

his hands, and under his protection. Note, Acts xiv. 23. ¶ *And to the word of his grace.* That is, to his gracious word; to his merciful promise. To his doctrine of salvation by Jesus Christ, which has been conferred on us by grace. Paul refers, doubtless, to the *gospel*—including its promises of support, its consoling truths, and its directions to seek all needful help and comfort in God. ¶ *Which is able.* Which has power. Τῷ δυναμένῳ. Which word, or gospel, has power to build you up. Heb. iv. 12, "For the word of God is quick [living, life-giving, ζῶν], and powerful, and sharper than any two-edged sword," &c. Comp. Isa. xlix. 2. Jer. xxiii. 29. "Is not my word like as a fire? saith the Lord: and like a hammer that breaketh the rock in pieces?" It is implied here, that the gospel is not a dead letter; that it has *power* to accomplish a great work; and that it is *adapted* to the end in view, the conversion and sanctification of the soul. There is no danger in representing the gospel as mighty, and as fitted by infinite wisdom to secure the renovation and salvation of man. Comp. Rom. i. 16. 1 Cor. i. 18. 2 Cor. x. 4. ¶ *To build you up.* The word used here is properly applied to a house which is reared and completed by slow degrees, and by toil. It here means to establish, make firm, or permanent; and hence to instruct, to establish in doctrine, and in hope. It here means that the word of God was able to confirm and establish them in the hopes of the gospel, amidst the dangers to which they would be exposed. ¶ *And to give you an inheritance.* To make you heirs; or to make you joint partakers with the saints of the blessings in reserve for the children of God. Those blessings are often represented as an inheritance, or heirship, which God will confer on his adopted children. Matt. xix. 29; xxv. 34. Mark x. 17. Heb. vi. 12. Rev. xxi. 7. Eph. i. 11; v. 5. Col. i. 12; iii. 24. Rom. viii. 17. Gal. iii. 29. ¶ *Among all them which are sanctified.* With all who are holy; with all the saints. Note, John x. 36. Those who shall be saved are made holy. They who receive a part in the inheritance beyond the grave, shall have it only among the sanctified and the pure. They must, therefore, be pure themselves, or they can have no part in the kingdom of Christ and of God.

33. *I have coveted.* I have not desired. I have not made it an object of my living among you to obtain your property. Thus (2 Cor. xii. 14) he says, "I seek not yours, but you." Paul had power to demand support in the ministry as the reward of his labour. 1 Cor. ix. 13, 14. Yet he did not choose to exercise it, lest it should bring the charge of avarice against the ministry. 1 Cor. ix. 12. 15. Paul also had power in another respect. He had a vast influence over the people. The early Christians were disposed to commit their property to the disposal of the apostles. See Acts iv. 34, 35. 37. The heathen had been accustomed to devote their property to the support of religion. Of this propensity, if the object of Paul had been to make money, he might have availed himself, and have become enriched. Deceivers often thus impose on people for the purpose of amassing wealth; and one of the incidental but striking proofs of the Christian religion, is here furnished in the appeal which the apostle Paul made to his hearers, that this had *not* been his motive for action. If it had been, how easy would it have been for them to have contradicted him! and who, in such circumstances, would have dared to make such an appeal? The circumstances of the case, therefore, prove that the object of the apostle was *not* to amass wealth. And this fact is an important proof of the truth of the religion which he defended. What should have induced him to labour and toil in this manner, but a conviction of the truth of Christianity? And if he really believed it was true, it is, in his circumstances, a strong proof that this religion is from heaven. See this proof stated in Faber's "Difficulties of Infidelity," and in Lord Lyttleton's "Letter on the conversion of St. Paul." ¶ *Or apparel.* Raiment. Changes of raiment among the ancients, as at present among the orientals, constituted an important part of their property. See Note, on Matt. vi. 19.

34. *Yea, ye yourselves know.* By your own acquaintance with my manner of life. In Corinth he had lived and labour-

unto my necessities, and to them that were with me.

35 I have showed you all things, how that so labouring ye ought to [a] support the weak; and to remember the words of the Lord

a Rom.5.11. Eph.4.28. 1Thess.5.14

ed with Apollos (Note, ch. xviii. 3); and he refers elsewhere to the fact, that he had supported himself, in part at least, by his own labour. 1 Cor. iv. 12. 1 Thess. ii. 9. 2 Thess. iii. 8. We may hence learn that it is no discredit to a minister to labour. Whatever it may be to a people who put him under a necessity to toil for his support, yet the example of Paul shows that a man should rejoice in the privilege of preaching the gospel, even if it is done while he is obliged to resort to labour for his daily bread. It is well when a minister of the gospel can make an appeal to his people like this of Paul, and say, "I have coveted no man's gold, or silver, or apparel." Every minister should so live that he can make this appeal to their own consciences of the sincerity and disinterestedness of his labours from the pulpit; or when called to separate from them as Paul did; or when on a dying bed. Every minister of the gospel, when he comes to lie down to die, will desire to be able to make this appeal, and to leave a solemn testimony there, that it was not for gold, or ease, or fame, that he toiled in the ministerial office. How much more influence can such a man have, than he who has been worldly-minded; who has sought to become rich; and the only memorials of whose life is, that he has sought "the fleece, not the flock," and that he has gained the *property*, not the *souls* of men. And every Christian, when he dies, should and will desire to leave a testimony *as* pure, that he has been disinterested, self-denying, and laborious in the cause of the Lord Jesus.

35. *I have showed you.* I have taught you by instruction and example. I have not merely *discoursed* about it, but have *showed* you how to do it. ¶ *All things.* Or, in respect to all things. In every thing that respects preaching and the proper mode of life, I have for three years set you an example, illustrating the design, nature, and duties of the office by my own self-denials and toil. ¶ *How that.* Or *that.* "Or, I have showed you *that* ye should by so labouring support the weak. ¶ *So labouring.* Labouring as I have done. Setting this example, and ministering in this way to the wants of others. ¶ *To support the weak.* To provide for the wants of the sick and feeble members of the flock, who are unable to labour for themselves. The *weak* here denote the poor, the needy, the infirm. ¶ *And to remember.* To call to mind for encouragement, and with the force of a command. ¶ *The words of the Lord Jesus.* These words are nowhere recorded by the evangelists. But they did not pretend to record *all* his sayings and instructions. Comp. John xxi. 25. There is the highest reason to suppose, that many of his sayings which are not recorded would be treasured up by those who heard them; would be transmitted to others; and would be regarded as a precious part of his instructions. Paul evidently addresses them as if they had heard this before, and were acquainted with it. Perhaps he had himself reminded them of it. This is one of the Redeemer's most precious sayings; and it seems even to have a peculiar value, from the fact that it is *not* recorded in the regular and professed histories of his life. It comes to us *recovered*, as it were, from the great mass of his unrecorded sayings; *rescued* from that oblivion to which it was hastening if left to mere tradition, and placed in permanent form in the sacred writings by the act of an apostle, who had never seen the Saviour before his crucifixion. It is a precious relic—a memento of the Saviour—and the effect of it is, to make us regret that more of his words were not recovered from an uncertain tradition, and placed in permanent form by an inspired penman. God, however, who knows what is requisite to guide us, has directed the words which are needful for the welfare of the church, and has preserved by inspiration the doctrines which are adapted to convert and bless man. ¶ *It is more blessed to give.* It is a higher privilege; it tends more to the happiness of the individual, and of the world. The giver is more blessed or happy than the receiver. This appears, (1.) Because it is a privilege to give to the wants of others; it is a condition for which we should be thankful when we are in a situation to promote their felicity. (2.) Because it tends to promote the happiness of the benefactor himself. There is pleasure in the act of giving when it is done with pure motives. It promotes our own peace; is followed by happiness in the recollection of it

Jesus, how he said, It [a] is more blessed to give than to receive.

36 And when he had thus spoken, he kneeled [b] down, and prayed with them all.

37 And they all wept sore, and [c] fell on Paul's neck, and kissed him;

38 Sorrowing most of all for the [d] words which he spake, that they should see his face no more. And they accompanied him unto the ship

a Luke 14.12-14. b c.21.5. c Gen.46.29. d ver.25.

and will be followed by happiness for ever. That is the most truly happy man, who is most benevolent. He is the most miserable, who has never known the luxury of doing good, but who lives to gain all he can, and to hoard all he gains. (3.) It is blessed in the reward that shall result from it. Those who give from a pure motive, God will bless. They shall be rewarded, not only in the peace which they shall experience in this life, but in the higher bliss of heaven. Matt. xxv. 34—36. We may also remark, that this is a sentiment truly great and noble. It is worthy of the Son of God. It is that on which he himself acted, when he came to *give* pardon to the guilty; comfort to the disconsolate and the mourner; peace to the anxious sinner; sight to the blind; hearing to the deaf; life to the dead; and heaven to the guilty and the lost. Acting on this, he *gave* his own tears to weep over human sorrows and human guilt; he *gave* his own labours and toils to instruct and save man; he *gave* his own life a sacrifice for sin on the cross; and he *gave* his Spirit to awaken and save those for whom he died. Loving to give, he has freely given us all things. Loving to give, he delights in the same character in his followers, and seeks that they who have wealth, and strength, and influence, should be willing to give all to save the world. Imitating his great example, and complying with his command, the church shall yet learn more and more to *give* its wealth to bless the poor and needy; its sons and its daughters to bear the gospel to the benighted heathen; and its undivided and constant efforts to save a lost world.—Here closes this speech of Paul; an address of inimitable tenderness and beauty. Happy would it be if every minister could bid *such* an adieu to his people, when called to part from them; and happy if, at the close of life, every Christian could leave the world with a like consciousness that he had been faithful in the discharge of his duty. Thus dying, it will be blessed to leave the world; and thus would the example of the saints live in the memory of survivors long after they themselves have ascended to their rest.

36. *He kneeled down.* The usual attitude of prayer. It is the proper posture of a suppliant. It indicates reverence and humility; and is represented in the Scriptures as the common attitude of devotion. 2 Chron. vi. 13. Dan. vi. 10. Luke xxii. 41. Acts vii. 60; ix. 40; xxi. 5. Rom. xi. 4. Phil. ii. 10. Eph. iii. 14. Mark i. 40.

37. *Wept sore.* Wept much. Greek, "There was a great weeping of all." ¶ *And fell on Paul's neck.* Embraced him, as a token of tender affection. The same thing Joseph did when he met his aged father Jacob. Gen. xlvi. 29. ¶ *And kissed him.* This was the common token of affection. Note, Matt. xxvi. 48. Luke xv. 20. Rom. xvi. 16. 1 Cor. xvi. 20.

38. *Sorrowing most of all*, &c. This was a most tender and affectionate parting-scene. It can be more easily imagined than described. We may learn from it, (1.) That the parting of ministers and people is a most solemn event, and should be one of much tenderness and affection. (2.) The effect of true religion is to make the heart more tender; to make friendship more affectionate and sacred; and to unite more closely the bonds of love (3.) Ministers of the gospel should be prepared to leave their people with the same consciousness of fidelity, and the same kindness and love, which Paul evinced. They should live such lives as to be able to look back upon their whole ministry as pure and disinterested; and as having been employed in guarding the flock, and in making known to them the whole counsel of God. So parting, they may part in peace. And so living, and acting, they will be prepared to give up their account with joy, and not with grief. May God grant to every minister the spirit which Paul evinced at Ephesus, and enable each one, when called to leave his people by death or otherwise, to do it with the same consciousness of fidelity which Paul evinced, when he left his people to see their face no more.

CHAPTER XXI.

AND it came to pass, that after
we were gotten from them, and
had launched, we came with a
straight course unto Coos, and the
day following unto Rhodes, and
from thence unto Patara:
2 And finding a ship sailing over
unto Phenicia, we went aboard, and
set forth.
3 Now when we had discovered
Cyprus, we left it on the left hand,
and sailed into Syria, and landed
at Tyre: for there the ship was to
unlade her burden.
4 And finding disciples, we tar-

CHAPTER XXI.

1. *After we were gotten from them.* After we had left the elders at Miletus. ch. xx. 38. They were on their way to Jerusalem. ¶ *Unto Coos.* This was a small island in the Grecian Archipelago, a short distance from the south-western point of Asia Minor. It is now called *Stan-co.* It was celebrated for its fertility, and for the wine and silk-worms which it produced. ¶ *Unto Rhodes.* This was an island in the Levant. On the island was a city of the same name, which was principally distinguished for its brazen Colossus, which was built by Chares of Lyndus. It stood across the mouth of the harbour, and was so high that vessels could pass between its legs. It stood fifty-six years, and was then thrown down by an earthquake. It was reckoned as one of the seven wonders of the world. When the Saracens took possession of this island, they sold this prostrate image to a Jew, who loaded 900 camels with the brass of it. This was A. D. 600, about 900 years after it had been thrown down. The ancient name of the island was Asteria. Its name *Rhodes* was given from the great quantity of *roses* which it produced. ¶ *Unto Patara.* This was a maritime city of Lycia, in Asia Minor, over-against Rhodes.

2. *Into Phenicia.* See Note, ch. xi. 19. Phenicia was on their way to Jerusalem. ¶ *Set forth.* Sailed.

3. *Had discovered Cyprus.* Note, ch. iv. 36. ¶ *Into Syria.* Note, Matt. iv. 24. ¶ *And landed at Tyre.* Note, Matt. xi. 21. ¶ *To unlade her burden.* Her cargo. Tyre was formerly one of the most commercial cities of the world; and it is probable, that in the time of Paul its commercial importance had not entirely ceased.

4. *And finding disciples.* Christians. This is the first mention of there being Christians at Tyre, but there is no improbability in supposing that the gospel had been preached there, though it is not expressly recorded by Luke. ¶ *Who said to Paul.* Comp. ver. 12. Their deep interest in his welfare, and their apprehension of his danger, was the reason why they admonished him not to go. ¶ *Through the spirit.* There is some difficulty in understanding this. In solving this difficulty, we may remark, (1.) That it is evident that the Holy Spirit is meant, and that Luke means to say that this was spoken by his inspiration. The Holy Spirit was bestowed on Christians at that time in large measures, and many appear to have been under his inspiring guidance. (2.) It was not understood by Paul as a positive *command* that he should not go up to Jerusalem—for had it been, it would not have been disobeyed. Paul evidently understood it as expressive of their earnest wish that he should *not go*, as apprizing him of danger, and as a kind expression in regard to his own welfare and safety. Comp. ver. 13. Paul was in better circumstances to understand this than we are, and his interpretation was doubtless correct. (3.) It is to be understood, therefore, simply as an *inspired prophetic warning*, that if he went, he went at the risk of his life; a prophetic warning joined with their individual personal wishes, that he would not expose himself to this danger. The meaning evidently is, that they said by inspiration of the Spirit, that he should not go unless he was willing to encounter danger, and the hazard of life as a consequence, for they foresaw that the journey would be attended with this hazard. Grotius renders it, "that he should not go, *unless he was willing to be* bound." Michaelis and Stolzius, "They gave him prophetic warning, that he should not go to Jerusalem." Doddridge, "If he tendered his own liberty and safety, not to go up to Jerusalem, since it would certainly expose him to very great hazard." The inspiration in the case was that of admonition and warning, not of positive command. Paul was simply apprized of the danger; and then left to the free determination of his own will. He chose to encounter the danger of which he was thus apprized. He did not despise the intimations of the Spirit; but he judged that his duty to God called him thus to encounter the

ried there seven days: who said
[a] to Paul through the Spirit, that
he should not go up to Jerusalem.
5 And when we had accomplished those days, we departed and
went our way: and they all brought
us on our way with wives and children, till *we were* out of the city:
and we kneeled [b] down on the shore,
and prayed.
6 And when we had taken our
leave one of another, we took ship;
and they returned home again.
7 And when we had finished *our*
course from Tyre, we came to
Ptolemais, and saluted the brethren,
and abode with them one day.
8 And the next *day*, we that were
of Paul's company departed, and
came unto Cesarea: and we enter-

a ver.12. b c.20.36.

hazards of the journey. We may be apprized of danger in a certain course, either by our friends or by the word of God, and still it may be our duty to meet it. Our duty is not to be measured by the fact that we shall experience *dangers*, in whatever way that may be made known to us. It is in following the will of God; and *encountering* whatever trials may be in our way.

5. *Had accomplished those days.* When those days were passed. ¶ *They all brought us on our way.* They attended us. Note, ch. xv. 3. Rom. xv. 24. 1 Cor. xvi. 6. 11. 3 John 6. This was an expression of tender attachment, and of a deep interest in the welfare of Paul and his fellow-travellers. ¶ *We kneeled down.* Note, ch. xx. 36. ¶ *On the shore.* Any place may be proper for prayer. Note, John iv. 21—24. God is every where, and can as easily hear the prayer of the humble on the sea-shore as in the most magnificent temple. This is an instance, as well as that in ch. xx. 36, where the apostle evidently prayed with the church without a form of prayer. No man can believe that he thus poured forth the desires of his heart at parting, and commended them to God, in a *prescribed form of words.* Besides that there is not the least evidence that such a form was then used in the Christian church, scenes like this show more clearly than abstract arguments could do, that such a form was not needed, and would not be used. Paul and his fellow Christians, on the sand of the sea-shore, would pour forth the gushing emotions of their souls in language such as their circumstances would suggest, and such as such a scene would demand. And it is presumed to be impossible that any man can read this narrative in a dispassionate manner without believing that they offered an *extempore* prayer.

7. *We came to Ptolemais.* This was a city situated on the coast of the Mediterranean, on the north angle of a bay which extends, in a semi-circle of three leagues, as far as the point of Mount Carmel. At the south and west sides the city was washed by the sea; and was surrounded by triple walls. It was in the tribe of Asher (Judg. i. 31), and was originally called ACCHO; but was called *Ptolemais* in honour of one of the *Ptolemies*, who beautified and adorned it. The Christian crusaders gave it the name of Acre, or St. John of Acre, from a magnificent church which was built in it, and which was dedicated to the apostle John. It is still called *Akka* by the Turks. The Syriac and Arabic render it *Accho* in this place. It sustained several sieges during the crusades, and was the last fortified place wrested from the Christians by the Turks. It sustained a memorable siege under Bonaparte, and since then it has been much increased and strengthened. Its present population is estimated at from 18,000 to 20,000. ¶ *And saluted the brethren.* Embraced them; gave them expressions of affection and regard.

8. *We that were of Paul's company.* From this it would appear that they had been attended thus far by some persons who were going only to Ptolemais. This clause, however, is wanting in many MSS., and has been omitted by Bengel, Griesbach, Knapp, and others, as spurious. It is also wanting in the Syriac and the Vulgate. ¶ *Unto Cesarea.* See Note, ch. viii. 40. ¶ *Into the house of Philip.* One of the seven deacons. ch. vi. 5. After his conversation with the eunuch of Ethiopia, he went to Cesarea, and probably there abode. ¶ *The evangelist.* This word properly means one who announces good news. In the New Testament it is applied to a preacher of the gospel, or one who declares the glad tidings of salvation. It occurs only in two other places. Eph. iv. 11. 2 Tim. iv 5. What was the precise rank of those who bore this title in the early Christian church, cannot perhaps be determined

ed into the house of Philip [a] the evangelist, [b] which was *one* of the seven; [c] and abode with him.

9 And the same man had four daughters, virgins, which [d] did prophesy.

10 And as we tarried *there* many days, there came down from Judea a certain prophet, named Agabus. [e]

11 And when he was come unto us, he took Paul's girdle, and bound his own hands and feet, and said, Thus saith the Holy Ghost, So [f] shall the Jews at Jerusalem bind the man that owneth this girdle, and shall deliver *him* into the hands of the Gentiles.

12 And when we heard these things, both we, and they of that place, [g] besought him not to go up to Jerusalem.

13 Then Paul answered, What mean ye to weep and to break mine heart? for I am ready [h] not to be

a c.8.26,40. b Eph.4.11. 2Tim.4.5. c c.6.5. d Joel 2.28. c.2.17. e c.11.28.

f ver.33. c.20.23. g Matt.16.22,23. h 2Tim.4.6.

It is evident, however, that it is used to denote the office of preaching the gospel; and as this title is applied to *Philip*, and not to any other of the seven deacons, it would seem probable that he had been intrusted with a special commission to *preach*, and that *preaching* did not pertain to him *as a deacon*, and does not properly belong to that office. The business of a deacon was, to take care of the poor members of the church. ch. vi. 1—6. The office of preaching was distinct from this, though, as in this case, it might be conferred on the same individual.

9. *Which did prophesy.* See Note, ch. ii. 17; xi. 27. That females sometimes partook of the prophetic influence, and foretold future events is evident from various places in the New Testament. See Note, ch. ii. 17.

10. *There came down.* Note, ch. xv. 1. ¶ *Named Agabus.* See Note, ch. xi. 28.

11. *He took Paul's girdle.* The loose, flowing robes, or outer garments, which were worn in eastern countries, were bound by a *girdle*, or *sash*, around the body, when they ran, or laboured, or walked. Such a girdle was, therefore, an indispensable part of dress. ¶ *And bound his own hands and feet.* As emblematic of what would be done by the Jews to Paul. It was common for the prophets to perform actions which were emblematic of the events which they predicted. The design was to make the prediction more forcible and impressive, by representing it to the eye. Thus Jeremiah was directed to bury his girdle by the Euphrates, to denote the approaching captivity of the Jews. Jer. xiii. 4. Thus he was directed to make bands and yokes, and to put them around his neck, as a sign to Edom and Moab, &c. Jer. xxvii. 2, 3. Thus the act of the potter was emblematic of the destruction that was coming upon the nation of the Jews. Jer xviii. 4. So Isaiah walked naked and barefoot as a sign of the captivity of Egypt and Ethiopia. Isa. xx. 3, 4. Comp. Ezek. iv., xii., &c. ¶ *So shall the Jews, &c.* This was fulfilled. See ver. 33, and ch. xxiv. ¶ *Into the hands of the Gentiles.* To be tried; for the Romans then had jurisdiction over Judea.

13. *What mean ye.* Gr. What do ye. A tender and affectionate, but firm reproach. ¶ *To weep and to break my heart?* To afflict me, and distract my mind by alarms, and by the expressions of tenderness. His mind was fixed on going to Jerusalem; and he felt that he was prepared for whatever awaited him. Expressions of tenderness among friends are proper. Tears may be inevitable at parting from those whom we love. But such expressions of tenderness and love ought not to be allowed to interfere with the convictions of duty in their minds. If they have made up their minds that a certain course is proper, and have resolved to pursue it, we ought neither to attempt to divert them from it, nor to distract their minds by our remonstrances or our tears. We should resign them to *their* convictions of what is demanded of them, with affection and prayer, but with cheerfulness. We should lend them all the aid in our power, and then commend them to the blessing and protection of God. These remarks apply especially to those who are engaged in the missionary enterprise. It is trying to part with a son, a daughter, or a beloved friend, in order that they may go to proclaim the gospel to the benighted and dying heathen. The act of parting—*for life;* and the apprehension of the perils which they may encounter on the ocean, and in heathen lands, may be painful. But if they, like Paul, have looked at it calmly

bound only, but also to die at Jerusalem for the name of the Lord Jesus.

14 And when he would not be persuaded, we ceased, saying, The will [a] of the Lord be done.

15 And after those days we took up our carriages, and went up to Jerusalem.

16 There went with us also *certain* of the disciples of Cesarea, and brought with them one Mnason of Cyprus, an old disciple, [b] with whom we should lodge.

17 And when we were come to Jerusalem, the brethren received [c] us gladly.

18 And the *day* following Paul

a Matt.6.10; 26.42. b Prov.16.31. c c.15.4.

candidly, and with much prayer; if they have come to the deliberate conclusion that it is the will of God that they should devote their lives to this service, we ought not to weep, and to break their hearts. We should cheerfully and confidently commit them to the protection of the God whom they serve, and remember that they are seeking his glory, and that the parting of Christians, though for life, will be short. Soon, in a better world, they will be united again, to part no more; and the blessedness of that future meeting will be greatly heightened by all the sorrows and self-denials of separation here, and by all the benefits which such a separation may be the means of conveying to a dying world. That mother will meet, with joy, in heaven, the son from whom, with many tears, she was sundered, when he entered on a missionary life; and surrounded with many ransomed heathen, heaven will be made more blessed, and all eternity more happy. ¶ *But also to die.* This was the true spirit of a martyr. This spirit reigned in the hearts of all the early Christians. ¶ *For the name of the Lord Jesus.* For his sake; in making his name known.

14. *Would not be persuaded.* To remain. He was resolved to go. ¶ *We ceased.* We ceased remonstrating with him, and urging him to remain. ¶ *The will of the Lord be done.* They were now assured that it was the will of God that he should go. And they were now ready to submit to that will. This is an instance and an evidence of true piety. It was the expression of a wish that whatever God might judge to be necessary for the advancement of his cause, might take place, even though it should be attended with many trials. They commended their friend to the protection of God, confident that whatever should occur would be right. Comp. Note, Matt. vi. 10; xxvi. 42.

15. *After those days.* After what had occurred, as related in the previous verses. ¶ *We took up our carriages.* This is a most unhappy translation. The word *carriage* we apply now exclusively to a vehicle for conveying any thing—as a coach, chariot, gig, cannon carriage, &c. The original word means simply, that they prepared themselves; made themselves ready; put their baggage in order, &c. Ἀποσκευασάμενοι. They prepared for the journey. The English word *carriage* was formerly used in the sense of *that which is carried*, baggage, burden, vessels, furniture, &c. Thus it was used in the time that our translation was made; and in this sense it is to be understood in 1 Sam. xvii. 22, "And David left his *carriage* (baggage) in the hand of the keeper of the carriage," &c. See ver. 20, margin. Isa. x. 28, "At Michmash he hath laid up his *carriages*," [his baggage, &c.]

16. *One Mnason of Cyprus.* The original in this place would be better translated, "And brought us *to* Mnason of Cyprus, an old disciple," &c. It is evident that, though Mnason was originally of Cyprus, yet he was now an inhabitant of Jerusalem, and was well known to the disciples at Cesarea. It is possible that he might have been at Cesarea, and accompanied Paul to Jerusalem; but the more correct interpretation of the passage is, that Paul and his fellow-travellers were conducted *to* his house in Jerusalem, and that he was not with them in the journey. ¶ *Of Cyprus.* Note, ch. iv. 36. ¶ *An old disciple.* An early convert to Christianity—perhaps one who was converted before the crucifixion of the Saviour. ¶ *With whom we should lodge.* In whose house we were to take up our abode. The rites of hospitality were shown in a distinguished manner by the early Christians.

17. *The brethren.* Christians. ¶ *Received us gladly.* They had been long absent. They had been into distant regions, and had encountered many dangers. It was a matter of joy that they had now returned in safety.

18. *Unto James.* James the Less. Note

went in with us unto James; [a] and all the elders were present.

19 And when he had saluted them, he declared particularly what [b] things God had wrought among the Gentiles by [c] his ministry.

20 And when they heard *it*, they glorified the Lord; and said unto him, Thou seest, brother, how many thousands of Jews there are which believe; and they are all zealous [d] of the law:

a c.15.13,&c. Gal.1.19. b Rom.15.18,19. c c.20.24. 2Cor.12.12.

d c.22.3. Rom.10.2.

ch. xv. 13. He resided at Jerusalem. Comp. Gal. i. 19. It is not improbable that he was the only one of the apostles then at Jerusalem; and there is reason to believe that the church at Jerusalem was left under his particular care. It was natural, therefore, that Paul and his travelling companions should take an early opportunity to see him. James was the cousin of our Lord, and in Gal. i. 19, he is called the Lord's brother. On all accounts, therefore, he was entitled to, and would receive particular respect from the early disciples.

19. *Had saluted them.* With the usual tokens of respect and affection. ¶ *He declared particularly*, &c. As an evidence that God had been with him. It is not improbable that there might have been some suspicion in regard to Paul among the disciples at Jerusalem, and he might have heard that they were prejudiced against him. This prejudice would be removed by his stating what had actually occurred under his ministry.

20. *They glorified the Lord.* They gave praise to the Lord for what he had done. They saw new proofs of his goodness and mercy, and they rendered him thanks for all that had been accomplished. There was no jealousy that it had been done by the instrumentality of Paul. True piety will rejoice in the spread of the gospel, and in the conversion of sinners, by whatever instrumentality it may be effected. ¶ *Thou seest, brother.* The language of tenderness in this address, recognising Paul as a fellow-labourer and fellow Christian, implies a wish that Paul would do all that could be done to avoid giving offence, and to conciliate the favour of his countrymen. ¶ *How many thousands.* The number of converts at this time must have been very great. Twenty-five years before this, three thousand had been converted at one time (ch. ii.), and afterwards the number had swelled to some more thousands. ch. iv, 4. The assertion, that there were, then, "many thousands," implies that the work so signally begun on the day of Pentecost in Jerusalem, had not ceased, and that many more had been converted to the Christian faith. ¶ *Which believe.* Who are Christians. They are spoken of as *believers*, or as having faith in Christ, in contradistinction from those who rejected him, and whose characteristic trait it was that they were *unbelievers.* ¶ *And they are all zealous of the law.* They still observe the law of Moses. The reference here is, to the law respecting circumcision, sacrifices, distinctions of meats and days, festivals, &c. It may seem remarkable that they should still continue to observe those rites, since it was the manifest design of Christianity to abolish them. But we are to remember, (1.) That those rites had been appointed by God, and that they were trained to their observance. (2.) That the apostles conformed to them while they remained in Jerusalem, and did not deem it best to set themselves violently against them. ch. iii. 1. Luke xxiv. 53. (3.) That the question about their observance had never been agitated at Jerusalem. It was only among the Gentile converts that the question had risen, and there it *must* arise, for if they were to be observed, they must have been *imposed* upon them by authority. (4.) The decision of the council (ch. xv.) related only to the *Gentile* converts. It did not touch the question, whether those rites were to be observed by the *Jewish* converts. (5.) It was to be presumed, that as the Christian religion became better understood—that as its large, free, and catholic nature became more and more developed, the peculiar institutions of Moses would be laid aside of course, without agitation, and without tumult. Had the question been agitated at Jerusalem, it would have excited tenfold opposition to Christianity, and would have rent the Christian church into factions, and greatly retarded the advance of the Christian doctrine. We are to remember also, (6.) That, in the arrangement of Divine Providence, the time was drawing near which was to destroy the temple, the city, and the nation; which was to put an end to sacrifices, and *effectually* to close for ever the observance of the Mosaic rites. As this destruction was so

21 And they are informed of thee, that thou teachest all the Jews which are among the Gentiles to forsake Moses, saying that they ought not to circumcise [a] *their* children, neither to walk after their customs.

22 What is it therefore? The multitude must needs come [b] together: for they will hear that thou art come.

23 Do therefore this that we say to thee: We have four men which have a vow on them;

a Gal.5.3. b c.19.32.

near, and as it would be so effectual an *argument* against the observance of the Mosaic rites, the Great Head of the church did not suffer the question of their obligation to be needlessly agitated among the disciples at Jerusalem.

21. *And they are informed of thee.* Reports respecting the conduct of Paul would be likely to be in circulation among all at Jerusalem. His remarkable conversion; his distinguished zeal; his success among the Gentiles, would make his conduct a subject of special interest. Evil-minded men among the Jews, who came up to Jerusalem from different places where he had been, would be likely to represent him as the decided enemy of the laws of Moses, and these reports would be likely to reach the ears of the Jewish converts. The reports, as they gained ground, would be greatly magnified, until suspicion might be excited among the Christians at Jerusalem, that he was, as he was reputed to be, the settled foe of the Jewish rites and customs. ¶ *That thou teachest all the Jews,* &c. From all the evidence which we have of his conduct, this report was incorrect and slanderous. The truth appears to have been, that he did not enjoin the observance of those laws on the Gentile converts; that the effect of his ministry on them was, to lead them to suppose that their observance was not necessary—contrary to the doctrines of the Judaizing teachers (see ch. xv.); and that he argued with the Jews themselves, where it could be done, against the *obligation* of those laws and customs, since the Messiah had come. They depended on that observance for justification and salvation. This Paul strenuously opposed, and this he defended at length in the epistles which he wrote. See the epistles to the Romans, the Galatians and the Hebrews. Yet these facts might be easily misunderstood and perverted, so as to give rise to the slanderous report, that he was every where the enemy of Moses and the law. ¶ *Which are among the Gentiles.* Who live in heathen countries. The Jews were extensively scattered, and settled in all the large towns and cities of the Roman empire. ¶ *To forsake Moses.* The law and authority of Moses. That is, to regard his laws as no longer binding. ¶ *To walk after the customs.* To observe the institutions of the Mosaic ritual. Note, ch. vi. 14. The word *customs* denotes the *rites* of the Mosaic economy—the offering of sacrifices, incense, the oblations, anointings, festivals, &c. which the law of Moses prescribed.

22. *What is it therefore?* What is to be done? What is it proper to do, to avoid the effects of the evil report which has been circulated? What they deemed it proper to do, is suggested in the following verses. ¶ *The multitude.* The multitude of Jews. ¶ *Must needs come together.* There will be inevitably a tumultuous assemblage. It will be impossible to prevent that. The reasons were, because their minds were exceedingly agitated that one of their own countrymen had, as they understood, been advising *apostasy* from the religion of their fathers; because it had been extensively done in many parts of the world, and with great success; and because Paul, having, as they believed, himself apostatized from the national religion, had become very conspicuous, and his very presence in Jerusalem, as in other places, would be likely to excite a tumult. It was, therefore, the part of friendship to him, and to the cause, to devise some proper place to prevent, if possible, the anticipated excitement.

23. *We have four men.* There are with us four men. It is evident that James and the elders meant to say, that these men were connected with them in the Christian church; and the fact shows that the Christians at Jerusalem did not disregard the institutions of Moses, and had not been so far enlightened in the doctrines of Christianity as to forsake yet the ceremonial rites of the Jews. ¶ *Which have a vow on them.* Which have made a vow. See Notes, ch. xviii. 18. From the mention of shaving the head (in ver. 24), it is evident that the vow

24 Them take, and purify thyself with them, and be at charges with them, that they may shave [a] *their* heads: and all may know, that those things, whereof they were informed concerning thee, are nothing, but *that* thou thyself also walkest orderly, and keepest the law.

a Num.6.2,13,18. c.18.18.

25 As touching the Gentiles which believe, we [b] have written, *and* concluded that they observe no such thing, save only that they keep themselves from *things* offered to idols, and from blood, and from strangled, and from fornication.

b c.15.20,29.

which they had taken was that of the *Nazarite;* and that as the time of their vow was about expiring, they were about to be shaven, in accordance with the custom usual on such occasions. See Note, ch. xviii. 18. These persons Paul could join, and thus show decisively that he did not intend to undervalue or disparage the laws of Moses, when those laws were understood as mere ceremonial observances.

24. *Them take.* Take with you. Join yourself with them. ¶ *And purify thyself with them.* Join them in observing the forms of purification prescribed by the law of Moses in the observance of the vow of the Nazarite. The *purifying* here refers to the vows of sanctity which the Nazarites were to observe. They were to abstain from wine and strong drink; they were to eat no grapes, moist or dried; they were to come near no dead body, nor to make themselves "unclean" for their father, mother, brother, or sister, when they died (Num. vi. 3—7); and they were to present an offering when the days of the vow were completed. Num. vi. 8. ¶ *And be at charges with them.* Share with them the expense of the sacrifices and offerings required when the vow is completed. Those offerings were a ram of a year old for a burnt-offering, a sheep of the same age for a sin-offering, a ram for a thank-offering, a basket of unleavened cakes, and a libation of wine. See Num. vi. 13—20. ¶ *That they may shave their heads.* The shaving of the head, or the cutting off the hair which had been suffered to grow during the continuance of the vow (Num. vi. 5), was an observance indicating that the vow had been performed. Paul was requested to join with them in the expense of the sacrifices and offerings, that thus the whole of the ceremonies having been observed, their heads might be shaved as an indication that every part of the vow had been complied with. ¶ *And all may know.* By the fact of your observance of one of the rites of the Mosaic religion, all may have evidence that it is not your purpose or practice to speak contemptuously of those rites, or to undervalue the authority of Moses. ¶ *Are nothing.* Are untrue, or without any foundation. ¶ *Walkest orderly.* That you live in accordance with the real requirements of the law of Moses. To *walk* in the Scriptures often denotes *to live, to act, to conduct,* in a certain manner. All, probably, that they wished Paul to show by this was, that he was not an enemy of Moses. They who gave this counsel were Christians, and they could not wish him to do any thing which would imply that *he* was not a Christian.

25. *As touching the Gentiles.* In regard to the Gentile converts. It might be expedient for Paul to do what could not be *enjoined* on the Gentiles They could not *command* the Gentile converts to observe those ceremonies, while yet it might be proper, for the sake of peace, that the converts to Christianity from among the Jews should regard them. The conduct of the Christians at Jerusalem in giving this advice, and of Paul in following it, may be easily vindicated. If it be objected, as it has been by infidels, that it looks like double-dealing; that it was designed to *deceive* the Jews in Jerusalem, and to make them believe that Paul actually conformed to the ceremonial law, when his conduct among the Gentiles showed that he did not; we may reply, (1.) That the observance of that law was not necessary in order to justification; (2.) That it would have been improper to have enjoined its observance on the Gentile converts as necessary, and therefore it was never done; (3.) That when the Jews urged its observance as necessary to justification and salvation, Paul strenuously *opposed* this view of it every where; (4.) Yet, that as a matter of expediency, he did not oppose its being observed either by the Jews, or by the converts made among the Jews. In fact, there is other evidence besides the case before us, that Paul himself continued to observe some at least

26 Then Paul took [a] the men; and the next day purifying himself with them, entered [b] into the temple, to signify the accomplishment [c] of the days of purification, until that an offering should be offered for every one of them.

27 And when the seven days were almost ended, the Jews [d] which were of Asia, when they

a 1Cor.9.20. b c.24.18. c Num.6.13. d ch.24.18.

of the Jewish rites, and his conduct in public at Jerusalem, was in strict accordance with his conduct in other places. See ch. xviii. 18. The sum of the whole matter is this, that when the observance of the Jewish ceremonial law was urged as necessary to justification and acceptance with God, Paul resisted it; when it was demanded that its observance should be enjoined on the Gentiles, he opposed it: in all other cases he made *no* opposition to it, and was ready himself to comply with it, and willing that others should also. ¶ *We have written.* ch. xv. 20. 29.

26. *Then Paul took the men.* Took them to himself; united with them in observing the ceremonies connected with their vow. To transactions like this he refers in 1 Cor. ix. 20, "And unto the Jews I became as a Jew, that I might gain the Jews; to them that are under the law, as under the law, that I might gain them that are under the law." Thus, it has always been found necessary in propagating the gospel among the heathen, not to offend them needlessly; but to conform to their innocent customs in regard to dress, language, modes of travelling, sitting, eating, &c. Paul did nothing more than this. He violated none of the dictates of honesty and truth. ¶ *Purifying himself with them.* Observing the ceremonies connected with the rite of purification. Note, ver. 24. This means evidently that he *entered* on the ceremonies of the separation according to the law of the Nazarite. ¶ *To signify.* Greek, Signifying or making known. That is, he announced to the priests in the temple his purpose of observing this vow with the four men, according to the law respecting the Nazarite. It was proper that such an announcement should be made beforehand, in order that the priests might know that all the ceremonies required had been observed. ¶ *The accomplishment,* &c. The fulfilling, the completion. That is, he announced to them his purpose to observe all the days, and all the rites of purification required in the law, in order that an offering might be properly made. It does not mean that the days *had been* accomplished, but that it was his intention to observe them, *so that* it would be proper to offer the usual sacrifice. Paul had not indeed, engaged with them *in the beginning* of their vow of separation; but he might come in with hearty intention to share with them. It cannot be objected that he meant to impose on the priests, and to make them believe that he had observed the whole vow with them; for it appears from their own writings (*Bereshith Rabba* 90, and *Koheleth Rabba* 7), that in those instances where the Nazarites had not sufficient property to enable them to meet the whole expense of the offerings, other persons, who possessed more, might become sharers of it, and thus be made parties to the vow. See Jahn's Archæology, § 395. This circumstance will vindicate Paul from any intention to take an improper advantage, or to impose on the priests or the Jews. All that he announced was, his intention to *share* with the four men in the offering which they were required to make; to divide the expenses with them; and thus to show his *approval* of the thing, and his accordance with the law which made such a vow proper, *as he had before done in a voluntary manner, when it could not be pretended that it was for double-dealing, or imposition.* ch. xviii. 18. ¶ *Until that an offering,* &c. The sacrifices required of all those who had observed this vow Note ver. 24. Num. vi. 13. It is a complete vindication of Paul in this case, that he did no more here than he had done in a voluntary manner (ch. xviii. 18.), and as appears then in a secret manner, showing that he was still in the practice of observing this rite of the Mosaic institution. Nor can it be proved that Paul ever, *in any way,* or *at any time,* spoke against the vow of the Nazarite, or that a vow of a similar kind in spirit would be improper for a Christian in any circumstances.

27. *And when the seven days were almost ended.* Gr. As the seven days were about to be fulfilled. Ἔμελλον συντελεῖσθαι. The seven days which were to complete the observance of the vow. ver. 26 Perhaps the whole observance in this case was intended to be but seven days as the *time* of such a vow was voluntary The translation, "were almost ended," is not quite correct. The Greek implies no more than that the period of the seven

saw him in the temple, stirred up all the people, and laid [a] hands on him.

28 Crying out, Men of Israel, help: this is the man that [b] teacheth all *men* every where against the people, and the law, and this place; and further, brought Greeks also into the temple, and hath polluted this holy place.

29 (For they had seen before with him, in the city, Trophimus [c] an Ephesian, whom they supposed that Paul had brought into the temple.)

30 And all the city was moved, and the people ran together; and they took Paul, and drew him out of the temple: and forthwith the doors were shut.

31 And as they were about to [d] kill him, tidings came unto the

a c.26.21. b c.6.13,14; 24.5,6. c c.20.4. d 1Cor.11.23,&c.

days was *about to be accomplished,* without implying it was near the close of them when he was seized. By comparing the following places, ch. xxi. 18. 26; xxii. 30; xxiii. 12. 32; xxiv. 1. 11, it appears that the time of his seizure must have been near the beginning of those days. (*Doddridge.*) ¶ *The Jews which were of Asia.* Who resided in Asia Minor, but who had come up to Jerusalem for purposes of worship. Comp. Notes on ch. ii.

28. *Men of Israel.* Jews. All who are the friends of the law of Moses. ¶ *This is the man, &c.* This implies that they had before given information to the Jews at Jerusalem that there was such a man; and they now exulted in the fact, that they had found him. They, therefore, called on all these to aid in securing and punishing him. ¶ *That teacheth, &c.* See Notes, ch. vi. 13, 14. ¶ *Against the people.* The people of the Jews. That is, they pretended that he taught, that the customs and laws of the Jewish nation were not binding, and endeavoured to prejudice all men against them. ¶ *And the law.* The law of Moses. ¶ *And this place.* The temple. Every thing against the law would be interpreted also as being against the temple, as most of the commandments of the law were celebrated there. It is possible also that Paul might have declared that the temple was to be destroyed. Comp. ch. vi. 13, 14. ¶ *And further, brought Greeks, &c.* The temple was surrounded by various areas called *courts.* Notes, Matt. xxi. 12. The outermost of these courts was called the court of the Gentiles, and into that it was lawful for the Gentiles to enter. But the word "temple" here refers, doubtless, to the parts of the area appropriated especially to the Israelites, and which it was unlawful for a Gentile to enter. See the area marked G. G. G. G. in the plan of the temple. Matt. xxi. 12. ¶ *And hath polluted, &c.* He defiled the temple by thus introducing a Gentile. No greater defilement, in their view, could scarcely be conceived. No more effective appeal could be made to the passions of the people than this.

29. *In the city.* In Jerusalem. As he was with Paul, it was *inferred* that he would attend him every where. ¶ *Trophimus.* He had accompanied Paul on his way from Ephesus. ch. xx. 4. ¶ *Whom they supposed, &c.* This is a most striking illustration of the manner in which accusations are often brought against others. They had *seen* him with Paul in the city; they *inferred,* therefore, that he had been with him in the temple. They did not even pretend that they had *seen* him in the temple; but the inference was enough to inflame the angry and excitable passions of the multitude. So in the accusations which men now often make of others. They *see* one thing, they *infer* another; they could *testify* to one thing, but they *conclude* that another thing will also be true, and that *other thing* they charge on them as the truth. If men would state facts as they are, no small part of the slanderous accusations against others would cease. An end would be made of most of the charges of falsehood, and error, and heresy, and dishonesty and double-dealing, and immorality. If a statement is made, it should be of the thing as it was. If we attempt to state what a man has done, it should not be what we *suppose* he had done. If we attempt to state what he believes, it should not be what we *suppose* he believes.

30. *The city was moved.* Was agitated; was thrown into commotion. ¶ *Drew him out of the temple.* Under the pretence that he had defiled it. The evident design was to put him to death. ver. 31. ¶ *The doors were shut.* The doors leading into the courts of the temple.

31. *And as they were about to kill him.* Gr. They *seeking* to kill him. This was

chief captain of the band, that all
Jerusalem was in an uproar:
32 Who [a] immediately took soldiers and centurions, and ran down
unto them: and when they saw
the chief captain and the soldiers,
they left beating of Paul.
33 Then the chief captain came
near, and took him, and commanded *him* to be bound [b] with two
chains; and demanded who he was,
and what he had done.
34 And some cried one thing,
some another, among the multitude; and when he could not know
the certainty for the tumult, he
commanded him to be carried into
the castle. [c]
35 And when he came upon the
stairs, so it was, that he was borne
of the soldiers, for the violence [d]
of the people.
36 For the multitude of the people followed after, crying, Away
[e] with him!
37 And as Paul was to be led
into the castle, he said unto the
chief captain, May I speak unto

a c.23.27;24.7. b ver. 11. c.20.23. Eph.6.20. c c.23.10,16 d Ps.55.9. Hab.1.3. e Luke 23.18. Jno.19.15. c.22.22. 1Cor.4.13.

evidently done in a popular tumult, as had been done in the case of Stephen. ch. vii. They could not pretend that they had a right to do it by law. ¶ *Tidings came.* The news, or rumour came; he was told of it. ¶ *The chief captain of the band.* This band or body of Roman soldiers was stationed in the tower Antonia, on the north of the temple. This tower was built by John Hyrcanus, high-priest of the Jews, and was by him called *Baris.* It was beautified, and strengthened by Herod the Great, and was called *Antonia,* in honour of his friend, Mark Antony. Josephus describes this castle as consisting of four towers, one of which overlooked the temple, and which he says was seventy cubits high. Jewish Wars, b. v. ch. 5, § 8. In this tower a guard of Roman soldiers was stationed, to secure the temple, and to maintain the peace. The commander of this cohort is here called "the chief captain." Reference is made to this guard several times in the New Testament. Matt. xxvii. 65, 66. John xviii. 12. Acts v. 26. The word translated "chief captain" (χιλίαρχος), denotes properly one who commanded a thousand men. The *band* (σπεῖρα) was the tenth part of a legion, and consisted sometimes of four hundred and twenty-five soldiers, at others of five hundred, and at others of six hundred, according to the size of the legion. The name of this captain was Claudius Lysias. ch. xxiii 26. ¶ *In an uproar.* That the whole city was in commotion.

32. *Centurions.* Captains of a hundred men.

33. *To be bound with two chains.* To show to the enraged multitude that he did not intend to rescue any one from justice, but to keep the peace. Paul's being thus bound would convince them of his determination that justice should be done in the case. Probably he was bound between two soldiers, his right arm to the left arm of the one, and his left arm to the right arm of the other. See Note, ch. xii. 6. Or, if his hands and feet were bound, it is evident that it was so done that he was able still to walk. ver. 37, 38. This was in accordance with the prediction of Agabus, ch. xxi. 11.

34. *Into the castle.* The castle or tower of Antonia, where the guard was kept. Note on ver. 31. Comp. ch. xxiii. 10. 16.

35. *Upon the stairs.* The stairs which led from the temple to the tower of Antonia. Josephus says (Jewish Wars, b. v. ch. 5, § 8), that the tower of Antonia "was situated at the corner of two cloisters of the court of the temple, of that on the west, and of that on the north; it was erected on a rock of fifty cubits [seventy-five feet] in height, and was on a great precipice. On the corner where it joined to the two cloisters of the temple, *it had passages down to them both, through* which the guards went several ways among the cloisters with their arms, on the Jewish festivals," &c. It was on these stairs, as the soldiers were returning, that the tumult was so great, or the crowd so dense, that they were obliged to bear him along to rescue him from their violence. ¶ *The violence of the people.* The *rush* of the multitude.

36. *Away with him!* That is, to death Comp. Luke xxiii. 18.

37. *May I speak unto thee?* May I have the privilege of making my defence before thee; or of stating the case truly, the cause of my accusation, of this tumult, &c. ¶ *Canst thou speak Greek?*

thee? Who said, Canst thou speak Greek?

38 Art not thou that [1] Egyptian, which before these days madest an

[1] This Egyptian rose A.D. 55. c.5.36.

Implying that if he could, he might be permitted to speak to him. The Greek language was that which was then almost universally spoken, and it is not improbable that it was the native tongue of the chief captain. It is evident that he was not a Roman by birth, for he says (ch. xxii. 28) that he had obtained the privilege of citizenship by paying a great sum. The language which the Jews spoke, was the Syro-chaldaic; and as he took Paul to be an Egyptian Jew (ver. 38.), he supposed from that circumstance also, that he was not able to speak the Greek language.

38. *Art not thou that Egyptian.* That Egyptian was probably a Jew, who resided in Egypt. Josephus has given an account of this Egyptian, which strikingly accords with the statement here recorded by Luke. See Josephus' Antiq. b. xx. ch. viii. § 6, and Jewish War, b. ii. ch. xiii. § 5. The account which he gives is, that this Egyptian, whose name he does not mention, came from Egypt to Jerusalem. and said that he was a prophet, and advised the multitude of the common people to go with him to the Mount of Olives. He said further, that he would show them from thence how the walls of Jerusalem would fall down; and he promised them that he would procure for them an entrance through those walls when they were fallen down. Josephus adds (Jewish War), that he got together thirty thousand men that were deluded by him, "these he led round about *from the wilderness* to the mount, which was called the Mount of Olives, and was ready to break into Jerusalem by force from that place." But Felix, who was apprized of his movements, marched against him with the Roman soldiers, and discomfited him, and slew four hundred of them, and took two hundred alive. "But the Egyptian escaped himself out of the fight, but did not appear any more." It was natural that the Roman tribune should suppose that Paul was this Egyptian, and that his return had produced this commotion and excitement among the people. ¶ *Madest an uproar.* Producing a sedition, or a *rising* among the people. Greek, "That Egyptian, who before these days having risen up." ¶ *Into the wilderness.* This corresponds remarkably with the account of Josephus. He indeed mentions that he led them to the Mount of Olives, but he expressly says that "he led them round about from the wilderness." This wilderness was the wild and uncultivated mountainous tract of country, lying to the east of Jerusalem, and between it and the river Jordan. See Note, Matt. iii. 1. It is also another striking coincidence showing the truth of the narrative, that neither Josephus nor Luke mention the *name* of this Egyptian, though he was so prominent and acted so distinguished a part. ¶ *Four thousand men.* There is here a remarkable discrepancy between the chief captain and Josephus. The latter says that there were thirty thousand men. In regard to this, the following remarks may be made. (1.) This cannot be alleged to convict Luke of a false statement, for his record is, that the *chief captain* made this statement, and it cannot be proved that Luke has put into his mouth words which he did not utter. All that he is responsible for is, a correct *report* of what the Roman tribune *said*, not for the truth or falsehood of his statement. It is certainly *possible* that that might have been the common estimate of the number then, and that the account given by Josephus might have been made from more correct information. Or it is possible, certainly, that the statement by Josephus is incorrect. (2.) If Luke *were* to be held responsible for the statement of the number, yet it remains to be shown that he is not as correct a historian as Josephus. Why should Josephus be esteemed infallible, and Luke false? Why should the accuracy of Luke be tested by Josephus, rather than the accuracy of Josephus by Luke? Infidels usually *assume* that Josephus and other profane historians are infallible, and *then* endeavour to convict the sacred writers of falsehood. (3.) The narrative of Luke is the more probable of the two. It is more probable that the number was only four thousand, than that it was thirty thousand. For Josephus says, that four hundred were killed, and two hundred taken prisoners; and that thus they were dispersed. Now, it is scarcely credible, that an army of thirty thousand desperadoes and cut-throats would be dispersed by so small a slaughter and captivity. But if the number was originally but four thousand, it is entirely credible that the loss of six hundred would discourage and

uproar, and leddest out into the wilderness four thousand men that were murderers?

39 But Paul said, [a] I am a man *which am* a Jew of Tarsus, *a city* in Cilicia, a [b] citizen of no mean city: and I beseech thee, suffer me to speak unto the people.

40 And when he had given him license, Paul stood on the stairs, and beckoned [c] with the hand unto the people: and when there was made a great silence, he spake unto *them* in the Hebrew tongue, saying,

CHAPTER XXII.

MEN, [d] brethren, and fathers, hear ye my defence, [e] *which I make* now unto you.

2 (And when they heard that he spake in the Hebrew tongue to them, they kept the more silence: and he saith,)

a c.9.11; 22.3. b c.22.25. c c.12.17.

d c.7.2. e 1Pet.3.15.

dissipate the remainder. (4.) It is possible that the chief captain refers only to the *organized Sicarii*, or murderers that the Egyptian led with him, and Josephus to the *multitude* that afterwards joined them, the rabble of the discontented and disorderly that joined them on their march. Or, (5.) There may have been an error in transcribing Josephus. It has been supposed that he originally wrote four thousand, but that ancient copyists, mistaking the Δ delta, *four*, for Λ lambda, *thirty*, wrote thirty thousand, instead of four thousand. Whichever of these solutions be adopted is not material. ¶ *Which were murderers.* Σικαρίων. *Sicarii.* This is originally a Latin word, and is derived from *Sica*, a short sword, or sabre, or crooked knife, which could be easily concealed under the garment. Hence it came to denote assassins, and to be applied to banditti, or robbers. It does not mean that they *had* actually committed murder, but that they were desperadoes and banditti, and were drawn together for purposes of plunder and of blood. This class of people was exceedingly numerous in Judea. See Notes, Luke x. 30.

39. *A Jew of Tarsus.* A Jew by birth. See Note, ch. ix. 11. ¶ *Of no mean city.* Not obscure, or undistinguished. He could claim an honourable birth, so far as the place of his nativity was concerned. See Note, ch. ix. 11. Tarsus was much celebrated for its learning, and was at one time the rival of Alexandria and Athens. Xenophon calls it *a great and flourishing city.* Anabasis. Josephus (Antiq. b. i. ch. vi. § 6) says, that *it was the metropolis, and most renowned city among them* [the *Cilicians*].

40. *License.* Liberty; permission. ¶ *On the stairs.* Note, ver. 35. ¶ *Beckoned with the hand.* Waving the hand as a sign that he was about to address them, and to produce silence, and attention. See ch. xii. 17. ¶ *In the Hebrew tongue.* The language which was spoken by the Jews, which was then a mixture of the Chaldee and Syriac, called *Syro-chaldaic.* This language he doubtless used on this occasion in preference to the Greek, because it was understood better by the multitude, and would tend to conciliate them if they heard him address them in their own language. The following chapter should have been connected with this. The division here is unnatural.

CHAPTER XXII.

1. *Men, brethren, and fathers.* This defence was addressed to the Jews; and Paul commenced it with an expression of sincere respect for them. Stephen began his defence with the same form of address. Note, ch. vii. 2. ¶ *My defence.* Against the charges brought against me. Those charges were, that he had endeavoured to prejudice men every where against the Jews, and the law, and the temple. ch. xxi. 28. In order to meet this charge, Paul stated (1.) That he had been born a Jew, and had enjoyed all the advantages of a Jewish education (ver. 3.); (2.) He recounted the circumstances of his conversion, and the reason why he believed that he was called to preach the gospel (ver. 4—16); (3.) He proceeded to state the reasons why he went among the Gentiles, and evidently designed to vindicate his conduct there (ver. 17—21); but at this point, at the name *Gentiles*, his defence was interrupted by the enraged multitude, and he was not permitted to proceed. What *would* have been his defence, therefore, had he been suffered to finish it, it is impossible to know with certainty. On another occasion, however, he was permitted to make a *similar* defence, and perhaps to complete the train of thought which he had purposed to pursue here. See ch. xxvi.

2. *The Hebrew tongue.* Note, ch. xxi. 40

3 I am [a] verily a man *which am* a Jew, born in Tarsus, *a city* in Cilicia, yet brought up in this city, at the feet of [b] Gamaliel, *and* taught according [c] to the perfect manner of the law of the fathers, and was [d] zealous towards God, as ye [e] all are this day.

4 And I persecuted [f] this way unto the death, binding and delivering into prisons both men and women.

5 As also the high-priest doth bear me witness, and all the estate of the elders: from whom also I received letters unto the brethren, and went to Damascus, [g] to bring them which were there, bound, unto Jerusalem, for to be punished.

6 And it came to pass, that as I made my journey, and was come nigh unto Damascus about noon, suddenly there shone from heaven a great light round about me.

7 And I fell unto the ground, and heard a voice saying unto me, Saul, Saul, why persecutest thou me?

8 And I answered, Who art thou, Lord? And he said unto me, I am Jesus of Nazareth, whom thou persecutest.

9 And they that were with me saw [h] indeed the light, and were afraid; but they heard not the voice of him that spake to me.

10 And I said, What shall I do, Lord? And the Lord said unto me, Arise, and go into Damascus; and there it shall be told thee of all things which are appointed for thee to do.

a c.21.39. 2Cor.11.22. Phil.3.5. *b* c.5.34. *c* c.26.5. *d* Gal.1.14. *e* c.21.20. Rom.10.2. *f* c.8.3;26.9-13. Phil.3.6. 1Tim.1.13. *g* c.9.2,&c. *h* Dan.10.7.

3. *Born in Tarsus.* Note, ch xxi. 39. ¶ *Brought up in this city.* In Jerusalem, sent there for the advantage of more perfect instruction in the law. ¶ *At the feet of Gamaliel.* As a scholar, or disciple of Gamaliel. The phrase *to sit at the feet of one,* is expressive of the condition of a disciple or learner. Comp. Deut. xxxiii. 3. Luke x. 39. It is probable that the expression arose from the fact that the learners occupied a lower place or seat than the teacher. The phrase is expressive of humility and a lower condition. On the character and rank of Gamaliel, see Note on ch. v. 34. Paul mentions his having been instructed in this manner, in order to show that he was entitled to the full privilege of the Jew, and that he had had every opportunity to become fully acquainted with the nature of the law. ¶ *According to the perfect manner.* Κατὰ ἀκρίβειαν. By strict diligence, or exact care; or in the utmost rigour and severity of that instruction. No pains were spared to make him understand and practise the law of Moses. ¶ *The law of the fathers.* The law of our fathers; i. e. the law which they received, and handed down to us. Paul was a Pharisee; and the law in which he had been taught was not only the *written* law of Moses, but the *traditional* law which had been handed down from former times. Note, Matt. iii. 6. ¶ *And was zealous towards God.* Gal. i. 14. He had a constant burning zeal for God and his law, which was expressed not only by scrupulous adherence to its forms, but by persecuting all who opposed it. ver. 4, 5.

4. *And I persecuted.* ch. viii. 3. ¶ *This way.* Those who were of this mode of worshipping God; that is, Christians Note, Acts ix. 2. ¶ *Unto the death.* Intending to put them to death. He did not probably put any to death himself, but he committed them to prison, he sought their lives, he was the agent employed in arresting them; and when they were put to death, he tells us that he gave his voice against them (Acts xxvi. 10); that is, he joined in, and approved of their condemnation. ¶ *Delivering into prisons, &c.* ch. viii. 3.

5. *As also the high-priest, &c.* Note. ch. ix. 2. ¶ *All the estate of the elders* Greek. All the presbytery; that is, the whole body of the sanhedrim, or great council of the nation. ¶ *Unto the brethren.* The *Jewish* brethren, who were at Damascus. Paul here speaks as a Jew, and regards his countrymen as his brethren.

6. *As I made my journey.* As I was on my journey. ¶ *About noon.* ch. xxvi. 13. "At mid-day." This circumstance is omitted by Luke in his account in ch. ix. Paul mentions it, as being the more remarkable since it occurred at mid-day, to show that he was not deluded by any meteoric or natural appearances, which usually occur at night.

6—11. See Notes, ch. ix. 3—7

11 And when I could not see for the glory of that light, being led by the hand of them that were with me, I came into Damascus.

12 And one Ananias, [a] a devout man according to the law, having a good [b] report of all the Jews which dwelt *there*,

13 Came unto me, and stood, and said unto me, Brother Saul, receive thy sight. And the same hour I looked up upon him.

14 And he said, The [c] God of our fathers hath chosen [d] thee, that thou shouldest know his will, and see [e] that Just [f] One, and shouldest hear the voice [g] of his mouth.

15 For thou [h] shalt be his witness unto all men, of what thou hast seen and heard.

16 And now, why tarriest thou? arise, and be baptized, and wash away thy sins, calling [j] on the name of the Lord,

17 And it came to pass, that when I was come again to Jerusalem, even while I prayed in the temple, I was in a trance;[k]

a c.9.17. b c.10.22. 1Tim.3.7. Heb.11.2. c c.3.13;5.30. d ch.c.9.15. Gal.1.15. e ver.18. 1Cor.9.1;15.8. f c.3.14;7.51. g 1Cor.11.23. Gal.1.12. h c.23.11, 26.16,&c. i Heb.10.22. 1Pet.3.21. j Rom.10.13. 1Cor.1.2. k 2Cor.12.2.

11. *The glory of that light.* The splendour, the intense brilliancy of the light. See this and its effects explained in the Note on ch. ix. 8.

12, 13. See Notes, ch. ix. 17, 18

14. *Shouldest know his will.* His will in the plan of salvation, and in regard to your future life. ¶ *And see that Just One.* The Messiah. Note, ch. iii. 14. As Paul was to be an apostle, and as it was the peculiar office of an apostle to bear witness to the person and deeds of the Lord Jesus (Note, ch. i. 21, 22.) it was necessary that he should *see* him, that thus he might be a competent witness of his resurrection. ¶ *Shouldest hear the voice of his mouth.* Shouldst hear and obey his commands.

15. *For thou shalt be his witness,* &c. As an *apostle* to testify to all men that the Messiah has come; that he has died; that he has risen; and that he is the Saviour of the world. ¶ *Of what thou hast seen and heard.* Of the remarkable proof which has been furnished you of the divine mission and character of the Lord Jesus.

16. *And now why tarriest thou?* Why dost thou delay, or wait any longer? These words are not recorded by Luke in ch. ix., where he has given an account of the conversion of Paul; but there is nothing here contradictory to his statement. ¶ *And wash away thy sins.* Receive baptism, as an act expressive of the washing away of sins. It cannot be intended that the external rite of baptism was sufficient to make the soul pure, but that it was an ordinance divinely appointed as *expressive* of the washing away of sins, or of purifying the heart. Comp. Heb. x. 22 Sinners are represented in the Scriptures as *defiled* or *polluted* by sin To *wash* away the sins, denotes the purifying of the soul from this polluted influence. 1 Cor. vi. 11. Rev. i. 5; vii. 14. Isa. i. 16. Ps. li. 2. 7. ¶ *Calling on the name of the Lord.* For pardon and sanctification. Rom. x. 13, "Whosoever shall call upon the name of the Lord shall be saved." It was proper that this calling on the name of the Lord should be connected with the ordinance of baptism. That ordinance was expressive of a purifying which the Lord only could produce. It is proper that the rite of baptism should be attended with extraordinary prayer; and that he who is to be baptized should make it the occasion of peculiar and very solemn religious exercises. The external rite will avail nothing without the pardoning mercy of God.

17. *When I was come again to Jerusalem.* That is, three years after his conversion. See Gal. i. 17, 18. ¶ *While I prayed in the temple.* Paul, like the other converts to Christianity from among the Jews, would naturally continue to offer his devotions in the temple. We meet with repeated instances of their continuing to comply with the customs of the Jewish people. ¶ *I was in a trance.* Greek, Ecstasy. Note, ch. x. 10. Perhaps he here refers to what he elsewhere mentions (2 Cor. xii. 1—5,) which he calls "visions and revelations of the Lord." In that place he mentions his being "caught up to the third heaven" (ver. 2) and "into paradise," where he heard words which it was "not possible for a man to utter." ver. 4. It is not certain, however, that he refers in this place to that remarkable occurrence. The narrative would rather imply that the Lord Jesus appeared to him in the temple in a remarkable manner, in a vision, and gave

18 And saw [a] him saying unto me, Make haste, and get thee quickly out of Jerusalem: for they will not receive thy testimony concerning me.

19 And I said, Lord, they [b] know that I imprisoned and beat in every synagogue them that believed on thee:

20 And when the blood of thy martyr Stephen was shed, I [c] also was standing by, and consenting [d] unto his death, and kept the raiment of them that slew him.

21 And he said unto me, Depart: for [e] I will send thee far hence, unto the Gentiles.

22 And they gave him audience unto this word, and *then* lift up their voices, and said, Away with such a *fellow* from the earth: for [f] it is not fit that he should live.

a ver.14. b ver.4. c c.7.58. d c.8.1. e c.13.2,47. Rom.1.5; 12.13; 15.16. Gal.2 7,8. Eph.3.7,8. 1Tim.2.7. f c.25.24.

him a direct command to go to the Gentiles. Paul had now stated the evidence of his conversion, which appears to have been satisfactory to them: at least they made no objection to his statement; he had shown by his being in the temple his respect for their institutions; and he *now* proceeds to show that in his other conduct he had been directed by the same high authority by which he had been called into the ministry, and that the command had been given to him in their own temple and in their own city

18. *And saw him.* Evidently the Lord Jesus. ver. 14. He had received his commission from him, and he now received a distinct command to go to the Gentiles. ¶ *For they will not receive.* The inhabitants of Jerusalem, probably including both Jews and Christians. The *Jews* would not listen to him, because he had become, in their view, an apostate, and they would hate and persecute him The *Christians* would not be likely to receive him. for they would remember his former persecutions, and would be suspicious of him, because he had been so long in Arabia, and had not sooner connected himself with them. See Note on ch. ix. 26. "And when Saul was come to Jerusalem, he assayed to join himself to the disciples; but they were all afraid of him, and believed not that he was a disciple."

19. *And I said, Lord.* This shows that it was the Lord Jesus, whom Paul saw in a trance in the temple. The term *Lord* is usually applied to him in the Acts. Note, ch. i. 24. ¶ *They know.* Christians know; and they will therefore be not likely to receive to their fellowship their former enemy and persecutor. ¶ *Beat in every synagogue.* Beating, or scourging, was often done in the synagogue. See Note, Matt. x. 17. Comp. Acts xxvi. 11. It was customary for those who were converted to Christianity, still to meet with the Jews in their synagogues, and to join with them in their worship.

20. *The blood of thy martyr Stephen was shed.* See ch. vii. 58; viii. 1. ¶ *I was standing by.* ch. vii. 58. ¶ *And consenting unto his death.* ch. viii. 1. ¶ *And kept the raiment.* The outer robes or garments which were usually laid aside, when they engaged in running or labour. See ch. vii. 58. All this showed, that though Paul was not engaged in stoning Stephen, yet he was with them in spirit, and fully accorded with what they did. These circumstances are mentioned here by him, as *reasons* why he knew that he would not be received by Christians as one of their number, and why it was necessary, therefore, for him to turn to the gentile world.

21. *And he said unto me, Depart.* Because the Christians at Jerusalem would not receive him. ¶ *Far hence.* Paul travelled far in the heathen nations. A large part of his time in the ministry was spent in remote countries, and in the most distant regions then known. See Rom. xv. 19.

22. *And they gave him audience.* They heard him patiently. ¶ *Unto this word.* The word *Gentiles.* ¶ *Away with such a* fellow. Greek, Take such a man from the earth; i. e. put him to death It is language of strong indignation and abhorrence. The reasons of their indignation were, not that they supposed that the Gentiles could not be brought into covenant with God, for they would themselves compass sea and land to make one proselyte; but they were, (1.) That they believed that Paul taught that they might be saved without conforming to the law of Moses; and, (2.) His speech implied that the Jews were more hardened than the Gentiles, and that he had a greater

23 And as they cried out, and
cast off *their* clothes, and threw
dust into the air,
24 The chief captain commanded him to be brought into the castle, and bade that he should be
examined by scourging; that he
might know wherefore they cried
so against him.
25 And as they bound him with
thongs, Paul said unto the centurion that stood by, Is it lawful for
you to scourge a man that is a Roman, [a] and uncondemned?
26 When the centurion heard
that, he went and told the chief
captain, saying, Take heed what
thou doest: for this man is a Roman.
27 Then the chief captain came,
and said unto him, Tell me, art
thou a Roman? He said, Yea.
28 And the chief captain answered, With a great sum obtained

a c.16.37; 15.16.

prospect of success in bringing them to God than he had in regard to the Jews.

23. *Cast off their clothes.* Their outer garments. Probably they did it now intending to stone him. ch. vii. 58. ¶ *And threw dust into the air.* As expressive of their abhorrence and indignation. This was a striking exhibition of rage and vindictive malice. Paul was guarded by Roman soldiers, so that they could not injure him; and their only way of expressing their wrath was by menaces and threats, and by these tokens of furious indignation. Thus Shimei expressed his indignation against David by cursing him, and throwing stones at him, and casting dust. 2 Sam. xvi. 13.

24. *The castle.* The tower of Antonia. He would be there removed entirely from the wrath of the Jews. ¶ *Should be examined.* Ἀνετάζεσθαι. The word *examine* with us commonly means to inquire, to question, to search for, or to look carefully into a subject. The word here used is commonly applied to *metals* whose nature is tested, or *examined* by fire; and then it means to subject to torture or torments, in order to extort a confession, where persons were accused of crime. It was often resorted to among the ancients. The usual mode has been by the *rack*, but various kinds of torments have been invented in order to extort confessions of guilt from those who were accused. The whole practice has been one of the most flagrant violations of justice, and one of the foulest blots on human nature. In this case, the tribune saw that Paul was accused violently by the Jews; he was ignorant of the Hebrew language, and had not probably understood the address of Paul; he supposed from the extraordinary excitement that Paul must have been guilty of some flagrant offence, and he therefore resolved to subject him to torture, to extort from him a confession. ¶ *By scourging.* By the scourge or whip. Comp. Heb. xi. 36. This was one mode of torture, in order to extort a secret from those who were accused.

25. *Bound him with thongs.* With cords, preparatory to scourging. ¶ *Is it lawful*, &c. It was directly contrary to the Roman law, to bind and scourge a Roman citizen. See Note, on ch. xvi. 36, 37.

28. *With a great sum obtained I this freedom.* This freedom, or privilege of Roman citizenship. From this it would seem, that the privilege of being a Roman citizen might be purchased. Perhaps he refers, however, to the expenses which were necessarily attendant in passing through the proper *forms* of becoming a Roman citizen. The argument of the tribune in this case is this:—'*I* obtained this privilege at a great price. Whence did you Paul, thus poor and persecuted, obtain the means of becoming a Roman citizen?' Paul had informed him that he was a native of Tarsus (ch. xxi. 39); and the chief captain supposed that that was not a free city, and that Paul could not have derived the privilege of citizenship from his birth. ¶ *But I was free-born.* I was born a Roman citizen, or I am such in virtue of my birth. Various opinions have been formed on the question, in what way or for what reasons Paul was entitled to the privilege of a Roman citizen. Some have supposed that Tarsus was a Roman colony, and that he thus became a Roman citizen. But of this there does not appear to be sufficient proof. Pliny says (5 27) that it was *a free city*. The city of Tarsus was endowed with the privileges of a free city by Augustus Cesar, after it had been greatly afflicted and oppressed by wars. (*Appian.*) Dio Chrysost. says to the people of Tarsus, "he (Augustus) has conferred on you every thing which any

I this freedom. And Paul said,
But I was *free* born.

29 Then straightway they departed from him which should have [1] examined him: and the chief captain also was afraid, after he knew that he was a Roman, and because he had bound him.

30 On the morrow, because [a] he would have known the certainty wherefore he was accused of the Jews, he loosed him from *his* bands, and commanded the chief priests and all their council to appear, and brought Paul down, and set him before them.

CHAPTER XXIII.

AND Paul, earnestly beholding the council, said, Men *and* brethren, I [b] have lived in all good

[1] or, *tortured him.* [a] c.13 38.

[b] c.24.16. 2Cor.1.12. Heb 13.18.

---

one could bestow on his friends and companions, a country (i. e. a free country), laws, honour, authority over the river (Cydranus), and the neighbouring sea." Free cities were permitted in the Roman empire to use their own laws and customs, to have their own magistrates, and they were free from being subject to Roman guards. They were required only to acknowledge the supremacy and authority of the Roman people, and to aid them in their wars. Such a city was Tarsus, and having been born there, Paul was entitled to these privileges of a free man. Many critics have supposed that this privilege of Roman citizenship had been conferred on some of the ancestors of Paul, in consequence of some distinguished military service. Such a conferring of the rights of citizenship was not unusual, and possibly might have occurred in this case. But there is no direct historical proof of it; and the former fact, that he was born in a free city, will amply account for his affirmation that he was free-born.

29. *Then straightway.* Immediately. They saw that by scourging him they would have violated the Roman law, and exposed themselves to its penalty. ¶ *Which should have examined him.* Who were about to torture him by scourging him. ver. 24. ¶ *Because he had bound him.* Preparatory to scourging him. The act of *binding* a Roman citizen, with such an intent, untried and uncondemned, was unlawful Prisoners who were to be scourged were usually bound by the Romans to a pillar or post; and a similar custom prevailed among the Jews. That it was unlawful to bind a man, with this intent, who was uncondemned, appears from an express declaration in Cicero (against Verres). "It is a heinous sin to *bind* a Roman citizen; it is wickedness to *beat* him; it is next to parricide to kill him, and what shall I say to crucify him?"

30. *On the morrow* After he had arrested Paul. Paul was still a prisoner; and if suffered to go at liberty among the Jews, his life would have been in danger. ¶ *And commanded the chief priests, &c.* Summoned a meeting of the sanhedrim, or great council of the nation. He did this, as he was prevented from scourging Paul, in order to know what he had done, and that he might learn from the Jews themselves the nature of the charge against him. This was necessary for the safety of Paul, and for the ends of justice. This should have been done without any attempt to *torture* him in order to extort a confession. ¶ *And brought Paul down.* From the elevated castle or tower of Antonia. The council assembled commonly in the house of the high-priest. ¶ *And set him before them.* He brought the prisoner to their bar, that they might have an opportunity to accuse him, and that thus the chief captain might learn the real nature of the charge against him.

CHAPTER XXIII.

1. *And Paul, earnestly beholding.* Ἀτενίσας. Fixing his eyes intently on the council The word denotes a fixed and earnest gazing; a close observation. See Luke iv. 20. Note, Acts iii. 4. Paul would naturally look with a keen and attentive observation on the council. He was arraigned before them, and he would naturally observe the appearance, and endeavour to ascertain the character of his judges. Besides, it was by this council that he had been formerly commissioned to persecute the Christians. ch. ix. 1, 2 He had not seen them since that commission was given. He would naturally, therefore, regard them with an attentive eye. The result shows, also, that Paul looked at them to see what was the character of the men there assembled, and what was the proportion of Pharisees and Sadducees. ver. 6. ¶ *The council.* Gr. The sanhedrim ch. xxii. 30. It was the great council composed of seventy elders, to whom was intrusted the affairs of the nation. See Note, Matt. i. 4

conscience before God until this day.

2 And the high-priest Ananias commanded them that stood by him to smite him [a] on the mouth.

a Jno.18.22.

¶ *Men and brethren.* Gr. 'Men, brethren;' the usual form of beginning an address among the Jews. See ch. ii. 29. He addressed them still as his *brethren.* ¶ *I have lived in all good conscience.* I have conducted myself so as to maintain a good conscience. I have done what I believed to be right. This was a bold declaration, after the tumult, and charges, and accusations of the previous day (ch. xxii.); and yet it was strictly true. His persecutions of the Christians had been conducted *conscientiously.* Acts xxvi. 9, "I verily thought with myself," says he, "that I *ought* to do many things contrary to the name of Jesus of Nazareth." Of his conscientiousness and fidelity in *their* service, they could bear witness. Of his conscientiousness *since,* he could make a similar declaration. And he, doubtless, meant to say, that as he had been conscientious in persecution, so he had been in his conversion, and in his subsequent course. And as they *knew* that his former life had been with a good conscience, they ought to *presume* that he had maintained the same character still. This was a remarkably bold appeal to be made by an accused man, and it shows the strong consciousness which Paul had of his innocence. What would have been the drift of Paul's discourse in proving this, we can only conjecture. He was interrupted (ver. 2); but there can be no doubt that he would have pursued such a course of argument as should tend to establish his innocence. ¶ *Before God.* Gr. To God. Τῷ Θεῷ. He had lived *to* God, or with reference to his commands, so as to keep a conscience pure in his sight. The same principle of conduct he states more at length in ch. xxiv. 16: "And herein do I exercise myself, to have always a conscience void of offence toward God and toward men. ¶ *Until this day.* Including the time *before* his conversion to Christianity, and after. In both conditions he was conscientious; in one, conscientious in persecution and error, though he deemed it to be right; in the other, conscientious in the truth. The mere fact, that a man is conscientious, does not prove that he is right, or innocent. See Note on John xvi. 2.

2. *And the high-priest Ananias.* This Ananias was, doubtless, the son of Nebedinus (Jos. Ant. xx. ch. v. § 3), who was high-priest when Quadratus, who preceded Felix, was president of Syria. He was sent bound to Rome by Quadratus, at the same time with Ananias, the prefect of the temple, that they might give an account of their conduct to Claudius Cesar. Josephus, Ant. b. xx. ch. vi. § 2. But in consequence of the intercession of Agrippa the Younger, they were dismissed, and returned to Jerusalem. Ananias, however, was not restored to the office of high-priest. For, when Felix was governor of Judea, this office was filled by Jonathan, who succeeded Ananias. Josephus, Ant. b. xx. ch. x. Jonathan was slain in the temple itself, by the instigation of Felix, by assassins who had been hired for the purpose. This murder is thus described by Josephus (Ant. b. xx. ch. viii. § 5): "Felix bore an ill-will to Jonathan, the high-priest, because he frequently gave him admonitions about governing the Jewish affairs better than he did, lest complaints should be made against him, since he had procured of Cesar the appointment of Felix as procurator of Judea. Accordingly, Felix contrived a method by which he might get rid of Jonathan, whose admonitions had become troublesome to him. Felix persuaded one of Jonathan's most faithful friends, of the name Doras, to bring the robbers upon him, and to put him to death." This was done in Jerusalem. The robbers came into the city as if to worship God, and with daggers, which they had concealed under their garments, they put him to death. After the death of Jonathan the office of high-priest remained vacant, until king Agrippa appointed Ismael, the son of Fabi, to the office. Josephus, Ant. b. xx. ch. viii. § 8. It was during this interval, while the office of high-priest was vacant, that the events which are here recorded took place. Ananias was then at Jerusalem; and as the office of high-priest was vacant, and as he was the last person who had borne the office, it was natural that he should discharge, probably by common consent, its duties, so far at least as to preside in the sanhedrim. Of these facts, Paul would be doubtless apprized; and hence what he said (ver. 5) was strictly true, and is one of the evidences that Luke's history accords precisely with the peculiar circumstances which then existed.

3 Then said Paul unto him, God
shall smite thee, *thou* whited wall:
for sittest thou to judge me after
the law, and commandest me to
be smitten [a] contrary to the law?

4 And they that stood by said,
Revilest thou God's high-priest?
5 Then said Paul, I wist not,
brethren, that he was the high-
priest: for it is written, [b] Thou

a Lev.19.35. Deut.25.1,2. Jno.7.51.

b Ex.22.28. Eccl.10.20. 2Pet.2.10. Jude 8.

When Luke here calls Ananias "the high-priest," he evidently intends not to affirm that he was actually such; but to use the word as the Jews did, as applicable to one who *had* been in that office, and who, on that occasion, when the office was vacant, performed its duties. ¶ *To smite him on the mouth.* To stop him from speaking; to express their indignation at what he had said. The anger of Ananias was excited, because Paul affirmed, that all that he had done had been with a good conscience. Their feelings had been excited to the utmost; they regarded him as certainly guilty; they deemed him to be an apostate: and they could not bear it that he, with such coolness and firmness, declared that *all* his conduct had been under the direction of a good conscience. The injustice of the command of Ananias is apparent to all. A similar instance of violence occurred on the trial of the Saviour. John xviii. 22.

3. *God shall smite thee.* God shall punish thee. God is just; and he will not suffer such a manifest violation of all the laws of a fair trial to pass unavenged. This was a remarkably bold and fearless declaration. Paul was surrounded by enemies. They were seeking his life. And he must have known that such declarations would have only excited their wrath, and made them more thirsty for his blood. That he could thus address the president of the council, was not only strongly characteristic of the man, but was also a strong proof that he was conscious of innocence, and that justice was on his side. This expression of Paul, "God shall smite thee," is not to be regarded in the light of an *imprecation*, or as an expression of angry feeling, but of a *prediction*, or of a strong conviction on the mind of Paul, that a man so hypocritical and unjust as Ananias was, could not escape the vengeance of God. Ananias was slain, with Hezekiah his brother, during the agitation that occurred in Jerusalem when the robbers, or *Sicarii*, under their leader, Manahem, had taken possession of the city. He attempted to conceal himself in an aqueduct, but was drawn forth and killed. See Josephus, Jewish Wars, b. ii. ch. xvii. § 8. Thus Paul's prediction was fulfilled. ¶ *Thou whited wall.* This is evidently a proverbial expression, meaning *thou hypocrite.* His hypocrisy consisted in his pretending to sit there to do justice; and yet, in commanding the accused to be smitten in direct violation of the law, he thus showed that his character was not what, by his sitting there, he professed it to be, but that of one determined to carry the purposes of his party, and of his own feelings. Our Saviour used a similar expression, to describe the hypocritical character of the Pharisees (Matt. xxiii. 27), when he compares them to whited sepulchres. A whited wall is a wall or enclosure that is covered with lime or gypsum, and that thus appears to be different from what it is, and thus aptly describes the hypocrite. Seneca (de Providentia, ch. 6) uses a similar figure to describe hypocrites: "They are sordid, base, and like their walls adorned only externally." See also Seneca, Epis. 115 ¶ *For sittest thou.* &c. The law required that justice should be done, and in order to that, it gave every man an opportunity of defending himself. See Note, John vii. 51. Prov. xviii. 13. Lev. xix. 15, 16. Ex. xxiii. 1, 2. Deut. xix. 15. 18. ¶ *To judge me after the law.* As a judge to hear and decide the case according to the rules of the law of Moses. ¶ *Contrary to the law.* In violation of the law of Moses (Lev. xix. 35), "Ye shall do no unrighteousness in judgment."

4. *Revilest thou.* &c. Dost thou reproach or abuse the high-priest of God? It is remarkable that they who knew that he was *not* the high-priest, should have offered this language. He was, however, in the place of the high-priest, and they might have pretended that respect was due to the office.

5. *Then said Paul, I wist not.* I know not; I was ignorant of the fact, that he was high-priest. Interpreters have been greatly divided on the meaning of this expression. Some have supposed that Paul said it in *irony;* as if he had said. 'Pardon me, brethren, I did not consider that this was the high-priest. It did not occur to me, that a man who could con

shalt not speak evil of the ruler of thy people.

6 But when Paul perceived that the one part were Sadducees,

duct thus, could be God's high-priest.' Others have thought (as Grotius) that Paul used these words for the purpose of mitigating their wrath, and as an acknowledgment that he had spoken hastily, and that it was contrary to his usual habit, which was not to speak evil of the ruler of the people. As if he had said, 'I acknowledge my error and my haste. I did not *consider* that I was addressing him whom God had commanded me to respect.' But this interpretation is not probable, for Paul evidently did not intend to retract what he had said. Dr. Doddridge renders it, "I was not aware, brethren, that it was the high-priest," and regards it as an apology for having spoken in haste. But the obvious reply to this interpretation is, that if Ananias was the high-priest, Paul could not but be aware of it. Of so material a point, it is hardly possible that he could be ignorant. Others suppose, that as Paul had been long absent from Jerusalem, and had not known the changes which had occurred there, he was a stranger to the person of the high-priest. Others suppose that Ananias did not occupy the usual seat which was appropriated to the high-priest, and that he was not clothed in the usual robes of office, and that Paul did not recognise him the high-priest. But these interpretations are not probable. It is wholly improbable that, on such an occasion, the high-priest, who was the presiding officer in the sanhedrim, should not be known to the accused. The true interpretation, therefore, I suppose is, that which is derived from the fact that Ananias was *not* then properly the high-priest; that there was a vacancy in the office, and that he presided by courtesy, or in virtue of his having been formerly invested with that office. The meaning then will be, 'I did not regard or acknowledge him as the high-priest. I did not address him *as such*, since that is not his true character. Had he been truly the high-priest, even if he had thus been guilty of manifest injustice, I would not have used the language which I did. The *office*, if not the *man*, would have claimed respect. But as he is *not* truly and properly clothed with that office, and as he was guilty of manifest injustice, I did not believe that he was to be shielded in his injustice by the law which commands me to show respect to the proper ruler of the people.' If this be the true interpretation, it shows that Luke, in this account, accords entirely with the truth of history. The character of Ananias, as given by Josephus; the facts which he has stated in regard to him, all accord with the account here given, and show that the writer of the "Acts of the Apostles" was acquainted with the history of that time, and has correctly stated it. ¶ *For it is written.* Ex. xxii. 28. Paul adduces this to show that it was his purpose to observe the law; that he would not intentionally violate it; and that, if he had known Ananias to be high-priest, he would have been restrained by his regard for the law from using the language which he did. ¶ *Of the ruler of thy people.* This passage had not any peculiar reference to the high-priest, but it inculcated the general spirit of respect for those in office, whatever that office was. As the office of high-priest was one of importance and authority, Paul declares here that he would not be guilty of showing disrespect for it, or of using reproachful language towards it.

6. *But when Paul perceived.* Probably by his former acquaintance with the men who composed the council. As he had been brought up in Jerusalem, and had been before acquainted with the sanhedrim (ch. ix. 2), he would have an acquaintance, doubtless, with the character of most of those present, though he had been absent from them for fourteen years. Gal. ii. 1. ¶ *The one part,* &c. That the council was divided into two parties Pharisees and Sadducees. This was commonly the case, though it is uncertain which had the majority. In regard to the opinions of these two sects, see Notes on Matt. iii. 7. ¶ *He cried out,* &c. The reasons why Paul resolved to take advantage of their difference of opinion were, probably, (1.) That he saw that it was impossible to expect *justice* at their hands; and he, therefore, regarded it as prudent and proper to consult his safety. He saw, from the conduct of Ananias, and from the spirit manifested (ver. 4), that they, like the other Jews, had prejudged the case, and were driven on by blind rage and fury. (2.) His object was to show his innocence to the chief captain. To ascertain that, was the purpose for which he had been arraigned. Yet that, perhaps, could be most directly and satisfactorily shown by bringing out, as he knew he could do, the real spirit

and the other Pharisees, he cried out in the council, Men *and* brethren, [a] I am a Pharisee, the son of a Pharisee: of [b] the hope and resurrection of the dead I am called in question.

a c.26.5. Phil.3.5.

b c.24.15,21; 26.6; 28.20.

which actuated the whole council, as a spirit of party-strife, contention, and persecution. Knowing, therefore, how sensitive they were on the subject of the resurrection, he seems to have resolved to do what he would *not* have done had they been disposed to hear him according to the rules of justice, to abandon the *direct* argument for his defence, and to enlist a large part, perhaps a majority of the council, in his favour. Whatever may be thought of the propriety of this course, it cannot be denied that it was a master-stroke of policy, and that it evinced a profound knowledge of human nature. ¶ *I am a Pharisee.* That is, I was of that sect among the Jews. I was born a Pharisee, and I ever continued while a Jew to be of that sect. In the main he agreed with them still. He did not mean to deny that he was a Christian, but that so far as the Pharisees differed from the Sadducees, he was in the main with the former. He agreed with *them*, not with the Sadducees, in regard to the doctrine of the resurrection, and the existence of angels and spirits. ¶ *The son of a Pharisee.* What was the name of his father is not known. But the meaning is, simply, that he was entitled to all the immunities and privileges of a Pharisee. He had, from his birth, belonged to that sect, nor had he ever departed from the great cardinal doctrines which distinguished that sect—the doctrine of the resurrection of the dead. Comp. Phil. iii. 5. ¶ *Of the hope and resurrection of the dead.* That is, of the hope that the dead will be raised. This is the real point of the persecution and opposition to me. ¶ *I am called in question.* Gr. I am judged; that is, I am persecuted, or brought to trial. Orobio charges this upon Paul as an artful manner of declining persecution, unworthy the character of an upright and honest man. Chubb, a British Deist of the seventeenth century, charges it upon Paul as an act of gross "dissimulation, as designed to conceal the true ground of all the troubles that he had brought upon himself; and as designed to deceive and impose upon the Jews." He affirms also, that "St. Paul probably invented this pretended charge against himself, to draw over a party of the unbelieving Jews unto him." See Chubb's Posthumous Works vol. ii p. 238. Now, in reply to this, we may observe, (1.) That there is not the least evidence that Paul denied that he had been, or was then, a Christian. An attempt to deny this, after all that they knew of him, would have been vain; and there is not the slightest hint that he attempted it. (2.) The doctrine of the resurrection of the dead *was* the *main* and *leading* doctrine which he had insisted on, and which had been to him the cause of much of his persecution. See ch. xvii. 31, 32. 1 Cor. xv. Acts xiii. 34; xxvi. 6, 7. 23. 25. (3.) Paul defended this by an argument which he deemed invincible, and which constituted, in fact, the principal evidence of its truth—the fact that the Lord Jesus *had* been raised. That fact had given demonstration to the doctrine of the Pharisees, that the dead would rise. As Paul had every where proclaimed the fact that Jesus had been raised up, and as this had been the occasion of his being opposed, it was true that he had been persecuted on account of that doctrine. (4.) The real ground of the opposition which the Sadducees made to him, and of their opposition to his doctrine was, the additional zeal with which he urged this doctrine, and the additional argument which he brought for the resurrection of the dead. Perhaps the cause of the opposition of this great party among the Jews—the Sadducees—to Christianity, was the strong confirmation which the resurrection of Christ gave to the doctrine which they so much hated—the doctrine of the resurrection of the dead. It thus gave a triumph to their opponents among the Pharisees; and Paul, as a leading and zealous advocate of that doctrine, would excite their special hatred. (5.) All that Paul said, therefore, was strictly true. It was because he advocated this doctrine that he was opposed. That there were *other* causes of opposition to him might be true also; but still this was the main and prominent cause of the hostility. (6.) With great propriety, therefore, he might address the Pharisees, and say, 'Brethren, the great doctrine which has distinguished you from the Sadducees, is at stake. The great doctrine which is at the foundation of all our hopes—the resurrection of the dead, the doctrine of our fathers of the Scriptures, of our sect, is in danger

7 And when he had so said, there arose a dissension between the Pharisees and the Sadducees: and the multitude was divided.

8 For the Sadducees [a] say that there is no resurrection, neither angel nor spirit: but the Pharisees confess both.

9 And there arose a great cry: and the scribes *that were* of the Pharisees' part arose, and strove, saying, We find [b] no evil in this man: but if a spirit [c] or an angel hath spoken to him, let us not [d] fight against God.

a Matt.22.23. Mark 12.18. Luke 20.27.

b c.25.25;26.31. c c. 22.17,18. d c.5.39.

Of that doctrine I have been the advocate. I have never denied it. I have endeavoured to establish it, and have every where defended it, and have devoted myself to the work of putting it on an imperishable basis among the Jews and the Gentiles. For my zeal in that, I have been opposed. I have excited the ridicule of the Gentile, and the hatred of the Sadducee. I have thus been persecuted and arraigned; and for my zeal in this, in urging the argument in defence of it, which *I* have deemed most irrefragable—the resurrection of the Messiah, I have been persecuted and arraigned, and now cast myself on your protection against the mad zeal of the enemies of the doctrine of our fathers. Not only, therefore, was this an act of policy and prudence in Paul, but what he affirmed was strictly *true*, and the effect was as he had anticipated.

7. *A dissension.* A dispute, or difference. ¶ *And the multitude.* The council. Comp. ch. xiv. 4. The Pharisees embraced, as he desired and expected, his side of the question, and became his advocates, in opposition to the Sadducees, who were arrayed against him.

8. *For the Sadducees say.* They believe. ¶ *No resurrection.* Of the dead. By this doctrine they also understood that there was no future state, and that the soul did not exist after death. See Note, Matt. xxii. 23. ¶ *Neither angel.* That there are no angels. They deny the existence of good or bad angels. See Note, Matt. iii. 7. ¶ *Nor spirit.* Nor soul. That there was nothing but matter. They were materialists, and supposed that all the operations which we ascribe to mind, could be traced to some modification of matter. The Sadducees, says Josephus (Jewish War, b. ii. ch. viii. § 14), "take away the belief of the immortal duration of the soul, and the punishments and rewards in Hades." "The doctrine of the Sadducees is this," says he (Ant. b xviii. ch. i. § 4), "that souls die with the bodies." The opinion that the soul is material, and that there is nothing but matter in the universe, has been held by many philosophers, ancient and modern, as well as by the Sadducees. ¶ *Confess both.* Acknowledge, or receive both as true; i. e. that there is a future state, and that there are spirits distinct from matter, as angels, and the disembodied souls of men. The two points in dispute were, (1.) Whether the dead would be raised and exist in a future state; and, (2.) Whether mind was distinct from matter. The Sadducees denied both, and the Pharisees believed both. Their belief of the latter point was, that spirits existed in two forms—that of angels, and that of souls of men distinct from the body.

9. *A great cry.* A great clamour, and tumult. ¶ *The scribes.* The learned men. They would naturally be the chief speakers. ¶ *Of the Pharisees' part.* Who were Pharisees; or who belonged to that party. The scribes were not a distinct sect, but might be either Pharisees or Sadducees. ¶ *We find no evil in this man.* No opinion which is contrary to the law of Moses; and no conduct in spreading the doctrine of the resurrection which we do not approve. The importance of this doctrine, in their view, was so great as to throw into the back ground all the *other* doctrines that Paul might hold; and provided this were propagated, they were willing to vindicate and sustain him. A similar testimony was offered to the innocence of the Saviour by Pilate. John xix. 6. ¶ *But if a spirit or an angel, &c.* They here referred, doubtless, to what Paul had said in ch. xxii. 17, 18. He had declared that he had gone among the Gentiles in obedience to a command which he received in a vision in the temple. As the Pharisees held to the belief of spirits and angels, and to the doctrine that the will of God was often delivered to men by their agency, they were ready now to admit that he had received such a communication, and that he had gone among the Gentiles in obedience to it, to defend their great doctrine of the resurrection of the dead. We are not to suppose that the Pharisees had be-

10 And when there arose a great dissension, the chief captain, fearing lest Paul should have been pulled in pieces of them, commanded the soldiers to go down, and to take him by force from among them, and to bring *him* into the castle.

11 And the night following, the Lord stood [a] by him, and said, Be of good cheer, Paul: for as thou hast testified of me in Jerusalem, so must thou bear witness also at Rome.[b]

12 And when it was day, certain [c] of the Jews banded together, and bound themselves [1] under a curse, saying, that they would

a Ps.46.1,7. c.18.9; 27.23,24. b c.28.30,31.Rom.1.15. c ver.21.30. c.25.3.

1 or, *with an oath of execration.*

come the friends of Paul, or of Christianity. The true solution of their conduct doubtless is, that they were so inflamed with hatred against the Sadducees, that they were willing to make use of *any* argument against their doctrine. As the testimony of Paul might be turned to their account, they were willing to vindicate him. It is remarkable too, that they *perverted* the statement of Paul in order to oppose the Sadducees. Paul had stated distinctly (ch. xxii. 17, 18.) that he had been commanded to go by *the Lord*, meaning the Lord Jesus. He had said nothing of "a spirit, or an angel." Yet they would unite with the Sadducees so far as to maintain that he had received no such command from the Lord Jesus. But they might easily vary his statements, and suppose that an "angel or a spirit" had spoken to him, and thus made use of his conduct as an argument against the Sadducees. Men are not always very careful about the exact correctness of their statements, when they wish to humble a rival. ¶ *Let us not fight against God.* See Note, ch. v. 39. These words are wanting in many MSS. and in some of the ancient versions. The Syriac reads it, "if a spirit or an angel have spoken to him, what is there in this?" i. e. what is there unusual or wrong.

10. *A great dissension.* A great tumult, excitement, or controversy. ¶ *Into the castle.* Note, ch. xxi. 34.

11. *The Lord stood by him.* Evidently the Lord Jesus. See Note, ch. i. 24. Comp. ch. xxii. 18. The appearance of the Lord in this case was a proof that he approved the course which Paul had taken before the sanhedrim. ¶ *Be of good cheer.* It would not be remarkable if Paul, by these constant persecutions, should be somewhat dejected in mind. The issue of the whole matter was as yet doubtful. In these circumstances, it must have been peculiarly consoling to him to hear these words of encouragement from the Lord Jesus, and this assurance that the object of his desires should be granted, and that he would be permitted to bear the same witness of him in Rome. Nothing else can comfort and sustain the soul in trials, and persecutions, but evidence of the approbation of God, and the promises of his gracious aid. ¶ *Bear witness also at Rome.* This had been the object of his earnest wish (Rom. i. 10; xv. 23, 24), and this promise of the Lord Jesus was fulfilled. ch. xxviii. 30, 31. The promise which was here made to Paul was not *directly* one of deliverance from the present persecution, but it *implied* that, and made it certain.

12. *Certain of the Jews.* Some of the Jews. They were more than forty in number. ver. 13. ¶ *Banded together.* Made an agreement, or compact. They conspired to kill him. ¶ *And bound themselves under a curse.* See the margin. The Greek is, "they anathematized them selves;" that is, they bound themselves by a solemn oath. They invoked a curse on themselves, or devoted themselves to destruction, if they did not do it. Lightfoot remarks, however, that they could be absolved from this vow by the Rabbins, if they were unable to execute it Under various pretences they could easily be freed from such oaths, and it was common to take them; and if there was any difficulty in fulfilling them, they could easily apply to their religious teachers and be absolved. ¶ *That they would neither eat nor drink.* That is, that they would do it as soon as possible. This was a common form of an oath, or curse, among the Jews. Sometimes they only vowed abstinence from particular things, as from meat, or wine. But in this case, to make the oath more certain, and binding, they vowed abstinence from all kinds of food and drink till they had killed him. Who these were—whether they were Sadducees or not—is not mentioned by the sacred writer. It is evident, however, that the minds of the Jews were greatly inflamed against Paul;

neither eat nor drink [a] till they had
killed Paul.
13 And they were more than
forty which had made this conspiracy.
14 And they came to the chief
[b] priests and elders, and said, We
have bound ourselves under a great
curse, that we will eat nothing until
we have slain Paul.
15 Now therefore ye, with the
council, signify to the chief captain
that he bring him down unto you
to-morrow, as though ye would inquire
something more perfectly
concerning him: and we, or ever
he come near, are ready [c] to kill
him.
16 And when Paul's sister's son
heard of their lying in wait, he
[d] went and entered into the castle,
and told Paul.

a Ps.31.13. b Hos.4.9. c Ps.21.11; 37.32,33. d 2Sam.17.17.

and as they saw him in the custody of the Roman tribune, and as there was no prospect that *he* would punish him, they resolved to take the matter into their own hands. Michaelis conjectures that they were of the number of the *Sicarii*, or cut-throats, with which Judea then abounded. See Note on ch. xxi. 38. It is needless to remark that this was a most wicked oath. It was a deliberate purpose to commit murder; and it shows the desperate state of morals among the Jews at that time, and the infuriated malice of the people against the apostle.

13. *Which had made this conspiracy.* This oath (συνωμοσίαν), this agreement, or compact. This large number of desperate men, bound by so solemn an oath, would be likely to be successful; and the life of Paul was therefore in peculiar danger. The manner in which they purposed to accomplish their design is stated in ver. 15.

14. *And they came*, &c. Probably by a deputation. ¶ *To the chief priests and elders.* The members of the great council, or sanhedrim It is probable that the application was made to the party of the Sadducees, as the Pharisees had shown their determination to defend Paul. They would have had no prospect of success had they attacked the castle, and they, therefore, devised this ingenious mode of obtaining access to Paul, where they might easily despatch him. ¶ *Under a great curse.* Greek, "We have anathematized ourselves with an anathema." We have made the vow as solemn as possible.

15. *Ye, with the council.* With the concurrence or request of the sanhedrim. It was only by such a request that they had any hope that the chief captain would remove Paul from the castle. ¶ *Signify to the chief captain.* Send a message or request to him. ¶ *That he bring him down unto you.* That he bring him from the castle to the usual place of the meeting of the sanhedrim. As this was at some distance from the castle, or tower of Antonia, where Paul was, they supposed it would be easy to waylay him, and take his life. ¶ *To-morrow.* This is wanting in the Syriac, Vulgate, and Ethiopic versions. It is, however, probably the correct reading of the text, as it would be necessary to convene the council, and make the request of the tribune, which might require the whole of one day. ¶ *As though ye would inquire*, &c. This request appeared so reasonable that they did not doubt that the tribune would grant it to the council. And though it was obviously a false and wicked pretence, yet these conspirators knew the character of the persons to whom they addressed themselves so well, that they did not doubt that they would prevail on the council to make the request. Public justice must have been deeply fallen, when it was known that such an iniquitous request could be made with the certain prospect of success. ¶ *Or ever he come near.* Before he comes near to the sanhedrim. The great council will thus not be suspected of being privy to the deed. We will waylay him, and murder him *in the way.* The plan was well laid; and nothing but the interposition of Providence could have prevented its execution.

16. *Paul's sister's son.* This is all we know of the family of Paul. Nor do we know for what purpose he was at Jerusalem. It is possible that Paul might have a sister residing there; though, as Paul had been sent there formerly for his education, it seems more probable that this young man was sent there for the same purpose. ¶ *Entered into the castle.* Paul had the privileges of a Roman citizen, and as no well-founded charge had been laid against him, it is probable that he was not very closely confined, and that his friends might have free access to him.

17 Then [a] Paul called one of the centurions unto *him*, and said, Bring this young man unto the chief captain; for he hath a certain thing to tell him.

18 So he took him, and brought *him* to the chief captain, and said, Paul the prisoner [b] called me unto *him*, and prayed me to bring this young man unto thee, who hath something to say unto thee.

19 Then the chief captain took him by the hand, and went *with him* aside privately, and asked *him*, What is that thou hast to tell me?

20 And he said, The Jews have [c] agreed to desire thee that thou wouldest bring down Paul to-morrow into the council, as though they would inquire somewhat of him more perfectly.

21 But do not thou yield [d] unto them: for there lie in wait for him of them more than forty men, which have bound themselves with an oath, that they will neither eat nor drink till they have killed him: and now are they ready, looking for a promise from thee.

22 So the chief captain *then* let the young man depart, and charged *him*, *See thou* tell no man that thou hast showed these things to me.

23 And he called unto *him* two centurions, saying, Make ready two hundred soldiers to go to Cesarea, and horsemen threescore and ten,

a Prov.22.3. Matt.10.16. b c.28.17. Eph.3.1; 4.1. Phil.9. c ver.12. d Ex.23.2.

17. *Called one of the centurions.* Who might at that time have had special charge of the castle, or been on guard. Paul had the most positive assurance that his life would be spared, and that he would yet see Rome; but he always understood the divine promises and purposes as being consistent with his own efforts, and with all proper measures of prudence and diligence in securing his own safety. He did not rest merely on the divine promise without any effort of his own; but he took encouragement from those promises to put forth his own exertions for security and for salvation.

18. *And prayed me.* And asked me.

19. *Took him by the hand.* As an expression of kindness and civility. He did it to draw him aside from the multitude, that he might communicate his message privately.

20. *And he said, &c.* In what way this young man had received intelligence of this, we can only conjecture. It is not improbable that he was a student under some one of the Jewish teachers, and that he might have learned it of him. It is not at all probable that the purpose of the forty men would be very closely kept. Indeed it is evident that *they* were not themselves very anxious about concealing their oath, as they mentioned it fully to the chief priests and elders. ver. 14.

21. *Waiting for a promise from thee.* Waiting for your consent to bring him down to them.

23. *And he called unto him two centurions, &c.* Each centurion had under him one hundred men. The chief captain resolved to place Paul beyond the power of the Jews, and to protect him as became a Roman citizen. ¶ *Two hundred soldiers.* These foot-soldiers were designed only to guard Paul till he was safely out of Jerusalem. The horsemen only were intended to accompany him to Cesarea. See ver. 32. ¶ *And horsemen.* These were commonly attached to foot-soldiers. In this case, however, they were designed to attend Paul to Cesarea. ¶ *And spearmen.* Δεξιολάβους. This word is found nowhere else in the New Testament, and occurs in no classic writer. It properly means *those who take, or apprehend by the right hand;* and might be applied to those who *apprehend prisoners*, or to those who hold a spear or dart in the right hand for the purpose of throwing it. Some have conjectured that it should be read δεξιοβόλους—those who cast or throw [a spear] with the right hand. So the Vulgate, the Syriac, and the Arabic understand it. They were probably those who were armed with spears or darts, and who attended on the tribune as a guard. ¶ *At the third hour of the night.* At nine o'clock. This was in order that it might be done with secrecy, and to elude the band of desperadoes that had resolved to murder Paul. If it should seem that this guard was very numerous for one man, it should be remembered, (1.) That the number of those who had conspired against him was also large, and

and spearmen two hundred, at the third hour of the night;

24 And provide *them* beasts, that they may set Paul on, and bring *him* safe unto Felix the governor.

25 And he wrote a letter after this manner:

26 Claudius Lysias unto the most excellent governor Felix *sendeth* greeting.

27 This man [a] was taken of the Jews, and should have been killed of them: then came I with an army, and rescued him, having understood that he was a Roman.

28 And [b] when I would have known the cause wherefore they accused him, I brought him forth into their council:

29 Whom I perceived to be accused of questions [c] of their law, but to have nothing [d] laid to his charge worthy of death or of bonds

30 And when [e] it was told me, how that the Jews laid wait for the man, I sent straightway to thee, and gave [f] commandment to his accusers also, to say before thee what *they had* against him. Farewell.

31 Then the soldiers, as it was commanded them, took Paul, and brought *him* by night to Antipatris.

32 On the morrow they left the horsemen to go with him, and returned to the castle:

33 Who, when they came to Cesarea, and delivered the epistle [g] to the governor, presented Paul also before him.

34 And when the governor had read *the letter*, he asked of what

a c.21.33; 24.7. b c.22.30. c c.18.15; 25.19. d c.26.31. e ver. 20,21. f 24. 8; 25.6. g ver.25–30.

(2.) That they were men accustomed to scenes of blood, of desperate characters, and who had solemnly sworn that they would take his life. In order, therefore, to deter them effectually from attacking the guard, it was made very numerous and strong, and nearly five hundred men were appointed to guard Paul as he left Jerusalem.

24. *And provide them beasts.* One for Paul, and one for each of his attendants. The word translated *beasts* (κτήνη) is of a general character, and may be applied either to horses, to camels, or to asses. The latter were most commonly employed in Judea. ¶ *Unto Felix the governor.* The governor of Judea. His place of residence was Cesarea, about sixty miles from Jerusalem. See Note, ch. viii. 40. His name was Antonius Felix, and was a freedman of Antonia, the mother of the emperor Claudius. He was high in the favour of Claudius, and was made by him governor of Judea. Josephus calls him Claudius Felix. He had married three wives in succession that were of royal families, one of whom was Drusilla, afterwards mentioned in ch. xxiv. 24. who was sister to king Agrippa. Tacitus (Hist. v. 9) says, that he governed with all the authority of a king, and the baseness and insolence of a slave. "He was an unrighteous governor, a base, mercenary, and bad man." (*Clarke.*) See his character further described in the Note on ch. xxiv. 25.

26. *Unto the most excellent governor Felix.* The most honoured, &c. This was a mere title of office ¶ *Greeting.* A term of salutation in an epistle wishing health, joy, and prosperity.

27. *Should have been killed of them.* Was about to be killed by them. The life of Paul had been twice endangered in this manner. ch. xxi. 30; xxiii. 10. ¶ *With an army.* With a band of soldiers. ver. 10.

29. *Questions of their law.* So he understood the whole controversy to be. ¶ *Worthy of death.* By the Roman law. He had been guilty of no crime against the Roman people. ¶ *Or of bonds.* Of chains, or of confinement.

31. *To Antipatris.* This town was anciently called Cafar-Saba. Josephus says (Antiq. xiii. 23.), that it was about seventeen miles from Joppa. It was about twenty-six miles from Cesarea, and of course about thirty-five from Jerusalem. Herod the Great changed its name to Antipatris, in honour of his father Antipater. It was situated in a fine plain, and watered with many springs and fountains.

32. *They left the horsemen.* As they were then beyond the danger of the conspirators, the soldiers who had guarded them thus far returned to Jerusalem

34. *Of what province he was.* Greek.

province he was. And when he
understood that *he was* of Cilicia; [a]
35 I will hear thee, said he, when
thine accusers [b] are also come. And
he commanded him to be kept in [c]
Herod's judgment-hall.

CHAPTER XXIV.

AND after five days, Ananias [d]
the high-priest descended with
the elders, and *with* a certain orator
named Tertullus, who informed
the governor against Paul.
2 And when he was called forth,
Tertullus began to accuse *him*, saying, Seeing that by thee we enjoy
great quietness, and that very worthy
deeds [f] are done unto this nation by
thy providence,
3 We accept *it* always, and in all
places, most noble Felix, with all
thankfulness.

a c.21.39. b c.24.1,&c. 25.16. c Matt.27.27. d c.23.2;25.2. e Ps.11.2. f Ps.12.2.

Of what eparchy (ἐπαρχίας) he was. He knew from the letter of Lysias that he was a Roman, but he was not informed of what place or province he was. This he doubtless did in order to ascertain whether he properly belonged to his jurisdiction. Roman provinces were districts of country which were intrusted to the jurisdiction of procurators. How far the jurisdiction of Felix extended is not certainly known. It appears, however, that it included Cilicia. ¶ *Was of Cilicia.* Tarsus, the birth-place of Paul, was in this province. ch. xxi. 39.

35. *In Herod's judgment-hall.* Greek, In the pretorium of Herod. The word here used denoted formerly the *tent* of the Roman prætor; and as that was the place where justice was administered, it came to be applied to halls, or courts of justice. This had been reared probably by Herod the Great as his palace, or as a place for administering justice. It is probable also, that prisons, or places of security, would be attached to such places.

CHAPTER XXIV.

1. *And after five days.* This time was occupied, doubtless, in their receiving the command to go to Cesarea, and in making the necessary arrangements. This was the twelfth day after his arrival at Jerusalem. See ver. 11. ¶ *Ananias, the high-priest.* See Note, ch. xxiii. 2. ¶ *Descended.* Came down from Jerusalem. This was the usual language when a departure from Jerusalem was spoken of. See Note, ch. xv. 1. ¶ *With a certain orator named Tertullus.* Appointed to accuse Paul. This is a Roman name, and this man was doubtless a Roman. As the Jews were, to a great extent, ignorant of the Roman customs and laws, and of their mode of administering justice, it is not improbable that they were in the habit of employing Roman lawyers to plead their causes. ¶ *Who informed the governor against Paul.* Who acted as the accuser, or who managed their cause before the governor.

2. *And when he was called forth.* When Paul was called forth from prison. See ch xxiii. 35. ¶ *We enjoy great quietness.* This was said in the customary style of flatterers and orators, to conciliate his favour, and is strikingly in contrast with the more honest, and straightforward introduction in the reply of Paul. ver. 10. Though it was said for flattery, and though Felix was in many respects an unprincipled man, yet it was true that his administration had been the means of producing much peace and order in Judea, and that he had done many things that tended to promote their welfare. In particular, he had arrested a band of robbers, with Eleazar at their head, whom he had sent to Rome to be punished (Jos. Ant. b. xx ch. viii.); he had arrested the Egyptian false prophet, who had led out four thousand men into the wilderness, and who threatened the peace of Judea (see Note, ch. xxi. 38); and he had repressed a sedition which arose between the inhabitants of Cesarea and of Syria. Jos. Jewish Wars, b. ii. ch. xiii. § 2. ¶ *Very worthy deeds.* Acts that tended much to promote the peace and security of the people. He referred to those which have just been mentioned as having been accomplished by Felix, particularly his success in suppressing riots and seditions; and as, in the view of the Jews, the case of Paul was another instance of a similar kind, he appealed to him with the more confidence that he would suppress that also. ¶ *By thy providence.* By thy foresight, skill, vigilance, prudence.

3. *We accept it always.* We *admit* that it is owing to your vigilance, and we accept your interposition to promote peace, with gratitude. ¶ *Always, and in all places.* Not merely in your presence, but we always acknowledge that it is owing to your vigilance that the land is secure,

4 Notwithstanding, that I be not further tedious unto thee, I pray thee that thou wouldest hear us of thy clemency a few words.
5 For we have found this man *a* pestilent *fellow*, [a] and a mover of sedition among all the Jews throughout the world, and a ringleader of the sect of the Nazarenes.
6 Who also hath gone about to profane [b] the temple: whom we took, and would have judged [c] according to our law:
7 But the chief [d] captain Lysias came *upon us*, and with great violence took *him* away out of our hands,
8 Commanding his accusers [e] to come unto thee: by examining of whom, thyself mayest take knowledge of all these things whereof we accuse him.

a Luke 23.2. c.6.13; 16.20; 17.6; 21.28. 1Pet.2.12.19. *b* c.19.37; 21.28.

c Jno.13.31. *d* c.21.33. *e* c.23.30.

"What we now do in your presence, we do also in your absence; we do not commend you merely when you are present." (*Wetstein.*) ¶ *Most noble Felix.* This was the title of office. ¶ *With thankfulness.* In this, there was probably sincerity, for there was no doubt that the peace of Judea was owing to Felix. But at the same time that he was an energetic and vigilant governor, it was also true that he was proud, and avaricious, and cruel. Josephus charges him with injustice and cruelty in the case of Jonathan, the high-priest (Ant. b. xx. ch. viii. § 5); and Tacitus (Hist. b. v. ch. 9), and Suetonius (Life of Claudius, ch. 28), concur in the charge.

4. *Be not further tedious unto thee.* By taking up your time with an introduction, and with commendation.

5. *We have found this man a pestilent* fellow. Λοιμὸν. This word is commonly applied to a plague, or pestilence, and then to a man who corrupts the morals of others, or who is turbulent, and an exciter of sedition. Our translation somewhat weakens the force of the original expression. Tertullus did not say that he was a pestilent fellow, but that he was *the very pestilence itself.* In this he referred to their belief, that he had been the cause of extensive disturbances every where among the Jews. ¶ *And a mover of sedition.* An exciter of tumult. This they pretended he did by preaching doctrines contrary to the laws and customs of Moses, and exciting the Jews to tumult and disorder. ¶ *Throughout the world.* Throughout the Roman empire, and thus leading the Jews to violate the laws, and to produce tumults, riots, and disorder. ¶ *And a ringleader.* Πρωτοστάτην. This word occurs nowhere else in the New Testament. It is properly a military word, and denotes one who stands first in an army, a standard-bearer, a leader, or commander. The meaning is, that Paul had been so active, and so prominent in preaching the gospel, that he had been a leader or the principal person in extending the sect of the Nazarenes. ¶ *Of the sect.* The original word here (αἱρέσεως) is the word from which we have derived the term *heresy.* It is, however, properly translated *sect,* or *party,* and should have been so translated in ver. 14. See Note, ch. v. 17. ¶ *Of the Nazarenes.* This was the name usually given to Christians by way of contempt. They were so called because Jesus was of Nazareth.

6. *Who also hath gone about.* Who has endeavoured. ¶ *To profane the temple.* This was a serious, but unfounded charge. It arose from the gross calumny of the apostle, when they pretended that he had introduced Greeks into that sacred place. ch. xxi. 28. To this charge the apostle replies in ver. 18. ¶ *And would have judged.* That is, would have condemned and punished. ¶ *According to our law.* Their law, which forbade the introduction of strangers into the temple.

7. *But the chief captain, &c.* Tertullus pretends that they would have judged Paul righteously, if Lysias had not interposed; but the truth was, that without regard to law or justice, they would have murdered him on the spot.

8. *Commanding his accusers, &c* ch. xxiii. 30. ¶ *By examining of whom.* That is, the Jews who were then present. Tertullus presented them as his witnesses of the truth of what he had said. It is evident that we have here only the summary or outline of the speech which Tertullus made. It is incredible that a Roman rhetorician would have, on such an occasion, delivered an address so brief, so meagre, and so destitute of display as this. But it is doubtless a correct summary of his address, and contains the leading points of the accusation. It is customary for the sacred writers, as for other writers, to give only the outline of discourses

9 And the Jews also assented,
saying that these things were so.
10 Then Paul, after that the [1]
governor had beckoned unto him to
speak, answered, Forasmuch as I
know that thou hast been of many
years a judge unto this nation, I
do the more cheerfully answer [a] for
myself:
11 Because that thou mayest

1 *Felix*, made Procurator over *Judea*, A. D. 53

a 1Pet.3.15

and arguments. Such a course was inevitable, unless the New Testament had been swelled to wholly undue proportions.

9. *And the Jews also assented.* The Jews who had accompanied Tertullus to Cesarea. They had gone as the accusers of Paul, and they bore testimony, when called upon, to the truth of all that the orator had said. Whether they were examined individually or not, is not declared. In whatever way their testimony was arrived at, they confirmed unanimously the accusation which he had brought against Paul.

10. *Had beckoned unto him to speak.* Either by a nod or by the hand. ¶ *Hast been of many years.* Felix and Cumanus had been joint-governors of Judea; but after Cumanus had been condemned for his bad administration of the affairs, the government fell entirely into the hands of Felix. This was about seven years before Paul was arraigned before him, and might be called *many years*, as he had been long enough there to become acquainted with the customs and habits of the Jews; and it might also be called *long* in comparison with the short time which any of his immediate predecessors had held the office. See Josephus, Ant. b. xx. ch. vi, vii. ¶ *A judge.* This word is evidently used here in the sense of *magistrate*, or one appointed to administer the affairs of government. To determine litigated matters was, however, one part of his office. It is remarkable that Paul did not begin his speech as Tertullus had done, by any flattering address, or by any of the arts of rhetoric. He founded his plea on the justice of his cause, and on the fact, that Felix had had so much experience in the affairs of Judea that he was well qualified to understand the merits of the case, and to judge impartially. Paul was well acquainted with his character (see Note, ch. xxiv 25), and would not by flattering words declare that which was not strictly true. ¶ *I do the more cheerfully,* &c. Since you are so well acquainted with the customs and habits of the Jews, I the more readily submit the case to your disposal. This address indicated great confidence in the justice of his cause; and was the language of a man, bold fearless, and conscious of his innocence

11. *Because that thou mayest understand.* Gr. 'Thou being able to know. That is, he could understand or know, by taking the proper evidence. Paul does not mean to say that Felix could understand the case, *because* he had been many years a judge of that nation. That fact would qualify him to judge correctly, or to understand the customs of the Jews. But the fact, that he had been but twelve days in Jerusalem, and had been orderly and peaceable there, Felix could ascertain only by the proper testimony. The first part of Paul's defence (ver. 11—13) consists in an express denial of what they alleged against him. ¶ *Are yet but twelve days.* Beza reckons these twelve days in this manner: The first was that on which he came to Jerusalem. ch. xxi. 15. The second he spent with James and the apostles. ch. xxi. 18. Six days were spent in fulfilling his vow. ch. xxi. 21. 26 On the ninth day the tumult arose, being the seventh day of his vow, and on this day he was rescued by Lysias. ch. xxi 27; xxii. 29. The tenth day he was before the sanhedrim. ch. xxii. 30; xxiii. 10. On the eleventh the plot was laid to take his life, and on the same day, at evening, he was removed to Cesarea. The days on which he was confined at Cesarea are not enumerated, since his design in mentioning the number of days was, to show the improbability that, in that time, he had been engaged in producing a tumult; and it would not be pretended that he had been so engaged while confined in a prison at Cesarea. The defence of Paul here is, that but twelve days occurred from the time that he went to Jerusalem till he was put under the custody of Felix; and that during *so short a time* it was wholly improbable that he would have been able to excite sedition. ¶ *For to worship.* This farther shows that the design of Paul was not to produce sedition. He had gone up for the peaceful purpose of devotion, and not to produce riot and disorder. That this was his design in going to Jerusalem, or at least a part of his purpose, is indicated by the passage in Acts xx. 16. It should be observed, however, that our translation con

understand that there are yet but
twelve days since I went up to [a]
Jerusalem for to worship.
12 And they neither [b] found me
in the temple disputing with any
man, neither raising up the people,
neither in the synagogues, nor in
the city.

a c.21.15. b c.25.8; 28.17.

13 Neither can they prove [c] the
things whereof they now accuse me.
14 But this I confess unto thee,
that after the way which they call
heresy, so [d] worship I the God of
[e] my fathers, believing all things
which are [f] written in the law and
[g] the prophets;

c 1Pet.3.16. d Mic.4.5. e 2Tim.1.3. f Luke 24.27. c.26.22; 28.23. g Matt.22 40. Luke 16.16 Jno.1.45. c.13.15. Rom.3.21.

veys an idea which is not necessarily in the Greek—that this was the *design* of his going to Jerusalem. The original is, 'Since I went up to Jerusalem *worshipping*' (προσκυνήσων); i. e. he was actually *engaged* in devotion when the tumult arose. But his main design in going to Jerusalem was, to convey to his suffering countrymen there the benefactions of the Gentile churches. See ver. 17. Rom. xv. 25, 26.

12. *And they neither found me*, &c. The first charge of Tertullus against Paul was (ver. 5), that he was "a pestilent fellow, and a mover of sedition." The charge of his being *a pest* was so general, that Paul did not think it necessary to attempt to refute it. To the *specification*, that he was a mover of sedition, he replies by a firm denial, and by a solemn declaration that they had not found him in any synagogue, or in the city, or in the temple, either disputing or exciting a tumult. His conduct there had been entirely peaceable; and they had no right to suppose that it had been otherwise any where.

13. *Neither can they prove the things*, &c. That is, that I am a mover of sedition, or a disturber of the peace of the people. This appeal he boldly makes; he challenges investigation; and as they did not offer to specify any acts of disorder or tumult excited by him, this charge falls of course.

14. *But this I confess*, &c. The next specification in the charge of Tertullus was (ver. 5), that he was "a ringleader of the sect of the Nazarenes." To this, Paul replies in this, and the two following verses. Of this reply we may observe, (1.) That he does not stoop to notice the contempt implied in the use of the word *Nazarenes*. He was engaged in a more important business than to contend about the *name* which they chose to give to Christians. (2.) He admits that he belonged to that sect or class of people. That he was a Christian, he neither denied, nor was disposed to deny. (3.) He maintains that in this way he is still worshipping the God of his fathers. Of this, the fact that he was engaged in worship *in the temple*, was sufficient proof. (4.) He shows them that he believed only what was written in the law and the prophets; that this involved the main doctrine of their religion—the hope of the resurrection of the dead (ver. 15); and that it was his constant and earnest desire to keep a pure conscience in all things. ver 16. These are the points of his defence to this second charge, and we shall see that they fully meet and dispose of the accusation. ¶ *After the way*. After the manner or mode of worship. ¶ *Which they call heresy*. This translation does not express to us the force of the original. We have attached to the word *heresy* an idea which is not conveyed by the Greek word, and now commonly understand by it, *error of doctrine*. In Paul's answer here, there is an explicit reference to their charge, which does not appear in our version. The charge of Tertullus was, that he was the ringleader *of the sect* (τῆς αἱρέσεως) of the Nazarenes. ver. 5. To this, Paul replies, 'After the way which they call *sect* (αἵρεσιν, not *error of doctrine*, but after a way which they maintain is producing *division* or *schism*) so worship I the God of my fathers.' Paul was not ashamed to be called a follower of that *sect* or *party* among the Jewish people. Nor should we be ashamed to worship God in a mode that is called *heresy* or *schism*, if we do it in obedience to conscience and to God. ¶ *So worship I*. I continue to worship. I have not departed from the characteristic of the Jewish people, the proper and public acknowledgment of the God of the Jews. ¶ *The God of my fathers*. My fathers' God, Jehovah; the God whom my Jewish ancestors adored. There is something very touching in this, and fitted to find its way to the heart of a Jew. He had introduced no new object of worship (comp. Deut. xiii. 1—5); he had not become a follower of a false or foreign God; and *this* fact

15 And have hope [a] toward God, which they themselves also allow, that there shall be a resurrection [b] of the dead, both of the just and unjust.
16 And herein do I exercise myself, to have [c] always a conscience void of offence toward God and *toward* men.
17 Now after many years, I came [d] to bring alms to my nation, and offerings.

a c.23.6,&c. 26.6,7; 28.20,&c. b Dan.12.2. Jno.5. 28,29. 1Cor.15.12-27. Rom.20.6,13. c c.23.1. d c.11.29,30; 20.16. Rom.15.25

was really a reply to their charge, that he was setting up a new *sect* in religion. The same thing Paul affirms of himself in 2 Tim. i. 3: "I thank God, whom I serve from my forefathers with a pure conscience." ¶ *Believing all things*, &c. Particularly respecting the Messiah. So he more fully explains his meaning in his speech before king Agrippa. ch. xxvi. 23. ¶ *In the law and in the prophets.* Commanded in the law of Moses, and foretold by the prophets. That Paul had ever disbelieved any of these things, they could not prove; and his whole course had shown that he fully credited the sacred records. Most of his arguments in defending Christianity had been drawn from the Jewish writings.

15. *And have hope toward God.* Having a hope of the resurrection of the dead, which arises from the promises of God. ¶ *Which they themselves*, &c. That is, the Pharisees. Perhaps he designated in this remark the Pharisees who were present. He held nothing in this great cardinal point, which they did not also hold. For the reasons why Paul introduced this point so prominently, and the success of thus introducing it, see Note on ch. xxiii. 1—9. ¶ *Both of the just, and of the unjust.* Of the righteous and the wicked; that is, of all the race. As *they* held this, they could not arraign him for holding it also.

16. *And herein.* In this, or for this purpose. ¶ *Do I exercise myself.* Ἀσκῶ. I accustom or employ myself; I make it my constant aim and endeavour. It is the purpose of my constant study. Paul often appeals to his conscientiousness as the leading habit of his life. Even before his conversion he endeavoured to act according to the dictates of conscience. See Acts xxvi. 9. Comp. Phil. iii. 5, 6. ¶ *To have always a conscience*, &c. To do that which is right, so that my conscience shall approve of it, and never reproach me. ¶ *Void of offence.* Ἀπρόσκοπον. That which is inoffensive, or which does not cause one to stumble or fall. He means, that he endeavoured to keep his conscience so enlightened and pure in regard to duty, and that he acted according to its dictates in such a way that his conduct should not be displeasing to God, or injurious to man. To have such a conscience implies two things: (1.) That it be enlightened or properly informed in regard to truth and duty; and, (2.) That that which is made known to be right should be honestly and faithfully performed. Without these two things, no man can have a conscience that shall be inoffensive and harmless. ¶ *Toward God.* In an honest endeavour to discharge all the duties of public and private worship, and to do constantly what he requires. In believing all that he has spoken; doing all that he requires; and offering to him the service which he approves. ¶ *Toward men.* In endeavouring to meet all the demands of justice and mercy; to advance their knowledge, happiness, and salvation; so that I may look back on my life with the reflection that I have done all that I *ought* to have done, and all that I *could* do, to promote the welfare of the whole human family. What a noble principle of conduct was this! How devoted, and how pure! How unlike the conduct of those who live to gratify debasing sensual appetites, or for gold or honour; and who pass their lives in such a manner as to offer the grossest offence to God, and to do the most injury to man! The great and noble aim of Paul was to be pure; and no slander of his enemies, no trials, persecutions, or perils, and no pains of dying could take away the approving voice of conscience. Alike in his travels, and in his persecutions; among friends and foes; when preaching in the synagogue, the city, or the desert; or when defending himself before governors and kings, he had this testimony of a self-approving mind. Happy they who thus frame their lives. And happy will be the end of a life where this has been the grand object of the journey through this world.

17. *Now after many years.* After many years absence. Paul here commences a reply to the charges of Tertullus, that he had endeavoured to profane the temple. ver 6 He begins, by saying that his

18 Whereupon certain Jews from
Asia found me purified in the temple,
neither with multitude, nor
with tumult:
19 Who ought to have been here
[a] before thee, and object, if they
had aught against me.
20 Or else let these same *here*
say, if they have found any evil-doing
in me, while I stood before
the council;
21 Except it be for this one voice,
that I cried standing among them,
Touching the resurrection of the
dead, I am called in question by
you this day.
22 And when Felix heard these
things, having more perfect know-

a c.25.16.

design in coming up to Jerusalem was, to bring to them needed aid in a time of distress. It would be absurd to suppose, therefore, that his object in coming was to violate the customs of the temple, and to defile it. ¶ *I came to bring.* See ch. xi. 29, 30. Note, Rom. xv. 25, 26. ¶ *Alms.* Charities; the gift of the churches. ¶ *To my nation.* Not to *all* the nation; but to the poor saints or Christians who were in Judea, and who were suffering much by persecutions and trials. ¶ *And offerings.* The word used here properly denotes an offering or gift of any kind; but it is usually applied to an oblation, or offering made to God in the temple—a thank-offering, a sacrifice. This is probably its meaning here. He came to bring aid *to his needy countrymen,* and *an offering to God;* and it was, therefore, no part of his purpose to interfere with, or to profane the worship of the temple.

18. *Certain Jews from Asia.* ch. xxi. 27. ¶ *Found me purified in the temple.* ch. xxi. 26, 27. They found me engaged in the sacred service of completing the observance of my vow. ¶ *Neither with multitude.* Not having introduced a multitude with me—in a quiet and peaceful manner.

19. *Who ought to have been here,* &c. They were the proper witnesses; as they had staved away, it showed that they were not prepared to undergo a strict examination. Paul, therefore, justly complains that the very persons who alone *could* testify against him were absent, and showed that there was really no well-founded charge against him. They alone could testify as to any thing that occurred in the temple; and as *they* were not present, that charge ought to be dismissed.

20. *Or else.* Since they are not here to witness against me in regard to what occurred in the *temple,* let these here present bear witness against me, if they can, in regard to *any other part* of my conduct. This was a bold appeal, and it showed his full consciousness of innocence. ¶ *Let these same here say.* The Jews who are here present. ¶ *Any evil-doing.* Any improper conduct, or any violation of the law. ¶ *While I stood before the council.* The sanhedrim. ch xxiii. 1—10. As they were present there Paul admits that they were competent to bear witness to his conduct on that occasion; and calls upon them to testify, if they could, to any impropriety in his conduct.

21. *Except it be for this one voice.* For this one expression, or declaration. This was what Paul had said before the council—the *main* thing on which he had insisted, and he calls on them to testify to this, and to show, if they could, that in this declaration he had been wrong. Chubb, and other infidels have supposed that Paul here acknowledges that he was *wrong* in the declaration which he made, when he said, that he was called in question for the doctrine of the resurrection of the dead (ch. xxiii. 6), and his conscience reproached him for appearing to be time-serving, and for concealing the true cause of offence against him; and for attempting to take advantage of their divisions of sentiment, and endeavouring to produce discord in the council. But against this interpretation we may urge the following considerations: (1.) Paul wished to fix their attention on the *main* thing which he had said before the council. (2.) It was true, as has been shown on the passage (xxiii. 1—10), that this was the principal doctrine which Paul had been defending. 3.) If they were prepared to witness against him for holding and teaching the resurrection of the dead as a false or evil doctrine, he called on them to do it. As this had been the *only* thing which they had witnessed before the council, he calls on them to testify to what they knew only, and to show, if they could, that this was wrong. ¶ *Touching the resurrection,* &c. Respecting the resurrection. ch. xxiii. 6.

22. *Having more perfect knowledge of that way.* Our translation of this verse

ledge of *that* way, he deferred them, and said, When Lysias [a] the chief captain shall come down, I will know the uttermost of your matter.

23 And he commanded a centurion to keep Paul, and to let *him* have liberty, [b] and that he should forbid none of his acquaintance to minister or to come unto him.

24 And after certain days, when Felix came with his wife Drusilla,

a ver.7.

b c.27.3; 28.16.

is very obscure, and critics are divided about the proper interpretation of the original. Many (Erasmus, Luther, Michaelis, Morus, &c.) render it, 'although he had a more perfect knowledge of the Christian doctrine than Paul's accusers had, yet he deferred the hearing of the cause till Lysias had come down.' They observe that he might have obtained this knowledge, not only from the letter of Lysias, but from public rumour, as there were doubtless Christians at Cesarea. They suppose that he deferred the cause, either with the hope of receiving a bribe from Paul (comp. ver. 26), or to gratify the Jews with his being longer detained as a prisoner. Others, among whom are Beza, Grotius, Rosenmuller, and Doddridge, suppose that it should be rendered, 'he deferred them, and said, after I have been more accurately informed concerning this way, when Lysias has come down, I will hear the cause.' This is doubtless the true interpretation of the passage, and it is rendered more probable by the fact that Felix sent for Paul, and heard him concerning the faith of Christ (ver. 24), evidently with a design to make himself better acquainted with the charges against him, and the nature of his belief. ¶ *Of that way.* Of the Christian religion. This expression is repeatedly used by Luke to denote the Christian doctrine. Note, ch. ix. 2. ¶ *He deferred them.* He put them off; he postponed the decision of the case; he adjourned the trial. ¶ *When Lysias, &c.* Lysias had been acquainted with the excitement and its causes, and Felix regarded him as an important witness in regard to the true nature of the charges against Paul. ¶ *I will know the uttermost, &c.* I shall be fully informed and prepared to decide the cause.

23. *And he commanded, &c.* It is evident from this verse, that Felix was disposed to show Paul all the favours that were consistent with his safe keeping. He esteemed him to be a persecuted man, and doubtless regarded the charges against him as entirely malicious. What was Felix's *motive* in this cannot be certainly known. It is not improbable, however, that he detained him, (1.) To gratify the Jews by keeping him in custody as if he were guilty; and, (2.) That he hoped the friends of Paul would give him money to release him. Perhaps it was for this purpose that he gave orders that his friends should have free access to him, that thus Paul might be furnished with the means of purchasing his freedom.

24. *Felix came, with his wife Drusilla.* Drusilla was the daughter of Herod Agrippa the elder, and was engaged to be married to Epiphanes, the son of king Antiochus, on condition that he would embrace the Jewish religion; but as he afterwards refused to do that, the contract was broken off. Afterwards she was given in marriage, by her brother Agrippa the younger, to Azizus king of Emesa, upon his consent to be circumcised. When Felix was governor of Judea, he saw Drusilla, and fell in love with her, and sent to her Simon, one of his friends, a Jew, by birth a Cyprian, who pretended to be a magician, to endeavour to persuade her to forsake her husband, and to marry Felix. Accordingly, in order to avoid the envy of her sister Bernice, who treated her ill on account of her beauty, "she was prevailed on," says Josephus, "to transgress the laws of her forefathers, and to marry Felix." Josephus, Antiq. b. xx. ch. vii. § 1, 2. She was, therefore, living in adultery with him, and this was probably the reason why Paul dwelt in his discourse before Felix particularly on "temperance," or chastity. Note, ver. 25. ¶ *He sent for Paul, and heard him.* Perhaps he did this, in order to be more fully acquainted with the case which was submitted to him. It is possible also that it might have been to gratify his wife, who was a Jewess, and who doubtless had a desire to be acquainted with the principles of this new sect. It is certain also that one object which Felix had in this, was to let Paul see how dependent he was on him, and to induce him to purchase his liberty. ¶ *Concerning the faith in Christ.* Concerning the Christian religion. Faith in Christ is

which was a Jewess, he sent for Paul, and heard him concerning the faith in Christ.

25 And as he reasoned of [a] righteousness, temperance, [b] and judgment [c] to come, Felix trembled, [d]

a Prov.16.12. Jer.22.15–17. Dan.4.27. Jno.16.8. b Prov.31.4,5. Dan.5.1–4. Hos.7.5. 1Pet.4.4. c Ps.50.3,4. Dan.12.2. Matt.25.31–46. 2Cor.5.10. Rev.20.12. d Ps.99.1. Is.52.11. Hab.3.16. Heb.4.1,18.

often used to denote the whole of Christianity, as it is the leading and characteristic feature of the religion of the gospel.

25. *And as he reasoned.* Greek, "And he discoursing." Διαλεγομένου δὲ αὐτοῦ. No argument should be drawn from the word that is used here, to prove that Paul particularly appealed to *reason,* or that his discourse was *argumentative.* That it *was* so is, indeed, not improbable, from all that we know of the man, and from the topics on which he discoursed. But the word used here means simply, as he *discoursed,* and is applied usually to making a public address, to preaching, &c. in whatever way it is done. Acts xvii. 2; xviii. 4. 19; xix. 8, 9; xxiv. 12. Felix and Drusilla intended this as a matter of entertainment or amusement. Paul readily obeyed their summons, as it gave him an opportunity to preach the gospel to them; and as they desired his sentiments in regard to the faith in Christ, he selected those topics which were adapted to their condition, and stated those principles of the Christian religion which were fitted to arrest their attention, and lead them to repentance. Paul seized every opportunity of making known the gospel; and whether a prisoner or at liberty; whether before princes, governors, kings, or common people, was equally prepared to defend the pure and holy doctrines of the cross. His boldness in this instance is the more remarkable as he was dependent on Felix for his pardon. A time-server or an impostor would have chosen such topics as would have conciliated the favour of the judge, and procured his pardon. He would have flattered his vanity or palliated his vices. *But such an idea never seems to have occurred to Paul.* His aim was to defend the truth; and to save, if possible, the souls of Drusilla and of Felix. ¶ *Of righteousness.* Περὶ δικαιοσύνης. Of justice. Not of the justice of God particularly, but of the nature and requirements of justice in the relations of life, the relations which we sustain to God and to man. This was a proper topic with which to introduce his discourse, as it was the office of Felix to dispense justice between man and man; and as his administration was not remarkable for the exercise of that virtue. It is evident that he could be influenced by a bribe (ver. 26), and it was proper for Paul to dwell on this as designed to show him the guilt of his life, and his danger of meeting the justice of a Being who cannot be bribed, but who will dispense equal justice alike to the great and the mean. That Paul dwelt also on the *justice* of God, as the moral governor of the world, may also be presumed. The apprehension of *that* justice, and the remembrance of his own guilty life, tended to produce the alarm of Felix, and to make him tremble. ¶ *Temperance.* ἐγκρατείας. The word *temperance* we now use commonly to denote moderation, or restraint in regard to eating and drinking, particularly to abstinence from the use of ardent spirits. But this is not its meaning here. There is no reason to suppose that Felix was *intemperate* in the use of intoxicating liquors. The original word here denotes a restraint of all the passions and evil inclinations; and may be applied to prudence, chastity, and moderation in general. The particular thing in the life of Felix which Paul had probably in view, was the indulgence of licentious desires, or incontinence. He was living in adultery with Drusilla; and for this, Paul wished doubtless to bring him to repentance. ¶ *And judgment to come.* The universal judgment; the judgment that was to come on all transgressors. On this topic Paul also dwelt when he preached before the Areopagus at Athens. Acts xvii. 31. These topics were admirably adapted to excite the alarm of both Felix and Drusilla. It evinced great boldness and faithfulness in Paul to select them; and the result showed that he correctly judged of the kind of truth which was adapted to alarm the fears of his guilty auditor. ¶ *Felix trembled.* In view of his past sins, and in the apprehension of the judgment to come. The Greek (ἔμφοβος) does not denote that his body was agitated or shaken, but only that he was alarmed, or terrified. That such fear usually shakes the frame, we know; but it is not certain that the body of Felix was thus agitated. He was alarmed and terrified; and looked with deep apprehension to the coming judgment. This was a remarkable instance of the effect of truth on the mind of a man unaccustomed to such alarms, and unused to hear such

and answered, Go [a] thy way for this time; when I have a convenient season, I will call for thee.
26 He hoped also that money

a Prov.1.24-32. Matt.22.5; 25.1-10.

b Ex.23.8.

truth. It shows the power of conscience, when thus under the preaching of a *prisoner*, the judge should be thrown into violent alarm. ¶ *And answered, Go thy way*, &c. How different is this answer from that of the jailor of Philippi when alarmed in a similar manner. *He* asked, "what must I do to be saved?" and was directed to him in whom he found peace from a troubled conscience. Acts xvi. 30, 31. Felix was troubled; but instead of asking what he should do, he sent the messenger of God away. He was evidently not prepared to break off his sins, and turn to God. He sought peace by sending away his reprover; and manifestly intended *then* to banish the subject from his mind. Yet, like others, he did not intend to banish it altogether. He looked forward to a time when he should be more at leisure; when the cares of office should press less heavily on his attention; or when he should be more disposed to attend to it. Thus multitudes, when they are alarmed, and see their guilt and danger, resolve to defer it to a more convenient time. One man is engaged in a career of pleasure, and it is not *now* a convenient time to attend to his soul's salvation. Another is pressed with business; with the cares of life; with a plan of gain; with the labours of office, or of a profession, and it is not *now* a convenient time for him to attend to religion. Another supposes that his time of life is not the most convenient. His youth he desires to spend in pleasure, and waits for a more convenient time in middle age. His middle life he spends in business, and the toils of the world, and *this* is not a convenient time. Such a period he expects then to find in old age. But as age advances, he finds an increasing disposition to defer it; he is still indisposed to attend to it; still in love with the world. Even old age is seldom found to be a convenient time to prepare for heaven; and it is deferred from one period of life to another, till death closes the scene.—It has been commonly supposed and said that Felix never found that more convenient time to call for Paul. That he did not embrace the Christian religion, and forsake his sins, is probable, nay, almost certain. But it is not true that he did not take an opportunity of hearing Paul further on the subject; for it is said that he sent for him often, and communed with him. But though Felix found this opportunity, yet (1.) We have no reason to suppose that the *main thing*—the salvation of his soul ever again occupied his attention. There is no evidence that he was again alarmed or awakened, or that he had any further solicitude on the subject of his sins. He had passed for ever the favourable time; the golden moments when he might have secured the salvation of his soul. (2.) Others have no right to suppose that their lives will be lengthened out that they may have *any* further opportunity to attend to the subject of religion. (3.) When a sinner is awakened, and sees his past sins, if he rejects the appeal to his conscience *then*, and defers it to a more convenient opportunity, he has no reason to expect that his attention will ever be again called with deep interest to the subject. He may live; but he may live without the strivings of the Holy Spirit. When a man has once deliberately rejected the offers of mercy; when he has trifled with the influences of the Spirit of God, he has no *right* or *reason* to expect that that Spirit will ever strive with him again. Such, we have too much reason to fear, was the case with Felix. Though he often saw Paul again, and "communed with him," yet there is no account tha he was again alarmed or awakened And thus sinners often attend on the means of grace after they have grieved the Holy Spirit; they listen to the doctrines of the gospel, they hear its appeals, and its warnings, but they have no feeling, no interest; and die in their sins. ¶ *A more convenient time.* Greek, 'Taking time.' I will take a time for this. ¶ *I will call for thee.* To hear thee further on this subject. This he did. ver. 26. It is remarkable that Drusilla was not alarmed. She was as much involved in guilt as Felix; but she, being a Jewess, had been accustomed to hear of a future judgment, until it caused in her mind no alarm. Perhaps also she depended on the rites and ceremonies of her religion as a sufficient expiation for her sins. She might have been resting on those false dependencies which go to free the conscience from a sense of guilt, and which thus beguile and destroy the soul.

26. *He hoped also.* He thought that by giving him access to his friends, and by often meeting him himself, and showing

should have been given him of Paul, that he might loose him: wherefore he sent for him the oftener, and communed with him.

27 But after two years, Porcius Festus came into Felix's room: and Felix, willing to shew [a] the Jews a pleasure, left Paul bound.

CHAPTER XXV.

NOW when Festus was come into the province, after three

a Mark 15.15. c.25.9.

kindness, Paul might be induced to attempt to purchase his freedom with a bribe. ¶ *That money should have been given him of Paul.* That Paul would give him money to procure a release. This shows the character of Felix. He was desirous of procuring a bribe. Paul had proved his innocence, and should have been at once released. But Felix was influenced by avarice; and he therefore detained Paul in custody, with the hope that, wearied with confinement, he would seek his release by a bribe. But Paul offered no bribe. He knew what was justice; and he would not be guilty, therefore, of attempting to purchase what was his due, or of gratifying a man who prostituted his high office for the purpose of gain. The Roman governors in the provinces were commonly rapacious and avaricious, like Felix. They usually took the office for the purpose of its pecuniary advantage, and they consequently usually disregarded justice, and made the procuring of money their leading object. ¶ *He sent for him the oftener.* It may seem remarkable that he did not fear again being alarmed. But the hope of money overcame all this. And having once resisted the reasoning of Paul, and the strivings of the Spirit of God, he seems to have had no further alarm or anxiety. He could again hear the same man, and the same truth, unaffected. When sinners have once grieved God's Spirit, they often sit with unconcern under the same truth which once alarmed them, and become entirely hardened and unconcerned. ¶ *And communed with him.* And conversed with him.

27. *But after two years.* Paul was unjustly detained during all this time. The hope of Felix seems to have been to weary his patience, and induce him to purchase his freedom. ¶ *Came into Felix's room.* As governor. ¶ *And Felix willing to show the Jews a pleasure.* Desirous of pleasing them, even at the expense of justice. This shows the principle on which he acted ¶ *Left Paul bound.* Left him in custody to the charge of his successor. His object in this was to conciliate the Jews; that is, to secure their favour, and to prevent them, if possible, from accusing him for the evils of his administration before the emperor. The account which Luke gives here coincides remarkably with that which Josephus has given. He says, that Porcius Festus was sent as successor to Felix by Nero. He does not indeed mention Paul, or say that Felix sought to conciliate the favour of the Jews. But he gives such an account as to make the statement by Luke *perfectly consistent* with his character while in office. He informs us that Felix was unpopular, and that there was reason to apprehend that the Jews would accuse him before the emperor; and, *therefore,* the statement in the Acts, that he would be willing to show the Jews a favour, is in perfect keeping with his character and circumstances, and is one of those *undesigned coincidences,* which show that the author of the Acts was fully acquainted with the circumstances of the time, and that his history is true. The account in Josephus is, that "when Porcius Festus was sent as successor to Felix by Nero, the principal inhabitants of Cesarea went up to Rome to accuse Felix; and he had been certainly brought to punishment, unless Nero had yielded to the importunate solicitations of his brother Pallas, who was at that time had in the greatest honour by him." Antiq. b. xx. ch. viii. § 9. The plan of Felix, therefore, in suppressing the enmity of the Jews, and conciliating their favour by injustice to Paul, did not succeed; and is one of those instances, so numerous in the world, where a man gains nothing by wickedness. He sought money from Paul by iniquity, and failed, he sought by injustice to obtain the favour of the Jews, and failed in that also. And the inference from the whole transaction is, that "honesty is the best policy," and that man in any office should pursue a course of firm, and constant, and undeviating integrity.

CHAPTER XXV.

1. *Now when Festus was come.* Note, ch. xxiv 27. ¶ *Into the province.* The province of Judea; for Judea at that time was a Roman province. ¶ *After three days.* Having remained three days at Cesarea. ¶ *He ascended.* This was

days he ascended from Cesarea to
Jerusalem.

2 Then the high-priest and the
chief of the Jews informed him
against Paul, and besought him,

3 And desired favour against
him, that he would send for him
to Jerusalem, laying [a] wait in the
way to kill him.

4 But Festus answered, that
Paul should be kept at Cesarea,
and that he himself would depart
shortly *thither*.

5 Let them therefore, said he,
which among you are able, go
down with *me*, and accuse this
man, if there be any wickedness
in him.

a c.23.14 15.

the usual language which described a journey to Jerusalem. Thus the English people speak of going up to London, because it is the capital. See Note, ch. xv. 1. ¶ *To Jerusalem.* The governors of Judea at this time usually resided at Cesarea; but as Jerusalem had been the former capital; as it was still the seat of the religious solemnities; as the sanhedrim held its meetings there; and as the great, and rich, and learned men, and the priests resided there, it is evident that a full knowledge of the state of the province could be obtained only there. Festus therefore, having entered on the duties of his office, early went to Jerusalem to make himself acquainted with the affairs of the nation.

2. *Then the high-priest.* The high-priest at this time was Ismael, the son of Fabi. He had been promoted to that office by Agrippa. Josephus' Antiq. b. xx. ch. viii. § 8. It is probable, however, that the person here intended was Ananias, who had been high-priest, and who would retain the name. Notes, ch. xxiii. 2. Some MSS. read *high-priests* here in the plural number, and this reading is approved by Mill and Griesbach. There is, however, no improbability in supposing that the high-priest Ismael might have been also as much enraged against Paul as the others. ¶ *Informed him against Paul.* Informed him of the accusation against him; and doubtless endeavoured to prejudice the mind of Festus against him. They thus showed their unrelenting disposition. It might have been supposed that after two years this unjust prosecution would be abandoned and forgotten. But malice does not thus forget its object; and the spirit of persecution is not thus satisfied. It is evident that there was here every probability that injustice would be done to Paul, and that the mind of Festus would be biassed against him. He was a stranger to Paul, and to the embittered feelings of the Jewish character. He would wish to conciliate their favour on entering on the duties of his office. And a strong representation therefore, made by the chief men of the nation, would be likely to prejudice him violently against Paul, and to unfit him for the exercise of impartial justice.

3. *And desired favour against him.* Desired the favour of Festus, that they might accomplish their wicked purpose on Paul. ¶ *Would send for him to Jerusalem.* Probably under a pretence that he might be tried by the sanhedrim; or perhaps they wished Festus to hear the cause there, and to decide it while he was at Jerusalem. Their *real* motive is immediately stated. ¶ *Lying wait in the way to kill him.* That is, they would lie in wait, or they would employ a band of Sicarii, or assassins, to take his life on the journey. See Notes, ch. xxi. 38; xxiii. 12. It is altogether probable that if this request had been granted, Paul would have been killed. But God had promised him that he should bear witness to the truth at Rome (ch. xxiii. 11), and his providence was remarkable in thus influencing the mind of the Roman governor, and defeating the plans of the Jewish council.

4. *But Festus answered, &c.* What induced Festus to refuse their request, is not known. It is probable, however, that he was apprized that Paul was a Roman citizen, and that his case could not come before the Jewish sanhedrim, but must be heard by himself. As Cesarea was also at that time the residence of the Roman governor, and the place of holding the courts, and as Paul was lodged there safely, there did not appear any sufficient reason for removing him to Jerusalem for trial. Festus, however, granted them all that they could reasonably ask, and assured them that he should have a speedy trial.

5. *Which among you are able.* Enjoy all the advantages of just trial, and exhibit your accusations with all the learn-

6 And when he had tarried
among them [1] more than ten days,
he went down unto Cesarea; and
the next day sitting in the judgment-seat, commanded Paul to be
brought.
7 And when he was come, the
Jews which came down from Jerusalem stood round about, and laid
many and grievous complaints
against Paul, which [a] they could
not prove.
8 While he answered for him
self, Neither against the laws of
the Jews, neither against the temple, nor yet against Cesar, have I
offended any thing at all.
9 But Festus, willing to do the
Jews a pleasure, answered Paul,
and said, Wilt thou go up to Jerusalem, and there be judged of these
things before me?
10 Then said Paul, I stand at
Cesar's judgment-seat, where I

[1] or, as some copies read, *no more than eight or ten days.*

a Ps.35.11. Matt.5.11,12. c.24.5,13.

ing and talent in your power. This was all that they could reasonably ask at his hands.

6. *More than ten days.* See the margin. The Syriac reads it, 'eight or ten.' The Vulgate, 'not more than eight or ten.' The Coptic, 'eight or ten.' Griesbach supposes this to be the true reading, and has admitted it into the text. ¶ *Sitting in the judgment-seat.* On the tribunal; or holding a court for the trial of Paul. ¶ *Commanded Paul to be brought.* To be brought up for trial. He had been secured, but was placed in the care of a soldier, who was commanded to let him have all the freedom that was consistent with his security.

7. *Grievous complaints.* Heavy accusations. Doubtless the same with which they had charged him before Felix. ch. xxiv. 5, 6. Comp. ch. xxv. 19. ¶ *Which they could not prove.* ch. xxiv. 13. 19.

8. *While he answered,* &c. See this answer more at length in ch. xxiv. 10—21. As the accusations against him were the same now as then, he made to them the same reply.

9. *But Festus, willing to do the Jews a pleasure.* Desirous of securing their favour, as he had just entered on his administration. Comp. ch. xxiv. 27. In this he evinced rather a desire of popularity than an inclination to do justice. Had he been disposed to do right at once, he would have immediately discharged Paul. Festus perceived that the case was one that did not come fairly within the jurisdiction of a Roman magistrate; that it pertained solely to the customs and questions among the Jews (ver. 18—20); and he therefore proposed that the case should be tried before *him* at Jerusalem. It is remarkable, however, that he had such a sense of justice, and law, as not to suffer the case to go out of his own hands. He proposed still to hear the cause, but asked Paul whether he was willing that it should be tried at Jerusalem? As the question which he asked Paul, was one on which he was at liberty to take his own course, and as Paul had no reason to expect that his going to Jerusalem would facilitate the cause of justice, it is not remarkable that he declined the offer, as perhaps Festus supposed he would.

10. *Then said Paul,* &c. The reasons why Paul declined the proposal to be tried at Jerusalem are obvious. He had experienced so much violent persecution from his countrymen; and their minds were so full of prejudice, misconceptions, and enmity, that he had neither justice nor favour to hope at their hands. He knew too that they had formerly plotted against his life, and that he had been removed to Cesarea for the purpose of safety. It would be madness and folly to throw himself again into their hands, or to give them another opportunity to form a plan against his life. As he was, therefore, under no obligation to return to Jerusalem; and as Festus did not propose it because it could be supposed that justice would be promoted by it, but to gratify the Jews, Paul prudently declined the proposal, and appealed to the Roman emperor. ¶ *I stand at Cesar's judgment-seat.* The Roman emperors after Julius Cesar were all called Cesar; thus, Augustus Cesar, Claudius Cesar, &c., as all the kings of Egypt were called Pharaoh, though they had each his proper name, as Pharaoh Necho, &c. The emperor at this time (A. D. 60) was Nero, one of the most cruel and impious men that ever sat on a throne. It was under him that Paul was afterwards beheaded. When Paul says, "I stand at Cesar's judgment-seat," he means to

ought to be judged: to the Jews have I done no wrong, as thou very well knowest.

11 For if I be an offender, or have committed any thing worthy of death, I refuse not to die; but if there be none of these things whereof these accuse me, no man

---

say that he regarded the tribunal before which he then stood, and on which Festus sat, as really the judgment-seat of Cesar. The procurator, or governor, held his commission from the Roman emperor, and it was, in fact, his tribunal. The *reason* why Paul made this declaration, may be thus expressed: 'I am a Roman citizen. I have a right to justice. I am under no obligation to put myself again in the hands of the Jews. I have a right to a fair and impartial trial; and I claim the protection and privileges which all Roman citizens have before their tribunals; the right of a fair and just trial.' It was, therefore, a severe rebuke of Festus for proposing to depart from the known justice of the Roman laws; and, for the sake of popularity, proposing to him to put himself in the hands of his enemies. ¶ *Where I ought to be judged.* Where I have a right to demand and expect justice. I have a right to be tried where courts are usually held, and according to all the forms of equity which are usually observed. ¶ *I have done no wrong.* I have not injured their persons, property, character, or religion. This was a bold appeal which his consciousness of innocence, and the whole course of proceedings enabled him to make, without the possibility of their gainsaying it. ¶ *As thou very well knowest.* Festus knew, probably, that Paul had been tried by Felix, and that nothing was proved against him. He had now seen the spirit of the Jews, and the cause why they arraigned him. He had given Paul a trial, and had called on the Jews to adduce their "able" men to accuse him, and after all, nothing had been proved against him. Festus *knew* therefore that he was innocent. This abundantly appears also from his own confession. ver. 18, 19. As he knew this, and as Festus was proposing to depart from the regular course of justice for the sake of popularity, it was proper for Paul to use the strong language of rebuke, and to claim what he knew Festus did not dare to deny him, the protection of the Roman laws. Conscious innocence may be bold; and Christians have a right to insist on impartial justice, and the protection of the laws. Alas, how many magistrates there have been like Festus, who, when Christians have been arraigned before them, have been fully satisfied of their innocence, but who, for the sake of popularity, have departed from all the rules of law, and all the claims of justice

11. *For if I be an offender.* If I have injured the Jews so as to deserve death. If it can be proved that I have done injury to any one. ¶ *I refuse not to die.* I have no wish to escape justice. I do not wish to evade the laws, or to take advantage of any circumstances to screen me from just punishment. Paul's whole course showed that this was the noble spirit which actuated him. No true Christian wishes to escape from the laws He will honour them, and not seek to evade them. But, like other men, he has rights; and he may and should insist that justice should be done. ¶ *No man may deliver me unto them.* No man shall be allowed to do it. This bold and confident declaration Paul could make, because he knew what the law required, and he knew that Festus would not *dare* to deliver him up contrary to the law. Boldness is not incompatible with Christianity; and innocence, when its rights are invaded, is always bold. Jesus firmly asserted his rights when on trial (John xviii. 23), and no man is under obligation to submit to be trampled on by an unjust tribunal in violation of the laws. ¶ *I appeal unto Cesar.* I appeal to the Roman emperor, and carry my cause directly before him. By the Valerian, Porcian, and Sempronian laws, it had been enacted, that if any magistrate should be about to beat, or to put to death any Roman citizen, the accused could appeal to the Roman people, and this appeal carried the cause to Rome. The law was so far changed under the emperors, that the cause should be carried before the emperor, instead of the people. Every citizen had the right of this appeal; and when it was made, the accused was sent to Rome for trial. Thus Pliny (Ep. 10. 97) says, that those Christians who were accused, and who, being Roman citizens, appealed to Cesar, he sent to Rome to be tried. The reason why Paul made this appeal was, that he saw that justice would not be done him by the Roman governor. He had been tried by Felix, and justice had been denied him, and he was detained a prisoner

may deliver me unto them. I appeal [a] unto Cesar.

12 Then Festus, when he had conferred with the council, answered, Hast thou appealed unto Cesar? unto Cesar shalt thou go.

13 And after certain days, king Agrippa and Bernice came unto Cesarea, to salute Festus.

14 And when they had been there many days, Festus declared Paul's cause unto the king, saying,

a c.26.32.

in violation of law, to gratify the Jews; he had now been tried by Festus, and saw that he was pursuing the same course; and he resolved, therefore, to assert his rights, and remove the cause far from Jerusalem, and from the prejudiced men in that city, at once to Rome. It was in this mysterious way that Paul's long cherished desire to see the Roman church, and to preach the gospel there, was to be gratified. Comp. Note on Rom. i. 9—11. For this he had prayed long (Rom. i. 10; xv. 23, 24), and now at length this purpose was to be fulfilled. God answers prayer; but it is often in a way which we little anticipate. He so orders the train of events; he so places us amidst a press of circumstances, that the desire is granted in a way which we could never have anticipated, but which shows in the best manner that he is a hearer of prayer.

12. *When he had conferred with the council.* With his associate judges, or with those who were his counsellors in the administration of justice. They were made up of the chief persons, probably military as well as civil, who were about him, and who were his assistants in the administration of the affairs of the province. ¶ *Unto Cesar shalt thou go.* He was willing in this way to rid himself of this trial, and of the vexation attending it. He did not *dare* to deliver him to the Jews in violation of the Roman laws; and he was not willing to do justice to Paul, and thus make himself unpopular with the Jews. He was, therefore, probably rejoiced at the opportunity of thus freeing himself from all the trouble in the case, in a manner against which none could object.

13. *And after certain days, king Agrippa.* This Agrippa was the son of Herod Agrippa (Acts xii. 1), and great grandson of Herod the Great. His mother's name was Cypros. Josephus' Jewish Wars, b. ii. ch. xi § 6. When his father died, he was at Rome with the emperor Claudius. Josephus says that the emperor was inclined to bestow upon him all his father's dominions, but was dissuaded by his ministers. The reason of this was, that it was thought imprudent to bestow so large a kingdom on so young a man, and one so inexperienced. Accordingly, Claudius sent Cuspius Fadus to be Procurator of Judea, and of the entire kingdom. Josephus' Antiq. b. xix. ch. ix. § 2. When Herod, the brother of his father Agrippa the Great, died in the eighth year of the reign of Claudius, his kingdom—the kingdom of Chalcis, was bestowed by Claudius on Agrippa. Josephus' Antiq. b. xx. ch. v. § 2. Afterwards he bestowed on him the tetrarchy of Philip and Batanea, and added to it Trachonitis with Abila. Antiq. b. xx. ch vii. § 1. After the death of Claudius, Nero his successor added to his dominions Julias in Perea, and a part of Galilee. Agrippa had been brought up at Rome; and was strongly attached to the Romans. When the troubles commenced in Judea which ended in the destruction of Jerusalem, he did all that he could to preserve peace and order, but in vain. He afterwards joined his troops with those of the Romans, and assisted them at the destruction of Jerusalem. After the captivity of that city, he went to Rome with his sister Bernice, where he ended his days. He died at the age of seventy years, about A. D. 90. His manner of living with his sister, gave occasion to reports respecting him very little to his advantage. ¶ *And Bernice.* She was sister of Agrippa. She had been married to Herod, king of Chalcis, her own uncle by her father's side. After his death, she proposed to Polemon king of Pontus and part of Cilicia, that if he would become circumcised she would marry him. He complied, but she did not continue long with him. After she left him, she returned to her brother Agrippa with whom she lived in a manner such as to excite scandal. Josephus directly charges her with incest with her brother Agrippa. Antiq. b. xx. ch. vii. § 3. ¶ *To salute Festus.* To show him respect as the governor of Judea.

14. *Festus declared Paul's cause.* He did this, probably, because Agrippa being a Jew, would be supposed to be interested in the case. It was natural that this

There is a certain man left in bonds by Felix.

15 About whom, when [a] I was at Jerusalem, the chief priests and the elders of the Jews informed *me*, desiring *to have* judgment against him.

16 To whom I answered, It is not the manner of the Romans to deliver any man to die, before that he which is accused have the accusers face to face, and have license to answer for himself concerning the crime laid against him.

17 Therefore when [b] they were come hither, without any delay on the morrow I sat on the judgment-seat, and commanded the man to be brought forth.

18 Against whom, when the accusers stood up, they brought none accusation of such things as I supposed:

19 But [c] had certain questions against him of their own supersti-

a ver.2,3. b ver.6. c c.18.15.

---

trial should be a topic of conversation, and perhaps Festus might be disposed to ask what was proper to be done in such cases. ¶ *Left in bonds.* Greek, "a prisoner." δέσμιος. He was left in custody, probably in the keeping of a soldier. ch. xxiv. 23. 27.

15 *About whom,* &c. See ver. 1—5. ¶ *To have judgment against him.* To have him condemned.

16. *It is not the manner,* &c. He here states the reasons which he gave to the Jews for not delivering Paul into their hands. In ver. 4, 5. we have an account of the *fact* that he would not accede to the requests of the Jews; and he here states that the reason of his refusal was, that it was contrary to the Roman law. Appian in his Roman history says, "it is not their custom to condemn men before they are heard." Philo de Præsi. Rom. says the same thing. In Tacitus (Annal. ii.), it is said, "a defendant is not to be prohibited from adducing all things, by which his innocence may be established." It was for this, that the equity of the Roman jurisprudence was celebrated throughout the world. We may remark that it is a subject of sincere gratitude to the God of our nation, that this privilege is enjoyed in the highest perfection in this land. It is the privilege of every man here to be heard; to know the charges against him; to be confronted with the witnesses; to make his defence; and to be tried by the *laws,* and not by the passions and caprices of *men.* In this respect our jurisprudence surpasses all that Rome ever enjoyed; and is not inferior to that of the most favoured nation of the earth. ¶ *To deliver.* To give him up as a favour (χαρίζεσθαι), to popular clamour and caprice. Yet our Saviour, in violation of the Roman laws, was thus given up by Pilate. Matt. xxvii. 18—25. ¶ *Have the accusers face to face* That he may know who they are, and hear their accusations, and refute them. Nothing contributes more to justice than this. Tyrants suffer men to be accused without knowing who the accusers are, and without an opportunity of meeting the charges. It is one great principle of modern jurisprudence, that the accused may know the accusers, and be permitted to confront the witnesses, and adduce all the testimony possible in his own defence. ¶ *And have license.* Greek, 'place of apology,' may have the liberty of defending himself.

17. *Therefore when they were come hither,* &c. See ver. 6.

18. *None accusation,* &c. No charge as I expected of a breach of the peace; of a violation of the Roman law; of atrocious crime. It was natural that Festus should suppose that they would accuse Paul of some such offence. He had been arraigned before Felix; had been two years in custody; and the Jews were exceedingly violent against him. All this, Festus would presume, must have arisen from some flagrant and open violation of the laws.

19. *But had certain questions.* Certain inquiries, or litigated and disputed subjects; certain points of dispute in which they differed. Ζητήματα τινα. ¶ *Of their own superstition.* Δεισιδαιμονίας. This word properly denotes the worship, or fear of demons; but was applied by the Greeks and Romans to the worship of their gods. It is the same word which is used in Acts xvii. 22. where it is used in a good sense. See Note on that place There are two reasons for thinking that Festus used the word here in a good sense, and not in the sense in which we use the word superstition. (1.) It was the word by which the worship of the Greeks and

tion, and of one Jesus, which was dead, whom Paul affirmed to be alive.

20 And because [1] I doubted of such manner of questions, I asked *him* whether he would go to Jerusalem, and there be judged of these matters.

21 But when Paul had appealed to be reserved unto the [2] hearing of Augustus, I commanded him to be kept till I might send him to Cesar.

22 Then Agrippa said unto Festus, I would also hear the man myself. To-morrow, said he, thou shalt hear him.

23 And on the morrow, when Agrippa was come, and Bernice, with great [a] pomp, and was entered into the place of hearing, with the chief captains, and principal men of the city, at Festus' commandment Paul [b] was brought forth.

24 And Festus said, King Agrippa, and all men which are here

[1] or, *I was doubtful how to inquire hereof.* [2] or, *judgment.*

a Ezek.7.24. b c.9.15.

Romans, and, therefore, of Festus himself, was denoted, and he would naturally use it in a similar sense in applying it to the Jews. He would wish simply to describe their worship in such language as he was accustomed to use when speaking of religion. (2.) He knew that Agrippa was a Jew. Festus would not probably speak of the religion of his royal guest as *superstition*, but would speak of it with respect. He meant, therefore, to say simply, that they had certain inquiries about their own *religion;* but accused him of no crime against the Roman laws. ¶ *And of one Jesus, which was dead.* Gr. 'Of one dead Jesus.' It is evident that Festus had no belief that Jesus had been raised up; and in this he would expect that Agrippa would concur with him. Paul had admitted that Jesus had been put to death; but he maintained that he had been raised from the dead. As Festus did not believe this, he spoke of it with the utmost contempt. 'They had a dispute about one dead Jesus, whom Paul affirmed to be alive.' In this manner a Roman magistrate could speak of the glorious truth of the Christian religion; and this shows the spirit with which the great mass of philosophers and statesmen regarded its doctrines.

20. *And because I doubted of such manner of questions.* See the margin. Because I hesitated about the right way of disposing of them; because I was ignorant of their nature and bearing, I proposed to go to Jerusalem, that the matter might be there more fully investigated. It is obvious, that if Paul was not found guilty of any violation of the laws, he should have been at once discharged. Some interpreters understand this as affirming that he was not satisfied about the question of Paul's innocence, or certain whether he ought to be set at liberty or not.

21. *But when he had appealed.* ver. 11. ¶ *To be reserved.* To be kept; not to be tried at Jerusalem, but to be sent to Rome for trial. ¶ *Unto the hearing.* Margin, "the judgment." That Augustus might hear and decide the cause. ¶ *Of Augustus.* The reigning emperor at this time was Nero. The name *Augustus* (Σεβαστος) properly denotes that which is *venerable*, or worthy of honour and reverence. It was first applied to Cesar Octavianus, who was the Roman emperor in the time when our Saviour was born, and who is usually called Augustus Cesar. But the title continued to be used of his successors in office, as denoting the veneration or reverence which was due to the rank of emperor.

22. *Then Agrippa said, &c.* Agrippa doubtless had heard much of the fame of Jesus, and of the new sect of Christians; and probably he was induced by mere curiosity to hear what Paul could say in explanation and defence of the doctrine of Christianity. This wish of Agrippa gave occasion to the noblest defence which was ever made before any tribunal, and to as splendid eloquence as can be found any where in any language. See ch. xxvi.

23. *With great pomp.* Gr. "With much phantasy" (φαντασίας); with much show, parade, and splendour. It was an occasion on which he could exhibit much of the splendour of royalty, and he chose to do it. ¶ *Into the place of hearing.* The court-room; or the place where the judges heard and tried causes. ¶ *With the chief captains.* Gr. The chiliarchs; the commanders of a thousand men. It means here, that the military officers were assembled. ¶ *The principal men of the city.* The civil officers, or the men of reputation and influence.

24. *Have dealt with me.* Have appeared

present with us, ye see this man,
about whom all [a] the multitude of
the Jews have dealt with me, both
at Jerusalem, and *also* here, crying
that [b] he ought not to live any
longer.
25 But when I found that he had
committed nothing [c] worthy of
death, and that he himself hath
appealed [d] to Augustus, I have determined to send him.
26 Of whom I have no certain
thing to write unto my lord. Wherefore I have brought him forth before
you, and specially before thee, O
king Agrippa, that, after examination had, I might have somewhat to
write.
27 For [e] it seemeth to me unrea
sonable, to send a prisoner, and not
withal to signify the crimes *laid*
against him.

a ver.3,7. *b* c.22.22. *c* c.23.9,29; 26.31. *d* ver.11,12. *e* Prov.18.13. Jno.7.51.

before me, desiring me to try him. They have urged me to condemn him. ¶ *Crying out*, &c. Comp. ch. xxii. 22. They had sought that he should be put to death.

26. *Of whom.* Respecting his character, opinions, manner of life; and respecting the charges against him. ¶ *No certain thing.* Nothing definite, and well established. They had not accused Paul of any crime against the Roman laws; and Festus professes himself too ignorant of the customs of the Jews to inform the emperor distinctly of the nature of the charges, and the subject of trial. ¶ *Unto my lord.* To the emperor; to Cesar. This name *Lord*, the emperors Augustus and Tiberius had rejected, and would not suffer it to be applied to them. Suetonius (Life of Augustus, v. 53.) says "the appellation of Lord he always abhorred as abominable and execrable." See also Suetonius' Life of Tiberius, v. 27. The emperors that succeeded them, however, admitted the title, and suffered themselves to be called by this name. Nothing would be more satisfactory to Nero, the reigning emperor, than this title. ¶ *I might have somewhat to write.* As Agrippa was a Jew, and was acquainted with the customs and doctrine of the Jews, Festus supposed that after hearing Paul, he would be able to inform him of the exact nature of these charges, so that he could present the case intelligibly to the emperor.

27. *For it seemeth to me unreasonable.* Festus felt that he was placed in an embarrassing situation. He was about to send a prisoner to Rome to be tried, who had been tried by himself, and who had appealed from his jurisdiction; and yet he was ignorant of the charges against him, and of the nature of his offences, if any had been committed. When prisoners were thus sent to Rome to be tried before the emperor, it would be proper that the charges should be all specified, and the evidence stated by which they were supported. Yet Festus could do neither; and it is not wonderful that he felt himself perplexed and embarrassed; and that he was glad to avail himself of the desire which Agrippa had expressed to hear Paul, that he might be able to specify the charges against him. ¶ *Withal.* Also; at the same time. ¶ *To signify.* To specify, or make them know. In concluding this chapter, we may observe:

(1.) That in the case of Agrippa, we have an instance of the reasons which induce many men to hear the gospel. He had no belief in it; he had no concern for its truth or its promises; but he was led by *curiosity* to desire to hear the minister of the gospel of Christ. Curiosity thus draws multitudes to the sanctuary. In many instances, they remain unaffected and unconcerned in regard to its provisions of mercy. They listen, and are unmoved, and die in their sins. In many instances, like Agrippa, they are almost persuaded to be Christians. ch. xxvi. 28. But, like him, they resist the appeals; and die uninterested in the plan of salvation. In some instances, they are converted; and their curiosity, like that of Zaccheus, is made the means of their embracing the Saviour. Luke xix. 1—9. Whatever may be the motive which induces men to desire to hear, it is the duty of the ministry cheerfully and thankfully like Paul, to state the truth, and to defend the Christian religion.

(2.) In Festus we have a specimen of the manner in which the great men, and the rich, and the proud, usually regard Christianity. They esteem it to be a subject of inquiry, in which they have no interest; a question about "one dead Jesus," whom Christians affirm to be alive. Whether he be alive or not; whether Christianity be true or false, they suppose is an inquiry which does not pertain to them. Strange that it did not occur to Festus that if he *was* alive, his religion

CHAPTER XXVI.

THEN Agrippa said unto Paul, Thou art permitted to speak for thyself. Then Paul stretched forth the hand, and answered for himself:

2 I think myself happy, king Agrippa, because I shall answer for myself this day before thee, touching all the things whereof I am accused of the Jews:

3 Especially, *because I know* thee

was true; and that it was possible that it *might* be from God. And strange that the men of this world regard the Christian religion as a subject in which *they* have no personal interest, but as one concerning which Christians *only* should inquire, and in which *they* alone should feel any concern.

(3.) In Paul we have the example of a man unlike both Festus and Agrippa. He felt a deep interest in the subject—a subject which pertained as much to them as to him. He was willing not only to look at it with curiosity, but to stake his life, his reputation, his all, on its truth. He was willing to defend it every where, and before any class of men. At the same time that he urged his rights as a Roman citizen, yet it was mainly that he might preach the gospel. At the same time that he was anxious to secure justice to himself, yet his chief anxiety was to declare the truth of God. Before any tribunal; before any class of men, in the presence of princes, nobles, and kings, of Romans and of Jews, he was ready to pour forth irresistible eloquence and argument in defence of the truth. Who would not rather be Paul than either Festus or Agrippa? Who would not rather be a *prisoner* like him, than invested with authority like Festus, or clothed in splendour like Agrippa? And who would not rather be an honest and cordial believer of the gospel like Paul, than, like them, to be cold contemners or neglecters of the God that made them, and of the Saviour that died, and rose again.

CHAPTER XXVI.

1. *Then Paul stretched forth the hand.* See Note, ch. xxi. 40. This was the usual posture of orators or public speakers. The ancient statues are commonly made in this way, with the right hand extended. The *dress* of the ancients favoured this. The long and loose robe, or outer garment, was fastened usually with a hook or clasp on the right shoulder, and thus left the arm at full liberty. ¶ *And answered for himself.* It cannot be supposed that Paul expected that his defence would be attended with a release from confinement; for he had himself appealed to the Roman emperor. ch. xxv. 11. This design in speaking before Agrippa was, doubtless, (1.) To vindicate his character, and obtain Agrippa's attestation to his innocence, that thus he might allay the anger of the Jews; (2.) To obtain a correct representation of the case to the emperor, as Festus had desired this in order that Agrippa might enable him to make a fair statement of the case (ch. xxv. 26, 27); and, (3.) To defend his own conversion, and the truth of Christianity, and to preach the gospel in the hearing of Agrippa and the attendants, with a hope that their minds might be improved by the truth, and that they might be converted to God.

2. *I think myself happy.* I esteem it a favour and a privilege to be permitted to make my defence before one acquainted with Jewish customs and opinions. His defence, on former occasions, had been before *Roman* magistrates, who had little acquaintance with the opinions and customs of the Jews, who were not disposed to listen to the discussion of the points of difference between him and them, and who looked upon all their controversies with contempt. See ch. xxiv. xxv. They were, therefore, little qualified to decide a question which was closely connected with the Jewish customs and doctrines; and Paul now rejoiced to know that he was before one, who, from his acquaintance with the Jewish customs and belief, would be able to appreciate his arguments and motives. Paul was not now on his trial; but he was to defend himself, or state his cause, so that Agrippa might be able to aid Festus in transmitting a true account of the case to the Roman emperor. It was his interest and duty, therefore, to defend himself as well as possible; and to put him in possession of all the facts in the case. His defence is, consequently, made up chiefly of a most eloquent statement of the *facts* just as they had occurred. ¶ *I shall answer.* I shall be permitted to make a statement, or to defend myself. ¶ *Touching,* &c. Respecting. ¶ *Whereof I am accused of the Jews.* By the Jews. The matters of the accusation were, his being a mover of sedition, a ringleader of the Christians, and a profaner of the temple. ch. xxiv. 5, 6.

3 *To be expert.* To be skilled, or well

to be expert [a] in all customs and
questions which are among the
Jews: wherefore I beseech thee to
hear [b] me patiently.
4 My manner [c] of life from my
youth, which was at the first among
mine own nation at Jerusalem,
know all the Jews;
5 Which knew me from the beginning,
if they would testify, that
after the most straitest sect of our
religion, I lived a Pharisee. [d]
6 And now [e] I stand and am
judged for the hope of the pro-

a Deut.17.18 b c.24.4. c 2Tim.3.10. d c.23.3. Phil.3.5. e c.23.6.

acquainted. ¶ *In all customs.* Rites, institutions, laws, &c. Every thing pertaining to the Mosaic ritual, &c. ¶ *And questions.* Subjects of debate, and of various opinions. The inquiries which had existed between the Pharisees, Sadducees, scribes, &c. Paul could say this of Agrippa without falsehood or flattery. Agrippa was a Jew; and had passed much of his time in the kingdom over which he presided; and though he had passed the early part of his life chiefly at Rome, yet it was natural that he should make himself acquainted with the religion of his fathers. Paul did not know how to flatter men; but he was not unwilling to state the simple truth, and to commend men as far as truth would permit. ¶ *Wherefore.* On this account; because you are acquainted with those customs. The Romans, who regarded those customs as superstitious, and those questions as matters to be treated with contempt, could not listen to their discussion with patience. Agrippa, who knew their real importance, would be disposed to lend to all inquiries respecting them a patient attention.

4. *My manner of life.* My opinions, principles, and conduct. ¶ *From my youth.* Paul was born in Tarsus; but at an early period he had been sent to Jerusalem for the purpose of education in the school of Gamaliel. ch. xxii. 3. ¶ *Which was at the first.* Which was from the beginning; the early part of which; the time when the opinions and habits are formed. ¶ *Know all the Jews.* It is not at all improbable that Paul was distinguished in the school of Gamaliel for zeal in the Jewish religion. The fact that he was early intrusted with a commission against the Christians (ch. ix.), shows that he was known. Comp. Phil. iii. 4—6. He might appeal to them, therefore, in regard to the early part of his life; and, doubtless, to the very men who had been his violent accusers.

5. *Which knew me.* Who were well acquainted with me. ¶ *From the beginning.* Ἄνωθεν. Formerly; or from the very commencement of my career. Who were perfectly apprized of my whole course. ¶ *If they would testify.* If they would bear witness to what they knew. ¶ *That after the most straitest.* The most rigid; the most strict; not only in regard to the written law of God, but the traditions of the elders. Paul himself elsewhere testifies (Phil. iii. 4—6), that he had enjoyed all the advantages of birth and training in the Jewish religion, and that he had early distinguished himself by his observance of its rites and customs. ¶ *Sect.* Division, or party. ¶ *I lived a Pharisee.* I lived in accordance with the rules and doctrines of the Pharisees. See Note, Matt. iii. 7. The reasons why Paul here refers to his early life are, (1.) As he had lived during the early period of his life without crime; as his principles had been settled by the instruction of the most able of their teachers, it was to be presumed that his subsequent life had been of a similar character. (2.) As he, at that period of his life, evinced the utmost zeal for the laws and customs of his country, it was to be presumed that he would not be found opposing or reviling them at any subsequent period. From the strictness and conscientiousness of his past life, he supposed that Agrippa might argue favourably respecting his subsequent conduct. A virtuous and religious course in early life is usually a sure pledge of virtue and integrity in subsequent years.

6. *And now I stand.* I stand before the tribunal. I am arraigned. ¶ *And am judged.* Am tried with reference to being judged. I am undergoing a *trial* on the point in which all my nation are agreed. ¶ *For the hope.* On account of the hope; or because, in common with my countrymen, I had entertained this hope, and now believe in its fulfilment. ¶ *Of the promise,* &c. See the references in the margin. It is not quite certain whether Paul refers here to the promise of the Messiah, or to the hope of the resurrection of the dead. When he stood before the Jewish sanhedrim (ch. xxiii. 6), he said that he was called in question on account of holding the doctrine

mise [a] made of God unto our fathers:
7 Unto which *promise* our twelve tribes, instantly serving [b] *God* [1] day and night, hope to come. For which hope's sake, king Agrippa, I am accused of the Jews.
8 Why [c] should it be thought a

a Gen.3 15; 22.18; 49.10. Deut.18.15. 2Sam.7.12. Ps. 132.11. Isa.4.2; 7.14; 9.6,7. Jer.23.5; 33.14–16. Ezek.34.23. Dan.9.24. Mic.7.20. Zech.13.1,7. Mal.3.1. c.13.32. Gal.4.4.
b Luke 2.37. 1Thess.3.10 [1] night and day
c 1Cor.15.12,20.

of the resurrection of the dead. But it may be observed, that in Paul's view, the two things were closely united. He hoped that the Messiah would come, and he hoped *therefore* for the resurrection of the dead. He believed that he *had* come, and had risen; and *therefore* he believed that the dead would rise. He argued the one from the other. And as he believed that Jesus was the Messiah, and that he had risen from the dead, and had thus furnished a demonstration that the dead would rise, it was evident that the subject of controversy between him and the Jews involved every thing that was vital to their opinions and their hopes. See ver. 8. ¶ *Made of God.* Made by God. See the marginal references. The promises had been made to the fathers of a Messiah to come, and that embraced the promise of a future state, or of the resurrection of the dead. It will help us to understand the stress which Paul and the other apostles laid on the doctrine of the resurrection of the dead, to remember that it involved the whole doctrine of the separate existence of the soul, and of a future state. The Sadducees denied all this; and when the Pharisees, the Saviour, and the apostles opposed them, they did it by showing that there would be a future state of rewards and punishments. See the argument of the Saviour with the Sadducees explained in the Notes, Matt. xxii. 23–32. ¶ *Unto our fathers.* Our ancestors, the patriarchs, &c.

7. *Unto which promise.* To the fulfilment of which promise, they hope to come: i. e. they hope and believe that the promise will be fulfilled, and that they will partake of its benefits. ¶ *Our twelve tribes.* This was the name by which the Jews were designated. The ancient Jewish nation had hoped to come to that promise; it had been the hope and expectation of the nation. Long before the coming of the Messiah, ten of the twelve tribes had been carried captive to Assyria, and had not returned, leaving but the two tribes of Benjamin and Judah. But the name, 'the twelve tribes,' to designate the Jewish people would be still retained. Comp. James i. 1. Paul here says that the hope had been that of the Jewish nation. Except the comparatively small portion of the Sadducees, the great mass of the nation had held to the doctrine of a future state. This Agrippa would well know. ¶ *Instantly.* Constantly; *with intensity;* with an effort (ἐν ἐκτενίᾳ); with zeal. This was true; for amidst all the sins of the nation, they observed with punctuality and zeal the outward forms of the worship of God. ¶ *Serving God.* In the ordinances and observances of the temple. As a nation, they did not serve him in their hearts; but they kept up the outward form of religious worship. ¶ *Day and night.* With unwearied zeal; with constancy and ardour. Luke ii. 37. The ordinary Jewish services and sacrifices were in the morning and evening, and might be said to be performed day and night. Some of their services, as the paschal supper were prolonged usually till late at night. The main idea is, that they kept up the worship of God with constant and untiring zeal and devotion. ¶ *For which hope's sake.* On account of my cherishing this hope in common with the great mass of my countrymen. See ch. xxiii. 6. If Paul could convince Agrippa that the main point of his offence was that which had been the common belief of his countrymen, it would show to his satisfaction that he was innocent. And on this ground Paul put his defence; that he held only that which the mass of the nation had believed, and that he maintained this in the only consistent and defensible manner—that God had, *in fact,* raised up the Messiah, and had thus given assurance that the dead should rise.

8 *Why should it be thought,* &c. The force of this question will be better seen by an exclamation point after *why* (τί). 'What! is it to be thought a thing incredible?' &c. It intimates surprise that it should be thought incredible; or implies that no reason could be given why such a doctrine should be unworthy of belief. ¶ *A thing incredible.* A doctrine which cannot be credited or believed

thing incredible with you, that God should raise the dead?

9 I [a] verily thought with myself, that I ought to do many things contrary to the name of Jesus of Nazareth.

10 Which thing I also did in [b] Jerusalem: and many of the saints did I shut up in prison, having received authority [c] from the chief priests; and when they were put to death, I gave my voice against *them*.

a 1Tim.1.13. b c.8 3. Gal.1.13. c c.19.14.

Why should it be regarded as absurd. ¶ *With you.* This is in the plural number; and it is evident that Paul here addressed not Agrippa alone, but those who were with him. There is no evidence that Agrippa doubted that the dead could be raised; but Festus, and those who were with him, probably did; and Paul, in the ardour of his speech, turned and addressed the entire assembly. It is very evident that we have only an *outline* of this argument, and there is every reason to suppose that Paul would dwell on each part of the subject at greater length than is here recorded. ¶ *That God should raise the dead.* Why should it be regarded as absurd that God—who has all power; who was the creator of all; who was the author of the human frame—should again restore man to life, and continue his future existence. The resurrection is no more incredible than the original creation of the human body, and it is attended with no greater difficulties. And as the perfections of God will be illustrated by his raising up the dead; as the future state is necessary to the purposes of justice in vindicating the just, and punishing the unjust; and as God is a righteous moral governor, it should not be regarded as an absurdity that he will raise up those who have died, and bring them to judgment.

9. *I verily thought.* I indeed (μὲν) supposed. Paul here commences the account of his conversion, and states the evidence on which he judged that he was called of God to do what he had done. He begins by saying that it was not because he was originally disposed to be a Christian, but that he was violently and conscientiously opposed to Jesus of Nazareth, and had been converted when in the full career of opposition to him and his cause ¶ *With myself.* I thought *to* myself; or, I myself thought. He had before stated the hopes and expectations of his countrymen. ver. 6—8. He now speaks of his own views and purposes. 'For myself, I thought,' &c. ¶ *That I ought to do.* That I was bound, or that it was a duty incumbent on me. Δεῖν. 'I thought that I owed it to my country, to my religion, and to my God, to oppose in every manner the claims of Jesus of Nazareth to be the Messiah.' We here see that Paul was conscientious, and that a man may be conscientious even when engaged in enormous wickedness. It is no evidence that a man is right because he is conscientious. No small part of the crimes against human laws, and almost all the cruel persecutions against Christians, have been carried on under the plea of conscience. Paul here refers to his conscientiousness in persecution, to show that it was no slight matter which could have changed his course. As he was governed in persecution by conscience, it could have been only by a force of demonstration, and by the urgency of conscience equally clear and strong, that could ever have induced him to *abandon* this course, and become a friend of that Saviour whom he had thus persecuted. ¶ *Many things.* As much as possible. He was not satisfied with a *few* things—a few words, or purposes, or arguments; but he felt bound to do as much as possible to put down the new religion. ¶ *Contrary to the name,* &c. In opposition to Jesus himself, or to his claims to be the Messiah The name is often used to denote the person himself. ch. iii. 6.

10. *Which thing I did,* &c. ch. viii. 3. *And many of the saints,* &c. Many Christians. ch. viii. 3. ¶ *And when they were put to death.* In the history of those transactions there is no account of any Christian being put to death, except Stephen. Acts vii. But there is no improbability in supposing that the same thing which had happened to Stephen, had occurred in other cases. Stephen was the first martyr, and as he was a prominent man, his case is particularly recorded. ¶ *I gave my voice.* Paul was not a member of the sanhedrim, and this does not mean that he *voted*, but simply that he joined in the persecution; he approved it; he assented to the putting of the saints to death. Comp. ch. xxii. 20. The Syriac renders it, "I joined with those who condemned them." It is evident also that Paul instigated them in this persecution, and urged them on to deeds of blood and cruelty.

11 And I punished them oft in [a] every synagogue, and compelled *them* to blaspheme; and being exceedingly mad against them, I persecuted *them* even unto strange cities.

12 Whereupon as I went [b] to Damascus, with authority and commission from the chief priests,

13 At mid-day, O king, I saw in the way a light from heaven, above the brightness of the sun, shining round about me, and them which journeyed with me.

14 And when we were are all fallen to the earth, I heard a voice speaking unto me, and saying in the Hebrew tongue, Saul, Saul, why persecutest thou me? *it is* hard for thee to kick against the pricks.

15 And I said, Who art thou, Lord? And he said, I am Jesus whom thou persecutest.

16 But rise, and stand upon thy feet: for I have appeared unto thee for this purpose, to make thee a minister [c] and a witness [d] both of

a c.22.19. b c.9.3. c Eph 3.7. Col.1.23,25. d c.22 15.

11. *And I punished them oft*, &c. See ch. xxii. 19. ¶ *And compelled them to blaspheme.* To blaspheme the name of Jesus, by denying that he was the Messiah, and by admitting that he was an impostor. This was the object which they had in view in the persecution. It was not to make them blaspheme or reproach *God*, but to deny that Jesus was the Messiah, and to reproach him as a deceiver and an impostor. It is not necessarily implied in the expression, "and *compelled* them to blaspheme," that he succeeded in doing it; but that he violently *endeavoured* to make them apostatize from the Christian religion, and deny the Lord Jesus. It is certainly not impossible that a few might thus have been induced by the authority of the sanhedrim, and by the threats of Paul to do it; but it is certain that the great mass of Christians adhered firmly to their belief that Jesus was the Messiah. ¶ *And being exceedingly mad.* Nothing could more forcibly express his rage and violence against the Christians. He raged like a madman; he was so indignant that he laid aside all appearance of reason; and with the fury and violence of a maniac, he endeavoured to exterminate them from the earth. None but a madman will persecute men on account of their religious opinions; and all persecutions have been conducted like this, with the violence, and fury, and ungovernable temper of maniacs. ¶ *Unto strange cities.* Unto foreign cities; cities out of Judea. The principal instance of this was his going to Damascus; but there is no evidence that he did not intend also to visit other cities out of Judea, and bring the Christians there, if he found any, to Jerusalem.

12—15. See this passage explained in the Notes on ch. ix. 5, &c.

16. *But rise*, &c. The particulars mentioned in this verse and the two following, are not recorded in the account o Paul's conversion in ch. ix. But it is not improbable that many circumstances may have occurred which are not recorded. Paul dwells on them here at length, in order particularly to show his authority for doing what he had done in preaching to the Gentiles. ¶ *To make thee a minister.* A minister of the gospel; a preacher of the truth. ¶ *And a witness.* Note, ch. xxii. 15. ¶ *Which thou hast seen.* On the road to Damascus; that is, of the Lord Jesus, and of the fact that he was risen from the dead. ¶ *And of those things*, &c. Of those further manifestations of my person, protection, and will, which I will yet make to you. It is evident from this, that the Lord Jesus promised to manifest himself to Paul in his ministry, and to make to him still further displays of his will and glory. Comp. ch. xxii 17, 18. This was done by his rescuing him from destruction and danger; by the intimation of his will; and by the growing and expanding view which Paul was permitted to take of the character and perfections of the Lord Jesus. In this we see that it is the duty of ministers to bear witness not only to the truth of religion in general, or of that which they can demonstrate by argument; but more especially of that which they experience in their own hearts, and which they understand by having themselves been the subjects of it. No man is qualified to enter the ministry who has not a personal and practical and saving view of the glory and perfections of the Lord Jesus, and who does not go to his work as a

these things which thou hast seen,
and of those things in the which I
will appear unto thee;
17 Delivering thee from the
people, and *from* the Gentiles, unto
[a] whom now I send thee;
18 To open [b] their eyes, *and* to
turn [c] *them* from darkness to light,
and *from* the power [d] of Satan unto
God; that they may receive forgiveness [e] of sins, and inheritance [f]
among them which are [g] sanctified,
by faith [h] that is in me.
19 Whereupon, O king Agrippa
I was not disobedient unto the
heavenly vision:
20 But showed [i] first unto them
of Damascus, and at Jerusalem,

a c.22.21. Rom.11.13. b Isa.35.5; 42.7. c Luke 1.79. Jno.8.12. 2Cor.4.6. Eph.1.18. d Col.1.13. 1Pet.2.9. e Luke 1.77. Eph.1.7. Col.1.14. f Eph.1.11. Col.1.12. 1Pet.1.4. g Jno.17.17. c.20 32. 1Cor.1.30. Rev.21.27. h Eph.2.8. Heb.11.6. i c.11.26,&c.

witness of those things which he has felt. And no man enters the ministry with these feelings, who has not, as Paul had, a promise that he shall see still brighter displays of the perfections of the Saviour, and be permitted to advance in the knowledge of him and of his work. The highest personal consolation in this work is the promise of their being admitted to ever-growing and expanding views of the glory of the Lord Jesus, and of experiencing his presence, guidance, and protection.

17. *Delivering thee from the people.* From the Jewish people. This implied that he would be persecuted by them, and that the Lord Jesus would interpose to rescue him. ¶ *And from the Gentiles.* This also implied that he would be persecuted and opposed by them—a prospect which was verified by the whole course of his ministry. This was expressed in a summary manner in ch. ix. 16. Yet in all he experienced, according to the promise, the protection and the support of the Lord Jesus. ¶ *Unto whom now I send thee.* ch. xxii. 21. As the opposition of the Jews arose mainly from the fact that he had gone among the Gentiles, it was important to bring this part of his commission into full view before Agrippa, and to show that the same Saviour who had miraculously converted him, had commanded him to go and preach to them.

18. *To open their eyes.* To enlighten or instruct them. Ignorance is represented by the eyes being closed, and the instruction of the gospel by the opening of the eyes. See Eph. i. 18. ¶ *And to turn them from darkness to light.* From the darkness of heathenism and sin, to the light and purity of the gospel. Darkness is an emblem of ignorance and of sin; and the heathen nations are often represented as sitting in darkness. Comp. Note, Matt. iv. 16. John i. 4, 5. ¶ *And from the power of Satan.* From the dominion of Satan. Comp. Col. i. 13. 1 Pet. ii. 9. Notes, John xii. 31; xvi. 11. Satan is thus represented as the prince of this world; the ruler of the darkness of this world; the prince of the power of the air, &c. The heathen world, lying in sin and superstition, is represented as under his control; and this passage teaches, doubtless, that the great mass of the people of this world are the subjects of the kingdom of Satan, and are led captive by him at his will. ¶ *Unto God.* To the obedience of the one living and true God. ¶ *That they may receive forgiveness of sins.* Through the merits of that Saviour who died; that thus the partition wall between the Jews and the Gentiles might be broken down, and all might be admitted to the same precious privileges of the favour and mercy of God. Comp. Note, Acts ii. 38. ¶ *And inheritance.* An heirship, or lot (κλῆρον); that they might be entitled to the privileges and favours of the children of God. See Note, Acts xx. 32. ¶ *Which are sanctified.* Among the saints; the children of God. Note, Acts xx. 32.

19. *Whereupon.* Whence (ὅθεν). Since the proof of his being the Messiah and of his resurrection, and of his calling me to this work, was so clear and plain, I deemed it my duty to engage without delay in the work. ¶ *I was not disobedient.* I was not incredulous, or unbelieving; I yielded myself to the command, and at once obeyed. See Acts ix. 6. Comp. Gal. i. 16. ¶ *To the heavenly vision.* To the celestial appearance; or to the vision which appeared to me manifestly from heaven. I did not doubt that this splendid appearance (ver. 13) was from heaven and I did not refuse to obey the command of him who thus appeared to me. He knew it was the command of God his Saviour; and he gave evidence of repentance by yielding obedience to it at once.

20. See ch. ix. 20—23. The 20th

and throughout all the coasts of
Judea, and *then* to the Gentiles, that
they should repent and turn to God,
and do works [a] meet for repentance.
21 For these causes the Jews [b]
caught me in the temple, and went
about to kill *me*.
22 Having therefore obtained help
of God, I continue unto this day,
witnessing both to small and great,
saying none other things than those
which [c] the prophets and Moses did
say should come.
23 That Christ should suffer, *and*
that he should be the first [d] that
should rise from the dead, and

a Matt.3.8 b c.21.30. c Luke 24.27,46. d 1Cor.15.23.

verse contains a *summary* of his labours in obedience to the command of the Lord Jesus. His argument is, that the Lord Jesus had from heaven commanded him to do this, and that he had done no more than to obey his injunction.

21. *Caught me in the temple.* ch. xxi. 30. ¶ *And went about, &c.* Endeavoured to put me to death.

22. *Having therefore obtained help of God.* Paul had seen and felt his danger. He had known the determined malice of the Jews, and their efforts to take his life. He had been rescued by Lysias, and had made every effort to avoid the danger, and to save his life; and at the end of all, he traced his safety entirely to the help of God. It was not by any power of his own that he had been preserved; but it was because God had interposed and rescued him. Those who have been delivered from danger, if they have just views, will delight to trace it all to God. They will regard *his* hand; and will feel that whatever wisdom *they* may have had, or whatever may have been the kindness of their friends to aid them, yet that *all this also* is to be traced to the superintending providence of God. ¶ *Witnessing.* Bearing testimony to what he had seen, according to the command of Christ. ver. 16. ¶ *To small.* To those in humble life; to the poor, the ignorant, and the obscure. Like his master, he did not despise them, but regarded it as his duty and privilege to preach the gospel to the poor. ¶ *And great.* The rich and noble; to kings, and princes, and governors. He had thus stood on Mars' Hill at Athens; he had borne testimony before the wise men of Greece; he had declared the same gospel before Felix, Festus, and now before Agrippa. He offered salvation to all. He passed by none because they were poor; and he was not deterred by the fear of the rich and the great from making known their sins, and calling them to repentance. What an admirable illustration of the proper duties of a minister of the gospel! ¶ *Saying none other thing, &c.* Delivering no new doctrine; but maintaining only that the prophecies had been fulfilled. As he had done this only, there was no reason for the opposition, and persecution of the Jews. ¶ *Should come.* Should come to pass; or should take place. Paul here evidently means to say, that the doctrine of the atonement, and of the resurrection of Christ, is taught in the Old Testament.

23. *That Christ.* That the Messiah expected by the Jews should be a suffering Messiah. ¶ *Should suffer.* Should lead a painful life, and be put to death. See Note, ch. xvii. 3. Comp. Dan. ix. 27 Isa. liii. ¶ *And that he should be the first, &c.* This declaration contains two points. (1.) That it was taught in the prophets that the Messiah should rise from the dead. On this, see the proof alleged in ch. ii. 24—32; xiii. 32—37. (2.) That he should be the first that should rise. This cannot mean that the Messiah should be the first dead person who should be restored to life, for Elijah had raised the son of the Shunammite, and Jesus himself had raised Lazarus, and the widow's son at Nain. It does not mean that he should be the first *in the order of time* that should rise, but *first in eminence*, the most distinguished, the chief, the head of those who should rise from the dead. Πρῶτος ἐξ ἀναστάσεως νεκρῶν. In accordance with this he is called (Col. i. 18), "the beginning, the first-born from the dead," having among all the dead who should be raised up, the rights and pre-eminence of the primogeniture, or which pertained to the first-born. In 1 Cor. xv. 20. he is called "the first-fruits of them that slept." This declaration is, therefore, made of him by way of eminence. (1.) As being chief, a prince among those raised from the dead; (2.) As being raised by his own power (John x. 18); (3.) As, by his rising, securing a dominion over death and the grave (1 Cor. xv. 25, 26); and, (4.) As bringing by his rising, life and immortality to light. He rose to return to death no more. And he thus secured an ascendancy over death and the grave, and was thus, by way of eminence, *first* among those raised from

should shew light unto the people,
and to the Gentiles.
24 And as he thus spake for
himself, Festus said with a loud
voice, Paul, thou art beside thy
self; much learning doth make thee
mad.[a]
25 But he said, I am not mad,

a 2Kings 9.11.

the dead. ¶ *And should show light unto the people.* To the Jews. Should be their instructor and prophet. This Moses had predicted. Deut. xviii. 15. ¶ *And to the Gentiles.* This had often been foretold by the prophets, and particularly by Isaiah. Isa. ix. 1, 2. Comp. Matt. iv. 14—16. Isa. xi. 10; xlii. 1. 6; liv. 3; lx. 3. 5; 11; lxi. 6; lxii. 2; lxvi. 12.

24. *Festus said with a loud voice.* Amazed at the zeal and ardour of Paul. Paul doubtless evinced deep interest in the subject, and great earnestness in the delivery of his defence. ¶ *Thou art beside thyself.* Thou art deranged; thou art insane. The reasons why Festus thought Paul mad were, probably, (1.) His great earnestness and excitement on the subject. (2.) His laying such stress on the gospel of the despised Jesus of Nazareth, as if it were a matter of infinite moment. Festus despised it; and he regarded it as proof of derangement that so much importance was attached to it. (3.) Festus regarded, probably, the whole story of the vision that Paul said had appeared to him, as the effect of an inflamed and excited imagination; and as the proof of delirium. This is not an uncommon charge against those who are Christians, and especially when they evince any unusual zeal. Sinners regard them as under the influence of delirium and fanaticism; as terrified by imaginary and superstitious fears; or as misguided by fanatical leaders. Husbands often thus think their wives deranged, and parents their children, and wicked men the ministers of the gospel. The gay think it proof of derangement that others are serious, and anxious, and prayerful; the rich, that others are willing to part with their property to do good; the ambitious and worldly, that others are willing to leave their country and home, to go among the Gentiles to spend their lives in making known the unsearchable riches of Christ. The really sober, and rational part of the world—they who fear God, and keep his commandments; who believe that eternity is before them, and who strive to live for it—are thus charged with insanity by those who are really deluded, and who are thus living lives of madness and folly. The tenants of a mad-house often think all others deranged but themselves; but there is no madness so great, no delirium so awful, as to neglect the eternal interest of the soul for the sake of the poor pleasures and honours which this life can give. ¶ *Much learning.* It is probable that Festus was acquainted with the fact that Paul had been well instructed, and was a learned man. Paul had not while before him manifested particularly his learning. But Festus, acquainted in some way with the fact that he was well educated, supposed that his brain had been turned, and that the effect of it was seen by devotion to a fanatical form of religion. The tendency of long continued and intense application to produce mental derangement, is every where known. ¶ *Doth make thee mad.* Impels, drives, or excites thee (περιτρέπει) to madness.

25. *I am not mad.* I am not deranged. There are few more happy turns than that which Paul gives to this accusation of Festus. He might have appealed to the course of his argument; he might have dwelt on the importance of the subject, and continued to reason; but he makes an appeal at once to *Agrippa*, and brings him in for a witness that he was not deranged. This would be far more likely to make an impression on the mind of Festus, than any thing that Paul could say in self-defence. The same reply, 'I am not mad,' can be made by all Christians to the charge of derangement which the world brings against them. They have come, like the prodigal (Luke xv. 17), to their right mind; and by beginning to act as if there were a God and Saviour, as if they were to die, as if there were a boundless eternity before them, they are conducting according to the dictates of reason. And as Paul appealed to Agrippa, who was not a Christian, for the reasonableness and soberness of his own views and conduct, so may all Christians appeal even to sinners themselves, as witnesses that they are acting as immortal beings *should* act. All men *know* that if there is an eternity, it is right to prepare for it; if there is a God, it is proper to serve him; if a Saviour died for us, we should love him; if a hell, we should avoid it, if a heaven, we should seek it. And even when they charge us with folly and derangement, we may turn at once upon *them*, and appeal to their own consciences,

most noble Festus, but speak forth the words of truth and soberness.

26 For the king knoweth of these things, before whom also I speak freely; for I am persuaded that none of these things are hidden from him; for this thing was not done in a corner.

27 King Agrippa, believest thou

---

and ask them if all our anxieties, and prayers, and efforts, and self-denials, are not right? One of the best ways of convicting sinners is, to appeal to them just as Paul did to Agrippa. When *so* appealed to, they will usually acknowledge the force of the appeal; and will admit that all the solicitude of Christians for their salvation is according to the dictates of reason. ¶ *Most noble Festus.* This was the usual title of the Roman governor. Comp. xxiv. 3. ¶ *Of truth.* In accordance with the predictions of Moses and the prophets; and the facts which have occurred in the death and resurrection of the Messiah. In proof of this he appeals to Agrippa. ver. 26, 27. Truth here stands opposed to delusion, imposture, and fraud ¶ *And soberness.* Soberness (σωφροσύνη, *wisdom*) stands opposed here to madness, or derangement, and denotes sanity of mind. The words which I speak are those of a sane man, conscious of what he is saying, and impressed with its truth. They were the words, also, of a man who, under the charge of derangement, evinced the most perfect self-possession, and command of his feelings; and who uttered sentiments deep, impressive, and worthy of the attention of mankind.

26. *For the king.* King Agrippa. ¶ *Knoweth.* He had been many years in that region, and the fame of Jesus and of Paul's conversion were probably well known to him. ¶ *These things.* The things pertaining to the early persecutions of Christians; the spread of the gospel; and the remarkable conversion of Paul. Though Agrippa might not have been fully informed respecting these things, yet he had an acquaintance with Moses and the prophets; he knew the Jewish expectation respecting the Messiah; and he could not be ignorant respecting the remarkable public events in the life of Jesus of Nazareth, and of his having been put to death by order of Pontius Pilate on the cross. ¶ *I speak freely.* I speak openly, boldly. I use no disguise; and I speak the more confidently before him, because, from his situation, he must be acquainted with the truth of what I say. Truth is always bold and free; and it is an evidence of honesty when a man is willing to declare every thing without reserve before those who are qualified to detect him if he is an impostor. Such evidence of truth and honesty was given by Paul. ¶ *For I am persuaded.* I am convinced; I doubt not that he is well acquainted with these things. ¶ *Are hidden from him.* That he is unacquainted with them. ¶ *For this thing.* The thing to which Paul had mainly referred in this defence, his own conversion to the Christian religion. ¶ *Was not done in a corner.* Did not occur secretly and obscurely; but was public, and was of such a character as to attract attention. The conversion of a leading persecutor, such as Paul had been, and in the manner in which that conversion had taken place, could not but attract attention and remark. And although the Jews would endeavour as much as possible to conceal it, yet Paul might presume that it could not be entirely unknown to Agrippa.

27. *King Agrippa.* This bland personal address is an instance of Paul's happy manner of appeal. He does it to bring in the testimony of Agrippa to meet the charge of Festus that he was deranged. ¶ *Believest thou the prophets?* The prophecies respecting the character, the sufferings, and the death of the Messiah. ¶ *I know that thou believest.* Agrippa was a Jew; and, as such, he of course believed the prophets. Perhaps too, from what Paul knew of his personal character, he might confidently affirm that he professed to be a believer. Instead, therefore, of waiting for his answer, Paul anticipates it, and says that he knows that Agrippa professes to believe all these prophecies respecting the Messiah. His design is evident. It is, (1.) To meet the charge of derangement, and to bring in the testimony of Agrippa, who well understood the subject, to the importance and the truth of what he was saying. (2.) To press on the conscience of his royal hearer the evidence of the Christian religion, and to secure if possible his conversion. 'Since thou believest the prophecies, and since I have shown that they are fulfilled in Jesus of Nazareth, that he corresponds in person, character, and work with the prophets, it follows that his religion is true.' Paul lost no opportunity of pressing the truth on every class of men. He had such a conviction

the prophets? I kno that thou believest.

28 Then Agrippa said unto Paul, Almost thou [a] persuadest me to be a Christian.

a James 1.23,24.

of the truth of Christianity, that he was deterred by no rank, station, or office; by no fear of the rich, the great, and the learned; but every where urged the evidence of that religion as indisputable. In this, lay the secret of no small part of his success. A man who *really* believes the truth will be ready to defend it. A man who truly loves religion will not be ashamed of it any where.

28. *Then Agrippa said unto Paul.* He could not deny that he believed the prophets. He could not deny that the argument was a strong one, that they had been fulfilled in Jesus of Nazareth. He could not deny that the evidence of the miraculous interposition of God in the conversion of Paul was overwhelming. And instead, therefore, of charging him as Festus had done with derangement, he candidly and honestly avows the impression which the proof had made on his mind. ¶ *Almost.* Except a very little. Ἐν ὀλίγῳ. Thou hast nearly convinced me that Christianity is true, and persuaded me to embrace it. The arguments of Paul had been so rational; the appeal which he had made to his belief of the prophets had been so irresistible, that he had been nearly convinced of the truth of Christianity. We are to remember, (1.) That Agrippa was a Jew, and that he would look on this whole subject in a different manner from the Roman Festus. (2.) That Agrippa does not appear to have partaken of the violent passions and prejudices of the Jews who had accused Paul. (3.) His character as given by Josephus is that of a mild, candid, and ingenuous man. He had no particular hostility to Christians; he knew that they were not justly charged with sedition and crime; and he saw the conclusion to which a belief of the prophets inevitably tended. Yet, as in thousands of other cases, he was not *quite* persuaded to be a Christian. What was included in the "almost;" what prevented his being *quite* persuaded, we know not. It may have been that the evidence was not so clear to his mind as he would profess to desire; or that he was not willing to give up his sins; or that he was too proud to rank himself with the followers of Jesus of Nazareth; or that, like Felix, he was willing to defer it to a more convenient season. There is every reason to believe that he was never *quite* persuaded to embrace the Lord Jesus; and that he was never nearer the kingdom of heaven than at this moment. It was the *crisis*, the turning point in Agrippa's life, and in his eternal destiny; and, like thousands of others, he neglected or refused to allow the full conviction of the truth on his mind, and died in his sins. ¶ *Thou persuadest me.* Thou dost convince me of the truth of the Christian religion, and persuadest me to embrace it. ¶ *To be a Christian.* On the name *Christian*, see Note, ch. xi. 26. On this deeply interesting case, we may observe, (1.) That there are many in the same situation as Agrippa—many who are *almost*, but not *altogether*, persuaded to be Christians. They are found among (*a*) Those who have been religiously educated; (*b*) Those who are convinced by argument of the truth of Christianity; (*c*) Those whose consciences are awakened, and who feel their guilt, and the necessity of some better portion than this world can furnish. (2.) Such persons are deterred from being altogether Christians by the following, among other causes. (*a*) By the love of sin—the love of sin in general, or some particular sin which they are not willing to abandon. (*b*) The fear of shame, persecution, or contempt, if they become Christians. (*c*) By the temptations of the world—its cares, vanities, and allurements—which are often prosecuted most strongly in just this state of mind. (*d*) The love of office, the pride of rank, and power as in the case of Agrippa. (*e*) A disposition, like Felix, to delay to a more favourable time the work of religion, until life has wasted away, and death approaches, and it is too late; and the unhappy man dies ALMOST *a Christian.* (3.) This state of mind is one of peculiar interest, and peculiar danger. It is not one of safety; and it is not one that implies any certainty that the 'almost Christian' will ever be saved. There is no reason to believe that Agrippa ever became *fully* persuaded to become a Christian. To be *almost* persuaded to do a thing which we ought to do, and yet not to do it, is the very position of guilt and danger. And it is no wonder that many are brought to *this* point—the turning point, the *crisis* of life—and then lose their anxiety, and die in their sins. May the God of grace keep us from resting in being almost persuaded to be Christians

29 And Paul said, I would [a] to
God that not only thou, but also all
that hear me this day, were both
almost, and altogether such as I
am, except these bonds.
30 And when he had thus spoken,
the king rose up, and the governor,
and Bernice, and they that sat with
them.
31 And when they were gone
aside, they talked between themselves,
saying, This man doeth nothing
worthy of death or of bonds.
32 Then said Agrippa unto Fes-

a 1Cor.7.7.

And may every one who shall read this account of Agrippa be admonished by his convictions, and be alarmed by the fact that *he* then paused, and that his convictions there ended! And may every one resolve by the help of God to forsake *every* thing that prevents his becoming an *entire* believer, and without delay embrace the Son of God as his Saviour!

29. *I would to God.* I pray to God; I earnestly desire it of God. This shows, (1.) Paul's intense desire that Agrippa, and all who heard him, might be saved. (2.) His steady and constant belief that none but God could incline them to become altogether Christians. Hence he expressed it as the object which he earnestly sought of God, that they might be true believers. Paul knew well that there was nothing that would overcome the reluctance of the human heart to be an entire Christian but the grace and mercy of God. He had addressed to them the convincing arguments of religion; and he now breathed forth his earnest prayer to God that these arguments might be effectual. So prays every faithful minister of the cross. ¶ *All that hear me.* Festus, and the military and civil officers who had been assembled to hear his defence. ch. xxv. 23. ¶ *Were both almost, and altogether,* &c. Paul had no higher wish for them than that they might have the faith and consolations which he had himself enjoyed. He had so firm a conviction of the truth of Christianity, and had experienced so much of its consolations and supports amidst all his persecutions and trials, that his highest desire for them was, that they might experience the same inexpressibly pure and holy consolations. He well knew that there was neither happiness nor safety in being *almost* a Christian; and he desired, therefore, that they would give themselves, as he had done, entirely and altogether to the service of the Lord Jesus Christ. ¶ *Except these bonds.* These chains. This is an exceedingly happy and touching appeal. Probably Paul, when he said this, lifted up his arm with the chain attached to it. His wish was, that they might be partakers of the pure joys which religion had conferred on him; that in all other respects they might partake of the effects of the gospel, *except those chains.* Those he did not wish them to bear. The persecutions, and unjust trials, and confinements which he had been called to suffer in the cause, he did not desire them to endure. True Christians wish others to partake of the full blessings of religion. The trials which they themselves experience from without in unjust persecutions, ridicule, and slander, they do not wish them to endure. The trials which they themselves experience from an evil heart, from corrupt passions, and from temptations, they do not wish others to experience. But even *with* these, religion confers infinitely more pure joy than the world can give; and even though others should be called to experience severe trials for their religion; still, Christians wish that all should partake of the pure consolations which Christianity alone can furnish in this world and the world to come.

31. *This man doeth nothing worthy of death.* This was the conclusion to which they had come, after hearing all that the Jews had to allege against him. It was the result of the whole investigation; and we have, therefore, the concurring testimony of Claudius Lysias (ch. xxiii. 29), of Felix (ch. xxiv.), of Festus (ch. xxv. 26, 27), and of Agrippa to his innocence. More honourable and satisfactory testimony of his innocence Paul could not have desired. It was a full acquittal from all the charges against him; and though he was to be sent to Rome, yet he went there with every favourable circumstance of being acquitted there also.

32. *Then said Agrippa unto Festus,* &c. This is a full declaration of the conviction of Agrippa, that Paul was innocent. It is an instance also where boldness and fidelity will be attended with happy results. Paul had concealed nothing of the truth. He had made a bold and faithful appeal (ver. 27) to Agrippa him-

tus, This man might have been set at liberty, if he had not appealed unto Cesar.

CHAPTER XXVII.

AND when it was determined that we should sail into Italy, they delivered Paul [a] and certain other prisoners unto *one* named Julius, a centurion of Augustus' band.

2 And entering into a ship of Adramyttium, we launched, mean-

a c.25.12,25.

---

self for the truth of what he was saying. By this appeal, Agrippa had not been offended. It had only served to impress him more with the innocence of Paul. It is an instance which shows us that religion may be commended to the consciences and reason of princes, and kings, and judges, so that they will see its truth. It is an instance which shows us that the most bold and faithful appeals may be made by the ministers of religion to their hearers, for the truth of what they are saying. And it is a full proof that the most faithful appeals, if respectful, may be made without offending men, and with the certainty that they will feel and admit their force. All preachers should be as faithful as Paul; and whatever may be the rank and character of their auditors, they should never doubt that they have truth and God on their side, and that their message, when most bold and faithful, will commend itself to the consciences of men.

CHAPTER XXVII.

1. *And when it was determined.* By Festus (ch. xxv. 12), and when the time was come when it was convenient to send him. ¶ *That we should sail.* The use of the term "we" here shows that the author of this book, Luke, was with Paul. He had been the companion of Paul, and though he had not been accused, yet it was resolved that he should still accompany him. Whether he went at his own expense, or whether he was sent at the expense of the Roman government, does not appear. There is a difference of reading here in the ancient versions. The Syriac reads it, "And thus Festus determined that he [Paul] should be sent to Cesar in Italy," &c. The Latin Vulgate and the Arabic also read "he" instead of "we." But the Greek manuscripts are uniform; and the correct reading is, doubtless, that which is in our version. ¶ *Into Italy.* The country still bearing the same name, of which Rome was the capital. ¶ *And certain other prisoners.* Who were probably also sent to Rome for a trial before the emperor. Dr. Lardner has proved that it was common to send prisoners from Judea and other provinces to Rome. Credibility, Part 1, ch. x. § 10. pp. 248, 249. ¶ *A centurion.* A commander of a hundred men. ¶ *Of Augustus' band.* For the meaning of the word "band," see Note, Matt. xxvii. 27. Acts x. 1. It was a division in the Roman army, consisting of from four to six hundred men. It was called "Augustus' band" in honour of the Roman emperor Augustus (Note, ch. xxv. 21), and was probably distinguished in some way for the care in enlisting or selecting them. The Augustine cohort or band is mentioned by Suetonius in his Life of Nero, 20.

2. *A ship of Adramyttium.* A maritime town of Mysia, in Asia Minor, opposite to the island of Lesbos. This was a ship which had been built there, or which sailed from that port, but which was then in the port of Cesarea. It is evident from ver. 6, that this ship was not expected to sail to Italy, but that the centurion expected to find some other vessel into which he could put the prisoners to take them to Rome. ¶ *We launched.* We loosed from our anchorage; or we set sail. See ch. xiii. 13. ¶ *By the coasts of Asia.* Of Asia Minor. Probably the owners of the ship designed to make a coasting voyage along the southern part of Asia Minor, and to engage in traffic with the maritime towns and cities. ¶ *One Aristarchus, a Macedonian.* This man is mentioned as Paul's companion in travel in ch. xix. 29. He afterwards attended him to Macedonia, and returned with him to Asia. ch. xx. 4 He now appears to have attended him, not as a prisoner, but as a voluntary companion, choosing to share with him his dangers, and to enjoy the benefit of his society and friendship. He went with him to Rome, and was a fellow-prisoner with him there (Col. iv. 10); and is mentioned (epistle to Philemon 24) as Paul's fellow-labourer. It was, doubtless, a great comfort to Paul to have with him two such valuable friends as Luke and Aristarchus; and it was an instance of great affection for him that they were not ashamed of his bonds, but were willing to share his dangers, and to expose them

ing to sail by the coasts of Asia; *one* Aristarchus,[a] a Macedonian of Thessalonica, being with us.
3 And the next *day* we touched at Sidon. And Julius courteously [b] entreated Paul, and gave *him* liberty to go unto his friends to refresh himself.
4 And when we had launched from thence, we sailed under Cyprus, because the winds were contrary.

5 And when we had sailed over the sea of Cilicia and Pamphylia, we came to Myra, *a city* of Lycia.
6 And there the centurion found a ship of Alexandria sailing into Italy; and he put us therein.
7 And when we had sailed slowly many days, and scarce were come over against Cnidus, the wind not suffering us, we sailed under Crete [1] over against Salmone;
8 And, hardly passing it, came

a c.19.29. *b* c.24.23; 28.16.

1 or, *Candy.*

selves to peril for the sake of accompanying him to Rome.

3. *We touched at Sidon.* Note, Matt. xi. 21. It was north of Cesarea. ¶ *And Julius courteously entreated Paul.* Treated him kindly, or humanely. ¶ *And gave him liberty,* &c. The same thing had been done by Felix. ch. xxiv. 23. ¶ *Unto his friends.* In Sidon. Paul had frequently travelled in that direction in going to, and returning from Jerusalem, and it is not improbable, therefore, that he had friends in all the principal cities. ¶ *To refresh himself.* To enjoy the benefit of their kind care, to make his present situation and his voyage as comfortable as possible. It is probable that they would furnish him with many supplies which were needful to make his long and perilous voyage comfortable.

4. *We sailed under Cyprus.* For an account of Cyprus, see Note, ch. iv. 36. By sailing "*under* Cyprus" is meant that they sailed along its coasts; they kept near to it; they thus endeavoured to break off the violent winds. Instead of steering a direct course in the open sea, which would have exposed them to violent opposing winds, they kept near this large island, so that it was between them and the westerly winds. The force of the wind was thus broken, and the voyage rendered less difficult and dangerous. They went between Cyprus and Asia Minor, leaving Cyprus to the left. Had it not been for the strong western winds they would have left it on the right. ¶ *The winds were contrary.* Were from the west, or southwest, which thus prevented their pursuing a direct course. See the map.

5. *The sea of Cilicia and Pamphylia.* The sea which lies off the coast from these two regions. For their situation, see the map, and Notes, Acts vi. 9, and xiii 13. ¶ *We came to Myra, a city of Lycia.* Lycia was a province in the southwestern part of Asia Minor, having Phrygia and Pisidia on the north, the Mediterranean on the south, Pamphylia on the east, and Caria on the west.

6. *A ship of Alexandria.* A ship belonging to Alexandria. Alexandria was in Egypt, and was founded by Alexander the Great. It appears from ver. 38, that the ship was laden with wheat. It is well known that great quantities of wheat were imported from Egypt to Rome; and it appears that this was one of the large ships which were employed for that purpose. Why the ship was on the coast of Asia Minor, is not known. But it is probable that it had been driven out of its way by adverse winds or tempests.

7. *Had sailed slowly.* By reason of the prevalence of the western winds. ver. 4. ¶ *Over against Cnidus.* This was a city standing on a promontory of the same name in Asia Minor, in the part of the province of Cana called Doris, and a little northwest of the island of Rhodes. ¶ *The wind not suffering us.* The wind repelling us in that direction, not permitting us to hold on a direct course, we were driven off near to Crete. ¶ *We sailed under Crete.* See ver. 4. We lay along near to Crete, so as to break the violence of the wind. For the situation of Crete, see Note, ch. ii. 11. ¶ *Over against Salmone.* Near to Salmone. This was the name of the promontory which formed the eastern extremity of the island of Crete.

8. *And, hardly passing it.* Scarcely being able to pass by it without being wrecked. Being almost driven on it. They passed round the east end of the island, because they had been unable to sail directly forward between the island and the main land. ¶ *The fair havens.* This was on the southeastern part of the island of Crete. It was probably not so much a harbour as an open kind of *road,* which afforded good anchorage for a time.

unto a place which is called the fair
havens; nigh whereunto was the
city *of* Lasea.
9 Now when much time was
spent, and when sailing was now
dangerous, because the fast [1] was
now already past, Paul admonished
them,
10 And said unto them, Sirs, I
perceive [a] that this voyage will be
with [2] hurt and much damage, not
only of the lading and ship, but
also of our lives.
11 Nevertheless, the centurion
believed the master and the owner
of the ship, more than those things
which were spoken by Paul.
12 And because the haven was
not commodious to winter in, the
more part advised to depart thence
also, if by any means they might
attain to Phenice, *and there* to win-

[1] *The feast was on the 10th day of the 7th month.* Lev.23.27,29. [a] 2Kings 6.9,10. Dan.2.20. Amos 3.7. [2] or, *injury.*

[b] Prov.27.12.

It is called by Stephen, the geographer, "the fair shore."

9. *When much time was spent.* In sailing along the coast of Asia; in contending with the contrary winds. It is evident, that when they started, they had hoped to reach Italy before the dangerous time of navigating the Mediterranean should arrive. But they had been detained and embarrassed contrary to their expectation, so that they were now sailing in the most dangerous and tempestuous time of the year. ¶ *Because the fast was now already past.* By "the fast," here is evidently intended the fast which occurred among the Jews on the great day of atonement. That was the tenth of the month *Tisri*, which answers to a part of September and part of October. It was therefore the time of the autumnal equinox, and when the navigation of the Mediterranean was esteemed to be particularly dangerous, from the storms which usually occurred about that time. The ancients regarded this as a dangerous time to navigate the Mediterranean. See the proofs in Kuinoel on this place. ¶ *Paul admonished them.* Paul exhorted, entreated, or persuaded them. He was somewhat accustomed to the navigation of that sea; and endeavoured to persuade them not to risk the danger of sailing at that season of the year.

10. *Sirs.* Gr. Men. ¶ *I perceive.* It is not certain that Paul understood this by direct inspiration. He might have perceived it from his own knowledge of the danger of navigation at the autumnal equinox, and from what he saw of the ship as unfitted to a dangerous navigation. But there is nothing that should prevent our believing also that he was guided to this conclusion by the inspiration of the Spirit of God. Comp. ver. 23, 24. ¶ *Will be with hurt.* With injury, or hazard. It is not meant that their lives would be lost; but that they would be jeoparded. ¶ *The lading.* The freight of the ship. It was laden with wheat. ver. 38. Paul, evidently, by this, intended to suggest the propriety of remaining where they were, until the time of dangerous navigation was past.

11. *The master.* The captain, or the pilot. The person who is here meant, was the helmsman, who occupied, in ancient ships, a conspicuous place on the stern, and steered the ship, and gave directions to the crew. ¶ *The owner of the ship.* Probably a different person from "the master." He had the general command of the ship as his own property, but had employed "the master," or the pilot, to direct and manage it. His counsel in regard to the propriety of continuing the voyage, would be likely to be followed.

12. *The haven.* The fair havens. ver. 8. ¶ *Was not commodious to winter in* Not safe or convenient to remain there. Probably it furnished rather a safe anchorage ground in time of a storm, than a convenient place for a permanent harbour. ¶ *The more part.* The greater part of the crew. ¶ *To Phenice.* This was a port or harbour on the south side of Crete, and west of the fair havens. It was a more convenient harbour, and regarded as more safe. It appears, therefore, that the majority of persons on board concurred with Paul in the belief that it was not advisable to attempt the navigation of the sea until the dangers of the winter had passed by. ¶ *And lieth toward.* Greek, *Looking* toward; i. e. it was *open* in that direction. ¶ *The southwest.* Κατὰ Λίβα Toward *Lybia*, or *Africa*. That country was situated southwest of the mouth of the harbour. The entrance of the harbour was in a southwest direction. ¶ *And northwest.* Κατα Χῶρον. This word denotes a wind blowing from the northwest. The harbour was doubtless

ter; *which is* an haven of Crete, [a]
and lieth toward the southwest and
northwest.
13 And when the south wind
blew softly, supposing that they
had obtained *their* purpose, loosing [b] *thence*, they sailed close by
Crete.
14 But not long after there [1]
arose against it a tempestuous [c]
wind, called Euroclydon.

15 And when the ship was caught,
and could not bear up into the wind,
we let *her* drive.
16 And running under a certain
island which is called Clauda, we
had much work to come by the
boat;
17 Which when they had taken up, they used helps, undergirding the ship; and fearing lest
they should fall [d] into the quic

a ver.7. b ver.21. 1 or *beat*. c Ps.107.25. d ver.41

curved. Its entrance was in a southwest direction. It then turned so as to lie in a direction towards the northwest. It was thus rendered perfectly safe from the winds and heavy seas; and in that harbour they might pass the winter in security.

13. *The south wind.* The wind before had probably been a head wind, blowing from the west. When it veered round to the south, and when it blew gently, though not entirely favourable, yet it was so that they supposed they could sail along the coast of Crete. ¶ *Had obtained their purpose.* The object of their desire; that is, to sail safely along the coast of Crete. ¶ *Loosing* thence. Setting sail from the fair havens. ¶ *Close by Crete.* Near the shore. It is evident that they designed, if possible, to make the harbour of Phenice, to winter there.

14. *Arose.* Beat violently. ¶ *Against it.* Against the island of Crete. ¶ *A tempestuous wind.* Turbulent, violent, strong. ¶ *Called Euroclydon.* Interpreters have been much perplexed about the meaning of this word, which occurs nowhere else in the New Testament. The most probable supposition is, that it denotes a wind not blowing steadily from any quarter, but a *hurricane*, or wind veering about to different quarters. Such hurricanes are known to abound in the Mediterranean, and are now called *Levanters*, deriving their name from blowing chiefly in the Levant, or eastern part of the Mediterranean. The name *Euroclydon* is derived probably from two Greek words, εὖρος, *wind*, and κλύδων, *a wave*; so called from its agitating and exciting the waves. It thus answers to the usual effects of a hurricane, or of a wind rapidly changing its points of compass.

15. *The ship was caught.* By the wind. It came suddenly upon them as a tempest. ¶ *Could not bear up*, &c. Could not resist its violence, or could not direct the ship. It was seized by the wind, and driven with such violence that it became unmanageable. ¶ *We let her drive.* We suffered the ship to be borne along by the wind without attempting to control it.

16. *And running under.* Running near to an island. They run near to it, where the violence of the wind was probably broken by the island. ¶ *Which is called Clauda.* This is a small island southwest of Crete. ¶ *We had much work.* Much difficulty; we were scarcely able to do it. ¶ *To come by the boat.* This does not mean that they attempted here to land in the boat, but they had much difficulty in saving the small boat attached to the ship from being staved to pieces. Whether it was carried in the ship or towed at the stern does not appear; but it is evident that it was in danger of being broken to pieces, or lost, and that they had much difficulty in securing it. The importance of securing the small boat is known by all seamen.

17. *Which when they had taken up.* When they had raised up the boat into the ship, so as to secure it. ¶ *They used helps.* They used ropes, cables, stays, or chains, for the purpose of securing the ship. The danger was that the ship would be destroyed; and they, therefore, made use of such aids as should prevent the loss of the ship. ¶ *Undergirding the ship.* The ancients were accustomed to pass cables or strong ropes from one side of the ship to another, to keep the planks from springing or starting by the action of the sea. The rope was slipped under the prow, and passed along to any part of the keel which they pleased, and made fast on the deck. See cases mentioned in Kuinoel on this verse. An instance of the same kind is mentioned in lord Anson's voyage round the world. Speaking of a Spanish man-of-war in a storm, he says, "they were obliged to throw overboard all their upper-deck guns, and take six turns of the cable round the ship, to prevent her opening" (*Clarke.*)

sands, strake sail, and so were
driven.
18 And being exceedingly tossed
[a] with a tempest, the next *day* they
lightened the ship.
19 And the third *day* we cast
out [b] with our own hands the tackling of the ship.
20 And when neither [c] sun nor
stars in many days appeared, and
no small tempest lay on *us*, all hope
[d] that we should be saved was then
taken away.
21 But after long abstinence,
Paul stood forth in the midst of
them, and said, Sirs, ye should
have hearkened [e] unto me, and not
have loosed [f] from Crete, and to
have gained this harm and loss.
22 And now [g] I exhort you to be
of good cheer: for there shall be
no loss of *any man's* life among
you, but of the ship.
23 For there stood by me this
night [h] the angel [i] of God, whose [j]
I am, and whom [k] I serve.
24 Saying, Fear not, Paul; thou
must be brought before Cesar: and,
lo, God hath given thee [l] all them
that sail with thee.

a Ps.107.27. *b* Job 2.4. Jon.1.5. *c* Ps.105.28. *d* Ezek.37.11. *e* ver.10. *f* ver.13. *g* Job 22.29. Ps.112.7. 2Cor.4.8,9. *h* c.23.11. *i* Heb.1.14. *j* Deut.32.9. Ps.135.4. Isa.44.5. Mal.3.17. Jno.17.9,10. 1Cor.6.20. 1Pet.2.9,10 *k* Ps.116.16. Isa.44.21. Dan. 3.17; 6.16. Jno.12.26. Rom.1.9. 2Tim.1.3. *l* Gen. 19.21,22.

¶ *Lest they should fall into the quicksands.* There were two celebrated *syrtes*, or quicksands on the coast of Africa, called the greater and lesser. They were vast beds of sand driven up by the sea, and constantly shifting their position, so that that they could not know certainly where the danger was, and guard against it. As they were constantly changing their position, they could not be accurately laid down in a chart. They were afraid, therefore, that they should be driven on one of those banks of sand, and thus be lost. ¶ *Strake sail.* Or rather, lowered, or took down the mast; or the yards to which the sails were attached. There has been a great variety of interpretations proposed on this passage. The most probable is, that they took down the *mast*, by cutting or otherwise, as is now done in storms at sea, to save the ship. They were at the mercy of the wind and waves; and their only hope was by taking away their sails. ¶ *And so were driven.* By the wind and waves. The ship was unmanageable, and they suffered it to be driven before the wind.

18. *They lightened the ship.* By throwing out a part of the cargo.

19. *The tackling of the ship.* The anchors, sails, cables, baggage, &c. That is, they threw over every thing that was not indispensable to its preservation, for it seems still (ver. 29) that they retained some of their anchors on board.

20. *Neither sun nor stars*, &c. As they could see neither sun nor stars, they could make no observations; and as they had no compass, they would be totally ignorant of their situation, and gave up all as lost.

21. *But after long abstinence.* By the violence of the storm, by their long-continued labour, and by their apprehension of danger, they had a long time abstained from food. ¶ *And to have gained this harm.* To have *procured* this harm, or have subjected yourselves to it. Had you remained there, you would have been safe. It seems to be bad English to speak of *gaining a loss*, but it is a correct translation of the original (κερδῆσαι), which expresses the idea of *acquiring* or *procuring*, whether good or evil. See ver. 9, 10.

22. *There shall be no loss.* This must have been cheering news to those who had given up all for lost. As Paul had manifested great wisdom in his former advice to them, they might be now more disposed to listen to him. The reason why he believed they would be safe, he immediately states.

23. *There stood by me.* There appeared to me. ¶ *The angel of God.* The messages of God were often communicated by angels. See Heb. i. 14. This does not mean that there was any *particular* angel, but simply *an* angel. ¶ *Whose I am.* Of the God to whom I belong. This is an expression of Paul's entire devotedness to him. ¶ *Whom I serve.* In the gospel. To whom and to whose cause I am entirely devoted.

24. *Fear not, Paul.* Do not be alarmed with the danger of the loss of life. ¶ *Thou must be brought*, &c. And therefore thy life will be spared. ¶ *God hath given thee all*, &c. That is, they shall all

25 Wherefore, sirs, be of good
cheer; for [a] I believe God, that it
shall be even as it was told me.
26 Howbeit, we must be cast
upon a certain island. [b]
27 But when the fourteenth
night was come, as we were driv-
en up and down in Adria, about
midnight the shipmen deemed that
they drew near to some country:
28 And sounded, and found *it*
twenty fathoms: and when they
had gone a little further, they
sounded again, and found *it* fifteen
fathoms.
29 Then fearing lest they should
have fallen upon rocks, they cast
four anchors out of the stern, and
wished [c] for the day.
30 And as the shipmen were
about to flee out of the ship, when
they had let down the boat into the
sea, under colour as though they
would have cast anchors out of the
foreship,
31 Paul said to the centurion

a Luke 1.45. Rom.4.20,21. 2Tim.1.12. b c.28.1. c Ps.130.6.

be preserved with thee. None of their lives shall be lost. It does not mean that they should be converted; but that their lives should be preserved. It is implied here that it was for the sake of Paul, or that the leading purpose of the divine interposition to rescue them from danger was, to save his life. The wicked often derive important benefits from being connected with Christians; and God often confers important favours on *them* in his general purpose to benefit his own people. The lives of impenitent men are often spared because God interposes to save his own people.

26. *Howbeit.* Nevertheless. ¶ *Upon a certain island.* Malta. See ch. xxviii. 1.

27. *The fourteenth night.* From the time when the tempest commenced. ¶ *In Adria.* In the Adriatic sea. This sea is properly situated between Italy and Dalmatia, now called the Adriatic gulf. But among the ancients the name was given not only to that gulf, but to the whole sea lying between Greece, Italy, and Africa, including the Sicilian and Ionian sea. It is evident from the narrative, that they were not in the Adriatic gulf, but in the vicinity of Malta. See the map. ¶ *Deemed.* Judged. Probably by the appearance of the sea.

28. *And sounded.* To *sound* is to make use of a line and lead to ascertain the depth of water. ¶ *Twenty fathoms.* A fathom is six feet, or the distance from the extremity of the middle finger on one hand to the extremity of the other, when the arms are extended. The depth, therefore, was about one hundred and twenty feet. ¶ *Fifteen fathoms.* They knew, therefore, that they were drawing near to shore.

29. *They cast four anchors.* On account of the violence of the storm and waves, to make if possible the ship secure. ¶ *And wished for the day.* To discern more accurately their situation and danger.

30. *The shipmen.* The sailors, leaving the prisoners. ¶ *Under colour.* Under pretence. They pretended that it was necessary to get into the boat, and carry the anchors ahead of the ship so as to make it secure, but with a real intention to make for the shore. ¶ *Out of the foreship.* From the prow, so as to make the fore part of the ship secure. The reason why they did this was, probably, that they expected the ship would go to pieces; and as all on board could not be saved in one small boat, they resolved to escape to a place of safety as soon as possible.

31. *Paul said to the centurion and the soldiers.* The centurion had, it appears, the general direction of the ship. ver. 11. Probably it had been pressed into the service of the government. ¶ *Except these.* These seamen. The soldiers and the centurion were unqualified to manage the ship, and the presence of the sailors was therefore indispensable to the preservation of any. ¶ *Abide in the ship.* Remain on board. ¶ *Ye cannot be saved.* You cannot be preserved from death. You will have no hope of managing the ship so as to be secure from death. It will be remembered that Paul had been informed by the angel, and had assured them (ver. 22—24), that no lives should be lost. But it was only in the use of the proper *means* that their lives would be safe. Though it had been determined, and though Paul had the assurance that their lives would be safe, yet this did not, in his view, prevent the use of the proper means to secure it. From this we may learn, (1.) That the certainty of an event does not render it improper to use means to obtain it. (2.) That though the event

and to the soldiers, Except these
abide in the ship, ye cannot be
saved.
32 Then the soldiers cut off
the ropes of the boat, and let her
fall off.
33 And while the day was coming on, Paul besought *them* all to
take meat, saying, This day is the
fourteenth day that ye have tarried, and continued fasting, having
taken nothing.
34 Wherefore I pray you to take
some meat; for this [a] is for your
health: for there [b] shall not an hair
fall from the head of any of you.
35 And when he had thus
spoken, he took bread, and [c] gave
thanks to God in presence of them
all: and when he had broken *it*, he
began to eat.
36 Then were they all of good

a Matt.15.32. 1Tim.5.23. b 1Kings 1.52. Matt. 10.30. Luke 12.7; 21.18. c 1Sam.9.13. Matt.15.36. Mark 8.6. Jno.6.11,23. 1Tim. 4.3,4.

may be determined, yet the use of the means may be indispensable. The event is rendered no more certain than the means requisite to accomplish it. (3.) That the doctrine of the divine purposes or decrees, making certain future events, does not make the use of man's agency unnecessary or improper. The means are determined as well as the end; and the one will not be secured without the other. (4.) The same is true in regard to the decrees respecting salvation. The end is not determined without the means; and as God has resolved that his people shall be saved, so he has also determined the means. He has ordained that they shall repent, shall believe, shall be holy, and shall *thus* be saved. (5.) We have in this case a full answer to the objection that a belief in the decrees of God will make men neglect the means of salvation, and lead to licentiousness. It has just the contrary tendency. Here is a case in which Paul *certainly* believed in the purpose of God to save these men; in which he was assured that it was fully determined; and yet the effect was not to produce inattention and unconcern, but to prompt him to use strenuous efforts to accomplish the very effect which God had determined *should* take place. So it is always. A belief that God has purposes of mercy; that he designs, and has always designed, to save some, will prompt to the use of all proper means to secure it. If we had no evidence that God had any such purpose, effort would be vain. We should have no inducement to exertion. Where we *have* such evidence, it operates as it did in the case of Paul, to produce great and strenuous endeavours to secure the object.

32. *Cut off the ropes*, &c. It is evident that the mariners had not yet got on board the boat. They had let it down into the sea (ver 30), and were about to go on board. By thus cutting the ropes which fastened the boat to the ship, and letting it go, they removed all possibility of their fleeing from the ship, and compelled them to remain on board.

33. *And while the day was coming on.* At daybreak. It was before they had sufficient light to discern what they should do. ¶ *To take meat.* Food. The word *meat* was formerly used to denote *food* of any kind. ¶ *That ye have tarried.* That you have remained or been fasting. ¶ *Having taken nothing.* No *regular* meal. It cannot mean that they had lived entirely without food; but that they had been so much in danger, so constantly engaged, and so anxious about their safety, that they had taken no *regular* meal; and that what they had taken had been at irregular intervals, and had been a scanty allowance. "Appian speaks of an army which for twenty days together had neither food nor sleep; by which he must mean that they neither made full meals, nor slept whole nights together. The same interpretation must be given to this phrase." (*Doddridge.*) The effect of this must have been, that they would be weak and exhausted; and little able to endure the fatigues which yet remained.

34. *Not an hair fall from the head*, &c. This is a proverbial expression, denoting that they should be preserved safe; that none of them should be lost, and that in their persons they should not experience the least damage. 1 Kings i. 52. 1 Sam. xiv. 45.

35. *And gave thanks*, &c. This was the usual custom among the Hebrews. See Note, Matt. xiv. 19. Paul was among those who were not Christians. But he was not ashamed of the proper acknowledgment of God, and was not afraid to avow his dependence on him, and to express his gratitude for his mercy.

cheer, and they also took *some*
meat.
37 And we were in all in the
ship, two hundred threescore and
sixteen souls.
38 And when they had eaten
enough, they lightened the ship,
and cast out the wheat into the
sea.
39 And when it was day, they
knew not the land: but they discovered a certain creek with a
shore, into the which they were
minded, if it were possible, to
thrust in the ship.
40 And when they had [1] taken
up the anchors, they committed
themselves unto the sea, and loosed
the rudder-bands, and hoisted up
the mainsail to the wind, and made
toward shore.
41 And falling into a place
where two seas met, they ran the
ship aground; and the forepart
stuck fast, and remained unmov-
able, but the hinder part was
broken with the violence of the
waves.

[1] or, *cut the anchors, left them in the sea, etc.*

38. *They lightened the ship.* By casting the wheat into the sea. As they had no hope of saving the cargo, and had no further use for it, they hoped that by throwing the wheat overboard, the ship would draw less water, and that thus they would be able to come nearer to the shore.

39. *They knew not the land.* They had been driven with a tempest, without being able to make any observation; and it is probable that they were entire strangers to the coast, and to the whole island. ¶ *A certain creek with a shore.* Greek, A certain *bosom* (κόλπον) or *bay*. By its having *a shore* is probably meant that it had a *level* shore, or one that was convenient for landing. It was not a high bluff of rocks, but was accessible. *Kuinoel* thinks that the passage should be construed, "they found a certain shore, having a bay," &c. ¶ *Were minded.* Were resolved.

40. *Had taken up the anchors.* The four anchors with which they had moored the ship. ver. 29. See the margin. The expression may mean that they slipped or cut their cables, and that thus they left the anchors in the sea. This is the most probable interpretation. ¶ *And loosed the rudder-bands.* The rudder in navigation is that by which a ship is steered. It is that part of the helm which consists of a piece of timber, broad at the bottom, which enters the water, and is attached by hinges to the stern-post on which it turns.—(*Webster.*) But what was the precise form of the rudder among the ancients, is not certainly known. Sometimes a vessel might be steered by oars. In most ships they appear to have had a rudder at the prow as well as at the stern. In some instances also, they had them on the sides. The word used here in the Greek is in the plural (τῶν πηδαλίων), and it is evident that they had in this ship more than one rudder. The *bands* mentioned here were probably the cords, or fastenings by which the rudder could be made secure to the sides of the ship, or could be raised up out of the water in a violent storm, to prevent its being carried away. And as in the tempest, the rudders had become useless (ver. 15. 17), they were probably either raised out of the water, or made fast. Now that the storm was passed, and they could be used again, they were *loosed*, and they endeavoured to direct the vessel into port. ¶ *The mainsail.* Ἀρτέμονα. There have been various explanations of this word. Luther translates it *the mast.* Erasmus, *the yards.* Grotius, who supposes that the mainmast had been cast away (ver. 17), thinks that this must mean the foremast or bowsprit. The word usually means the *mainsail.* The Syriac and Arabic understand it of a *small sail,* that was hoisted for a temporary purpose.

41. *And falling.* Being carried by the wind and waves. ¶ *Into a place where two seas met.* Gr. Into a place *of a double sea.* Διθάλασσον. That is, a place which is washed on both sides by the sea. It refers properly to an isthmus, tongue of land, or a sand-bar stretching out from the main land, and which was washed on both sides by the waves. It is evident that this was not properly an *isthmus* that was above the waves, but was probably a long sand-bank that stretched far out into the sea, and which they did not perceive. In endeavouring to make the harbour, they ran on this bar or sand-bank. ¶ *They ran the ship aground.* Not designedly, but in endeavouring to reach the harbour. ver 39

42 And the soldiers' counsel [a] was to kill the prisoners, lest any of them should swim out, and escape.

43 But the centurion, willing to save Paul, [b] kept them from *their* purpose; and commanded that they which could swim should cast *themselves* first *into the sea*, and get to land:

44 And the rest, some on boards, and some on *broken pieces* of the ship. And so [c] it came to pass that they escaped all safe to land

CHAPTER XXVIII.

AND when they were escaped, then they knew that the island [d] was called Melita.

a Ps.74.20. b 2Cor.11.25. c Ps.107.28,30. ver.22. d c.27.26.

¶ *The hinder part was broken.* The stern was broken or staved in. By this means the company was furnished with boards, &c., on which they were safely conveyed to the shore. ver. 44.

42. *And the soldiers' counsel*, &c. Why they gave this advice is not known. It was probably, however, because the Roman military discipline was very strict, and if they escaped, it would probably be charged on them that it had been done by the negligence and unfaithfulness of the soldiers. They therefore proposed, in a most cruel and bloodthirsty manner, to kill them, though contrary to all humanity, justice, and laws; presuming probably that it would be supposed that they had perished in the wreck. This is a remarkable proof that men can be cruel even when experiencing the tender mercy of God; and that the most affecting scenes of divine goodness will not mitigate the natural ferocity and cruelty of those who delight in blood.

43. *But the centurion, willing to save Paul.* He had at first been disposed to treat Paul with kindness. ver. 3. And his conduct on board the ship; the wisdom of his advice (ver. 10); the prudence of his conduct in the agitation and danger of the tempest; and not improbably the belief that he was under the divine protection and blessing, disposed him to spare his life. ¶ *Kept them from their purpose.* Thus, for the sake of this one righteous man, the lives of all were spared. The instance here shows, (1.) That it is possible for a pious man, like Paul, so to conduct in the various trying scenes of life—the agitations, difficulties, and temptations of this world—as to conciliate the favour of the men of this world; and, (2.) That important benefits often result to sinners from the righteous. Paul's being on board was the means of saving the lives of many prisoners; and God often confers important blessings on the wicked for the sake of the pious relatives, friends, and neighbours with whom they are connected. Ten righteous men would have saved Sodom (Gen. xviii. 32); and Christians are in more ways than one the salt of the earth, and the light of the world. Matt. v. 13, 14. It is a privilege to be related to the friends of God—to be the children of pious parents, or to be connected with pious partners in life. It is a privilege to be connected with the friends of God in business; or to dwell near them; or to be associated with them in the various walks and dangers of life. The streams of blessings which flow to fertilize *their* lands, flow also to bless others; the dews of heaven which descend on their habitations, descend on all around; and the God which crowns them with loving-kindness, often fills the abodes of their neighbours and friends with the blessings of peace and salvation. ¶ *And commanded.* Probably they were released from their chains.

44. *And the rest.* Those who could not swim. ¶ *They escaped all safe to land.* According to the promise which was made to Paul. ver. 22. This was done by the special providence of God. It was a remarkable instance of divine interposition to save so many through so long continued dangers; and it shows that God can defend in any perils, and can accomplish all his purposes. On the ocean, or the land, we are safe in his keeping; and he can devise ways that shall fulfill all his purposes, and that can protect his people from danger.

CHAPTER XXVIII.

1. *They knew.* Either from their former acquaintance with the island, or from the information of the inhabitants. ¶ *Was called Melita.* Now called Malta. It was celebrated formerly for producing large quantities of honey, and is supposed to have been called *Melita* from the Greek word, signifying honey. It is about twenty miles in length from east to west, and twelve miles in breadth from north to south, and about sixty miles in circumference. It is about sixty miles

2 And the barbarous [a] people
shewed us no little kindness: for
they kindled a fire, and received
us, [b] every one, because of the
present rain, and because of the
cold.
3 And when Paul had gathered
a bundle of sticks, and laid *them*
on the fire, there came a viper out
of the heat, and fastened on his
hand.
4 And when the barbarians saw
the *venomous* beast hang on his
hand, they said among themselves,
No doubt [c] this man is a murderer,
whom, though he hath escaped the

a Rom.1.14. Col.3.11. b Matt.10.42. Heb.13.2. c Jno.7.24.

---

from the coast of Sicily. The island is an immense rock of white soft free-stone, with a covering of earth about one foot in depth, which has been brought from the island of Sicily. There was also another island formerly called *Melita*, now called *Meleda*, in the Adriatic sea, near the coast of Illyricum, and some have supposed that Paul was shipwrecked on that island. But tradition has uniformly said that it was on the island now called Malta. Besides, the other Melita would have been far out of the usual track in going to Italy; and it is further evident that Malta was the place, because, from the place of his shipwreck, he went directly to Syracuse, Rhegium, and Puteoli, thus sailing in a direct course to Rome. In sailing from the other Melita to Rhegium, Syracuse would be far out of the direct course. The island now is in the possession of the British.

2. *And the barbarous people.* See Note, Rom. i. 14. The Greeks regarded all as barbarians who did not speak their language; and applied the name to all other nations but their own. It does not denote, as it does sometimes with us, people of savage, uncultivated, and cruel habits, but simply those whose speech was unintelligible. See 1 Cor. xiv. 11. The island is supposed to have been peopled at first by the Phœcians, afterwards by the Phœnicians, and afterwards by a colony from Carthage. The language of the Maltese was that of Africa, and hence it was called by the Greeks the language of barbarians. It was a language which was unintelligible to the Greeks and Latins. ¶ *The rain.* The continuance of the storm. ¶ *And of the cold.* The exposure to the water in getting to the shore, and probably to the coldness of the weather. It was now in the month of October.

3. *Had gathered a bundle of sticks.* For the purpose of making a fire. ¶ *There came a viper.* A poisonous serpent. Note, Matt. iii. 7 The viper was, doubtless, in the bundle of sticks or limbs of trees which Paul had gathered, but was concealed, and was torpid. But when the bundle was laid on the fire, the viper became warmed by the heat, and ran out, and fastened on the hand of Paul. ¶ *And fastened on his hand.* Καθῆψε. This word properly means to join one's-self to; to touch; to adhere to. It might have been by coiling around his hand and arm; or by fastening its fangs in his hand. It is not expressly affirmed that Paul was *bitten* by the viper, yet it is evidently implied; and it is wholly incredible, that a viper, unless miraculously prevented, should fasten himself to the hand without biting.

4. *The* venomous *beast.* The word *beast* we apply usually to an animal of larger size than a viper. But the original word (θηρίον) is applicable to animals of any kind, and especially applied by Greek writers to serpents. (See *Schleusner.*) ¶ *No doubt.* The fact that the viper had fastened on him, and that, as they supposed, he must now certainly die, was the proof from which they inferred his guilt. ¶ *Is a murderer.* Why they thought he was a *murderer* rather than guilty of some other crime, is not known. It might have been, (1.) Because they inferred that he must have been guilty of some very atrocious crime, and as murder was the highest crime that man could commit, they inferred that he had been guilty of this. Or, (2.) More probably, they had an opinion that when divine vengeance overtook a man, he would be punished in a manner similar to the offence; and as murder is committed usually with the hand, and as the viper had fastened on the hand of Paul, they inferred that he had been guilty of taking life. It was supposed among the ancients, that persons were often punished by divine vengeance in that part of the body which had been the instrument of the sin. ¶ *Whom though he hath escaped the sea.* They supposed that vengeance and justice would still follow the guilty; that though he might escape one form of punishment, yet he would be exposed to another. And this, to a certain extent, is true. These bar-

sea, yet vengeance suffereth not to
live.
5 And he shook off the beast into
the fire, and felt [a] no harm.
6 Howbeit, they looked when he
should have swollen, or fallen down
dead suddenly: but after they had
looked a great while, and saw no
harm come to him, they changed
their minds, and said [b] that he was
a god.
7 In the same quarters were possessions of the chief man of the
island, whose name was Publius;
who received us, and lodged us
three days courteously.
8 And it came to pass, that the
father of Publius lay sick of a fe-
ver, and of a bloody flux: to whom
[c] Paul entered in, and prayed, and
laid [d] his hands on him, and healed
him.
9 So when this was done, others
also, which had diseases in the
island, came, and were healed:
10 Who also honoured [e] us with

a Mark 16,18. Luke. 10.19. b c.14.11.

c James 5.14,15. d Matt.9.18. Mark 6.5-7.32;16.18. Luke 4.40. c.19.11. 1Cor.12.9,28. e 1Thess.2.6. 1Tim 5.17.

---

barians reasoned from great original principles, written on the hearts of all men by nature, that there is a God of justice, and that the guilty would be punished. They reasoned incorrectly, as many do, only because that they supposed that *every* calamity is a judgment for some particular sin. Men often draw this conclusion; and suppose that suffering is to be traced to some particular crime, and to be regarded as a direct judgment from heaven. See Notes, John ix. 1—3. The general proposition, that all sin will be punished at some time, is true; but we are not qualified to affirm of particular calamities always that they are direct judgments for sin. In some cases we may. In the case of the drunkard, the gambler, and the profligate, we cannot doubt, that the loss of property, health, and reputation is the direct result of specific crime. In the ordinary calamities of life, however, it requires a more profound acquaintance with the principles of divine government than we possess, to affirm of each instance of suffering, that it is a particular judgment for some crime. ¶ *Yet vengeance.* Ἡ δίκη. *Diké,* or justice, was represented by the heathen as a goddess, the daughter of Jupiter, whose office it was to take vengeance, or to inflict punishment for crimes. ¶ *Suffereth not to live.* They regarded him as already a dead man. They supposed the effect of the bite of the viper would be so certainly fatal, that they might speak of him as already in effect dead. *Beza.*

5. *And he shook off,* &c. In this was remarkably fulfilled the promise of the Saviour (Mark xvi. 18): "They shall take up serpents," &c.

6 *When he should have swollen.* When they expected he would have swollen from the bite of the viper. The poison of the viper is rapid; and they expected that he would die soon. The word rendered "swollen" (πίμπρασθαι) means properly to burn; to be inflamed; and then to be swollen from inflammation. This was what they expected here, that the poison would produce a violent inflammation. ¶ *Or fallen down dead suddenly.* As is sometimes the case from the bite of the serpent, when a vital part is affected. ¶ *They changed their minds.* They saw he was uninjured, and miraculously preserved; and they supposed that none but a god could be thus kept from death. ¶ *That he was a god.* That the Maltese were idolaters there can be no doubt. But what gods they worshipped is unknown, and conjecture would be useless. It was natural that they should attribute such a preservation to the presence of a divinity. A similar instance occurred at Lystra. See Notes, ch. xiv. 11.

7. *In the same quarters.* In that place, or that part of the island. ¶ *Possessions.* Property. His place of residence. ¶ *The chief man.* Gr. The *first* man. Probably he was the governor of the island.

8. *A bloody flux.* Gr. Dysentery. ¶ *And laid his hands on him,* &c. In accordance with the promise of the Saviour. Mark xvi. 18. This miracle was a suitable return for the hospitality of Publius, and would serve to conciliate further the kindness of the people, and prepare the way for the usefulness of Paul.

10. *Who also honoured us.* As men who were favoured of heaven, and who had been the means of conferring important benefits on them in healing the sick, &c. Probably the word "honours" here means *gifts,* or marks of favour. ¶ *They laded us.* They gave us, or con-

many honours; and when we departed, they laded *us* with such things [a] as were necessary.

11 And after three months we departed in a ship of Alexandria, which had wintered in the isle, whose sign was Castor and Pollux.

12 And landing at Syracuse, we tarried *there* three days.

13 And from thence we fetched a compass, and came to Rhegium: and after one day the south wind blew, and we came the next day to Puteoli;

14 Where we found brethren, and were desired to tarry with them seven days: and so we went toward Rome.

15 And from thence, when the brethren heard of us, they came [b] to meet us as far as Appii Forum, and the Three Taverns: whom when Paul saw, he thanked God, and took courage. [c]

a Matt.6.31-34; 10.8-10. 2Cor.2.5-11. Phil.4.11,12.

b c.21.5. 3Jno.6,8. c Josh.1.6,7.9. 1Sam.30.6. Ps. 27.14.

ferred on us. They furnished us with such things as were necessary for us on our journey.

11. *And after three months.* Probably they remained there so long, because there was no favourable opportunity for them to go to Rome. If they arrived there, as is commonly supposed, in October, they left for Rome in January. ¶ *In a ship of Alexandria.* See Note, ch. xxvii. 6. ¶ *Whose sign.* Which was ornamented with an image of Castor and Pollux. It was common to place on the prow of the ship the image of some person, or god, whose name the ship bore. This custom is still observed. ¶ *Castor and Pollux.* These were two semi-deities. They were reputed to be twin brothers, sons of Jupiter and Leda, the wife of Tyndarus, king of Sparta. After their death, they are fabled to have been translated to heaven, and made *constellations* under the name of *gemini*, or the twins. They then received divine honours, and were called the sons of Jupiter. They were supposed to preside over sailors, and to be their protectors; hence it was not uncommon to place their image on ships. See authorities in Lempriere's Dictionary.

12. *And landing at Syracuse.* Syracuse was the capital of the island of Sicily, on the eastern coast. It was in the direct course from Malta to Rome. It contains at present about 18,000 inhabitants.

13. *We fetched a compass.* We coasted about; or we coasted along the eastern side of Sicily. The course can be seen on the map. ¶ *And came to Rhegium.* This was a city of Italy, in the kingdom of Naples, on the coast near the south-west extremity of Italy. It was nearly opposite to Messina, in Sicily. It is now called *Reggio.* See the map. ¶ *The south wind.* A wind favourable for their voyage. ¶ *To Puteoli.* The wells. It was celebrated for its warm baths, and from these, and its springs, it is supposed to have derived its name of *the wells.* It is now called *Pozzuoli*, and is in the campania of Naples, on the northern side of the bay, and about eight miles northwest from Naples. The town contains at present about 10,000 inhabitants.

14. *Brethren.* Christian brethren. But by whom the gospel had been preached there, is unknown.

15. *And from thence.* From Puteoli ¶ *When the brethren heard of us.* The Christians who were at Rome. ¶ *As far as the Appii Forum.* This was a city about 56 miles from Rome. The remains of an ancient city are still seen there. It is on the borders of the Pontine marshes. The city was built on the celebrated Appian way, or road from Rome to Capua. The road was made by Appius Claudius, and probably the city also. It was called the *forum* or *market-place* of Appius, because it was a convenient place for travellers on the Appian way to stop for purposes of refreshment. It was also a famous resort for pedlars and merchants. See Horace, b. i. sat. 5. 3. ¶ *And the Three Taverns.* This place was about eight or ten miles nearer Rome than the Appii Forum. Cicero ad Att. ii. 10. It undoubtedly received its name because it was distinguished as a place of refreshment on the Appian way. Probably the greater part of the company of Christians remained at this place, while the remainder went forward to meet Paul, and to attend him on his way. The Christians at Rome had doubtless heard much of Paul. His epistle to them had been written about the year of our Lord 57. or at least five years before this time. The interest which the Roman Christians felt in the apostle was thus manifested by their coming so far to meet him, though he was a prisoner. ¶ *He thanked God.* He had long ardently desired to see the Chris-

16 And when we came to Rome, the centurion delivered the prisoners to the captain of the guard: but Paul was suffered to dwell by himself [a] with a soldier that kept him.

17 And it came to pass, that after three days Paul called the chief of the Jews together: and when they were come together, he said unto them, Men *and* brethren, though [b] I have committed nothing against the people, or customs of our fathers, yet was I delivered [c] prisoner from Jerusalem into the hands of the Romans:

18 Who, [d] when they had examined me, would have let *me* go, because there was no cause of death in me.

19 But when the Jews spake against *it*, I was constrained to appeal [e] unto Cesar; not that I had aught to accuse my nation of.

20 For this cause therefore have I called for you, to see *you*, and to speak with *you*: because that for the hope [f] of Israel I am bound with this chain. [g]

21 And they said unto him, We neither received letters out of Judea concerning thee, neither any of the brethren that came showed or spake any harm of thee.

a c.24.25; 27.3. b c.24.12,13; 25.8. c c.21.33, &c. d c.24.10; 26.31.

e c.25.11. f c.26.6,7. g c.26.29. Eph.3.1: 4.1: 6.20. 2Tim.1.16; 2.9. Philem.10,13.

tians of Rome. Rom. i. 9—11; xv 23. 32. He was now grateful to God that the object of his long desire was at last granted to him, and that he was permitted to see them, though in bonds. ¶ *And took courage.* From their society and counsel. The presence and counsel of Christian brethren is often of inestimable value in encouraging and strengthening us in the toils and trials of life.

16. *The captain of the guard.* The commander of the Pretorian cohort, or guard. The custom was, that those who were sent from the provinces to Rome for trial were delivered to the custody of this guard. The name of the prefect or captain of the guard at this time, was Burrhus Afranius. Tacit. Ann. 12. 42. 1. ¶ *But Paul was suffered*, &c. Evidently by the permission of the centurion, whose favour he had so much conciliated on the voyage. See ch. xxvii. 43. ¶ *With a soldier that kept him.* That is, in the custody of a soldier, to whom he was chained, and who, of course, constantly attended him. See ch. xxiv. 23. Note, ch. xii. 6.

17. *Paul called the chief of the Jews.* He probably had two objects in this: one was to vindicate himself from the suspicion of crime, or to convince them that the charges alleged against him were false; and the other, to explain to them the gospel of Christ. In accordance with his custom every where, he seized the earliest opportunity of making the gospel known to his own countrymen; and he naturally supposed that charges highly unfavourable to his character, had been sent forward against him to the Jews at Rome by those in Judea. ¶ *Against the people.* Against the Jews. ch. xxiv. 12. ¶ *Or customs*, &c. The religious rites of the nation. Note, ch. vi. 14. ¶ *Was I delivered prisoner*, &c. By the Jews. ch. xxi. 33, &c.

18. *When they had examined me*, &c. ch. xxiv. 10—27; xxv. xxvi. 31, 32. ¶ *No cause of death.* No crime worthy of death.

19. *The Jews spake against it.* Against my being set at liberty. ¶ *I was constrained.* By a regard to my own safety and character. ¶ *To appeal unto Cesar.* Note, ch. xxv. 11. ¶ *Not that I had aught*, &c. I did it for my own preservation and safety; not that I wished to accuse my own countrymen. It was not from motives of revenge, but for safety. Paul had been unjustly accused and injured; yet with the true spirit of the Christian religion, he here says that he cherished no unkind feelings towards them.

20. *Because for the hope of Israel.* On account of the hope which the Jews cherished of the coming of the Messiah; of the resurrection; and of the future state through him. See this explained in the Note on ch. xxiii. 6. ¶ *I am bound with this chain.* See Note, ch. xxvi. 29. Probably he was attached constantly to a soldier by a chain.

21. *We neither received letters*, &c. Why the Jews in Judea had not forwarded the accusation against Paul to their brethren at Rome, that they might continue the prosecution before the emperor is not known. It is probable that they

22 But we desire to hear of thee
what thou thinkest: for as concerning this sect, we know that
every where [a] it is spoken against.
23 And when they had appointed him a day, there came many to
him into *his* lodging; [b] to whom he
expounded [c] and testified the kingdom of God, persuading them concerning Jesus, both [d] out of the
law of Moses, and *out of* the prophets, from morning till evening.
24 And some [e] believed the
things which were spoken, and
some believed not.
25 And when they agreed not
among themselves, they departed,
after that Paul had spoken one
word; Well spake the Holy Ghost
by Esaias [f] the prophet unto our
fathers,
26 Saying, Go unto this people,
and say, Hearing ye shall hear,
and shall not understand; and
seeing ye shall see, and not perceive:
27 For the heart of this people
is waxed gross, and their ears are
dull of hearing, and their eyes have
they closed; lest they should see
with *their* eyes, and hear with *their*
ears, and understand with *their*
heart, and should be converted,
and I should heal them.
28 Be it known therefore unto
you, that the salvation of God is

a Luke 2.34. c.24.5,14. 1Pet.2.12; 4.14. b Philem. 2. c Luke 24.27. c.17.3; 19.8. d c.26.6,22. e c.14.4; 17.4; 19.9. Rom.3.3. f Ps.81.11. Isa.6.9. Jer.5.21. Eze.3.6,7; 12.2. Matt.13.14,15. Rom.11.8.

regarded their cause as *hopeless*, and choose to abandon the prosecution. Paul had been acquitted successively by Lysias, Felix, Festus, and Agrippa; and as they had not succeeded in procuring his condemnation before them, they saw no prospect of doing it at Rome, and chose therefore not to press the prosecution any farther. ¶ *Neither any of the brethren that came.* Any of the Jews. There was a very constant intercourse between Judea and Rome, but it seems that the Jews who had come before Paul had arrived, had not mentioned his case, so as to prejudice them against him.

22. *What thou thinkest.* What your belief is; or what are the doctrines of Christians respecting the Messiah. ¶ *This sect.* The sect of Christians. ¶ *Spoken against.* Particularly by Jews. This was the case then; and to a great extent, is the case still. It has been the common lot of the followers of Christ to be spoken of with contempt. Comp. ch. xxiv. 5.

23. *Appointed him a day.* A day when they would hear him. ¶ *To his lodging.* To the house where he resided. ver. 30. ¶ *He expounded.* He explained or declared the principles of the Christian religion. ¶ *And testified the kingdom of God.* Bore witness to, or declared the principles and doctrines of the reign of the Messiah. See Note, Matt. iii. 2. ¶ *Persuading them concerning Jesus.* Endeavouring to convince them that Jesus was the Messiah. ¶ *Both out of the law of Moses.* Endeavouring to convince them that he corresponded with the predictions respecting the Messiah in the books of Moses. (See Gen. xlix. 10. Deut. xviii. 18.) and with the types which Moses had instituted to prefigure the Messiah. ¶ *And out of the prophets.* Showing that he corresponded with the predictions of the prophets. See Note, ch. xvii. 3. ¶ *From morning until evening.* An instance of Paul's indefatigable toil in endeavouring to win his own countrymen to Jesus as the Messiah.

24. *And some believed, &c.* See Note, ch. xiv. 4.

25 *Had spoken one word.* One declaration of solemn prophecy, reminding them that it was the characteristic of the nation to reject the testimony of God, and that it was to be expected. It was the last solemn warning which we know Paul to have delivered to his countrymen the Jews. ¶ *Well spake.* Or he spoke the truth; he justly described the character of the Jewish people. The passage here quoted was as applicable in the time of Paul as of Isaiah. ¶ *The Holy Ghost.* A full proof of the inspiration of Isaiah. ¶ *By Esaias.* By Isaiah Isa. vi. 9, 10.

26, 27. *Saying, &c.* See this passage explained in the Notes on Matt. xiii. 14 and John xii. 39, 40.

28. *The salvation of God.* The know ledge of God's mode of saving men. ¶ *Is sent unto the Gentiles.* Since you have rejected it, it will be offered to them See Note, ch. xiii. 46. ¶ *And that they will hear it.* They will embrace it. Paul was never discouraged. If the gospel

sent unto the Gentiles, [a] and *that*
they will hear it.
29 And when he had said these
words, the Jews departed, and
had great reasoning among themselves.
30 And Paul dwelt two whole
years in his own hired house, and
received all that came in unto him.
31 Preaching [b] the kingdom of
God, and teaching those things
which concern the Lord Jesus
Christ, with all confidence, no man
forbidding him.

a Matt.21.41. c.13.46,47; 18.6.; 22.21; 26.17,18. Rom. 11.11

b c.4.31. Eph.6.19.

was rejected by one class of people, he was ready to offer it to another. If his own countrymen rejected and despised it, he never allowed himself to suppose that Christ had died in vain, but believed that others would be inclined to embrace its saving benefits. How happy would it be if all Christians had the same unwavering faith and zeal as Paul!

29. *And had great reasoning*. Great discussion or debates. That is, the part which believed that Jesus was the Messiah (ver. 24) discussed the subject warmly with those who did not believe. This whole verse is wanting in the Syriac version, and in some Greek MSS., and is supposed by Mill and Griesbach to be spurious.

30. *Paul dwelt two whole years*. Doubtless in the custody of the soldiers. Why he was not prosecuted before the emperor during this time is not known. It is evident, however (ver. 21), that the Jews were not disposed to carry the case before Nero, and the matter, during this time, was suffered quietly to sleep. There is great probability that the Jews durst not prosecute him before the emperor. It is clear that they had never been in favour of the appeal to Rome, and that they had no hope of gaining their cause. Probably they might remember the former treatment of the Roman emperor of their people (Note, ch. xviii. 2); they might remember that they were despised at the Roman capital, and not choose to encounter the scorn and indignation of the Roman court; and as there was no prosecution, Paul was suffered to live in quietness and safety. Lardner, however, supposes (vol. v. p. 528, 529. Ed. 8vo. Lond. 1829) that the case of Paul was soon brought before Nero, and decided; and that the method of confinement was ordered by the emperor himself. Lightfoot also supposes that Paul's "accusers, who had come from Judea to lay their charge against him, would be urgent to get their business despatched, that they might be returning to their own home again, and so would bring him to trial as soon as they could." But nothing certainly is known on the subject. It is evident, indeed, from 2 Tim. iv. 16, that he was at *some time* arraigned before the emperor; but when it was, or what was the decision, or why he was at last set at liberty, are all involved in impenetrable obscurity. ¶ *In his own hired house*. In a house which he was permitted to hire and occupy as his own. Probably in this he was assisted by the kindness of his Roman friends. ¶ *And received all*, &c. Received all hospitably and kindly who came to him to show him kindness, or to listen to his instructions. It is evident from this, that he was still a prisoner, and was not permitted to go at large.

31. *Preaching the kingdom of God*. Note, ch. xx. 25. ¶ *With all confidence* Openly and boldly, without any one to hinder him. It is known also, that Paul was not unsuccessful even when a prisoner at Rome. Several persons were converted by his preaching even in the court of the emperor. The things which had happened to him, he says (Phil. i. 12, 13, 14), had fallen out rather to the furtherance of the gospel, so that his bonds in Christ were manifested in all the palace, and in all other places; and many brethren in the Lord, says he, waxing confident by my bonds, are much more bold to speak the word without fear. In this situation he was remembered with deep interest by the church at Philippi, who sent Epaphroditus to him with a contribution to supply his wants. Of their kindness he speaks in terms of the tenderest gratitude in Phil. ii. 25; iv. 18. During his confinement also, he was the means of the conversion of Onesimus, a runaway slave of Philemon, of Colosse in Phrygia (Philem. 10); whom he sent back to his master with a letter to himself, and with an epistle to the church at that place. See epistle to the Colossians iv. 8, 9. 18. During this imprisonment, he wrote, according to Lardner, the following epistles, in the following order and time, viz:

Ephesians, April, A. D 61
2 Timothy, May 61
Philippians, before the end of... 62
Colossians 62
Philemon 62
Hebrews, spring of 63

Here closes the inspired account of the propagation of Christianity, of the organization of the Christian church, and of the toils and persecutions of the apostle Paul. Who can but be deeply affected when he comes to the conclusion of this inspired book of revivals, and of the history of the spread of the Christian religion, and of the account of that wonderful man—the apostle Paul? Who can help heaving the sigh of regret, that this interesting historian did not carry forward the history of Paul till his death, and that henceforward, in the history of the church, we want this faithful, inspired guide; and that, from the close of this book, every thing becomes at once so involved in obscurity and uncertainty? Instead, however, of pouring forth the sigh of unavailing regret that the sacred historian has carried us no farther onward, we should rather speak the language of praise that he has given, by the inspiration of the Holy Ghost, a history of the church for thirty years after the ascension of the Saviour; that he has recorded the accounts of the first great revivals of religion; that he has presented us the examples of the early missionary zeal; that he has informed us how the early Christians endured persecution and toil; that he has conducted us from land to land, and from city to city, showing us every where how the gospel was propagated, until we are led to the seat of the Roman power, and see the great apostle of Christianity there proclaiming, in that mighty capital of the world, the name of Jesus as the Saviour of men. Perhaps there could be no more appropriate close to the book of the inspired history, than thus to have conducted the apostle of the Gentiles, and to have recorded the spread of Christianity, to the capital of the Roman world, and to leave the principal agent in the establishment of the Christian religion in that seat of intelligence, and influence, and power. It is the conducting of Christianity to the very height of its earthly victories; and having shown its power in the *provinces* of the empire, it was proper for the inspired author of this ecclesiastical history to close the account with the record of its achievements in the capital.

Why Luke closed his history here is not known. It may have been that he was not afterwards the companion of Paul; or that he might have been himself removed by death. It is agreed on all hands that he did not attend Paul in his subsequent travels; and we should infer from the conclusion of this book, that he did not survive the apostle, as it is almost incredible, if he did, that he did not mention his release and death It is the uniform account of antiquity, that Luke, after the transactions with which the Acts of the Apostles closes, passed over into Achaia, where he lived a year or two, and there died at the age of eighty-four years.

Every thing in regard to the apostle Paul, after the account with which Luke closes this book, is involved in doubt and uncertainty. By what means he was set at liberty is not known; and there is a great contradiction of statements in regard to his subsequent travels, and even the time of his death. It is generally agreed, indeed, that he was set at liberty in the year of our Lord 63. After this, some of the fathers assert, that he travelled over Italy, and passed into Spain. But this account is involved in great uncertainty. Lardner, who has examined all the statements with care, and than whom no one is better qualified to pronounce an opinion on these subjects, gives the following account of the subsequent life of Paul. (Works, vol. v. 331—336. Ed. Lond. 1829.) He supposes that after his release, he went from Rome to Jerusalem as soon as possible; that he then went to Ephesus, and from thence to Laodicea and Colosse; and that he returned to Rome by Troas, Philippi, and Corinth. The reason why he returned to Rome, Lardner supposes was, that he regarded that city as opening before him the widest and most important field of labour; and that, therefore, he proposed there to spend the remainder of his life.

In the year of our Lord 64, a dreadful fire happened at Rome which continued for six or seven days. It was generally supposed that the city had been set on fire by order of the emperor Nero. In order to divert the attention of the people from this charge against himself, he accused the Christians of having been the authors of the conflagration, and excited against them a most furious and bloody persecution. In this persecution, it is generally supposed that Paul and Peter suffered death; the former by being beheaded, and the latter by crucifixion. Paul is supposed to have been beheaded rather than crucified, because he was a Roman citizen, and because it was unlawful to put a Roman citizen to death on a cross. Lardner thinks that this occurred in the year 65. Where Paul was beheaded is not certainly known. It is generally supposed to have occurred at a place called the Salvian Waters, about three miles from Rome, and that he was buried in the Ostian Way, where a magnificent church was afterwards built. But of this there is no absolute certainty.

It is far more important and interesting for us to be assured, from the character which he evinced, and from the proofs of his zeal and toil in the cause of the Lord Jesus, that his spirit rested in the bosom of his Saviour and his God. Wherever he died, his spirit, we doubt not, is in heaven. And where that body rested at last, which he laboured "to keep under," and which he sought to bring "into subjection" (1 Cor. ix. 27), and which was to him so much the source of conflict, and of sin (Rom. vii. 5. 23), is a matter of little consequence. It will be watched and guarded by the eye of that Saviour whom he served, and will be raised up to eternal life. In his own inimitable language, it was sown in corruption; it shall be raised in incorruption; it was sown in dishonour, it shall be raised in glory; it was sown in weakness, it shall be raised in power; it was sown a natural body, it shall be raised a spiritual body. 1 Cor. xv. 42—44. And in regard to him, and to all other saints, when that corruptible shall have put on incorruption, and that mortal shall have put on immortality, then shall be brought to pass the saying that is written, death is swallowed up in victory. 1 Cor. xv. 54. To Paul now, what are all his sorrows, and persecutions, and toils in the cause of his Master? What but a source of thanksgiving that he was permitted thus to labour to spread the gospel through the world? So may we live—imitating his life of zeal, and self-denial, and faithfulness, that when he rises from the dead we may participate with him in the glories of the resurrection of the just.

THE END.